W9-BJQ-969

BEACHAM'S ENCYCLOPEDIA OF
POPULAR FICTION

Editor
Kirk H. Beetz, Ph.D.

 BEACHAM PUBLISHING CORP.

BEACHAM'S ENCYCLOPEDIA OF POPULAR FICTION

Editor
Kirk H. Beetz, Ph.D.

Cover Design
Amanda Mott

Cover Art is "Pierrot," 1947,
by William Baziotes
Oil on Canvas, 42 1/8 x 36
Donated by the Alisa Mellon
Bruce Fund, ©, 1996

Reproduced with Permission
from the Board of Trustees,
National Gallery of Art,
Washington, D.C.

Library of Congress
  Cataloging-in-Publication Data
Beacham's Encyclopedia of Popular Fiction
  Includes bibliographical references and index
  Summary: A multi-volume compilation of analytical essays on and study activities for the works of authors of popular fiction. Includes biography data, publishing history, and resources for the author of each analyzed work.

ISBN 0-933833-41-5 (Volumes 1-3, Biography Series)
ISBN 0-933833-42-3 (Volumes 1-8, Analyses Series)
ISBN 0-933833-38-5 (Entire set, 11 volumes)

1. Popular literature—Bio-bibliography. 2. Fiction—19th century—Bio-bibliography. 3. Fiction—20th century—Bio-bibliography. I. Beetz, Kirk H., 1952-

Z6514.P7B43 1996
[PN56.P55]
809.3—dc20   96-20771 CIP

Printed in the United States of America
First Printing, November 1996

CONTENTS

VOLUME 7, ANAYLSES SERIES

Contents

THE SEA-WOLF

Novel

1904

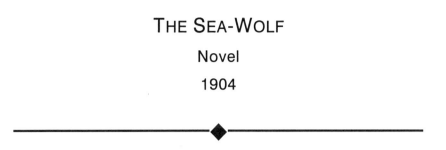

Author: Jack London

◆ Characters ◆

Humphrey van Weyden and Wolf Larsen of *The Sea-Wolf* are complementary opposites that allow London to examine extremes of background, behavior, and belief, and their conflict provides the dramatic energy in the novel.

Humphrey van Weyden is a physically incompetent aesthete who suddenly finds himself trapped in a violently competitive world, an environment in which his social standing counts for nothing. Renamed "Hump" and set to work as a cabin boy aboard the *Ghost*, van Weyden begins his initiation into "the world of the real," a struggle through which he builds a new self. Although van Weyden is weak and naive at the start of the novel, his latent adaptability makes him better suited for survival than Wolf Larsen. Unlike Larsen, van Weyden's optimistic intelligence and his ability to love move him toward life.

Wolf Larsen is undoubtedly London's most memorable character, a materialistic nihilist, a negative version of Nietzsche's superman. Ambrose Bierce wrote that "the hewing out and setting up of such a figure is enough for a man to do in a lifetime," and other critics have compared Larsen to Shakespeare's Hamlet, Milton's Satan, and Melville's Ahab. Despite his domineering brutality, Larsen has many sympathetic qualities. He is sensitive, intelligent, uninhibited, and terribly alone, but without belief or purpose to guide him, Larsen is frustratingly disoriented. Alienated from the natural and human world by his hyperrational sensibility and the disease of self, Larsen engages in senseless violence that is ultimately self-destructive.

Maud Brewster, the American poet who is brought on ship midway through the novel is not so successful; however, she plays an important role in van Weyden's development, for his love for her is the catalyst that leads him to break free of Larsen. Moreover, her presence in the novel allows London to imply that a true life must encompass both male and female as well as real and ideal.

The Sea-Wolf is a highly structured novel, and it is not, therefore, surprising that secondary characters are used to mirror the conflict between protagonist and antagonist. The young seaman Johnson, for example, is a lesser version of van Weyden, an idealistic and courageous sailor willing to die for manhood. Similarly, Thomas Mugridge, the cowardly and mean-spirited cook, embodies Larsen's violent nihilism but lacks his intelligence and sensitivity.

◆ Social Concerns ◆

At the age of seventeen, Jack London shipped out on a seven-month voyage aboard the sealing schooner *Sophia Sutherland*. Out of this experience, London created *The Sea-Wolf*, a powerful, symbolic novel of action and ideas in which he examines the class structure of American society, the conflict between materialism and idealism, the effective social limits of Nietzschean philosophy, and the function of the artist.

London remembered the hardships of his own years as a laborer, and the schooner *Ghost* is a microcosm of American industrialized society, a place in which the crewmen are brutalized by the conditions of their work and the cruelty of Captain Wolf Larsen. But by introducing the wealthy artists Humphrey van Weyden and Maud Brewster, London shows that the safety of privilege can also be debilitating.

The philosophical conflict between the protagonist Humphrey van Weyden and the antagonist Wolf Larsen explores the merits of idealism and materialism, and the self-destructiveness of Larsen's will to power underscores the dangers of Nietzschean individualism.

◆ Themes ◆

The Sea-Wolf is an example of symbolic naturalism, a novel that is simultaneously a study of environmental conditioning and a symbolic tale of initiation, a ritual of death and rebirth. Saved from drowning by Wolf Larsen, Humphrey van Weyden is shanghaied and set to work as a cabin boy. Conditioned by the violent "world of the real" aboard the *Ghost*, van Weyden is transformed from an elitist aesthete into a man of courageous action. In contrast, Wolf Larsen, the bullying materialist, is gradually incapacitated by raging headaches.

The conflict between van Weyden and Larsen is as much a war of ideas as it is a physical battle. Van Weyden is an idealist for whom "life had always seemed a peculiarly sacred thing," but he discovers that on the *Ghost* "it counted for nothing." In contrast, Larsen is a complete materialist who sees life as a "yeast, a ferment, a thing that moves . . . but that in the end will cease to move." Van Weyden triumphs because he learns to temper his naive idealism without embracing Larsen's misanthropy; thus, London suggests that the true path lies between the extremes.

Larsen displays the isolation and alienation inherent to Nietzschean individualism, and his decline expresses London's belief that modern society's complexity demands interdependence. London admired the will that drives some men to great individual accomplishments, but *The Sea-Wolf* shows that he recognized that greater strength results from cooperation.

Through the transformation of Van Weyden, London shows that an artist who is separated from work or struggle cannot develop fully. He suggests that the artist's function must, to some extent, be social.

◆ Techniques ◆

In *The Sea-Wolf* London uses his

vigorous, plain prose to dramatize his theories of environmental determinism through action and character. However, the novel's tight structure makes it seem formulaic at points, and London's preoccupation with matter over manner results in some static debates between van Weyden and Larsen.

Although Maud Brewster has an important function in terms of the novel's ideas, her improbable introduction off the coast of Japan and the sexless love affair that develops between her and van Weyden mark the weakest aspect of the novel. London is unable to describe their prudish passion in terms that significantly distinguish the prose of the final chapters from the sentimental claptrap common to the popular magazine fiction of his day.

◆ Literary Precedents ◆

In the character of Wolf Larsen, London bridges the gap between the Byronic hero and the modern anti-hero, and critics have drawn parallels with Shakespeare, Milton, Nietzsche and others. Yet the most important American literary precedent is Melville's *Moby Dick* (1851). Wolf Larsen is literary naturalism's Ahab. Like Melville's captain, Larsen is an intelligent man who has questioned too deeply. Refusing to comfort himself with beliefs he cannot get his hands on, Larsen, like Ahab, courageously confronts the natural and human worlds alone. However, unlike Ahab, whose life is directed by his mad quest to seek revenge on the white whale, Larsen has no purpose toward which to direct his energy. His increasingly severe headaches represent the way in which he is consumed by his own consciousness.

◆ Related Titles ◆

The tyranny of Wolf Larsen's rule aboard the *Ghost* foreshadows London's direct attack on fascist dictatorship in *The Iron Heel* (1908), and the attention given to the function of the artist in the novel foreshadows London's autobiographical novel Martin Eden (1909) in which the title character is a thinly veiled portrait of the author.

◆ Adaptations ◆

The Sea-Wolf has been the basis for more film adaptations than any of London's other novels. Some examples are *The Sea Wolf* (1913) with Hobart Bosworth; *The Sea Wolf* (1920) with Noah Berry; *The Sea Wolf* (1926) with Ralph Ince; *The Sea Wolf* (1930) with Milton Sills; *The Sea Wolf* (1941) directed by Michael Curtiz and starring Edward G. Robinson, Ida Lupino, John Garfield, Gene Lockhart, and Barry Fitzgerald; *Vik Larsen* (1947), a Czechoslovakian production; *Barricade* (1950), reworked as a western with Raymond Massey; *Wolf Larsen* (1958) with Barry Sullivan; and *Wolf of the Seven Seas* (1975), an Italian film starring Chuck Connors. Certainly, Edward G. Robinson's portrayal of Wolf Larsen is most memorable.

Carl Brucker
Arkansas Tech University

THE SECOND CHRONICLES OF AMBER

Four Novels

Trumps of Doom, 1985
Blood of Amber, 1986
Sign of Chaos, 1987
Knight of Shadows, 1989

◆

Author: Roger Zelazny

◆ Social Concerns/Themes ◆

The first Chronicle of Amber ends at the Courts of Chaos, where Corwin, Prince of Amber, meets for the first time his son Merlin. Indeed the reader learns that the whole five-novel sequence has been a story told by Corwin to Merlin — a kind of autobiography and apologia. The second chronicle is Merlin's story.

Merlin is the son of Corwin and Dara, Princess of Chaos, Corwin's one-time lover and more recently his bitter enemy. Thus he is a son both of Amber and Chaos and a pivotal figure in the ongoing struggle between those two opposed realms. While the plot defies easy summary, it turns on Merlin's attempt to discover who is trying to kill him, a quest that involves him in a dizzying array of political machinations, family feuds, and lovers' vendettas. The struggle culminates in what appears to be an ultimate conflict between the powers of the Logrus and the Unicorn, the rival metaphysical entities underlying Chaos and Amber.

If this sounds confusing, it is, and Zelazny further complicates the plot by adding characters and plot twists at virtually every turn.

The reader has the strong sense of a writer delighting in making up his story as he goes along, but at least one reviewer has unflatteringly compared the novels to a television soap opera, with the frequent cliffhanger endings, the discovery of new relatives every few episodes, and the general sense of an author writing himself in and out of corners.

The principal theme of the first Amber sequence is the need for a dynamic balance between freedom (or chaos, energy) and pattern (or law, order, form), which are represented by Chaos and Amber. Chaos is the primordial condition of existence; Amber, long thought by its inhabitants to be the original world, is an offshoot of Chaos, the product of the genius of a rebel Lord of Chaos who created a Pattern. Zelazny is here playing a variation on numerous creation accounts which portray the beginning of the universe not as a creation from nothing, but as the triumph of order over chaos. What makes Zelazny's version different is his celebration of balance. There is no suggestion that he regards order as morally or metaphysically superior to Chaos; it is a mistake to regard Chaos as evil and Amber as good. More precisely, his pairs are freedom and law, energy and pattern. None of the Amber books offers the opposition between good and evil seen in Christian-based fantasies like J. R. R. Tolkien's *The Lord of the Rings* (1954-1955). On the contrary, the ideal requires a continuous balance between opposites, not the triumph of one over the other.

While it is impossible to make a definitive pronouncement on the themes of a novel sequence still in progress, Merlin's parentage is perhaps suggestive of the main thematic line. As a child of both Chaos and Amber, one whose sole allegiance has been demanded by each side, Merlin plays a critical thematic role. Through the fourth novel he has resisted efforts of the Logrus and the Unicorn to recruit him, insisting upon his dual allegiance to Amber and Chaos. It is likely that the ultimate resolution of the plot will revolve around Merlin's choices and that the precarious balance of Chaos and Amber will depend upon his ability and willingness to be true to both sides of his heritage, to both poles of his being.

◆ Characters ◆

The growth of the protagonist — or his failure to grow — is at the heart of virtually all of Zelazny's fiction. In most genre fiction the protagonist solves a problem or defeats an enemy. If there is any hint of moral, emotional, or psychological growth, it may seem merely formulaic or simply incidental to the plot. In Zelazny's best work, however, the development of the protagonist is both central and problematic. His heroes are always attractive, but they are usually morally flawed or psychologically stunted. Their problem is not only to complete a quest or defeat an enemy, but to deepen their own humanity.

Merlin, despite the fact that he is a sorcerer, a warrior, and a prince of two magical realms, faces some rather prosaic problems. He is a young man trying to come to terms with his family: a famous (and absent) father who is a stranger yet intimately familiar; a protective mother who hates his father; and a jealous and resentful step-brother. In addition, Merlin's former lover now bitterly resents him because (as he is beginning to understand) he was unable to trust her or confide in her. Merlin is also trying to discover himself, to learn who he is and what he believes. Zelazny has transposed these common human problems to the level of high fantasy.

Merlin's step-brother Jurt and former lover Julia are both actively engaged in trying to kill him, using assassins, supernatural creatures, and a variety of magical spells. His mother saddles him with a guardian spirit which can temporarily possess any handy body to save Merlin from harm. And his father, though never actually present, still seems hauntingly near at hand. His family difficulties, moreover, involve concerns over the succession to the two major thrones of the universe. His own choices are apt to affect countless lives and the political and ontological balance of that universe. Nonetheless, the problems with which Merlin has to deal are recognizably human ones: Can he be true to others and remain true to himself? Will his level of moral maturity match his power? Will he grow to meet the challenges he faces?

◆ Techniques/Literary Precedents ◆

The second Amber sequence, like the first, is structured in part as a mystery story. Merlin attempts to discover who is trying to kill him and learns that there may be more enemies and more plots than he first imagined and that there are threats to more than just Merlin himself. Again, as in the first series, the hero spends a good deal of time listening to the stories of other characters — friends, enemies, and those who switch sides — as he tries to piece together a coherent account from their partial and contradictory tales. There is less reliance on the epic techniques of the first sequence and a greater concentration on magic and court intrigue.

Zelazny's wide reading is reflected in his highly allusive style. Echoes of dozens of other works permeate the novel's texture. For example the name Merlin for a young sorcerer is at the very least suggestive, though it is not yet clear how much Zelazny will exploit the Arthurian parallel. There is a sustained allusion to Lewis Carroll's *Alice in Wonderland* (1865), especially in a lengthy dream passage, and perhaps the invocation of Carroll suggests something of the novel's playful and often satiric tone.

◆Related Titles◆

Zelazny's principal precedent is his own first sequence of Amber novels. Although he introduces new elements, Zelazny mainly elaborates on his previously created universe. Amber/ Chaos/Shadow are not as fully realized as Tolkien's Middle Earth or Stephen R. Donaldson's The Land, for example. One has the sense that while there may be a good deal of vivid action going on in the foreground, the rest of the stage is decked with rather flimsy and ill-assorted props dredged from a theatrical company's archives. And yet there are hints, especially in the recent *Knight of Shadows* (1989), that Zelazny intends to explore the underlying significance of Amber and Chaos in much greater depth. Zelazny's fans may well hope so, for Amber has lost much of its original freshness and excitement.

Another problem with the second series is the fact that thus far Merlin is a less interesting character than Corwin. He lacks Corwin's maturity and painful experiences; as yet his emotional and psychological growth is more anticipated than real. Thus far, Zelazny seems to be capitalizing, admittedly in a generally entertaining way, on a previous success. Up to this point, the new Amber novels share the fate of most sequels: to be compared to the original and found wanting.

Kevin P. Mulcahy
Rutgers University

THE SECOND COMING

Novel

1980

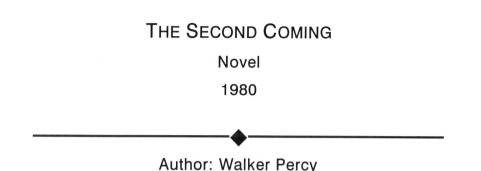

Author: Walker Percy

◆ Characters ◆

Will Barrett, the central character of *The Last Gentleman* (1966), is also the central character of *The Second Coming* (Percy wryly observed "the title refers to that, among other things"). Will, although older than in the earlier novel, is still a typical Percy hero: able to manage, but confused about what to do about life. The surprise of the novel is Allison. She is not the typical weak woman that Percy usually creates; some critics have speculated that Percy created her as a conscious response to critical attacks on his female characters. Allison does have problems: she has escaped a mental ward where she has undergone shock therapy, which has, among other things, impaired her ability to speak. But for Percy her awareness of her alienation is a virtue, as it is for his male characters. As Allison phrases it in her delightful, zany way: "our lapses are not due to synapses" (with Percy's theological pun on "lapse" for "fallen"). Will responds: "No, they are as they should be."

Allison is not a totally independent person: She needs Will "to give her the words." Yet their need is mutual (he falls, she hoists him up). In having her need him to provide words for her, Percy is not only following his own interest in semiotics (his own younger daughter was born deaf), he is following the "intersubjectivity" concepts of the Christian existentialist Gabriel Marcel: Consciousness must be shared, through language and symbol, before it can truly come into being. In sharing language, Will and Allison create a shared consciousness.

◆ Social Concerns ◆

In *The Second Coming*, as in many of his novels, Percy is more concerned with the attempts of two individuals to overcome their personal alienation from themselves, from others, and from God, than with their attempts to overcome their alienation from society. But these attempts are interrelated, and, in *The Second Coming*, Percy makes his clearest statement of the traditional belief that marriage is the basic social unit. At the end of the novel, Will and Allison have, to some extent, overcome their alienation, are preparing to marry, and, significantly, are planning to help others build a community.

The novel is also a satiric attack on

Christendom. Percy comments that his central character "lives in the most Christian nation in the world, in the most Christian part of that nation, the south, in the most Christian state in the south, North Carolina, in the most Christian town in North Carolina." Yet the people live in a "death-in-life" trance of greed, lust, and hate. Will's Pentecostal daughter and Jack Curl, the Episcopal priest who wears jump suits and is uncomfortable with "religious talk," are particular targets of Percy's satire.

◆ Themes ◆

Love — both human and divine — is a constant theme in Percy's novels, but in *The Second Coming*, Percy provides his most thorough analysis of love and marriage as a way through the alienation of the fallen world. Will Barrett, the central character, consciously (and comically) searches for God, or at least a sign of God, in this novel, but, instead of finding Him, he literally "falls" into love with a woman named Allison. Will and Allison are both alienated, which is to say "fallen" human beings, but by coming together they find a way back to their true selves and each other: "She was moving against him, enclosing him, wrapping her arms and legs around him, as if her body had at last found the center of itself outside itself." Their love is described in allegorical language that recalls both the Christian doctrine of the Fall and the neo-Platonism of Dante: He is a "faller" and she is a "hoister," but Percy is also simple, direct, colloquial: "His need of her was as simple and urgent as drawing the next breath."

Their love is sexual, but it is also sacramental. At the conclusion of the novel, Will asks for a sacramental (in this case, interestingly enough, Episcopal) marriage. In the traditions of the Catholic church, the sacrament of marriage is not complete until it is consummated, and, in the allegorical tradition of the Church, the physical act of intercourse is taken as a symbol of the hypostatic union of the human and the divine. It is in that context that Percy can have Will say, at the conclusion of the novel, as he looks at the priest: "Is she a gift and therefore a sign of a giver? Could it be that the Lord is here, masquerading behind this simple holy face? Am I crazy to want both, her and Him? No, not want must have. And will have." This is the most profoundly optimistic conclusion that Percy ever wrote: Will Barrett has found both love and the sign he had searched for so desperately.

◆ Techniques ◆

The novel begins with a chapter on Will, then one on Allison. Chapters alternate, occasionally linked very directly: one chapter ends, "He remembered everything" and the next begins, "She remembered nothing." The novel seems to conspire to bring these two lovers together, using coincidences that strain credibility (for example, it turns out that Allison is the daughter of Kitty Vaught, Will's girlfriend in *The Last Gentleman*). Percy may have intended to make a point with this string of coincidences; in a similar way, *The Last Gentleman* seems to conspire to baptize Jamie, whether he likes it or not. However, critics have complained that this technique and the unabashedly optimistic ending makes the novel overly sentimental.

◆ Literary Precedents ◆

The Second Coming, in providing a concrete, physical situation for philosophical and theological concerns, follows Percy's general approach, borrowed from the French existentialists. Again, much of the philosophical framework is provided by Kierkegaard, although the theme of love as a redemptive power is certainly related to neo-Platonic thought, as seen in Dante's *Divine Comedy*, and the action of the novel is a reworking of the Christian myth of the Fall. A subplot — Will's attempt to come to terms with the suicide of his father, and his realization that his father had intended to kill him — is handled in a Faulknerian way, even though Percy is one of the few modern southern writers who was not strongly influenced by Faulkner.

◆ Related Titles ◆

The most obviously related novel is *The Last Gentleman*, in which a younger, more confused Will is the central character. This Will Barrett has made a fortune as a lawyer in New York, has married into an even larger fortune, and has retired early. Percy's point is that Will's metaphysical problems are certainly not related to an inability to deal successfully with the world.

Also, even though *The Second Coming* is a more thorough consideration of the redemptive power of love and marriage, the optimism of this conclusion recalls a similar joyous conclusion to *Love in the Ruins* (1971): "To bed we go for a long winter's nap, twined about each other as the ivy twineth, not under a bush or in a car or on the floor or any such humbug as marked the past peculiar years of Christendom, but at home in bed where all good folk belong."

James Reynolds Kinzey
Virginia Commonwealth University

THE SECRET LIFE OF WALTER MITTY

Short Story

1939

◆

Author: James Thurber

◆ Characters ◆

In his daydreams, Mitty is a heroic, skillful, commanding character. While in the real world he is subject to defeat in the conflict with his wife and his society, in his imagination he can existentially create himself. He can take on the characteristics that he would like to embody (and which are the reverse of his actual nature), and he can be what he wants to be. This is a juvenile trait, but one that is defensive and necessary for his mental survival.

Mrs. Mitty represents the devouring force of domesticity; she brooks no heated passions or heroics that might endanger her comfortable home and lifestyle. In some ways, then, the male and female in Thurber's writing reverse literary stereotypes and include some of the characteristics exemplified in the heroes and heroines of William Faulkner's novels and the dramas of George Bernard Shaw, but Mitty, Mr. Munroe, and the other Thurber Little Men who cannot remove snow chains from their car tires and who suffer because of their overbearing wives do not have the strength of the Shavian Life-Force to drive them to true antihero status. Instead, and ironically, they defeat their unimaginative wives and restrictive society by exercising their imaginations.

◆ Social Concerns ◆

Throughout his writing career, Thurber was concerned about the misfit in society. Usually Thurber's misfits are simple, sensitive, imaginative men caught in a mundane world that they do not completely understand and over which they have little or no control. Typically, the world is too caught up in its own concerns to have much patience with such men, or to recognize their nature. Instead, it merely steamrolls over them. By extension, in examining the place of the imaginative Little Man in society, Thurber is metaphorically considering the conflict between an artist and his society. Another extension of this concept appears in the relationship between men and women in the author's stories, with the practical women dominating their wimpish spouses. In "The Secret Life of Walter Mitty" (March 18, 1939), these concerns come together as forces that, consciously or unconsciously, exert pressure on Mitty to make him conform to their images respectively of a solid, no-nonsense member of society or a manageable spouse.

◆ Themes ◆

Thematically, Thurber touched upon all aspects of society, from language to love and from art to war. Often he was more politically oriented than most of his humorist contemporaries. His favorite topic was the exploitation and mistreatment of the Little Man by women, creatures that he posited may have diverged from man's evolutionary path and thus actually belong to another race (a subject explored in Norris W. Yates's *The American Humorist*). Machines also are a source of the Little Man's downfall. Incidentally, although not present in "The Secret Life of Walter Mitty," observing many of the incidents depicted in his short stories and especially prevalent in his cartoons were dogs, independent, objective observers who see through pretense and bravado to vulnerability, yet who wisely seldom offer comments.

The theme of overcoming a humdrum everyday life by opposing it with fanciful images of a fantasy life is developed from the opening lines of "The Secret Life of Walter Mitty" as Mitty is found at the controls of a storm-tossed seaplane. Reality soon intrudes, though, and the heroic image is replaced by a description of Mitty, the husband, driving his wife to her regular visit with the hairdresser. Adventurous segments alternate throughout the tale of the couples' trip to town, as when Mitty's fantasy about being a skilled surgeon taking command in a hospital operating room life-and-death situation dissolves when he is confronted by a parking lot attendant who clearly is capable of managing Mitty's car better than Mitty himself can. As the story progresses, Mitty also imagines himself in the role of the world's greatest pistol shot, a bomber captain on a mission over enemy territory, an army captain about to lead his men into combat, and a proud, disdainful figure facing a firing squad.

◆ Techniques ◆

"The Secret Life of Walter Mitty" is one of the best known and most popular short stories in American literature. When it was printed it aroused more reaction than anything else ever published in the *New Yorker* — which, considering the brouhaha over Shirley Jackson's "The Lottery" (1949), and the fact that John Hersey's *Hiroshima* (1946) and Rachael Carson's *The Silent Spring* (1962) appeared in the journal, is intriguing in itself.

The tale is a classic fantasy in which the Little Man husband, Mitty, escapes from the realities of his mundane world by imagining himself performing heroic deeds in a variety of romantic situations with the action accompanied by a "pocketa-pocketa-pocketa" sound. According to Thurber, he was trying to "treat the remarkable as commonplace," in this piece. This approach to his material, and its obverse, is at the center of a great deal of his humor.

Because he was dealing with a common experience, one that his audience would find particularly familiar, all that Thurber had to do was to establish a pattern; he did not need to expand the plot very far (as was done in the movie version, or in a recent retelling in the British novel *Billy Liar*). The fantasy tone of the tale is offset to some extent by the inclusion of specific unifying details, such as the appearance of a Webley-Vickers automatic pistol in two of the dream sequences. The use of such details is also realistic in two ways. First, dreams frequently include elements that are incorporated from outside the dreamer (the ring of a telephone, for instance). Second, the details tie Mitty to reality, as when the use of the word "cur" in one imaginative segment suddenly propels Mitty back into reality and he remembers the item that he had not yet bought — puppy biscuits.

Interestingly, as Thurber's career evolved, two major elements of his style developed in different directions, yet they were interrelated. His penchant for rewriting never diminished. Although occasionally pieces such as "File and Forget" (January 8, 1949, reprinted in *Alarms and Diversions*), were dashed off in the course of one afternoon, even these exceptions were not the rarities that they seemed, according to Thurber. In an interview with George Plimpton and Max Steele, he explained that "File and Forget" came easily "because it was a series of letters just as one would ordinarily dictate." Even so, he acknowledged, the last letter took him a week — "It was the end of the piece and I had to fuss over it." He also recounted that his second wife took a look at a first version of something that he had written and said, "'Goddamn it, Thurber, that's high school stuff.' I have to tell her to wait until the seventh draft, it'll work out all right. I don't know why that should be so, that the first or second draft of everything I write reads as if it was turned out by a charwoman." It took Thurber about eight weeks and fifteen complete rewrites before he was satisfied with "The Secret Life of Walter Mitty," which is approximately four

thousand words long.

There are two reasons for Thurber's rewrites. To begin, he has said that "the whole purpose is to sketch out proportions. I rarely have a very clear idea of where I'm going when I start. Just people and/or a situation. Then I fool around — writing and rewriting — until the stuff jells." The second reason has to do with the author's "constant attempt . . . to make the finished version smooth, to make it seem effortless . . . With humor you have to look out for traps. You're likely to be very gleeful with what you've first put down, and you think it's fine, very funny. One reason you go over and over it is to make the piece sound less as if you were having a lot of fun with it yourself. You try to play it down."

As he grew increasingly blind, Thurber relied on a secretary to do the mechanical transcribing of his work. By the time he became totally blind he was so skilled at rewriting and his memory was so accurate that he could compose a two thousand-word story in his mind at night and then edit it as he dictated it to this secretary the next morning. Thus, the loss of his sight had little affect on his ability to polish, although there does seem to have been a reduction in the visual images incorporated in his stories that paralleled his diminishing vision.

Many critics have discussed Thurber's style and themes. Richard C. Tobias, for example, has written about the humorist's use of comic masks to explore common twentieth-century American subjects in his first efforts, how he uses conventional, social, and literary types later, and how he develops old comic plots in new ways. Like his colleagues White and Perelman, Thurber loved language — the way it sounds, the way it is used to mean something. His style depends on his precise usage, and much of his humor is based on an application of the literal meaning of words. Some of the techniques that Thurber employed include puns, artistic allusions, an exquisite sense of timing, and so forth. He also utilized both hyperbole and under-statement, frequently emphas-izing a point by juxtaposing these devices. He was also fond of reversal and other ironic forms.

Typically, Thurber's settings, circum-stances, and characters were normal, conventional middle-class American. Among his greatest talents was the ability to take these elements and to emphasize one or two minor details in his description to create an indelible image of the situation.

Thurber told Plimpton and Steele that "the act of writing is something the writer dreads or actually likes, and I actually like it. Even rewriting's fun." (Parenthetically, he did not consider himself an artist, because he did his cartoons "for relaxation, and . . . I do them too fast for them to be called art.") Moreover, in "The Case for Comedy," he had concluded, "As brevity is the soul of wit, form, it seems to me, is the heart of humor and the salvation of comedy." He had no trouble following Ross's admonition to "Use the rapier. not the bludgeon." However, in "Preface to a Life," which was added to the book version of *My Life and Hard Times* (1933), Thurber described himself as a typical professional writer of light pieces running from a thousand to two thousand words thusly: "The notion that such persons are gay of heart and carefree is curiously untrue. They lead, as a matter of fact, an existence of jumpiness and apprehension. They sit on the edge of the chair of Literature. In the house of Life they have the feel-ing that they have never taken off their overcoats. Afraid of losing themselves in the larger flight of the two-volume novel, or even the one-volume novel, they stick to short accounts of their misadventures because they never get so deep into them but that they feel they can get out. This type of writing is not a joyous form of self-expression but the manifestation of a twitchiness at once cosmic and mundane."

Ross and Thurber felt great affection for one another, and there can be no doubt that Ross's tutelage was a major factor in developing the humorist's precise style. The other primary influ-ence on Thurber's style was E. B. White. No longer under the time pres-sures of newspaper writing, Thurber could take advantage of White's guid-ance while writing segments of "The Talk of the Town." A simpler style emerged. As he admitted in an inter-view, "After the seven years I spent in newspaper writing, it was more E. B. White who taught me about writing, how to clear up sloppy journalese. He was a strong influence, and for a long time in the beginning I thought he might be too much of one. But at least he got me away from the rather curious style I was starting to perfect — tight journalese laced with heavy doses of Henry James."

◆ Related Titles ◆

As indicated above, even some of Thurber's later casuals reflect the sus-tained craftsmanship and humor of his early and middle periods. "Midnight at Tim's Place" (November 29, 1958), for instance, is a tightly written piece about a conversation in a bar. As light and well-paced as his stories from thirty years previous, this tale is about a young couple who intrude upon the narrator and his wife to involve them in a domestic quarrel. During the evening the young husband recounts an audience that he recently had with his old philosophy professor. The young man, suffering from depression, sought enlightenment only to be dismayed at finding the professor wearing two hats. When this detail is revealed, there is a long pause. "In his study?" the narrator asks incredulously. The timing and incongruity of the narrator's response is pure Thurber. There are two possible implied concepts underlying the question: Either it is completely unrelated to the event described and humor comes from the suddenness and incongruity, or it implies that wearing two hats is acceptable, although not, perhaps, in the study, an amusing thought. In either case the narrator's reaction is the focus of the humor.

Thurber then takes his story a step further, though; the narrator's wife, in her realistic fashion, is seized by the thought of the number of hats involved. Once more the Little Man and the Thurber Woman are present. The piece also contains the puns, literary allusions, and foreign phrases (see "Department of Correction: Re-Latin phrase in 'Midnight at Tim's Place,'" February 7, 1959) that Thurber enjoyed using.

Thurber's 307 drawings, most of which were cartoons, brought him almost as much fame as his prose did, though the first attempts to place his art work in the *New Yorker* were as inauspicious as had been the efforts with his short stories. The first Thurber line drawing to be formally submitted to the *New Yorker* was not even submitted by its creator; White had long been an admirer of Thurber's sketches and, unbeknown to his colleague, White presented to the art staff a picture of a seal looking at some black dots in a barren landscape and announcing, "Hm, explorers!" Thurber had drawn the sketch in 1929 and White had inked it in. Some months later Harper's published Thurber and White's collaboration, *Is Sex Necessary?* (1929), complete with Thurber's illustrations, which White had collected and insisted on having included. After the book became a best seller, Ross agreed to publish Thurber's cartoons, which became extraordinarily popular. Many reflected the view of life that occupied Thurber's attention in his prose (White identified Thurber's two major themes as the "melancholy of sex" and the "implausibility of animals"). One of the most famous of the cartoons is a rendering, published in January 1932, of a man and a woman in bed, with a seal looking over the headboard behind them. The woman is saying: "All Right, Have It Your Way — You Heard a Seal Bark!"

Thurber's whimsy comes through in a cartoon in which a startled man in the witness chair next to the judge's bench is confronted by an attorney pointing at a kangaroo and exclaiming, "Perhaps This Will Refresh Your Memory!" In a drawing exposing what Thurber calls the war between men and women, a man is depicted sitting at a table with a heavyset woman who glares at him while a younger woman sitting across from him presses his foot with hers over the caption, "Well, What's Come Over You Suddenly?" Elsewhere, a wife, lying on a divan and speaking on the telephone while her husband watches from a nearby chair, demands, "Well, if I Called the Wrong Number, Why Did You Answer the Phone?" And, if man cannot understand woman's logic, neither does he understand either her relationship to the universe or her emotions and sensitivity. For instance, in one cartoon a couple is about to be engulfed by a giant being surrounded by black and speeding toward them from space as the man says, "You and Your Premonitions!" while in another the woman in bed snarls "Well, it Makes a Difference to Me!" at the man standing next to the bed and dressed in pajama tops decorated with spots and bottoms that have a striped pattern.

◆ Adaptations ◆

Thurber's forte is the interesting combination of imaginative concepts, insights, and approaches to life expressed in strikingly clear images that depend on a careful manipulation of words. Because his writing appeared in magazines, his style is journalistic in nature; that is, it is most effective when he captures and condenses the essence of a thought within the limits imposed by the short story format. Because of his immense popularity, it is no surprise that there would be attempts to transpose his work to the movie screen or to television, but as might be expected, the very elements that characterize his writing work against a successful translation of that work into other media. His most famous creation, Walter Mitty, appeared in the film, *The Secret Life of Walter Mitty* (1947), directed by Norman Z. McLeod and starring Danny Kaye, but the result is only moderately effective. His play *The Male Animal* was a Broadway hit, and possibly because he had been working in a visual medium to begin with, the 1942 screen adaptation (directed by co-author Elliott Nuggent and starring Henry Fonda, Olivia de Havilland, and Jack Carson) is entertaining and was well received. A second cinematic treatment, the mediocre musical *She's Working Her Way Through College*, was released in 1952 (it was directed by H. Bruce Humberstone and starred Virginia Mayo and Ronald Reagan). On the other hand, the 1969 television series based on *My World — and Welcome to It*, starring William Windom, while occasionally amusing, demonstrated again that the humor in Thurber's sketches could not be sustained indefinitely since the original content was not intended to be sketched.

Steven H. Gale
Missouri Southern State College

THE SECRET PILGRIM

Novel

1991

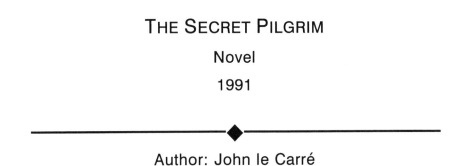

Author: John le Carré

◆ Social Concerns ◆

Although *The Secret Pilgrim* focuses on the conflict between the free and Communist worlds, it does not present many comparisons between Western and Eastern societies. The novel acknowledges Communist governments' torture and abuses of human rights, but it is more concerned with how deception affects individual people. The practice of spying is shown to be necessary for Western democracies; they need to know how to fend off threats to their sovereignty and liberties. On the other hand, characters such as Ned and Smiley note that some aspects of spying are antithetical to the ideals of freedom which form the moral foundation of their democratic government. They want to see themselves as secret protectors of the public good, but they wonder whether such aspects of domestic spying as wiretaps, investigations into people's private lives, and the Official Secrets Act actually help or harm the people they are supposed to serve. Overall, the novel suggests that even though spying can be destructive to the personality of individual spies, it is necessary in a world in which many powerful countries have no respect for the rights of others.

◆ Themes ◆

In a series of loosely connected episodes in the career of ace field spy Ned, *The Secret Pilgrim* examines how people behave under extreme stress. The most dramatic of these episodes is the one in which Ned is tortured by Polish agents. With all his courage he resists giving them what they want. He is beaten and loses teeth; he is tied to a rack and worked over. Typical of the melancholy tone of the novel, Ned's determination and endurance turn out to have no real meaning. He thinks that the colonel in charge of torturing him is after important secrets that could cost the lives of agents working for the British; instead, the colonel is only testing him to see how tough he is. It turns out that the colonel wishes to betray the Communist government, and in a bizarre twisting of motivations, he has tortured Ned in order to work for him; the colonel wants a tough man to be in charge of his own spying for the British.

The colonel is in search of a kind of perverse truth: He wants to find an honest man who would be true to his commitment to him. Throughout the novel, people seek truth, knowledge, and reassurance. A curious contrast to Ned's episode with the Polish colonel occurs when an old British war hero visits Smiley, who works in an office where citizens can report what seem to be suspicious activities that may involve spying against their country. The old war hero has come to find out whether his son worked for British intelligence. When he visited his son in prison, his son had claimed that being in prison was only a cover for his being out of the country, spying on Russia. After his son is stabbed to death, he comes to Smiley in hopes of finding the truth. After investigating the case, Smiley learns that the son was a nasty, vicious criminal who had led a life of crime, and who had died as he lived, in a vicious stabbing. Yet, when the old war hero returns with his wife, Smiley lets him believe that his son was involved in ultra-secret work, and gives the couple cufflinks that are supposed to symbolize their son's rank in British intelligence; the cufflinks are actually a pair given to Smiley by his wife before she had an affair with a vile double-agent, precipitating the break up of their marriage. Ned speculates on why the hard-nosed Smiley would allow the old couple to believe a falsehood — that their degenerate son was actually a heroic secret agent. In the convoluted world of secret intelligence, the falsehood actually gave Smiley a kind of truth. In the world of espionage, agents seldom know how their work will turn out; the case of the bereaved parents of a criminal son gave Smiley a moment of certainty in an otherwise uncertain career.

◆ Characters ◆

Ned's memoirs provide the foundation of the novel. He reminisces about aspects of his career as he listens to Smiley give a talk to a class of future spies whom Ned teaches. Ned believes that the world is changing as nations form new relationships made possible by the Soviet Union's collapsing empire. It is his hope — and Smiley's belief — that old brutal practices of the Cold War have become obsolete, that future British secret agents will lead lives that will be less hypocritical and dehumanizing than were the lives of the agents of his own generation. From episode to episode, Ned traces his own growth into a top secret agent. He begins as an idealistic young man. In training he is paired off with Ben, one of British intelligence's leading lights. He feels himself inferior to his partner, and his superiors also seem to think that Ben is much better. Once in the field, Ben transgresses and betrays his government; from this, Ned learns a hard lesson about what spying can do to people. He also learns not to trust people the way he had trusted Ben.

Ned decides that his life is "to be a search." He dedicates himself to ferreting out information and looking for truth. In one episode after another, he learns that absolute truth is hard to find. Almost nothing is ever what it seems to be in spying. Why does Jerzy, the Polish colonel, torture him? Obviously, it must be to force Ned to give him secret information; yet, in truth, the obvious is wrong. Jerzy tortures Ned not to receive information but rather so he can give it. Ned comes to suspect betrayal from any source. After all, Smiley had revealed that one of Britain's most trusted secret agents was actually working for the Soviet Union.

The response of Smiley's superiors was to punish him by relegating him to insignificant work. By the 1980s, Ned has become tired and unsure of what he has accomplished in life. He dislikes spying, being uncertain of its value. He hopes the kind of life he led will no longer be necessary in the future because of new arrangements with the Soviet Union. Even so, when he follows the news about how the Baltic republics are trying to break away from the Soviet Union, he wonders whether his government is now "diligently breaking" a Cold War promise to help the Baltic peoples.

Ned's memories and questions are triggered by George Smiley, a master spy of the generation before Ned's own. In some ways, Ned sees a parallel between their two careers, each having shared similar rewards and punishments. As Smiley chats with Ned's students, he seems to be a repository of wisdom. He scoffs "at the idea that spying was a dying profession now that the Cold War had ended." On the other hand, at the novel's end Smiley declares that his way of doing things is outdated and that therefore he will no longer come to the school for spies; the world will require new approaches to espionage. Still, when Ned studies his students, he sees in them what he and Smiley once were. Smiley represents what happens to a good man who must almost daily take charge of other people's lives and how having to lie to them, use them, and discard them — often without ever allowing them to know exactly what they are risking their lives for — can generate self-doubt and self-reproach inside the best of men. Among his students, Ned sees idealists like himself and the young Smiley; he sees the iconoclasts and the emotionally unstable who are nonethe-less necessary to British intelligence because of their special talents; and he sees women, who now attend previously all-male classes, as a sign of changing times. The careers of Ned and Smiley represent a past that they hope the new secret agents will not have to follow. Ned's own weary, melancholy attitude suggests that this hope may be as elusive as finding truth or happiness in the necessarily deceitful world of spying.

◆ Techniques ◆

The Secret Pilgrim is one of le Carré's most brilliantly written novels. It is a "framed" story, with an outer story that surrounds the main story; the frame is Smiley's talk with Ned's students. This frame allows for three different generations of spies to interact. Smiley represents the World War II generation, which joined British intelligence when anything seemed possible, when the world seemed ready to be made good, peaceful, and safe, with the British Empire still intact. For Smiley's generation, the 1950s and 1960s were profoundly disillusioning. Ned represents the generation that joined British intelligence during the height of the Cold War, when spying was a murderously desperate contest between nations. His students represent the future; they are the hope for better days, when it may be possible that spying will become less of a deadly war for national self-preservation. The interactions among these characters provide perspective on the main narrative. Ned is able to refer to comments made by Smiley and his students in order to provide insights into the tales of human suffering that make up the bulk of the novel.

The novel is episodic, with the character of Ned providing most of the links from one event to another. Like Smiley, Ned has become sensitive to humanity. He feels the losses of those he has known deeply and remembers their hopes having been dashed just as his own were. He calls his life a search, but as he tells it, it is more of an education in human strengths and weaknesses. The episodic organization of the novel allows him to examine several different kinds of people, such as Jerzy, who believes that his own cruelty has cost him his emotional life. Jerzy concludes that "by ceasing to feel he was ceasing to exist," so he spies for the British in part just to generate feelings and thus feel alive. Bella, the beautiful and sexually dynamic Soviet expatriate who is suspected of being a double-agent, turns out to be exactly what she seems, a strong, honest woman; Hansen, the brilliantly talented agent who survived the horrors of the genocidal war waged by Pol Pot in Cambodia, sees his daughter's personality destroyed by Marxist ideology, and now lives with her while she follows the only life that gives her a feeling of belonging, that of a brothel prostitute. These are colorful people whose portrayal makes them also realistic.

The episodic novel has at least three potentially significant weaknesses: the characters may not be well developed and may be merely one-dimensional stereotypes; the characters may become confused with one another and be easily forgotten; and the narrative may not flow, encouraging readers to close the novel after an episode and not reopen it. In *The Secret Pilgrim*, the characters are brilliantly realized. Ned's narrative has a stark, documentary feel to it, making the novel's events seem as though they may have

actually happened. This carefully controlled realistic tone, enhanced by well-observed details of locale and local customs, provides a fine background for the characters who are made more real by the world they inhabit.

Ned's primary interest is in what happens to people who risk their lives to serve others and he studies them in depth. For instance, Hansen emerges as a compelling figure. His life is a great modern tragedy played out against the most horrifying events of his time. His treatment at the hands of the Communists points out that there are vital reasons why he and Ned must ply their trade. Hansen himself is a complex man, talented yet whimsical. Something of a lost soul, he finds an anchor for himself in a bizarre and out-of-control environment, and it is this humane anchor that the novel implies is essential for survival. He loves his daughter and gives himself to her. Ultimately, the essential aspect of working for the public good demands that one focus on individuals and their welfare.

◆ Literary Precedents ◆

The Secret Pilgrim is in the tradition of le Carré's *The Spy Who Came in from the Cold* (1963). It is a typically gritty account of the work of spies, with an emphasis on the human cost of the Cold War.

◆ Related Titles ◆

The Secret Pilgrim takes place in the British intelligence community that le Carré has included in most of his earlier work. It is more clearly linked to his earlier work than *The Russia House* (1989) because of the inclusion of George Smiley, who appears prominently in earlier novels, most notably the "Smiley trilogy" of *Tinker, Tailor, Soldier, Spy* (1974), in which Smiley unmasks a Soviet agent working in a high position for British intelligence, an event that is discussed in *The Secret Pilgrim; The Honourable Schoolboy* (1977), in which Smiley helps the British intelligence community recover from the chaos created by the enemy agent; and *Smiley's People* (1980), in which Smiley pursues his archenemy, the Soviet master spy Karla.

◆ Ideas for Group Discussions ◆

The Secret Pilgrim is likely to generate rip-roaring discussions: some readers are likely to be outraged by the novel, others are likely to be dismayed, disappointed, encouraged, excited, or made meditative. The novel is a powerful study of the effects deception has on the human spirit, and it suggests that people need certainties in their lives — that they need truths. Exactly what these truths may be could be a good topic for discussion. The one-time spy whose daughter becomes a prostitute offers a challenging interpretation of what is good for individual people and a hard-edged look at what wounded spirits must do to find meaning in their lives. Throughout the novel, le Carré invites close examination of what motivates people who lie for their living and of the implications for societies that encourage lying and subterfuge. In *The Secret Pilgrim*, individual lives matter, and the novel implies that individual lives matter more than social standards.

1. How does the classroom setting provide a frame for the narrative? How does it link episodes together? Does le Carré take full advantage of the possibilities his classroom setting offers?

2. How does Ned grow during the narrative? Why does he recollect the particular episodes that he does? Does he like what he has become?

3. Why would Smiley believe that he has no more to offer modern students of espionage? How is this attitude a reflection of his personality? Is he right?

4. What important aspects of individual humanity seem to be universally lost by professional spies?

5. How do various characters find truth? Ned seems to be hunting for it everywhere. Does he find it? Is there more than one truth to be found?

6. Why does Ned dwell on ambiguities rather than his clear-cut successes and clear-cut failures?

7. What motivates Ned and Smiley? Do they have ideals? Do they believe that they serve just causes?

8. Will there always be a need for spies? Who would they spy on? Who would be the Western world's enemies?

9. It is important to note that the spies in *The Secret Pilgrim* are often spiritually crippled by the immense evil they must combat, as well as by the deceptions they are expected to formulate. What is the nature of the evil they fight? Is there ever any doubt that communism in particular is ever anything but far worse than the West-

ern alternative?

10. How resilient is the human spirit in *The Secret Pilgrim*? How do wounded spirits cope? Is le Carré's examination of the human spirit profound?

11. The novel is presented in episodes. Why would le Carré use this format to present his characters and themes?

12. What is the novel's most important theme? How closely linked is it to the novel's characterizations?

13. Who are the most memorable characters in the novel? What makes them come alive?

14. What are the dangers the novel suggests are inherent in a life of deception? Which of these dangers poses the greatest threat to the individual person? Which poses the greatest threat to Western societies?

Kirk H. Beetz

THE SECRET SHARER

Short Story

1912

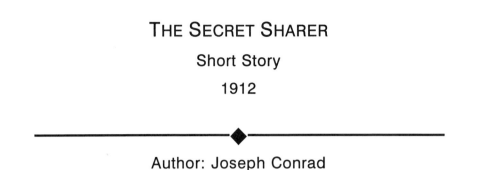

Author: Joseph Conrad

◆ Social Concerns ◆

While at work on his third political novel, *Under Western Eyes* (1911), Conrad returned imaginatively to his seafaring days in the East and his first command as Captain of the *Otego* to create his most powerful short story, "The Secret Sharer"; this and his earlier masterpiece, "The Lagoon" (1898) are his most widely read short stories. The social concerns in the story — the punishment for taking a life, the righting of a social imbalance arising therefrom, and the preservation of order in the orderly world of merchant mariners — take second place to the personal concerns of the captain-narrator and of Leggatt, the secret sharer of his thoughts and his life. The social concerns that, in other contexts, might have received major attention are entirely overshadowed by the Captain's moral initiation. It is as if his quest after verisimilitude in depicting life in Tsarist Russia and the lives of emigrés in Geneva in *Under Western Eyes* occupied his thoughts so intensely that he sought respite from it by returning to his own past and depicting an awakening. In one sense then, this story may be seen as a gloss on *Under Western Eyes*, a gloss in which humanity triumphs over social concerns and leads to freedom instead of disaster.

◆ Themes ◆

The principal theme of the story is the rite of passage, the captain's initiation into his new responsibility of command so that instead of perceiving himself an alien on his ship he can finally achieve the "perfect communion of a seaman with his first command." The captain reaches this communion in part by harboring Leggatt and sharing his first apprehensive hours of command with him and in part by risking the ship among the reefs and shoals to bring Leggatt close enough to the land so that he can strike out for a new destiny. His communion with the ship is mediated by Leggatt, shared by him for a time; and this sharing of danger is a common bond that unites them and that strengthens the captain once Leggatt has departed.

◆ Characters ◆

The captain has some autobiographi-

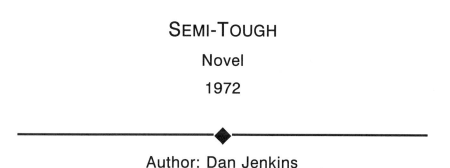

SEMI-TOUGH

Novel

1972

◆

Author: Dan Jenkins

◆ Characters ◆

The narrator-hero of *Semi-Tough* is Billy Clyde Puckett, star half-back for the New York Giants and unregenerate Texan. He and his teammates are preparing for the Super Bowl, and he has been commissioned to keep a journal for publication. It is a mark of Billy Clyde's intelligence that he sees the comedy of preserving the innermost thoughts of a football player for posterity even as he does it. Billy Clyde is profane, street smart, hard living, intelligent though hardly an intellectual, and possessed of a nature that is surpassingly sweet. His best friends are Marvin "Shake" Tiller, his teammate and childhood buddy, and Barbara Jane Bookman, every man's fantasy — gorgeous, rich, smart-mouthed, one of the boys. These three are one another's family; they live together, defend one another, love one another. In addition, there are Billy Clyde's teammates, his casual friends of both sexes, his opponents, Barbara Jane's parents, Big Ed and Big Barb Bookman — a grand collection of eccentric, larger-than-life characters derived from traditional satire or comedy.

Although there are hints that both Shake Tiller and Barbara Jane Bookman have hidden depths (Shake, for example, is clearly a closet intellectual and the only one troubled by the violence of the game that employs him and by the curious relationship the three share), Billy Clyde is the only character readers come to know completely. No deep thinker, he relies on instinct and triumphs. He is, in a very real sense, a figure of wish-fulfillment and fantasy; in his athletic prowess, his success with women, his talent for friendship, his careless lifestyle based on immediate self-gratification, he is what almost every Southwesterner has wished to be, in more frivolous moments.

The characters who inhabit *Semi-Tough* are from the comic tradition; rather than psychological depth and complexity, they offer the reader a series of social and moral positions personified. In Billy Clyde Puckett, for example, readers have a spokesman for good — in professional sports, in social intercourse, and in love.

◆ Social Concerns ◆

The central social concern in all of Jenkins's writing is the place and function of sports in American culture. *Semi-Tough* is concerned with professional football and the craziness that surrounds and defines it. The world of professional football is casually racist, profligate of humans and money. Jenkins, loving the sport, is not in the least reverent about its place in culture, and he has an insider's knowledge of the excesses that haunt it. As social satire, *Semi-Tough*, comically exposes human vice and folly and the "sins" of a small segment of society — the closed world of football players, their women, families, owners, and hangers-on.

Additionally, the novel depicts certain social values identifiable as uniquely Texan. *Semi-Tough* celebrates Texan brashness, boastfulness, hard-headedness; it also displays Jenkins's pleasure in the idiom of Texas — profane, inventive, comic.

◆ Themes ◆

Jenkins develops the idea of an unadulterated, although not naive, joy in sports values. These values are largely male-oriented in *Semi-Tough*, but they are also human values: the pleasure of competition, fair play, and team loyalty. Buried underneath the locker room horseplay, there is a complex fabric of affection and unspoken male bonding that makes race differences, the cynicism that arises from being treated as an object, and wild disparities in intelligence and skill peripheral.

In the very best sense, Jenkins's novel celebrates boys' values; his narrator ends almost every chapter with some ritualized taunt aimed at the opposing team: "Death to the dog-ass Jets." A man playing a boy's game triumphs by exhibiting a boy's strengths:

enthusiasm; a simple, unquestioned loyalty to teammates and friends; a love for the game that transcends the dross that threatens to overcome it; boundless, undirected energy; and an inexhaustible capacity for good-spirited naughtiness.

◆ Techniques ◆

Semi-Tough is written in the form of a journal or diary that Billy Clyde has been commissioned to keep as a record of the team's preparation for the Super Bowl. In fact, it is a highly personal, impressionistic book of days interspersed with memories of Billy Clyde's past. The tension between what the journal is supposed to accomplish and what it actually does is a comment upon the sports world that Billy Clyde inhabits. His preparation for the big game consists of nonstop parties, lots of sex and laughs, and sheer good times.

There is not a tightly-structured plot; the novel is episodic, anecdotal. There are two central actions which function as unifying elements: the Super Bowl game and the ultimate declaration of love between Billy Clyde and Barbara Jane Bookman. The novel, in the tradition of comedy, ends with the promise of a marriage.

◆ Literary Precedents ◆

Semi-Tough, a comic sports novel, rests upon both of those traditions. Ring Lardner is an obvious influence. The novel is also a good example of regional fiction; much of the humor of language and characterization is specifically Texan. The pleasure exhibited in the eccentric and flamboyant behavior of the characters has its roots in the Southwestern folklore of the cowboy/ wildcatter/good old boy/outlaw hero. In addition, the novel depends heavily on the tradition of wish fulfillment that is characteristic of romance; Billy Clyde is a fantasy figure of wish-fulfillment; in a less noble way, Barbara Jane Bookman is also. In the Giants' triumph over the Jets in the Super Bowl, one confronts the fantasy of the sports fan: his team, long a loser, wins it all. Jenkins's novel, written in 1972 in the spirit of wish fulfillment, provides the contem-porary reader with one of the few examples of romance and reality meeting and becoming one.

as Billy Clyde, Kris Kristofferson as Shake Tiller, and Jill Clayburgh as Barbara Jane Bookman. It was released in 1977 to generally favorable reviews. The only reservation that critics expressed was that the film was less an adaptation of the novel and more a vehicle for Burt Reynolds's brand of arch comedy. There was a television situation comedy adaptation of *Semi-Tough* that did not last a full season.

Elizabeth Buckmaster
Pennsylvania State University

◆ Related Titles ◆

In 1984, Jenkins published *Life Its Ownself*, whose subtitle is *The Semi-Tougher Adventures of Billy Clyde Puckett & Them*. It continues the story of "them," telling of Billy Clyde's career change, from football hero to color commentator, and of the troubles of Billy Clyde and Barbara Jane's marriage which are, according to Barbara Jane, "nothing that a faith healer can't fix."

The hero of Jenkins's 1974 novel, *Dead Solid Perfect*, is professional golfer, Kenny Puckett, Billy Clyde's uncle and role model. In all three novels, frequent reference is made to Herb's Cafe, a bar in Fort Worth that is Billy Clyde's emotional home. Herb's Cafe is the setting of the 1981 novel, *Baja Oklahoma*.

◆ Adaptations ◆

Semi-Tough was made into a very successful film starring Burt Reynolds

SEMPER FI

Novel

1986

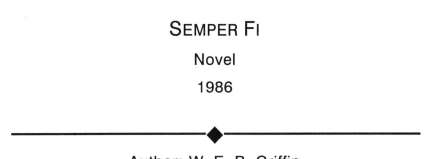

Author: W. E. B. Griffin

◆ Social Concerns ◆

The novel *Semper Fi* takes place in the year before the attack on Pearl Harbor and follows through the very early days of the war. Social issues, then, are typical of late prewar attitudes. For example, the main character, Kenneth "Killer" McCoy, is stationed in the Marine Corps in China in late 1940. Attitudes toward Chinese and Japanese, as well as toward other Europeans living in China, are shown through McCoy's eyes, particularly the atmosphere of antagonism evident in China before the beginning of the war. Smaller social commentary and social vignettes are also shown, such a glimpse at the world of the very wealthy in the form of the Pickering and Foster families.

◆ Themes ◆

Themes in *Semper Fi* are similar to those in other Griffin novels. Loyalty is especially important, given especially the Marine Corps' tradition as an elite force. The theme of change — rapid and dramatic change — also runs through the novel, be it a readjustment in attitudes (such as the reevaluation of Japanese fighting ability after the Pearl Harbor attack), a change in weapons (Griffin spends considerable time discussing the differences between the Springfield and Garand rifles), a change in status (both McCoy and Master Gunnery Sergeant Jack Stecker are raised from noncommissioned to commissioned rank, and Stecker will be a Brigadier General six novels in the series later).

◆ Characters ◆

In *Semper Fi*, Griffin's characters again largely adhere to broad but definite parameters. Ken "Killer" McCoy is a kid from a rough family in just-as-rough Bethlehem, PA, who seems always to have been a fast riser — into the Corps at eighteen, Corporal after only four years (the interwar promotion rate was very slow for both officers and enlisted personnel), lieutenant only a year later. His best friend, Malcolm "Pick" Pickering, is the grandson of a wealthy hotelier, accomplished in all the details of the hotel business, son of the owner of a steamship line, and he and McCoy are soul mates, not externally — one is a touchy, tough scrapper, and the other a debonair, insouciant playboy. But both seem born to rise to occasion, as Ken earlier proved through killing three Italian Marines in self-defense, and as they both prove in officer training school. Ellen Feller, wife of an uninspiring (and larcenous) missionary, brings out something new in a Griffin female character — a touch of imperfection. She is in cahoots with her husband in the removal of Chinese artifacts — illegally — from China, and it is significant that on this point McCoy, who has a brief affair with her, does not pass judgment on her. Jack NMI (No Middle Initial) Stecker, the epitome of the perfect Marine senior noncommissioned officer — immaculate, fair, demanding, and regal — for whom, in the novel, a mass of side information — his vehicle, his reputation, his Medal of Honor — substitute for direct description and narrative dialogue in creating his character.

◆ Techniques ◆

Sybil Steinberg, in *Publishers Weekly*, states, in commenting on *Battleground* (1992), that Griffin's prose is an:

> . . . effective alternative to military fiction's usual foxhole perspective — he places the characters on the fringes, rather than in the thick of the action, skirting familiar events and offering opportunities for exploring the Pacific War's less familiar byways. As he created a framework of coherent subplots and interesting personalities, he reveals WWII arcana, including the principles for establishing travel priorities and the status of

enlisted Marine pilots.

This is the most evident element of Griffin's prose — the considerable detail spent on description of the environment in which the characters operate, such that the environment almost becomes a character as well.

◆ Literary Precedents ◆

All of Griffin's books fit within a long tradition of twentieth-century military fiction; more specifically, Griffin has precedents in writers such as C. S. Forester, author of the Horatio Hornblower series; Douglas Reeman, author of a number of British seafaring novels, most treating the Second World War; and Max Hennessy, author of trilogies about the British cavalry and the RAF. In the work of all these authors, the protagonists are men who know themselves when put in positions of command. All these authors as well treat the relationships between the men in war. Perhaps most obviously, though, Griffin and the above-mentioned authors share a liminal connection to the modern "techno-thrillers" of Tom Clancy, Dale Brown, Stephen Coonts, and others. All provide a look into the technique of war — not simply the workings of a nuclear submarine (or an eighteenth-century man-of-war, or an Army helicopter) but of the techniques of making war, the techniques of living as a warrior, and the interactions of warriors. Like these other authors, Griffin provides considerable detail regarding the arcana of war, be it uniforms, aircraft, protocol, attitudes, or history. Unlike Forester's Hornblower, however, Griffin's characters are not long tormented by what they must do as soldiers; they do their jobs and move on.

Through the *Corps* series (*Semper Fi*, 1986; *Call to Arms*, 1987; *Counterattack*, 1990; *Battleground*, 1992, *Line of Fire*, 1992; *Close Combat*, 1992; *Honor Bound*, 1994) we see the development of a large number of officers and men; there are considerably more characters who are given some development than in the *Brotherhood of War* (1983-1988) or *Badge of Honor* (1988-1995) series. The focus shifts between novels; for example, in the latest novel in the series the action takes place in Argentina, not Europe or the Pacific, and few of the previously major characters — the McCoy brothers, the Pickerings (father and son) among them — are featured prominently. Other venues for action in the series include Australia, Guadalcanal, the U.S., and New Guinea. Some characters rise through the military hierarchy, such as Stecker and Pick's father Fleming Pickering.

◆ Ideas for Group Discussions ◆

Griffin introduces characters who are not as clearly "good" or "bad" as those in *The Aviators* (1988). As they cross the line between admirability and questionable behavior — or in the case of the coward and bully Lieutenant Macklin, despicability — their behavior, reactions, and attitudes and beliefs draw into focus the way we react to them as well as the things they react to; we as readers either mirror their reactions or recoil from them.

1. Describe the attitude toward Chinese in the novel. How is it different from the attitude toward Europeans? Is it xenophobic?

2. Why do you think Lieutenant Macklin and others disregard McCoy's advice regarding the Japanese troops and their plans to spy on them?

3. Describe the character of Lieutenant Macklin. What is his function in the novel? Is he a flat or a round character?

4, Are there really any round characters in the novel, or are they all, to a certain extent, flat?

5. Is Corporal McCoy's killing of the Italian marines justified? If so, why or how?

6. What are the similarities between Malcolm "Pick" Pickering and Ken McCoy? What are the differences? To what extent are the differences and similarities a function of the characters' respective environments? Why do they get along so well together?

Robert D. Whipple, Jr.
Creighton University

SENT FOR YOU YESTERDAY

Novel

1983

◆

Author: John Wideman

◆ Social Concerns ◆

At the center of John Wideman's work is the issue of race: what it means to be black in America. *Sent for You Yesterday*, the third volume of *The Homewood Trilogy*, weaves a rich tapestry exploring family, community, and culture, with the issue of race a striking part of the design.

Characters grapple with the social and personal tensions of race, striving to understand their own identities and the cultural history which has affected them. As in life, the people in the novel come in varying shades, from Brother, an albino, to his lover, Samantha, reminiscent of a Zulu woman in stance and color. Wideman encapsulates the tension between black and white in the character of Junebug, the son of Brother and Samantha, who dies in a kerosene fire, perhaps pushed by his black brothers and sisters. "People ain't easy to see," says Carl French (himself a light-skinned character), and the novel constitutes an attempt to see clearly the physical makeup and psychological aspects of its characters.

The interplay between shades of black and white is almost entirely centered in the African-American ghetto of Homewood in Pittsburgh, but the reverberations extend beyond the black community. The novel is a meditation on identity, a concept important to people of any color, in any community.

Equally important is the issue of family. *Sent for You Yesterday* embeds story within story as Doot, the narrator, limns the boundaries of his family history. In retelling the stories he has heard, Doot constructs his family and his own place in it. This act constitutes an emotional foundation for the novel and is a springboard for the reader to do the same, using his or her own family stories as a basis.

Another thread in the tapestry of the book is the idea of community. Homewood is described in detail, with street names, stores, particular houses, and an atmosphere of disintegration in which Brother thinks he can feel the "dry hot stale wind of thousands of trifling souls, old souls stuffed in drawers." The community, dilapidated but rich with memories and stories, echoes a vibrant past and anticipates a dissolute future. The portrait, then, is both hopeful and despairing, all the while offering a realistic look at an urban ghetto and its population.

◆ Themes ◆

Wideman's work is unique in its layering of themes, all connected yet echoing distinct aspects of human life. The central theme becomes that connection — the drawing together of disparate experiences in a shimmering kaleidoscope of emotion, history, meditation, and narrative. Making up the kaleidoscope are these themes: the fragility of ties, the construction of identity, the basis of heritage, and the nature of reality.

Fragile ties, to life and between people, are deftly rendered. Characters enter and then leave the world, their departures a commentary on the vulnerability of life. The death of Albert Wilkes, a blues pianist and cop killer, is implicit in his reappearance in Homewood. Junebug perishes in a fire on the Fourth of July. Brother is hit by a train, supposedly dead beforehand. The link to life is tentative in this novel, with characters wounded, crazy, and dead, veering off like tops.

Likewise, ties between people are shifting and unconstrained by traditional markers. For instance, Carl French, Brother Tate, and Lucy Tate are inextricably bound together, but they all drift in different directions and reunite sporadically. Albert Wilkes rejoins his white lover after seven years away, severing and then jauntily renewing his ties with her. Strong bonds exist, but they are unconventional, internal loyalties, marked by shifts and changes rather than continuity.

Continuity is found in the larger perspective of the novel, in the examination of heritage and its components of family, stories, and race. While individual family members may veer in radically different directions, the *idea* of family remains intact. Doot traces his family through their intertwining stories, and the family structure sustains the narrative.

Similarly, the act of storytelling continually informs the search for heritage. By recounting events from his family history, Doot envisions his heritage (simultaneously created and shared by the characters in the stories). This form of family storytelling is one of the binding elements of the novel.

The struggle to understand oneself is another constant of *Sent For You Yesterday,* and that search is aided by family and by story. The novel demonstrates how identity is formed and how it shifts over time, affected by external and internal events.

Finally, the nature of reality is an important theme of the novel. Memories, dreams, and time overlap, forming a reality which is not linear. Doot re-creates Homewood from stories he has been told as well as the slender details he remembers from living there at five or six years old. Dreams and reality echo one another, as in the images of trains: An unnamed narrator describes his nightmare of being stuck on a train at the beginning of the book; Brother dreams of being trapped inside a rattling boxcar; Albert Wilkes rides a train; Brother and Carl play a scare game, waiting to jump out in front of trains; and Brother dies in front of a train. The train images, manifested in dream and reality, mesh together. Similarly, time shifts and drifts throughout the narrative. Events are told, retold, flashed behind and in front. The past becomes the present, the future embedded in the past.

Taken together the themes resonate and play off one another. The whole becomes a vibrant kaleidoscope which offers a unique perspective of human existence — jumbled, piercing, and moving — which affects the reader on an almost subliminal level.

◆ Characters ◆

The narrator of *Sent for You Yesterday* slips in and out of other people's perspectives as easily as he downs a can of Iron City beer. Doot holds the book together, juggling all of the stories, memories, and points of view in his attempt to understand his family and identity. A minor character in some of the stories, Doot mainly serves to enact the literary devices which weave through the novel. By the end of the book Doot holds past and present, dead and living characters, in himself, learning "to stand, to walk, learning to dance."

Doot tells stories divided into three sections: The Return of Albert Wilkes, the Courting of Lucy Tate, and Brother. Within those three parts, with their multitude of inhabitants, the perspective shifts from character to character, mainly encompassing Albert Wilkes, John French, Carl French, Lucy Tate, Brother Tate, and Samantha.

Albert Wilkes is a jaunty, free-wheeling piano player who killed a white policeman and fled Homewood, to return seven years later and take up where he left off. His music infuses the narrative and offers a way to transcend despair. His friendship with John French links the first two sections of the book. John French is a man torn between lifestyles: He loves his family but remains drawn to Albert's penchant for staying up all night gambling and playing music. These two represent the elder generation of the book, the lords of a Homewood which used to be full of promise.

John's son Carl French spans the time frame of the novel. We see him as a young boy, sent out by his mother to search for his wayfaring father. He courts Lucy Tate and is shadowed by Brother Tate, and he recounts their years as "The Three Musketeers." At the end of the book, an old man on methadone, he cheers on his nephew Doot. An older version of Doot, he is both a participant in and narrator of events.

Like Carl, Lucy Tate spans the book. We see her as a girl described by Carl's mother as "fast," and then as Carl's friend and lover. She also remains at the end of the book as a link between Albert Wilkes, whose music she loved and whose death she witnessed, and Brother, whose life and death she struggles to understand.

The most compelling character in *Sent for You Yesterday* is Brother Tate, who does not speak and who has "no color," according to Carl. Other characters see Brother as an albino, a ghost, a shadow. He bests Carl at scare games, learns to play the piano without instruction, draws portraits of Homewood residents with wings on them, and, while he does not speak, never misses a thing. In him are embodied the tensions of race and cultural decay, and when he stakes his emotional life on his son, Junebug, it seems inevitable that both die young.

Junebug is the son of Brother and Samantha, a Zulu-like woman who labors to produce black children to replace the ones taken by society. When she gives birth to a white child by Brother, she loves the child desperately but cannot set herself against the remainder of her children who hate him. She wants to "teach them all to love," and when Junebug dies her mind falters and she isolates herself.

It would seem easy to get lost in this myriad of characters but they are coherent, especially in the context of the trilogy. Wideman set the basis for this unfolding in *Damballah* (1981) and followed it up in *Hiding Place* (1981). The characters, whether they are mentioned once or explored in depth, do form a meaningful pattern. By offering such a mixture of perspective, across characters and through time, Wideman evokes a rich personal and collective history.

◆ Techniques ◆

The hallmarks of Wideman's style in *Sent for You Yesterday* are the shifts in point of view and in time, and in the combination of Black English and Standard English. Critics have split in their opinions about the success of these techniques, with some finding the devices confusing and others hailing them as vivid and poetic.

Doot, the narrator who opens and closes the book, begins by describing Brother Tate, a "silent, scat-singing albino man who was my uncle's best friend." Then, in the space of a sentence, the point of view shifts: "I am not born yet. My Uncle Carl and Brother Tate hurry along the railroad tracks . . ." Later shifts do not even contain a small marker; the stories are simply told from Carl's point of view, or Albert Wilkes's, or Samantha's. In one section the perspective shifts so that Lucy Tate describes Doot who was describing Lucy and Carl telling stories.

This nimble juggling act sets Wideman in the tradition of Faulkner and Welty. In some of his other books, the shifts in point of view are distracting or confusing, but in *Sent for You Yester-*day Wideman utilizes Doot to maintain a stable core. The shifts are not distracting but meaningful; they place the reader in each character's head, offering intimate (sometimes contrasting and sometimes corroborating) portraits of events.

Likewise, the shifts in time might seem to fragment the story; in actuality they create a sense of time beyond our typical understanding. Time for the characters in *Sent for You Yesterday* is not linear. Stories pile upon stories, not necessarily in chronological order. The past is as close as the present, as when Doot will not wear his grandfather's hat because he wants to ask him if it is all right. Carl French compares time to a "circle going round and round so you getting closer while you getting further away and further while you getting closer." This circularity gives the novel a timeless quality.

Another hallmark of Wideman's work is his ability to intertwine Black English and Standard English. In his earlier novels, *A Glance Away* (1967) and *Hurry Home* (1970), Wideman relied more upon traditional, formal English. In *Sent for You Yesterday* he begins with colloquial speech:

Hey Bruh.
Hey man.
What you thinking, man?
I had this dream. This real bad dream.
Nightmare?
Worse than that. Night mare. Day mare. Afternoon mare. Every damn time-of-day mare. Whatever you want to call it. That dream had me by the nuts.

Contrast this with a later passage:

If he closes his eyes he can see an

ocean, red and wild as his blood, an ocean surging past the shimmering curtain of heat rising from the steel rails, an ocean rushing to the end of the world. He would run away that far if he could.

In both instances Wideman is in complete control of the prose. He demonstrates agility in balancing stream-of-consciousness, dialogue, description, and lyricism — surely part of the reason he was awarded the prestigious PEN/Faulkner award for *Sent for You Yesterday*.

◆ Literary Precedents ◆

Given Wideman's concern with heritage, it is fitting to trace his own literary heritage. His literary ancestors are both black and white, including renowned African-American writers like Richard Wright, James Baldwin, and Toni Morrison, and Caucasians like Mark Twain, Eudora Welty, and William Faulkner.

In the generational span of his novels and in the illumination of family ties, Wideman might be compared to Toni Morrison. Like her, he renders a variety of characters over an extended period. Also like Morrison, he admits ghosts as characters whose presence is strange but not extraordinary. The dialect is similar to that used in Alice Walker's *The Color Purple* (1982), but the book also echoes the colloquial language used in the works of Mark Twain and John Steinbeck.

Wideman's other literary connections may be found in Southern writers like Welty and Faulkner. In the lyrical, unhurried rendering of family relationships, Wideman might be compared to Welty. In his deft rendering of place,

his ability to evoke a whole community and people in it with realistic characters, Wideman is often compared to Faulkner. Critic Don Strachan has called Wideman "the black Faulkner, the soft-cover Shakespeare".

◆ Related Titles ◆

Sent for You Yesterday is Part III of *The Homewood Trilogy*. The characters, setting, and stories in *Sent for You Yesterday* have their beginning in *Damballah* and *Hiding Place*, the two books which Wideman wrote because he had trouble with *Sent for You Yesterday*.

Throughout the trilogy, Homewood is the central setting, although *Damballah* begins in Africa and in *Hiding Place* Tommy, the main character, visits Aunt Bess's cabin outside of Homewood. Characters resurface in all three books, as do stories. John French is a staple, with his gadabout ways examined from several perspectives. John's daughter Lizabeth appears more than once, usually linked with the caterpillar story (she eats a bite of caterpillar and John French eats the rest). Reba Love Jackson, a blues singer, is given her own story in *Damballah* and mentioned in passing in another part of the trilogy.

As the characters resurface they do not change identities, they are simply portrayed more fully. Aunt Bess and Uncle Carl appear briefly in *Damballah* and become main characters in *Hiding Place* and *Sent for You Yesterday*, respectively. The overlapping stories allow characters to surface, once or many times, and by the end of *Sent for You Yesterday* Homewood and its inhabitants have become a part of the reader's internal landscape.

Wideman is credited with having a unique voice in contemporary American literature because of his experimentation with literary techniques and his ability to evoke simultaneously a family, community, and cultural history. *Sent for You Yesterday* is a lyrical book, brimming with pride and emotion. Readers will enjoy discussing its multitude of characters and the connections between stories.

1. In *Damballah* "A Begat Chart" is included; in *Hiding Place* a genealogical chart prefaces the book. Using this material, trace the relationships between characters in *Sent for You Yesterday*. How are they related?

2. Many of the characters engage in unsavory or illegal activities. Which characters gain the reader's sympathy? Why?

3. Brother Tate has no color and no speech. What statement is Wideman making in this character about race, suppression, and identity?

4. Junebug encapsulates the conflict of white and black. What do you make of his brief life and death?

5. Look at the women characters in the book (Lucy, Samantha, Freeda, Old Mrs. Tate, Albert Wilkes's lover). What is your reaction to Wideman's portrayal? Are the goals and ambitions of the women different from those of the men?

6. Consider the portrait of Homewood. What picture of life for urban blacks does it offer? Is that picture relevant for contemporary African-Americans?

7. For whom is Wideman writing? Blacks, whites, people of all color?

8. Examine the conception of race in the book. Would you characterize the conception as bitter, realistic, or optimistic?

9. Why is storytelling so important to Doot? What place do stories have in modern society?

10. What stories might be told in tracing your own family heritage?

Amber Dahlin
Metropolitan State College of Denver

A SEPARATE PEACE

Novel

1960

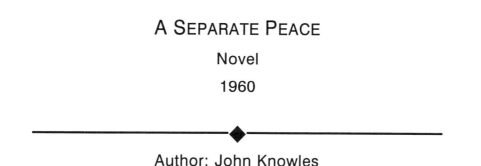

Author: John Knowles

◆ Social Concerns ◆

It is a testament to Knowles's ability that a story about relatively privileged young men in the 1940s, written from the perspective of the quiet, almost humdrum days of the Eisenhower era, has not become dated. Knowles has written in *A Separate Peace* what appears to be a real "classic" of youthful ardor that so perfectly captures the poignancy of a young man's feeling that it will continue to transcend its temporal and social bounds. The book's portraits of youthful aspirations, fears, frustrations, and revelations remain apt decades after Knowles painted them. Gene's progress from the protected environment of a friendly, unified school setting to his first encounters with the demands of an indifferent or hostile world has the resonance of an archetype of human behavior.

Yet, there is one aspect of the relationship between Gene and Phineas that looks a bit different now than it did thirty years ago. In the 1940s, it would be very unusual for boys of this background to discuss sex at all, and the absence of women from their thoughts is a function of the cultural reservations more than anything else, a fact still essentially operative in 1960 as well. Also, the virtual elimination of any interest in women might be regarded as Knowles's choice to remove a factor that would not particularly contribute to the themes he is considering. Still, the absence of any sexual curiosity tends to be conspicuous in the 1990s, in which sexual awakening is almost a requisite theme in many young adult stories. In addition, the almost total exclusion of any women from the narrative (besides a comment on "Hazel Brewster the professional town belle"), combined with several derogatory references to unattractive women, skews the male focus a bit further. An obligatory pinup of Betty Grable appears, but it does not elicit much interest compared to the boys' passionate responses to so many other things.

◆ Themes ◆

A Separate Peace was recognized immediately as a sensitive account of a young man's self-discovery through the process of maturation, and the passage of time has not lessened its universal appeal. John Knowles identifies and examines some of the crucial questions a young man might ask about himself and the world during his later teen-age years. Knowles's evocation of the moods of developing manhood is deeply felt, precisely rendered, and exceptionally incisive. The novel captures a period of life in which everything seems intense and important, in which decisions must be made that may affect one's entire life, in which action is seen with rare moral clarity, and in which an almost desperate sense of potential loss (of innocence, of uniqueness, of importance) underlies every act.

In addition, Knowles uses an effective method for organizing this narrative of self-discovery. At the core of the story, the narrator undergoes an epiphany, a moment of irrevocable displacement that haunts the remainder of his life and reverberates throughout the book. Unsure of its meaning at the instant it occurs, the narrator finds that the incident symbolizes for him the awesome power of revelation, the moment of vision that shapes a life and defines existence, offering access to the secrets of the innermost self. The progress of the narration is controlled by a concentration on the full meaning of this incident and, by implication, on the universality of such events.

Beyond this, *A Separate Peace* may recall for older readers the special qualities of existence in those years when one is "green and dying," in Dylan Thomas's words. The novel reconnects the mature reader to that period in life when the demands and rewards of friendship and love were new and noble, and it helps to explain why idealism is so valuable a quality, and one so difficult to sustain. At the same time, the book articulates these feelings for all readers who may have been unable to express them.

The values that John Knowles emphasizes in *A Separate Peace* reveal his belief that an appreciation of nature's wonders is fundamental to a life of moral integrity and spiritual satisfaction. Consequently, the novel is set in the beautiful countryside of New England, not far from the Atlantic coastline at a New Hampshire prep school called Devon. The year is 1942 and the United States is increasing its involvement in World War II. The early reverses the Allies suffer seem to imperil the very values of Western civilization. The war is presented first as a distant source of uneasiness, but its presence gradually grows into an emblem of the encroachment of the adult world's most mundane elements onto an unspoiled realm of youth and beauty.

That realm lies within the protected sanctuary of the school, a place of privilege run by quasi-British masters who espouse "continuity" but have ceased to provide the inspirational energy that keeps tradition vital. Although Knowles admires the school's overall aims and holds it in higher esteem than he does most other institutions in American life, he also recognizes its tendencies to mold and limit its students, draining them of the creativity and spontaneity that make life so vivid for his exceptional, artistic, and slightly eccentric characters. Still, in the "gypsy summer" that produces the book's freest and happiest moments, it is the school grounds, glowing like a marvelous garden of Eden, that provide the setting for the idyll that precedes the "fall" into the "real" world. Knowles sees this moment in history, this place in the country, as the last vestige of a vanishing era, and the school's location on the banks of two rivers — the clean, pure Devon and the "turbid, saline Nagaumsett" — illustrates its pivotal place at a turning point in time.

◆ Characters ◆

Knowles has created a friendship that parallels that of Nick Carraway and Jay Gatsby in F. Scott Fitzgerald's novel *The Great Gatsby* (1925). Gene, like Nick, records his friend's exceptional qualities and singular style. The parallel is particularly appropriate since Knowles, like Fitzgerald, is writing about the American dream and the loss of idealism. Gene's involvement with Phineas, however, is more intimate than Nick's relationship with Gatsby, and his own actions are more intricately connected with Finny's destiny. Gene's participation in Finny's fate irrevocably changes his own character.

This change in Gene's character structures the narrative and gives it a sense of progression, but the central core around which it revolves is the character of Phineas, Gene's roommate and best friend. In creating Phineas, Knowles builds a character upon an idea of excellence that a young man might aspire to, and he has succeeded in making Phineas a plausible person where he might easily have remained a wooden icon or symbol. Finny is the center of all social situations, the energy-giver who instigates and directs action. His wild imagination makes him a bold explorer of new possibility, and his sheer joy in existence contributes to his natural leadership. He is most at home in the world of sport — triumphing in traditional games with an almost casual competence, serving as the spirit of inspiration in games he creates to enchant his friends. Because

he is so good at handling conventional social arrangements, he loves a challenge and often dares himself to go beyond the limits set by authorities. He is both a rebel and a faithful supporter. He loves Devon School "truly and deeply," and he directs his rebellion against blind order that prohibits the establishment of the perfect order he envisions. Clever and audacious, he enjoys the effect of proclaiming the unsayable, yet he always remains within the bounds of genuine good taste as defined by the totally democratic (that is, not class-conscious) world he longs for. The tree was tremendous, an irate, steely black steeple beside the river.

The reader sees Phineas in the book through the eyes of his closest friend, Gene, who adores and, unfortunately, also envies him. Gene is Knowles's projection of his own early artistic consciousness. While reconstructing the formation of this creative intelligence, Knowles concentrates on the contradictions and uncertainties of a young man gradually coming to terms with the imperfections of his character and of the world. Because of Gene's doubts, he cannot fully and freely accept Finny's gift of unrestricted friendship and unrestrained candor, hiding his own fear behind a shield of fashionable sarcasm. Because he is unable to express his own feelings, he distrusts Finny's motives and ascribes to Finny his own competitive ambitions.

At the beginning of the narrative, Gene has a sense of himself as the center of the world. By the conclusion, he has been compelled to accept his own relatively insignificant position in a vast cosmos. Interestingly, this adjustment, essential to the process of maturity, enables him to understand Finny's gift for empathy and sharing.

A Separate Peace

This understanding is the beginning of a real strength in Gene's character — a strength born of disappointment, pain, and loss, as well as insight.

While a confrontation with the dark dimensions of his own psyche is crucial for Gene's growth, it is only one aspect of his life. To balance the psychic struggle, Knowles skillfully evokes the beauty of a New England summer for a young man temporarily transfixed by a perfect moment in time. Gene is the embodiment of the heightened emotion, instinct, and candor that make youth such a poignant, precious, and, of course, temporary state of existence. The fleeting nature of these qualities is underscored by Gene's degree of change at the end of the book. At the end of the school year in June, Gene has prepared himself for the adult world — specifically the war — by consciously creating a gulf between his former pure joy in existence and his newly-formed guarded attitude as he faces the coming tumult.

But in a final reflection on Devon, the bruised, wary seventeen-year-old merges with the adult's narrative consciousness to try to come to terms with the transforming power of his friendship with Finny. What remains with him is Finny's wonderful and singular presence. The legacy of their shared moments is Gene's sense of the best side of himself and his understanding that one does not have to give in to the worst ways of the world to survive. The "separate peace" that Gene arranges is with that part of himself that was corrupted by fear, and as he realizes on his return, he remains at least somewhat at peace because of this accommodation. And although he will always resent the world that drove him to compete with and not fully accept Finny, Gene has made peace with that

enemy also, recognizing that resistance through hate is negative and self-destructive, an impediment to the preservation of Finny's finest and most cherished gift, the life he bequeathed to his friend.

◆ Techniques ◆

None of the books John Knowles has written since *A Separate Peace* has achieved nearly the critical or popular success of his first novel. The reason is not that Knowles has exhausted his knowledge of the world but that *A Separate Peace* has a rare unity of subject and style. Knowles is a graceful and lucid writer, but his ability to use language most effectively seems to require a specific focus to prevent style from becoming merely decorative, an end in itself. Knowles's task in *A Separate Peace*, to establish the authenticity of Gene's sensibility — that is, his heightened sensitivity to the beauty of the natural world and his capacity for intense feeling about human nature — required the creation of a lyric voice to register the range of emotional response with poetic precision. His vivid descriptions of the countryside through four seasons enable him to echo the psychic landscape of his narrator in powerful imagery, and the clarity of his descriptions of certain key locations — a marble staircase, the testing tree, the pure river — offers an anchor and a context for the novel's most important events. Because Gene's voice throughout the narrative is generally sober and reflective, when Knowles shifts into a different rhythm the effect is often striking by contrast.

Knowles also knows the atmosphere of the school very well, and his unobtrusive presentation of details gradually gives the reader a full sense of the school's grounds. The other boys in Finny's "circle" are not presented with much depth, but they are drawn from familiar types, and Knowles has invested each one with enough personality to make him distinct. Knowles masterfully recreates the conversation of young men in groups, complete with all of the self-conscious, artificial linguistic apparatus. His ear for the telling phrase or the right slang gives his depiction of life in the dorms a convincing authenticity. As Gene grows throughout the year, the other boys are also affected by the changing times; but their transformations are mostly background for Gene's development. Still, the sense that they have grown, too, reinforces Gene's progress.

The first-person narrative draws the reader very close to Gene, an identification crucial to a full involvement in his quest. Knowles's skillful alternation between action and reflection, confrontation and relaxation, and seasons of ease and seasons of stress, prevents Gene's story from becoming routine or too predictable. Against these changes of pace, Gene's engaging desire to learn everything he can about all he encounters drives the narrative forward. Because Gene is such an open vessel, each setback has serious consequences, but because he has an essentially positive outlook, he can rebound quickly. The structure of the book follows this pattern of crisis and resolution until its conclusion, at which point it has been established that Gene will eventually become the man who can tell the story.

◆ Related Titles ◆

Knowles based *A Separate Peace* on a short story entitled "Phineas" that he had written about ten years earlier. The short story ends at the point where Gene goes to confess to Finny that he is responsible for Finny's fall from the tree. Knowles published "Phineas" in 1968 as part of the short story collection *Phineas: Six Stories*. The follow-up novel to *A Separate Peace, Peace Breaks Out*, serves as an interesting commentary on the post-World War II era.

◆ Adaptations ◆

In 1972 *A Separate Peace* was filmed by Paramount. The studio was unable to find a writer or director with the requisite cinematic genius to find images to correspond to the moods of Knowles's writing. Aside from the title and some scenes taken directly from the book, the film bears little resemblance to the novel and has been deservedly forgotten.

◆ Ideas for Group Discussions ◆

The opening pages of *A Separate Peace* serve as a prologue in the "present" when the book is being written, fifteen years after 1942, the critical year in the life of the novel's narrator, Gene Forrester. A mood of philosophical reflection develops as the narrator describes a visit back to his prep school. His memory soon takes him back to the days of his seventeenth year, at the convergence of youth and manhood in a timeless moment when "feeling was stronger than thought." This return enables Knowles to place the action within an introspective frame so that both "feeling" and "thought" are employed in the service of understanding. In addition to the perspective provided by the passage of time, another kind of framework emerges as Gene, the central subject of his own narrative, also becomes the narrator of a hero's life, the poetic story of the extraordinary Phineas.

1. How do the boys at Devon feel about the adults they know?

2. Why and how is the school and its setting important for Gene and the other boys at Devon?

3. What is the meaning of war for Gene and his friends? How does their attitude change? Does it affect all of the boys the same way?

4. How does the concept of friendship control and influence the lives of the boys at Devon?

5. Why does Gene fear the tree that Finny wants him to climb? How does his behavior in the tree reflect this fear?

6. What is the "separate peace" that Gene feels he has achieved? How has it affected the rest of his life?

7. Find several examples of the way in which Knowles uses the natural world (e.g., the tree, the rivers) to introduce and express the novel's important themes. Do you think these images work well as symbolism? Why?

8. What is the place of sports in the life of the boys at Devon? How does Knowles use sports to help portray his characters?

9. What kind of picture of American society does Knowles develop in his portrait of the United States in the early days of World War II? How might his writing the book in the 1950s affect his description of the 1940s?

10. Gene is described with considerable psychological insight, but Phineas is presented primarily from Gene's perspective. How does Phineas see himself? How might Phineas's self-image differ from Gene's image of him?

Leon Lewis
Appalachian State University

SERMONS AND SODA-WATER

Novellas

1960

◆

Author: John O'Hara

◆ Characters ◆

The unifying consciousness in the three novellas comprising *Sermons and Soda-Water* is that of Jim Malloy, who narrates all three in the first person. Malloy is O'Hara's most closely autobiographical character; he first appeared in the title story of O'Hara's first collection of short stories, *The Doctor's Son* (1935), as the son of a small-town doctor who, like O'Hara, resists the pressure to follow in his father's professional footsteps and instead becomes a journalist. In *Sermons and Soda-Water*, Malloy, like O'Hara, is in a reflective mood; each novella is composed of a personal reminiscence in which other characters take center stage for a time, but in which Malloy is a consistent presence and voice. Some of the same characters appear in "The Girl on the Baggage Truck" and "We're Friends Again," the first and third novellas, especially Junior and Polly Williamson, a Long Island socialite couple whose lifestyle recalls that of Fitzgerald's Gatsby. The novella's focus on a few characters allows O'Hara to develop some memorable individuals — particularly women — and among the more inter-esting are the film star Charlotte Sears, whose real life begins when her film career is cut short by a disfiguring car accident, and Bobbie McCrea, in "Imagine Kissing Pete," who becomes almost an heroic figure as she endures economic deprivation and an unfaithful husband.

◆ Social Concerns ◆

The three novellas that comprise *Sermons and Soda-Water* all deal in various ways with human relationships as they are affected by time and social conditions. In the first, "The Girl on the Baggage Truck," the setting is primarily New York in the 1930s, a world of speakeasies and vast differences between the rich and the poor. O'Hara uses his knowledge of the film industry in presenting the figure of Charlotte Sears, a movie star whose position as a public figure prevents her from having a normal love relationship and involves her with a snobbish, back-biting crowd. In "Imagine Kissing Pete," O'Hara turns again to Gibbsville, to chronicle the decline of Bobbie and Pete McCrea from a position in the Gibbsville social scene to near-poverty through drinking and infidelity, and their slow struggle to regain respectability. The third novella "We're Friends Again" returns to New York and to the excesses and superficiality of the affluent. Major portions of each of the three stories are set in the 1930s, the era of Prohibition, and alcohol consumption and abuse is a common activity for the characters, a fact that demonstrates the failure of the "Great Experiment" and also recalls O'Hara's own heavy drinking before he gave up alcohol in 1953.

◆ Themes ◆

Central to *Sermons and Soda-Water* is a concern for the fleeting nature of time. In his foreword to the collection, O'Hara refers to his own aging and to his sense of urgency about his own work: "I want to get it all down on paper while I can. . . . at fifty-five I have no right to waste time." What O'Hara wants to "get down on paper" is the story, from his perspective, of the decades between 1920 and 1950, which he was not willing to leave "in the hands of the historians and the editors of picture books." For the characters in these three novellas, time is an almost tangible quantity: youth is too short; life is measured by marriages, births, and funerals; the past is more vivid than the present. As always, O'Hara is also concerned here with the difficulty of forming and maintaining honest, warm relationships. People at all social levels marry for the wrong reasons, are unfaithful to their spouses, and seek meaning in money and alcohol. These two themes — the rapid passing of time, and human loneliness — are closely related in O'Hara's presentation of a period of

rapid social change in American life.

◆ Techniques ◆

O'Hara's use of the novella form influences both the tone and the perspective of *Sermons and Soda-Water*. One of the common characteristics of the novella is the use of a narrator whose limited interaction with the other characters necessarily limits the reader's knowledge of them to only those moments of greatest drama or conflict. Instead of the panoramic sweep of the typical O'Hara novel, in which a central character is presented through multiple points of view, the novellas offer glimpses of characters at widely-spaced intervals, so that character development is suggestive rather than exhaustive. The narrator, Jim Malloy, makes this approach explicit in "Imagine Kissing Pete," when he remarks, "Such additions I made to my friends' dossiers as I heard about them from time to time; by letters from them, conversations with my mother, an occasional newspaper clipping." This technique enhances the tone of nostalgic memory and makes Gibbsville a small town from which some people move away, rather than the center of the universe it often seems to be in O'Hara's novels. Similarly, the contrast between people of power, wealth, and prestige and those who live average, middle-class lives is sharpened by Malloy's movement between the worlds of New York and Hollywood, on the one hand, and his hometown of Gibbsville on the other.

◆ Literary Precedents ◆

In form, these three novellas are

reminiscent of the shorter works of Henry James, such as "Daisy Miller." James referred to the novella form as "the idea happily developed," which is similar to O'Hara's desire to "get it all down," and both use the narrator as a controlling device, providing a limited, personal perspective on the central characters. In theme, *Sermons and Soda-Water* provides a reflective summation of many of O'Hara's earlier concerns: the tension among people of various social classes, the difficulty of maintaining meaningful human relationships, and the resultant sense of human isolation in a rapidly-changing culture.

◆ Related Titles ◆

The reappearance of characters and places from O'Hara's other fictional works relates *Sermons and Soda-Water* to the rest of his canon. Especially striking is O'Hara's use of the autobiographical character Jim Malloy as his narrator; the young boy in the 1935 story "The Doctor's Son" is here a man of O'Hara's age, reflecting on the changes the years have brought to Gibbsville, its inhabitants, and himself.

Nancy Walker
Stephens College

SEVEN FOR A SECRET

Novel

1992

Author: Victoria Holt

◆ Social Concerns ◆

As she grew older, Holt increasingly integrated contemporary social issues into her novels. Her continuing concern with female independence is illustrated in *Seven for a Secret* by the narrator Frederica Hammond's dissatisfaction with village life after she finishes her education. Frederica is saved from the fate of governess or paid companion by the offer of a position as an assistant on the St. Aubyn's estate. More striking though is Holt's integration of a variety of modern concerns about social relations and religious belief. Loveless, mistaken marriages, divorce, and long-term, loving relationships without marriage are all present and are treated with Holt's customary lack of moralizing.

Especially interesting is the depiction of the relationship between Frederica's father and Karla that Frederica finds when she travels halfway around the world to meet him. Karla is the woman with whom he has shared happiness and tragedy, but they have chosen not to marry. Frederica is not at all shocked. The relationship is given another layer of interest by Karla's status as "half native, half Anglo-Saxon." The subject of miscegenation is not mined, but Holt touches interestingly on colonial attitudes and the questionable role of religion in colonialism. The portrayal of Luke Armour and his fellow missionaries allows an exploration of two types of proselytizing, one, stern and aesthetically dry, the other, humane and filled with beauty. Even the rejection of marriage by Frederica's father holds the implication that true love does not need religious sanction, though they are protected from disapproval by the native culture they live in and, ironically, by Karla's half-caste status. In an event that offers a parallel to this gentle rejection of the institution of marriage, Frederica leaves England because of the discovery that the first wife of Crispin St. Aubyn, whom she has come to love, is not dead. Crispin wishes to marry anyway, insisting that the wife who used and deserted him can be bribed. Frederica leaves rather than staying to be tempted. She returns to him, however, before she learns that his first marriage has been voided because his wife was already married. The question of whether she returned to marry him despite the prohibition or to face up to the temptation is left open.

The connection between religious zeal and corruption is made in the portrayal of Mr. Dorian, the uncle and guardian of Frederica's childhood friend, Rachel. Both girls are made uneasy not only by his zealotry but also by the undue interest he shows in them, especially when they are praying in their nightgowns. After he attempts to attack Frederica, from which she is saved by Crispin St. Aubyn, Dorian commits suicide from fear of exposure. Frederica's Aunt Sophie explains, "He wanted to be a saint, but he had certain instincts. He tried to suppress them and they came out this way."

♦ Themes ♦

Seven for a Secret is about the destructive power of secrets and the healing power of honesty and love. The title refers to the children's rhyme that ends, "And seven for a secret/never to be told." The poem and the picture of seven magpies that illustrates it help suppress the truth about the novel's principal secret: the death of a child under extraordinary circumstances and the substitution of another child. If a secret is breached by an unscrupulous person, such as Gaston Marchmont who marries Tamarisk St. Aubyn, it gives him or her dangerous power. The effects of secrecy are particularly noticeable in the relationship between Frederica and Crispin. Secrecy destroys because it erects walls between people, like the bitterness of Lucy, Crispin's real mother, and like the wall that Frederica feels between herself and Crispin even after their marriage. "There are times when I can forget it," she says. Yet, "I can't get close to you while it is there."

The attempted molestation of Frederica by Dorian is the secret that brings the fourteen-year-old girl and the young man together. The secret that Crispin carries inside him about his own birth nearly drives them apart. Disclosure, while it may be painful and difficult, as is Crispin's revelation of his parentage to Tamarisk, who has grown up believing they are siblings and that he is the heir to the estate, always brings relief and is rewarded with greater happiness. Frederica forces her husband to reveal his secret to Tamarisk who re-affirms her love for him, his control of the estate, and her desire that this revelation never make a difference between them.

Effectively intertwined with the concern for the negative power of secrecy are the ideas of lost innocence and the instability of material things. Frederica's move from a home filled with unhappy memories to her aunt's Wiltshire cottage in the village of Harper's Green is seemingly a move away from tragedy and into a world of innocence. Soon she becomes aware of the confusing and frightening reality hidden by its placid façade. The unwelcome attention and violence of Dorian steals her youth and his suicide reveals to the village its own dark side. Frederica says of her experience, "I grew up in that moment." Increasingly, as Frederica becomes aware of the village's secret history, it is apparent that innocence was only a delusion. It is a delusion also if the characters believe that material things, houses like Cedar Hall and St. Aubyn's, and fortunes like those associated with Crispin's tenuously-held estate, are a firm foundation for identity and future hopes. The experience of both Frederica and her friend Tamarisk proves that only love built on a foundation of "trust, faith and understanding," can give strength and stability, while mansions and fortunes may slip away in a moment.

◆ Characters ◆

Frederica, who narrates the story, is not clearly differentiated from most earlier Holt heroines. The character remains nearly unchanged from *Mistress of Mellyn* (1960) onward. Only the social issues with which she comes into contact change. Frederica Hammond is an independent spirit, not unduly concerned with the opinions of others, and is unwilling to be constricted by limits on her life and happiness. As with earlier Holt heroines, curiosity is a dominant feature of her personality and at one point she must be warned, "Sometimes it can get you into trouble." Frederica is not unshockable, but she recovers quickly from shocks and her practical, compassionate nature takes over. She accepts with only brief surprise the news that Rachel Grey is expecting the child of Gaston Marchmont, who has recently wed their friend Tamarisk. She begins immediately to calculate a way out of this disaster. Within moments she sets the plan in action. Frederica is an action heroine. Practical yet passionate, she is ultimately rewarded for the traits that "can get you into trouble."

Crispin St. Aubyn, too, is not essentially different from Connan TreMellyn, although Holt's male protagonists have become more sensitive and less stern over the years. He keeps his problems to himself, which leaves his actions open to misinterpretation. Even as he proposes to Frederica and holds her in his arms, she is filled with "fear and suspicions." Her mind constantly returns to Crispin's violence toward Dorian when he interrupted the older man's attack on her. He is a tender lover, but capable of violent emotion and action. There is the mystery of his first wife's desertion and death, and the murder of Gaston Marchmont, neither of which he can fully explain or clear himself of the implication that he is somehow responsible. When his first wife re-appears and he is seen with her by Aunt Sophie, his character comes into greater clarity. Against all reason, he believes that he can bribe the ex-wife, a scheming former actress, to leave him alone, and marry Frederica. What surprises Frederica is not the violation of religious or legal boundaries, but that Crispin would have kept these arrangements secret from her. He is a man defined by secrets until the most fundamental secret, the secret of his birth, is revealed.

There is more drama in the secondary characters of Tamarisk St. Aubyn and Rachel Grey. These are Frederica's childhood friends, each of whom has a well-defined personality. More importantly, they have complex emotional responses and are given the ability to learn and change. Tamarisk, rich and frivolous, must first make an impulsive and ill-advised match with Gaston Marchmont, which teaches her about suffering, before she can meet Luke Armour and learn dedication to a cause beyond herself. As she falls in love with Luke and decides to stay behind on Casker's Island to help with the mission school she retains the gaiety and "comedy turn" of her personality, but replaces frivolity with a sense of purpose that she never had before. Rachel Grey's fate is tied to Tamarisk's by Gaston Marchmont and her fate has its more melancholy aspects. Marchmont leaves Rachel pregnant and marries Tamarisk. Rachel, an orphan who as a girl slept with her door locked to keep her Uncle Dorian out, has few reserves against both heartbreak and more intimate betrayal. Frederica arrives just in time to prevent Rachel's suicide and introduce the hope of a solution to Rachel's seemingly insoluble problem. She convinces Daniel Grindle, who loves Rachel and has been rejected by her, that he must marry Rachel and accept her child as his own. This particular incident reveals more about Frederica than about Daniel or Rachel. As she discloses Rachel's secret to Daniel, Frederica thinks, "I was going too far. That sense of the important part I must play — had been chosen to play — in this tragedy was fast disappearing. I was trying to arrange other people's lives. It was arrogant. It was meddling . . ." The solution is not without its complications and setbacks. Rachel does not love Daniel as she loved Gaston and Daniel, a gentleman farmer, is not a gentleman. Daniel himself has more difficulty accepting the child than he foresaw. They overcome their problems, though, with a love that matures and deepens over time.

◆ Techniques ◆

Secrecy is the dominant theme of *Seven for a Secret*, and those secrets are enclosed in, and closely associated with, a series of houses. Interestingly, as the covers of Holt novels have moved from showing a windswept, forbidding mansion toward portraits of the imposing heroines, the houses in the novels have proliferated to carry a complex symbolic load. Lavender House, actually a cottage, houses the "genteel poverty" left to Frederica's mother after her profligate father's

death and her husband's desertion when the child was one year old. The bitterness and anger never leave her mother. They are fueled by the view of Cedar Hall, the grand house where she was raised, which she sees constantly from her windows. The Hall now houses the *nouveau riche* Carter family. The contrast between the two residences exerts an effect that is nearly physical.

After a dispute with Mrs. Carter about who will arrange flowers in the church, a dispute won by Mrs. Carter, Frederica's mother has a stroke. Her illness precipitates Frederica's move to Wiltshire and her Aunt Sophie. Frederica moves to her aunt's comfortable cottage, The Rowans, but this modest dwelling is overshadowed by St. Aubyn's, the mansion where Crispin and Tamarisk have been reared by a series of nannies and governesses. The Rowans houses the secret of the real character and whereabouts of Frederica's father and his relationship with her aunt before his ill-advised marriage to her mother. The answers to these mysteries are gradually revealed to Frederica, shaping her impressions of the father she never knew.

Bell House, "red brick and gracious," has an external appearance that belies its suffocating atmosphere of religious mania and perverse sexuality. Their experience with the owner of Bell House forces both Rachel and Frederica to grow up quickly and gives Rachel's life a sad spin, which she finds hard to overcome. St. Aubyn's saw the neglected upbringing of Tamarisk and Crispin, an upbringing involving parents so unfamiliar with their infant son that another baby could be exchanged for him when he is killed in a bizarre accident.

In contrast to all of these is the

house on Casker's Island where Ronald Hammond and his friend Karla live. It is a cool, light and open, native-style home surrounded by flowers. The profusion of flowers on the island and Tamarisk's successful introduction of flowers into the dour religious atmosphere of the mission offer a bright contrast to the incident that caused Mrs. Hammond's stroke.

The central secret and solutions to the remaining mysteries are found in the house that Frederica calls "The House of the Seven Magpies." This cottage is home to the sisters, Lucy and Flora Lane, both Crispin's former nannies. Lucy, the earlier nanny, is aloof and bitter. Her character is attributed to the fact that she must care for her sister, Crispin's second nanny, whose mind became mysteriously unhinged many years earlier. Slowly it becomes apparent that the cottage and Flora's confused mind can provide the key to the mystery of Crispin's birth, "the secret never to be told," the death of the true heir to St. Aubyn's, and Gaston Marchmont's death. The solutions to the mysteries are not widely shared and any need to make painful decisions about blame or punishment are rendered moot when the cottage burns and Flora dies.

In the final act of the novel, Crispin and Frederica, now happily married, find in the ruins of the Lanes's cottage the picture of seven magpies that hung in the nursery. This picture and its cautionary rhyme were a daily reminder to Flora not to reveal the secrets of the cottage. They destroy the picture and all of the need for secrecy that the picture and house represent.

◆ Literary Precedents ◆

Seven for a Secret shares with Holt's earlier novels a background in the gothic and romance fiction of the eighteenth and nineteenth centuries. The contemporary appeal of her stories is enhanced with the introduction of modern concerns, such as child abuse and the proper role of women, and a reduced reliance on the possibility of the supernatural for the chill of fear. The title of the novel is taken from a children's rhyme in which Holt was quick to note the dark implications, which she draws out in the story. Frederica, as she herself notes, has the character of a "romancer." When she first sees the picture of the magpies that illustrates the rhyme, she is struck by the tinge of evil given to the message by the birds. Frederica is attuned to these feelings of uncanniness as others are not. As Tamarisk St. Aubyn writes in her letter to Frederica from Casker's Island, "One wouldn't have thought it would happen to real people . . . especially those in Harper's Green. Life goes on in a dreary sort of pattern for years, and suddenly drama strikes." The novel illustrates that Tamarisk is only half right, though. It is a characteristic of the romance that it deals with the eruption of drama, the unusual, into life. But the exposure of the dark subplot only appears to be sudden. Behind that "dreary sort of pattern" is a long-standing web of deceptions and in this we see the novel's gothic literary background. In the truth about Lucy's indiscretion and Crispin's birth, the past returns to haunt the present and the lives of "real people."

In the same letter, Tamarisk notes that the surprising truth about "Flora and the babies" is "like something out of the Bible or Shakespeare." She is correct in pointing out the connection of the story to plots, such as that of *The Winter's Tale* (c.1610-1611), that revolve around mistaken identity, misplaced children, separated twins, or orphans who are discovered to be royalty. Such tales exercise a fascination that seems to be akin to the attraction of the Oedipus myth or the feeling popularly supposed to be common among children that they must be orphans or the lost children of famous parents. The story has in common with the Bible its air of providentiality, exemplified by Frederica's statement that she has a part she "must play," that she "was chosen to play," as if total revelation were inevitable. Harper's Green seems a paradise, until its fallen character is exposed and its innocents see clearly what the face of evil looks like.

◆ Ideas for Group Discussions ◆

Seven for a Secret offers a good opportunity to approach the topic of the clash of cultures from several perspectives. Casker's Island is a microcosm of colonial activity, with the focus on religious beliefs. Explicit value judgments are rarely expressed, but events and attitudes on the island can be compared to events in England with an eye toward determining the novel's implied values. Readers who have read Holt's early novels might be interested in comparing the male characters of this novel to earlier male protagonists like Connan TreMellyn of *Mistress of Mellyn* (1960) or Napier Stacy of *The Shivering Sands* (1969). In the later novels, these characters seem to have become more sensitive and less inclined to violence, even less sexually active. The novels are themselves a record of cultural changes in the last thirty-five years.

1. Frederica describes herself as a "romancer." She agrees that she "mak[es] up stories about people . . . and half of them without a trace of truth to them." How important is this facet of her personality? How does it blend with her practical and truth-loving nature? What role does it play in the plot?

2. What are the points of comparison and contrast between Mrs. Hammond's experience with the vicar and the church in England and the missionaries' encounters with the chief, Olam, and the religious rituals of Casker's Island?

3. The attack on Frederica in Barrow's Wood plays a central role in the novel. What are some of the ways that it influences relationships in the story and the development of the plot?

4. Is the handling of the issue of child abuse — its perpetrators and its intended victims — psychologically persuasive?

5. Does the youthful character of Tamarisk contain the seeds of the mature woman? Is the change in her outlook presented in a way that makes it believable?

6. The marriage of Rachel Grey and Daniel Grindle is a marriage of necessity. What stages does their relationship go through? How do they resolve their problems?

7. In *Seven for a Secret* parents are often absent, through death, desertion or neglect. What kind of parent is Ronald Hammond? Can he be compared with Mrs. Hammond or Mrs. St. Aubyn? With surrogate parents like the Dorians and Aunt Sophie?

8. Frederica is unhappy with the knowledge that Crispin did not intend to tell her of his first wife's return. In a discussion with her father, she says, "It is dishonest." He responds, "It is love, and did we not agree that there is nothing in life so wonderful as true love?" Does the book make completely convincing the argument that "true love" requires total honesty?

9. What kind of a man is Crispin St. Aubyn? Are he and Frederica a good match, considering their experiences, personalities, values, and expectations about love?

10. Through Frederica's observations, the novel offers a critique of Christian conversion efforts on the island. What are the problems she sees? What does she think of them? Can the problems be overcome?

11. Are the characters' attitudes toward pedophilia and sex outside of marriage consistent with modern expectations about Victorian attitudes and beliefs?

Rebecca E. Martin
Pace University

SEVENTH SON

Novel

1987

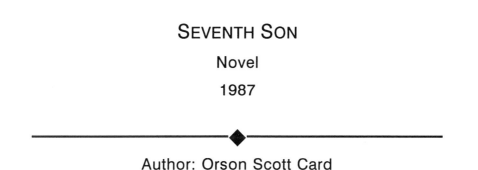

Author: Orson Scott Card

◆ Social Concerns ◆

In *Seventh Son* Card has created an alternate universe with an alternate history of the settlement of the American colonies. In addition, magic works in this alternate universe and exists side by side with Christianity. Social problems arise because of the existence of both religion and magic — much as the witch hunts of earlier times arose from the belief in magic and the churches' insistence that magic was evil. So, Alvin, the main character of the book, and all of his family, who have strong magical gifts, are looked on with suspicion by religious people, even though they go to church and never flaunt their talents. Alvin's older sister is forbidden by her husband from practicing even the most basic household magics, such as warding off evil or making bread rise and cheese age. She is forced to practice surreptitiously, and her husband never notices because he has forbidden, on the basis of his religious beliefs, a practice he has never seen or experienced. The local preacher even convinces himself that it is his duty to kill Alvin to pro-tect his community, although all signs point towards Alvin's being a major benefit to the community. Thus fundamentalist religious beliefs condemn people with magical gifts as "unnatural" even though the gifts are clearly natural and not derived from any source other than Nature.

◆ Themes ◆

The main theme of *Seventh Son* is the conflict between good and evil. Alvin Miller is a "maker," so endowed with magical talent that he can create from raw material without tools. He discovers his opponent is "The Unmaker," a being that desires destruction of all living things. Alvin Miller, then, is a god-figure and because of his persecution at the hands of the religious authorities, he is also an analogue of Jesus Christ. The subtheme of *Seventh Son* is persecution of those different from the norm and religious encouragement of that persecution.

The theme of persecution of "different" people is not a new one. The twist here is that those persecuted are not different looking but differently endowed with magical talent in a world where everyone has some magical talent. Alvin and his family differ from other people in the strength of their magical gifts and their contact with natural elements. This causes other not-so-gifted people at best to feel uncomfortable around them and at worst to actively wish them harm. They are persecuted by believers not because they are unbelievers but because they possess a strong talent and choose not to deny or suppress it at the whim of others. Ironically, the talent is beneficial to society but condemned as evil by the very people, the clerics, who should recognize its beneficence.

◆ Characters ◆

The main character of *Seventh Son* is Alvin Miller. The rest of his family and the character Taleswapper exist as types: the stern-but-loving father and mother, the patient older brother, the wild brothers, and the prim sister. To be sure, there is some interplay between the parents, the siblings, and the wandering minstrel Taleswapper aimed at setting the stage, but ultimately only Alvin's actions count in moving the plot forward. Even Alvin is not a rounded character, mostly because he is still too young, even at the close of this novel, to be fully formed. Alvin is a "maker," the highest type of magical talent, and to some extent a Christ figure. He has such perfect rapport with natural elements that he can shape stone, wood, and other elements without tools. These elements are so in tune with Alvin that they cannot be used to hurt him because they simply will not cooperate. For example, a beam accidentally dropped on his head

splits itself apart before it lands.

Alvin is very aware of his gifts and the responsibility they demand. He knows he must use his talent for the benefit of the community and that there is an elemental force he calls the "Unmaker" who will try to unmake the world just as hard as Alvin will try to make it. The book ends as Alvin is about to be apprenticed to a smith, another maker of a sort, to get him away from the suspicious community of Vigor.

◆ Techniques ◆

In order to convey the rusticity of the Millers and most of the other characters in the story, the writer adopts a country accent for most of his characters but not the third person narrator. The characters use nonstandard English of the type usually associated with the Appalachian area of the United States. For instance, they refer to "hetting up the stove a mite." Card also provides a type of Greek chorus in the character of Taleswapper, a wandering-minstrel type, who spouts poetry by William Blake because in this alternate universe, he is Blake. Taleswapper provides a different, more cosmopolitan viewpoint than is usually available in Vigor. He also acts as a catalyst, helping Alvin to see his true calling, without interfering with Fate.

◆ Literary Precedents ◆

Like much of Card's work, this story is steeped in biblical tradition. Alvin is a Christ-figure, capable of working miracles and clearly guarded by some higher power. As the established Pharisees in the Bible distrusted Jesus, so the Reverend Thrower in *Seventh Son* distrusts Alvin and his family. The reverend manages to influence much of Alvin's own community to regard the Miller family and Alvin in particular as suspicious, much as Jesus was persecuted by his own people. The wandering minstrel as Greek chorus is a familiar figure also. The minstrel guild of Anne McCaffrey's Pern series comes to mind. Like Taleswapper, the minstrels in Pern bring news and trade secrets; they also help people to understand their roles in life and show courses of action, without demanding that action be taken.

◆ Related Titles ◆

The story of Alvin's struggles with the "Unmaker" are continued in *Red Prophet* (1988) and *Prentice Alvin* (1989). In each of the books Alvin has increasingly difficult encounters with the "Unmaker." He also journeys toward union with his soulmate, Peggy Guesler. He must overcome the spiritual obstacles to this union. Each encounter with the Unmaker increases Alvin's strength and understanding.

◆ Ideas for Group Discussions ◆

Alvin Miller is clearly a Christ-figure. As such, he is persecuted by his own people as well as pursued by a supernatural being, the "Unmaker." Religious leaders encourage this persecution, much as the Pharisees in the Bible encouraged the persecution of Christ and his followers. There is also a suggestion that religious fundamentalists often miss the connection between Nature and Religion, a failure of perception that led to the witch hunts

of centuries not so long past.

1. What parallels can you draw between Jesus Christ and Alvin?

2. What parallels can you draw between the "Unmaker" and the devil as he appears in the Bible?

3. What parallels between today's social discrimination can you see in the persecution of the Millers and other strong magical talents?

4. The Reverend Thrower wants to be a good man, but he fails because of misperceptions. Explain his misperceptions and discuss what led to them.

5. Do you see any parallels between Reverend Thrower and the historical persecutors of witches in Salem, Massachusetts?

6. Envy of property or prosperity often triggered historical witchhunts. Do you think this is a factor in Seventh Son?

7. The Mullers' "talents" are looked on suspiciously by the less talented. Do you see any parallels between the Mullers' talents and modern science, both often at odds with organized religion?

Margery L. Brown
State University of New York
at Farmingdale

THE SHADOW KNOWS

Novel

1974

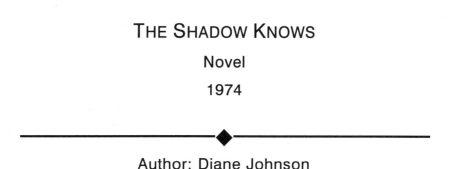

Author: Diane Johnson

◆ Social Concerns/Themes ◆

Set in northern California, in the suburbs of Sacramento, *The Shadow Knows* deals with such universal themes and social concerns as race relations, especially between whites and blacks; relations between household help and the people who employ them; and the eternal triangle of husband-wife-mistress. Without pushing any special feminist agenda, Johnson is particularly concerned in this novel with the efforts of a divorced woman trying to look after her small children, earn an advanced degree, hang on to her lover, and keep her sanity.

Race relations come into focus through the relations between household help and their employers: Both social concerns are intertwined. Mrs. N. Hexam first employs Osella Barnes to help clean and cook and look after her four small children. Recently widowed, Osella is an enormous black woman still in her forties who had been Gavin Hexam's mammy long ago. Osella takes a dislike to N., apparently goes mad, and is dismissed. Evalin Wilson, another black woman, but shy and handsome, replaces her. She is genuinely devoted to N. and her chil-

dren, and looks after everyone well but herself. N.'s concern for Ev is also real and they become still closer after N.'s marriage to Gavvy breaks up and she moves with Ev and the children into a small unit in a housing development on the outskirts of Sacramento. Their relationship demonstrates that whites and blacks can overcome racial antagonisms, although Ev's lover, A. J. Harper, seems menacing and mean not only to Ev, whom he physically abuses, but to N. as well.

The affair that N. has with her husband's colleague, Andrew Mason, seems to awaken in Andrew a sense of passion and sexual intensity he did not know he possessed after years of marriage to his wife, Cookie. N.'s husband finally suspects something and leaves when N. refuses to end the affair. When, on Christmas Eve, Andrew sends N. a note ending the affair, she is nearly crushed, but this is not the main, or at least the only, cause of her emotional state a week later when strange events begin to occur, such as the front door of her unit being slashed, a dead cat thrown on her doorstep, and shadowy figures apparently lurking about the place. The conflict between appearance and reality, or reality taking ambiguous form as shadowy presences, is really the main theme of the novel. It transcends the feminist concern, which is also evident, of a single, not affluent, mostly isolated woman trying to make a life amidst a dreary set of experiences.

◆ Characters ◆

N. Hexam (she never reveals her first name) is the principal character and first-person narrator of the novel, which takes place over a period of eight days, Wednesday, January 1, to Wednesday, January 8. During this period, N. also looks back over her life with Gavin, her former husband; her affair with Andrew Mason; Osella's entrance into their lives; Evalin's marriage to Clyde Wilson, her estranged husband; and other significant events of the past. She does this as part of her attempt to sort out what is happening to her now. Her feeling that someone is trying to kill her or Evalin or all of them increases as the threats increase, including the harassing phone calls from Osella and the "phantom caller," who is never identified. In fact, Evalin does die, ostensibly the result of chronic pancreatitis aggravated by New Year's Eve celebrating, but possibly accelerated by the beating she receives in the laundry room two nights later.

Ev's death brings out both the best and the worst in N. — her genuine love for the handsome black woman and her inability to cope with her problems effectively enough to forestall disaster. For all of her sensitivity, intelligence, and education (she is earning an M.A. in linguistics), N. emerges as something of a klutz when it comes to dealing with the practical side of life as well as her own personal relationships.

What redeems her, apart from a wry sense of humor, is her relentless search to find reality and truth.

Gavin, or Gavvy, N.'s husband, is a mean-spirited, regressive man whom N. helped put through law school but who sees no need to finance her further education after their divorce. N. learns to despise him, with cause. Her lover, Andrew Mason, whom she adores, turns into the kind of philanderer her friend, Bess Harvill, describes — the kind that never leaves his wife after all. He cruelly ends the affair with N. with an abrupt note, then soon afterwards calls her, promising to take up with her again, but never shows up. Nor are the other men in the novel shown to be much better. Evalin's husband is a good-for-nothing whom she is well rid of, although he keeps coming around; A. J., her lover, is brutal at times and unreliable, but Ev loves him and keeps going back to him; Inspector Dice of the Police Department is patronizing and finally impatient when N. tries to convince him that a crime has been committed (Ev's death) and that danger still lurks.

Women emerge as being not much better. N.'s best friend, Bess, turns out to be someone who envies and hates N.; Osella is a constant threat and helps drive the Hexams apart; Cookie Mason is a stereotyped middle-class house-proud wife desperately trying to hang on to her husband. Only Evalin appears as a woman fully deserving N.'s (or anyone's) love and devotion, and she herself is careless and ineffectual when it comes to her own well-being.

◆ Techniques/Literary Precedents ◆

The Shadow Knows aptly takes its title

from the old radio mystery play that used to begin with a frightening voice saying, "Who knows what evil lurks in the hearts of men? The Shadow knows." The foregoing analysis suggests that there is plenty of evil in everyone's heart, even N.'s, but the vehicle Johnson uses for its presentation is a mixture of the detective novel, the Gothic romance, and the surreal fiction of Franz Kafka (whose best known protagonists are named "K.").

As one reviewer described the novel, it is like "Charlotte Brontë filtered through Kafka, or like a strange dream in which Agatha Christie is transformed into a feverish metaphysician." Johnson uses many different devices to develop her fiction, chief among them the withholding of details after they have first been mentioned. For example, N. mentions Andrew's letter twice before revealing the actual contents sometime later. Similarly, she mentions that Gavvy — like everyone else, one of her suspects — once hurt Ev, but only later does she say how or when. This is standard detective novel procedure, which Johnson uses along with other devices that build suspense. She even consciously parodies the genre by introducing "The Famous Inspector," a character who appears only in N.'s mind, as she tries to imagine what he will do and, near the end, attempts to impersonate him herself by tracking down Ev's "murderer." The strange sounds that N. hears as the door to her unit in the housing complex is attacked recall the sounds Jane Eyre hears, and N.'s meditations share the qualities of both K.'s and Jane's broodings on events.

Except for the fact that the principal character and narrator is a woman, and it is her life the novel is mainly concerned with, *The Shadow Knows* is not otherwise a feminist novel, for Johnson does not try to develop N. as a kind of exemplary heroine, and she is as much concerned with the nature of reality and perception as she is with her protagonist.

Jay L. Halio
University of Delaware

THE SHADOW RIDERS

Novel

1982

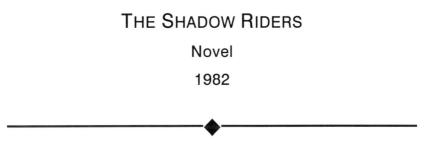

Author: Louis L'Amour

◆ Characters ◆

The three Traven brothers — Dal, Mac and Jesse — are dark, tall, tough, and indistinguishable. In fact, the three are very similar to the three Sackett brothers Orrin, Tell, and Tyrel (the same three actors, Sam Elliott, Tom Selleck, and Jeff Osterhage played the Traven brothers in the TV version of *The Shadow Riders* and the Sackett brothers in the TV miniseries *The Sacketts*).

The love interest in the novel, Dal's fiancée Kate Connery, is a stronger, cleverer, more plucky woman than Angie Lowe in the earlier *Hondo* (1953). This increased strength and intelligence for a L'Amour heroine may have resulted from the influence of the women's liberation movement on American society. As Kate is more active in the novel than earlier L'Amour heroines, she is also more violent: She stabs one man in the throat with a pointed stick and leaves another to drown. Also, although Kate is more resourceful, the knowledge she uses comes from a male. Before she acts, she constantly asks herself what Dal would do in the same situation and tries to remember what he has taught her.

More interesting in *The Shadow Riders* are the minor characters: Happy Jack Traven, Martin Connery, and Maddy Wyatt. Jack Traven, the independent black sheep of the family, is obviously a favorite of L'Amour. Although a man of questionable — possibly even criminal — background, he nevertheless preaches L'Amour's moral doctrines. The character Martin Connery is not fully developed but is interesting historically: He is a pirate rancher. In an interview printed in *The Shadow Riders*, L'Amour tells of reading about pirates who worked the Gulf and then settled down to become ranchers in Texas. Maddy Wyatt, a great contrast to Martin, is the typical motherly soul upon whom all the neighbors can depend, but the warmth and spirit of her dialogue makes her character rise above the stereotype. When the Traven brothers arrive at her home, she welcomes them enthusiastically, "Light an' set!" She then describes how she avoided capture by the slavers: she "bellied down in the ol' rifle pit up yonder" and stayed hidden until the marauders left. It is characters like Happy Jack, Martin and Maddy who color the otherwise sketchy background of this book.

The Shadow Riders

With the publication of the first Sackett novel *The Daybreakers,* in 1960, L'Amour changed his focus from a single man on the frontier to families, especially brothers, working together to establish and maintain their communities. The Sackett novels now number eighteen, and L'Amour has created other families, including the Talons, Chantrys and, in *The Shadow Riders,* the Travens. L'Amour's concentration on the family reinforces traditional middle-class values and the growing concern with the state of the family in American society of the 1970s and 1980s.

In an interview published along with *The Shadow Riders,* L'Amour explained his views on the importance of the family, past and present: "A lot of people think the family's going downhill. I don't think so at all . . . In those days the family was a unit, you see, and they worked together . . . it gave a whole lot of unity and a whole lot of strength to the country itself."

◆ Themes ◆

Building on the theme of the importance of the family, L'Amour tries to show that the caring of a family can spread outward to the community. When little Susan Atherton's mother, for example, is captured by rebel slave traders, the Travens take Susan with them and leave her in the care of their neighbor Maddy Wyatt who lovingly welcomes the girl.

Another important theme, a natural to a Civil War story, is slavery. Although L'Amour does not explore to the moral depths possible the irony of white slavery after the emancipation by the whites of black slaves, he does take the opportunity to give the history of the word slave (early Roman slaves coming from Slavic countries), to explain that whites as well as blacks have been slaves, and to condemn those who have enslaved their own people and races.

Still another theme of *The Shadow Riders* is the greed and corruption which follows war. Colonel Ashford, a rebel unwilling to give up the cause, steals women and animals to trade for munitions to mount another campaign. L'Amour exposes Ashford's idealism as a front for greed. Happy Jack Traven, uncle to the Traven brothers, speaks for L'Amour: "There's some folks will justify anything if it will make them a dollar. Commonest excuse is that if they don't do it somebody else will." Although L'Amour understands how hard times were after the war with men returning home to ruined plantations and three men available for every job, he sees no excuse for dishonesty and thievery. His solution for unemployed men is to set them to work farming, to create rather than destroy.

◆ Techniques ◆

Perhaps because *The Shadow Riders* was written to turn immediately into a television movie, it skimps on L'Amour's typically strong portrayal of setting. For every evocative description like that of the town of Refugio — "a muddy, rutted alleyway between two rows of nondescript shacks, sodden with rain" — there are several clichéd descriptions empty of sensual or emotional content. The narrator at one point, for example, tells his readers, "It was almighty still, and there was nobody around a body could see." L'Amour is working with a setting other than the West — the gulf coast of Texas — but, aside from writing about whooping cranes and having one villain fall in a swampy pit, fails to take full advantage of this new setting.

Another related change is an increase in dialogue. This, too, may be rooted in the quick conversion to a television script, but it also has roots in the nature of the heroes. In a family novel the characters must talk to each other, whereas earlier L'Amour novels with the lone man against the wilderness and hostile forces need more description of action and setting — there can only be so much interior monologue.

◆ Literary Precedents ◆

Fiction on the corruption following the Civil War abounds. It ranges in quality from Margaret Mitchell's extraordinarily popular *Gone with the Wind* (1936) to Faulkner's portraits of the Compson, Sartoris, Snopes, Stevens, and Sutpen clans in his short stories and novels. L'Amour's fiction does not reach the level of Margaret Mitchell's nor even approach that of Faulkner in intellectual depth, emotional power, and artistry. There are, nevertheless, similarities. All are interested in families, the relationships between their members, and depiction of the postwar South. All depict the mixture of races and nationalities — whites, blacks and Hispanics — both in friendship and hatred. All value those who exhibit courage, who endure and who fight the battle of good over evil. All emphasize the importance of the land and the strength that it gives to those who possess it.

◆ Related Titles ◆

L'Amour has not written of the Traven family again, although, as mentioned before, his Sackett novels are very similar. Similar character types and plot elements can also be found in other L'Amour novels. The sweet little girl figure (Susan Atherton in *The Shadow Riders*) also appears in *Down the Long Hills* (1968). L'Amour has used semi-retired pirates like Martin Connery in *The Shadow Riders* twice before, in *Lando* (1962) and *The Sackett Brand* (1965). The pathos L'Amour tries to create with the Travens finding their loyal family dog butchered when they return home after the war plays on the same emotions he tried to create in Hondo when Hondo's dog is slaughtered while trying to protect him.

◆ Adaptations ◆

The Shadow Riders was made into a successful television movie in 1982. A sign of its popularity and relative quality as a television movie is its reshowing numerous times since its first broadcast. The movie starred Sam Elliott (Dal), Tom Selleck (Mac), Jeff Osterhage (Jesse) as the Traven brothers and Katherine Ross (Kate Connery) as the love-interest. The first half of the movie follows the book rather closely, but the second half veers off, especially when Kate dresses as a nun to visit the imprisoned women to tell them of the escape plan. In an interview published at the end of *The Shadow Riders*, L'Amour expressed general satisfaction with the movie, although he felt that the action he provided in the novel needed no expansion.

Ann W. Engar
University of Utah

SHADOWS

Novel

1986

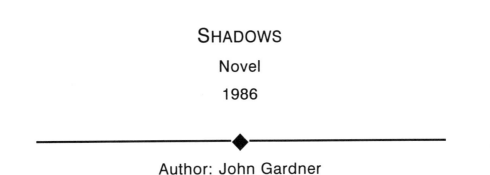

Author: John Gardner

◆ Social Concerns/Themes ◆

Unlike *Stillness,* his other unfinished novel, *Shadows* was never really abandoned. Gardner began work on it the mid-1970s, but not long before his death he told his fiancée, Susan Thornton, that he had "figured out how to fix *Shadows.*" Editors and critics agree that he must have meant that he felt he would be able to complete the plot and to resolve the problems the text had created. What he left behind, two fairly complete sections and seven coherent fragments, suggests that this may have been, like his other two variations on the detective genre, another of Gardner's ambitious, "big" novels.

Both *The Sunlight Dialogues* (1972) and *Mickelsson's Ghosts* (1982) allude insistently to the conventions of detective romance. Officer Fred Clumly and Professor Peter Mickelsson must employ those ratiocinative skills and the tenacity associated with the detective hero to solve a mystery and thereby bring some order to a community. Gerald Craine, the hero of *Shadows,* is a professional detective. Once extraordinarily successful in Chicago, he has, in semi-retirement, opened a small office in peaceful Carbondale, Illinois.

The name of the town, however, suggests something less than a pastoral setting, and both Craine and Gardner have fun punning with this name. It is no Eden in its recent crime statistics either. Although Craine has had only trivial crimes to investigate for the past few years, a series of six serial murders has recently disturbed the community. Craine is dragged into these when a mysterious local character, Two-heads Carnac, warns Craine that he is being watched. He also has a paranoid suspicion that the local police may intend to pin the killings on him. The person watching Craine proves to be a client, a young lady who fears that she may be an intended victim of the serial killer.

Beyond the themes of restoring a fallen world, or a dale of carbon, which are not worked out fully because the crime is not solved, *Shadows* meditates on two themes, one traditional and even central to Gardner's fiction and the other new for his work. Unlike traditional fictional detectives, Craine is a deliberate amnesiac. His intentionally repressing memories is a rejection of his past and the experiences that have made up his identity; hence some of the "shadows" of the title, which one character defines as those healthy images children create for their future, which beckon them toward their ideal selves, while other "shadows," people's unworthy acts, haunt and oppress them.

This is an individuated version of a kind of estrangement that permeates Gardner's later fiction. For Craine, the ontology of human fear derives from this estrangement. He tells his client that human beings felt fear for the first time when they killed a creature and ate its flesh; for the second time when someone killed another person. In both cases, Craine argues, people invented gods to explain their sense of separation from the world. Eden, that archetype that images human existence before this estrangement took place, Craine calls this "terrible, terrible place" because it reminds human beings, whether or not they repress the memory, of their fallen condition.

The theme new to *Shadows* has to do with computers and artificial intelligence. One suspect and one victim were associated with the Computer Center at the university, and a body has been dumped in a vehicle belonging to the center's director, who later dies in an accident or suicide. In the only section of which the "fragments" offer two distinct versions of the same scene, Craine discusses the technology and threat of computers with a specialist, Professor Weintraub. This seems to be an important clue to the mystery, and had the novel been completed, Gardner might have been able to pursue this concern with electronic information in the pastoral settings this novelist prefers.

◆ Characters/Techniques ◆

In all detective fiction, the work proceeds from the characterization of the hero. Craine seems almost a parody of the traditional fictional detective: Whereas Sherlock Holmes and Hercule Poirot forget nothing, Craine practices voluntary amnesia; whereas Ross Macdonald's Lew Archer has eagle eyes and subtle powers of observation, Craine is near-sighted; whereas Robert B. Parker's Spenser is physically fit, Craine is decrepit, out of shape, and recovering from an operation for colon cancer; whereas Raymond Chandler's Philip Marlowe is a two-fisted drinker, Craine is an alcoholic who is surprised in one of the fragments to discover that he has gotten through half a day without a drink. Like Rex Stout's Nero Wolfe (whom he in no other way resembles), Craine is an avid reader of esoteric texts. He buys a used Bible and a book on Sanskrit; he also steals one on clairvoyance. Unlike Wolfe, however, Craine forgets most of what he reads.

Craine, like many detectives, surrounds himself with individuals who complement or tolerate his eccentricities. His secretary, Hannah, exhibits a maternal care to protect him from his drunkenness; his associate Tom Meekins, as his name implies, suggests a kindly alternative to the tough world Craine inhabits. His other associate, pistol-brandishing Emmitt Royce, who threatens to kill Craine and resigns from his office, is a psychopathic version of the American television detective.

Why Gardner should write so deliberate a parody of the detective genre can only be guessed at, but it is likely that this was part of a vast meditative design approximating that of *Mickelsson's Ghosts*. The association of existential freedom and Craine's profession would seem to support this hypothesis.

Detectives are abnormally free characters in fiction; but poet-suspect Ira Katz challenges the freedom Craine and other fictional detectives claim for themselves as well as Craine's claim that as a detective he is a man outside time. The "problem" with existentialists, Katz sermonizes, is that they assume a freedom that does not exist; they obey "the age-old law of mammals, the law that precedes our particular existence: Try not to get hurt." This idea, which Gardner may have been able to explore fully after he found a way to "fix" *Shadows*, might have proved a valuable synthesis of the techniques of detective fiction with the concerns of the serious novel.

David C. Dougherty
Loyola College in Maryland

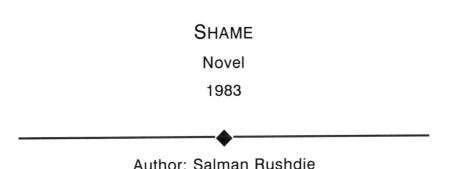

SHAME

Novel

1983

Author: Salman Rushdie

◆ Social Concerns/Themes ◆

Unlike the sprawling nature of *Midnight's Children* (1981; please see separate entry), *Shame* is a tightly controlled narrative. The novel begins with the strange birth of its "peripheral hero," Omar Khayyam Shakil, jointly born to three sisters named Chhunni, Munnee, and Bunny. Shakil is a peripheral hero because he is relegated to the margins of the action after the first three chapters. The focus then shifts abruptly to the linked destinies of two other families, the Harappas and the Hyders, and especially to the men who dominate these families, Iskander Harappa and Raza Hyder.

Iskander Harappa, a gambler and womanizer turned politician, is removed from power by General Hyder, the man he had promoted to a high public position when he became prime minister. On this level *Shame* is the story of the political rivalry between two men who were once in collusion but who inevitably become antagonists. However, Rushdie goes beyond this rivalry to highlight the tragic fortunes of Sufiya Zinobia, daughter of Hyder, and wife of Shakil. Although a brain-sick girl since infancy, Sufiya is preter-

naturally aware of the shameful deeds being committed all around her by the men of her country. Ultimately metamorphosed into a beast of shame, a violent agent of retribution, not unlike Nemesis, she becomes a savage killer. As in an Elizabethan revenge play, the stage is littered with corpses in the final scenes as men who had pursued power in immoral ways face horrible deaths. Other women join Sufiya in becoming instruments of vengeance. Hyder, for instance, is killed by Shakil's three mothers sometime after he has had Harappa executed. Shakil, too, meets a violent death when Sufiya decapitates him. She then reverts to the retarded girl she was before the shamelessness around transformed her into a Beast of Shame.

If *Shame* resembles an Elizabethan revenge play or a Gothic novel, Rushdie, appearing throughout the novel as the author-narrator, tells his readers quite clearly that the events of his story are only "at a slight angle to reality." In fact, he leaves no doubt that *Shame* is an attempt to recreate the history of the state of Pakistan in the imaginative mode. Thus the novel must first of all be seen as a political allegory. Iskander Harappa is based on

Zulfiqar Bhutto, prime minister of Pakistan in the 1970s, while Hyder is modelled on General Ziaul Huq, who usurped power from Bhutto in a military coup and had him hung. While there are no historical equivalents of Shakil and Sufiya, Harappa's daughter, Arjumand, an ambitious and sophisticated woman, clearly resembles Benazir Bhutto, who subsequently became Pakistan's prime minister. Rushdie's major premise is that the history of Pakistan is a shameful one, filled with coups, massacres, rigged elections, religious hypocrisy, and power-hungry, treacherous, mean-minded men who violated the ideals that led to the formation of a state meant to embody purity of faith. Rushdie attacks, among other things, "the mutually advantageous relationships between the country's establishment and it's armed forces" and emphasizes the psychic damage to that section of the population that must bear the brunt of the tyranny. Death and destruction, Rushdie appears to be saying in the apocalyptic conclusion, will spread throughout a land when a country's leadership is taken over by successive unscrupulous, repressive regimes. As far as Rushdie is concerned, Pakistan's history reads like a chapter from a book about the Middle Ages or any period when barbarians vied for power and left ruin in their wake. To make this point, Rushdie dates his story according to the hegerian calendar so that the novel's events literally take place in the fourteenth century.

◆ Characters ◆

As in *Midnight's Children*, *Shame* contains a gallery of fantastic, even bizarre characters, the most striking being Sufiya Zinobia. Made to blush at her birth by the disappointment of her father at the birth of a daughter, infected with brain fever at the age of two, married off to a man who does not care about her, confined to an attic to prevent her from walking the streets, and eventually transformed into the fiery, ravening beast of shame, Sufiya retains our sympathy throughout her strange, troubled story. Shakil, her husband, always at the edge of things, clearly embodies shamelessness. Obese, drunk, and an opportunist, he is also believably grotesque.

Besides those characters modeled on historical figures, some are purely imaginary beings that advance Rushdie's allegorical points. Talver Ulhaq, Iskander Harappa's chief of secret police, for instance, is so clairvoyant that he can read people's thoughts before they can translate them into action. Still other characters stand out because they are given distinctive touches. Harappa's wife, Rani, embroiders a shawl to cope with the humiliation of being cast aside by her playboy-husband. The shawl is her way of getting revenge on him and it documents his political wrongdoings. Rushdie's characterization in *Shame* thus runs the gamut from the complex to the simple, from the psychologically realistic to the emblematically representative. All of the characters embody various forms of shame or shamelessness.

However, the most interesting of all the characters one encounters in *Shame* is the author-narrator. The novel contains not only the stories of the Shakils, the Harappas, and the Hyders, but also the ruminations, the likes and dislikes of a man driven to write about a country to which he is tied, as he puts it, with "elastic" bonds. As a matter of fact, there is a great deal about Rushdie's own life in the novel. The first five pages of the second chapter, for example, reads like an extract from Rushdie's own diary. There is nothing gratuitous about Rushdie's presence or his dark musings on Pakistan in the novel; his presence is needed to steer us through the bewildering series of events with our sense of reality intact.

◆ Techniques ◆

"I'm only telling a fairy story," says the author-narrator at one point. On another occasion he affirms that he is telling the truth, mainly, with only some "off-centering" of it. At still another point he confesses that he is forced to reflect Pakistani history in his narrative "in fragments of broken mirrors" since a straight realistic novel about his country would be too fantastic for most people. Such comments not only indicate Rushdie's self-consciousness about his narrative technique but also underlines the constant oscillation between fantasy and history that takes place in *Shame*. As in *Midnight's Children*, Rushdie has drawn from a variety of narrative forms: political allegory, revenge tragedy, the gothic-oriental tale, postmodernist metafiction, the fairy tale, the personal essay, and the moral fable. By turns serious and farcical, tragic and playful, surrealistic and realistic, eloquent and loquacious, Rushdie again displays in this novel his control over a wide range of fictional techniques. His prose shows his mastery of different levels of discourse: sophisticated English syntax, Indian English, bureaucratese, idioms based on Urdu, and words of Indian origin. Not surprisingly, Rushdie has been criticized for his stylistic excesses and self-indulgent prose, but that is the risk involved in his commitment to experimental fiction.

◆ Literary Precedents ◆

Many of the texts which were important in the literary genealogy of *Midnight's Children* remain primary for a work like *Shame*. The digressions, authorial interventions, and attempts to lay bare storytelling devices again bring to mind Laurence Sterne's *Tristram Shandy* (1759-1767). The technique of exaggeration, of fantasy put to use in the service of realism, the apocalyptic violence of the ending, the political consciousness, and the preoccupation with powerful families continues to echo García Márquez's *One Hundred Years of Solitude* (1967) and other works of the "magical realism" tradition. The fabulous, phantasmagoric nature of most of the episodes continue to evoke the "Thousand and One Nights"; in fact, Rushdie alludes to that work quite clearly in his novel.

Shame also recalls two other writers as influences on Rushdie at this stage of his career. The savage irony of sections of the novel and satiric distinctions, such as that between the one-godly (Muslims) and the stone-godly (Hindus), show the influence of Jonathan Swift. (Swift made fun of Lilliputian factions by calling them Big Endians and Little Endians.) Rushdie's techniques and fictional concepts also show similarities to those of the Czech novelist, Milan Kundera, who alternates his "fairy tale" with an expatriate's comments on the politics of a country. Like Kundera, too, Rushdie is able to express his pain at what goes on in the name of ideology in his country without abandoning the comic mode.

Fakrul Alam
University of Dhaka

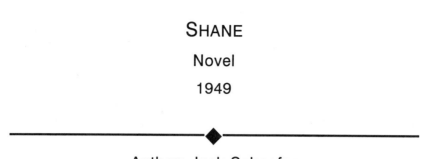

SHANE

Novel

1949

◆

Author: Jack Schaefer

◆ Social Concerns ◆

Much of *Shane's* early popularity may be traced to the fact that it addresses societal changes on a vast scale, a theme which speaks tellingly to the concerns of postwar generations. In the tradition of Stephen Crane's "The Bride Comes to Yellow Sky," *Shane* treats the *fin de siècle* American West in which an era of lawless individualism is being supplanted by the rooted, domesticated values of an intrusive and inexorable civilization. Ironically, both the gunfighter Shane and his antagonist Luke Fletcher, a pioneering and land-hungry cattleman, are among those who are being shunted aside by the urgent drift of historical progress; both men are fated to be subsumed by the legions of civilized farmers represented in the story by the Starrett family.

Throughout the novel, Shane struggles desperately to associate himself with the values and visions of these homesteaders, and he becomes their staunchest champion in their final stand against Fletcher. But Shane is ultimately unable to deny his own heroic role within the fading age that molded him; appropriately enough, his desertion of the Starretts has him riding alone into a Western sky from which the sun has already departed.

◆ Themes ◆

Shane is told from the point of view of young Bob Starrett; the novel involves the adolescent narrator's initiation into the positive moral values of both Shane, whom he idolizes, and of his own stalwart father, Joe. These two men reflect opposing approaches to life: Joe Starrett represents the civilizing ethos of domesticity, while Shane is the archetypal loner, irretrievably cut off from the burgeoning society that he momentarily serves. Nonetheless, Bob's two "fathers" share a common conviction that life is a persistent struggle in which the mettle of a man is tested and shaped by the overcoming of contentious obstacles.

As Bob witnesses Joe and Shane's epic battle with a monstrous tree stump, Shane's inner struggle to conform to the life of the farmer, and the gunfighter's expert dispatching of Fletcher and Wilson, he learns to appreciate and adopt the best values of both the "Old" and "New" West.

◆ Characters ◆

Shane is peopled by stock characters: the stolid-but-honest farmer, the "house-proud" farm wife, the enigmatic and black-clad gunfighter, the rapacious land baron. In the case of *Shane,* however, the familiarity of these characters serves to lend mythic dimensions and a certain timelessness to Schaefer's overtly simple plot. Still, the archetypal patterns of ancient myth are reversed here: Shane's quest is not so much to enter a dark wood of violent adventure as it is to divest himself of his heroic past and to take on the trappings of the new order. In this sense, therefore, Shane is the one dynamic character in the novel. He struggles valiantly to deny his true calling and to assume the factitious role of homesteader, even to the point of dressing the part, putting away his ebony Colt, and falling half in love with Marian, Joe's wife. But that domestic role is artificial at its heart for Shane, a fact which he ultimately acknowledges when he answers the siren call of Wilson, Fletcher's hired gun. Shane again straps on his revolver, thereby becoming "complete" and at one with his heroic stature, a lone rider into the dark depths of the soul's hidden violence. As in classical myth, Shane-as-hero vanquishes the evil forces threatening the larger community, revivifying the agricultural village from which he himself is permanently (and ironically) barred.

◆ Techniques ◆

Schaefer was a newspaper editor for many years, and the journalist's penchant for clear, simple, and emphatic language is apparent throughout *Shane.*

This simplicity of style, however, harbors a variety of complex literary devices — including foreshadowing, symbolism, and counterpoint — all of which add immeasurably to the work's appeal. The central conflict in the novel is not so much the literal one of cattleman vs. homesteader as it is the struggle that rages within Shane himself; the reader of *Shane* is absorbed from the outset by the question of whether the loner, provoked by Fletcher's outrages against the Starretts, will take up his gun and revert to his former ways. The first time Shane appears in the novel, he is seen hesitating at a symbolic fork in the road; finally he chooses to ride on toward the Starrett's farm and its life of happy domesticity. But Shane's brief career as a farmer is punctuated by recurring episodes that reveal the insistent pull of the life he has tried to renounce. For example, Shane at one point gazes longingly at the wild mountain ranges that border the farm; he coaches Bob lovingly in the use of a gun; he bridles as Fletcher's assaults begin to focus on Joe. By the time Shane reassumes his former identity, therefore, the reader has been well prepared for his critical decision; nonetheless, Schaefer's craftsmanship as a storyteller is such that this foreshadowing does not diminish the plot's informing texture of suspense.

◆ Literary Precedents ◆

Early reviewers of *Shane* likened Schaefer's novel to the works of Owen Wister (especially *The Virginian,* 1902), Mary Hallock Foote, and Helen Hunt Jackson. To a certain extent, *Shane* is an apotheosis of the Western story as it has become known to generations of movie goers, pulp novel readers, and television viewers: the conflict between society and outlaw, culminating inevitably in a fiery showdown, has become so familiar as to have permanently entered the American mythic consciousness. As mentioned above, however, Schaefer's themes are more closely linked with Stephen Crane's; Schaefer deals repeatedly with that twilight era of the Old West in which frontier individualism and values are being usurped by Eastern notions of order and degree. In his substantial canon of novels and stories, Schaefer increasingly strikes an elegiac chord, lamenting the passage of those giants who once walked the American West and finding fault with the so-called "civilized" life that effectively eradicated them.

◆ Adaptations ◆

Shane was made into a justly famous motion picture in 1953 (produced and directed by George Stevens for Paramount; screenplay by A. B. Guthrie, Jr.). The film starred Alan Ladd in the title role and featured such well-known actors as Van Heflin, Jean Arthur, Brandon De Wilde, and Jack Palance (who brilliantly portrayed the malevolent Wilson).

The production received general praise from critics. Although the film lacks the novel's complexity of characterization, internalized descriptions, and mythic dimensions, it nonetheless follows Schaefer's plot faithfully as it graphically depicts Shane's essential separation from the farmers whom he champions. In one scene, for example, Shane stands outside in the rain while talking to Marian, who remains inside the snug Starrett house; the soundtrack plays "Beautiful Dreamer" at this point, accentuating the unreality of Shane's desire to fit in with the homesteaders.

William Ryland Drennan
University of Wisconsin Center
Baraboo/Sauk County

SHARDIK

Novel

1974

Author: Richard Adams

◆ Social Concerns/Themes ◆

Shardik tells how the presence of a monstrous bear inspires a subject island people to overthrow the ruling empire. Confident that this bear is Shardik, the promised incarnation of divine power, the Ortelgans capture the capital of Bekla. They are led by Kelderek, who first discovered Shardik. While Kelderek ministers to the captive bear, the Ortelgans consolidate power throughout the empire and begin to rule harshly. Shardik suddenly escapes from Bekla. Following him into the countryside, Kelderek discovers that Ortelgans have allowed the slave trade to flourish. When Shardik perishes in the act of saving some children from a slaver, Kelderek believes that this is God's revelation: children must be cared for if society is to flourish.

Fundamentally *Shardik* is a novel about human misery. From the opening description of a forest fire, destruction is the constant occurrence of the novel. *Shardik* is the antithesis of *Watership Down* (1972), showing the ravaging rather than the reestablishment of community. The novel is filled with riveting scenes of death and devastation: the sack of the capital city, the slaughter of a Beklan army, Shardik's destruction of his temple, and Genshed's torture of enslaved children. Although the novel ends with Shardik's revelation about children, this commandment is only a hope rather than an accepted principle.

Thematically, the novel is a puzzle. Shardik may or may not be divinely ordained. The bear's actions in overthrowing the empire and freeing the children can be interpreted as deliberate or as accidental. If Shardik is divine power incarnate, this power is both awesome and murderous; it is responsible for the death of thousands of innocent people and allows the Ortelgans to act for ill as well as good. Insofar as they are a chosen people, the Ortelgans are unstoppable. They are also uncontrollable, using their newly acquired power to act more imperiously than the Beklan empire.

The central conflict in the novel is between the Ortelgans and the Beklans who represent intuitive and rational ways of knowing. The Ortelgans accept the divinity of Shardik on faith; they act instinctively, without thinking of consequences, trusting to providence. The Beklans determine their actions by weighing pros and cons, by taking logical steps to perceived ends. The Ortelgans lack a sense of history and aesthetic appreciation; the Beklans possess a strong sense of civic identity and cultivate civilized pleasures. Ambiguity and polarity have led reviewers to speculate about Adams's meaning. Is *Shardik* a historical commentary, an allegory of the coming of Christ, and of the impact of Christianity upon a pagan Roman empire? Is *Shardik* a contemporary tract about revived religious fundamentalism in a technological world which thinks it left the idea of faith far behind? Is *Shardik* a philosophical meditation upon the power that myth holds upon human imagination even in a scientific age? Is *Shardik* a timeless warning, the book of a new prophet who lashes a society that, despite its notable accomplishments, continues to abuse and neglect its children?

◆ Characters ◆

The main characters reflect both the tensions and the ambiguities of the novel. Shardik is a powerful creature, but whether his power stems from God or Nature is never clear. Shardik is always viewed from afar. The author (although he knows what happens in the minds of rabbits and dogs) never takes the reader inside Shardik. Thus his actions occur without clear motivation.

Shardik's chief priest and priestess, Kelderek and the Tuginda, profess no doubts. They sense the bear's divine power and plan, and they entrust their lives to it. Kelderek is the more developed of the two; in the course of the novel he undergoes an interesting transformation. Before Shardik comes, Kelderek is a mere hunter, despised by the Ortelgans as a permanent adolescent whose nickname is Kelderek-Play-with-the-Children. As soon as Kelderek identifies the bear as the long awaited Shardik, he gains stature: He becomes first priest, then chief priest, and ultimately king. He directs the Ortelgans to victory. He surrenders those titles willingly when Shardik flees Bekla, interpreting the flight as the god's abandonment of an unworthy people. Kelderek wanders in despair until Shardik saves the children; with this revelation Kelderek senses that the divine purpose has been accomplished. Although Kelderek is the character whose thoughts the reader most often shares, he is curiously unreflective. It is clear that he does not realize all the implications of the unfolding events.

Some of those implications are realized instead by a series of Beklan leaders. The first is the Beklan Commander at the Battle of the Foothills. He is a good man, a wise leader, and an officer loyal to his duty; he is as ready to use his troops on construction projects that benefit small villages as he is to take them on campaign. Nonetheless, he is slaughtered by Shardik. The second is Elleroth, a Beklan nobleman who leads the battle against the Ortelgans after the capital falls. Elleroth is handsome, cultivated, and brave. He fights to preserve civic order rather than personal power; he fearlessly confronts those he regards as fanatics and plots intelligently (although unsuccessfully) to topple the Ortelgan rulers with a minimum of bloodshed. The last is Siristro who oversees the efforts to rebuild society after Shardik's death and the Ortelgan's collapse. These three characters offer an admirable view of a cultivated society striving to maintain order.

◆ Techniques ◆

Shardik presents, in one way, a microcosm like the lapine universe of *Watership Down*. Bekla is a completely realized alternate world. Adams gives it language, culture, geography, and history. The novel offers therefore a total involvement and immersion in a world strange, wonderful, and terrible.

Shardik, like *Watership Down*, offers frequent natural description. Adams's prose is filled with long passages of scenic description, and the narrative often pauses for a paragraph-long metaphor or simile. Its purpose in *Shardik*, though, is to create the sublime rather than the pastoral. The landscape, like the events unfolding on it, is beyond human control. Whether it is divine wrath or lucky political rebellion that is ravaging Bekla, the reader is aware that the action is a life-and-death struggle. *Shardik* is the epic of Bekla, the story of a turning point in the history of a civilization.

◆ Related Titles ◆

Maia (1985) is an odd sequel to *Shardik*. It tells of events in Bekla, but the story occurs at a time before Shardik's coming. It continues the theme of the enslavement of children, but instead of depicting physical cruelty, it recounts the hedonistic life of a fifteen-year-old concubine named Maia. Although this novel explores the corrupt core of a civilized empire, it totally lacks the attention to natural landscape and the epic vocabulary that gives *Shardik* its power. Almost twelve hundred pages long, *Maia* reads like a combination of Robert Graves's *I, Claudius* (1934) and Jacqueline Susann's *Valley of the Dolls* (1966). That this mix-ture of ceaseless political intrigue and constant amorous adventure will attract the same favorable response from readers and critics as *Shardik* seems doubtful. *Maia* is ultimately redeemed at the novel's end, but after more than a thousand pages no one may care. *Maia* seems to lack a strong central conflict upon which an elaborate plot can be erected.

Robert M. Otten
Marymount University

IRWIN SHAW'S SHORT FICTION

Short Stories: Five Decades

1978

◆

Author: Irwin Shaw

◆ Characters ◆

Irwin Shaw's characters are a gallery of interesting, usually likable characters whose plight is not of their own making. Their diverse personalities, familiar difficulties, and awkward efforts to extract themselves account for the popularity of his stories. To read the collected stories is to read *la comedie humaine* of America in the middle decades of the century. Shaw possesses a keen eye for the way people look or gesture, and a knack for spotting what makes them tick.

Shaw's stories pulse with the life of the American city. Characters from varied professions crowd his pages: salesman, cab driver, soldier, sailor, prize fighter, football player, writer, farmer, bartender, deputy sheriff, nurse, student. They are any and all ages: adolescent boys, marriageable girls, middle-aged husbands and wives, long term bachelors and career women, aged mothers and ancient fathers. They poise along all life's milestones: making plans for work or love, anxious to leave home, newly employed or married, stuck in dead-end job or relationship, lamenting a dead parent or absent lover.

Although the lives of Shaw's characters are most often shaped by chance, some of them cooperate unwittingly in their fate because they are ignorant of their own best interest. Shaw's most deliciously malicious vision of human self-deception and self-destruction is the aptly titled "A Wicked Story." Robert and Virginia Harvey are dining at a restaurant after attending the theater. They are talking about one of the actresses when she enters the room. Immediately and inexplicably Virginia begins to insist that Robert has been eyeing the woman all night and wants to have an affair with her. Virginia uses the occasion to pour out her fears about Robert's infidelity and her jealousy of his physical attractiveness. Robert vehemently denies Virginia's allegations, but as they leave the restaurant, he eyes the actress. She eyes him back. Robert decides to let ripen the seed which Virginia planted.

◆ Social Concerns ◆

Shaw wrote over eighty short stories, sixty-three of which are included in this collection written between 1937 and 1978. The stories chronicle the career of a generation from struggling adolescence during the Depression to uneasy maturity in the 1970s. They depict a generation that is never able to relax its vigilance or take things for granted. These stories portray the literal and metaphorical battles this generation fought.

The literal battlefield is Europe in the 1940s. Typical of Shaw's wartime tales is the poignant "Walking Wounded" which recounts the plight of Peter, a British soldier, who cannot, after two years at the front, remember what his wife looks like. Although he finds a friendly pilot willing to take him home, he cannot find his commanding officer. Without orders he cannot leave. Bureaucratic red tape triumphs.

An important pseudo-battlefield for this generation is the football field. It is the setting for the satiric, "March On, March On Down the Field." The story tells of the sorry plight of a professional football team working for a stingy owner. When the crowd is smaller than anticipated, he insists the players take a pay cut; as an economy measure he refuses to provide helmets. Yet, having played the hardheaded accountant, he pleads with them just before game time to play in a college-like, enthusiastic spirit.

Hard times force even gentle people into economic conflict. A number of Shaw stories recount the poverty of the Depression era. In "Second Mortgage" a penniless Brooklyn family that cannot pay its bills receives weekly visits from an elderly widow who holds the second mortgage on the property. She sits pathetically for a couple of hours in the living room as if some miracle will put money into the family's pockets before her eyes. At first sympathetic to her, the family comes to hate her hopeless vigil.

The bedroom is no more placid a place for Shaw's generation than the battlefield, stadium, or marketplace. Representative of the battle between the sexes is the famous "Girls in Their Summer Dresses." Michael and Frances Loomis are trapped in a loveless marriage but manage not to think about it often. One beautiful Sunday they set out for a stroll with unusually light hearts. Soon Frances notices that Michael is eyeing every pretty girl in a summer dress. She complains about his old habit, and soon they are enmeshed in a familiar quarrel. The mood is ruined; they decide to spend time with acquaintances they do not like in order to avoid each other.

◆ Themes ◆

Three themes recur frequently in Shaw's short fiction. The first is the role of chance and accident in shaping human life. In "Small Saturday" Christopher meets and dates the girl who will become his wife only after both miss the chance to go out with others. Unknown to them, a lusty Swiss flying into New York, a police bust of several con artists, and a middle-aged man's passion for a young actress have helped mold their destiny. In "Noises in the City" a man's affection for his pregnant wife is rekindled after he meets a man whose wife was murdered. The victim died when a stable husband and father went unaccountably berserk. In Shaw's world lives are changed by a thoughtless word, a careless glance, or an unplanned meeting. Tales about people whose fates are sealed by chance and coincidence strike readers with wonder; unexpected convergence is one of the staple devices of the best-selling storyteller.

The second recurring theme is the longing of the individual to maintain a sense of purpose and self-worth amid the twists of fate. In "God Was Here, But He Left Early," Rosemay Maclain returns to Paris. A department store buyer who visits Europe on occasion, and the divorced mother of a teen-age girl, Rosemary became pregnant as the result of a one-night stand with a young married Frenchman. Seeking legal abortion, she is interviewed by a French psychologist, who refuses her request. Rosemary seeks out her lover, but he offers only a vague hope of a doctor in Zurich. Later, she dines with friends who lead her to Rodney Harrison, an Englishman as young as her French lover. His attentions, her fear of the wine at dinner, and the atmosphere of Paris encourage her to seek consolation in Rodney's arms. Instead of love, however, he has only mild sadism to offer her. Rosemary retreats into a bewildering, self-mocking, but ultimately protective hysteria.

The third recurring theme is the American predilection for building a sense of self-worth on athletic or economic success. The archetypal story elaborating this theme is "The Eighty Yard Run." The story tells of the decline of Christian Darling. Taking the classic path to success, he married the boss's daughter, but the stock market crash of 1929 ruined both the boss and the inherited business. Surprisingly, his wife Louise is successful in the Depression job market as an editor while Christian is forced to sell suits to undergraduates at his alma mata. The job brings him close to a haunting image of the man he might have become. As a collegiate football player, Darling once ran eighty yards for a touchdown. The memory has sustained him — until he goes out, in jacket and tie, onto the field of the deserted stadium to reenact the moment. When undergraduates unexpectedly observe him, Darling flees the stadium in embarrassment, recalling that he ran the play in practice, not in a game.

◆ Techniques/Literary Precedents ◆

As the outlines of these stories suggest, Shaw's artistry rests upon an ability to place two characters in a deceptively ordinary setting, put them in conflict, allow them to talk at cross purposes, and send them finally in opposite directions. Such scenes work only if the narrator can quickly sketch the crucial characteristics of these colliding personalities and cast their exchange in rapid dialogue. The technique relies upon dramatic irony, with the audience realizing more implications to each speech than either the speaker or the listener. In some stories the interior monologue of the central character replaces dialogue as the main device for exposing the personalities in conflict.

Shaw does not rely on the device which O. Henry, the nineteenth century master of short fiction, popularized: the unexpected plot twist revealed in the final paragraph or sentence. Shaw's method is closer to that of James Joyce who articulated the concept of epiphany. Joyce strove to create in a short story a moment at which the character has a revelation about, an insight into, his own nature. The epiphany is more striking, Joyce argued, if it results from the familiar rather than from the extraordinary. Many of Shaw's best stories — "Girls in Their Summer Dresses," "The Eighty Yard Run," "A Wicked Story" — are clearly tales of epiphany.

◆ Adaptations ◆

Four of Shaw's stories were filmed in the 1940s and 1950s. "Educating the Heart" was filmed as *Easy Living* (RKO, 1949), directed by Jacques Tourneur and starring Victor Mature and Lucille Ball. The film was released as a home video in 1989. "Tip on a Dead Jockey was filmed under the original title (MGM, 1957) by Richard Thorpe and starred Robert Taylor and Dorothy Malone. "The Walking Wounded" and "Act of Faith" were also filmed. None of these last three were commercial or critical successes, and none is available on video now.

In 1981 three stories were adapted by Kenneth Cavender for television: "The Girls in Their Summer Dresses," "The Man Who Married a French Wife," and "The Monument."

"The Eighty Yard Run" is available as part of the anthology *The Esquire Collection of Great Fiction* on audio cassette (Esquire Audio, 1985). The reader captures beautifully the staccato rhythm of Shaw's style built on the simple, short sentences.

◆ Ideas for Group Discussions ◆

With their focus on the seemingly endless battles in human existence, Shaw's stories make ideal readings for discussion groups. His short fiction, especially those tales about conflicts between men and women, cause readers to take sides with one character or the other. Differing sympathies give rise to lively debate.

The time of Shaw's stories also leads to an area of discussion. The America of Shaw's 1930-1960 stories and the America of the turn-of-the-century is much different. Contrasting aspects of Shaw's America — its business climate, its leisure activities, its military life — with their contemporary state will generate lively conservation about the degree and cause of change. It is a rich topic to explore with readers of different generations who will inevitably view social and economic changes differently. Those who believe that contemporary America is in decline from a more heroic, more stable, more moral post-World War II America will especially find Shaw's writing a challenge to their assumptions.

A discussion group leader could approach the short fiction by grouping stories. Each discussion session might treat a group of four or five stories that center on a theme or topic. Among possible topics are the relations between the sexes, the means to, and meaning of, economic success, and professional football as a reflection of social values.

1. How is the experience of reading a short story different from reading a novel? Edgar Allan Poe attributed the power of short fiction to its ability to create one dominant impression in a reader who could devour a story in one, uninterrupted setting. Does each Shaw story create a dominant impression?

2. How clear is Shaw's opinion of each character in a story? Can readers easily tell whose side the author is on?

3. Whether the subject is career or sexuality, Shaw's attitude seems to be that it is an arena of human conflict. Which of the following describes Shaw's vision? (a) Gender conflicts are part of a never-ending conflict that is incapable of decisive victory or (b) A battle in which there will be a victor

and a vanquished?

4. Shaw's stories are filled with characters expressing their failed dreams, exploded hopes, and disappointed expectations. Is there prospect for human happiness in Shaw's world?

5. Read one of Shaw's stories aloud. How does hearing the story affect the listener's interpretation of themes and conflicts?

6. Are there certain topics in Shaw's fiction that seem very outdated? Are there topics that seem both contemporary and timeless?

7. Shaw has a knack for catchy, arresting titles. Which titles are especially striking? What aspect of a story does he emphasize with the title? Does he always explain the title?

8. In the Introduction to his collected stories, Shaw writes, "In a collection of stories you can be all the men or fragments of men, worthy or unworthy, who in different seasons abound in you." What are the most noteworthy character traits that abound in Shaw's fiction? Which are worthy/unworthy? What seasons, do you sense, Shaw's life has passed through?

9. *Short Stories: Five Decades* is arranged in chronological order, which offers an opportunity to trace the development of Shaw's vision of America and the development of his art. Choose two or three early stories and contrast them to two or three late stories. What changes are immediately apparent?

Robert M. Otten
Marymount University

SHELTER

Novel

1994

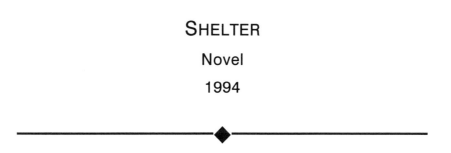

Author: Jayne Anne Phillips

◆ Characters ◆

In the novel *Shelter,* Jayne Anne Phillips has chosen to balance four points of view, describing the events of this novel as they are experienced and reflected upon by Lenny, Alma, and Buddy (in eleven sections each) and by Parson (in ten sections). Of the other major characters, Carmody seems too angry and inarticulate to express himself, and Delia has retreated into passivity in order to escape the pain of her father's death.

Lenny Swenson, the first character introduced, is a fifteen year old Girl Guide at Camp Shelter. Since this year is probably her last as camper, she lives in one of the tents at the upper fringe of the camp. In this section of the camp, called Highest, the campers are given little direct supervision; so she and Cap have little difficulty sneaking away to go skinny-dipping in Turtle Hollow, the forbidden swimming hole.

Poised on the boundary between childhood and maturity, Lenny still retains some physical characteristics of a child. Her long, loose hair is "the color of bleached hay that has weathered in fields," and most of the time she wears it in "a silky, blunt cut ponytail that swings when she moves." Again, however, appearances are deceptive; Lenny has reached the point of sexual awakening, although she still is somewhat confused by the emotions she is feeling. She now sleeps naked, her games with Cap have taken on a sexual quality, and she has begun to realize the true character of the "touching" incidents in her parents' bedroom. Moreover, she has the most objective view of the sexual hostility between her parents, Wes and Audrey. In the course of the novel, Lenny matures most, as she comes to recognize sexual attraction and learns how to deal with it.

Lenny provides most of the information about her best friend, Catherine Briarley, known as Cap. Also fifteen, Cap is nonetheless several months older than Lenny and more advanced sexually, perhaps because she has witnessed the frequent verbal battles between her parents, Henry and Catherine. For Cap, it is essential that she maintain control of people and situations, and she knows precisely how to manipulate Lenny. After deliberately frightening Lenny by taking her to the bat cave, Cap agrees to a midnight swim only if Lenny will swim nude. It is she who draws Frank's attention to the naked Lenny, and it is she who orchestrates the sexual encounter between the two. When she attempts to repeat the incident with Alma and Delia as observers, Alma innocently foils her plan, and having lost control of the situation, Cap is unable to act decisively when Carmody appears. As Lenny assumes the position of authority, Cap's dominance appears to have ended.

Alma Swenson, Lenny's sister, was accepted in the Junior (twelve year old) Level of Camp Shelter only because the camp director was reluctant to separate her from Delia. Believing her friend is better off at camp and away from the gossip in Aunt Bird's beauty shop, Alma works hard to avoid anything that will call the counselors' attention to Delia; thus she tries to prevent Delia's sleepwalking, and she completes all the chores and craft projects assigned to the two of them. In fact, still a week short of her twelfth birthday, Alma has already assumed a number of adult responsibilities. Throughout Audrey's two-year affair with Nickel, Alma has been her unwilling confidante, and although Audrey insists that Alma is the daughter who most resembles her, Alma seems actually more mature than her mother. It is Alma who worries that someone from Gaither will see Audrey and Nickel together during their rendezvous in Winfield, and Alma is also the only one who seems concerned about how Delia will be affected by knowledge of her father's infidelity and suicide. When she believes that Lenny has violated the camp rules by writing a letter to Frank, Alma quickly removes the letter from Frank's mailbox and destroys it.

After Nickel Campbell's death, Alma observes a dramatic change in his daughter and her best friend. Delia, who does not share Alma's enthusiasm for reading, seemed never to notice or reflect upon the meaning of anything taking place around her. Now, however, she seems "eminently puzzled, suspicious, distracted"; she cynically insists that Mrs. Thompson-Warner makes up all the material presented in Heritage Class. Obviously depressed, Delia has begun to sleepwalk, and during a recent episode, she fell and cut her lip badly. Furthermore, she refuses to participate in camp activities, preferring to wander in the woods, alone or with Alma, but when Parson extracts the snake's egg and shows it to the girls, for the first time Delia reacts with strong emotion, screaming hysterically and running deeper into the woods. Likewise, during the Carmody episode, Delia remains the most conventional of the girls, as she first suggests notifying the authorities and later says the prayer over Carmody's body. Sobbing, Delia acknowledges her fear, but overcomes it when she enters the hidden cave with Buddy and the other girls. Noting similarities between her father's death and Carmody's, she must accept the truth about Nickel's suicide before she can also comprehend their differences.

Until this summer, Buddy has always preferred the woods in winter, when he and his mother are the only residents on the Camp Shelter Road. To Hilda Carmody's young son, Camp Shelter then seems like his private realm, where he can find sanctuary among the trees. Now, though, he is beginning to admire the campers; in fact, he develops a crush on Lenny and steals one of Mrs. Thompson-Warner's rings, intending it as a present for Lenny. Buddy's plan fails, however, because for the first time in his memory, the man he calls Dad is home from prison. Carmody not only takes the ring but insists that Buddy steal the other rings as well. More than ever, Buddy is aware of the need to hide, whether alone in the woods, or with his mother at the local church. He fears his abusive stepfather, especially after Carmody threatens to force Buddy to accompany him when he leaves Shelter County for good. Despite his quickness and cunning, Buddy feels powerless to escape Carmody until he meets Parson, the one person Carmody seems to fear.

All of his life, Parson has been an outsider. As a child at the orphanage at Huntingdon, he was called a "guinea kid" because his complexion and hair were very dark and even at age sixteen he had a "swarth of beard." Selected as a foster son by Harkness, the alcoholic postal worker, Parson soon discovered that Harkness had taken two foster sons into his home only in order to abuse them sexually. After setting the fire that killed Harkness and burned his house, Parson was sent to the Industrial School for Boys at Proudytown, even though he was beginning to gain the reputation of being crazy. Before long, however, he became Preacher Summers's foster son and a young evangelist at Summers's Calvary Church. A gambler and womanizer, Summers was shot at a card game, and driving erratically as he raced to get Summers home, Parson struck and killed a young girl. Sentenced to prison for vehicular homicide, Parson believed he was always surrounded by the "legion of the vapor world," as he called the dead. His "legion" accompanies him as he simply walks away from prison in order to follow his cellmate, Carmody, whom he considers fallen and vicious, but also capable of leading

him to grace. Living in an abandoned shack, Parson works on a construction crew during the day, but at night he hears the walking of the Devil, whom he thinks of as "a fallen child, lost, abandoned." Both Lenny and Buddy are drawn to Parson: For Lenny, he seems to represent entrance into the adult world, and he gives Buddy hope of escaping Carmody. Ultimately Parson intervenes not only to thwart Carmody's attacks upon Lenny and Buddy and to prevent similar attacks upon the other girls, but to take upon himself the responsibility for Carmody's death.

Carmody, whose first name is never mentioned, is described as "long and lank," with "faded, wheat-colored hair and squinty eyes." His face is "not young," but he has a "callow, unfinished look, showing always an edge of the rabbity anger that caused him to hang back, scheming while his cohorts preened and strutted." Childhood abuse and his experiences as a prisoner of war have left him mentally unbalanced, and he has spent the past five years in prison, sometimes beating the walls. Hilda explains to Buddy that Carmody reacts violently because he is afraid of everything. When he is killed, Buddy assures the girls that no one will miss him.

Among the minor characters who figure prominently in the thoughts of the girls is Frank, the camp bugler. Many of the junior and senior campers flirt with Frank, who habitually ignores them. As Lenny discovers during their midnight encounter at Turtle Hole, he is almost a man. Alma also devotes much time to considering the reactions of Mrs. Thompson-Warner, the widowed camp director, whose husband reportedly committed suicide. Likewise, concern for Delia leads Alma to reflect upon the affair between her mother, Audrey, and Delia's father, Nickel Thackery Campbell. In contrast, Lenny's memories involve her relationship to her father, Wes Swenson. The center of Buddy's universe is his mother, Hilda Carmody, described by the girls as "a big woman gone to fat." When Buddy thinks of her, he recalls her lingering vanilla scent and the religious fervor which seems to cut her off from him.

◆ Social Concerns ◆

Phillips recreates the mood of America in late July through early November 1963, choosing to conclude her novel just before the assassination of John Kennedy. Nevertheless, there is an obvious parallel between the shattering events at Camp Shelter, West Virginia, in late July and those in Dallas in late November. Just as the death of President Kennedy ended the era of America's postwar innocence, the death of Carmody marks the end of childhood for four Girl Guides and the camp cook's young son.

In keeping with her emphasis upon portraying the attitudes of 1963, Phillips accurately portrays the Cold War mentality of the era. Mrs. Thompson-Warner, the camp director, regularly teaches a Heritage Class where she lectures on the dangers of trusting Kruschev, introduces former Russian political prisoners, and shows films of the atrocities inflicted upon Russian political dissidents. Each evening one of the campers is assigned to make a "supper speech" on the subject of freedom.

The novel also reflects the changes in American family life which were beginning to become obvious in the early 1960s, as the role of women slow-ly evolved. While women like Hilda Carmody had always been required to hold menial jobs in order to support their families, until the 1960s work outside the home was not considered a reasonable alternative to remaining in an unhappy marriage, as *Shelter* shows it to be for Audrey Swenson and Catherine Winthrop (Briarley). Thus, divorce became not only possible, but actually prevalent, as suburban housewives found means of escape other than Mina Campbell's alcoholism or Audrey Swenson's assignations. Babyboomers were impatient, unwilling to endure the misery of a failing relationship; thus, while single parenthood was still considered unfortunate, it did not carry the severe social stigma of earlier generations. This shift in attitudes is most obvious as Mina and Hilda build new lives when circumstances force them to be single parents, while Audrey and Catherine choose the role.

Among the current social issues raised is the failure of the criminal justice system, especially in dealing with the mentally ill. Both Carmody and Parson have spent much of their lives in reformatories and prisons, when they undoubtedly should have been in mental institutions. Childhood sexual abuse and mistreatment in a Manchurian prisoner of war camp have left Carmody paranoid and abusive, and his incarcerations at a youth farm and in prison have only made him more violent, then paroled him again into society. Considered retarded, Parson is, in fact, schizophrenic. Several times he used fire to combat manifestations of the Devil, whom he sees pursuing him, but no one believed his confessions, and he was not jailed until he killed a young girl in a traffic accident. Because he talks about the "legion" of the dead (at least two of whom he has killed), both the other convicts and the prison authorities leave him alone, and he is able to walk away from a prison work detail and follow Carmody to Shelter County.

Carmody also provides the most striking example of another contemporary social problem — domestic violence. As a teen-ager, after years of neglect and abuse, he turned on his alcoholic mother and beat her until she was nearly dead. As an adult, he continues the pattern, subjecting Hilda to marital rape and abusing Buddy sexually and verbally. Carmody enjoys the power his brutality gives him; both Hilda and Buddy fear him and wish he would leave home forever.

◆ Themes ◆

Shelter develops Phillips's recurring theme of disintegrating families. Although clearly the most dysfunctional, the Carmody family differs only in degree from the Briarleys, the Campbells, and the Swensons. None is these families is stable, as the recollections of Alma and Lenny reveal. Long before the novel opens, reenacting the Briarleys' fights has become a game for Cap and Lenny. Catherine Winthrop has already left Henry Briarley, returned to her family home in Connecticut, and taken back her maiden name. Audrey Swenson and Nickel Campbell have come to believe their marriages are mistakes, and they have engaged in a two-year affair. Moreover, throughout the affair, Audrey has detailed all her feelings in conversations with her younger daughter, Alma. Meanwhile, Lenny has begun to remember incidents of sexual "touching," presumably by her drunken father. Trapped by

Mina's psychological dependence, and tortured by guilt about what he is doing to his children, Nickel has killed himself. The epilogue to this novel reveals that finally the Swensons too have separated; Audrey and her daughters live in New York state, where Audrey works in the admissions department of the private school Lenny and Cap attend.

In keeping with the dysfunctional family theme is the family secrets motif. Each of the major characters is privy to a secret which must remain hidden, often even within the family. Cap and Lenny cloak themselves in Catherine's discarded rabbit coats and make the telling of secrets a game, but Lenny quickly learns that truth can still be concealed if told in a way that defies belief. On the other hand, when secrets such as their smoking and drinking are revealed, Catherine will no longer allow Lenny to spend the night with Cap. Lenny also is careful to make certain that Audrey does not know about the incidents with Wes. Alma feels compelled to conceal Audrey's affair with Nickel and to protect Delia from knowledge of the affair and of Nickel's apparent suicide. During each day's camp activities, Alma completes Delia's tasks as well as her own, so that the counselors will not realize how troubled Delia actually is. More dangerous, though, is Buddy's need to hide from Carmody. This man, whom he calls Dad, threatens to add beating and kidnapping to his usual sexual abuse. Finally, there is Parson, the escaped convict, who hides by living in an abandoned shack and joining an isolated work crew. At the climax of the novel, all of these characters are linked by the most sinister of secrets, one they vow never to disclose.

Involved in this secret is the theme

of initiation, another important concern in *Shelter*. Initially the subject is maturation, as Lenny's naked, midnight swim becomes an introduction to sexuality and a step toward definition of her sexual identity. Later, however, Lenny and her friends become part of a more sinister initiation, as these five young people experience their first direct encounter with the corruption of the adult world and learn not only to recognize evil, but to deal with its consequences. Isolated physically and psychologically from home and parents, they can rely only on the assistance of Parson, the mad prison escapee who already sees the Devil every night. Parson represents the contradictory nature of human personality. Although he has killed two people, he becomes a kind of savior, first when he intervenes to save the youngsters from Carmody, and again when he assumes the guilt of their crime.

The motif of appearance and reality also figures prominently in this novel. Initially these young people seem innocent, but through their thoughts and recollections, Phillips gradually reveals that each of them has experienced some prior brush with a powerful, corrupting force. As her mother's confidante, Alma considers herself almost a participant in Audrey's affair with Nickel Campbell; in fact, Alma recognizes a greater spiritual affinity with Nickel than with either of her own parents. Her guilt causes her to be extremely protective of her surrogate step-siblings, Delia and John-John. In Delia's case, her psychological balance has been upset by a growing recognition of the circumstances surrounding her father's death. Her parents' bitter and prolonged fights have caused a similar dislocation for Cap, making her cynical and manipulative, especially sexually.

In contrast, Lenny has become passive. She knows about her mother's affair, and she vaguely recalls childhood experiences of a clearly sexual nature. Her response has been to share her father's beer and to participate in Cap's implicitly sexual games. Buddy, the youngest of the group, has been the most victimized, as Carmody has repeatedly abused him sexually.

♦ Techniques ♦

Phillips employs the Faulknerian technique of multiple narrative perspectives, allowing four different characters to convey their individual thoughts and actions in forty-three separate sections. By providing the reader with diverse interpretations, Phillips presents the most comprehensive and accurate account of the various incidents leading up to the climactic conclusion when all the characters converge at Turtle Hole, the swimming area off-limits to the campers. Since the horror of that experience is shared by characters of divergent personalities and backgrounds, the reader accepts their action as a valid response.

Perhaps even more than Phillips's earlier fiction, *Shelter* is a highly symbolic novel. For example, the snake captured by Parson serves as a multidimensional symbol associated with nature, atonement, and sexuality in addition to the traditional link with evil. Similar connections exist between Turtle Hole and the dangers of the adult world, and the various earlier secrets foreshadow the ultimate secret of what happened to Carmody.

♦ Literary Precedents ♦

The development of a character

whose limited mental capacity is at odds with his physical strength may be influenced by John Steinbeck's *Of Mice and Men* (1937). The crisis of a group of young people forced to confront evil without the support of civilized society is reminiscent of William Golding's novel *Lord of the Flies* (1954), and the climactic scene in which a major character can save himself or herself only by killing a depraved oppressor may owe something to *Deliverance* (1970) by James Dickey. The sacramental tone may also reflect that of Flannery O'Connor's *Wise Blood* (1952). Like William Faulkner, Phillips develops multiple perspectives by presenting different characters' viewpoints in separate sections. While Phillips's individual sections are less complex rhetorically, they also suffer from Faulkner's problem of too much similarity in voice.

◆ Related Titles ◆

Shelter explores many of the same family and social issues as other Phillips novels such as *Machine Dreams* (1984; see separate entry) and *Fast Lanes* (1987; see separate entry). For example, in personality Wes Swenson strongly resembles Mitch Hampson, and — though she is the product of a very different era — Lenny is somewhat like Danner Hampson, especially in her relationship with her younger sibling.

◆ Ideas for Group Discussions ◆

1. The 1960s were a time of upheaval in American families; the divorce rate soared as people examined their relationships in terms of the happiness and fulfillment they provided. Why did this change take place? Was there a change in society's attitude toward concepts such as responsibility and commitment?

2. In the late 1950s and early 1960s, camps such as the Girl Guides' Camp Shelter were extremely popular with campers and parents alike. Why did these camps appeal to each group?

3. Observing that *Shelter* is set in the summer and fall immediately preceding the assassination of John F. Kennedy, reviewers immediately pointed out the parallel between the girls' initiation into adult evil and America's loss of innocence with the death of President Kennedy. Do you think Phillips intended the girls' experience to be interpreted in this way? Is the symbolism too subtle? Too obvious?

4. Mrs. Thompson-Warner presides over a daily Heritage Class in which she lectures and shows filmstrips about the dangers of "trusting the Russians." During the Cold War years, did most Americans share her attitudes? How did Americans react when Nikita Krushchev visited the United States?

5. Mina and Nickel call their baby John-John in honor of President Kennedy's son. As this choice of names suggests, both John and Robert Kennedy were very popular in West Virginia. What was the reason for their popularity? Why do you think Phillips chose to emphasize this link to the Kennedy family?

6. The roots of the 1970s women's movement can be found in the growing discontent of women during the 1960s. In what ways do Audrey Swenson and

Catherine Briarley exemplify that discontent? How do they differ from Mina Campbell and Hilda Carmody?

7. The behavior of *Shelter's* characters — parents and their children — suggests that maturity is not a matter of age. What is the basis of genuine maturity? In what ways does the girls' experience hasten the growth of their maturity?

8. Phillips repeatedly demonstrates that people and situations are not always what they seem. Point out examples of this disparity? How does each contribute to the development of the novel's theme?

9. Clearly both Parson and Carmody are mentally ill. Has society helped them by incarcerating them? What purpose has been served by sentencing them to prison? Is this use of the penal system justified?

10. Implicit in *Shelter* are two traditional views of the wilderness: as a savage place and as the site of innocence and purity. How does Phillips use these two attitudes to develop her principal theme?

11. Why is Alma especially drawn to Delia and Johnny, with the urge to protect them?

12. What incidents reveal Lenny's awakening sexuality? What is Cap's role in this transformation?

13. Cite specific examples of irony in this novel — e.g., the fact that the girls have been sent to camp to keep them out of trouble.

14. Should the girls have told what happened to Carmody? What would have been the result? Why did they decide to keep the secret?

15. What are the various secrets in this novel? How do childhood secrets differ from those of adults? Are the girls to be considered adults simply because they keep adult secrets?

16. Is Alma a believable preadolescent? Why or why not?

17. Has Carmody been subjected to more brutalizing experiences than someone of his background is likely to have encountered? Why have his reactions differed so markedly from those of Parson?

18. Is Parson an instrument of cosmic justice? What probably would have happened if he had not been at Turtle Hole?

19. Discuss Alma's role as the central link, pulling together all of the novel's characters and incidents.

20. How might the Turtle Hole incident have been different if Alma had not intercepted Cap's note to Frank?

Charmaine Allmon Mosby
Western Kentucky University

THE SHEPHERD OF THE HILLS

Novel

1907

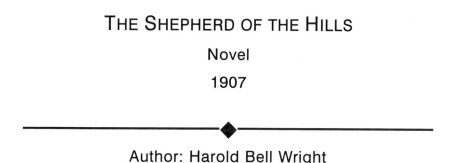

Author: Harold Bell Wright

◆ Characters ◆

Luckily for Wright, at the time he wrote laws did not require the disclaimer that all characters were fictitious and any resemblance to people, living or dead, was purely coincidental. Many of his characters were based on living people; many of those people were friends. And many times, he was one of his own characters. In *The Shepherd of the Hills,* he is the shepherd, the preacher who has gone to find peace in the healing powers of the woods and hills and streams, just as Wright returned, time and time again, to nature for spiritual and physical renewal.

Wright's characters may have been based on actual people, but they were bigger than life and he was criticized for his artificiality in characterization. Young Matt is a giant of a man, a perfect physical specimen, intelligent, fearless, frank, kind, gentle and honest. Sammy Lane is even more splendid, for she strives to become a better person through learning the finer graces of life, but never forgets that inner qualities alone determine whether or not a woman is a lady. Through these and lesser characters, Wright develops the principle of manhood and womanhood, that being a man or lady comes from quality of character. Both should be thoughtful, sympathetic, fun-loving and always desire to help others.

Wright characterizes Sammy as "not to be described." Although he details her womanly appearance, it can not capture the real woman. He lets another character reveal her magnificence: "That gal o' Jim Lane's jest plumb fills th' whole house. What! An' when she comes a-ridin' up t' th' office on that brown pony o' hern, I'll be dad-burned if she don't pretty nigh fill th' whole outdoors, ba thundas!"

It is not difficult to see the color of the hats in Wright's novel. The "bad guys" are drunken, slovenly, dirty, sweaty, rude and boastful. The "good guys" are always concerned for the other person. They may be dusty and grimy from working in the field, but they always have clear eyes and walk with a sure step.

◆ Social Concerns ◆

Not only did Wright record life as it happened, he passed judgment on it. In *The Shepherd of the Hills* he contrasted, in his slanted way, city dwellers with the hill people of the Ozarks, and the hill people come out the winners. Although one may attain the mask of city sophistication, Wright believed, if one is a ruffian, it will be apparent and, on the other hand, if one is a true lady or gentleman, even illiterate speech will not conceal it.

Wright stressed the importance of nature as "God's other book." Too often in the hurry and busyness of city life, greed and hypocrisy take over, but if one takes the time to commune with nature, the healing spirit will help him see the important things of life.

Wright also criticized churches. At this time in history, social consciousness was being raised, and many leaders asserted that the poor were not always to blame for their condition. If one looked to the church for help, the church would look the other way. Wright believed that too often organized religion produced folly and hypocrisy, fulfilling the pretense of religion, but not addressing the actual social abuses around it.

◆ Themes ◆

It must be remembered that Wright saw his writing as a ministry to the people and all his works have a moralistic overtone. *The Shepherd of the Hills*, although no exception, is his most plotted story, based on an old legend about a city dweller who came to the hills and seduced, then deserted a young woman, who died shortly after her child was born. While this relationship was viewed as a crime, the overriding theme is one of renewing faith in God and man.

A stranger who comes to the Ozarks is the father of the city dweller, but conceals this fact and also the fact that he was a preacher at a big city church. Instead, he becomes the Shepherd in Mutton Hollow, tending the sheep as he once tended his congregation, but gaining strength and peace in his solitude, instead of false pride and shallow egotism. The internal struggle of the Shepherd, to rediscover the God he has lost, dominates the book, but other characters face internal conflicts as well. Young Matt, the young mountain man, struggles to overcome the animal side of himself and become a real man, and Sammy Lane, the young mountain woman, searches within herself for a lady's heart. Through this moralistic story Wright builds up faith in man to show his readers that there is always hope for a finer life.

◆ Techniques ◆

Wright's tale is told in the third person with occasional lapses when, as author, he speaks to the reader. During these times he moralizes and touches on the preachy tone his early critics noted. He begins this book talking to the reader with an allegory about the two trails of life — one leading to the higher, sunlit fields — and one leading to lower ground. Always, not just in *The Shepherd of the Hills*, there is a guiding element for mankind in Wright's writing.

Wright's use of dialect is very accurate, for he listened to the people of the Ozarks and recorded it faithfully. He uses it to distinguish the various characters and insert local color. He also used it to discern the various levels of book learning. When Sammy begins her studies from the "character-forming" books, her speech pattern changes as she assimilates knowledge. When her boyfriend Ollie returns from the city, his vocabulary and speech patterns also have improved.

While description is a useful tool to a writer, leading the reader to visualize the setting and understand characters' reactions, Wright is guilty of overusing description. His flowery pictures of events, people, and the Ozarks themselves bog down the narrative and leave the reader skimming ahead to pick up the plot once more.

◆ Literary Precedents ◆

There were others before Wright who wrote in the evangelical mode. Edward Payson Roe was also a minister who turned to print. His books followed the pattern of a religious hero's or heroine's efforts to convince a doubter (usually of the opposite sex) to become a Christian. The hero was always successful with the help of a great catastrophe as a climax.

Wright more directly followed the work of Charles M. Sheldon, also a preacher, who had written a series of essays that he read to his congregation and developed into *In His Steps* (1896), which predicted how Jesus would live if he lived today. Wright acknowledged Sheldon's influence in his first work, *That Printer of Udell's*, but even the critics agreed that Wright's work was better. Neither Sheldon nor Roe matched the prolific writings of Harold Bell Wright.

◆ Related Titles ◆

Although *The Shepherd of the Hills* has a more intriguing and interwoven plot than any of his other books, it contains the same criticism of the church manifested in his first book, *That Printer of Udell's* and in his two other books featuring Dan Matthews, *The Calling of Dan Matthews* (1909) and *God and the Groceryman* (1927).

The *Calling of Dan Matthews* was Wright's third book and followed *The Shepherd of the Hills* in the prescribed two year interval. Wright attacks the institutional church where Dan Matthews has become minister and the closed-minded elders, who by their constant interference, make it impossible for him to minister to the people. Finally Dan decides he cannot work under such control and returns to the Ozarks to enter another sort of ministry in his work as a businessman.

In *God and the Groceryman,* Dan Matthews feels he has not attained a true ministry through his work in developing the Old Baldy Mine. His efforts to achieve a ministry through his business that serves mankind is the central theme. Through Dan Matthews, Wright calls on the church to accept more social responsibility toward those less fortunate. He also lectures Christians against bowing to the doctrines of denominations instead of striving for a true life of service to others.

◆ Adaptations ◆

The Shepherd of the Hills was first made into a movie in 1919. Remakes were filmed in 1928, 1941, 1951, and 1963. The 1941 Paramount Pictures Technicolor filming starred the rising young actor, John Wayne, as young Matt.

Several stage versions of *The Shepherd of the Hills* have been performed through the years. Prior to 1931, Wright produced the play, at his own expense, with all proceeds to go to charity. In 1960 a group in Branson, Missouri formed The Shepherd of the Hills Historical Society. They built an outdoor theater and staged the novel, declaring eighty-five percent of the dialogue was from the book. The play, produced from May to October each year, complete with live horses and a burning cabin, has an average annual attendance of a quarter of a million people. The Institute of Outdoor Drama in Chapel Hill, North Carolina, has recognized it as America's most attended outdoor theater.

Veda Rae Jones

SHILOH AND OTHER STORIES

Short Stories

1982

◆

Author: Bobbie Ann Mason

◆ Characters ◆

The title story of the collection, *Shiloh and Other Stories*, is typical of the development of Mason's characters throughout the volume. In "Shiloh," Leroy Moffit has suffered a leg injury which has curtailed his career as a truck driver. He and his wife, Norma Jean, live in a small, nondescript house in Kentucky, while he pursues dreams of building a log cabin for himself and his wife. Norma Jean embarks on a course of self-improvement, pursuing programs in everything from physical fitness to English composition. Like many of Mason's characters, Norma Jean's aspirations for individual development appear somewhat naive and limited; however, they do have real consequences.

Norma Jean's mother has constantly urged Norma Jean and Leroy to visit the Civil War battlefield at Shiloh, the site of her own honeymoon, and when they do visit the site, partly to escape from their own disintegrating relationship, Norma Jean announces that she is leaving Leroy. Typical of Mason's characters, this breakdown seems both inevitable and pathetic. Neither is able to grow in the present circumstances, yet Leroy is unable to formulate the means to make their relationship a ground for real individual development.

Much the same dilemma is faced by the older couple Mary Lou and Mack Skaggs in "Rookers." While Mary Lou plays cards with older women friends and socializes in town, Mack stays home with the woodworking projects that are both his livelihood and his refuge from the world. He tries to read to keep up with their daughter who is away at college, but when she comes home before her exams, Mack is largely unable to communicate with her. This attitude is best captured at the end of the story by his telephone calls to the weather recording, which allows him to feign communication without speaking.

This sense of estrangement also characterizes Mason's women. The young girl, Peggy Jo, in "Detroit Skyline," visits her aunt and uncle in Detroit with her mother shortly after the introduction of television in America. During this visit her mother suffers a miscarriage, while Peggy Jo learns of the nascent world of television and about the "red scare" that is worrying her uncle and jeopardizing his job. For

Peggy Jo, the promise of Detroit's skyline seems both alluring and threatening, and her experiences are very distant from her home in Kentucky.

Much the same distance is described in "Drawing Names," when Carolyn Sisson attends a Christmas dinner with her family. She and her sisters try to maintain a sense of familial harmony, but this often means placating their husbands or boyfriends, and Carolyn's own lover, Kent, fails to show up for the occasion. Most difficult of all are Carolyn's father and Pappy, her mother's father. Carolyn ultimately elicits a compassionate response from Jim, the man living with her sister, Laura Jean, whose presence at this family dinner is not entirely well received, particularly by the other men. Jim's outsider status as a Northerner and as someone who is morally suspect in this conservative family gives him insight into Carolyn's feelings of alienation. And although Carolyn feels closer to Jim at the end of the story and somewhat free of her family's often oppressive judgments, her estrangement from this supposed harmony is not diminished.

In the story "Nancy Culpepper," the title character searches for a photo of her namesake great-great-aunt, and this search becomes emblematic of a larger attempt to connect herself to her ancestors. She, like other female figures in Mason's work, feels distanced from her family, but Nancy's distance has been caused by her move to the North and her advanced education.

On the whole, Mason's stories depict characters who are experiencing both a transformation of the family and a dissolution of the ways of economic life that had traditionally defined their families. Within this context, they are forced to establish a separate identity to achieve reconciliations, however temporary, with their lovers, parents, and siblings.

◆ Social Concerns/Themes ◆

Typical of realistic writing generally, Mason's first collection of short stories is strongly oriented toward documenting the social lives of her characters. In Mason's version of life in western Kentucky, these concerns are predominantly economic and familial. On the one hand, Mason demonstrates at great length the disjunction between the limited horizons of predominantly rural Kentucky life and the world of television and consumer culture with which it collides. This generates one of Mason's often repeated themes, that of the person who desires to flee a constraining environment. On the other hand, she also asserts the powerful pull of familial connections upon these often frustrated individuals.

The emotional world of Mason's fiction is one that is governed frequently by disappointment, compromise, divorce, and diminished expectations. This, however, is principally true of those figures who grew up under the shadow of the end of provincial life and the arrival of mainstream America in western Kentucky. Typically, they have factory jobs in an increasingly threatened industrial base, or they pursue a living on the low-paying fringes of commercial life. The older generation, frequently rural and seemingly innocent of or indifferent to the contemporary world, is the source of familial affiliations, and many of Mason's female characters find themselves torn between the roles of daughter and independent woman in a transformed social world.

The female characters are also usually the focus of the narration, and her work is in this respect characteristic of recent women's fiction in America. But what is perhaps distinctive about Mason's fiction is her singular preoccupation with popular culture. Her frequent references to television programs, popular music, brand names, and fads is used to suggest the limitations of the characters she explores, but it is also a means of demonstrating the emotional sophistication of the responses and the wit of her characters, who exploit this range of references often as an ironic counterpoint to and commentary upon their lives.

◆ Techniques ◆

Mason's fiction has been described by one reviewer as "shopping mall realism," and one of its most conspicuous achievements is its overall appearance of artlessness. This avoidance of obvious stylization is consistent with the aspiration of a realistic writer to present fiction as an accurate and faithful transcription of the real world, not as an elaborate and contrived story. To substantiate this claim to authenticity, Mason dwells upon the circumstantial details of the experience she describes, and this is particularly true of her use of popular culture. In contrast to those writers who depend upon references to other literary works to give their texts resonance, Mason relies upon popular culture as source of many of her allusions. For example, Norma Jean of "Shiloh," as the narrator notes, bears the real first names of Marilyn Monroe.

Shiloh and Other Stories belongs to the literary tradition of the related short story series. James Joyce's *Dubliners* (1914) is a good example of such a text, but much closer to Mason is Er-

nest Hemingway's first book of short stories, *In Our Time* (1925). With respect to her contemporaries, Mason is squarely within the tradition of recent American minimalist writing, and one might compare *Shiloh and Other Stories* with the similar collection by Raymond Carver, *Cathedral* (1983).

◆ Related Titles ◆

While *Shiloh and Other Stories* might be said to anticipate much of Mason's subsequent fiction in its thematic concerns and technical strategies, at least one story foreshadows a subsequent work. The Culpepper family is the subject of Mason's second novel *Spence + Lila* (1989), which is in many a ways a metaphoric extension of the events outlined in Mason's story, "Nancy Culpepper."

◆ Ideas for Group Discussions ◆

Abundant opportunity for discussion of familial and social relationships exists in the various stories Mason presents in this collection. Readers might want to list the many themes they encounter, such as parenthood, sibling relationships, spousal relationships, forgiveness, the power of memory, etc., then go back and find such themes in individual stories to note how the varied plots can focus upon identical themes. Most readers will see themselves in one or more of Mason's characters, or at least an aspect of themselves. An enjoyable exercise is the discussion of which character individual group members are most strongly attracted to and why.

1. Discuss the effects of depressed

economic conditions upon the various characters of Mason's short stories.

2. How does television work as a negative influence in the lives of Mason's short stories.

3. Choose one female character from a Mason story who you think best represents Mason's idea of a "heroine". Explain why.

4. Choose one male character from a Mason story who you think best represents Mason's idea of a "hero". Explain why.

5. In "Drawing Names", why is Carolyn attracted to Jim? How can you defend this aspect of Mason's plot as realistic?

6. Explain which of the stories is your favorite and why.

7. Can any positive message be drawn from the dissolution of the relationship between Leroy and Norma Jean in "Shiloh"?

8. Discuss the theme of communication seen in "Rookers."

9. In "Nancy Culpepper", the theme of personal identity is seen in Nancy's curiosity regarding her ancestors. Does she ever reach "closure" regarding her own identity and place in the family?

10. Which, if any, of Mason's short story characters seems determined to carry on family traditions? Analyze why each feels this necessity.

Thomas Carmichael
University of Western Ontario
[Ideas for Group Discussion
by Virginia Brackett,
University of Kansas]

THE SHINING

Novel

1977

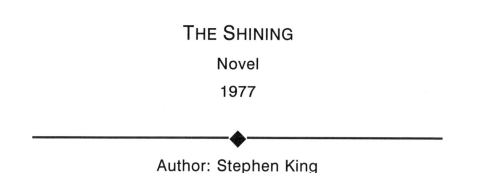

Author: Stephen King

◆ Characters ◆

The Shining has a relatively limited cast of characters for a novel of its length and scope. At the work's core, at the place where all thematic and structural lines intersect, is Jack Torrance — a man ridden by guilt and failure in his roles of husband, father, teacher, and aspiring author. Haunted by memories of his own alcoholic, violent father, Jack's career has been largely that of a man caught in the throes of Poe's "Imp of the Perverse," and the opportunity to serve as the winter caretaker of a luxury hotel deep in the heart of the Rocky Mountains is for him, literally, a last chance to set his life in order. Instead of providing the opportunity to become the man he wishes to be, however, Jack's sojourn in the Overlook Hotel becomes a nightmarish descent into the depths of subhuman depravity, and a large part of the novel's appeal rests with the skillful manner in which its author depicts the gradual disintegration of this character's personality.

Danny Torrance, Jack's five-year-old son, is an interesting but somewhat imperfectly realized character. Children and adolescents figure prominently in many of King's works as highly creditable and thematically central characters, but in *The Shining* Danny's principal function seems to be that of a somewhat esoteric potential victim. Danny is possessed of "The Shining," an essentially precognitive and telepathic talent, which seems to be the ultimate objective of the collective evil which infests the hotel. Although he can foresee certain critical events, he seems largely unable to interpret them correctly, and, with the exception of his final confrontation with the hotel in the form of his transformed father, he is able to do little to affect their outcome.

Ever growing in intensity as the novel develops pace is its most diffuse and disquieting character, The Overlook Hotel, and the force which inhabits and animates the place. Through a host of manifestations, in word and in action, it gradually assumes the form of a vast and threatening antagonistic force, rendering it perhaps the most memorable and highly personified of all haunted houses.

◆ Social Concerns ◆

The Shining, Stephen King's third

published novel, avoids the sweeping social concerns manifest in such apocalyptic visions as *The Stand* (1990) and *The Mist* (1985), or even the more limited examination of society's treatment of the "outsider" figure prevalent in so much of his fiction from *Carrie* (1974) onward. Despite its powerful supernatural elements, careful readers of this novel have long noted that a great deal of its core interest lies in its examination of a family attempting to function under conditions of extreme stress, and, perhaps most particularly, in the manner in which it depicts the gradual and ultimately total disintegration of its central character, Jack Torrance. Within this context, a number of motifs common to King's depiction of parent-child relationships in a great many of his works, in particular alcoholism, child abuse, obsessive behavior of one sort or another, and destructive guilt, are strongly evident in *The Shining*. Still, the largely naturalistic stance which seems to underlie the novel's basic movement forces attention to a somewhat different plane of understanding and provides an essentially nonsocially oriented frame of reference from which to explore its thematic implications.

◆ Themes ◆

When asked by his girlfriend about the subject of a book he is writing, Ben Mears, the protagonist of King's *'Salem's Lot* (1975), replies: "Essentially, it's about the recurrent power of evil." He might well have been speaking of *The Shining*, another work featuring a writer as its central character, for a large portion of the latter novel's thematic impact seems to derive from the notion that evil is both eternal and periodic in its ascendancy. It is more complex than merely that, however, for to this basic concept King harnesses two corollary and archetypal premises — a) the concentration of evil's power in what, presumably not requiring a more precise term, is most frequently referred to simply as a "Bad Place," and b) the ability of evil to act and sustain itself only through the subjugation and ultimate absorption of human subjects. The magnificent Overlook Hotel, primary setting of *The Shining*, is the primal "Bad Place" of this novel's action, and within its confines Jack Torrance is transformed from a flawed but empathetic human character into a monstrous pawn of evil. And, as if to emphasize the horrible inevitability of this darkly naturalistic trap, Jack is ultimately forced to accept the hotel's pronouncement upon him: "You've always been the caretaker."

◆ Techniques ◆

King's basic plotting technique in *The Shining* is similar to that found in many of his novels: A long, leisurely buildup is used to inculcate in his readers the sense of a disarmingly normal human situation, during which time — with the exception of an occasional foreshadowing — little is done to suggest the nature of the horrors to come. Thus, when the strange events do begin to manifest themselves — frequently about one-third through the novel — they come with the shock of sudden reversal, and from that point onward accrue with ever greater intensity as the narrative accelerates toward its climax.

King frequently uses small towns (often situated in Maine) as relatively closed settings within which to pursue his plots, but in *The Shining* he does himself one better by choosing the claustrophobic expedient of a totally isolated, snowbound hotel as the setting for one of his most inward-looking, psychologically-oriented novels. Character, plot, theme — all are vastly enhanced by this choice, and it is one of the novel's most successful technical features.

Other elements of technique which King uses to good purpose in the novel include multiple points of view, a limited but highly effective set of symbols ranging from the conventional (snow) to largely innovative (topiary animals), and pointed allusions to other literary works, principally E. A. Poe's "The Masque of the Red Death" (1842), and Shirley Jackson's *The Haunting of Hill House* (1959).

◆ Literary Precedents ◆

What is generally considered to be the first gothic novel, Horace Walpole's *The Caste of Otranto* (1764), features at its heart a haunted castle, and of all the elements which have come to be regarded as conventional in the roughly 200 years of gothic tradition linking Walpole and Stephen King, the haunted house has surely been the most frequently employed. To note that King has written a haunted house novel in *The Shining* is thus to immediately place him in the distinguished company of such writers as Nathaniel Hawthorne, Edgar Allan Poe, Henry James, and Shirley Jackson, to name but several, and in his or her own way each of them has contributed something vital to the texture of King's work.

King's frontispiece to *The Shining* includes a lengthy quotation from Poe's "The Masque of the Red Death," and he both quotes from and alludes to it on frequent occasions in the novel. Though such homage is certainly appropriate given the novel's context, it is another of Poe's works, "The Fall of the House of Usher" (1839), which, though never explicitly mentioned in *The Shining*, seems most clearly linked to a number of the author's themes and techniques. From the use of similar details of descriptive personification (including eyelike windows and a palpable, vital atmosphere) to cataclysmic endings involving the total devastation of the respective structures, the works share a great many features in common, although most telling of all is undoubtedly the manner in which each author forges a ghastly symbiotic bond between house and character. This is not to suggest, of course, that *The Shining* is little more than an updated version of Poe's classic tale: to do so would be to absurdly oversimplify a work which addresses itself to a wide variety of issues not in any way a part of the earlier narrative. Still, some knowledge of this important precedent is useful in any attempt to thoroughly evaluate King's aims and accomplishments in *The Shining*.

◆ Related Titles ◆

King has created one other memorable haunted structure — the Marsten House in *'Salem's Lot* — and utilizes this convention as a motif in several other works (e.g., the Black Hotel of *The Talisman*, 1984). The notion of the "Bad Place" in contexts other than that of the haunted house per se is explored in various ways in *Cujo* (1981), *Christine* (1983), *Pet Sematary* (1983), and a number of short stories.

Paranormal mental powers, or "Wild Talents," as they are sometimes called, are recurring elements in King's fiction, and are frequently explored with greater depth and sensitivity than is the case in *The Shining*. Most notable in this regard are *Carrie, Firestarter* (1980), and what is in many respects King's best effort in this mode, *The Dead Zone* (1979).

The interlocking themes of recurring evil and of the ability of evil to subjugate human endeavor to its own ends, so essential to an understanding of *The Shining*, are pervasive elements in much of Stephen King's work. They lie, for instance, at the heart of such seemingly diverse novels as *'Salem's Lot, The Stand, Christine*, and *Pet Sematary*, and form one major strand of a vision which, despite occasional forays into the realms of the hopeful (e.g., *Firestarter*), essentially contemplates a world in the process of being eclipsed by Matthew Arnold's darkling plain.

◆ Adaptations ◆

King's novels and short stories have formed the basis for a large number of film adaptations and have attracted the attention of such innovative directors as Brian De Palma, Tobe Hooper, John Carpenter, George A. Romero, and Lewis Teague. Perhaps none has been so controversial, however, as the 1980 film version of *The Shining*, directed by the celebrated Stanley Kubrick. King himself was clearly disappointed with Kubrick's handling of his novel (an attitude which he has not, incidentally, expressed with regard to most adaptations of his work), and critics have generally tended to view it as the sort of grand failure which men of genius are occasionally permitted. Kubrick's

essential method was to reduce the novel's themes and structures to several monolithically sustained effects. This involved, among other things, a vastly simplified notion of character, which may be seen quite clearly in the stripped down versions of Jack and Wendy Torrance played by Jack Nicholson and Shelley Duvall. On the other hand, Kubrick enhances, rather than deemphasizes, a number of the novel's other features, so that, for instance, the setting (the Overlook Hotel) assumes monumental significance through the manipulation of the film's impressive sets, while the symbolism inherent throughout the novel is given additional vigor in the film's reiterative use of mirrors, mazes, and other powerfully suggestive elements. Whether *The Shining* is the most effective of Stephen King's film adaptations is, to say the least, open to serious debate: Nonetheless, it remains in all probability the most interesting.

◆ Ideas for Group Discussions ◆

The Shining ranks with *'Salem's Lot, The Stand*, and *The Dead Zone* as the best novels by Stephen King. Remarkably, these also appeared within the first decade of his publishing career. *The Shining* is probably his most literary as well, demonstrating King's understanding of the scope and nuances of the American canon, as well as his specific study of the various genres of literature *fantas tique*—literature of the imagination, which encompass horror, science fiction, fantasy, even mainstream literature. These characteristics make *The Shining* the most-taught novel of King's collection, a reputation which was enhanced by Kubrick's film. While some purists criticize the film, particularly suggesting that the characters are not accurate to King's text, the film catapulted Stephen King to brand-name status in American fiction, while bringing his unique horror images to life.

1. King builds on the Gothic tradition of the haunted house. For King, a haunted house has more than a creepy history and a rumor of ghosts; it is a physical structure that embodies psychic evil. But he carries this image on step further, giving the house ill will and malevolent impulses. How does King give the Overlook Hotel a personality, and the power to act? What descriptions and images illuminate its nature?

2. One of the prevailing themes in King's novels is the breakdown of the family, particularly from the child's perspective. What normal stresses does the Torrance family suffer? What supernatural stresses? How do these stresses interact? What is at stake for Danny? for Wendy? for Jack?

3. King's continuing fascination with writing about writing is also evident in *The Shining*. Based on Jack's failed experiences with writing, what connections can you draw between writing and madness?

4. *The Shining* is one of a few novels by King that does not take place in Maine. In fact, the Overlook Hotel is based on the Stanley Hotel in Estes Park, Colorado. How has he transplanted the New England gothic landscape of Hawthorne, Poe and Lovecraft?

5. While King draws extensively from contemporary fiction, he also makes some unique contributions to the powerful and enduring images and scenes in American horror fiction. What images stand out from your reading? How is it unique? How does it adapt previously-existing images and motifs?

Richard E. Meyer
Western Oregon State College
[Ideas for Group Discussions
by Lynne Facer]

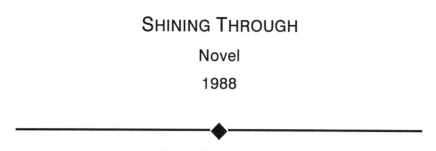

SHINING THROUGH

Novel

1988

◆

Author: Susan Isaacs

◆ Characters ◆

As the novel *Shining Through* opens, Linda Voss, the protagonist, seems to be a typical 1930s working girl. She worries about her alcoholic mother and spends lunch hours gossiping with the other secretaries, trying to conceal her crush on her handsome boss. But, like Isaacs's other female protagonists, she is witty, irreverent, and aware of her own sexuality. When war propels her into the midst of momentous events, she discovers her own inner resources and courage (which she deprecatingly calls foolhardiness).

The two men in her life, members of the Wall Street law firm where she works, handle levers of power which influence the entire nation. Through Linda's eyes, however, they are shown as vulnerable human beings. John Berringer, whom she marries, seems truly gifted by the gods; his intelligence, charm, and good looks impress everyone he meets. Only gradually does Linda — and the reader — discover the obsession which makes him unable to love. Edward Leland, an aristocrat and World War I hero who has the trust of the president himself, at first intimidates Linda. As the story proceeds she

comes to know him as a man whose bravery and humane concern shows his true nobility to be of the spirit.

Many other characters touch Linda's life during the course of the novel. Almost all of them are developed at least two-dimensionally, rather than being mere stereotypes.

◆ Social Concerns/Themes ◆

Shining Through tells the barely credible tale of an obscure "old-maid" legal secretary, who volunteers for a hazardous spy mission to Nazi Germany. She carries it out successfully — shining through — to find both safe haven in Switzerland and true love waiting for her at the end of the novel. The book thus mixes major elements from several different genres.

The romance motif holds the perennial appeal of the Cinderella story, but in a version shaped to the lost innocence of the twentieth century. It is not enough for this heroine to be beautiful and deserving; she must also prove herself in a harrowing ordeal before the happy ending is attained. Her previous marriage to a man who outwardly has all the attributes of the handsome prince, but who cannot love her, adds another nonstandard twist.

Linda Voss's adventures in wartime Germany not only provide excitement and suspense in the tradition of the spy novel but they offer the added satisfaction of a brave protagonist and a just cause. The Nazi regime's evil is vividly portrayed in the many brief episodes of disappearances and torture. Linda's part-Jewish identity increases the danger she faces. It also provides oblique commentary on the bigotry of the era, since even in America it makes her unwelcome in some circles.

Both the New York-Washington and the Berlin segments of the novel reflect much of the texture of ordinary life during the World War II years. As a story which provides the vicarious adventure of a historical novel, along with a glimpse of events which most of its readers' parents or grandparents lived through, the book has a unique appeal.

Finally, before Linda's entry into the world of intrigue, she works as a secretary and then lives as the "outsider" wife of a privileged Wall Street lawyer. These segments give an in-depth look at two settings which might be pictured as mere "ordinary life" in many types of fiction. Here those settings are shown to be equally as rich in the cross-currents of suspicion, masked identities, and sudden disaster as are the halls of power on either side of the Atlantic. Besides providing ongoing developments which put her in "the right place at the right time" to take on the espionage assignment, these episodes illustrate that similar human reactions and political machinations must be coped with no matter what the milieu.

◆ Techniques ◆

Isaacs uses first-person narration throughout the novel. This intensifies the horror and anxiety of Linda's experiences in wartime Berlin; the reader feels the dislocation and fear almost as immediately as the narrator does.

Like Isaacs's previous novels, *Shining Through* exuberantly mixes story-lines and formulas. It borrows "action" and suspense elements from the espionage novel, but its protagonist is an amateur, and is both more ethical and less prone to heroics than such culture-idol spies as James Bond.

As a historical novel it aims to place its characters in a plausible setting and situation, rather than to show them as participants in "Great Events." The Normandy invasion is the only actual military operation referred to, and its impact in the story is offstage and indirect.

As a love story, *Shining Through* rather resembles the modern Gothic romance in keeping both reader and heroine guessing about which man in her life will be worthy of her. It also has a mysterious and injured hero, a frequent feature in Gothic romances from the Brontë sisters' works to the present. However, it lacks a stately or haunted house, a brooding atmosphere, and several other elements of the Gothic genre.

◆ Related Titles/Literary Precedents ◆

In looking at Isaacs' first four novels, some interesting patterns begin to emerge. Perhaps "non-patterns" would be a better description, because two are patterns of surprise rather than predictability.

Shining Through draws on a variety of

one, all well and good, if you know what it means and what to do with it. If you are aiming to take up the writing trade, you need different equipment from that which you will need for the art, or even just the profession of writing."

Critics who faulted *Ship of Fools* for its lack of conventional plot disagreed with Porter's foregoing statement, but she was not shaken in her belief that thematic concerns were the basis of all serious fiction. In her own novel, Porter chronicles the alternate attractions and repulsions among the passengers and crew of the *Vera* which finally erupt in violence at the climactic gala.

Throughout the book, the use of the omniscient narrator gives Porter the freedom to roam among her large cast, looking into interior lives when appropriate and showing the limitations of individual perspectives. For example, early in the voyage, Porter mocks Frau Rittersdorf's efforts to record reality in her journal; the treatment is doubly ironic since Porter herself kept a journal during her own 1931 voyage, jotting notes for this very novel. By means of her omniscient voice, Porter provides a narrative voice less self-involved than any one passenger could provide.

◆ Literary Precedents ◆

At the outset of her book, Porter frankly pays homage to Sebastian Brant's *Das Narrenschiff* (1495; *Ship of Fools*), a medieval moral allegory about a voyage. Both the author and reader know that the *Vera* is headed into disaster, but Porter is interested in investigating how the destination is unavoidable, not in offering alternatives. Her pessimism about human nature and society, as well as the voyage structure itself, have a notable literary precedent also in Jonathan Swift's *Gulliver's Travels* (1726), in which the characters' physical grossness or abnormalities embodied their interior qualities.

One of Porter's favorite writers, Henry James, often used the voyage and cross-cultural conflicts as the basis of his work. In her own fiction, Porter had depicted in some detail the cross-cultural voyage twice before. *Hacienda* (1934) takes a North American writer to Mexico to watch a Russian film crew at work. "The Leaning Tower" takes the American painter Charles Upton to Berlin before World War II. In both these works Porter clearly shows the interests which would keep her working off and on for close to thirty years on *Ship of Fools*.

◆ Adaptations ◆

In 1965, *Ship of Fools* was adapted for the motion picture screen. Abby Mann wrote the screenplay and Stanley Kramer directed it. A prestigious international cast including Vivien Leigh, Simone Signoret, and Oskar Werner ensured the movie wide distribution, but the only Academy Awards it won were for black and white cinematography and art direction. Critics faulted the movie for its characterization of the proto-Nazis as dupes or fools.

Emilie F. Sulkes

THE SHIPPING NEWS

Novel

1993

Author: E. Annie Proulx

◆ Characters ◆

The main and only fully developed character in *The Shipping News* is Quoyle. As the omniscient narrator tells the story, Quoyle was born into a family that seemed to care nothing for him. His older brother abusively belittled him and his father thought of him as nothing but a failure. If that were not enough to make him insecure, his hideous appearance — "head shaped like a crenshaw, no neck, reddish hair ruched back" — further diminished his sense of self worth. What is surprising is that Quoyle did not turn mean himself. Instead, he suffered in silence, lacked ambition as a result of his family's attitude toward him, and did not bother to set goals for himself other than to try to make a living. Alone as he was, despite the presence of family, Quoyle seemed rudderless. As such, he drifted into his friendship with Partridge who steered him toward becoming a newspaperman. Partridge helped Quoyle land a job at *The Mockingburg Reporter*, where Quoyle worked unless it was vacation time for the editor's kids. Then Quoyle would lose his job to those kids until college was in session again.

Hired, fired; fired, hired, over and over — that seemed to be the repetition of Quoyle's life in Mockingburg whether it was as reporter or as husband. Ed Punch, editor, thought nothing of casting Quoyle out when Quoyle was not needed or was in the way; likewise, Quoyle's wife, Petal Bear (who came into Quoyle's life about the time Partridge and his wife, Mercalia, left Mockingburg for California) did the same. A caricature of an oversexed and loose woman, Petal Bear bore Quoyle two daughters, Bunny and Sunshine. She had no interest in mothering the girls; rather, she would take off by car for weeks or months at a time, sailing up and down east coast highways and byways, seemingly employed, but quite literally tramping from one relationship to another while Quoyle patiently and passionately begged her to come home. At the same time that Quoyle longed for Petal Bear, he gave the appearance of being spineless in his marriage, reflexively cowering behind his receding chin whenever he was verbally abused by her dismissive and bruising nonchalant attitude toward him.

However, Quoyle is not a spineless character. Unmanned though he has been by his wife's unfaithfulness, he becomes a new breed of man by necessity and by his own innate goodness — one who not only does the fathering but the mothering as well. While Petal Bear is off with one male after another, Quoyle is home raising the girls, going to work, earning a living — juggling modern society's roles. When the marriage ends — by accident with the violent death of Petal Bear in a car crash — Quoyle quite naturally continues the dual roles. Ironically, the most balanced family of the book emerges from Quoyle's linking up with his aunt, Agnis Hamm, to make a home for his two girls whom he has precipitously retrieved from a pornographic photographer (to whom they had been sold by their mother) in the nick of time before they became his subjects. Quoyle's restructured family functions very well as it builds a new life, quite aptly in the place called Newfoundland.

On course as a newspaperman, Quoyle lands the position of reporter of the shipping news for *The Gammy Bird* by following his own lead and not what has been dictated to him. He submits a different article from the one which has been requested by the editor. Instead of being chastised, Quoyle is finally praised for doing something right. The narrator notes that it is the first time in his life. He is thirty-six. Over the course of the remainder of the novel, he tells the news while he makes the news as the novel's central character. On the ship of life, Quoyle moves from passive passenger to active deck hand. Encountering one storm after another, literally and figuratively, Quoyle overcomes them.

◆ Social Concerns ◆

In *The Shipping News*, Proulx tells more than a story; it is news, ultimately good news. Metaphorically, Quoyle is on the ship of life. Proulx's fictional *The Shipping News* frames Quoyle's nonfictional shipping news in that Proulx's novel — in the telling — paradoxically and ironically reports the real news about humanity (and inhumanity), the same as that which is told daily in late twentieth century newspapers and on radio and television news shows, such as dysfunctional families, parental and spousal abuse, incest, extramarital sexual encounters, rape, murder, and even the presence of child pornography.

Quoyle's life begins in a dysfunctional abusive family, verbally abusive if not physically; yet, he survives the abuse and grows up and into a loving, kindly, and functional adult. Quoyle not only does what is right as a responsible human being but he also does what is right because he cares for his fellow human beings.

The predominant setting of the novel, Killick-Claw, Newfoundland, provides the backdrop for a dwindling breed of men and women, those who have withstood the harsh northern seacoast while they drew their livelihood from the sea. The remaining residents of Killick-Claw, quirky though they may be, ply on not only against the elements but also against the modern world, realizing (some more, some less) that the twenty-first century, as Proulx observes, "hangs over Newfoundland like a clenched fist." The yield from the sea is shrinking, and the hard life of the northland is not what some of the older generation want for their younger ones. On the other hand, the culture of the cities to the south is encroaching as a new generation looks to Newfoundland for hidden treasures in offshore oil beds and mineral deposits, those treasures which contemporary society needs in order to support modern technology. While the novel, like many before it, implicitly affirms the natural and quickening world of the "outport," in contrast to the unnatural and demeaning world of asphalt and concrete, the novel also knots the two worlds together. Neither is self-sustaining any longer.

◆ Themes ◆

As a *bildungsroman*, the novel builds the main character as he moves from one world to another. While those worlds contrast with one another, they are also interrelated. The contrasts are of south to north (the United States to Canada), Quoyle's unnatural urban life of the early novel against nature holding sway over human interactions in Newfoundland, and the dysfunctional with the functional family. The contrasting worlds are not separated along two distinct lines; they overlap. In fact, they are lashed together by the interconnectedness which comes from the unfolding of human lives and the dependencies of one world upon another.

Unlike the typical *bildungsroman, The Shipping News* is the story of a man whose life begins in a world in which the trappings are those of a late twentieth-century exposé. It is a world which seems totally devoid of innocence, peopled by a brother who is meanness personified, by unloving and self-centered parents whose suicide message is left on Quoyle's answering machine, by a newspaper boss who hires and fires Quoyle at will, and by a wife who sells herself over and over to men up and down the east coast and finally, just before her fatal car crash, even sells their two young daughters to a porno-graphic photographer. Quoyle's growth out of that ugly world is a movement toward expressing and affirming his more kindly nature and a "gaining of innocence," according to critic Natasha Walter. Paradoxically, then, the novel reverses the traditional *bildungsroman.*

While Quoyle's life in Mockingburg, New York, is generally devoid of human kindnesses, he does encounter some kindliness there when he meets and is helped by Partridge, a newspaperman. Partridge (who bears a name which is symbolic of the bringer of peace and love) sets Quoyle on course. Then Quoyle's aunt steers him toward his new home in Newfoundland where he finds his life work. Dropping anchor in Killick-Claw (meaning anchor hook), Quoyle puts together his family with the aunt (as she is most often called in the book) and his daughters in Newfoundland. Having removed himself from the frenetic and screeching harshness represented by the Mockingburg of New York, Quoyle has returned to the land of his forebears, to his roots. It is not a return to a simplistic innocence of unknowing, but rather it is a movement into an understanding and appreciation of the simpler joys of life. Certainly, in the realism of the novel's form, the author does not deny the complications of life. They are there in the harshness of that northern landscape as well. With growing self-assurance, Quoyle faces them, usually with his chin up rather than in an earlier way of reflexively shielding his receding chin.

The simpler joys are those derived from being with family and friends and from being anchored to a place. The dysfunctional family of Quoyle's childhood and young adulthood is not that of his life in Newfoundland. He builds a functioning family when he sets up housekeeping with his aunt and daughters; he develops a relationship with a woman, Wavey Prowse, which grows into a marriage in the last pages of the novel; and he connects with his neighbors, befriended by them and befriending them through their shared experiences in the outport of Killick-Claw and inside the offices of *The Gammy Bird*.

The contrast of the dysfunctional with the functional is reflected in the differences between Mockingburg and Killick-Claw, between *The Mockingburg Record* and *The Gammy Bird*, between New York and Newfoundland. New York, devoid of the harshness of nature, should be an easier environment in which to function. Yet it is in the harsh ice-covered, bitter cold, squally north of Newfoundland where Quoyle and his aunt Agnis Hamm make a warm and caring home for themselves and Quoyle's daughters, Bunny and Sunshine. Proulx's novel, though, is not so simplistic as to suggest that New York is all bad and Newfoundland naturally good. The people of Killick-Claw can do evil things as well as those of Mockingburg. Certainly Agnis Hamm's rape by her brother, Quoyle's father, and Nutbeem's pursuit of sex stories and car crashes and all sorts of bloody events for *The Gammy Bird*, and the apparent murder and dismemberment of Bayonet Melville by his wife — are tied to Newfoundland even if they do not all occur there. Nevertheless, *The Shipping News* never becomes dark and brooding in its presentation of the tragic moments of life, but in the essence of comedy ends in a marriage, with Proulx closing the novel by saying that "love sometimes occurs without pain or misery."

◆ Techniques ◆

As the tale unravels, Quoyle quite literally learns the ropes of life. Chapters are introduced by quotations from Clifford Warren Ashley's *The Ashley Book of Knots* (1944), which Proulx acknowledges provided her with the inspiration for making the novel into more than "just the thread of an idea." Quoyle, whose name means a coil of rope, experiences the various knots or themes of life as he either uncoils (or unravels) or coils himself from childhood into adulthood.

Knots are strung throughout the novel, pictured at the openings of most of the chapters, and one type of knot appears in chapter after chapter, separating smaller units of each chapter. The knots which introduce the chapters are symbolic of the focus of the chapter or an event in the chapter: half hitches, rolling hitches, slippery hitches, lanyards, cats cradles, marriage knots and more. Knots relate to Quoyle but also to other characters as well. Knots serve as symbol and knots are purposeful in the workaday world of Killick-Claw. A distant cousin of Quoyle's who is thought to be not quite right in his head and who mysteriously hovers in the coves and corners near Quoyle's Point leaves knots for the unsuspecting Quoyle to discover (an overhand on Quoyle's car seat or another often used rope, twisted and kinked, under the boat seat and more and more here, there, and everywhere) as if they were hexes, seemingly winding Quoyle's life in their symbolically knotted tale. Agnis Hamm speaks of her friend and lover, Irene Warren, as "all knotted up" when Warren succumbs to cancer. On the other hand, knots have a real purpose not only for the young Bunny who takes pleasure from learning the knots of shipping from an old sea captain but also for her father, Quoyle, who must learn knots for the mere safety of sailing his small boat and for the aunt, too, who must learn knots as part of her education in stitchery for the success of her sewing business, Hamm's Custom Yacht Interiors and Upholstery.

Despite the sometimes mysterious or caricatured behavior of the peculiar characters, such as the old Quoyle cousin or *The Gammy Bird* newspaper staff: Buggit, Nutbeem, and Card, and a raft of other types, who people the novel (Dickensian though they may be), *The Shipping News* is realistic in its portrayal of human nature. Proulx spent a number of years — making nine trips in fact — going back and forth to Newfoundland from New England to study the people of the region, to learn their manner of speaking, to learn their way of life. Her characters, then, are drawn from true studies.

Much in the way that characters move in and out of our lives from day to day, some present more often than others, so they weave in and out of Quoyle's daily life. The more they enter his life and he theirs, the more intertwined and connected their lives become. Yet Quoyle's growth in Proulx's *bildungsroman* comes not only from connecting himself with others who live in Killick-Claw and with his Quoyle roots at Quoyle Point but also from detaching himself from the dysfunctional twinings of his earlier life with family, wife, work. Proulx's writing is much like her symbolic use of knotting. She uses language made dense by tersely knotted phrases — kinky, crimped, twisted — interspersed among a full sentence here or there. The writer dispenses with any extraneous words, tightening the language as tautly as knots tighten to serve their specific purposes. Quoyle's story is never strung out in long and easy-going sentences even though Proulx takes more pleasure from writing a novel than a short story for the very reason that she can go on at length. But the length is not due to verbiage; rather it allows for more characters, a broader swath of the coil of humanity, and for more about locale as it affects and effects character.

◆ Literary Precedents ◆

When *The Shipping News* was published in hard cover, it was hailed by *The Boston Globe* as being in the tradition of George Eliot, the two writers alike in their love of observation, and their understanding of place in relation to person. George Eliot's classic statement defining her intent to be realistic in her writing, to focus on the common life and everyday experiences, is representative of what Proulx has done as well. Like her nineteenth-century British predecessor, Proulx has a sharp eye for setting as well as a good ear for regional voices. The dialogue of the novel makes character reflect region. However, Proulx's portrayal of character seems more in the manner of Dickens than in the vein of George Eliot. From Dickensian-like names to similarly caricatured personalities, the people of Killick-Claw (and Mockingburg as well) call to mind the Uriah Heeps and the David Copperfields or even the Pickwickian types and the Pips of a previous century. Likewise, Proulx's education of Quoyle follows in the line of a Dickensian *bildungsroman*. Like a Copperfield or a Pip, Quoyle's education comes from his encounters with quirky one-dimensional characters and not from more fully-developed supporting characters such as those of Eliot's novels.

The novel's forebears are not only British; Proulx's work has been likened to that of the American writer Wallace Stegner. Verlyn Klinkenborg traces Proulx's interest in landscape and in work to Stegner; accuracy of setting and authenticity of historical evidence place Proulx, like Stegner, within the tradition of American realism. In that respect, place, voice, and person reflect the work of Twain as well. The terseness of Proulx's sentences (with language clipped, pithy, and aphoristic) like that of the poet Emily Dickinson further secures Proulx within the tradition of realism.

Yet Proulx is thoroughly modern in her inclusion of once taboo characters such as the lesbian aunt and the pornographic photographer. Even by including young Herry, Wavey Prowse's son who is born with Downs Syndrome, the author places herself within the spirit of modernism which does not deny the range of human aberrations. That range includes grotesqueries as well. For example, the Melvilles — Bayonet and Silver, gross in their slovenly and drugged state of overconsumption — show up initially in their battering ram of a boat, Hitler's elegantly outfitted *Botterjacht*, obnoxiously loud and abusive toward one another, and return a second time, at least part of Bayonet does, in a suitcase, dismembered apparently by his wife, Silver. The talk can be blatantly frank, too, whether it comes from Petal Bear's vulgarities or Bunny's innocent bluntness; Nutbeem's call for stories about car crashes, shipwrecks, or spousal beatings; or an aunt who tells it like it is. Behaviors, too, touch on the forbidden or reflect the extremes of human responses. Agnis Hamm takes pleasure in knowing that her brother's ashes are in the bottom of the privy where she put them, retribution for his long past rape of her, yet long suffered and long remembered by her.

As modern as Proulx is, her novels do not do what the modern novel does over and over: explore the psychological depths of the characters. The reader is not allowed to understand what impulses are at work. However, in detailing their responses to work, place, and one another, the author presents real folks with real drives and real desires.

◆ Related Titles ◆

In *Postcards* Proulx uses a technique similar to that used in *The Shipping News*. She signals the reader to note the intent of the chapter by opening each with a postcard, pictured and inscribed, just as she opens each chapter in *The Shipping News* with a quotation from *The Ashley Book of Knots* as well as the drawing and naming of the knot inscribed. Referred to by some critics as Proulx's *double ouevre*, both books focus on the chronicling of the protagonist's family, the disintegration of the dysfunctional family unit, the place which produced that family, and the significant changes occurring in that place and how they affect the lives of those living there.

Accordion Crimes (1996) uses another device, an accordion, to tie a fragmented story together. An ambitious Sicilian immigrant in 1890 attempts to bring his family to America, but a series of bizarre ailments kills all but the father, an accordion maker, and youngest son, who eventually make their way to New Orleans. They find a city that is seething with corruption and hate, and they eventually die in an anti-Italian riot. In a wildly ironic sequence of freak accidents, weird suicides, odd coincidences and poor judgment, the accordion surfaces in North Dakota, Texas, Maine and Chicago, where it gives voice to the laments and dreams of African, German, Mexican, French, and Polish immigrants. Proulx's theme is the malleability and insidiousness of prejudice and lost past.

◆ Ideas for Group Discussions ◆

Proulx has come to publishing novels later in life than most contemporary authors. Yet her fame has been immediate and her work has won significant literary awards which most critics and reviewers think are merited. Lauded for the density of her language, the wealth of lore which the books reveal, and the encyclopedic range of subjects addressed, Proulx's books have much to say. Just as they are about the realities of life and are set in a real place, so too they make use of symbolism and metaphor. Consequently, they provide a variety of topics for discussion.

In *The Shipping News*, Proulx is interested in such topics as knots, the sea, the small town newspaper trade, saltwater fishing lore, the rules of sailing, shipwrecks, weather and its effects on the Newfoundlanders, their patois, their superstitions, and their saga. Discussion of the setting alone would appeal to the traveler since Newfoundland is not the place where a majority of novels are situated; however, the lore which Proulx explores in relation to that setting makes it much richer for the traveler and the historian as well.

Readers who search for metaphorical relationships and symbolical meaning, those who find delight in words or phrases which carry double meanings or signals which act as clues will take pleasure in discussing what their detective work has uncovered in a name or a knot.

1. To begin, then, at the beginning of the novel, which is where the reader encounters knots first, what is the significance of them and how are they used in *The Shipping News*? They not only open each chapter and define segments of chapters, but one also closes the book. What do they mean?

2. Likewise, what is the significance of the naming of characters and places? While Quoyle's name links him to the knots, what about the names of the other characters and the names of the places where they live or work?

3. Proulx seems to set up a contrast between Mockingburg and Killick-Claw. Do the names indicate differences between the two? What about the newspapers which represent the two places? How are they alike; how do they differ?

4. The contrast goes further than that of two towns; it extends to regions and to nations. What are those contrasts between the coastal region of Newfoundland and that of Long Island, between Canada and the United States — and how are those contrasts significant to the story line?

5. What other contrasts are there in the book? Between characters? Between mannerisms? In what ways are the contrasted characters, work places, regions alike? In the parallelisms which

the book explores, what are the truths which Proulx seems to be establishing about person and place?

6. If *The Shipping News* does represent the ship of life and Quoyle the protagonist of a *bildungsroman*, what is it that Quoyle learns as he sails through life? Is he a passenger on the ship or does he steer his own way?

7. Does Quoyle really change very much from his days in Mockingburg to his life in Newfoundland? If so, what are the events or words which cause or signify the changes?

8. Why does Proulx invent an oddly demented old cousin as one of the novel's characters and have him shadow Quoyle and his family, apparently hexing them with knots? What do the old man's knots mean? And, what do his ghostly appearances suggest in a realistic novel? Could the novel be said to have a gothic quality as well?

9. What societal concerns is Proulx addressing when she has a lesbian aunt replace a promiscuous mother as the adult female figure in the family? Are there any other instances of societally-determined aberrancy supplanting the norm? If so, what meaning can be drawn from the topsy-turvy displacements?

10. Does the house at Quoyle Point carry any symbolical meaning?

11. Why are the Melvilles in the novel? Do they represent more than a couple of sensational moments in a good story?

12. With the conclusion of the novel, is it fair to say that it is a novel of realism? That it is gothic? Modern? More? Does Proulx pack her novel with characteristics from various prose fictions? If so, what is the effect? Does the novel hold together as an integrated and comprehensive work of art?

Alice Conger Patterson
Salem College

SHOELESS JOE

Novel

1982

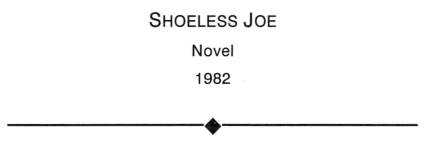

Author: W. P. Kinsella

◆ Social Concerns/Themes ◆

Somewhat similar to what he does in his Cree Indian stories, Kinsella hints in *Shoeless Joe* that the world changes rapidly and that these changes often destroy some irreplaceable treasures and resources. Within the novel's plot, for instance, Ray Kinsella's (no relationship to author Kinsella intended) small Iowa farm is in danger of being taken over by a computer-farming conglomerate, a fate that has befallen other neighboring farms. In addition are oblique contempts for academe, religion, and "all the forces that control our lives." In the main, however, *Shoeless Joe* is basically an entertaining narrative, or, as Kinsella admits: "I am an old-fashioned storyteller. I try to make people laugh and cry. A fiction writer's duty is to entertain. If you then sneak in something profound or symbolic, so much the better."

Kinsella claims that *Shoeless Joe* is not a novel about baseball but rather about the "power of love in all directions." This theme becomes evident, for example, when protagonist Ray Kinsella lists the loves of his life: his wife Annie, his daughter Karin, Iowa, and the "great god Baseball." J. D. Salinger, a fictionalized characterization of the author of *The Catcher in the Rye* (1951), also is a great lover of baseball. In its more universal implications, the love of baseball is typified by those old-time players who have long since died but who mysteriously appear to play on Ray's field and who all love baseball for its own sake.

◆ Characters ◆

Shoeless Joe has two protagonists, Ray Kinsella and J. D. Salinger, both of whom are devotees of baseball. Ray quits his lucrative insurance business and buys a small Iowa farm from Eddie Scissons who lies about being the "oldest living Chicago cub." Ray loves the natural beauty of his farm, or as he says, "Once you've been touched by the land, the wind never blows so cold again, because your love files the edges off it." Ray's being "touched by the land" is evident when he refuses to sell his debt-ridden farm to Martin, his brother-in-law, who needs the farm to complete a computer-farming conglomerate that would make the land "neat and clean and sterile and heartless."

Ray's devotion to and love for baseball is underscored when a mysterious voice says that if he builds a baseball field on his farm, the late Joseph Jefferson (Shoeless Joe) Jackson, a former 1919 White Sox player, will appear. In a labor of love and buoyed by Annie's love, Ray constructs the diamond where he, Annie, and Karin watch ghostly players including Shoeless Joe. Moreover, when Ray hears another voice exhorting him to "Ease his pain," he intuitively knows that his refers to the now reclusive Salinger whose childhood dream had been to play baseball at the now defunct Polo Grounds. After kidnapping Salinger and taking him to a Boston Red Sox game where both hear another voice — "Fulfill the dream" — they travel to Minnesota, meet the now deceased Moonlight Graham, an ex-New York Yankee who never caught a ball or had a time at bat, and the three of them return to Ray's farm.

Once back at the farm, the ghostly games resume, and Moonlight Graham fulfills his wish to play professional baseball. Besides Shoeless Joe and Graham, other ghostly players are Ray's father and the other White Sox players who, along with Shoeless Joe, were banished forever from baseball because of being involved in the 1919 World Series scandal. The novel's point is, of course, that all of these old-time players are chosen because they loved baseball for itself, or, as Shoeless Joe says: "I loved the game . . . I'd have played for food money. I'd have played free and worked for food. It was the game, the parks, the smells, the sounds." Similarly, Ray, Annie, Karin, Salinger, and Scissons are the chosen few because of their love for baseball and thus can see the games while unbelievers like Martin and Ray's identi-

cal twin, Richard, see nothing.

In the final analysis, dreams do come true on Ray's magical baseball diamond. Ray sees his father and the legendary Joe Jackson play on the same team; Moonlight Graham fulfills his wish of actively playing in major league games; and Eddie Scissons finally plays for the Chicago Cubs. Furthermore, in the novel's conclusion, when he exits with the ghostly players, Salinger fulfills his wish of playing at the Polo Grounds.

◆ Techniques ◆

Kinsella combines both fantasy and reality and fact and fiction to create an entertaining and suspenseful narrative. Simply stated, the plot centers upon Ray's magical baseball diamond where dreams do come true, and once the fantasy begins, the details are so vivid that the reader is swirled along by the characters and the narrative events. Moreover, by alternating his scenes between the fantasy baseball games and the reality in the characters' lives, Kinsella captures the transient nature of dreams while emphasizing the grace and essence of baseball, a sport that is peculiarly an American constant, or as Salinger says: "It is a living part of history, like calico dresses, stone crockery, and threshing crews waiting at outdoor tables. It continually reminds us of what it once was, like an Indianhead penny in a handful of new coins."

◆ Literary Precedents ◆

Kinsella's *Shoeless Joe* belongs to the American sports-literature tradition that includes poems, essays, short stories, and novels about all forms of sports. Among the sport novels are, to suggest a few, Lawrence Shainberg's *One On One* (basketball); Leonard Gardner's *Fat City* (boxing); *Peter Gent's North Dallas Forty* (1973, football); Bernard Malamud's *The Natural* (1952) and Robert Coover's *The Universal Baseball Association* (1968, baseball). These novels expose some of the unsavory aspects of their various sports; for example, the doom inherent in *Fat City* for boxers, the excessive violence for the sake of corporate enterprise in professional football, Roy Hobbs's personal failure in baseball. Generally, these works and others of their ilk emphasize how the particular sport is a metaphor for the world and even life itself. In juxtaposition to these starker renderings of the sporting world, Kinsella's novel is devoid of any violence or hardened villains and simply recaptures the beauty, grace, and essence of baseball as a sport. In this sense, the novel entertains the reader while permitting him to escape temporarily and to experience the mythic baseball world, still the oldest sport in the American heritage.

◆ Related Titles ◆

The major themes in *The Iowa Baseball Confederacy* (1986) are a love for baseball and the nature of dreams. The theme is evident in Gideon Clarke's quest to prove that in 1908 the Chicago Cubs played a game with the All Stars of the amateur Iowa Baseball Confederacy in Big Inning, Iowa. Stan Rogalski, Gideon's friend and aging triple A ballplayer, has loved the game and hopes someday to play in the major leagues. Similar to the dream motifs in *Shoeless Joe,* both Gideon and Stan fulfill their dreams when they slip

through the "cracks in time" to the "gauzy dreamland that separates the past from the present."

Gideon and Stan are the novel's protagonists and both of them are baseball fanatics. Within the plot, Gideon is indoctrinated into baseball lore by Matthew, his father, whose lifetime quest has been to prove that the game between the Chicago Cubs and the Iowa Baseball Confederacy took place, knowledge that is mysteriously seared into his imagination when he is making love to a carnival dancer under a tree and is struck by lightning. Despite scoffers and disbelievers, Matthew pursues his quest and even writes a doctoral dissertation about the history of the Iowa Baseball Confederacy, a dissertation rejected by his dissertation committee who recommend that Matthew major in creative writing. When Matthew is ironically killed by a line-drive at a Milwaukee baseball game, his knowledge and desires are transferred to Gideon, who assumes his father's quest. Stan Rogalski has also loved baseball since he was a child and although he eventually plays triple A ball in Salt Lake City, he desperately wants to play in the major leagues. Discovering an old piece of track appropriately named the Baseball Spur, Gideon and Stan slip through the "cracks in time" from 1978 to 1908 and the legendary game between the Chicago Cubs and The Iowa Baseball Confederacy, a game that lasts for forty days and more than 2,000 innings and which the Confederacy win. Even though both Gideon and Stan love the past — Stan plays well for the Confederacy and has an offer to play for the Cubs — they both decide that they must return to the present.

Kinsella is not particularly interested in social concerns in *The Iowa Baseball*

Confederacy. Gideon is contemptuous of big business, conglomerate farming, academia, and religion. His sister, Enola Gay — she was named "a full year before the bomber droned over Hiroshima" — becomes America's first urban guerrilla when she and her cohorts bomb a Chicago Dow Chemical subsidiary, thus being years ahead of the Chicago Seven, the Weather Underground, and the Symbionese Liberation Army. The narrator's contempt and Enola Gay's exploits are only secondary, however, and again Kinsella is primarily interested in storytelling and entertaining the reader.

As he has done in *Shoeless Joe*, Kinsella combines fact with fiction and reality with fantasy to create an entertaining novel. Moreover, the plot elements are even more fantastic than those of *Shoeless Joe*. In *The Iowa Baseball Confederacy*, for example, the Black Angel, a huge cemetery statue, plays field for the Confederacy; Teddy Roosevelt appears and takes his time at bat; Leonardo da Vinci drifts through the skies in a striped balloon and claims that he actually invented baseball; the mythical Indian Drifting Away materializes to hit the winning run; during the forty-day game, a torrential rain and flood destroys Big Inning, Iowa; and Gideon falls in love with Sarah who is killed by one of the few automobiles in town.

Kinsella uses the time-machine motif — e.g., H. G. Wells's *The Time Machine* (1895) — to transport his characters back and forth through the cracks in time. Even though the past for Gideon and Stan may be a wondrous place where dreams may come true, they decide to return to the present where things are real.

◆ Adaptations ◆

In 1984 *Field of Dreams*, the movie adaptation of *Shoeless Joe*, premiered. Directed by Phil Alden Robinson, the film received mostly favorable reviews and starred Kevin Costner as Ray Kinsella, Amy Madigan as Annie Kinsella, Burt Lancaster as Doc Graham, and James Earl Jones as Terrence Mann, a character that was substituted for J. D. Salinger's role in the novel.

Edward C. Reilly
Arkansas State University

SHOGUN

Novel

1975

◆

Author: James Clavell

◆ Characters ◆

John Blackthorne, pilot of the Dutch expedition to prey on Spanish shipping, and open up trade for Holland in unknown, probably dangerous lands and waters, is as skilled and as daring as sea-captains in literature are meant to be. He brooks no opposition from the enemy or his own men. Only the forces of nature can humble him and he fights even those to his utmost. Not only is he brave, however, he is intelligent, tolerant and eager to learn. These qualities save his life, when thoughtless bravery alone would insure his death and the deaths of his men. Because of his lack of rigidity, he is capable of adapting to a thoroughly alien culture and creating a place for himself in it. He is not a stereotype, in that he does not vanquish all enemies and succeed immediately; perhaps he will never sail back to England in triumph, but he will have led a thrilling life and made some contribution to the betterment of the human condition. Tall, handsome, and strong, he learns that there are other kinds of beauty and other kinds of strength than his own. He comes to recognize that these are not to be despised but enjoyed.

His adversary is Toranaga, who wants to be dictator of all of Japan, and will sacrifice anyone who prevents him from doing this. Clavell makes readers see that Toranaga is not an evil man, because while he causes pain to individual people, he will bring peace and well-being to his country. He acts honorably according to his lights, and he is too intelligent to be intolerant; he, like Blackthorne, is willing to learn.

Lady Mariko, has made the best of her marriage to a man she hates by becoming a Christian and learning all the languages the missionaries could teach her. Because of her ability, she becomes Blackthorne's translator, his teacher, and then his lover. Her self-respect, her intelligence and her strength, as well as her selflessness and beauty, typify the best of Japanese culture, yet she is more than a stereotype.

The minor characters are always memorable: Buntaro, Mariko's husband, who is a brute but the master of the delicate and complex tea ceremony, and Yabu, the brave Japanese aristocrat who savors poetry and military strategy, yet is a sadist and a traitor. The female characters are equally memorable: Kiku, the beautiful prostitute, and

Gyoko, her mentor; Kiri, Toranaga's consort and political advisor; Fujiko, Blackthorne's consort, who runs his household. These women manage to tip the balance of power in the government by their intelligence, persistence, and bravery. It is not only the Japanese characters who are presented so vividly. The Catholic diplomat-missionaries, who believe that their duty to save souls exempts them from the claims of ordinary morality, are memorable, as is Rodrigues, Blackthorne's fellow captain-pilot who is torn between his respect for Blackthorne and fear of the danger he represents.

There are no ordinary villains in this novel. What distinguishes Clavell's sympathetic characters from the others is simply that these characters are willing to learn and willing to act for the common good.

♦ Social Concerns ♦

In all his novels, Clavell stresses the differences in values and behavior among different cultures. A superb teacher, he explains the clash of lifestyles and values between seventeenth-century Japan and seventeenth-century Europe very clearly. The fact that certain habits of action and thought still influence the Japanese as well as the West makes his explanations important. Because his facts are presented so dramatically, they are fascinating. Clavell manages to tell the reader about the Japanese class system, the history of the samurai, and the meaning of *Bushido*, the samurai code. He also explains Japanese politics, family life and sexual practices. In addition, he supplies a great deal of information on daily life in Elizabethan England, Catholic-Protestant strife in Europe,

and seventeenth-century seafaring and exploration. His novels are based on serious research and according to critics, are a fund of accurate information.

♦ Themes ♦

Set in Japan in 1600, Shogun is concerned with ageless questions of the price and the uses of power. How does one lead men? What methods are permissible to use even for glorious ends? How much personal insult can one accept in order to triumph ultimately? Can one deny moral, ethical and religious principles for what he considers to be the "greater good"? As abstract questions these factors are mildly interesting. When dramatized by a superb storyteller, these questions become all-absorbing.

Toranaga, the Japanese leader who wishes to rule the entire country and become Shogun, or dictator of Japan, will betray anyone, including his "friend" Blackthorne, to unify his country under his domination, something that would save his country from the dire effects of civil war and bring its citizens peace and prosperity, but will certainly harm his unsuspecting friend. Is Toranaga a good man or an evil man? Clavell intimates that his actions are understandable given his circumstances.

Clavell also addresses the question of whether the representatives of the Church are justified in using chicanery in order to achieve their goal — converting the Japanese to Christianity. He brings the reader to understand their actions too, even when he cannot approve.

A related theme has to do with cultural values. The English hero Blackthorne, as a product of Western civilization and a good man, believes that life must be preserved at any cost. He will not take a life unnecessarily and he acts to save the lives of others. He will even accept humiliation rather than cause loss of life. The Japanese find his behavior utterly incomprehensible. Blackthorne also assigns responsibility for events and suffers guilt. The Japanese believe in the influence of Karma, fate, and do not accept the fact that sin or guilt can exist if one has behaved correctly, that is, obediently to one's master. The Japanese consider loyalty and obedience to one's overlord as paramount values and life itself as worthless.

◆ Techniques ◆

Clavell's techniques are highly cinematic. *Shogun,* for example, contains a great deal of dialogue interspersed with scenes of exciting action: ambushes, hand-to-hand combat, storms at sea, earthquakes. There is certainly suspense, too. The reader does not know whether Toranaga will succeed or whether Blackthorne will ever get home, but he certainly cares.

◆ Literary Precedents ◆

The tale of the heroic traveler wrecked at sea, who finds strange lands with strange customs and must struggle wearily to get home to his own land, his wife and his family is, of course, as old as Homer's *Odyssey* (c. 1050-850 B.C.), the story of Odysseus' ten year journey home. Blackthorne's fate, as a helpless giant, in a land of small but powerful people who are embroiled in political dissension is a variant of Jonathan Swift's "Voyage to Lilliput" in *Gulliver's Travels* (1726). The fact that Blackthorne's adventures are not the stuff of myth or legend ties *Shogun* to "true" adventure stories such as *The Travels of Marco Polo* (1298), a record of the impressions made by a European of a different, but not at all savage, Oriental culture.

◆ Related Titles ◆

Tai-Pan (1966) discusses the history of China's trade with the West and the establishment and growth of Hong Kong, while dramatizing the conflict between Dirk Struhan, the head of a vast trading company and his chief rival, Tyler Brock. Again the clash of Oriental and Western customs underlies the action-filled plot as history is explained. Clavell's theme remains the proper uses of power and the behavior necessary to seize and retain it. A very popular novel, *Tai-Pan* remained on the best seller list for ten months.

Noble House (1981) brings the history of Western trade with China, and the history of Hong Kong, up to date, as the latest *Tai-Pan*, Ian Struan Dunross, a descendent of Dirk Struan, struggles to maintain the solvency of his company in the face of the Brock clan's machinations now engineered by Quillen Gornt, its latest descendent. Dunross is also faced with modern political and financial problems. This novel was even more successful than its predecessor, leading the best seller list and remaining on it for eleven months.

◆ Adaptations ◆

NBC presented *Shogun* as a television miniseries in September 1980. It was shot in Japan at a cost of twenty-two million dollars. Richard Chamberlain, as Blackthorne, headed a cast of fifteen Europeans and twenty-eight Japanese. *Shogun* had the second largest television audience in the United States up to that time. The miniseries was also made into a two-and-one-half-hour film which was shown internationally.

Barbara Horwitz
Long Island University
C.W. Post Campus

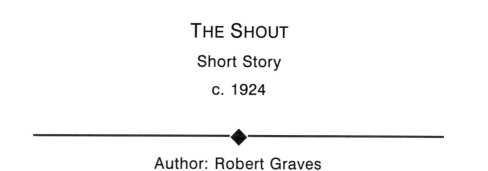

THE SHOUT

Short Story

c. 1924

Author: Robert Graves

♦ Characters ♦

Crossley describes himself as "of middle age, and tall; his hair grey; his face never still for a moment; his eyes large and bright, sometimes yellow, sometimes brown, sometimes grey." He is an uncertain image, dreamlike. As the storyteller, he is a powerful force: "'My story is true,' he said, 'every word of it. Or, when I say that my story is "true," I mean at least that I am telling it in a new way. It is always the same story, but I sometimes vary the climax and even recast the characters. Variation keeps it fresh and therefore true.'" Crossley here represents himself as a storyteller, having all of a storyteller's destructive and creative powers. He can kill everything in his tale with a shout, and he shapes and reshapes the marriage of Rachel and Richard at will.

If Crossley is symbolic of the storyteller, then Rachel and Richard may be fragments of him. Rachel is inspiration; she both commands and obeys. When Crossley says to her, "At ten o'clock, Rachel, you and I sleep together," Rachel responds submissively: "Why, of course, my dear." Then she slaps Richard "with all her strength." Later she denies all this had happened and tells Richard that "it was part of his dream." The image of woman as inspiration or creative muse is common in Graves's writings; Rachel embodies the frustrations inspiration presents for the storyteller. Sometimes she gives on command, sometimes she refuses, and other times she commands the storyteller.

Richard is analytical and tries to make sense out of the mad attraction Rachel and Crossley have for each other. The relationship between the three shifts from the mundane to the impossible and back again. The destructive powers of the storyteller frighten Richard, yet as a rational man he denies that Crossley can have such powers. Terrified by Crossley, bewildered by his wife's capriciousness, Richard concludes that the irrational events he witnesses are products of his own imagination and that he is therefore mad. Unwilling to acknowledge the existence of his irrational self, he becomes self-destructive and tries to kill himself by smashing the stone that is his soul. Instead, he mistakenly smashes that of Crossley, fragmenting it into four parts, shattering the storyteller's magic save for his power to destroy.

◆ Social Concerns ◆

The marriage of Richard and Rachel is an open one; by mutual agreement, neither is obligated to remain faithful to the other "because they wished to feel themselves bound by love rather than ceremony." The absence of certainties in their relationship makes them ready victims for Charles Crossley, who insinuates himself into their house and divides the two.

Although the idea of "open marriage" became a social issue in the 1970s, Graves uses the possibility of sanctioned infidelity to set up a psychological study of his characters. Morality is not at issue; rather the demonic forces that can enter relationships, causing the partners to delude each other. The elements of illusion and reality beckon the characters to make excuses for their behavior, thus allowing destructive forces the potential to propel them apart.

◆ Themes ◆

Madness, superstition, and magic are mixed together in "The Shout." Charles Crossley is either a deluded madman who thinks he has magical powers or is a "devil" who can kill by shouting. The tale is an uncertain one because Crossley tells it; it is either a lunatic's fantasy or a chilling account of a battle between souls.

Dreams play an important role in "The Shout," which is itself dreamlike because it wanders in and out of everyday reality and even changes events the way a dream might. For instance, Crossley's powers seem frightening when he commands Rachel to sleep with him, yet later she says she heard no such command. Both Rachel and Richard first meet Crossley in their dreams, and the whole story may be an extension of their dreams. For instance, early on, Rachel remarks that "when I am asleep I become, perhaps, a stone with all the natural appetites and convictions of a stone." Later, "Richard went again to the sand hills, to the heap of stones, and identified the souls of the doctor and the rector." This may be no more than a fantasy evolved out of Rachel's account of her dream, or it could be as real as Crossley says it is.

◆ Techniques ◆

"The Shout" is told within a "frame"; that is, the actual narrator retells a story he heard Crossley tell at a cricket match, which "frames" the beginning and ending of the story. It is the presence of the outside narrator that gives the story its mixture of reality and unreality. The Crossley that the narrator meets is "a man of unusual force" who knows that he is insane and in an asylum. In the narrator's world, Richard and Rachel know of Crossley only through seeing a magic act he put on at the asylum as the "Australian Illusionist"; Crossley's detailed description of Rachel and scant one of Richard may have the ordinary explanation that Crossley "looked at [Rachel] all the time" during his performance. The tale may be no more than a madman's fantasy. On the other hand, Crossley and his physician get into a pushing match when a thunderstorm breaks up the cricket game and are supposedly killed instantly by a bolt of lightning. Yet, "Crossley's body was found rigid, the doctor's was crouched in a corner, his hands over his ears. Nobody could understand this because death had been instantaneous, and the doctor was not a man to stop his ears against thunder." Thus the story is at once the merest fantasy and real; it is a shout.

an eighty-seven minute motion-picture adaptation of "The Shout." Also titled *The Shout,* the film alters the plot but succeeds in conveying the dread of the story. It stars Alan Bates and was directed by Jerzy Skolimowski.

Kirk H. Beetz

◆ Literary Precedents ◆

The horror story has long been a staple of popular fiction. For instance, Edgar Allan Poe's "A Tale of the Ragged Mountains" (1844) is "framed" and has a main character who recounts to the narrator a tale that may be a hallucination or real. The idea that dreams symbolize the creative side of human nature is also commonplace, as in H. P. Lovecraft's *The Dream-Quest of Unknown Kadath* (1939; c. 1926). The image of a woman representing inspiration dates back at least to the Ancient Greeks' Muses of the arts, and perhaps even earlier according to Graves's own *The White Goddess* (1948).

◆ Related Titles ◆

Graves's stories were gathered in *Collected Short Stories* in 1964. In 1978, Penguin Books brought out a paperback edition titled *The Shout: And Other Stories.* They tend to be whimsical and much shorter than "The Shout," and they reflect Graves's interest in creativity and history, sometimes combining the interests as in the Roman story "Epics Are Out of Fashion," in which it is better to be a good runner than a good poet.

◆ Adaptations ◆

In 1979, Columbia Pictures released

SIDDHARTHA

Novel

1923

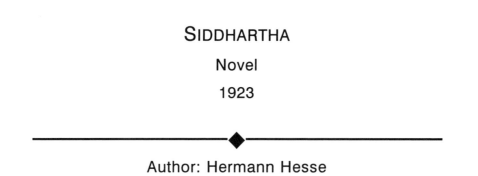

Author: Hermann Hesse

◆ Characters ◆

The protagonist of the novel is Siddhartha, who takes his name from the historical Buddha (563-483 B.C.) whose given name was Siddhartha and whose family name was Gautama. The word "Buddha" comes from the Sanskrit and means "the enlightened One." It is precisely this enlightenment which Hesse's main character is seeking, although not entirely in accordance with the life of the actual Buddha.

The remaining characters are: Govinda, Siddhartha's boyhood friend, confidant, and religious follower; Gautama Budda himself; Kamala, the embodiment of sensuality and the mother of Siddhartha's son; Kamaswami, a wealthy merchant; and, Vasudeva, the ferryman with whom Siddhartha later lives. The importance of these characters lies, however, not in their enumeration, but in what they each represent: Govinda, who is Siddhartha's other self; the Buddha, who is the Eastern ideal; Siddhartha himself, who is the Western ideal; Kamala, who represents the art of sensual love; Kamaswami, whose very name means "master of the material world"; and, Vasudeva, saintly reincarnation of the Hindu god Vishnu. The representations of the characters can be seen as exhibiting opposites which make up some Whole: ego/alter ego; East/West; spiritual love/earthly love; spirituality/ materiality; god/man.

◆ Social Concerns ◆

A Westerner disillusioned by the attitudes which brought about and sustained World War I, Hesse sought meaningfulness in the Orient. Raised in a family of Pietist missionaries to India and living amidst the artifacts of Eastern culture, he said he often felt more at home surrounded by the thoughts and accouterments of the East than he did in his hometown of Calw.

Deeply introspective, Hesse was intent upon discovering the very kernel of his being; his hope was that he might find a way to affirm life. Whatever answers he might come across he did not consider as material for proselytizing, but as fuel for his own inner development. This ideal found its expression in the character *Siddhartha* (based on the Buddha Gautama Siddhartha), who achieves self-realization at the end.

Ever fascinated by opposites, Hesse saw much in the East that was diametrically different in the West and sought to wrest from the former the most useful aspects for the latter. At the top of the list stood meditation, an uncommon practice in the West calculated to achieve a knowledge of one's relationship to reality, called in Buddhism "enlightenment" (*bodhi*) and Nirvana, i.e. the attainment of a higher state of being. In this enlightenment there is no time in the face of all history and the future. Every moment, every individual life is indestructible; there is no "was," no "will be." Any moment is part of a continuum reaching into the past and future simultaneously. In a sense more religious than philosophical, Hesse offers all individuals who would know themselves this statement of faith in mankind and life at large.

In *Siddhartha* two ideals are presented: the Eastern Gautama Buddha and the Western Siddhartha. Where the first ideal incorporates essentially a rejection of self and life, the other adopts a positive attitude toward both. Hesse undoubtedly hoped that *Siddhartha's* message would be clear: There is no panacea for life's problems — solutions cannot be found wholly in the East or in the West — but within oneself as an example for all. Hesse was certain that only by influencing the individual can the world be improved.

◆ Themes ◆

Siddhartha contains four prominent themes, all of which are related to a discovery of Self. The first of these, the father-son theme, would strike most the readers as familiar — perhaps even in their own personal lives. Although Siddhartha admires and loves his father, an orthodox Brahmin, he knows he cannot rely on his father's wisdom but must seek his own way to truth. Siddhartha is, therefore, a conventional rebel within his family. He knows that no one — not even his learned father — can lead him to find his true Self. He calls into question the effectiveness of his father's attempts at cleansing away guilt by frequent ablutions in the river and leaves home in his search for *Atman*, that individual spirit within each human being. For Siddhartha it is a search which is based on personal experience, not on secondhand knowledge. The father-son theme reappears at the end of the novel when Siddhartha's son leaves him for many of the same reasons.

The river is mentioned in the very first sentence of the novel and provides the setting for the beginning chapter. At this sacred stream gather family and friends for the rite of purification. At its simplest level, the river represents tradition and permanence. But rivers flow and thus contain an element of movement and change. For this reason the symbolic effect of the river is strong, for in his search for Self, Siddhartha underwent much change, yet clung to traditional values of permanence. Siddhartha is not always aware of the significance of the river, as, for example, when the ferryman Vasudeva takes him across and tells him all that the river can teach him. Later, as ferryman himself, Siddhartha sees the river as a symbol of the commingling of all things.

Govinda, Siddhartha's childhood companion and closest friend is often described as his shadow, his most ardent follower. But he symbolizes more than that as the embodiment of the struggle in Siddhartha's soul. Govinda completes the picture of Siddhartha; he is, as it were, his exterior. At the same time he exemplifies the series of "opposites" that permeates the work and demonstrates the theme of unity that binds all persons and things.

On top of all the foregoing themes rests the theme of timelessness, that state achieved when true enlightenment is reached. Hesse has combined artistically all aspects of nature, their physical substance and their mind and soul, under the umbrella of arrested time. Each individual thing or person is archetypal — Siddhartha's father, his mother, the eternal river, the wisdom of Buddha, Siddhartha's own iconoclastic side — and delineated in a set, formalized way down to the oversimplified language of the book, prayerlike, almost a ritual.

◆ Techniques ◆

Throughout his writings, from poetry to essays to long prose, Hesse employs several characteristic general techniques. One might even say that the order of influence begins in his love of poetry, which then permeates all his prose. His sentences, usually direct and often short and grammatically uncomplicated, read like poetry. Their rhythmic flow is like a melody, the words like musical notes. This poetic, musical quality to his prose gives it a loftiness befitting the meditative and philosophical content.

Although poetic imagery informs his writing, there is no evidence of an unconventional or avant garde style. He himself averred he never strove for the new in form, but remained traditional in his use of language. The unconventionality is evident primarily in his thoughts.

The substance of Hesse's thoughts is always tempered by the admission of an opposite. Such duality is the very fiber of all his works. Even the titles of his novels state or elicit an awareness of duality: for example, *Narcissus and Goldmund, Demian* (Emil Sinclair), *Siddhartha* (Govinda), *Steppenwolf* (sheep). His works therefore evoke such dichotomies as meditation and action, pleasure and pain, love and hate, heterosexual love and homosexual love, peer love and mother love, the bourgeoisie and the artist's world, introversion and extroversion, God and Satan. His technique entails combining these and other opposites in an attempt to create a totality of person. In the Cabinet of Mirrors in the Magic Theater of *Steppenwolf* he even utilizes mirrors to reflect the innermost secrets of the individual so that a reconstitution of the psyche can be accomplished. He explained: "Any work of art that is not faked has this provocative, smiling dual face, this male-femaleness, this togetherness of naked drives and pure spirituality." The combination of all these polarities results in a work which is psychologically real, but in actuality merely symbolic.

The subject of all Hesse's works is, at bottom, people and their interrelationships, particularly as touching friendship and love. It is upon this foundation that Hesse tries to erect the total person out of his various polarities in a language that instructs seductively through the cadences of poetic prose.

◆ Literary Precedents ◆

Although the crystallization of Hesse's thought came only after his trip to India in 1911, the groundwork had been laid earlier in his readings in Kierkegaard, Nietzsche, and Jakob

Burckhardt. Hesse appreciated the artist in Nietzsche but rejected much of his philosophy. In Basel, Hesse replaced Nietzsche with Burckhardt as the dominant intellectual force in the second half of his life. Jakob Burckhardt's namesake, good and wise Pater Jakobus of *Magister Ludi*, is to Josef Knecht what Burckhardt must have represented in his writings for Hesse.

During the 1930s Hesse also read and studied Goethe and the German romantics, as well as others as diverse as Maeterlinck, Dante, Meyer, Fontane, and Bohme. Although he saw no future for naturalism, he admitted the artistry and depth of Ibsen, Hauptmann, Turgenev, and Zola. Because he also associated Dostoevsky and other Russian writers with this sordid, near-nihilistic movement, he rejected them.

His relations with contemporary authors were cordial, even close. There are photographs of him with such famous men as Thomas Mann, Jakob Wassermann, Bertolt Brecht, Henry Miller, and Stefan Zweig. Many journeyed to Montagnola to visit him.

The collection of literary and philosophical influences upon Hesse is numerous and varied. It is more difficult to point to particular works as establishing literary precedents for him than it is to see certain general characteristics that might have been borrowed or absorbed. Philosophical in content, Hesse's works are romantic in spirit, introspective, inwardly conflictive, autobiographical, mystical, unresolved. A loner, a visionary, a musician of words, a craftsman of his art, Hesse combined all these aspects of his personality and work to produce truly new and unprecedented writings.

Donald D. Hook
Trinity College Hartford

THE SILENCE OF THE LAMBS

Novel

1987

◆

Author: Thomas Harris

◆ Characters ◆

In *The Silence of the Lambs*, Clarice Starling's character is one of several to whom we are given privileged entry (other sections are rendered through the central consciousnesses of Special Agent Jack Crawford, Hannibal Lecter, and Buffalo Bill/Jame Gumb), but there seems little question that we are intended to consider Starling the main character. The book begins and ends with her and follows her quest to find Buffalo Bill, employing hints provided by Dr. Lecter. Clarice is bright, ambitious, and talented: an honors graduate from the University of Virginia with a double major in criminology and psychology. Although the daughter of a small-town lawman who was killed by criminals, she is also, as Lecter observes, driven by the plight of those less fortunate.

Jame Gumb (or "Buffalo Bill," as he is called in the press) is the serial killer Clarice and the rest of the law enforcement community is tracking. Like the *Red Dragon* (1981), his killings are intended to aid him in transforming himself, but Gumb's transformation is much more easily understood: He is killing and skinning women with the intention of putting together a "woman suit" for himself. A drifter who has a terrible self-image and consequently wants to be anyone but himself, Gumb is another of Harris's villains with plenty of societal and psychological reasons for becoming the monster he is, although Harris also resists simple solutions: "At least two scholarly journals explained that this unhappy childhood was the reason he killed women in his basement for their skins. The words crazy and evil do not appear in either article."

Hannibal Lecter assumes much more importance and a much more active role in this novel than in *Red Dragon*. His meetings with Starling represent the core of the novel, and in their give and take, he comes to respect and even like Starling. This spark of humanity makes Lecter fascinating, because unlike Gumb, no attempt is ever made to explain why he became what he became. He is presented as purely evil, and when he escapes from captivity in a bloody but brilliant fashion, we are reminded of his complex character, a man of civility and refinement who killed and ate at least nine human beings.

The Silence of the Lambs, like *Red Dragon,* centers on the hunt for a serial killer, one of American society's most frightening nightmares. However, this novel emphasizes from the very outset the trials of an intelligent and capable woman, FBI trainee Clarice Starling, in a patriarchal system, and as such should be considered a work with strong feminist sensibilities. Clarice is treated differently from Will Graham, the hero of *Red Dragon,* and not simply because she is a trainee at the FBI Academy; she is consistently treated with less respect because she is female. Underlying all Clarice's trials in the novel is the reason for her involvement with the case, the murder spree of the serial killer "Buffalo Bill," who kills and mutilates women so that he can construct a costume of their skins. This combination of female hero and female victims means that *The Silence of the Lambs* makes a strong point about the victimization of women in our society.

◆ Themes ◆

With the character of Clarice Starling, Harris moves away from his usual emphasis on the similarities between the hunters and the hunted. Unlike Will Graham in *Red Dragon,* who had a strange identification with those he hunted, Clarice's empathy works differently; she does not see things through the eyes of the serial killer who objectifies his victims. Her connection, instead, is to the victims. She goes through the rooms and possessions of the victims to learn more about the women Bill took, to see things through their eyes, and her ability to see through their eyes proves to be the decisive element in locating Buffalo Bill.

The transactions between Hannibal Lecter and Starling also reflect a continuing concern of Harris, the creation of sympathetic and psychologically complex characters of all sorts. Although Lecter originally greets Clarice Starling with malevolent civility, from their first scene meeting, Starling treats Lecter as an authority and perhaps even a teacher, emphasizing his professional title in each conversation, instead of dealing with him as we know many others have, as a case study or a non- (or extra-) human aberration. Lecter appreciates and reciprocates this courtesy. Whether unconsciously or consciously, Clarice, who knows what it is to be an object, treats Lecter as human rather than object, and the lesson is not lost on him.

Clarice is most concretely Harris's representation of good in the struggle with evil, and perhaps because Clarice's character does not partake of the ambiguity of other Harris heroes, she is the least affected by the evil she combats. She does not lose her life like Kabakov or nearly lose life and sanity, like Will Graham. Although she is not unaffected by the events of the novel, at the conclusion of the novel she has earned the "silence of the lambs," which at least for the time being represents peace.

◆ Techniques ◆

The Silence of the Lambs is Harris's most perfectly-realized novel. In its expert use of the omniscient narrator to present the thoughts and emotions of principal characters, in its riveting dialogue, in its psychological acuity, and in its authentic use of police procedure, *The Silence of the Lambs* is considered by many critics to be a book which ultimately bridges the gap between popular fiction and literary fiction, a book which can be read for enjoyment or reflection. Harris again creates suspense by having his heroes work against a deadline, this time days instead of weeks, and by moving back and forth between the principals of his story, this time weaving in Lecter as a subsidiary storyline to the cat and mouse game between Buffalo Bill and the authorities pursuing him.

◆ Literary Precedents ◆

In *The Silence of the Lambs,* Harris creates a perfect combination of the detective and horror novels: We want Clarice Starling to solve the crime, and at the same time, we do not want her to come in contact with Buffalo Bill. The tension created by these diametrically opposed forces makes for a delicious unease.

Hannibal Lecter, as portrayed in this novel, is built even further into a sort of ultimate and insoluble evil like that of Fu Manchu in the novels of Sax Rohmer or Dr. Moriarty in the Sherlock Holmes tales of Arthur Conan Doyle. More than a fit nemesis for Starling, who knows she survives on the strength of Lecter's courtesy, Dr. Lecter is the embodiment of rational evil, an even more frightening prospect than the psychotic evil represented by Buffalo Bill.

◆ Related Titles ◆

The development of Hannibal Lecter into one of the great fictional villains sets this book apart from *Red Dragon,* where Lecter first appears. Of the other characters common to both novels, Jack Crawford, head of the Behavior Science division which tracks serial killers, has a considerably more important role in *The Silence of the Lambs,* both as Starling's mentor and as a husband dealing with the death of his wife.

Like *Red Dragon,* this novel shows Harris moving in a decidedly more literary direction, with epigrams, literary references, and archetypal characters who achieve both personal and symbolic significance. Given this movement in his work, the competent writer of thrillers who produced *Black Sunday* (1975) is long gone, replaced by a writer of great sensitivity and style who just happens to know how to weave a great thriller.

◆ Adaptations ◆

The 1991 adaptation of *The Silence of the Lambs* directed by Jonathan Demme became one of the most talked-about films of the year and one of the most critically-successful of all time, winning Academy Awards in five major categories including Best Film and Best Screenplay. Anthony Hopkins's portrayal of Hannibal Lecter justifiably made him a household word, while Jodie Foster won her second Academy Award for her sensitive turn as Clarice Starling. Although the film differs little from Harris's novel, Demme, Foster, and screenwriter Ted Tally take the book as a starting point and then go beyond it to reinforce the idea that women must be seen as people rather than objects. By accenting Starling's harassment, by removing male helpers present in the novel, and by stressing Starling's resistance to the attempts of men to objectify her, the film creates, in Foster's words, an "incredibly strong feminist hero" as well as an even stronger statement about the various forms of female victimization in our society.

An abridged version of the novel is available as a book on tape from Simon & Schuster. The reading by Kathy Bates is as powerful in its immediacy as the film adaptation and has the benefit of retaining much of Harris's actual language.

♦ Ideas for Group Discussions ♦

In this, Harris's most popular novel, we find many of his trademarks: psychological insight, the inclusion of authenticating details, and villains who genuinely frighten us. Discussion on any of Harris's works might consider his penchant for humanizing the inhuman, for suggesting the depths of good and evil in each of us, and for arguing that although good may triumph over evil it often does so only at great cost. In *The Silence of the Lambs*, specific areas of interest include Harris's creation of a strong female protagonist, his psychological insight into major characters as diverse as Jame Gumb, Catherine Baker Martin, and Clarice Starling, and the strange appeal of Dr. Hannibal Lecter.

1. Why does Hannibal Lecter capture our interest so strongly? What qualities of his character are so intriguing?

2. This novel suggests that the question of evil is problematical in connection with individuals like Jame Gumb. Do you believe that any societal or personal factors can explain such monstrous evil? Are any such explanations advanced for Lecter?

3. In what ways does the film version of *The Silence of the Lambs* seem to you to be superior to the novel? In what ways inferior?

4. Does Jack Crawford's character seem to differ in any ways from his portrayal in *Red Dragon*? Does he treat his chief investigators, Graham and Starling any differently? What are the implications of these differences?

5. In what ways does Starling have to deal with sexism and prejudice because she is a woman in a traditionally male world?

6. Why does Lecter talk to Starling? What about her character appeals to him? And why does he tell her he has no plans to call on her, "the world being more interesting with you in it"?

7. How does the character of Dr. Chilton come to stand for male arrogance and incompetence?

8. Are the serial killers in *Red Dragon* and *The Silence of the Lambs* similar in any ways? Which do you find more horrifying? Why?

9. How does Clarice Starling's empathy serve her better than the technology of the law enforcement agencies tracking Gumb? What clues does she discover that male agents might have missed?

Greg Garrett
Baylor University

THE SILVER PILLOW

Novella

1987

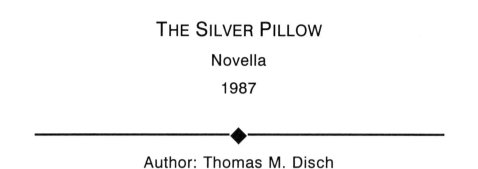

Author: Thomas M. Disch

◆ Social Concerns/Themes ◆

At the age of seventy-one, "too dilapidated to be considered an active menace to society," Mrs. Ostrowsky has been paroled into the care of her son from the State Hospital for the Criminally Insane at Northhampton. She is a nasty person who believes that her killing of her husband was his fault. Disch uses the problems society has in warehousing and caring for the mentally ill as part of the background for his tale.

The Silver Pillow: A Tale of Witchcraft focuses on a mother and her grown child. Although their relationship is a perverse one, its exaggerated tensions reflect common psychological aspects of mother-son relationships. Mrs. Ostrowsky is domineering, constantly bossing her son around. In this, she represents the role mothers must play if a small child requires constant supervision. On the other hand, as an old and frail woman, she is really at her son's mercy. After she has lived in his home for a few years, her son Bill realizes that he is more her jailer than her servant. Their roles have reversed, with Bill controlling much of his mother's life. Tension is created by Mrs. Ostrow-

sky's desire to continue to control her son, who has a quiet, sad life of work and sexual denial that he tries to keep distinct from his life with his mother. A preternaturally evil woman, Mrs. Ostrowsky slowly exerts psychological pressure on her son through her constricting personality. Her death should liberate him, but through her silver pillow her spirit remains, talking to him, badgering him, and demanding to accompany him when he goes out.

The pillow symbolizes that part of a mother that remains a permanent part of her child. It is a common part of adult experience to find oneself repeating parental mistakes and advice, as well as remembering the rules of conduct learned during one's childhood. In the case of Mrs. Ostrowsky, the rules were nasty ones that stunted Bill's growth and maturity. He becomes a regular patron of a pornographic movie theater; ugly and socially maladjusted, he cannot have a mature relationship with a woman. Under the pillow's influence, he becomes more and more like his mother. The pillow constricts his life and demands that he harm women. At the last, the theme of the mother-son relationship is resolved logically. To become an adult, Bill must assert his own selfhood as a man responsible to himself, not his mother. When the pillow commands him to murder a prostitute, he defies it, thus asserting his own mature moral code over the debased one of his mother. By attacking the pillow, he symbolically kills the Mrs. Ostrowsky within himself. Her killing him is a hollow victory, because he dies not merely as an extension of herself, but as a grown man who chooses to do what is right, even though it is contrary to his mother's wishes.

◆ Characters ◆

This tale features two characters: Bill Ostrowsky, the main character and focus of the action, and his mother, Mrs. Ostrowsky. *The Silver Pillow* is a psychological study, with most of the action taking place in Bill's confused mind. He does not love his mother, yet he takes care of her. When he can, he escapes into the fantasies of pornographic movies. He has enough self-awareness to know that he does not appeal to women; the tale implies that his miserable personality and ugly looks are the product of his upbringing by an insanely hateful woman. He seems to lack the energy to hate deeply, but at the same time lacks the insight to fully understand how hateful his mother is.

Mrs. Ostrowsky is a demonic force in the tale. If a parent through wise judgment and loving actions can raise a strong, well-adjusted child, then a blindly hateful and cruel parent can raise a warped child. Instead of becoming an angry, hateful adult, which might seem the logical result of a nasty upbringing, Bill becomes a nonentity who drifts through life, going in whatever direction he is pushed. His mother's domineering personality has almost crushed his. During the tale, Bill struggles to become an individual who is responsible to himself, not his mother. But the spirit of his mother, through the pillow, seeks to completely take over Bill's life and make him a mere copy of herself. There are no redeeming qualities to Mrs. Ostrowsky — she is utterly selfish.

◆ Techniques ◆

The tale is told simply. Its atmosphere of suppressed rage is created primarily through ambiguity. Mrs. Ostrowsky plainly oppresses her son, but exactly how she does it is not clear. The action takes place in a psychological world; thoughts and motivations in a person's mind are often vague, confused, and tied up with other feelings from unidentifiable sources. Bill's mind is more than usually confused, so his feelings and thoughts are more than usually vague. His world is suffused with his mother's evil, but how she makes him miserable is not always plainly shown. After her death, when her pillow exerts its influence on Bill, it is not clear whether Bill is deranged and is actually hearing his mother's voice from inside himself, or whether the pillow is indeed possessed by a demonic spirit. Bill himself does not believe in the supernatural and thinks that he probably is going mad, but he does not regard the pillow's influence on him as particularly alarming. No one takes an interest in what he does, anyway, so he believes his delusions can be kept to himself and secret. The ambiguous nature of Mrs. Ostrowsky's malevolent influence helps build suspense for *The Silver Pillow*'s climactic scene in which Bill finally chooses between his mother's personality and his own.

◆ Literary Precedents ◆

The Silver Pillow is a gothic tale, featuring ghostly influences and psychological insight. From its inception, the gothic literary genre has used superstitions about the supernatural world to symbolize personality traits. The monster in Mary Shelley's *Frankenstein* (1818) is a complicated being, but among other aspects of the personality of his creator, he represents the reckless lust to acquire knowledge without understanding it. In Robert Louis Stevenson's *The Strange Case of Dr. Jekyll and Mr. Hyde* (1886), the character of Mr. Hyde represents the evil that lurks within every personality. The subject of the crazed mind is also common in gothic literature. For instance, Edgar Allan Poe presents such characters in several of his tales such as "The Cask of Amontillado" (1846), and "The Black Cat" (1843). A more recent writer, H. P. Lovecraft, often sets his fiendish characters in urban locales, just as Disch does in his tale.

Kirk H. Beetz

SING DOWN THE MOON

Novel

1970

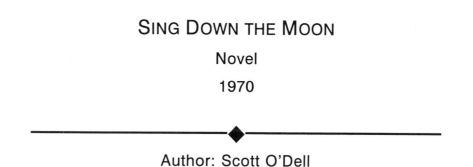

Author: Scott O'Dell

◆ Characters ◆

Bright Morning is one of the strong, resourceful and independent young Indian women that O'Dell creates in his novels. She has a fierce desire for freedom which makes her refuse to give up and adapt to the ways of her Spanish captors. Instead, she stubbornly bides her time and takes the first chance to escape. This independent streak also characterizes her relationship with Tall Boy who later becomes her husband. Critics of O'Dell have mentioned the stoicism and absence of emotion in Bright Morning, but this is not quite true. Although the girl does not express her emotions easily, something considered inappropriate among her people, she has a deep bond with the young man and understands his feelings. When he is crippled by a bullet during his attempt to help her escape from the Spaniards, she carefully rebuilds his self-esteem, knowing that his pride is deeply hurt by his inability to hunt and do the work of other men. "Tall Boy rode through the field on his way home, but did not stop. 'You think that I went to the white man's village just to rescue you,' he said as he passed. 'You are wrong. I went there for another reason.' I watched him ride away, sitting stooped in the saddle, one shoulder lower than the other, and my heart went out to him."

A similar, unspoken but deep relationship exists between Bright Morning and her mother. Although her mother taunts her about Tall Boy's inability to provide, there is concern only that her daughter would be making a mistake, and when she sees that Bright Morning is determined, she accepts her decision unquestioningly. "Every week my mother and I went to visit Tall Boy and his family. She never again said anything about his arm and when he had trouble, when it was awkward for him to do something, she always looked away in pity."

Bright Morning is the central character of the novel, and all others are seen in relationship to her. Tall Boy, the young Navajo brave who eventually becomes her husband, is proud but lacks the strength of the young woman. Wounded during the rescue of Bright Morning from the Spanish slavers, he eventually loses the use of his right arm. Although he learns to compensate for his physical injury, his emotional recovery is much more difficult. He overcompensates by denying that he is crippled, but underneath he is well aware that the others in the tribe consider him with pity. When the tribe is relocated on the reservation, however, most of the other men are also quickly giving up. As Bright Morning says scornfully, they become the worst gossips, doing nothing all day except sit around and talk. It is the women such as Bright Morning and her mother who still carry on and dream. When Tall Boy is thrown into prison for beating an Apache, he escapes, but lacks the will to go any further than his reservation home. Only the combined efforts of his mother-in-law, who taunts him, and Bright Morning, who plans for him, get him to flee the reservation and take his wife back to their old home in the Canyon de Chelly. There, Bright Morning and her family have again hopes for the future.

The remaining characters of the novel have marginal roles in the life of the protagonist. Running Bird, her friend, shares her captivity, Bright Morning's mother is a forceful example of the Navajo women, and the Spanish townspeople, the members of the tribe, and the white soldiers only serve to promote the action. Scott O'Dell uses an omniscient point of view, yet we do not see into the minds of these characters. Even Bright Morning is shown mainly through her actions and statements. Indeed, what she does not say is sometimes more eloquent than what she does.

◆ Social Concerns ◆

Much of O'Dell's fiction revolves around two major areas of interest: the history of the Southwest and the conflict between Native Americans and white people. *Sing Down the Moon* deals

with the canyons and deserts of Arizona and the attempts to resettle the Navajo people from these, their homelands. Bright Morning, a fourteen-year-old Navajo girl, leads a simple but happy life, caring for her mother's sheep and sharing in the work and celebrations of her community. Her first encounter with whites almost brings an end to this way of life, as Bright Morning and her friend Running Bird are captured by Spanish slavers and taken south to a large city. There the girls are sold as household help and meet young Indian girls from several tribes, even from as far north as the Nez Perce, an indication of the widespread trade in Indian slaves by the Spanish. While some of the young women have adjusted and even enjoy the softer city life, Bright Morning's fierce desire for freedom helps her and Running Bird to escape and return home. This episode, which serves both as an introduction to the abuse of the Indians by the whites and as a demonstration of the determination and love of freedom of the Navajo, deals with a widespread practice of the Spanish in the Southwest to use and abuse the native population for labor. The seemingly idyllic life of the old Spanish families is based on such exploitation of the natives, often under the guise of making them converts to Christianity. But while Rosarita, another captured Navajo girl, goes willingly to the white man's church, Bright Morning refuses stubbornly during her captivity to have anything to do with the god of her captors.

The second part of the confrontation between whites and Indians occurs when the army, "the Long Knives," forcibly relocates the Navajo and marches them to a reservation, a long, painful journey reminiscent of the

Cherokee's Trail of Tears to Oklahoma. This treatment of the Native Americans is even harsher, and some of Bright Morning's people suspect that the army tries to eliminate them and does not wish them to survive. Illness, starvation, and lack of shelter take a terrible toll of the Indians at Bosque Redondo, the inhospitable desert where their new reservation is located.

◆ Themes ◆

Living in harmony with the environment is a theme that appears in several of Scott O'Dell's stories about Native Americans. Just as Karana, the heroine of *Island of the Blue Dolphins* (1960), manages to live and even find satisfaction in a hostile environment, Bright Morning, her family and people lead a frugal but satisfying life in Canyon de Chelly, raising sheep, fruit, vegetables, and corn. There is pleasure in watching the sheep prosper, as well as responsibility for their welfare. Bright Morning recalls an episode where she was frightened by a storm and went home, leaving the flock to fend for itself. She is not punished, but her mother refuses to trust her for a year and treats her as an irresponsible child.

The Navajo life is meaningful because everyone knows his place in it, but when this way of life is disturbed, so is the social balance. After the soldiers have forcibly settled the Indians on the reservation, they try to turn them into wheat farmers, not a natural activity for the Indians. Their natural seasonal rhythm is destroyed, and they merely exist on the food they are handed, lacking any will to work because they have lost their role and purpose in life. Totally demoralized, they lose their self-respect and will to survive.

"My mother and sister and I, like all the other women, had little to do. There was no corn to grind. Wagons came filled with flour. White soldiers stood in it up to their knees and passed it out to us on big wooden shovels. There were no sheep to tend or wool to shear and weave into blankets. There were no hunters to bring in hides to scrape and stretch and make into leggings. We were idle most of the time."

The domination by a foreign culture leading to the destruction of an ancient way of life is another, related theme of *Sing Down the Moon*. The colorful rites of becoming a woman that Bright Morning undergoes in the early part of the novel are in stark contrast to the apathy and lethargy of reservation existence. It is only when Bright Morning refuses to give up her old ways, represented by her sheep, that she is able to escape and recapture her former existence. In this, she is the leader, and her husband Tall Boy, the follower, just as in the Navajo culture the women are the keepers of tradition. and guardians of the home and the flocks.

◆ Techniques ◆

Scott O'Dell's style and narrative technique are very original, and both have drawn high praise as well as criticism from his reviewers. He is a master of understatement. Rarely do his characters express their emotions, although the perceptive reader will find that they may run deep. The love between Bright Morning and Tall Boy is never expressed except for brief comments such as "I stood there and felt like crying," or "My heart hurt for him." Yet although she feels sorry and understands Tall Boy's despair, when her mother taunts her husband and says: "He will soon have to change his name again . . . What do you think it should be? Boy-Who-Sits-at the Fire? Boy-Who-Sleeps-Standing-up?"she comments drily, "I will need to think hard." This seeming stoicism and lack of emotion is derived from older stereotypical pictures of the Indian, but in Scott O'Dell's writing it becomes a powerful and effective tool. The strength of his protagonists comes from an inner core and does not need outward confirmation.

As spare and unemotional as his style are his descriptions, but they are extraordinarily evocative due to effective uses of comparisons and metaphors. The first day of spring is described as the day the waters came. High on the mesa, Bright Morning first hears them as a whisper like the wind among the dry corn stalks, then as a sound of the feet of warriors dancing, and finally as a roar that shakes the earth. Metaphors and comparisons are drawn from the world of the characters, and underscore the Indian way of life.

◆ Literary Precedents ◆

The Indian as the "noble savage" is an age-old concept used by many writers, ranging from Cooper's Leather Stocking Tales to modern Westerns such as Dorothy Johnson's "The Lost Sister." The eighteenth century saw the American native as a person living in a state of innocence, in a natural paradise unspoiled by civilization. Unfortunately, the European world often destroyed this paradise. Scott O'Dell uses this theme when he describes the happy, productive life of Bright Morning and her people in the Canyon de Chelly, a life that is abruptly ended when

they are moved to the reservation by the white government. Yet O'Dell still sees hope for the future when the courageous Navajo woman and her husband return to their home and start life over. Later such a hope is no longer possible, as in *Thunder Rolling in the Mountains* (1992), where the Nez Perce under Chief Joseph have no chance to return to their beautiful Wallowa mountains.

◆ Related Titles ◆

Both *Island of the Blue Dolphins* and *Streams to the River, River to the Sea* (1985), have young female Indian protagonists who overcome obstacles through their courage and persistence. Karana builds herself a life on a solitary island, yet she never forgets the revenge for her brother who was killed by wild dogs. And Sacajawea, the young woman who guides Lewis and Clark, has lived through years as a captive, yet never gives up hope and eventually manages to escape her kidnappers. The same resourceful and courageous young women also appear in O'Dell's novels about other cultures such as Bright Dawn, an Eskimo girl in *Black Star, Bright Dawn* (1988), and Sarah Bishop in the novel of the same title which is set in Colonial America.

◆ Ideas for Group Discussions ◆

When Scott O'Dell first submitted his manuscript for *Island of the Blue Dolphins*, it was rejected because the protagonist was a young woman. O'Dell's agent suggested that he change the sex of the main character, but the writer refused to do so. In what way does his preference for young female protagonists affect his novels? Would the theme and story evolve the same way if Karana was a boy or Bright Morning a young man? It is interesting that in *Sing Down the Moon*, only the women play an important role. The men may brag or give up, but the Navajo women are the ones that carry on the traditions and tasks of everyday life. Why would a male author show such preferences? Are his girls feminine or masculine? Does the fact that the Navajo culture is largely maternal — the women own the sheep, the backbone of the economy of the tribes — explain the strength of character of the protagonist, or are there other explanations?

1. *Sing Down the Moon* actually consists of two plots — the kidnapping of Bright Morning by Spanish slavers and the relocation of the Navajo by the U.S. Army. Why did O'Dell bring in these two plots? Are they related? What is the function of the kidnapping and rescue story?

2. What is the purpose of the detailed description of the Womanhood Ceremony? Why is it placed between the two tragic stories? How is this ceremony related to O'Dell's overall theme? What is its importance in the life of Bright Morning? Does it explain her character? Her standing in the tribe? The role of women in Navajo society?

3. What significant role do sheep play in Bright Morning's life? O'Dell uses them almost in a symbolic manner. What is their purpose beyond factual detail?

4. What is the relationship between Tall Boy and Bright Morning in their marriage? When they escape from the reservation, he rides their horse and she has to walk. She says that "someday I hoped to have a horse of my own and then I would ride beside my husband. Perhaps he would not own a horse by this time, then it would be he who would have to walk." How does the Navajo concept of marriage differ from the one of the white society?

5. How does O'Dell handle emotion in this story? Are the Indians simply stoic? What about the teasing that Bright Morning refers to with her friends? Are we to take everything she says literally? Is this true also for her relationship with Tall Boy?

6. Why does Bright Morning destroy the toy spear Tall Boy has made for his son? Does this illustrate her vision of the future, and what does this vision promise? Why does she call the rain at the end of the book "Navajo rain"?

Ingeborg Urcia
Eastern Washington University

SINGING GUNS

Novel

1928-1929

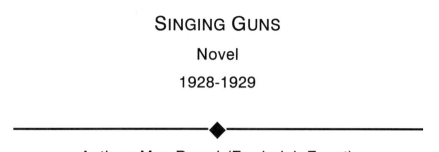

Author: Max Brand (Frederick Faust)

◆ Themes/Characters ◆

Two of the most memorable characters in popular western fiction appear in *Singing Guns* — the courageous but guileless outlaw giant, Annan Rhiannon, and his canny Welsh friend, Sheriff Owen Caradac. Although masculine friendship or "bonding" is an ancient theme of the frontier story — as old as Hawkeye and Chingachgook in James Fenimore Cooper — and some versions of this theme may be found in Faust's predecessors, like Grey and Clarence Mulford, the intense comradeship that develops between an outlaw and sheriff is an original contribution of this story. The friendship between Caradac and Rhiannon springs up after an opening confrontation in the mountains where Caradac, trying to track down the legendary outlaw Rhiannon, is wounded and then nursed back to health by the bearded and half-savage Rhiannon. Rhiannon, a brave and skillful warrior who lives alone in the mountains, has a kind heart and suffers from loneliness. The reason for his becoming an outlaw is never clearly explained, but it is obvious that Rhiannon is a Max Brand hero in the manner of the archetypal outsider, Whistlin' Dan Barry, in Faust's first western, *The Untamed* (1919). Rhiannon is clearly too independent to adjust to civilization easily, and he lacks the guile that enables a man like Caradac (a fighter of the same mettle) to accommodate himself successfully to a life in society. Both Rhiannon and Caradac recognize that there is a curious kinship between them, which goes beyond the circumstances of their meeting: the outlaw and the manhunter are alike in their love of danger and their willingness to take life threatening risks, and this quality, or this need to test one's courage and prowess regularly, sets them apart from the commonplace middle class citizens whom Rhiannon robs and Caradac tries to protect. The similarities between Caradac and Rhiannon are symbolically emphasized by Faust's giving them the names of Welsh heroes.

Caradac's guile and essential humanity are demonstrated in his plan to help Rhiannon find a new life as a small rancher, while his cleverness and wisdom are also expressed in his effort to keep a fatherly eye on Rhiannon during his probationary period. Even more admirably, Caradac proves himself a master of intrigue in his ability to outwit the cunning Nancy Morgan, the female trickster who plays damsel in distress in order to manipulate Rhiannon into leading her to the cavern where a fortune lies hidden. As a wise and tutelary older figure, Caradac becomes the archetype of experienced and pragmatic characters who aid Faust's heroes in the later westerns, like Lanky, who guides the naive Nelson Gray through perils in *Dead or Alive* (1938) and, of course, Jim Silver or Silvertip, the mythic figure who helps younger characters in the Silvertip series. Caradac is also a prototype of the wise but disenchanted Dr. Gillespie in the Dr. Kildare novels and films.

Rhiannon represents the hero of Max Brand westerns learning to come to terms with society, or at least making a negotiated truce with it. In many earlier Max Brand westerns, the hero is not only an "untamed" figure like Dan Barry — who never learns to accept society and is finally killed by his pursuers in the final Dan Barry novel, *The Seventh Man* (1921) — but the hero's acceptance of civilization, and the concomitant marriage that often goes with such acceptance, is an extremely tenuous act, often entered reluctantly. Sometimes, in fact, the endings of earlier Max Brand westerns are clearly cynical concessions to the audience's expectations of a happy ending in the manner of Zane Grey (marriage and monetary success for the hero) — as in *The Border Bandit* (1926), where the hero's enjoyment of the freedom he finds in outlawry does not seem likely to prepare him to accept a tame, domestic life with his sweetheart. In Rhiannon, however, Faust created an "untamed" Dan Barry type, who, despite his independence and energy, manages to avoid Barry's fate. Rhiannon may have learned to live on acceptable terms with society, despite the

longing for adventure that allows him to succumb to Nancy Morgan's wiles. For all his courage and skills with guns, the loneliness Rhiannon has endured in the mountains drives him to a conventional life when Caradac offers it. It is Caradac's friendship, as much as Rhiannon's need for Isabella Dee, that brings him to a life of honest toil.

The secondary characters, though less memorable, are fairly well drawn. Nancy Morgan, the cunning minx from the East who is finally unmasked as a villainess, is a convincing confidence woman, perhaps suggested by Morgan le Fay, in Arthurian stories. Her temptress role is played convincingly, and almost leads Rhiannon to his death. Indeed, Faust may have been the first popular western writer to portray women as major villains. In this regard, Faust's characterization of women proves to be similar to that of his celebrated contemporary and fellow pulp writer, Dashiell Hammett in *The Maltese Falcon* (1930).

Equally successful is Faust's depiction of the wealthy but unpretentious Dee family, who operate the largest ranching operation in the Laurel Mountain country. Oliver Dee, the patriarch, is a credible millionaire of the Rocky Mountain West, a weather-beaten old man who wears down-at-the-heels clothes and talks like his ranch hands. Charlie Dee, the male scion of the family, is one of the irresponsible scapegraces who people numerous Faust westerns. The best character in this family, however, is Isabella Dee, the heroine, whose candor and charm are both winning and durable. In this regard, Faust's westerns tend to break with the conventional stereotype of the heroine of westerns as a calico-clad innocent or as a foolish and pretentious ingenue from the East. Isabella, like the best of Faust's heroines, is neither a reform-minded schoolmarm nor a saloon girl, but a young lady of spirit with some traits of the tomboy.

◆ Techniques/Literary Precedents ◆

Faust's earlier westerns about outlaws and adventurers on the edge of the law are the main precedents for *Singing Guns*. To a certain degree, Faust created his own conventions for the genre. The outline of the Max Brand hero was established in archetypal form in *The Untamed*, and except for the addition of guile and a conscience, the pattern is repeated with variations for the next fifteen or twenty years. Indeed, Silvertip, roaming the West in 1933, is remarkably similar in important ways to Dan Barry in 1919. Some variations on the pattern include heroes who use ropes instead of guns, like Reata, or kung fu, like Speedy the tramp, or simply rely on their bare fists, like Harry Gloster in *Dan Barry's Daughter* (1924). (The major exception is a character like Eddie Clewes, in *The Iron Trail* [1926], a tramp who uses glibness and guile to manipulate and control others.)

Nevertheless, there are some precedents for *Singing Guns* both within the genre of the western and outside of it. Although numerous earlier Max Brand heroes managed to win a pardon for their transgressions as Rhiannon does, the classic pattern for the redemption of the lone wolf outlaw is established in Zane Grey's *The Lone Star Ranger* (1915), where Buck Duane is given a second chance by the stern but kindly Captain McNelly of the Texas Rangers. It is well known, of course, that Faust was encouraged to read Grey's pub-lished works by Bob Davis, the Munsey editor who urged him to concentrate his career on producing westerns.

Another important source is Welsh mythology, and specifically the Mabinogion, the collection of classic tales which Faust probably read in the famous Charlotte Guest translation. In the opening of *Singing Guns*, Faust alludes to the Welsh goddess Rhiannon, whose songs could bring death to men, as a way of establishing his hero's legendary and heroic stature. It should also be noted that the names of nearly all the principal characters are Welsh, or at least Celtic. Faust often reminded his friends and confidants that his mother was Irish in descent, and he showed an abiding interest in Celtic mythology for most of his professional life. Finally, Nancy Morgan's name suggests Morgan le Fay as a source.

◆ Adaptations ◆

In the late 1940s, when, after his death, Faust had become a Hollywood legend, several of the Max Brand westerns were adapted for film. Republic did a version of *Singing Guns* which was released in 1950 with a popular singer of that era, Vaughan Monroe, as Rhiannon and the lovely Ella Raines as the female lead. A bearded Monroe did a passable job as a western hero, and the script showed some fidelity to its original, but the production is undeniably second rate and of little importance in the tradition of the western film. Ironically, a 1943 film western, *The Desperadoes*, based on an original story by Faust, comes closer to the spirit of *Singing Guns*. This big budget technicolor film, with Glenn Ford and Randolph Scott as an outlaw and sheriff who share a lasting friendship, is a spirited action film which has worn fairly well. Curiously, *The Desperadoes* uses the plot of *Singing Guns* in reverse, by making Cheyenne Rogers, the outlaw played by a youthful Ford, into a clever trickster, while his honest friend, a sheriff played by Randolph Scott, is somewhat too trusting and naive. The climactic sequence in which Ford uses a wild horse stampede to rescue Scott is very exciting.

Edgar L. Chapman
Bradley University

SISTER LIGHT, SISTER DARK

Novel

1988

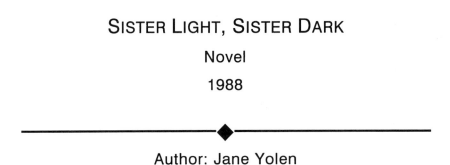

Author: Jane Yolen

◆ Social Concerns ◆

In *Sister Light, Sister Dark* Yolen addresses post-1960s feminist concerns by means of a narrative set in a fantasy world. Mountain clans of warrior women have established self-contained communities called Hames, in order to maintain themselves in a patriarchal Garunian age. The child protagonist Jenna resides in Selden Hame, one enclave among many. These clans arose when men rid themselves of large numbers of superfluous women, and when many female babies were abandoned to die. The women, called Altites, worship a female deity named Great Alta, and are helped by "dark sisters" who magically appear as facets of themselves. The conception is provocative in areas of women's multiple identities, self-development, mutual support, and potential for impact upon society and culture.

The nurturing of Jenna by Selden Hame foster mothers reflects the social concerns of single parenthood, child care, and the pauperization of many women. The maturation process of Jenna bears upon the issue of socialization for girls in an unstable, even threatening climate. Jenna's emergence into qualities of independence, leadership and strength underscores the call for better role models for girls, for competent heroines in literature and all avenues of mass culture.

◆ Themes ◆

As Jenna's life is followed from babyhood to teens, the theme of alienation and quest for identity functions on several levels. Jenna is troubled by her foster mothers' beliefs that events surrounding her birth and life identify her as the prophesied savior during the Garunian Gender Wars. The novel begins with prophecy. A virgin will give birth to a "white babe" with black eyes. Homage will be paid to her by ox, hound, bear, and cat. "Holy, holy, holiest of sisters," all will say; "who is both black and white, both dark and light, your coming is the beginning and it is the end." Three times will her mother die.

Jenna's situation explores questions about the making of myths, legends, heroes/heroines. Jenna has white hair and dark eyes. She had a mother who died at her birth, a midwife-mother figure killed while trying to find her another home, and a foster mother murdered while taking her from her Hame. Eventually Jenna defeats men named for beasts — the Hound, the Bull or Ox — thus unwittingly encouraging the Gender Wars, men's attacks on the Hames. The theme of Jenna's quest for self-identity, which often takes the form of challenge to her society's values, eventually meshes with that of social duty. Jenna seeks self through her impact upon social good.

Altite women see this good as the preservation of their autonomous communities. Through the story of Jenna's coming-of-age, Yolen explores the theme of bonding among women through a self-contained society of diverse personalities. Each Hame is managed by a priestess, a Mother Alta. Rituals are observed, tasks doled out. Games for the young develop strategy, skill, self-sufficiency in demonstration of the theme of value in socialization and education, including self-defensive techniques, for girls. The thematic conception of independence, assertiveness, and competence in women is markedly apparent in this fantasy, as it is in many of Yolen's fantasies for children or adults.

Although the novel's center is the women's culture, *Sister Light, Sister Dark* points toward social redemption attainable through balanced gender relationships, a theme developed in the sequel, *White Jenna* (1989). *Sister Light, Sister Dark* establishes that not all men are like those bent upon destruction of the women's groups; women enjoy occasional dalliances with men outside the Hames. "We choose to use men but not to live with them." Jenna encounters a mild-mannered boy who kindles her awakening womanhood and love.

The themes of self-definition, alienation, women's bonding and cultural life incorporate another theme commonly found in Yolen's fictional works. Yolen seeks to show the value to social stability of myth, folklore, and other products of the creative imagination — women's, in this case. The theme is stressed through Jenna's acquiescence in the poetry, balladry, and myth that surround her role. The thematic concept is also developed through inserted sections of fictitious scholarly discourse on the Garunian age. Typically the studies are stuffy and askew. Dialogue includes this subtle commentary, spoken in regard to the boy Carum: "They say he is a scholar and in danger, though what danger a scholar could possibly get into, only Alta knows."

◆ Characters ◆

In *Sister Light, Sister Dark,* the focal character is Jenna, traced from her birth through her early teens. Her special status as a prophesied savior is reflected in the images and various names attached to her: Jo-an-nna, Ann-uenna, the white babe, White Goddess, and more. "And so Great Alta made the Anna, the White One, the Holy One." The charm of Jenna's story is the play between the ordinary in life and the extraordinary, the tug between a gifted girl wanting to belong and an impressionable folk isolating the heroine of its myth. "I am not the White Babe," Jenna insists for years. "I am just a girl."

But Jenna is a girl blessed from babyhood with exceptional human qualities. She is tall, superior at games and lessons, quick of hand, excellent with the bow, throwing knife, and sword. She is inquisitive, assertive, strong, and rather rebellious against Hame social values. She dares to doubt the

Alta-worship scripture, the Book of Light. She questions the absolute moral and social value supposed to obtain from the magical presence of a dark sister. "Do all loneliness and all jealousy and all anger end when your sister is called forth?"

In many ways Jenna is the heroic young character of fantasy convention, although it is crucial to the novel's conception that she is female. Jenna is engaged in a quest, forced into heroism as she confronts a duality common to fantasy, a battle for social good against anarchic evil. The Hames are imperiled by armies of evil men. Jenna is typical in her ambivalent but worthy qualities. She escapes prophesied pitfalls of drowning, death by fire. She matures in the process, reconciles self with social duty. She sees that she *is* different at the core. "Did that make her a savior, an avatar, the Anna? She did not know." But "whether she believed or not," events would move on. "Sisters," Jenna capitulates, "I am the Anna."

The issues raised by Jenna's situation are reinforced by a rich cast of characters. Primary are the Hames-dwellers, warrior women, and girls. The girls demonstrate themes of maturation, alienation, and search for self. The adults reinforce the theme of women's competence, self-sufficiency, and sisterly bonding. Amalda is one of the story's several mother figures. With dark sister Sammor, she is known for kindness to her young birth-daughter Marga, nicknamed Pynt, who calls her A-ma. Amalda is the mother Jenna wishes she had had.

Jenna was named Jo-an-enna by Selna, the warrior woman and huntress who found and first nurtured her. Selna's characterization introduces the reader to the concept of sisters, light and dark. Selna is paired by dark Marjo who was called forth at a magical maturation rite for girls. Like all the dark sisters, Marjo becomes visible in the light of moon or candle to aid and complete the self. Selna's murder relates to themes of woman's integrity through inner strength and bonding with the group. Selna was absorbed in foster-mothering to Marjo's detriment, and was killed by a man while stealing baby Jenna from the Hame.

The novel presents two mother figures who oversee sisterhoods, the blind, mild-mannered Nill's Hame's Mother Alta, and Selden Hame's Mother Alta whom the girls nickname "old Serpent Mouth." Selden's Mother Alta is the novel's dominant mother figure, and the kind girls typically like to defy: "you will do as I say, for . . . I know what is best for you." This Mother Alta's characterization blends the wicked stepmother of fairy-tale tradition with the authority figure who may possess wisdom.

Mother Alta is a stock character, the aging woman who fears displacement. Jenna has questioned the authority which is absolute to Mother Alta. "If I am not thy priestess," Mother Alta prays to goddess Alta, "I am nothing. It is all my life." To Mother Alta, Jenna represents youth and change. In order to "begin the world anew," after all, "one must destroy the old."

Young characters Pynt and Petra illustrate the point of sisterly bonding, but with balance. First one girl, then the other, forges a tight-knit tie to Jenna. "I am your shadow," Pynt says. Her male literary prototype is Don Quixote's Sancho Panza, or the hero's sidekick in many western stories. Pynt's ejection from her "shadow" role by Jenna's romantic interest and evocation of a personal dark sister reflects themes of strength from within self, and a potential balance in relations with men.

Petra, a priestess-in-training, resembles the bard of medieval lore. She sings Jenna's praises on their travels, and illumines the way legends grow and folk heroes/heroines are made. When doubt is cast on Jenna's place as savior or the Anna, Petra instantly composes rhymes that reinforce but subtly enhance prophetic images. The theme is reinforced that society needs such cultural services.

The novel's few notable male characters indicate that male brutishness, not men, must be rejected. This concept is evidenced by Jenna's killing of the violent, beastly man Barnoo, "The Hound" of Garunian prophecy. The possibilities for a new kind of gender relationship are reflected in the character Carum Longbow, a teenager described as reasonably good-looking and not of barbarian stock. Carum is a prince in flight from the evil Lord Kalas and his men, who include the Hound, the Bull, the Bear, and the Cat of prophecy. Unlike the prince of traditional fantasy, Carum is a sensitive scholar who seeks the heroine Jenna's help.

◆ Techniques ◆

Sister Light, Sister Dark is a novel of fantasy constructed by cleverly interwoven and related parts. Jenna's story is accompanied by sections of myth, legend, poetry, parable, and even song, complete with musical notation. This approach enriches the storytelling, emphasizes the social and cultural value of the imagination, and illumines the way myths and legends can grow. The topics of the songs and poetry reinforce themes pertaining to women's

cause. History sections which satirize dry, misguided scholarly studies add to the novel's witty tone.

Yolen's conception of the mythic deity Great Alta is an inspired stroke relating to the complexities of women's lives. Alta's creative process displays Yolen's usage of symbolic form. Alta made light and dark sisters as mirror images from the golden and dark sides of her flowing hair, twining them as one within her intricate braids. Yolen's capacity for poetic imagery is apparent also in Alta's depiction as a goddess whose words were like "slivers of glass" which, when spoken, "reflected back the mind of the listener." Effective descriptive imagery is evident in the characterization of Nill's Hame's Mother Alta. Her fingers were "like little breezes," her hands wove "dark fantasies in the air."

Deftly wrought dialogue, attention to detail, and an easy, rhythmic style engage the reader. Character's names, such as Donya, Doey, Marna, Alinda, Brenna, are carefully chosen to enhance folkloric flavor. Yolen endows Jenna and her peers with typical little-girl and teen-age longings, enhancing believability despite the fantasy setting. Jenna's ambivalence and alienation strike a recognizable chord. She feels a growing, "odd sense of distance from the other girls." She wants to be "ordinary." The depiction illustrates Yolen's technique of reinforcing theme through characterization.

◆ Literary Precedents ◆

Sister Light, Sister Dark has roots in centuries-old fantasy and folk tradition. Nineteenth- and twentieth-century antecedents can be found in the works of Andrew Lang and the Brothers Grimm, as well as J. R. R. Tolkien who wrote fantasies based upon medieval lore. The novel's break with tradition lies in reversal of the male point of view and depiction of strong female characters. The warrior women, such as Jenna's swordplay teachers Catrona and dark sister Katri, and Jenna herself, have roots in legendary male counterparts.

Yolen's depiction of a society of women has some precedent in the works of speculative-fiction writers Marion Zimmer Bradley and Anne McCaffrey. The particular concept of light and dark sisters arises from the fantasy tradition of symbolic color usage and the maturation theme. In her *A Wizard of Earthsea* (1968), for example, part of the "Earthsea Trilogy," author Ursula K. Le Guin has the character Ged meet his shadow, unite with it, and achieve a point of maturity.

Yolen's work belongs to a broad feminist literary trend. Yolen herself is a significant force in the fantasy and fairy-tale genre. She has expressed in print her frustration with the modern versions of Cinderella, especially Disney's, which portray a passive, obedient girl awaiting rescue by a prince. Yolen may be best categorized among a number of post-1960s writers like Angela Carter, Roald Dahl, John Gardner, Richard Gardner, Judith Viorst, and Tanith Lee, who have written revised fairy tales or fantasies in order to subvert patriarchal values.

◆ Related Titles ◆

Yolen's *White Jenna,* a sequel to *Sister Light, Sister Dark,* takes up Jenna's tale from the point of her departure to warn and save the Hames. In the course of her adventures Jenna undergoes further development as a woman, and becomes a leading force in social reconstruction. Yolen's literary fairy tale "The Moon Ribbon" provides an example of a tough heroine, one who defeats a stepmother figure. The tale "The Undine" involves betrayal by men and autonomy for women.

◆ Ideas for Group Discussions ◆

A significant aspect of Yolen's fiction is concern for topical questions of patriarchy and feminism. Because of this, and because of her easy, flowing style, her fiction should provoke enjoyable discussion. The novel is centered in women's lifestyles, values, child-rearing and socializing issues. Comparisons between these fictive treatments and contemporary women's problems are good lines to pursue. Also useful for discussion are questions about the state and worth of scholarly research and discourse, which should arise from the fictitious "History" sections. Yolen has been a strong advocate of fantasy as the medium for hidden truths. Her application of the genre and her techniques should constitute effective topics for discussion.

1. The novel presents a view of an exclusively women's community. What are the positive aspects of Hame life? Are there negative aspects? Discuss in light of contemporary women's issues.

2. The Hame women claim to use men for pleasure, then casually dismiss them. What do you make of this approach to the gender relationship?

3. What happens on the ceremonial Night of Sisterhood? What do you make of the concept of dark sisters?

4. Discuss the games played by girls (the Eye-Mind game, the game of wands), and breathing exercises. What qualities do they teach that apply especially to the mature life of women? Are these preparations valuable for girls only?

5. Consider Jenna as a character. Is she really the prophesied child of Great Alta her supporters claim? Does every facet of her life coincide with prophecy?

6. What do you think of the form of the novel? Do you find the shifts from section to section, especially the shifts back and forth in time, to be an effective enhancement of the narrative, or a disruption?

7. What are some of the many plays on words used by Yolen, and what do they contribute to the tale? The Book of Light, for example, was so called because the Dalites were surprised how small the book was, and how light.

8. Follow the academic discussion in the sections entitled "The History." How accurate are the conclusions? How well constructed are these studies for getting to the truth as depicted in the "Story" sections? What can be said about the use of scientific methods and the search for truth in contemporary society?

9. Classic fairy tales like "Cinderella" and "Snow White," or "Snow White and the Seven Dwarfs" as it is known in the Disney version, portray young girls confronting mature female figures who thwart the maturation process. Is young Jenna's situation comparable? Consider tensions in her relationship with Mother Alta, and Catrona's reasons for Mother Alta's behavior.

10. The mirror used on the Night of Sisterhood is a significant symbol. How do you interpret it?

Marilyn A. Perlberg

Skinny Legs and All

Novel

1990

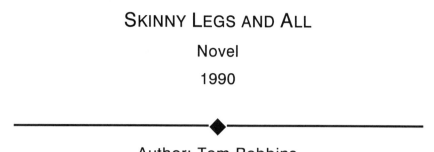

Author: Tom Robbins

◆ Characters ◆

As in his earlier works, Robbins employs an eccentric cast of characters. The protagonist in *Skinny Legs and All*, Ellen Cherry Charles, is tied to a double vocation as artist and waitress; her redneck husband, Boomer Petway, holds a similar twin calling as welder and artist. After the Airstream van that Boomer has welded into a giant roast turkey to win Ellen as his wife becomes the latest sensation in the New York art world and Boomer gains overnight celebrity status, the marriage, which Ellen entered with some uncertainty, rapidly disintegrates. To support herself, Ellen takes a job as a waitress at Isaac's and Ishmael's, a pacifist restaurant opened by an Arab and a Jew across from the United Nations. Joining Ellen and Boomer are additional outlandish characters, including Turn Around Norman, an artist whose creative expression leads him to rotate in front of St. Patrick's Cathedral so slowly his movements are imperceptible except to his devotees and inanimate objects; Buddy Winkler, a fundamentalist preacher intent on bringing about the second coming of Christ by fomenting war in the Middle East; and Salome, a virginal Lebanese nursing student by day, sexually charged belly dancer by night. Yet Robbins is not content with creating this odd assortment of human characters; his novel also includes a cast of inanimate characters: Conch Shell, Painted Stick, Sock, Spoon, and Can O'Beans. This unlikely group follows Ellen Cherry Charles and Boomer Petway across the United States to New York and, with the exception of Sock, makes its way across the Atlantic to Israel. The interaction between these unusual characters produces the fantastic situations which delight Robbins's fans.

◆ Social Concerns/Themes ◆

As he does in *Another Roadside Attraction* (1971) and *Even Cowgirls Get the Blues* (1976), Robbins chronicles the failure of western society to live in harmony and peace with itself. He believes modern Western culture, particularly as it is represented in Christian fundamentalism, is responsible for much human unhappiness and social discord. According to Robbins, modern man has been deceived by a culture that has impaired his spiritual vision. To illustrate his position, Robbins uses the Middle Eastern Dance of the Seven Veils as a means to present seven illusions which keep the naked facts of life from our eyes. As the veils drop in the course of the dance, Robbins reveals his philosophical position: that through ignorance or dissembling our purpose in life is hidden; that we do not have dominion over plants, animals, and inanimate objects; that political expediency is often advertised as virtue; that organized religion diminishes rather than enhances our spiritual life; that valuing money clouds our minds as much as valuing organized religion; that living as if only the afterlife were important keeps us from fulfillment in the here and now; and that every individual is responsible for his or her spiritual growth.

Robbins believes that the cure for the diseased Western cultural system is a return to earlier and healthier feminine principles, like the veneration of Astarte, the pre-Christian goddess of fertility once worshipped across the Middle East. Additionally, he suggests that much of the political discord in the Middle East is a result of the various groups — whether Jews, Arabs, or Christians — losing touch with the older religious system they once shared. Cultural veils lead us to prefer dry spirit in place of fertile soul, the easy power of money in place of the mysterious creative power of magic which produces art.

Overlaying Robbins's social concerns is a tale of two artists who attempt to come to terms with art and each other. *Skinny Legs and All* develops the relationship between beautiful painter Ellen Cherry Charles and lame welder Boomer Petway, a twentieth-century romance between Venus and Vulcan.

This love story connects the political, class, religious, and artistic themes of the novel.

◆ Techniques ◆

Skinny Legs and All is divided into seven major sections, each one corresponding to one of the seven veils dropped by Salome as she performs the Dance of the Seven Veils on Superbowl Sunday. As with each of Robbins's novels, this one manifests its author's delight with the written word, a delight reflected in his verbal humor, puns, stretched metaphors, and wordplay. Unlike his previous works, however, this novel is less experimental. The metafictional intrusion of the author into the work, which has been noted in *Another Roadside Attraction, Even Cowgirls Get the Blues*, and *Still Life with Woodpecker* (1980), has given place to more traditional methods of exposition. Still, Robbins's latest fiction successfully merges fantasy with many of the elements of popular culture as a means of articulating his views on Western sexuality and spirituality.

◆ Literary Precedents ◆

Robbins has indicated that he appreciates works by E. L. Doctorow, Günter Grass, Thomas Pynchon, Ishmael Reed, and Alice Walker. *Skinny Legs and All*, although less innovative than his earlier work, still expresses the playful style and literary techniques reminiscent of Kurt Vonnegut.

◆ Related Titles ◆

Robbins's protagonist, Ellen Cherry

Charles, plays a cameo role in his earlier novel *Jitterbug Perfume* (1984), in which she first appears as one of the "Daughters of the Daily Special" who receives a grant from her sister-waitresses to pursue her interest in painting. More importantly, the author's treatment of issues concerning personal freedom, spirituality, organized religion, human sexuality, and art which appear in *Skinny Legs and All* have been previously introduced in earlier works. Robbins's experience as art critic for the *Seattle Times* and his research on Jackson Pollack appear to have provided him with much of the background for Ellen Cherry Charles's artistic philosophy, the character of Ultima Sommervell, the art dealer, and the New York setting. Once again, Robbins directs some biting satire toward his birthplace, the Richmond, Virginia, area. His fictional Colonial Pines, actually Colonial Heights, Virginia, is depicted as the constricting home of Ellen Cherry Charles and the home base for misguided fundamentalist preacher Buddy Winkler. The area fosters an atmosphere that drives out art and encourages soul-deadening religion.

Kenneth B. Grant
University of Wisconsin Center
Baraboo/Sauk County

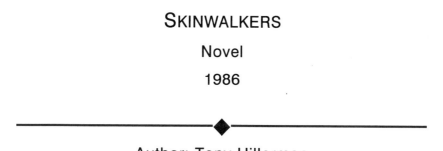

SKINWALKERS

Novel

1986

Author: Tony Hillerman

◆ Characters ◆

Although Joe Leaphorn dominates three earlier novels — *The Blessing Way* (1970), *Dance Hall of the Dead* (1973), and *Listening Woman* (1977) — Hillerman adds still more depth to his characterization of Leaphorn in *Skinwalkers*. Described in detail is Leaphorn's corkboard-mounted office map of "Indian Country" with his written annotations and the colored pins with which he marks crime locations. A symbol of Leaphorn's legendary eccentricity and rationalism, the map proves invaluable when it reveals connections between three seemingly unrelated killings.

Jim Chee also appears in his own set of early Hillerman novels. A police officer whose interest in his heritage is so strong that he is learning to perform a complicated Navajo ceremonial sing, Chee ironically is mistaken for a skinwalker and nearly killed. The attempt on his life precipitates the investigation that brings him together with Leaphorn to work on the same case. Chee is described physically from Leaphorn's point of view as "destined to be a skinny old man." This depiction is consistent with Hillerman's preferred method of characterization — the succinct description or personality sketch.

Minor characters are delineated with a phrase or two or a brief description of physical traits or characteristic speech patterns. In some cases, a character is labeled by a distinguishing costume, attitude, or posture — thus Janet Pete, the lawyer, is initially introduced from Chee's perspective as "Silk Shirt," and the no-nonsense owner of a remote trading post is known as "Iron Woman."

◆ Social Concerns ◆

In *Skinwalkers*, Hillerman highlights the clash between Navajo beliefs and white skepticism, a conflict caused by the intrusion of the modern world into traditional native American culture. At issue is the Navajo belief in the *skinwalker*, a witch who possesses the power to fly, to run faster than the wind, and to become a dog or a wolf. Joe Leaphorn and Jim Chee, both Navajos, educated in state universities in the white man's world, and both policemen, embody the collision between old tribal beliefs and modern-day skepticism as they investigate a series of killings seemingly perpetrated by a skinwalker. Leaphorn represents logical thinking, rational questioning, and a healthy doubt about the existence of skinwalkers. Chee is more involved with traditional culture and religion, more intuitive and idealistic, more troubled at the encroachment of Western culture, and more inclined to attach importance to stories about the existence of skinwalkers.

Also personifying the conflict between white and Native Americans are Irma Onesalt, a social worker and one of the murder victims, and Dr. Bahe Yellowhorse, founder and chief benefactor of the Bad Water Clinic that provides free medical care on the reservation. Onesalt seems to have spent her last days investigating possible Medicare abuses at the clinic; Yellowhorse justifies overcharging the government by reminding himself that the Native American population has yet to receive most of what the government promised them in the Fort Sumner treaty.

◆ Techniques ◆

As in his earlier novels, Hillerman interweaves the beliefs and customs of the Navajo throughout the plot of *Skinwalkers*, creating a tapestry of culture that forms the backdrop to the often violent and puzzling incidents that demand the investigative talents of Leaphorn and Chee. Incorporated into the narrative are clan tales, genealogies, local folklore, even words and phrases in the Navajo tongue — all elements that lend authenticity to the novel and depth to the characters.

Hillerman also uses interior monologue — in this novel to characterize a desperate mother whose baby is dying from a congenital defect and to provide motivation for Jim Chee's often impulsive decisions — and impressionistic description — to evoke the dry beauty of the desert, the blackness of night, the smell of rain over a butte. Most characteristic of Hillerman's prose is its evocation of locale, its creation of the ambiance and moods of the Southwest desert country with its dry creek beds, mesas and buttes, rocky peaks, and dramatic sunrises and sunsets. Hillerman peoples his fictional landscape with characters whose stark lives he sketches in the vivid detail that he uses to highlight human presence in a vast landscape.

◆ Literary Precedents ◆

Like much of Hillerman's work, *Skinwalkers* owes something to the mystery subgenre, the police procedural novel. Leaphorn and Chee are law enforcement professionals dedicated to discovering the truth as they work within the restricting rules and procedures of a frustrating bureaucracy. Leaphorn is a descendant of a long line of fictional policemen whose careful methodology and incisive thinking are distinct assets in the crime-solving game. He belongs with other famous police officers characterized in fiction — Tibbett, Wexford, Beef, Alleyn, and their colleagues. Chee, on the other hand, represents the maverick cop, the individualist who gets results by bending the rules and trusting his own intuition. In his tendency to involve himself deeply in a case he resembles Martha Grimes's Richard Jury; in his unorthodox approaches to problems he joins the fraternity of the gifted and curious amateur sleuth — men like Carolus Dean and occasionally Lord Peter Wimsey.

Previous Hillerman novels featured either Lt. Joe Leaphorn or Officer Jim Chee, but in *Skinwalkers* the two policemen are brought together to work on a peculiar group of murders that point to the involvement of Navajo witchcraft. Hillerman pairs Leaphorn's legendary reluctance to give credence to things occult with Chee's strong affinity for Navajo tradition and ceremony, thus creating an investigative team that combines the best of two cultures.

Throughout the novel, Jim Chee is forced to examine his feelings about Mary Landon, the blond, blue-eyed schoolteacher with whom he has been emotionally involved but who has returned to her native Wisconsin. Their relationship, which flourished in the earlier Chee novels, is disintegrating under the weight of their individual cultural loyalties. Chee's attempts to come to terms with Mary's refusal to live on the reservation and her insistence that he learn to live in her world are complicated by his growing friendship with an attractive young Navajo lawyer, Janet Pete.

Emma Leaphorn, whose calming presence and direct approach to life have helped her husband work his way through several difficult cases, is slowly succumbing to what Leaphorn believes to be Alzheimer's disease. She no longer recognizes him and his anguish at watching her deterioration threatens to undermine his famed objective and intellectual approach to crime-solving.

◆ Ideas for Group Discussions ◆

Hillerman's novels about Chee and Leaphorn are fun to discuss, as well as to read. Mystery fans love the interaction of the main characters with the sometimes conflicting cultures of the Navajo and America-at-large. *Skinwalkers* offers ample material for stimulating discussions of cultural beliefs at variance with one another, for instance the Navajo supernatural beliefs that differ from those of Leaphorn and other police investigators. By placing Chee and Leaphorn in the same novel, Hillerman emphasizes the differing approaches to living represented by Chee's immersion in the Navajo culture and Leaphorn's rationalistic views. The characterizations are fun, the conflicts are interesting, and the mystery is engrossing, making *Skinwalkers* ideal for group discussions.

1. Should Chee learn to live in Landon's world? Should Landon learn to live in his? Which one is right?

2. How well depicted is cultural conflict in the novel? Does Hillerman take sides?

3. What is the Fort Sumner treaty?

4. Who is the better detective, Chee or Leaphorn?

5. How important is Navajo folklore to the plot of the novel?

6. How good are Hillerman's descriptions in *Skinwalkers*? Do you have a favorite one? What do you like about it?

7. Is the mystery complicated? Would it be interesting even without the cultural setting Hillerman provides?

E. D. Huntley
Appalachian State University

SLAN

Novel

1946, Revised 1951

◆

Author: A. E. van Vogt

◆ Characters ◆

Readers often complain that van Vogt's characters are poorly developed. For instance, in *Slan* the ruthless Joanna Hillory shifts from being Jommy Cross's implacably murderous enemy to wanting to be his wife, because, she says, he brought her hope by showing concern for the welfare of human beings. This shift of character is not credible, although it serves as a contrast late in *Slan* to Jommy Cross's change into a calculatedly ruthless manipulator of people.

Ideas dominate the narrative of *Slan*, and it is not surprising that characters seem under-developed and poorly motivated. Some like Joanna Hillory shift personalities as the requirements of the plot dictate. Her change of faith enables Jommy Cross to escape certain death. On the other hand, Kier Gray turns out to be a special kind of slan who is actually working for a better future primarily to give *Slan* a happy ending. That in *Slan's* imaginative world humanity is too stupid to know and to work for its own good cannot excuse Kier Gray's reign of terror and his brutal treatment of his daughter. Thus his happy ending is unsatisfying.

Other characters, such as the lecherous councilor Jem Lorry and the pathologically greedy Granny are stereotypes that could have been lifted out of Charles Dickens's *Oliver Twist* (1837-1839); they are stick figures that serve the needs of the plot.

Van Vogt devotes special attention to only two characters: Jommy Cross and Kathleen Layton. Cross views society from the outside. He is a renegade. Layton views society from the inside. She is Kier Gray's special slan who is preserved for study by ordinary humans. Both characters are outsiders; Layton is as intellectually and spiritually apart from the people she lives among as the hunted Cross. Both she and Cross live in fear. He fears discovery and death. She fears persecution, sexual abuse, and murder. Both characters are kinds of supermen endowed with special powers that set them apart from ordinary human beings. These two point-of-view characters see that from inside and outside, human civilization is a failure. Exactly why it is a failure is uncertain, although the reason may be inherent in human nature.

Cross is an impressive creation. His growth from Granny's thief to self-assured adulthood seems to parallel that of Oliver Twist in Dickens's novel, but he grows into a unique creation, embodying many of the contradictions and compromises of a well-drawn character. Strong, intelligent, and determined, he remains vulnerable to love; this vulnerability makes him a sympathetic character and prevents him from becoming too remote from readers. His successes and failures are credible because van Vogt has carefully shown his growth from one event to the next. The idealistic child becomes the cynical man; the early idealism makes his joyful response to Kathleen Layton as believable as his cold-blooded response to her father and the cruel reality of slans. Layton, on the other hand, retains her innocence. Her upbringing is detailed enough to make her compassionate nature believable in spite of her harsh surroundings. She embodies the notion that the slan are an evolutionary step beyond homo sapiens — that they resulted from a broad biological change wrought by nature in humanity. As Kier Gray puts it, the slans were the result of "the web of biological forces [that] struck everywhere across the Earth." Jommy Cross represents the idea that character "is a matter of training." These two ideas conflict, which may be why Cross's response to the revelations of Kier Gray is revealed, but Kathleen Layton's is not. Environment in the person of Cross seems to triumph over biology in the person of Layton.

◆ Social Concerns ◆

Van Vogt's fiction nearly always criticizes society to some degree. What sets him apart from most social critics is that he does not merely focus on current American society but instead analyzes Western Civilization as a whole and sometimes the "human condition" in its broadest sense. In *Slan*, his first and most famous novel, some of the principal social themes of van Vogt's career are brought forward, although they are sketchy and confused.

The situation of *Slan* seems borrowed from the events of World War II, during which the novel was written. The "slans" — millions of mutated humans who are telepathic — are systematically hunted down and murdered by the agents of a worldwide police state. The persecution of the slans is similar to the persecution of European Jews by Nazi Germany, and the secret police resemble those of Nazi Germany and the Soviet Union. The world government itself is led by a ruthless Hitler-like dictator, Kier Gray, and the government's structure resembles that of the Soviet Union, including a chief governing board that operates like the Politburo. The Nazis blamed the Jews for Germany's military disaster in World War I, and so too the slans are accused of creating "a wave of terror that swept the world into war." In addition, the slans — because they are mutations — are rumored to mutilate human babies in order to make more slans.

These elaborate parallels to twentieth-century tyrannies and their victims are poorly developed in *Slan* and in fact are abandoned about three quarters of the way through the novel. Even so, the novel contains many small motifs that will become great ideas in van Vogt's later fiction. The protagonist Jommy Cross develops "a deep philosophical sense of the profound tragedy of life." The mysterious tendrilless slan Joanna Hillory asserts, "A normal life must include marriage." In his diary, the great scientist Samuel Lann asserts, "Morality, after all, is a matter of training." When Kier Gray explains how the cataclysm of the last worldwide war came about, he claims it was "a reaction to the countless intolerable pressures that were driving men mad, because neither their minds nor their bodies were capable of withstanding modern civilization." In *Slan* van Vogt touches on issues such as the inherent tragedy of human life, the difficulty of defining a "normal life," the effect of environment on morality, and the insanity fostered by Western Civilization. In this early novel, however, these ideas lack a coherent philosophical framework, and they therefore remain undeveloped. By the time he writes *The World of Null-Å* (1948; rev. 1970), van Vogt has found the framework he needs to give his social themes resonance and depth.

◆ Themes ◆

Slan focuses on two main themes. The first is the question of what makes a person fully human. The second is the problem of truth in a world in which there is far more that is knowable than any single person could ever know. These are important questions. One of the qualities that makes van Vogt's work stand out from most popular fiction is its working out challenging ideas in detail. This careful thinking through of complicated ideas unifies van Vogt's novels and gives his elaborate plots meaning beyond simple entertainment. This same working out of ideas has sometimes infuriated critics who disagree with them, as well as befuddling others who do not understand them.

When examining *Slan's* theme of what makes a person fully human, one can readily see why van Vogt's fiction is controversial and capable of arousing fierce passions in readers. Critics have failed to recognize that *Slan* is a part of the "Modernist" literary movement that has dominated the "serious" fiction of the twentieth century. Among Modernism's most significant traits are its depiction of alienation, loss, and despair, and its rejection of history and traditional values. From *Slan's* beginning, its protagonist Jommy Cross, a nine-year-old slan, suffers the loss of loved ones — his mother is murdered by the secret police, just as his father had been. For survival, he becomes a thief. Despair tempers him; every disillusionment and every loss of a loved one hardens him. He discovers that to be human is to fear what one does not understand and to be a pawn that is easily manipulated by propaganda. The slans are supposed to be the next evolutionary step after homo sapiens. They are supposed to be "by nature antiwar, antimurder, antiviolence." Even so, the slans' response to the problems of humanity is coldly calculated; they willingly sacrifice the lives of millions of slans and homo sapiens in order to secure their own future — a future that offers a more efficient law and order than the past, because the slans' superior brains are more efficient than those of homo sapiens.

The problem of truth in a dishonest world is less disturbing than the notion that people are inherently cruel and selfish. Even so, van Vogt's handling of the theme of truth suggests that people prefer ignorance that supports simple prejudice rather than the research and thinking that lead to compassion and understanding. The story of Jommy Cross is one of a search for truth. He discovers several different versions of the history of relations between homo sapiens, "true" slan, and tendrilless slan. The absolute truth of history eludes him. In his young imagination, he views true slans, like himself, as embodiments of such traditional values as honesty, courage, selflessness, and honor. When these hopeful views are proven false, he focuses on himself as his one truth; he is the one slan who can save the world from a disastrous conflict. Even this proves false. In *Slan,* truth is elusive. It is glimpsed but never understood.

♦ Techniques ♦

Van Vogt's plots are always intricate and often confusing. Readers often complain that his transitions from one scene to the next are abrupt and bewildering. For instance, a character at one moment may be looking at a docked spaceship and the next be landing it at some faraway planet — with no explanation of how he got in the spaceship and how he piloted it. Van Vogt explains that such gaps are meant to be filled in by his readers. Such gaps are understandable because of van Vogt's focus on the development of ideas rather than on plot; but the absence of coherent transitions nonetheless shows a lack of consideration for the reader.

Perhaps the awkward and sometimes nonexistent transitions stem from van Vogt's adherence to a pattern of plot development propagated by John W. Gallishaw in *Only Two Ways to Write a Short Story* (1912). The pattern consists of scenes of about 800 words each. Within each scene are five steps: First, establish the setting. Second, establish the purpose of the scene's principal character. Third, present the character's struggle to achieve his purpose.

Fourth, show the success or failure of the character. Fifth, show that the character faces even worse problems. To this day, van Vogt professes to follow this pattern in his fiction. So mechanical is this approach to writing a narrative that it may well create abrupt breaks between one 800-word scene and the next.

The techniques that van Vogt employs in *Slan* to hold the interest of the reader are commonplace. The novel portrays a violent and menacing world in which characters are in constant danger; this creates suspense. The violence is both calculated and capricious. Readers can observe the menacing plans of villains developing toward a dangerous future, thus creating anticipation of excitement to come. Furthermore, violence sometimes explodes without warning and sometimes without reason, lending excitement to every scene because of the potential for dramatic surprises. The menacing plans and violent acts take many forms. For instance, the head of the secret police John Petty plans for most of the novel to murder Kathleen Layton. Her struggle to thwart his efforts make all of her scenes suspenseful. In addition, sex is added to the complicated intrigues. Jem Lorry, whose good heart has been twisted by the cruel politics of a police state, schemes to make Layton one of his mistresses. In order to evade him, she may fall into Petty's clutches, but to evade Petty may require Lorry's help. Sex is a tease in *Slan* but is worked believably into the plot. The random violence is less credible because it seems more appropriate to the twentieth century than the thirty-sixth century; it uses bullets and bombs instead of more advanced technology.

The technique that has assured *Slan* lasting popularity among young adult readers is its focus on an alienated teen-ager. Jommy Cross is goodhearted but misunderstood. He is isolated and an outcast. Such unhappy feelings are often shared by young people who find themselves growing into an adult world with which they are not yet fully prepared to cope. In addition, Cross has super powers: He can read minds; he can out-think ordinary people; and he is physically stronger and more agile than nonslans. His basic nobility in the face of persecution makes him an attractive protagonist. The shy and unhappy teen-ager is wiser than those who misunderstand him and able to outwit and outfight a society that persecutes him.

◆ Literary Precedents ◆

The idea of mutation was not new when van Vogt wrote *Slan*, but he transformed the motif into a broader view of the world than before. For instance, in *The Island of Dr. Moreau* (1896), H. G. Wells portrays animals that were made into grotesque copies of human beings by the experiments of a mad scientist; but these were not truly mutations in the Darwinian sense. Van Vogt deserves credit for more fully grasping the implications of Charles Darwin's theory of natural selection than had earlier writers. In *Slan*, mutations appear throughout the world in the twenty-first century. Many of the mutations are hideous failures. Many others are the slan, beings who look like humans except for golden tendrils on the backs of their heads. These tendrils enable slans to communicate telepathically. The mutation is an evolutionary leap, not a matter of isolated freaks of nature or the misguided experiments of scientists. Slans are the

after-men — the next evolutionary step after homo sapiens. In that sense, *Slan* is an exploration of how humanity would respond to its own biological evolution. No one before *Slan* had so fully used biological evolution in fiction. Therefore, *Slan* is a seminal work: It set the precedent that other writers imitated.

◆ Ideas for Group Discussions ◆

Slan has a strong appeal for young adult readers. Thus one potentially fruitful approach to discussing it would be to identify those aspects of it that make it particularly attractive to them and whether the book panders to any of the baser aspects of young adult mentality. *Slan* is also a book of ideas. In it, van Vogt explores notions of Darwinian evolution, social injustice, tyranny, and the effects of environment versus biology in individual growth and development. The subject of Darwinian evolution would be particularly interesting to explore. In *Slan*, van Vogt depicts evolution as species-wide leaps; change does not come from an individual mutated being, but from many people at once. New ideas in evolutionary theory of the 1980s and 1990s would seem to support the idea of sudden changes in a species, rather than slow accumulation of changes, as part of the mechanism of evolution. Does van Vogt develop his notions of evolution coherently in *Slan*? How do his ideas fit in with modern theories of evolution?

1. Is the development of Jommy Cross's character fully depicted? Is anything missing? Is the person he becomes as attractive as the person he was at the novel's beginning? Is van

Vogt making any moral judgments when Cross's attitudes change?

2. Biological evolution is an inescapable theme in *Slan*. Does evolution show up in a small scale; do any individual characters evolve physically or in their personalities?

3. In what ways does *Slan* comment on twentieth-century society? Is its depiction of tyranny believable? What points does van Vogt make about modern social conflicts, such as racism?

4. Joanna Hillory asserts, "A normal life must include marriage." Must it? What does this remark tell us about Joanna Hillory? How might other characters in the novel regard her assertion?

5. Scientist Samuel Lann asserts, "Morality, after all, is a matter of training." Is it? Does *Slan* show this? Does this account for Cross's development throughout the novel?

6. Kier Gray claims that the last worldwide war came about as "a reaction to the countless intolerable pressures that were driving men mad, because neither their minds nor their bodies were capable of withstanding modern civilization." This sounds like *future shock*, a term coined about thirty years after *Slan* was published. Does *Slan* anticipate modern social issues? Does modern civilization in and of itself drive people insane?

7. Are the slans human beings? Are nonslans right to fear them?

8. What happens to homo sapiens if the slans take over the world?

9. Are any of the slans racists?

10. What is the true history of relations between homo sapiens, "true" slan, and tendrilless slan?

11. Are slans morally superior to homo sapiens?

12. What aspects of *Slan* suggest that it is part of the Modernist literary movement? What aspects of the novel suggest that it is not?

Kirk H. Beetz

SLAUGHTERHOUSE-FIVE:

OR, THE CHILDREN'S CRUSADE

Novel

1969

◆

Author: Kurt Vonnegut

◆ Social Concerns ◆

Vonnegut was a prisoner of war in Dresden on February 13, 1945, when the city, a cultural center of no military value, was destroyed by Allied incendiary bombs, and in *Slaughterhouse-Five* Vonnegut, who was born on Armistice Day 1922, focuses on the particularly human madness of war. He consciously wanted to avoid writing a novel that glamorized the brutality of war, so as his subtitle suggests, he portrays wars as being fought by young and uncomprehending innocents. He is equally appalled by a technology that can destroy 135,000 people in two hours and the absence of an adequate moral response to such destruction.

The novel, which was published as America was escalating its involvement in Southeast Asia and nightly newscasts were filled with body counts and bloody footage from the field, makes explicit and implicit references to Vietnam. This was also a time of widespread experimentation with mind-altering drugs. Thus, the novel's mixture of fantasy and antiwar philosophy made the book particularly popular.

◆ Themes ◆

Slaughterhouse-Five describes man's inhumanity to man, and the mass destruction of Dresden by Allied forces serves as Vonnegut's primary example. Although a humanist at heart, Vonnegut repeatedly demonstrates the human aptitude for cruelty, and he shows how technology magnifies this cruelty beyond human control.

At a deeper level the novel explores the moral vacuum in which contemporary human life exists. Vonnegut's outrage over Dresden was as much a result of the lack of attention given to this event as it was to the bloodshed, but there are no villains in Vonnegut's novels, and he fully recognizes the ambiguous connection between agent and victim. Thus, in one of the novel's many Biblical allusions he sympathizes with Lot's wife who looks back at the destruction she is escaping before being turned to stone.

Slaughterhouse-Five, which is about Vonnegut's effort to tell his story as much as it is about Billy Pilgrim, explores the ambiguous nature of communication, a recurrent theme in his work. In *Mother Night* (1961), Howard Campbell's Nazi propaganda broadcasts are also strategically coded messages to the Allies, messages that even he does not understand. In the end it is uncertain whether his strategic assistance to the Allies has outweighed the moral support his broadcasts gave the Nazi regime. Accordingly, Vonnegut approached the narration of his war experiences cautiously, fearful that by retelling his adventures he would inadvertently glamorize war. The result is a mix of historical and fantastic perspectives that discourages suspension of disbelief.

Finally, the novel explores the irreconcilable conflict between free will and determinism. Billy Pilgrim's motto — "God grant me the serenity to accept the things I cannot change, courage to change the things I can, and wisdom always to tell the difference" — is undercut by the narrator's comment that "among the things Billy Pilgrim could not change were the past, the present, and the future." The book accepts the logic of Tralfamadorian determinism, but it is nevertheless clear that Vonnegut cannot excuse the fire-bombing of Dresden as fated, and although Billy Pilgrim escapes into the Tralfamadorian belief that the perpetual existence of all moments of time eliminates the negation of death, he still finds himself at times inexplicably shedding tears.

◆ Characters ◆

As though to emphasize his vision of the life-denying nature of most modern existence, Vonnegut abandons the mimetic effort to develop character through motivation and causality. He explains that "there are almost no characters in this story, and almost no dramatic confrontations, because most of the people in it are so sick and so much the listless playthings of enormous forces."

Slaughterhouse-Five was Vonnegut's conscious leap toward a more personally revealing fiction. However, he directly presents himself as the spokesman only in the opening and closing chapters. Inside this autobiographical framework, the protagonist is Billy Pilgrim. Born in Vonnegut's version of Schenectady, New York (Ilium) in the year of Vonnegut's birth (1922), Billy also experiences the fire bombing of Dresden as a prisoner-of-war. He later marries Valencia Merble, becomes a successful optometrist, and fathers two children, including a Green-Beret son. Billy has been described as one of Vonnegut's "crucifieds," a passive, suffering character who fights brutality by shutting it out of his mind.

Slaughterhouse-Five is a self-conscious novel, and Vonnegut tries to insure that his readers will remember that it is only a novel. He emphasizes the artificial nature of his book by populating it with characters from his earlier work: Eliot Rosewater, Kilgore Trout, Howard Campbell, the Rumfoords, and the Tralfamadorians.

◆ Techniques ◆

On the title page Vonnegut says that *Slaughterhouse-Five* is written in the "telegraphic schizophrenic manner" of the Tralfamadorians, a self-deprecating, but fairly accurate description of the author's nontraditional approach. Actually, *Slaughterhouse-Five* was the first broadly popular work to completely abandon traditional restrictions of linear time and fixed space. Billy Pilgrim's time travel is paralleled by Vonnegut's free movement through narrative time, mixing descriptions of historic Dresden and his personal wartime experiences with Tralfamadorian fantasy and bits from his earlier fiction to create fragments of meaning. Similarly, Vonnegut uses stream of consciousness to portray Billy's difficulty in fully adopting the Tralfamadorian objectivity toward the Dresden bombing and to underscore the inexplicable interrelatedness of experience.

◆ Literary Precedents ◆

Slaughterhouse-Five's numerous references to other books emphasize the multiplicity of Vonnegut's vision. The books, actual and fictional, that become part of *Slaughterhouse-Five* range from documentary studies such as *The Bombing of Dresden* and William Bradford Huie's *The Execution of Private Slovik* (1970), through realistic portrayals such as Stephen Crane's *Red Badge of Courage* (1895) to Kilgore Trout's fantastic *Maniacs in the Fourth Dimension*. The stylistic conflict between these books echoes the novel's examination of fact, fancy, and the place of art in society.

The protagonist's name suggests a connection with Bunyan's allegory *The Pilgrim's Progress* (1678), and like Bunyan's Christian, Billy is exposed to the evils of the world. Unlike Christian, however, Billy is not supported by the vision of a Celestial City at the end of his journey; instead he envisions the moment of his own death.

◆ Related Titles ◆

Just as Vonnegut mixes history and fantasy in *Slaughterhouse-Five*, he combines his new material with characters and references to his earlier fiction. The city of Ilium was the setting for *Player Piano* (1952); the Tralfamadorians were the central focus of *The Sirens of Titan* (1959); Howard Campbell was the protagonist of *Mother Night*; and Eliot Rosewater and Kilgore Trout return from *God Bless You, Mr. Rosewater* (1965).

The apocalyptic nature of *Slaughterhouse-Five* is echoed in many of Vonnegut's other works: In *Mother Night*, Howard Campbell defends the holocaust; in *Cat's Cradle* (1963), the earth is destroyed by Dr. Hoenniker's ice-nine; in *Deadeye Dick* (1982), the citizens of Midland City are inadvertently killed by a neutron bomb; and *Galapagos* (1985) is narrated from a distant future long after man has been all but wiped out by an AIDS-like virus.

◆ Adaptations ◆

The film version of *Slaughterhouse-Five*, directed by George Roy Hill, starring Valerie Perrine, Michael Sacks, and Ron Leibman, with a screenplay by Stephen Geller, was released by Universal in 1972. The film won a special jury prize at the 1972 Cannes Film Festival.

Carl Brucker
Arkansas Tech University

SLEEPING BEAUTY

Novel

1973

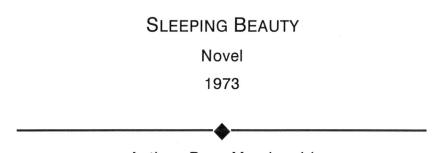

Author: Ross Macdonald

◆ Characters ◆

As with the other Archer books, the characters in *Sleeping Beauty* are grouped around a central family; the biggest difference lies in the fact that all of these figures are associated in one way or another with various elemental forces. Five of the men were in the navy and the novel keeps coming back to the sea; fire consumes characters and covers up the first crime; and the elements of air and land act in counterpoint with the sea to provide a rounding out of the four elements. The sailors gravitate to the ocean; most of the women are tied to the land; the central figure, Laurel, is associated with the air — not only through her connection with the oil-slicked gull — but also since she is the most innocent, the most angelic, and the most wraith-like. It is an interesting set of associations and one which makes this novel particularly tight symbolically.

◆ Social Concerns ◆

Like the other Lew Archer books, *Sleeping Beauty* deals with such matters as the intrusion of the past into the present, family guilt and decline, money and sex, the class struggle, and violent death. But it also focuses on an environmental issue as a metaphor for the despoliation which is going on in the human community. The plot is constructed around an oil spill off the California coast. The poetic image Macdonald uses is one of seeing the oil pumping station as a giant knife plunged into the earth with the black blood flowing out around the puncture wound. The natural environment, like the human one, has been attacked and violated, leaving a gaping hole.

Macdonald's use of the natural disaster caused by human error, which in turn was motivated by greed and power, provides a perfect image of a world gone wrong. It also supplies the necessary interconnected structure of events and motivations which characterize Lew Archer's world. Only this time, rather than stopping with the immediate past, Macdonald has metaphorically, at least, delved deeply into a primordial prehistory, a subconscious depth which produces a blackness that oozes over the sea onto the beaches and covers everything with a sticky reminder of human evil and greed.

◆ Techniques ◆

Macdonald has written in *Sleeping Beauty* the most metaphorically unified novel of the Lew Archer series. The integration he achieved by using the central symbol of the oil spill both draws the fiction together and expands its meaning outward. The circularity of the plot, actions brought full circle, as well as forward in time, are reflected in the ebb and flow, ever more menacing because of the free floating oil, of the sea which echoes the diurnal regularity of nature. The natural associations of the characters with various elements and the order of birth and death also add to the symbolic associations within the novel. Here there is little quarrel with Macdonald's use of poetic metaphor. It all seems right, in harmony with the larger literary structure of the story. Even the fairy tale suggested in the title adds to the resonance of the book. With a passing nod to Claude Levy-Straus, *Sleeping Beauty*, in concert with most fairy tales, contains a text deeply woven into the psychic fabric of the human unconscious. The novel is a stunning *tour de force*, one greatly underappreciated and all too much neglected.

◆ Literary Precedents ◆

Along with John D. MacDonald whose novels are set primarily in South Florida, Ross Macdonald came to feature in his books an ongoing concern for the environment. Like the other MacDonald, Ross watched as a virtual paradise along the southern California coastline became increasingly despoiled by over-development driven by over-population and money which transformed the natural beauty of the

state into a sprawling, urban nightmare. Like the "sleeping beauty" of the title of this early seventies Lew Archer tale, the environment perhaps only awaited a passing prince to awaken it to its former grandeur. John D. MacDonald had been railing against a similar destruction in South Florida by similar forces of development and greed. As environmental awareness became more prominent following the various political activities of the 1960s, both Ross and John D. increased their attention to environmental questions.

For Ross Macdonald treating the environment naturally coincided with his ongoing concerns for family histories and the impact of the past on the present. The Edenic qualities of the myth of California, as both the final frontier and the promise land, dovetailed nicely with such questions as ancestral sin being meted out in the present.

◆ Related Titles ◆

For similar treatment of the environment a cursory look at almost any the Travis McGee novels by John D. MacDonald or the more contemporary Florida writer Carl Hiaasen will provide some useful comparisons to the Archer stories. In addition, California has provided the original site for the development of the hard-boiled detective novel particularly those of Dashiell Hammett in Northern California and Raymond Chandler in the L.A. region. An examination of how these two predecessors of Macdonald treated the same environment would yield valuable insights into how the later writer saw the same landscape. Both Walter Mosely and James Ellroy, among others, have also dealt with L. A. and environs in more recent crime novels.

◆ Adaptations ◆

Although Macdonald's Archer has appeared on both television and in the movies, neither medium has proved especially successful in portraying him. Brian Keith played Archer in the TV series "Archer," and Peter Graves portrayed him in the made-for-TV movie of *The Underground Man;* but neither seemed quite right for the job. Paul Newman played Archer twice on the large screen, in *Harper* (1966) and later in *The Drowning Pool* (1976). Newman's performances probably came closer to capturing the diffident qualities of Macdonald's reluctant hero than did the television projects. Given the popularity of the Macdonald books it is odd that more films were not made.

◆ Ideas for Group Discussions ◆

1. As the title for this book suggests, many of Macdonald's Archer novels deal with dreamscapes and recall Freud's analysis with what he called "dream work." How is this novel especially psychological?

2. *Sleeping Beauty* also suggests something about awaking or reviving out of sleep as in the fairy tale. How do these ideas work in the fiction as well?

3. Using an oil spill against which to set the story places it in a contemporary world and recalls similar disasters occurring at the time of the novel. What does the plot say about such events and what does it say about modern life?

4. The events of this novel go back to the previous war and involve a ship which was destroyed by fire. How does this event provide the background against which the current events of the novel play out?

5. Parents and children again form a nexus of the plot in *Sleeping Beauty* and raise all sorts of questions about loss of innocence and failures within families to safeguard the young from past sins. Discuss how these ideas shape the narrative.

6. The question of infidelity works on several levels in this novel with friends, family, duty. What is the importance of this theme here?

7. How are women treated in this novel? How are women depicted in the Archer series?

8. Is there any progression or change throughout the Lew Archer series that you can see? Does the central character mature, see life differently from novel to novel?

9. What does the fairy tale reference in the title suggest for the development of the story? Are there other fairy tale elements in the fiction?

10. Why does Lew Archer never seem to become permanently involved with any of the characters in the series? Is it more than just to keep him free to investigate another case later on?

Charles L. P. Silet
Iowa State University

SMALL GODS

Novel

1992

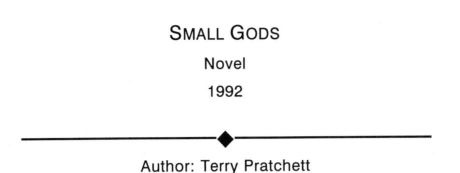

Author: Terry Pratchett

◆ Social Concerns ◆

Small Gods focuses on religion: why people need it, how they abuse it, what makes it work. By setting the tale in his imaginary Discworld, Pratchett avoids some of the minefields that tend to bedevil the path of those who explore such issues. "Omnianism" is a broad parody of Christianity, but Pratchett is less interested in ridiculing religion than in examining how it affects people. Although many of his allusions are to practices and conflicts of the distant past, his concerns are contemporary, stirred by the persistence of fanaticism and intolerance.

◆ Themes ◆

The central theme of the novel might be expressed as follows: gods need people, and people need gods. This theme comes through most consistently and effectively in the ever-evolving relationship between Brutha and Om. Brutha is the only genuine believer left to the (formerly) great god Om. Everyone else is too caught up in the machinery of Omnianism to remember the god; some devote their energies to crushing infidels and heretics, while the rest scramble to observe all the ceremonies; they pray, if at all, only to be spared the attentions of the "Quisition." Brutha progresses from unthinking fundamentalism and blind obedience through doubt to a humane, philosophical Omnianism of which he is the reluctant prophet. He never abandons his god, despite unusually concrete reasons for doing so; instead, he rejects his old, bad religion, and helps to make a new one by thinking for himself.

Om, a god fond of manifesting himself as a trampling bull or lightning-slinging smiter during his glory years, has fallen on hard times. As worship of Omnianism gradually took over from worship of Om, the god dwindled. Finally, he has become trapped in the body of a tortoise and only remembers his own divine nature when a preposterous coincidence brings him close to Brutha. Thereafter he is almost completely dependent on his last remaining worshipper. As he often does, Pratchett offers a mock-scientific explanation: all gods start off as small gods, mere sparks of yearning, buzzing around single-mindedly like insects. Those lucky enough to attract followers grow in proportion to the number of believers and the fervor of their belief. Gods need people; Om has sunk so low that he needs Brutha to rescue him from a mess of soup ingredients. By the time Om finally regains his lost stature, he has learned a few lessons himself and seems likely to take a more enlightened and informed interest in his worshippers than in the past.

The wrongness of Omnianism is incarnated in its most powerful figure, the sinister Deacon Vorbis. He is a man who only hears and sees what is inside his own head. His religion consists of an immovable but not passionate determination to stamp out all heresy, and then to spread such fear through all the neighboring lands that heresy will never arise again. In a work of literature written in our tradition, it is inevitable that such a man and such a system should lose. But Pratchett does not dismiss Vorbis as just another would-be tyrant; rather, he shows his wrongness on all levels, and then wipes him out by having an eagle drop Om (still in the form of a tortoise) on his bald head. This is hilarious, and Pratchett has been setting up this little joke from the beginning. There is a point, however: The absurdity of the death seems to be a comment on the putridity of Vorbis's life and beliefs.

◆ Characters ◆

Brutha is a sort of idiot savant at first, a lowly novice in the Citadel relegated to tending melons because he is not up to much else. He is tolerated because of his absolute humility and obedience, and he attracts the attention of Vorbis because of his phenomenal memory. Brutha is simply incapable of forgetting anything, except for a few mysterious childhood traumas. He solves the Labyrinth of Ephebe by recalling and retracing every step; he absorbs the entire contents of the great library of Ephebe before it is burned. He cannot read, but he can nonetheless recall every symbol he saw. All the information stored in his astonishing brain interacts with his new and transforming experiences to galvanize his essential goodness for action. Always fleshy, passive, and lumpish, always unquestioningly obedient to authority, he begins to think. Carrying his god around in the form of an irascible tortoise, hearing to his horror how much of his religion has simply been invented by the prophets without reference to Om, Brutha somehow keeps his faith, and adds wisdom to it. He stops obeying anyone or anything but his own sense of what is right; thus, he gains the moral authority to become the lawgiver and prophet of the new Omnianism, a religion of basic decency, tolerance, and forgiveness.

As a virtually helpless but constantly wrathful tortoise, Om combines features of several stock comic characters. He is the fiery midget goading the gentle giant, the street-smart hustler carping at the innocent he has decided to protect. He is so helpless for so long that he remains amusing even after he is restored to his old avatar: It has become impossible to take seriously his repeated curses and threats. Although he could smite anyone he liked, and though he has a long list of enemies made during his time in the shell, he has grown in other ways, grown too large for petty revenge.

◆ Techniques/Literary Precedents ◆

In a sense, the entire novel is built

around a favorite anecdote from classical times, the yarn about the philosopher who was killed when an eagle mistook his bald head for a rock and dropped a tortoise on it. All the rest falls rather neatly in place around the central joke. The philosopher turns into Ephebe, a whole city full of marvelous parodies of Greek thinkers. The tortoise naturally calls to mind the galactic turtle on which the Discworld muddles through the universe, which in turn suggests a new religion for the Omnians to persecute. Once the philosophical and religious conflicts are established as central concerns, Pratchett has ample scope for his whimsy, and the pages are full of allusions which are opposite to the story and at the same time a delight for the educated reader, references to Galileo, the Church Fathers, Greek mythology and history, invariably funny, and invariably with a thought worth noting wrapped in the humor.

Pratchett may be the most accomplished parodist since Cervantes. He carries on a tradition dating back at least to Aristophanes and Lucian, both of whom showed the same outrageous disrespect for gods, philosophers, and other institutions. An interesting precursor of Brutha is the mnemonic Ireneo Funes of the story "Funes el memorioso" (Funes the Memory Man) by Jorge Luis Borges. Borges's protagonist is eventually destroyed by the sheer weight of all that memory, however, whereas Brutha is able to keep his balance.

◆ Related Titles ◆

The entire Discworld series will interest readers of *Small Gods*; it is especially interesting to contrast its

more restrained humor and more unified action with the early novels. Those interested by Pratchett's views on religion might prefer to read *Good Omens* (1990), a comic novel about the Apocalypse set in our own place and time.

◆ Ideas for Group Discussions ◆

Pratchett's fiction is extraordinarily rich in allusion, incident, and ideas, and thus offers innumerable starting points for discussion. It would be both challenging and instructive to try to get past the jokes and identify the few principles in which Pratchett unequivocally believes. There is some danger of heated disagreements, in view of the subject matter and Pratchett's irreverence, but it is by no means necessary to confine the discussion to religion, since the book also has interesting things to say about politics and technology, to name only two alternatives.

1. What is the point of the most-repeated line in the novel: "There's very good eating on one of these, you know"?

2. Commenting on Omnia's version of the Inquisition, Pratchett observes: "there are hardly any excesses of the most crazed psychopath that cannot easily be duplicated by a normal, kindly family man." Are we to take this comment literally? Is it just a casual gibe, or does it reflect a continuing theme in the novel?

3. Early in the book, a character describes the sport of surfing, and Pratchett hints at its symbolic value. Would it be reasonable to speak of Pratchett's approach to philosophy and religion in this book as ideological

surfing?

4. In discussing the Discworld Athens, Ephebe, Pratchett does not hide the warts; he points out that only a minority can actually vote. What makes Ephebe preferable to Omnia, then? How do his experiences there help to open Brutha's eyes?

5. Brutha's total recall is useful in the plot of *Small Gods*. How does it form his character? How does it aid or hinder his search for truth? How does it set him apart from other people?

6. Pratchett's half-joking theory of divine mechanics — that the size and power of gods depends on human belief — can be interpreted in different ways. An extreme view, for example, would regard it as a brief for atheism. What other readings seem possible to you?

7. Brutha believes in the same god throughout, but his religion changes profoundly. What is Pratchett trying to say? Does his humorous approach enhance or confuse the message?

8. Since classical times, writers have found the Labyrinth a powerful image, and have explored its symbolic possibilities again and again. What does Pratchett add to this tradition?

9. Clearly, Vorbis represents all that is wrong with Omnianism. Are the opposite, good characteristics all concentrated in Brutha, or spread among several characters?

Philip Krummrich
Drury College

Small Gods

SNAKE EYES

Novel

1992

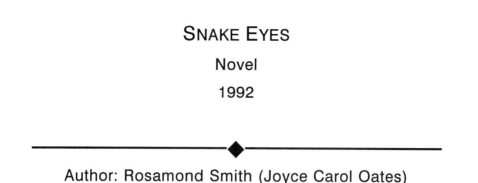

Author: Rosamond Smith (Joyce Carol Oates)

◆ Social Concerns/Themes ◆

Oates caused a stir when she submitted a novel under the pseudonym Rosamond Smith to Simon and Schuster. She has said that she was not trying to deceive, but that she wanted to find a new identity as a writer to see if that identity might generate a new voice. To date, she has published four novels under the pseudonym, a play on her husband's name, Raymond Smith: *Lives of the Twins* (1987), *Soul/Mate* (1989), *Nemesis* (1990), and *Snake Eyes* (1992).

Reflective of her choice of pseudonym, all of the novels pursue the theme of double identity. All portray a murderer whose charismatic exterior masks his psychopathic self. Centering on the most disturbing dimensions of madness, which cannot be traced solely to sociological origins, Oates suggests that the forces that compel the psychopath to kill involve dimensions of brain functioning that lie outside cognition. But the double identity of these charismatic madmen represents more than the split between the public and the private persona. Such a split also can occur as part of the creative process when the creator has no control over the unconscious forces that initiate the process.

Oates draws the connection between the psychopathic impulse and the artistic by making the murderer in *Snake Eyes* a released convict who is placed in an art therapy program and who is most proud of the snake tattoo he designed out of a "fever dream" he had in a Vietnam jungle. By connecting the psychopathic mind with the creative via the image of a snake, and, later in the novel, with increasingly pornographic statues, Oates also shows how the creative force may turn on itself to become a destructive force, particularly susceptible to the violent sexuality that has controlled the twentieth century's version of the psychopath.

◆ Characters ◆

Lee Roy Sears, the artist-murderer in *Snake Eyes,* is saved from the electric chair largely because of the efforts of Michael O'Meara, a lawyer whose *pro bono* work has introduced him to Sears and his art. O'Meara defends him because Sears's guilt is unclear and his poverty has caused the justice system to fail him. He also defends him because of his own sense of guilt for something he cannot pinpoint, but that we learn involves the drowning of his own twin when they were two years old.

Once Michael negotiates the release of Lee Roy Sears, Sears gradually works his way into the community and into the O'Meara family, seducing or almost seducing, various women, including Michael's sister Janet and his wife Gina. Worse, Sears befriends the O'Meara's twin boys, secretly teaching them to curse and fascinating and intimidating them with his tattoo. By adding the image of the invaded and corrupted children, Oates cranks up the threatening, sinister quality of this novel. She portrays Sears, Michael, and Gina internally, revealing the processes of their minds in various states of collapse: Sears becomes more and more vicious; Michael becomes more and more dependent on drugs; and Gina breaks down after Sears attacks her, scarring her face and the mind that hides behind it.

◆ Techniques/Literary Precedents ◆

Given her grounding in realistic fiction and her fascination with the obsessed or disintegrating mind, it is quite in keeping with her work that Oates has chosen to write a series of thrillers. She wants these to be popular novels, thus she writes linear, suspenseful plots that build tension by slowly increasing the level of madness in the characters. Precedents for Oates's techniques include Edgar Allan Poe's madmen in stories like "The Tell-Tale Heart" (1843), "The Black Cat" (1843), and "The Cask of Amontillado"

(1846), and Henry James's invaded children in "The Turn of the Screw" (1898). Oates also draws on various religious and cultural beliefs in such images as twins, cats, and snakes and in concepts embodied in such abstractions as the nemesis and the soul.

◆ Related Titles ◆

Snake Eyes and the three other novels Oates has written under the pseudonym Rosamond Smith can all be classified as thrillers. What distinguishes them from the thrillers of other novelists is their insistence on the idea of the double. Oates may be drawing on the work of Julian Jaynes, her colleague at Princeton, whose book *The Origins of Consciousness in the Breakdown of the Bicameral Mind* argues that the human mind once consisted of two parts, the speaking part and the hearing part. The mind, in other words, evolved from a split or double brain, with one part having an authoritative, commanding function and the other part an obeying function. Jaynes suggests that the schizophrenic brain may still be divided this way and Oates writes enough passages in each of these thrillers to suggest that she is using this theory to develop her artistic portrayal of the psychopathic mind.

Like *Snake Eyes*, *Lives of the Twins*, *Soul/Mate*, and *Nemesis* all use images of doubles and of commanding voices. Twins appear in *Lives of the Twins*, *Nemesis*, and *Snake Eyes*; the title *Soul/Mate* captures the idea of the double; images get doubled in tortoise shell cats, which have an unborn twin integrated in their genes (*Lives of the Twins*); the minds of characters retreat from themselves into an imagined Blue Room (*Soul/Mate*); and fugue-states provide an impulse to murder (*Nemesis*). These are terrifying novels because Oates captures in them minds out of control, unable ever to become integrated into a society that is itself dangerously fragmented and violent.

◆ Ideas for Group Discussions ◆

Those who read a great deal of popular thrillers are likely to enjoy *Snake Eyes* and groups can be encouraged to draw on their expertise to assess the value of this genre and to compare Oates's novel to others they have read. They could measure Oates against the standard for these novels to see whether or not she surpasses that standard.

1. How terrifying is this novel? Can you describe in what ways it is terrifying?

2. What other images of the snake do you find besides on Lee Roy's arm? How does the image connect to the idea of evil? Who is evil? How do people become evil?

3. How well does Oates capture Michael's gradual breakdown?

4. Is Michael's revenge against Lee Roy justified? Would you call him a murderer?

5. Was Michael responsible for his twin's death? Why does Oates make him a twin? What does the fact of Michael's twinness tell us about his sons?

6. Why does Oates have Michael find the quote from The Book of Matthew about an "eye for an eye"?

7. What kind of a mother is Mrs. O'Meara? What kind of a father is Michael?

8. What kind of a marriage do the O'Mearas have?

9. Why does Oates make Janet O'Meara a television personality?

10. Besides the twins and the image of the snake eyes, what other images of the double do you find in the novel? Why is Oates so fascinated with the double?

Sharon L. Dean
Rivier College

THE SNOW QUEEN

Novel

1980

Author: Joan D. Vinge

◆ Social Concerns ◆

Tiamat, the world ruled by Arienrhod, the eponymous Snow Queen, is technologically backward. Although it is clear to the reader that Tiamat was, at one time, a high tech world, it is equally clear that Tiamat must now purchase its high tech equipment from the off-world Hegemony. The Hegemony extracts a high price for its high tech wonders — it demands payment in a fountain-of-youth extract made from the blood of an indigenous species, the mers. Arienrhod will do anything to preserve her access to the high tech wonders of the Hegemony: She plans to subvert the succession to the throne by both artificially prolonging her life with the youth preserving elixir and by making an illegal clone of herself whom she hopes to control. She allows the wanton slaughter of the mers, despite the protests of those who argue that the mers may be sentient, to expand production of the elixir. Arienrhod's actions raise questions about the worth of technology as well as its cost. These questions are valid in today's society as well as Tiamat's society: Even if it were possible to preserve one's youth and life indefinitely, what limits should be placed on access to such technology? Even if cloning of a human being becomes possible, should it be allowed? Even if slaughtering animals benefits humans, when and where should the line be drawn? Is it ethical for a high tech society, such as the Hegemony, to extract unreasonable payment for its wares? In *The Snow Queen*, Vinge tries to show the disastrous consequences to a society whose ruling class values technology over ethics.

◆ Themes ◆

One major theme of *The Snow Queen* is that the indiscriminate pursuit and use of technology is immoral and can be disastrous. The other major theme is that wanton slaughter of any creature diminishes all humans and can also be disastrous. At the beginning of the book, Arienrhod subverts Hegemony technology to obtain an illegal clone of herself. Her goal is to use the clone to continue her own life once the fountain-of-youth elixir ceases to work on her original body. Arienrhod is also determined to make sure Tiamat becomes and remains a self-sufficient high tech world, a goal the Hegemony is equally determined to thwart since its rulers are dependent on the fountain-of-youth elixir. To obtain her goal, Arienrhod also plans to defy the traditions of her world as well as its natural laws. Tiamat's orbit between twin suns and a black hole causes major climatic changes every century and a half. When the planet is in winter phase, the black hole can be used by Hegemony traders as a gateway to Tiamat. During winter phase, Tiamat is ruled by the Winter People and enjoys a high tech lifestyle centered on its main city, Carbuncle. During summer phase, the black hole is unusable as a gateway, and the planet reverts to a low tech lifestyle ruled by the Summer People. At the juncture of the two phases Carnival is celebrated. The Winter queen goes voluntarily to her death, and a new queen is chosen from the Summer People. Arienrhod is determined not to die, but to live on in the body of her clone. She also plans to use a genetically engineered virus to kill off the Summer People. To maintain her high tech city, Arienrhod has been stockpiling high tech goodies which she obtains by selling the elixir to the Hegemony. To keep the elixir flowing, she encourages the slaughter of the mers despite objections by many who have begun to suspect that the mers are not animals but sentient beings. Ironically, Arienrhod does not know that the mers are genetically engineered sentient beings that are the one link to the knowledge of the ancient rulers of the universe, knowledge that would change Tiamat to just the sort of world she desires. Arienrhod's indiscriminate slaughter of the mers could damage the entire universe. Ultimately, Arienrhod is killed, and her plans are thwarted by her own clone, Moon Dawntreader who understands the relationship between the mers and the ancient knowledge — which will give Tiamat high tech without the Hegemony.

◆ Characters ◆

Arienrhod, Moon Dawntreader, and Sparks Dawntreader are three of the more important major characters in *The Snow Queen*. Moon Dawntreader, Arienrhod's clone, has been raised by her unwitting host-mother, a fisherwoman of the Summer People. As a result, she does not share Arienrhod's love and need for technology. Moon sees herself in the future as the wife of her maternal cousin, Sparks Dawntreader. Moon is a determined young woman who also wants the privileged position of a sibyl, a person who can communicate directly with a higher power when asked the right question. (The higher power is a computer of some sort). Would-be sibyls must make a pilgrimage to a designated spot where they are mysteriously tested and chosen or rejected. Sibyls travel with impunity throughout Tiamat but are specifically banned from Arienrhod's city of Carbuncle. When Moon and Sparks arrive at the test site, Moon is chosen and Sparks is rejected. In a fit of pique, Sparks demands that Moon abandon her calling, and when she refuses, departs for Carbuncle. In Carbuncle, Sparks attracts the attention of Arienrhod and quickly rises to the position of her official lover and mer-killer. Soon after this, Sparks begins to despise himself for killing the mers and for being Arienrhod's toy. When Arienrhod discovers that Moon is Sparks's former lover, she sends for Moon in his name. She soon discovers that Moon has left Tiamat involuntarily, a fact that enrages her. Moon journeys to the Hegemony where she begins to discover what a sibyl really is — a human interface with a computer. Moon returns to Tiamat to save Sparks because she still loves him. In the course of her journey to Carbuncle, she uncovers the true nature of the mers and determines to make Arienrhod conform to custom and die at the end of Carnival. Of course, such a determined woman gets what she wants. Arienrhod dies, and Tiamet gets high technology without the Hegemony.

◆ Techniques/Literary Precedents ◆

The Snow Queen is more or less a straightforward third-person narrative, although the author occasionally uses italics to set off her characters' thoughts from the narrative.

Vinge says in the foreword that *The Snow Queen* is an adaptation of Hans Christian Andersen's fairy tale of the same name. She also acknowledges a debt to Robert Graves's *The White Goddess* (1948). There is also an overlay of Celtic mythology, mostly evidenced in the names of some of the characters: Arienrhod, Blodwed, and Herne among others. The basic plot is a twist on the usual rescue of a damsel in distress by the fair young knight. In this case the evil ruler is a woman, not a man, who figuratively locks up a young man, not a young woman, in her fairy tale castle. The rescuer is the princess, not a prince. All the sub-plots are basic science fiction: the mysterious voices that turn out to be a computer, the heroic smugglers defying the powers that be, and the genetically engineered, angelic race.

◆ Related Titles ◆

In *World's End* (1984), a former Hegemony lawman and would-be lover of Moon Dawntreader, BZ Gundhalinu, journeys to a frontier-style planet to search for his lost brothers. While there, he uncovers a ruined city which may hold the key to interstellar travel by a means other than a gateway — and a future in which Tiamat no longer need to depend on Hegemony technology.

The Summer Queen (1991) continues the adventures of Moon Dawntreader and Sparks Dawntreader. Moon becomes the Summer Queen with Sparks as her consort. All is not smooth, however; the Summer People resist Moon's attempts at reform, and the Winter People plot to kill her. Even Sparks reverts to his previous vices learned while he was Arienrhod's lover. BZ Gundhalinu turns up also with news of his technological find. Moon ultimately through self-sacrifice and personal bravery resolves all problems — for now.

◆ Ideas for Group Discussions ◆

Vinge has opened up a great many concerns about ethics that are reflected in today's society. Some of these concern the ethics of bio-engineering. Among the questions are: How far should bio-engineering be allowed to advance? Should a procedure, such as cloning, be performed simply because scientists are able to perform it? How ethical is bio-warfare? Other ethical questions focus on economics: Is it morally right for a high tech society to impede a low tech society's growth for its own economic gain? Can the lower tech society justifiably rebel against this economic oppression? Other moral questions are echoed today by animal rights groups: Can the killing of animals for the benefit of humans ever be justified? If so, under what circumstances?

1. Do you think the Hegemony has the right to keep Tiamat in a low tech state by withholding certain high tech items and by building obsolescence into others?

2. Do you think that killing the mers can be justified in any circumstances?

3. Do you see any parallels between current concerns about the perils of science run amok and the situation on Tiamat?

4. Do you see any parallel between the Hegemony's trade relationship with Tiamat and the U.S. trade relationship with underdeveloped countries such as Mexico?

5. What major points about technology and society do you think the author is trying to make?

Margery L. Brown
SUNY at Farmingdale

SNOW WHITE

Novel

1967

Author: Donald Barthelme

◆ Characters ◆

There are no characters as such in Barthelme's fiction. Instead, there are names, voices, words. The characters in *Snow White* appear shallow, like the characters in a fairy tale. Even their psychologies seem to be lifted from a basic psychology textbook. *Snow White*, for example, is an updated urban version of the Grimms' Brothers figure, with more than a dash of the Walt Disney animated version tossed in for intertextual (as opposed to psychological) depth. She is known chiefly by her long black hair, which she likes to hang out the window, by her dissatisfaction, and by her longing to be something more than the "horsewife" she has become in her *ménage à huit* with the seven men with whom she lives and who, she claims, add up to only "two real men."

When not washing the windows, tending the vats of Chinese baby food, or manufacturing plastic buffalo humps to get in on "the leading edge of the trash phenomenon," the men — Bill (the withdrawn leader, later executed for "vatricide"), Kevin, Edward, Hubert, Henry, Clem, and Dan — contemplate their loss of equanimity since Snow White's arrival and more especially since the onset of her bout of longing to be something other, something more. Paul is the novel's "prince figure," torn between acting in a princely manner and eating "a-duck-with-blue-cheese sandwich." After a brief stint as a monk, he performs his own parodically princely deed, drinking the poisoned vodka gibson which the novel's wicked stepmother figure, Jane, intended for Snow White, because her lover, the "Loathesome" Hogo de Bergerac, née Roy, has taken a fancy to Snow.

◆ Social Concerns ◆

Snow White, Barthelme's second book and first novel, brilliantly combines metafictional techniques with a highly refracted critique of contemporary culture. Approached one way, the novel is about democratization in all its manifestations — political, sexual, economic, literary, and above all linguistic. Equality may be the novel's subject, perhaps even its aim, but it is an equality that invariably becomes reductive, in which nothing and no one is any better than anything or anyone else. The desire for equality may easily degenerate (just by substituting and deleting a few letters of the alphabet) into a low-grade longing for equanimity. In the world of *Snow White,* which is the world of consumerism, dissatisfaction is omnipresent. The characters yearn not only for commodities but for romance.

In its own peculiarly perverse way, the novel attempts to affirm an individualism that has been all but lost to modern society. Snow White's twin longings — for sexual equality and romantic adventure — take the form of neither a feminist tract nor a Harlequin romance but of a desire to be other than a "horsewife." Playfully yet insightfully, the novel depicts a world rapidly moving toward pure noise and complete trash, a world of "dreck" and "blague." By exploiting language, the novel calls the reader's attention to the fate of words and of word-users in a consumer society that manipulates language and people as if they were commodities. *Snow White* startles the reader into an awareness that the novel itself is an object that is both familiar and strange. As a short book about a familiar fairy tale, the novel should be eminently consumable, yet it resists the reader's efforts to understand and thus dispose of the text. Like a trash heap or a Calder mobile, it is simply there, a source of wonder and anxiety.

◆ Techniques/Literary Precedents ◆

Snow White is one of several works of the 1960s and 1970s that recycles myths and fairy tales: John Gardner's *Grendel* (1971), John Barth's *Chimera* (1972), Robert Coover's *Pricksongs and Descants* (1969), and Angela Carter's *The Bloody Chamber* (1979). In defense of James Joyce's high-modernist novel, *Ulysses* (1922), T. S. Eliot defined what he called "mythic method" — "the drawing of a continuous parallel between the ancient and the modern in order to make sense of the enormous panorama of anarchy and futility which is contemporary life." The postmodern writers are interested less in a continuous parallel (and the depth and resonance it implies) than in the factitiousness of the original story as a convention worthy of exploitation as well as exploration, a semiotic code worth cracking in order to sift through what Coover has called the "mythic residue." What results is not so much parallelism as anachronism, divergence, discontinuity, and intertextual play. Even the novel's "source" begins to blur as the fairy-tale Snow White merges with the Disney character, as well as with Rapunzel and Little Red Riding Hood. Barthelme's novel bears a certain similarity to the works of Jorge Luis Borges, Samuel Beckett, and the French New Novelists, but also to the kind of books that the dwarfs prefer, "books with a lot of dreck in them."

Snow White proceeds not in terms of its attenuated plot but through accretion, combination, and collage. Not only are the chapters exceptionally short, they are often stylistically and typographically distinct. At times they read like nothing more than summaries, captions, and headlines in boldface. Following a principle of more or less free substitution, the novel mixes a wide variety of opposing languages — high and low, old and new, standard and slang. The reader cannot with any assurance claim that the author speaks any more clearly in the chapter, "ANATHEMIZATION OF THE WORLD IS NOT AN ADEQUATE RESPONSE TO THE WORLD," than in the questionnaire situated between the first two of the novel's three parts, which mocks the reader in his or her efforts to understand the novel according to interpretive conventions which no longer apply but which cannot be forgotten or easily replaced.

◆ Related Titles ◆

Barthelme's allusive postmodern style also plays an important part in "A Shower of Gold" (1964) and "The Indian Uprising" (1965). An early story, later retitled "Me and Miss Mandible" (1961) makes use of comic disparity (an adult misassigned to an elementary school classroom) in a way that anticipates *Snow White* (modern characters attempting to live out fairy tale roles). "The Balloon" focuses on the interpretive indeterminacy which characterizes so many of Barthelme's stories and novels, especially the summarily ended *Snow White*.

◆ Adaptations ◆

A "rehearsed reading" of Barthelme's then in-progress "play" of *Snow White* took place at The American Place Theatre, New York, on June 10, 1976, with Wynn Handman, director and Julia Miles, associate director.

Robert A. Morace
Daemen College

SOLDIER BOY

Short Stories

1982

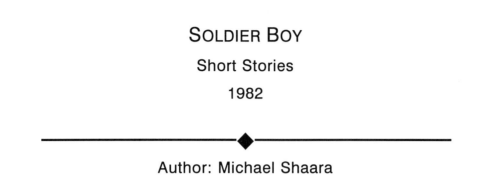

Author: Michael Shaara

♦ Social Concerns/Themes ♦

*S*oldier Boy contains some of Shaara's finest moments in fiction, and in his "Introduction" and his "Afterword" he hints at how they came out of his life and into his art. For Shaara, "writing has always meant . . . going for a while into another, real world," where flashes of insight are waiting, like Michelangelo's shapes, for the artist to set them free. Just as Chamberlain in *The Killer Angels* (1974) could not grasp the meaning of tragedy until he had lived it, at his best Shaara can make his reader share those times, a communication that he says has been, after his writing, "the best moment[s] in living as a writer: to know that somebody else has seen what you see, felt what you felt."

Ten of *Soldier Boy's* stories are science fiction, dating from the 1950s. The genre allowed Shaara to distance himself from what he calls "this incomprehensible mess" where most human beings live and to create hypothetical milieus to isolate and explore human griefs and growths. The title story dates from 1953, but it eerily forecasts the turbulent Vietnam era when some people had been taught "peace" so thoroughly that they despised the soldiers who had to maintain it; Shaara grimly observes that "no peace-loving nation in the history of the earth had ever kept itself strong." The same darkness that pervades many of Shaara's fictional universes prevailed in the Old Norse myth from which he drew the epigraph to "Soldier Boy" — the deadly certainty that evil will eventually vanquish good, and all that matters is the courage a man finds to meet his fate. The one saving grace in Shaara's valleys of the shadow is his sense of "a path going somewhere," just as the one common denominator of all his work is his belief that some human beings are able to choose it.

♦ Characters ♦

Shaara says that he writes about damaged people. Most often, as in "Soldier Boy," "Grenville's Planet," and "Wainer," society has wounded his protagonists, striking at the innate differences which mark them as superior but misunderstood or even hated. Their talents generally estrange Shaara's lonely ones from the rest of society, as with "Wainer," a man born —

and despised — as man's first evolutionary step to the stars. Shaara says that "Wainer was hope," leading him to his novel *The Herald* (1981), where he develops a disturbing variation on the end-of-the-world theme, a device lethal to most of humanity which will spare those gifted individuals capable of a new beginning. Most of Shaara's protagonists share Wainer's alienation and his "herald's" Promethean dilemma: Can the new world be worth the destruction of the old and the price the individual who brings it about must pay? For Wainer, a composer rejected by his society, it was; he died in the happy knowledge that his physical abnormalities foreshadowed new men, able to live in alien atmospheres, just as Chamberlain in the carnage of Gettysburg rejoiced at what Lincoln would call "a new birth of freedom."

The five mainstream short stories Shaara included in *Soldier Boy* also deal with characters whom life has hurt into insight. "Come to My Party" was the first story Shaara based on an actual experience, in which he lost a professional bout "to a guy . . . who boxed, but couldn't hit" and won on rules that never would have applied in a real life brawl. Shaara's hero Morgan loses a similar fight, but he lives out the ending Shaara says the story ought to have had, a soul-satisfying obliteration of the opponent who had made a fool of him in front of the woman he loved. Like all of Shaara's suffering heroes, Morgan pays his price willingly; badly beaten but victorious, he returns to her in a movingly inarticulate reconciliation. The unspeakable tenderness between them is one of the major motivations for Tom McClain, hero of Shaara's coming-of-age novel *The Broken Place* (1968), about a soldier-boxer who kills a man in the ring. In balancing Mc-

Clain's love for Lisa against the violence of his nature, Shaara evokes all the love a man can have for a woman in one terse unforgettable image: "I was the meteor. She was the earth." Like falling stars, Shaara's men consume themselves in one brief streak of glory; Shaara's women wait, sorrowing, inscrutable, silent. From Shaara's first story, "All the Way Back" to his latest, "Starface," the major preoccupation of his literary career is consistently the intricate human personality gifted with talents the world makes it pay for owning — because the world knows too well it cannot do without them.

♦ Techniques ♦

Shaara's excellence in the short story form accounts not only for the success of the kaleidoscopic presentation of *The Killer Angels* but for some difficulty in the larger scope of the traditionally narrated novel. As reviewer John Pine has pointed out, *The Broken Place* attempted to cover too much — war, love, boxing, travel; and in *The Herald*, Shaara seemed unable to concentrate on a single point of view, a disturbing problem in a novel with a single unsettling message. In the burning focus of a short story, however, Shaara conveys the intensity of his vision supremely well, since the genre demands that he choose his words with artistic inevitability. His diction often resembles Beethoven's chord sequences: no other choice seems possible.

♦ Literary Precedents ♦

Although Hemingway's influence is also apparent in the short stories of *Soldier Boy*, especially in the compactness of their dialogue, they also have a distinctly Nietzschean flavor — not the popularized and misread Nietzsche who claimed "God is dead," but the Nietzsche who celebrated the birth of tragedy in the equilibrium between man's rationality and his powerful emotional drives, and the Nietzsche who rejoiced in the belief that modern men could be "overcome," by abandoning pride and foolishness and stupidity and grow into greater beings, the sons of men to come. In *The Broken Place*, Shaara's autobiographical hero voiced his paradoxical view of the human condition today: "In all this world there are no signs and no miracles and nobody watching over and nobody caring. But I believe anyway." Throughout his work, Shaara's stubborn, wounded heroes go on believing anyway, an affirmation of the humanity that is their hope. It is hard to see how any writer of contemporary fiction can say it better.

Mitzi M. Brunsdale
Mayville State College

SOMETHING HAPPENED

Novel

1974

Author: Joseph Heller

◆ Social Concerns ◆

Like *Catch-22* (1961), *Something Happened* exposes the moral vacuity of American society. In this later novel, the targets of Heller's satire are two: the cutthroat corporate realm and the suburbanite middle-class family.

Through the eyes of his narrator/ protagonist Bob Slocum, Heller presents the hierarchical relationships and the social and sexual intrigues of the employees of an unidentified company — a company that Heller has suggested in conversation has affinities with Time, Incorporated, where he worked as an advertising copywriter from 1952 to 1956. In portraying the corporate world, the author uses stereotyped situations: the executive burnout in the upper ranks, the incompetent secretary whom everyone is afraid to fire, the office party flirtations and sexual misconduct at company conventions, and the requisite golf games. Fear and distrust flourish as department competes with department and individual vies against individual for promotion. In such a high-pressured atmosphere, nervous breakdowns are the norm, and suicides are an anticipated health hazard, as proven when Slocum nonchalantly reports: "We average three suicides a year: two men, usually on the middle-executive level, kill themselves every twelve months, almost always by gunshot, and one girl, usually unmarried, separated, or divorced, who generally does the job with sleeping pills."

Home life provides no more satisfaction than the corporate realm. The typical American middle-class family, embodied by the Slocums, is in decline. Bob Slocum ironically observes, "We are a two-car family in a Class A suburb in Connecticut. Advertising people of the U.S. Census Bureau . . . prepare statistics that include us in the categories of human beings enjoying the richest life." Such chapter titles as "My wife is unhappy," "My daughter's unhappy," and "My little boy is having difficulties," however, negate the statistical conclusion. Among the ills of modern family life that Heller diagnoses are marital infidelity, alcoholism, teen-age resentment of parents, children's lack of self-esteem or inability to compete in a brutal world, boredom, and coping with having a brain-damaged child.

Both Heller's depictions of the corporate world and domestic life reflect a larger disillusionment with America —

an America of lost innocence. An America that, according to Heller, has only improved in two areas — "smut and weaponry." Slocum complains:

> From sea to shining sea the country is filling with slag, shale, and used-up automobile tires. The fruited plain is coated with insecticide and chemical fertilizers. Even pure horseshit is hard to come by these days. They add preservatives. You don't find fish in lakes and rivers anymore. You have to catch them in cans. Towns die. Oil spills. Money talks. God listens. God is good, a real team player. 'American the Beautiful' isn't: it was over the day the first white man set foot on the continent to live.

The passage, however, is less a statement of Heller's concerns about the American environment than it is a reflection of the moral debris within Slocum's interior landscape.

◆ Themes ◆

The title of Heller's second novel reveals its major theme — that there is an unidentifiable something that happened to create anxiety and disillusionment in its Everyman protagonist. Through Bob Slocum's middle-age crisis, Heller confronts us with the truth that as humans age, they lose innocence and confidence in their ability to shape their destinies. Success in the corporate world does not guarantee happiness. Dreams of family affection and harmony are quickly dispelled by the realities of combativeness, insecurity, and guilt that characterize the Slocum family's interactions. Bob Slo-

cum's idealism becomes transformed into acceptance of life's banalities. As Heller explains, Something Happened "is a very bleak book, a melancholy illumination on the part of a man in his forties who looks at his past and looks at his present and tries to see some kind of future and sees not much of any."

Moreover, not only does the novel suggest there is a haunting, amorphous "something" that must have directed our fate, but there is an equally amorphous "something" that forebodes disaster, a paranoia-inspired presentiment that Slocum terms "the willies." It is the willies that make Slocum fearful about his job security despite salary raises and promotions, that make him fantasize that his children will drown, choke, or be murdered, that evoke disturbing sexual memories, and that compel him in an unforgettably horrible scene to hug his injured son so tightly in an attempt to protect and comfort him that he causes the boy's death by asphyxiation.

Ultimately as do Catch-22 and Closing Time (1994), Something Happened confronts human fallibility and mortality. The narrative is permeated with references to disease, disasters, the aging process, and death. One of the most poignant passages is when Bob Slocum realizes that his elder son is growing distant from him as the boy matures. As his son leaves the room and closes the door behind him, reminding us of the novel's opening sentence in which Slocum revealed his fear of closed doors, Slocum confides: "I don't want him to go. My memory's failing, my bladder is weak, my arches are falling, my tonsils and adenoids are gone, and my jawbone is rotting, and now my little boy wants to cast me away and leave me behind for reasons he won't give me. What else will I have?" He then predicts a future with nothing to look forward to except incontinence and then death. When Slocum laments that he wants his son back, he is also lamenting the loss of his own youth. The inexorable march of time is a realization that many of Heller's characters and indeed Heller himself have difficulty accepting.

Another of Heller's concerns, which links his second novel with *Catch-22*, is an emphasis upon the failure of meaningful communication. According to Sanford Pinsker in *Understanding Joseph Heller*, "Communication in *Something Happened* is always on the edge of breaking down, of dissolving, of deconstructing itself into meaninglessness." Slocum confesses, "All my life, it seems, I've been sandwiched between people who will not speak." These include his mother, condemned to silence before she died, his brain-damaged son who is unable to articulate ideas, and various relatives with whom he does not converse. Slocum himself is tormented by dreams that he cannot speak, and he does indeed stammer. When he speaks within the workplace, he mimics the person he is speaking with in terms of pace, volume, vocabulary, and dialect. When he speaks to his family, he is often taunting or evasive. Even his narration often seems empty verbosity, for it is filled with repetition and contradiction, particularly in its long parenthetical passages.

◆ Characters ◆

Bob Slocum's psyche directs the novel. As Heller explained in an interview with George Plimpton, *Something Happened* is about Slocum's "interior, psychological survival," in counterpart to Yossarian's exterior, physical sur-

vival in *Catch-22*. There is a war in Slocum's soul. One side of him is the cynical seeker of self-gratification — the sex-obsessed consort of whores, the chooser of promotion over friendship. However, the other side is the mourner of lost innocence — haunted by memories of the little boy inside himself, frustrated by his unfulfilled desire for the allegorical Virginia, and deeply attracted to his oldest son's generosity and ability to love. In one sense Slocum is the consummate corporate man eager to climb the ladder to success; yet conversely in his Happiness Charts he notes that those individuals who most closely identify with the corporation are the least happy, he attacks his company's practices, although participating in them, and he occasionally expresses longings to be powerless. Contradictions in Slocum's character abound. He is both insensitive and tender, concealing and revealing of his narcissism, sexism, and racism. Slocum laments, "The problem is that I don't know who or what I really am"; however, he is often remarkably self-perceptive, particularly in his parenthetical asides. The only consistency in Slocum's character is his paranoia. Heller has admitted that he originally intended Bob Slocum to be despicable but that he became a more sympathetic character as the narrative unfolded. Perhaps Slocum's most significant characteristic is, as Heller says, that "[h]e *is* very human." Indeed, it is that human fallibility that makes his dehumanization in the last chapter of the novel so chilling.

Other characters in the narrative are not deeply developed. For instance, there are the stereotyped employees Slocum works with, including Green, White, Black, and Brown. Neither his wife, eldest son, nor daughter are named; only his brain-damaged youngest son Derek, whose birth his father would like to deny. The family members are meant to serve typical roles rather than to be highly individualized characters. Thus Heller presents readers with the aging wife who attempts to use flirting and alcohol as defense mechanisms against boredom and loneliness, the disputatious fifteen-year-old daughter who resents any signs of affection from her father, and the nine-year-old son whose innate goodness renders him helpless in a success-oriented, back stabbing world. These characters function primarily as reflectors of Slocum himself, with his wife representing the desire for family unity and loyalty, his daughter representing the skeptical recognition of his self-deceptions, and his older son representing his idealism.

◆ Techniques ◆

Abandoning the multiple points of view of *Catch-22*, Heller in *Something Happened* experiments with a first person interior monologue. Related in the present tense, Bob Slocum's monologue, however, is less important for advancing the action than for conveying his memories of key events in the past, his dire presentiments of the future, and his confessions of anxieties and moral failings. The time shifts in the narration, which occur with greater frequency as the monologue unfolds, reflect Slocum's psychological breakdown. Heller has explained, "*Something Happened* is written from the point of view of someone so close to madness that he no longer has the ability to control what to think about." Perhaps the most interesting dimension of the narrator's monologue is that it shows

his avoidance of painful realities. For example, whenever, he starts discussing Derek, he digresses, most often to sex reveries. As in *Catch-22*, repetition is significant, with Slocum's recollections of his adolescent gropings with Virginia being the major unifying device revealing the futility of his efforts to romanticize his past.

The narrative structure relates closely to Heller's treatment of point of view. The monologue is divided into nine sections, which follow an orderly sequence of psychologically introducing Slocum, then portraying his company and each member of his family, then depicting two climactic events in Slocum's life — his acceptance of his colleague Kagle's job and his unwittingly causing the death of his son, the fulfillment of Slocum's fears throughout the novel — and finally presenting Slocum assuming command of his company in a brief epilogue. The structure moves us from the protagonist's tenuous control in his work and domestic environments to accelerating angst and narrative chaos to a return to an insidious control achieved only by Slocum's concealing the facts of his son's death.

That structure, in turn, directly relates to Slocum's style. In an interview Heller noted that Slocum's style reflects his mental condition: "At the beginning, the prose is very orderly, very precise, very controlled. But as you move into the middle, as Slocum becomes more emotional, the prose gets less orderly and the sentences get longer." Oxymorons increase, as do parenthetical expressions that qualify or contradict what Slocum has just said and that turn readers' grammatical expectations upside down since the seemingly nonessential parenthetical asides seem more meaningful than the nonparenthetical expressions. Furthermore, the dialogue Slocum presents bristles with disagreement and tension. The ending of the novel then returns to short declarative sentences, fewer parenthetical statements, and dialogue that depicts a surface politeness.

Throughout the novel the tone is flat and ordinary. Whether articulating deep-seated insecurities or describing his bedroom exploits, Slocum's voice remains devoid of passion. Many readers and critics have found the tone boring, yet one should note that the effect is intentional. Wedding content and form, Heller crafted Slocum's speeches to reflect the monotony of his life.

◆ Literary Precedents ◆

The major influence upon *Something Happened* is William Faulkner's *The Sound and the Fury* (1929). Stylistically, Heller has adopted from Faulkner the use of a first person monologue, which in its fragmented chronology reveals the constant impinging of the past upon the present. Thematically, the similarities between the two works are quite apparent. Both chart the disintegration of a family, satirize the commercial orientation of the modern world, and lament lost innocence. Most obvious is the parallel between Heller's Derek Slocum and Faulkner's Benjy Compson, and in fact, Heller actually refers to Benjy in the section entitled "It is not true." Also Bob Slocum — in his bitter diatribes about modern life and his mistreatment of his wife and daughter — resembles Jason Compson.

In his penetrating self-diagnosis, Slocum is reminiscent of Dostoevsky's Underground Man and T. S. Eliot's Prufrock. Heller has said in concentrating upon the processes of Bob Slocum's mind he was trying to achieve a similar technique to Samuel Beckett in his trilogy *Molloy* (1951), *Malone Died* (1951), and *The Unnamable* (1953). He also has asserted that he was trying to create a sense of the horrifying in the familiar, "the same sense of imprisonment, of intimidation, of psychological paralysis and enslavement" as in Kafka's works, but without Kafkaesque symbolism.

When questioned about the influences from his reading upon *Something Happened*, Heller mentioned the minor influence of Henry James. In a scene in which Slocum visits a psychiatrist, the psychiatrist repeatedly says, "Ah?" That response, Heller claims, was inspired by James's *The Ambassadors* (1903). Critics have linked Heller's portrayal of the corporate world to such books as Sloan Wilson's *The Man in the Gray Flannel Suit* (1955) and William Whyte's *The Organization Man* (1956).

◆ Related Titles ◆

Something Happened is most closely related to Heller's fourth novel, *God Knows* (1984), in the use of a first-person monologue that through memory links the past to the present and its moving depiction of the love and pain involved in the father/son relationship.

◆ Ideas for Group Discussions ◆

Readers who delighted in Heller's verbal wit and exposure of bureaucratic absurdities in *Catch-22* may be disappointed in *Something Happened*. Often animated debate results between those who find reading the over five hundred-page pessimistic novel an exercise in tedium and those who view the book as a penetratingly accurate capturing of the stultifying routines of middle-class life and a brilliant rendering of psychic disintegration. Discussion groups may also consider whether they find successful Heller's use of a first person monologue.

Discussion of this novel make take a personal turn as participants compare Heller's depiction to their own experiences and perceptions of the corporate world and family life, especially the changing dynamics between husband and wife, parents and children as time passes.

1. Some reviewers complained that in *Something Happened*, nothing happens. Is that complaint fair?

2. Does Bob Slocum seem a reliable or unreliable narrator? Does his paranoia affect our evaluation of the trustworthiness of his perceptions?

3. Do you think Heller suggests that the events in Slocum's life are, as Slocum himself contends, beyond his control or that Heller condemns Slocum for avoiding responsibility for his decisions and actions?

4. How has Virginia Markowitz affected Slocum's life? Of what significance is her name?

5. Why does Heller not give the name of the company that Slocum works for nor specify its product? If Slocum believes the company is "benevolent," then why is fear in the workplace so pervasive?

6. Slocum confesses that he worries about the decline of American civilization. What evidences of that decline does Heller present?

7. Is Slocum's fixation on sexual misconduct a sign of a midlife crisis, perhaps revealing anxiety over his virility?

8. What impact does the namelessness of Slocum's wife, daughter, and elder son have upon the reader?

9. Do you think Slocum loves Derek?

10. Does Slocum's relationship with his older son change your conception of the protagonist?

11. What is your reaction to the final chapter entitled "Nobody knows what I've done"? Does Slocum finally achieve success and take command of his life?

12. Is this a novel without hope?

13. Do you agree with Heller's assertion that Bob Slocum is "the most contemptible person I've ever found in literature"?

Lynne P. Shackelford
Furman University

SOMETHING IN THE AIR

Novel

1985

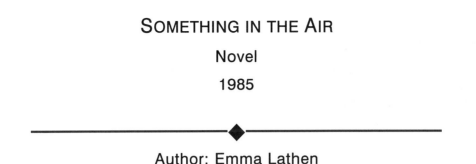

Author: Emma Lathen

◆ Social Concerns ◆

Like previous Thatcher stories, *Something in the Air* deals with a single financial enterprise—in this case, a no-frills commuter airline. While clearly accepting the capitalist system with all its implications, the novel raises questions about the relationship of labor and management that go beyond the treatment of this topic in Lathen's earlier books. Sparrow Flyways has an innovative profit sharing system and horizontal management, both of which become inconvenient for its founder during a period of proposed expansion. He then seeks to replace the system with a more conventional top-down management scheme. In the ensuing power struggle no faction is free of self-interest. The potential role of women also comes in for a greater share of attention than before, since one of the founding partners of Sparrow and the fiery leader of the workers' group are both female. By the end of the novel, Thatcher is wondering what will happen if and when his grown daughter—or his invaluable secretary, Miss Corsa—awakens to the kind of power which he sees wielded so ably by Eleanor Gough. Strong women have appeared in earlier Thatcher novels, but it is rare for Thatcher himself to think about what their strength may imply. The reviewer for the *New York Times Book Review*, not a habitual reader of mysteries, focused on this aspect throughout much of her review and concluded, "This no-frills mystery is quite a feminist tale."

◆ Themes ◆

As always, John Putnam Thatcher lives, works, and detects in a world motivated primarily by greed. Though the characters of *Something in the Air* pursue money just as eagerly as their counterparts in the earlier books, Lathen makes an explicit connection here between money and power that in the past was more often implicit, or sometimes not mentioned at all. Thus the murderer acts out of fear that something he did many years ago will be revealed, and in the belief that by removing his blackmailer he can continue to suppress the past. The fact that his old crime was itself based on greed is entirely secondary, and no financial benefit can come from the murder.

In addition to the murderer, other

characters in *Something in the Air* seek out and use power as an end in itself. Phoebe Fournier, the outspoken representative of the Sparrow workers, uses her ten thousand shares of Sparrow stock as political leverage and urges the Sloan Guaranty Trust as trustee to do the same; money is useful in buying power, whereas in many earlier Thatcher books the power was the means and the money the end.

Critics have mentioned Thatcher's (and evidently Lathen's) admiration for work, implying a value system in which hard work is a virtue in itself. *Something in the Air* continues this idea, often playing off superficial, image-conscious characters against solid workers. Intelligence, charm, and even success are lower in Lathen's world of values than work.

◆ Characters ◆

As always, John Putnam Thatcher, vice president of Sloan Guaranty Trust, is wise, urbane, and tolerant. Over the years he has become somewhat more removed from the concerns and ways of the young; a visit with his daughter and her extended family leaves him happy to return to his quiet widower's life, and he clearly appreciates the mature personality of Eleanor Gough more than the dynamic youth of Phoebe Fournier. For the first time in the series, an important part of the detective work is actually done by one of the other characters.

Of the Sloan staff, only Everett Gabler plays as large a role as usual, traveling to Boston to use his formidable accounting skills to ferret out secrets in the victim's financial records. The other Sloan characters put in only cameo appearances when Thatcher checks in at his home office, and they play no part in the action, probably because so much of the action takes place in Boston or at various airports.

Within Sparrow Flyways itself, flamboyant characters abound. Mitch Scovil, founder of Sparrow, is a typical boy wonder with little patience for the day-to-day operations which he leaves to his less colorful partners, Clay Batchelder and Eleanor Gough. The victim, Alan Whetmore, embodies the image of the egotistical, high-living commercial pilot, while Phoebe Fournier represents a combination of an idealistic approach with sound common sense and (perhaps most important) fiscal conservatism.

◆ Techniques ◆

Once again, Lathen cleverly uses a single financial body, this time a small commuter airline, to make the "closed society" of the classic detective story plausible. The death of the victim, a rather unpopular bachelor pilot, has no possible benefit for anyone outside of Sparrow Airways—but could be enormously useful to many within the company. Unlike most earlier novels in the series, however, *Something in the Air* has a variety of settings. Locale is not restricted to company headquarters and the Sloan, but includes two stunning airport scenes and a memorable boat excursion. This opening-up gives the action of the book a less contrived, more varied effect. Lathen had experimented with varying the scene with *When in Greece* (1969), much of which takes place on the road, but *Something in the Air* is a more successful effort. A comparison with Agatha Christie's classic *Death in the Air* (1935), in which all the important action takes place inside a plane in flight, shows how far Lathen has departed from the usual limitations of a closed-world setting.

Even though she varies the usual cast of characters by removing most of the Sloan staff, and departs from the closed aspect by focusing on travel, Lathen nevertheless retains most of the essentials of the classic mystery. As in all the previous Thatcher books, Lathen draws attention to the formal structure of the work, and to the ironic, game-like quality of the classic puzzle-mystery, by a series of humorous chapter titles. This time, they are drawn from the language of bird watchers: "Labored Flapping" for negotiations gone wrong, "Helpless on Land" for airport closures after a walkout, "Sighted in Louisiana" for a misleading journey by one suspect, and so on. The minor false suspect (introduced early) and then the major false suspect (near the end), the exciting climax in the next to last chapter, and the concluding explanation by Thatcher, all satisfy the reader's expectations for the classic genre.

◆ Related Titles ◆

A popular author with a winning formula tends to repeat it, and Emma Lathen is no exception. Every Thatcher novel starts at the Sloan and ends with Thatcher's exposition of the crime in the last or next to last chapter; every Thatcher novel has comic relief by the supporting cast at the Sloan; and every Thatcher novel has as its unsung heroine Rose Theresa Corsa, secretary *par excellence.*

For the most part, the novels concern themselves with management and owners more than with workers (except in very special kinds of businesses, for example, the hockey players in *Murder*

Without Icing, 1972). Only one previous novel has explored the nature of management-employee relations in any detail: *The Longer the Thread* (1971). In this book, set in Puerto Rico in politically troubled times, it is clear that the reader, and Thatcher, should support management and oppose a radical power base at the factory; indeed, a funny but wholly admirable ILGWU negotiator, Annie Galiano, is brought in: she is one of Lathen's ultra-competent, middle-aged female characters. In *Something in the Air,* however, the wants and needs of management and workers are more evenly balanced and the reader's sympathies are divided with excellent effect.

Another previous book with close ties to *Something in the Air* is its immediate predecessor, *Green Grow the Dollars* (1982). Here too, money is more than an end in itself; the murderer is motivated as much by his need for fame and continuing reputation as he is by simple greed. As a research scientist who has not had a breakthrough in ten years, he must produce or retire—a prospect which he clearly cannot face. His brilliant past controls his mediocre present just as much as the criminal past of the murderer of *Something in the Air* controls his.

In the only previous Lathen title involving the murder of a blackmailer, *By Hook or By Crook* (1975), the motive differs greatly. The murderer's initial "crime" falls under the heading of illegality but not, in any ordinary sense, of wrongdoing; he is forced to kill only because, with his grasp on his company and on his fortune threatened already by family feuding, his position both in his company and in his family depends on maintaining his false identity.

Finally, Thatcher's admiration for the

formidable Eleanor Gough resembles Congressman Benton Safford's long-standing alliance with Congresswoman Elsie Hollenback, "the scourge of the Department of Defense," in the R. B. Dominic series by the same authors. For the first time in the Thatcher series, another character—and a female character, at that—appears who, though less central in the novel, is fully Thatcher's equal.

◆ Ideas for Group Discussions ◆

Once again, Lathen takes her ideas from the headlines of the financial pages — here, they are airline deregulation and employee-run corporations. One need only recall the brief career of People Express airlines in the mid 1980s to see how "realistic" Lathen's portrait of Sparrow Flyways is. In fact, these issues still remain in the world of business, and small airlines constantly appear, endanger the giants, then disappear, and one of the major U.S. carriers was recently bought out by its employees. The issue of drug money financing also recurs with regularity.

1. Discuss the characters of Eleanor Gough and Phoebe Fournier as representatives of women in the modern work force. Do they differ significantly from the male characters in terms of how and why they operate? How do the male characters below and above them in the hierarchy of power deal with them?

2. Examine Mitch Scovil as representative of the modern entrepreneur and Fritz Diehl as representative of the modern corporate officer. Are they positive or negative characters? Are there other ambiguous characters in the novel? What is the purpose behind the ambiguity in terms of the plot? In terms of the portrait Lathen is painting of the business world?

3. Examine Lathen's ability to create a memorable scene, as in the Thanksgiving Day crisis at the Pittsburgh airport. What are the tools Lathen uses here? Look, for example, at her use of humor, her introduction of minor characters, and her switching of perspective.

Caroline Hunt
College of Charleston
[Ideas for Group Discussions
by Jane M. Kinney
Valdosta State University]

SOMETHING OF VALUE

Novel

1955

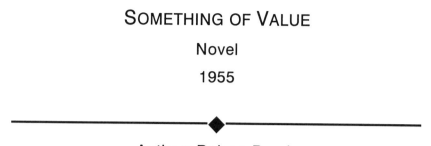

Author: Robert Ruark

◆ Characters ◆

Something of Value focuses on Peter, the son of a land-owning white settler, and Kimani, the son of a Kikuyu chief. When it begins, they are fifteen-year-old foster-brothers and best friends. Peter had been cared for as an infant by Kimani's mother after his own mother's death. Now they play war games together. However, because he is white, Peter expects the deference which Kimani is loathe to give. When Peter's future brother-in-law Jeff slaps Kimani for insolence, Kimani believes his family may be cursed. When his father and two of his father's wives are jailed for infanticide, he is certain of this and attempts to kill Jeff in order to remove the curse.

He then flees, and after some experience with petty crime, becomes a Mau Mau leader who eventually kills Jeff and two of his children. He severely wounds Jeff's wife, leaving her for dead. Kimani is presented as a weak, half savage creature, who is led into terrorism for lack of strong guidance from either the elders of his family, from whom he is separated, or from the white man. He has no political principles and kills only out of envy and hatred of the white man.

Peter, on the other hand, is handsome, intelligent and good. He is an excellent hunter, the best leader of safaris in Africa. Even his faults, drinking too much in Nairobi and engaging in mindless sexual activity with the women who are always throwing themselves at him, are what might be considered manly peccadillos. He is terribly macho, yet elegant, as good a fighter as he is a ballroom dancer.

He marries the woman he has loved since childhood and plans to devote himself to farming, but he is recalled from his honeymoon when he is notified of the slaughter of his sister's family by Kikuyu terrorists. The Mau Mau uprising has begun.

Peter hunts the Mau Mau with the same ferocity they exhibit, but he is sickened by the violence and his own brutality comes close to destroying him. He drinks too much; his wife leaves him. When he nearly murders an acquaintance of his wife, he realizes that only a return to hunting in the African wilderness can save him. This time, Kimani will be his prey. He kills Kimani with his bare hands but refuses to kill Kimani's baby son. Instead he brings the baby boy back to civilization to be raised by his sister with her own newborn baby. Presumably, these babies may bring about a better world.

Peter's father, Henry MacKenzie, may be the most interesting character in the book. He has worked excruciatingly hard and suffered great hardships, including the loss of his beloved wife, in order to establish a farm in Africa. He has learned a great deal, however, including a respect for African traditions and magic, which he uses when necessary.

Kimani's father, Karanja, is wise too, but he is faithful to the ways of his tribe and cannot live when the white man insists he disobey these laws. The white government jails him for abetting an infanticide which he believed was necessary and he dies from the tuberculosis he contracts in prison. His death, like the deaths of other tribal leaders either of old age or at the hands of a foolish and imperceptive white government, paves the way for the Kikuyu leadership to be dominated by savage terrorists.

The women in this novel count for very little. The white women are either staunch helpmates on the African farm or vehicles of corruption in Nairobi. The Kikuyu women are depicted as being perfectly content with their state of semislavery.

◆ Social Concerns ◆

Ruark loved Africa, its landscape, its animals and its people. The plight of those people, black natives and white settlers, disturbed him greatly. He believed that the white man had robbed the tribesmen of their traditional culture and given them nothing of value with which to replace it. Wise white settlers used the Kikuyu and Masai customs to ensure a settled and productive life for the natives, but government bureaucrats, well-meaning yet ignorant do-gooders, and London politicians undid their efforts.

According to Ruark, the African, bereft of his traditions, and still savage at heart had come to envy the material wealth of the white man and hoped to wrest it from him by violence. He then became prey to Communist and other anti-British agitators such as the Indians who organized and funded his rebellion.

Out of their love for secret societies, according to Ruark, the Kikuyu formed the Mau Mau conspiracy to kill and torture both white people and blacks who refused to endorse mayhem. Ruark justifies the brutal tactics of the white settlers as necessary for the defense of their wives, their children and their homes. However, the atrocities they are forced to perform destroy their own lives. The paradise that had been Kenya, Ruark believes, has been turned into a slaughterhouse.

Ruark denies he is a racial bigot and does point out that however horrifying their culture, the African natives did live in harmony with their environment. He believes, though, that it is the white man's duty and burden to civilize the black man and to keep him under careful supervision until this is accomplished, if it ever is. He seems to find it impossible to conceive of honest, effective, government under black rule in the foreseeable future.

◆ Themes ◆

The relationship between life and death in the wild as mediated by the hunter concerns Ruark. He notes that the lion shot by the hunter for sport provides a trophy for the white man, meat for the natives, and food for the hyenas and the vultures. Their leavings enrich the earth. The earth nourishes the vegetation on which the smaller animals, killed and used for bait with which to attract the lion, feed. Life and death are intertwined and interdependent.

Ruark also believes in the healing quality of the wilderness and the nobility of hunting. Cities, which are dominated by women, corrupt a man. In the wilderness, a man can purify himself and become almost godlike through suffering hardship while devoting himself to the hunt. Hunting itself serves to weed out the unfit and keep the animal population manageable, thus insuring not only the survival of the species but the improvement of the breed. Ruark insists that the environment must be respected and that ecologically sound practices must be maintained.

Indeed, ecologically sound practices must be applied to people as well as to nature. In Africa before the white man came, the population was controlled by constant warfare between the tribes, endemic disease, and periodic natural disasters such as drought. The white man prevented war between the tribes, mitigated disease and natural disaster and so caused overpopulation, urbanization, poverty, social unrest, and crime.

If there are any solutions to these problems, they must be implemented, Ruark believes, by white men who know the land and its people. Because of the forces of history, and the foolishness of those who do not understand Africa, the novel holds out only the faintest glimmer of hope that solutions will be found.

◆ Techniques ◆

Ruark dramatizes action very effectively. The reader is made to feel a participant in everything from a Kenyan wedding reception to an elephant hunt to ritual torture and murder. The narration is straightforward and exciting which creates and sustains suspense. The dialogue seems plausible enough and the characters are just realistic enough to keep the reader's sympathy although they do tend toward extremes of villainy or heroism.

Ruark is an accomplished journalist who presents facts accurately and describes events with great skill. Using language sparely but graphically, he brings the landscape alive — in the wilderness, on the farms and in the city. He also manages to describe with great clarity what it means to live in a country beset by civil war.

◆ Literary Precedents ◆

In his use of the African setting, in his appreciation of the great white hunter, in his pared down literary style, Ruark is the heir of Hemingway. Not only in his writing, but in his style of living, he attempted to emulate his literary hero. His style differs from that of Hemingway in its more graphic depictions of violent actions, an approach used by such writers as William Burroughs. His writing is certainly in the tradition of the novelists who wrote about World War II, such as Norman Mailer and James Jones.

His social philosophy has been compared to that of Ayn Rand, in its insistence on the privileges and responsibilities of the strong man. His literary techniques, as well as his interest in contemporary society, have been compared to that of John O'Hara. His belief in the moral and educative value of hunting is very similar to that of William Faulkner. To Ruark, as well as to Faulkner, a boy becomes a man when he makes his first difficult kill.

◆ Related Titles ◆

Uhuru (1962) shares the setting and concerns of *Something of Value*. Ruark's hero, Brian Dermott, like Peter McKenzie, a white hunter whose marriage has failed, believes the whites of Kenya should resist its independence and the consequent domination of the government by blacks. "Uhuru" means freedom. To Dermott, and the white settlers who share his point of view, Kenyan independence is more frightening than the Mau Mau uprising which had taken place several years earlier. Other whites, such as Dermott's Aunt Charlotte, welcome independence; still others hate and fear it but they feel it is useless to resist and plan to return to England.

Ruark believes that the African leaders are inept, cynical, and self-aggrandizing villains who will destroy Kenya if they are allowed to rule. He would thwart their struggle for independence, even if it meant abrogating the rule of law and resorting to violence, fighting the black man's terrorism with an even more brutal counterterrorism.

This is an exciting novel with distinctive characters. It gains plausibility because it reflects Ruark's familiarity with the East African landscape and with Kenyan life or at least with the life lived by Kenya's whites. Obviously, Ruark loves the land, but has little faith in its people.

◆ Adaptations ◆

In 1957, after paying $300,000 for the film rights, Metro-Goldwyn-Mayer Studios made *Something of Value* into a film starring Rock Hudson as Peter, and Sidney Poitier as Kimani. It was praised by critics for the stars' performances and its evenhandedness; Bosley Crowther of the *New York Times* thought it just missed being a great motion picture. He faulted it for its sentimentality and conventionality. To him, it appeared too similar to an ordinary cowboy and Indian movie, and he also believed that too much of the film was shot in a studio rather than in the wild, thus accentuating its lack of realism.

Barbara Horwitz
C. W. Post Center
Long Island University

SOMETHING WICKED THIS WAY COMES

Novel

1962

◆

Author: Ray Bradbury

◆ Social Concerns/Themes ◆

Based on the short story "Nightmare Carousel" (1962), *Something Wicked This Way Comes* has been enormously popular but has received wide criticism for the self-indulgence of its language and the weakness of its plot structure. The novel focuses in part on the same theme of nostalgia for a Midwestern small-town childhood as did Bradbury's earlier nonfantasy novel *Dandelion Wine* (1957), which it somewhat resembles. It adds, however, a strong *bildungsroman* theme and explores some of the darkest fantasies of childhood.

When Cooger and Dark's Pandemonium Shadow Show comes to Green Town, the book's protagonists, thirteen-year-old boys named Jim and Will, quickly discover that there is something evil riding with the carnival. A variety of frightening and bizarre transformations occur, many of them centered on the carnival's carousel which has the power to turn adults into children and children into adults. Much of the novel is simply good scary fun in a fairly high Gothic mode but, on a more serious level, Bradbury is talking about maturity and the various ways it can be achieved.

For Bradbury, the great danger of growing up is that one tends to lose one's imagination. When the Pandemonium Shadow Show begins to spread its evil spell through Green Town only three people appear to be capable of coming to grips with that evil. Two of them, of course, are Jim and Will, whose birthdays, one minute before midnight and one minute after midnight on Halloween, clearly symbolize their fitness to deal with a supernatural menace. The third person, and the only adult able to recognize the evil in town, is the aptly named Charles Halloway, Will's father and the janitor at the town library, an intelligent man who has nonetheless chosen, in the opinion of Green Town's more somber citizens, to read and daydream his life away, a man who has in some ways never grown up. By carefully contrasting Charles Halloway, the apparent failure who can see the truth, with the other adults in Green Town, Bradbury seems to be making the point that much of what the world thinks of as maturity is, in fact, nothing of the sort. Rather it is a kind of half life, a form of arrested development.

Cooger and Dark entrap people by offering them their fondest dreams, by promising to fulfill all the petty desires and end all the frustrations they have built up over the years. Those whom the town considers mature, the humorless people who work hard and have no time for fun and whimsy, are among the first to fall victim to the Shadow Show's lure because, by giving up the ability to dream, they have given up the ability to change. Thus they are stuck in their own pasts, unable to come to terms with or outgrow their frustrations. Their souls are stunted and it is only fit that the Pandemonium Shadow Show should turn them visibly into the twisted freaks and dwarfs they already are on the inside. Charles Halloway, still flexible, still possessing a sense of humor, has the imagination to deal with the evil that Mr. Dark represents, and by laughing at that evil, robs it of its power. True maturity is thus redefined by Bradbury as the ability to combine the experience of adulthood with the open-minded imagination of youth.

◆ Characters ◆

Bradbury, more than any other writer of fantasy and science fiction, has remained closely in touch with his own childhood. The children who appear in "Homecoming," "The Veldt," Dandelion Wine, and innumerable other Bradbury stories are invariably well drawn, and Jim and Will of Something Wicked This Way Comes are no exception. Although imbued with some of the old-photograph nostalgia that fills so much of the author's work, they are complex and interesting characters, basically good, but with believable imperfections. Indeed, it is the very fact that both boys seem susceptible to the evil that Cooger and Dark's repre-

sents that gives the novel its tension. Jim and Will are at risk, not just physically but spiritually.

Will's father, Charles, easy to like as a person, is Bradbury's secular version of the holy fool, but his very innocence makes him somewhat less successful as a character than are the two boys. At times Charles seems simply too good. It is hard to see him as being as thoroughly at risk as the boys are, and this robs the climax of Something Wicked This Way Comes of some of its force.

◆ Techniques ◆

Bradbury's use of ornate, elaborately metaphoric language reaches its extreme in Something Wicked This Way Comes and, as in many of his stories, those metaphors are required to carry a heavily allegorical freight. Characters with last names like Nightshade, Dark, and Halloway move through a realistically detailed, but frequently symbolic landscape. Jungian archetypes and Gothic transformations abound. Nothing is quite what it seems. Critics who appreciate the novel have argued that it is much more complex, and much more complexly structured, than its denigrators realize.

◆ Literary Precedents ◆

Many mainstream and genre writers influenced Bradbury's work. Of special interest in connection with Something Wicked This Way Comes are Poe, such German Romantic writers as E. T. A. Hoffmann and Ludwig Tieck with their frequent symbolic use of mirrors and mysterious transformations, and, most directly, Charles Finney, whose The Circus of Dr. Lao (1936) Bradbury had himself anthologized some six years earlier. Dr. Lao is a basically beneficent character, but his circus, like Bradbury's, features a number of supernatural and potentially dangerous attractions. His role seems to be primarily to force those who visit his circus into facing and coming to terms with their own imperfections.

It should also be noted that *Something Wicked This Way Comes* may well be Bradbury's most influential work. Any number of circus fantasies published over the last two decades show a considerable debt to it, among them Peter Beagle's clearly superior novel *The Last Unicorn* (1968), as well as Tom Reamy's *Blind Voices* (1978), Alan Ryan's *Dead White* (1983), and Al Sarrantonio's *Totentanz* (1985).

◆ Adaptations ◆

A film version of *Something Wicked This Way Comes* was made in 1983. Directed by Jack Clayton from Bradbury's own screenplay and starring Jason Robards, it received generally poor reviews. The sets and special effects were excellent but critics found the plot confusing and overly sentimental. Indeed, Bradbury's stories are so dependent on language and metaphor for their effect that it might well be argued that the successful transference of much of his work to the screen should be nearly impossible. It is probably not coincidental that *Fahrenheit 451* (1953), the Bradbury story which has been filmed with the greatest success, is also one of the author's most restrained works in terms of language use.

◆ Ideas for Group Discussions ◆

Although *Something Wicked This Way Comes*, is Gothic fantasy at an extreme, Bradbury comments on realistic issues, as well. For instance, he expresses an understanding of the family, and more than anything, the novel relates the positive aspects of friendship and the often difficult process of growing-up.

1. What is the significance of the salesman who comes to sell Jim and Will a lightning rod at the beginning of the novel?

2. Jim and Will realize the wicked nature of the carnival. Why is Charlie, Will's father, the only other character who understands the danger?

3. Some of the characters are named for traits which they embrace. List some of these people and explain why they are named as they are.

4. What is the significance of the lightning rod? Why is it "finely scratched and etched with strange languages, names that could tie the tongue or break the jaw, numerals that added to incomprehensible sums, pictographs of insect-animals all bristle, chaff, and claw?"

5. Discuss Will's relationship with his father.

6. Why are Will and Jim such close friends? Is this purely a small-town phenomenon?

7. What first convinces you that the carnival has an underlying wicked element to it?

8. Jim and Will get accused of robbery by Miss Foley. Will thinks, "No one'll believe anything we say from now on! Not about carnivals, not about carousels, not about mirrors or evil nephews, not about nothing!" How do Jim and Will convince people that they are telling the truth?

9. What is a calliope? What is its significance in the novel?

10. Church bells are mentioned more than once in the novel. Why are they important? Discuss their role in the plot.

11. Bradbury places three epigraphs in the front of his book — a line from the poet W. B. Yeats, a proverb, and a line from Herman Melville's *Moby Dick* (1851). Why are they there? How are they relevant to the novel?

12. Time is an issue in this novel. Charlie Halloway says, when he cannot sleep, "We are blind to continuity, all breaks down, falls, melts, stops, rots, or runs away." Refer to chapter 14, and explain what Charlie means by this.

13. Read *Dandelion Wine* and comment on the novels' similarities. What does each have to say about childhood?

14. In Chapter 22, Robert, Will, and Jim are running from Miss Foley. The narrator comments, "And so they ran, three animals in starlight. A black otter. A tomcat. A rabbit." Why are these three boys characterized in such terms. Where else in the novel do animal motifs appear?

15. Charles Halloway hears a Christmas carol in October:

Then pealed the bells more loud and deep: "God is not dead, nor doth He sleep! The Wrong shall fail, The Right Prevail. With peace on earth, good will to men!"

What is the significance of the verse and why is it appropriate that it should appear at the beginning of the novel? Does it give you a sense of what is to come?

Michael M. Levy
University of Wisconsin-Stout

SOMETIMES A GREAT NOTION

Novel

1964

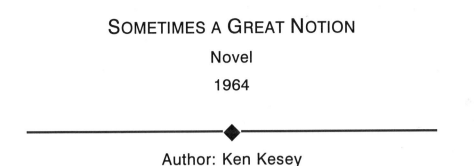

Author: Ken Kesey

◆ Characters ◆

The protagonists of *Sometimes a Great Notion* are Hank and Leland Stamper, half-brothers who are the opposites of each other. These characterizations evolved from Kesey's self-exploration, for he has confessed, "The two Stamper brothers in the novel are each one of the ways I think I am." The "woodsy, logger side" of Kesey is represented by Hank, the older brother by twelve years. A modern version of the western frontier hero, Hank is independent, courageous, and stoical, possessing almost superhuman strength in swimming and fighting. However, his most striking characteristic is his indomitable will that allows him, even in the midst of great work pressures and the loss of his best friend and his wife, not to give up. In contrast is Lee, articulate whereas Hank is taciturn, who represents the intellectual side of Kesey. Raised in the East from the time he was twelve, Lee has none of Hank's frontier spirit. Indeed, his main recollection of his western birthplace is the haunting vision of his mother having sexual intercourse with Hank. As Stephen Tanner observes in his study of Kesey, "In his portrayal of Hank, Kesey ex-

plores the nature of strength — its values, obligations, and costs. His portrayal of Lee explores the nature of weakness — its sources, manifestations, and consequences." Suicidal, paranoid, impotent, and cowardly, Lee is unable to trust anyone or to act effectively. He is controlled by an inner voice that constantly warns "WATCH OUT" and is motivated solely by a desire to get revenge on his brother by seducing his wife. Afflicted by the envious desire of the weak to see the strong brought low, Lee must stop blaming others for his problems and start developing his own strength. And Hank, in turn, must acknowledge his vulnerability, both physical and emotional. Resolution of their conflict comes in a cathartic fist fight, in Kesey's words, "the oh so long overdue dance of Hate and Hurt and Love." Then in the final picture of Hank and Lee working together to get the logs down the river, Kesey concludes his parable of brotherly love.

The cast of characters in *Sometimes a Great Notion* is large, including the townspeople of the Snag, union officials, and various members of the Stamper family. It also is diverse. As Stephen Tanner notes, "The range of characters runs from a Yale graduate student to an idiosyncratic Indian prostitute." Among the most important secondary characters are Henry Stamper, Hank and Leland's father, who is a seemingly indestructible individual with a will of iron; Joe Ben, Hank's relative and best friend, who offers loyalty and optimism; and Viv, Hank's wife and Lee's lover, who at the novel's end leaves the community to forge a new life.

◆ Social Concerns ◆

Ken Kesey's friend Ken Babbs once remarked, "A man should have the right to be as big as he feels it's in him to be." So taken was Kesey with Babbs's comment that he quoted it in *Sometimes a Great Notion*. Babbs's observation reveals the novel's primary social concern: that self-reliance must not be destroyed by a collectivist force, in this case a logging union. In the Emersonian tradition, Kesey advocates rebellion against pressures to conform. Evoking his favorite mythic hero, the cowboy, Kesey creates first in Henry Stamper, then in his son Hank, and ultimately in his younger son Lee the frontier blend of independence, courage, irrepressible determination, and ardent defense of personal freedom that the writer so admires.

◆ Themes ◆

Like *One Flew Over the Cuckoo's Nest* (1962), *Sometimes a Great Notion* examines the individual's battle against repressive forces. The plot centers on the Stamper family's attempts to fulfill a logging contract made with Wakonda Pacific. Led by Hank Stamper, who was raised according to his father's motto "NEVER GIVE AN INCH," the Oregon family resists the pressures put upon them by the striking logging union. Because they subscribe to the code of rugged individualism, they bravely face ostracism by the townspeople, illegal scare tactics, including arson, planned by the local union leader Floyd Evenwrite, and the coldly intellectual manipulations of Jonathan Draeger, a union negotiator from California. Echoing *One Flew Over the Cuckoo's Nest*, *Sometimes a Great Notion* reflects Kesey's advocacy of freedom over control by a collectivist system.

Another repressive force in Kesey's novel is nature. The western Oregon coast with its wild forests, its torrential rains, and its raging rivers tests the human spirit. There man is placed in an adversarial relationship with nature, which Kesey emphasizes in his descriptions of the Wakonda Auga River, eroding its banks, each day threatening to destroy the Stamper house. Nowhere does the river's strength seem more horrifying than in Joe Ben's slow death by drowning. Yet Kesey asserts that one must confront nature's challenges, as the Stamper brothers do at the end of the novel when they tackle the herculean task of getting the log booms down the river.

The most dangerous force in *Sometimes a Great Notion* is the human psyche. As indicated by the novel's epigraph from the song "Good Night, Irene," which includes the lines "Sometimes I get a great notion/To jump into the river . . . an' drown," some people cannot endure the pain and loneliness of life. A number of characters in the novel either attempt or contemplate suicide, including Myra Stamper, Lee Stamper, and Williard Eggleston. Kesey shows great sensitivity to festering psychic wounds — from Henry Stamper's indignation at his father's deserting the family and returning to Kansas, to Myra Stamper's depression at being entrapped in a loveless marriage with an aged husband, to Indian Jenny's hatred of Henry because he would not marry her. The most significant of the psychologically disturbed characters, however, is Lee Stamper, whose oedipal resentment of Hank almost destroys his capacity to love.

In *Sometimes a Great Notion*, Kesey presents three solutions for alleviating human suffering — the same solutions, in fact, that he presented in his earlier novel. One is discovering one's self-identity rather than being defined by appearance or role. This theme is seen most dramatically in Viv's realization that both Stamper brothers have used her as a pawn and she must now be herself, not what others want her to be. The second is giving and receiving brotherhood, that is, learning to forgive and to express love. To develop that theme Kesey depicts the literal brotherhood of Hank and Lee, ultimately showing the spiritual growth in both characters as they teach each other about their strengths and weaknesses. The third solution is affirming life, no matter how difficult that may be. As Kesey writes in his preliminary notes for *Sometimes a Great Notion*, "You have to fight for life and freedom and individuality and then fight to keep it."

♦ Techniques ♦

Sometimes a Great Notion is a highly complex novel in its time scheme, point of view, and imagery. The panoramic narrative begins and ends on Thanksgiving Day of 1961; but between its starting point and its conclusion, it moves back and forth in time to depict the lives of three generations of Stamper males, with the earliest events occurring in 1898. As Tony Tanner explains in *City of Words: American Fiction 1950-1970*, Kesey dissolves chronological time "so that past and future events swim into each other . . ." In the first chapter of the novel, Kesey himself gives the reader advice about his treatment of time. He cautions, "Truth doesn't run on time like a commuter train, though time may run on truth. And the Scenes Gone By and The Scenes to Come flow blending together in the sea-green deep while Now spreads in circles on the surface. So don't sweat it." Later in the novel he further clarifies his technique by observing, "Time overlaps itself." Often the author will intersperse the narration of an event in the present with the relating of a closely associated event from the past. For example, he interrupts the exposition of Hank's rescue of Lee from teen-aged bullies on Halloween of 1961 to record a Halloween from Lee's childhood when Hank rescued him from a pit. Such a method of presentation in which everything seems to happen at once demands multiple readings of the novel for the reader to comprehend fully the temporal sequence. In addition to mixing the past and present, Kesey also uses a spatial simultaneity, a cinematic technique in which he reveals what various characters in different locations were doing at the same moment.

The most experimental technique of the novel is Kesey's use of multiple points of view. The eleven unnumbered chapters begin with the author's or, in some cases, the persona's direct addresses to the reader, which are indented and italicized. Some are descriptive; some anecdotal; some philo-sophical. Most of the narrative is con-veyed in the third person omniscient point of view, but there are frequent first person passages. To complicate matters further, the novel uses a varie-ty of first person narrators. However, the two most important are Hank and Lee Stamper. Like Faulkner, Kesey often employs stream of consciousness. He also uses the epistolary method as Lee writes letters about Oregon to Peters, his former roommate in the East.

Sometimes a Great Notion is filled with motifs — in fact, many of the same ones Kesey used in *One Flew Over the Cuckoo's Nest*. Descriptions of hands and animal imagery enhance the char-acterizations. Like McMurphy, Hank has scarred hands and is associated with the lone goose and the dog. Lee, on the other hand, has soft hands and is linked to the crafty fox and the treacherous werewolf. Another similar-ity to *One Flew Over the Cuckoo's Nest* is the influence of folk tales and pop culture. Like Murphy, Hank is related to the cowboy and Captain Marvel; whereas Lee is like Billy Batson, hop-ing to evoke the magic of the word "Shazam." Biblical allusions are not used as extensively in *Sometimes a Great Notion* as in the earlier novel, but there are several, including the parallels between Joby and Job and between Lee and the prodigal son. Kesey again uses the motif of suicides; however, this time he shifts from Crucifixion and castration images to those of drowning. Also reflecting the despair of the char-acters are images of imprisonment, most notably the bird cages belonging to Myra and Viv. The essential stylistic difference between the two novels is that *Sometimes a Great Notion* contains more literary allusions. This is primar-ily because Lee, as a former English graduate student, enjoys displaying his intellect by referring to the Bible, my-thology, and Shakespeare.

◆ Literary Precedents ◆

Kesey's notes to *Sometimes a Great Notion* illuminate his literary prece-dents. In them he confesses that he wanted his second published novel to be "a cross between Faulkner and Bur-roughs and also me," and he reminds himself to study the panoramic effects in John Steinbeck's novel, *The Grapes of Wrath* (1939), Stephen Vincent Benet's poem, *John Brown's Body* (1928) and Dylan Thomas's play, *Under Milk Wood* (1953). Technically, particularly in terms of time scheme and point of view, the writer to whom he seems most indebted is William Faulkner. Kesey's beginning the novel with the last events of his plot and then going back in time to develop his characters and explain how those events hap-pened recalls Faulkner's *Light in August* (1932). His use of multiple points of view was probably influenced by *The Sound and the Fury* (1929), *Absalom, Absalom!* (1936), and *As I Lay Dying* (1930), and Lee Stamper's characteriza-tion seems modeled upon Quentin Compson.

In an interview with Robert Faggen (*Paris Review* 36, no. 130 [Spring 1994]: 58-94), Kesey credited Orson Welles's film *The Magnificent Ambersons* with providing the major inspiration for his narrative experimentation. Kesey ob-serves that the film taught him to move along narrative by going from one situation to another with just a few lines of a character's dialogue as a bridge. Kesey explains, "The first part of *The Magnificent Ambersons* covers a long period in a very short time, and you get to see the characters in a structured, stylized way — they step out on stage and deliver lines that help with the exposition. That influenced me in terms of structure."

◆ Related Titles ◆

Thematically, *Sometimes a Great Notion* bears a close resemblance to *One Flew Over the Cuckoo's Nest* in presenting the battle between the individual and a repressive system. It also reflects Kesey's ongoing interest in the frontier hero, an interest seen also in *One Flew Over the Cuckoo's Nest*, *Sailor Song* (1992), and *Last Go Round* (1994).

◆ Adaptations ◆

In 1971 a two-hour film version of *Sometimes a Great Notion* was released. Directed by Paul Newman, the movie had a talented cast, including Newman as Hank Stamper, Michael Sarrazin as Lee, Henry Fonda as Henry Stamper, and Lee Remick as Viv. Newman made no attempt to transfer the complex techniques of the novel to the film medium; thus the movie merely presents the plot of Kesey's book. A badly edited version of the film, retitled *Never Give an Inch*, was later shown on network television.

◆ Ideas for Group Discussions ◆

With its epic sweep and radical experimentation with narrative techniques, *Sometimes a Great Notion* is not a novel easily grasped in a casual reading. Indeed, it almost demands a second or even a third perusal. Discussion of this book will likely center on individuals' responses to the intellectual demands Kesey places upon them. Literarily sophisticated readers will probably react most favorably to Kesey's Faulknerian treatment of multiple points of view and Lee's allusions, reflecting his Yale education. Serious students of film will probably appreciate Kesey's adaptation of cinematic devices that relate this novel to a screenplay.

1. Do you find Kesey's combination of the vernacular and intellectual idioms an artistic achievement or an awkward yoking of two disparate traditions?

2. Are Kesey's experiments with rendering time, his multiple points of view, and his use of cinematic techniques effective for rendering full reality or too ambitious and innovative for most readers to appreciate?

3. What do you think is Kesey's attitude to the great notion "to jump into the river an' drown"? Why do some of the characters contemplate or commit suicide?

4. How does Kesey characterize the Wakonda Auga River? How does that characterization differ from Twain's portrayal of the Mississippi River in *The Adventures of Huckleberry Finn*?

5. Do you find the rivalry that Lee Stamper feels for his brother Hank psychologically plausible? Do you believe the parallelism of Lee's seeing through a hole in the wall Hank and Lee's mother Myra making love and, years later, Hank's witnessing through the same hole the lovemaking of Lee and Hank's wife Viv, who looks like

Myra, too contrived?

6. What is the function of Joe Ben in the novel? Indian Jenny? Jonathan Draeger?

7. Do you find the device of Henry Stamper's severed arm shockingly grotesque and distasteful or a meaningful symbol of individualistic defiance?

8. Do you think the major females in this novel are well-developed characters or serve merely as sexual objects? How do you respond to Kesey's statement made in an interview with Paul Krassner: "Women's Lib was the real issue in *Notion*. I didn't know this when I wrote it, but think about it: It's about men matching egos and wills on the battleground of Vivian's unconsulted hide. When she leaves at the end of the book, she chooses to leave the only people she loves for a bleak and uncertain but at least *equal* future"?

9. In a letter to Ken Babbs, Kesey said of *Sometimes a Great Notion*, "It's a big book. . . . Certainly a remarkable book. Perhaps even a great book." Would you label Kesey's second published novel "a great book"?

Lynne Shackelford
Furman University

A SON OF THE CIRCUS

Novel

1994

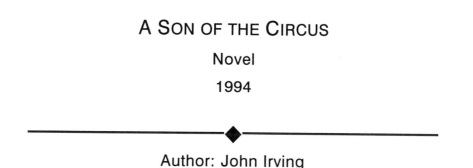

Author: John Irving

◆ Characters ◆

A *Son of the Circus* teems with characters. Farrokh Darawalla serves as the hero. He is the son of Dr. Lowji Darawalla, a famous orthopedist who founded the Hospital for Crippled Children in Bombay and who was killed by a car bomb because of his atheism. Farrokh Darawalla and his wife Julia have no children, but Darawalla plays surrogate father to various dwarfs and crippled children in Bombay and to his father's adopted son, John D. Anonymously, he writes screenplays for John D., turning him into the controversial movie star Inspector Dhar.

John D./Inspector Dhar and his twin Martin Miller are separated at birth when their mother, an actress, decides to marry one of her lovers and pass Martin off as this lover's child. Where Dhar loses his identity in the roles Darawalla creates for him, Martin seeks his in studying for the priesthood at age thirty-nine. The twins finally meet — on a plane trip scripted by Darawalla — and acknowledge their homosexuality, a sign that they are finding a more authentic sense of personal identity.

Embedded within *A Son of the Circus* is a murder mystery involving the search for a serial killer who draws pornographic elephants on the victims' bellies. Just as Darawalla creates the screenplays for Dhar, he orchestrates the search for the "real" murderer. Dhar, the actor-detective, helps solve the crime as much as does the real detective, Inspector Patel. Patel's wife Nancy, a hippie from Iowa, witnessed the first murders of her drug-smuggling pimp and a prostitute. The villain of the murder-mystery is Rahul Rai, son of Promila Rai who used to fondle him in a country club bathroom that contained elephant fixtures. Besides the legacy of abuse, Rahul is led to murder by his thwarted sexual identity. Without body hair, he is mocked by Promila and eventually completes a sex-change operation, returning to India as a woman and marrying Mr. Dogar, a member of the country club where his/her early abuse took place.

Irving develops the characters involved in the murder plot most fully though he tends to explain their motives rather than to develop them interiorly. Numerous other characters people the novel: Mr. Sethna, the country club steward who eavesdrops to help catch Rahul; Vinod, a circus dwarf, and his full-grown wife Deepa; Garg, nicknamed Acid Man because of a facial scar, who marries a child prostitute with AIDs; Ganesh, a crippled boy who falls to his death trying to learn the circus act that was supposed to save him from the streets; Suman, an aerialist who performs without a net; Tata Two, an obstetrician like his father, who gives quick and inaccurate blood tests. Irving's characters function like a circus cast, multiple, exaggerated, and glimpsed only in costume.

◆ Social Concerns/Themes ◆

At over six hundred pages, *A Son of the Circus* is a huge book, as if Irving wanted to pack into it something about all of the themes he has addressed in his previous novels. This is a book about religion: about how Christians and Parsis and Muslims cope with the problem of good and evil; how followers of these religions come to their faith; how cultural practices and prejudices arise from different religious views; how the religious person fulfills social responsibility by caring for those who need love and aid. For example, the novel's main character, Dr. Farrokh Darawalla, born a Parsi and descended, therefore, from the Zoroastrians who came to India in the seventh and eighth centuries to escape Muslim persecution, rejects both his Parsi background and his father's atheism. He converts to Christianity when he interprets a bite on his toe as inflicted by the ghost of a Christian instead of the bite of the novel's serial killer that it actually is. As a physician, Darawalla fulfills his Christian sense of social responsibility by healing the sick, by searching for a cure for dwarfism, and by rescuing children from the streets and brothels of India and delivering them to the circus.

This is also a novel about exile, about how and where one finds and defines home. Darawalla divides his time between Toronto and India, feeling out of place in both parts of the world and coming to realize by the end of the novel that his home is the circus, the place of dreams. Darawalla is the orphan who saves orphans and, through him and numerous other characters, Irving continues to explore his major thematic concern of what constitutes family.

As in all his novels, Irving places his big themes into contemporary cultural context. Questions about the nature of religious experience become questions about the relationship between reality and imagination that are examined through a narrative method that foregrounds the omniscient narrator as a god-concept. Questions about the nature of good and evil become questions about violence, which become, more specifically, questions about violence against women, violence against children, and, with a particularly contemporary twist, the violence of terrorist bombers leveled against those who do not follow the terrorists' version of religion. Questions about exile are grounded in cultural tensions surrounding immigration, with Darawalla, for example, being feared in Canada merely because of his dark skin.

A John Irving novel would seem incomplete without some focus on the theme of sexuality. Set primarily in India, *A Son of the Circus* exploits that country's more disturbing sexual practices, such as child prostitution and the practice of castrating males into androgynous *hijras*. It is rife with sexual images: a dildo, phallic statues, erect penises compared to elephants' trunks, naked bodies, and an array of sexual positions. Although many accuse Irving of using sexuality to shock, he wants to remind us not only that sexuality promotes disease and violence, but also that sexual orientation may be genetically determined and that, whether homosexual or heterosexual, sex can be an act of connection, of healing, and of love.

Like his characters, Irving's technique recalls the circus. This is a busy, chaotic book. Characters come on and off stage, plots surface and disappear only to surface again later, the atmosphere is at once funny, confusing, frightening, bizarre, dirty, and sad. Stories occur within stories with Darawalla/Irving playing the ringmaster god. At one point, the omniscient narrator asks if the "creative process [has] eclipsed his common sense." Like a child enthralled by the circus, Irving has given himself over to the chaos. Yet for all its chaos, the novel is still highly choreographed and the careful reader will find an intricate web of connections among the scenic performances.

One example of the web of connections in *A Son of the Circus* occurs in Irving's use of the vampire theme. Darawalla (here, Dracula) extracts blood from dwarfs, not that he may live but that they might live. Rahul preys on the blood of his victims, biting Darawalla's toe and the lips of Nancy and of his murder victims, not because he wants to harm them but because he cannot stop himself. But blood in the age of AIDs is not often a source of life: If Darawalla finds a

genetic marker for dwarfism, blood can transmit healing, but blood, especially in a country with the sexual practices of India, is also a vehicle of death.

Irving nods to various literary influences in *A Son of the Circus*, to Graham Greene especially and his treatment of Catholicism. He dedicates the novel to Salman Rushdie and embedded in its story is his concern for what happens to the artist who oversteps the bounds of what his or her culture or religion allows.

◆ Related Titles ◆

A Son of the Circus echoes images and concerns that Irving has addressed throughout his writing career. Its circus imagery recalls the zoo in *Setting Free the Bears* (1969); its concern with gender identity recalls *The World According to Garp* (1978); its over-the-edge sexual content and chaotic plot seem most like *The Hotel New Hampshire* (1981). Where *The Cider House Rules* (1985) pursues the orphan theme by connecting it to abortion and *A Prayer for Owen Meany* (1989) pursues it in Johnny's search for the father, *A Son of the Circus* pursues it in all the orphaned children of India. Like *The World According to Garp* and *The Hotel New Hampshire*, *A Son of the Circus* foregrounds issues of violence against women and sexual identity and like *A Prayer for Owen Meany*, it foregrounds questions of religious faith.

◆ Ideas for Group Discussions ◆

Given its pervasive sexual content and its chaotic plot, *A Son of the Circus* is apt to turn away readers. But its very intricacy can lead to avenues for discussion that should be lively and productive.

1. The main plot of *A Son of the Circus* involves the search for Rahul, the serial killer. How does this plot connect to some of the subplots, for example the search for the genetic marker for dwarfism and the search for a place within the circus? Which of the plots interests you the most and why?

2. Why is the novel called *A Son of the Circus* rather than *"The" Son of the Circus*? Who qualifies as a son?

3. How does the circus become a metaphor in the novel? A metaphor for what?

4. How does the novel address what it means to be a religious or spiritual person? How does religion serve as both a positive and a negative force in life?

5. How does Irving address the idea of fate? If he is the author controlling the text, can fate be possible?

6. Irving's novel is filled with references to contemporary social problems: religious intolerance, racism, homophobia, cultural identity, media exploitation, to name only a few. How does the novel help you to see the influence of these problems in your own life?

7. Do you find the novel too sexual? Is Irving being sensational?

8. Why does Irving include twins? What twin images can you find besides those embodied in Inspector Dhar and Martin Miller?

9. Irving never lived in India. Is his India convincing? What have you learned about this country? Do you like what you have learned?

10. How does the Epilogue pull the various threads of the novel together? In particular, how does Darawalla's encounter with the child and his mother serve as a gloss on the issues of the novel?

Sharon L. Dean
Rivier College

SONG OF SOLOMON

Novel

1977

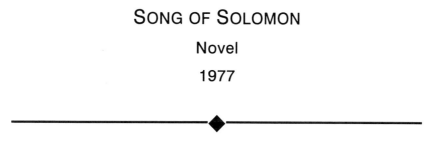

Author: Toni Morrison

◆ Social Concerns ◆

Morrison's place in American literature was assured with the publication of her third novel, *Song of Solomon*, by far her most penetrating inquiry into the sources and causes of cultural alienation among African-Americans. The book earned many awards and established her as both a popular and as a serious novelist. Few writers of her generation would be so simultaneously admired by the critics and by the Book-of-the-Month Club. Building on the critique of materialism and racism in American society developed in *The Bluest Eye* (1970) and *Sula* (1973), with this novel Morrison deepened her understanding of the causes of African-American cultural malaise. Although her emphasis remains on discrimination and limited opportunities for minorities, the problem central to *Song of Solomon* concerns strategies among the fragmented African-American community to deal with institutional racism. Each generation of her central family attempts strategies to deal with minority status in America, but the novel as a whole indicates that these are dead ends without a rediscovery of the lore and legends of African-American culture.

These tactics correspond with the generations of the main family, whose eldest male heir is always named Macon Dead. The eldest Macon received this as his name when a drunk reconstruction officer registered the ex-slave as a free man. Entries on the wrong lines resulted in the new free-man's first name being listed as that of a city, and his family name was listed as the condition in which his parents were believed to be. The cracker who made the error thought it was funny, but the family persisted, perhaps perversely, in keeping the strange name. As Guitar Baines, another character whose destiny mingles with that of the youngest Macon, argues later in the novel, ex-slaves were given the names of the oppressors, and denied their own (a theme Morrison will develop fully in *Beloved*, 1987) — thus the central confusion in the book about the three names of the legendary Solomon: In contemporary songs he is called "Sugarman"; a Virginia town named after him is "Shalimar." If names are one public symbol for identity, as Morrison argues in this and subsequent novels, African-Americans are uniquely encumbered by names that belong to

Euro-Americans and were imposed as residual vestiges of slave culture, or have been verbally garbled in the oral transmission of "ourstory."

The eldest Macon Dead responded to white economic power by establishing an African-American enterprise separate and equal economically if not socially with the majority culture. Establishing himself as a freed slave in Danville, Pennsylvania — having fled the overt racism of the south — he enacted the pioneer ideal by converting a piece of land no one else thought tillable into a model farm he called, in honor of the great Emancipator, "Lincoln's Heaven." But as his enterprise succeeded, white neighbors came to envy his success and to covet his riches. When Macon resisted a takeover by the Butler clan, then took up arms to protect his home, they murdered him on the very fence that symbolized his effort at separatism while his children watched in horror.

Scarred emotionally by watching his father die, Macon Dead II did not attempt to compete with white America, but chose to outscramble his fellow African-Americans for what white people leave behind. He emigrated to Detroit and eventually became a slum lord. He married the daughter of the town's only black physician and transformed his struggling real estate firm into an investment company that buys up unwanted properties and rents them, at exorbitant rates, to blacks. During the novel he evicts sympathetically drawn characters: Guitar Baines's widowed mother, whose husband dies in a sawmill accident implicitly because of the white owners' negligence, defaults on her rent, so out she and her children go; Howard Porter, Macon's daughter First Corinthians's lover, is evicted because, as laborer and lover,

he represents a threat to the respectability Macon so desperately craves. Macon's pride is in the fine automobiles he drives; his dream is to develop a beach-front community for wealthy blacks in a section of lakefront whites do not want anyway.

Macon's material success, while impressive, is a hollow victory, won at the expense of other struggling African-Americans. Because his power is merely materialistic, he does not command respect or love from his family, and his son, whom he grooms to follow in his footsteps as he believes he follows in his father's, is so bound up by materialism that he lacks a strong self-concept. He sees little value in himself or in his family. As he accepts his role as his father's successor, he finds no happiness or meaning in his role as landlord and collector. Throughout the first half of the novel, Milkman (so called because of his mother's nursing him beyond his infancy, suggesting her reluctance to grant him freedom and autonomy) unwittingly struggles with his father's materialistic aesthetic, in which ownership is the only way to establish parity with the whites, but, with no idea that his real enemy is materialism, not just Euro-American culture, seeks to find happiness by adding possessions: autos, fine clothes, money, women. He is, however, locking himself more inescapably into the cycle of materialism, which cost his grandfather his life and his father his soul. Morrison's point is that a materialism emulating that of Euro-American culture will not liberate black American culture from the delayed effects of slavery.

Finally, Morrison treats the growing militancy of some African-American groups of the 1970s, such as the Black Panthers and SNCC, through her creation of a radical, militant, vigilante group "the Seven Days." Drawing on historical accounts of injustice, in cases like the Scottsboro Boys and Emmett Till (Morrison later wrote a play, *Dreaming Emmett*, 1986), the Seven Days concoct a desperate, mad plan for responding to racist terrorism. Basing their theory on the (racist) assumption that only white people are capable of deliberate violence, Guitar and other men Milkman believes to be sensible commit themselves to systematic, passionless acts of violence in retaliation for that done to blacks by whites. The act must be taken against a randomly-chosen white victim, and it must emulate the crime against the blacks. The Days concoct a theory of numbers to justify their protocols, claiming that if white violence against blacks is not answered in kind, over many generations the numerical majority that now permits injustice will lead to genocide.

Morrison represents the Days as a desperate effort to respond to cruelty by whites, but she also shows that their way is flawed and a form of racism itself. Although two fundamental codes of the Days are that blacks must never commit violence against blacks, and that materialism is the basis of social injustice, Guitar, representing the Days, becomes so obsessed with gold he believes Milkman is keeping from the Days for selfish ends, that he makes repeated attempts on Milkman's life, eventually taking the life of the novel's most sympathetic character, Milkman's aunt Pilate. Morrison suggests that, although the anger driving the militant Days is real, their solution is inherently flawed. Like materialism, militancy is another false solution to the problem of finding an African-American identity in European-American culture.

◆ Themes ◆

In *Song of Solomon*, Morrison's suggested solution can be summed up in the transformation that occurs as Milkman goes on his quest for what he believes is gold his father and his aunt Pilate hid shortly after his father's death. As an alienated Detroit African-American youth of the 1960s, Milkman seeks wealth, the white culture's symbol of power and freedom. He wants to possess things, to control people, and to become free of the influence of his father's materialism. Milkman never finds gold; what he finds is true wealth, knowledge of and pride as well as delight in stories about his ancestors — his family's and his culture's myth.

As a youth wanting power and wealth, Milkman was far more like Macon Dead II than he ever believed. As his sister Magdalena charges, in a very funny but powerful scene, Macon III, like Macon II, has been pissing on everyone he knew all his life. True to form, Milkman undertakes the quest for selfish reasons. He and Guitar attempted to rob his aunt Pilate, and even Guitar's reason, while troublesome, was less selfish than Milkman's. He wanted money to finance the Days' operations, while his friend robbed the only relative who ever treated him well so he could leave town. Milkman was also in an exploitative relationship with Pilate's granddaughter Hagar, whose suicidal love he was incapable of returning. It is only as his quest imposes its shape on Milkman that he learns that knowledge is more valuable than gold, and that obligations to the family history are more liberating than physical freedom.

His quest forces him into several redefinitions, all of which involve renewed appreciation for the importance of narrative as cultural myth. When he gets to his father's childhood home in Danville, he learns through the old men's stories the value his grandfather had as a cultural hero. Although a martyr, Macon I left a legacy of successful competition with the whites in the agricultural and economic arenas, and his death created a legend of heroic defiance. Milkman had heard all this from his father, but he had refused to understand how the stories of the ancestors function practically as narratives of heroes. Before he leaves Danville, he tells stories of his own father's success to an eager audience, not out of arrogance, but out of an awareness that Macon II's stories can have a similar effect for these old men. Although Morrison quite clearly does not endorse it, Milkman now sees his father's grasping materialism differently.

One final symbolic event in Danville helps prepare Milkman for his redefinition of myth and his ancestral legacy. While seeking information about his grandfather and the gold Pilate supposedly hid, Milkman is instructed by the ancient Circe to find his grandfather's grave. On this journey he falls in a stream, soaking his money, tearing his suit, and breaking his watch. With these assaults pointing out the puniness of his emblems of wealth and power, he is prepared for a more fundamental encounter with his history in Virginia, the heart of the slave country from which his grandfather escaped.

In Virginia Milkman is astonished to learn that the very symbols of his power and influence that served him well in Detroit now emphasize his alienation. He must fight, hunt, bond with the men there, and learn to listen to the earth — it saves his life by warning him of Guitar's first assault — to

prepare himself for the final discovery, the pride and lore of his ancestors. Decoding a variety of Shalimar texts, he learns that his grandfather was "Jake" before he was Macon Dead, and that Jake was the youngest son of the legendary Solomon, who flew back to Africa. Solomon was unable to carry Jake with him, although he tried. For Milkman, Solomon's flight is liberating. From a man possessing little self-esteem except what his possessions could bestow, he experiences Dionysian joy in discovering his past. While swimming in a pool, another significant bond with nature, Milkman articulates his glee: "He didn't need no airplane. He just took off; got fed up. *All the way up.* No more cotton! No more bales! No more orders! No more shit! He flew, baby!"

Morrison has told interviewers that she did not intend Solomon's flight as a metaphor, but as a literal homage to slave stories of Africans who repudiated slavery and flew back home. In Solomon's flight she encodes the longing to escape the horrors of slavery, but more significantly for the novel the importance of myth, which transmits the extraordinary doings of heroes. Milkman is liberated by this knowledge, and he returns to Detroit with a far more other-directed vision. He seeks to understand and communicate with his father, whom he now understands to have been too much affected by materialism. He returns eager to share his pride in their ancestors with Pilate, whom he takes to Shalimar to bury her father, whose bones she has unwittingly carried all her adult life. But their return to Shalimar leads to Guitar's final attempt on Milkman's life, and Pilate is his unintended victim. As the novel ends, Milkman "surrenders to the air" and flies to meet his old friend, now his nemesis, in a battle to the death. Whether his flight is literal, thus re-enacting Solomon's legendary exit, or figural, suggesting his own liberation, is left for readers to decide.

Finally, Morrison complicates the issue of flight by acknowledging that for liberation there is a cost. Her epigraph suggests that the fathers "may soar" but that the remaining children "may know their names." The story of Solomon's flight is also the story of Jake's abandonment; the twenty-first of Solomon's children must learn his adulthood alone, and Shalimar's legend of "Ryna's Gulch" grows from the abandoned wife's lamentations. Thus, while Morrison emphasizes that the flight legend is liberating, she also makes it clear that liberation is not without its costs, and on Milkman's return he must acknowledge his responsibility in Hagar's despair and death. Pilate's dying by a bullet Guitar meant for Milkman compounds the costs associated with freedom. But the central theme of *Song of Solomon* is that only by knowing and celebrating the legends of the past can a culture learn freedom.

♦ Characters ♦

The special appeal of *Song of Solomon* is its well-developed characters, and the principal male characters articulate variations on the theme of materialism and transcendence. Minor characters, including members of the Days, the hunting party in Shalimar, and especially the old men Milkman meets in Danville, are deftly and effectively drawn.

The female characters also create an impressive enrichment on the roles of minorities in a white and male-dominated role. Except for Pilate, none of these efforts could be called successful, but Morrison offers them as sympathetic portraits of women trapped in a culture that does not respect their autonomy.

Milkman's mother is the most submissive, and her deference to white culture and to her father's respectability in the white community is a constant source of friction with her husband. Her behavior, which she explains to Milkman as a result of her feeling "small," suggests resistance to change and desire to exert control. Her nursing Milkman well past his infancy results in his nickname and expresses a reluctance to let her son develop his autonomy. His father tells him of her unnatural reverence for her dead father's hands, a perversity Ruth denies. Milkman later discovers, however, that she makes nocturnal pilgrimages to Dr. Foster's grave site decades after his death.

Another female character who cannot let go of the past is Circe, the wraith-like inhabitant of the mansion owned by the Butlers, who killed Milkman's grandfather in Pennsylvania. She rescued Macon and Pilate after the murder occurred, but she remained a servant of that evil family, and tenaciously keeps the mansion after the final Butler's death — to watch with her own eyes the downfall of the oppressors.

Ruth Dead's daughters, Magdalene and First Corinthians, like their mother, are trapped in ethnic and gender roles from which they do not escape. Both are well educated and able, but Magdalene lives in enraged memory of Macon II's and Milkman's assumptions of male power, and First Corinthians aspires to be a colleague of, but is really a maid for, Michigan's Poet Laureate. Corinthians falls reluctantly in love with a laborer, an attraction she feels demeaning but compelling. Her love, however, may be ennobling. Porter has by the end of the novel resigned from the vigilante group the Seven Days.

The pattern of submission and its consequences, to both ethnic and gender roles, is represented at its extreme by Macon's niece Reba and her daughter Hagar, who is Milkman's lover as well. Both women, while sharing Pilate's unconventional lifestyle and life-affirming qualities, cannot escape from their own perceived need for male approval. Reba cannot keep her self-esteem without its being reflected in a lover, and her dependency leads to her being exploited and occasionally abused. In a powerful scene, Pilate forcefully persuades Reba's lover that he must cease to harm her daughter or face death at Pilate's hands. Hagar's love for Milkman is, like her mother's dependence, finally suffocating. Guitar warns that Hagar's repeated attempts to kill Milkman represent an obsessive kind of love. When her efforts to force his attention fail and Milkman departs on his quest, Hagar loses all self-esteem. Convinced that she is ugly and poor, she seeks to "improve" herself, to make herself worthy of Milkman's love, by buying clothes and having her hair styled. Her disappointment as these accessories fail leads to despair, then to wasting away and eventually death.

The female character with a healthy self-esteem depends neither on ethnic models nor on men's approval for her self-idea. Always the outcast because orphaned by her mother's death in birthing her, her father's death, and Macon II's disappearance, then consistently ostracized because of her biolog-ical anomaly (she has no navel), Pilate is through her life's journey rejected by lovers and communities. She creates her life on the periphery of respectability; in Detroit she sells homemade wine with the result that her brother shuns her.

Yet Pilate is the novel's source of life and forgiveness. She does not despise the men and communities that reject her, and she aids Ruth in her efforts to bring Milkman into the world. Macon II sought to force a spontaneous abortion. Pilate later assumes an Aunt Jemima's role to get Milkman and Guitar out of jail after they have robbed her. Morrison implies that Pilate is capable of genuine metamorphosis when Milkman believes she actually diminished in stature when acting deferential toward the white cop, then resumes her natural height. Although she fails to prevent Hagar's plunge into despair, her song at the funeral is one of the novel's finest moments, affirming the distinction between eros, in this novel generally a destructive emotion, and agape, or universal love. Her epitaph for Hagar is "And she was *loved!*" She echoes this sentiment with her own dying words. Shot by Guitar, she tells Milkman her one regret: "I wish I'd a knowed more people . . . If I'd a knowed more, I would a loved more."

Thus the novel's most ostracized character is its apostle of love. Morrison supports this paradox by showing that Pilate differs from other characters in her veneration for the past and her respect for places. She mentions frequent ghostly visits from her father and mother and she looks to these ghosts for guidance (Morrison also spoke often with her dead father while writing *Song of Solomon*). From every place she stays, she keeps a rock as remembrance and her confused obedience to her father's ghost's comment, "You just can't fly off and leave a body" — actually a complaint against his father, Solomon — leads her to carry her father's skeleton for years in the mistaken belief that they are those of a man she thinks her brother inadvertently killed. By design Morrison associates Pilate's respect for the past and for places with her powers of love and forgiveness.

♦ Techniques/Literary Precedents ♦

By most standards, *Song of Solomon* is technically conservative for the author of *The Bluest Eye* and *Sula*. It is unique in Morrison's canon because it takes an essentially masculine view of the quest and in that the central figure is a male. It follows the logic of the quest, one of literature's true archetypes. The hero sets out looking for one thing, but learns as the quest develops that what he really needs to find is something else. Traditional variations on the quest motif involve some form of renewal — the grail quest behind much modern literature leads to a cultural and agricultural renewal — and as Milkman reshapes and defines his quest, he brings back to Detroit a new and vital appreciation for African-American culture and folklore, presumably something that liberates his life and can empower others as well. Morrison, however, qualifies this traditional quest result by introducing the killing of Pilate and the ambiguity of the final confrontation between Milkman and Guitar; will their embrace, surely resulting in the death of one, prevent Milkman from taking his new view back to Detroit?

The novel is organized into two quests, one false and one true. While Milkman seeks gold, he commits to an end that compounds rather than solves his problem. Discovering, through perils reminiscent of traditional quests such as caves, mansions haunted by ghostlike figures, hostile strangers, night-hunts, and attempts on his life, that his goal is destructive, Milkman adapts his quest to one for sources and knowledge.

During the 1970s, a large movement toward discovery of the familial and cultural origins of African-Americans took place. Perhaps the most spectacular commercial success was Alex Haley's *Roots* (1976), which was later adapted as a television miniseries, about a family's discovering its origins in Africa. Although Morrison does not take her characters back to Africa, she offers us a very sophisticated version of the quest for roots in American postslave culture.

The final unifying symbol of the novel is flight. The epigraph mentions the fathers' flight as a matter of legend, and Milkman is energized by learning the story of Solomon's flight. His own birth took place in a white hospital because Ruth went into labor when a man tried to fly but fell to his death, an event accompanied by Pilate's song about "Sugarman," which we eventually learn is a corruption of the song of Solomon. Milkman's low self-esteem as a child is traced to his discovery that he could not fly. Solomon's flight is a legendary defiance of the slave code, and Milkman may literally or figurally take flight to confront Guitar. The figure's full implications, like many themes and motifs in *Song of Solomon*, are manifested by Pilate, who, Milkman realizes as she dies, could fly all along — because of her transcendent love and forgiveness.

Because *Song of Solomon* is an accessible novel, and because it involves an exciting version of the quest for cultural solidarity, it should provoke lively discussions on matters like gender and ethnic stereotyping and variations on economic independence for minorities. Another focus for conversation might be Morrison's treatment of the Seven Days. She does not defend the attitudes and values of the group, but to what degree does she suggest that such groups are inevitable in a climate of racism? To what degree are Guitar and his associates creations of a repressive white economic culture?

1. What are we to make of the irony that Milkman's first other-directed deed in the novel, helping a man load a crate in the Danville station, convinces Guitar that he deserves to be hunted down and killed?

2. Is Circe, the ancient crone he encounters in the Butler mansion, a living anomaly, or has Milkman encountered a ghost (note her youthful voice and see *Beloved* for another ambivalent treatment of a ghostlike presence)? What readings of the novel are implicit in either response?

3. What specific experiences liberate Milkman in Shalimar? Which are the most important, and why?

4. Is Milkman responsible for Hagar's death? Pilate seems to think so, but she later forgives him. Do we as readers hold him accountable for Hagar's dependence? If so, is his carrying her hair, presumably accepting his role in her death, an adequate gesture of responsibility?

5. What does happen as the novel ends? Does Milkman fly? Will he defeat or be killed by Guitar? What understanding of the novel is implicit in either reading? Why does Morrison end the book on such an ambiguous note?

David Dougherty
Loyola College in Maryland

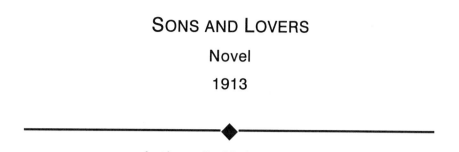

SONS AND LOVERS

Novel

1913

Author: D. H. Lawrence

◆ Characters ◆

*S*ons and Lovers is rich in character portrayals, but its focus is Paul Morel. All other characters are portrayed in their relationship to him: his mother, his lovers — Miriam Leivers and Clara Dawes — and Clara's husband Baxter. In the early chapters Paul's older brother William is the central focus. William dies, in part because he cannot break the Oedipal bond with his mother; his death foreshadows the relationship between his mother and Paul. The other two children, Annie and Arthur, are foils, incidental to the plot. Paul's father serves to introduce the male-female struggle through an account of the deterioration of his marriage with Gertrude Morel; he is also a study in well-meaning but clumsy brute vitality, a victim of society but also a type that Lawrence came into sympathy with in later years.

Paul cannot mature into manhood until he has freed himself from his mother. He loves her almost incestuously, however, and can barely face the fact that she is an older woman. In the climax of the book she gets cancer and Paul (with his sister Annie's collusion) finally administers an overdose of morphine because he can no longer stand her suffering. In the book's last chapter he is overcome by a yearning to join her in death — the darkness which until now his father the coal-miner has represented — but chooses the life-principle, almost by a sheer act of will.

Paul is vitally in touch with the life-force throughout the book, at times almost to the point of narcissism. His mother's love encourages such preoccupation with self, for she lives through her son. Once he becomes established in the world, however, her possessiveness becomes a barrier to his further maturation. A similar pattern becomes apparent in Paul's relationship with Miriam. She admires him and promotes him. In return he instructs her; in her presence his intellectual and spiritual idealism flourishes. But she is virtuous and physically untouchable, unable to enjoy a sensual apprehension of the world and unwilling to consummate their relationship. When she finally offers herself to Paul, it is as a sacrifice. For Lawrence she represents the attempt of modern Christian civilization to possess a man in his soul but to deny him the fullness of his being.

About halfway through the book

Paul deserts Miriam for Clara Dawes. Clara is full of life. She satisfies Paul's desire for sensual fulfillment; their lovemaking is impersonal, almost spiritual, because it awakens Paul to deep vitalistic forces beyond the intellect. However, she is still married and will not fully give herself to Paul, and he is still bound to his mother. In addition, in Paul's mind their sexual experimentation leads to debasement; Clara becomes the harlot to Miriam's nun. Paul finally befriends the pathetic Baxter Dawes, Clara's estranged husband, and arranges for a reconciliation. The reconciliation is a sign that a marriage relationship is not impossible, but Paul cannot achieve a lasting union with another woman until his mother dies. Her death brings Paul face-to-face with the yearning for obliteration implicit in their relationship. Unlike his older brother, he chooses to live in the world of men rather than to join her in death.

◆ Social Concerns ◆

This novel is worthy of study for several reasons. Not only is it accessible, but it is one of Lawrence's more successful and representative novels. The background of the novel is socially realistic; it reveals the way a novelist uses and transforms autobiographical material. The coming of age of Paul Morel parallels Lawrence's own successful but ambivalent escape from his working-class destiny as a coal-miner's son. The book is also an example of psychological realism heightened by poetic language — the novel evokes the inner lives of its main characters, especially Paul. His mother nurtures him but compensates for a disappointing marriage (and the loss of William, her older son) by projecting all of her love

and ambition into him. This bond between mother and son is so strong and instinctive that the book can be read as a case study of the Oedipal conflict. Paul futilely attempts to free himself from this mother-son bond by finding a suitable mate, first Miriam Leivers, a childhood friend of whom his mother disapproves, and then Clara Dawes, a sensual woman separated from her husband. He cannot break the Oedipal bond with his mother, and the ensuing conflicts dramatize the archetypal Lawrentian theme of friction between man and woman, making it a good introduction to his work.

◆ Themes ◆

Lawrence is always concerned with the relation between men and women, specifically with the struggle between the male and female principles. The duality inherent in life is thus one of his main themes. In *Sons and Lovers* this struggle concerns Paul Morel's allegiance to his mother, who couldn't bear to think that any of her sons would be condemned to manual labor, over the semi-literate robustness of his father, who "hated books, hated the sight of anyone reading or writing."

As in many of his works, Lawrence also dramatizes his hatred of industrialism. Here he does so by depicting Walter Morel, Paul's father, as a man brutalized by the life of the mines. The father's vitality has been subverted by mechanization, and the mother's love of her children warped into neurotic possessiveness by modern civilization. She attempts to realize her life through the achievements of her sons. Paul's need for sensual and erotic knowledge conflicts with such maternal idealism, although he, too, has a desire to possess his lovers. Lawrence constantly emphasizes the idea that a balance must be found between male and female principles if happiness is to be achieved. In later writings he supports this idea by calling upon the ancient vitality of pre-Christian ritual, by asserting the male principle or by announcing a truce between sexuality and the intellect. Here he is content to call for a recognition of the life of the blood by dramatizing several eternal conflicts: the conscious versus the subconscious life, instinctive desires versus idealistic yearnings, and a mechanized bourgeois society (with its repression and conditioned behavior) versus the impulse toward freedom and individual regeneration.

◆ Techniques ◆

Sons and Lovers is an excellent example of a realism heightened by poetic intensification, such as a symbolic identification of character with animals and nature. Of Miriam, for example, Lawrence writes that "It could never be mentioned [around her] that the mare was in foal," and he symbolically identifies her with the madonna lily. Flower imagery is frequently used to identify the nature of a character. In addition, Lawrence used organic metaphors to define character; he particularly favored the image of a plant which either grows to full bloom and then naturally decays, or, conversely, a plant which somehow denies its own nature and chokes itself. Such symbolism becomes more mordant in later novels such as *Women in Love* (1920), and more explicit in later allegorical fables such as *The Fox*, but here it effectively textures and structures the story.

Such techniques were necessary to Lawrence's purpose, for he proposed to reveal the passional side of character, which did not reflect simply a social class or family background, but instead articulated an impersonal flow of being. The description of natural phenomena, such as a river in flood, was intended to represent human relationships in a context which gave primacy to nonhuman standards. The use of symbolic description was not Lawrence's invention, but in his hands it became not only a tool of characterization but also a structural device. In addition, the repetition of key phrases and motifs achieves a similar sort of heightening. Such repetition is effective in *Sons and Lovers* and the best of his short stories, such as "The Rocking-Horse Winner" (1915), but is overused in books like *The Rainbow* (1915).

Lawrence's impulses were as much religious and prophetic as social. Sometimes his characters or the narrative voice become preachy and shrill. In *Sons and Lovers* such preachiness is usually integrated into the consciousness of its characters; in later work, such as *Aaron's Rod* (1922) or *Kangaroo* (1923), such didacticism results in thinly-sketched straw dogs or mouthpieces. The technique, however, often results in a powerful polemic which short-circuits ordinary rational criticism; it has attracted as many readers to Lawrence as it has repelled.

◆ Literary Precedents ◆

Critics often point to Thomas Carlyle's apocalyptic writings as a strong influence on the didactic strain in Lawrence's work, and to Thomas Hardy's pastoral anti-industrialism as formative of his themes (although Hardy, unlike Lawrence, defeats his heroes). It is important to note that Lawrence read widely and intensely (often, in his early years, with Jessie Chambers, the prototype of Miriam in *Sons and Lovers*). He admired writers who could be both savagely satirical of modern manners, particularly English manners, and fully alive.

Lawrence stands firmly in a long tradition of iconoclasts and revolutionaries: commentators have mentioned Swift, Thoreau, Voltaire, and Whitman. Swift and Voltaire hated cant and gloried in their hatred. They produced bracing satires — for Lawrence, clearly seen and felt hatred was more valuable than orthodox affection. Thoreau always spoke from his whole being, and gave at least as much respect to nature as to man; like Lawrence, he saw man not as primal but as only one element in a cosmic matrix. Although Whitman was too willing (for Lawrence's tastes) to argue that an overarching love of humankind was a kind of salvation, he didn't separate the life of man into flesh and spirit, but wrote passionately on behalf of a new nondualistic morality.

Lawrence is often categorized as a Modernist, along with Yeats, Joyce, Proust, Pound, Mann and Eliot (among others). Like them, he had contempt for modern civilization, in which "Things fall apart; the center cannot hold" (Yeats). The certainties of nineteenth-century society, with its traditions and its "realism," were gone, but Lawrence felt they had been replaced by something worse: mentalism, a permissiveness which allowed anything but valued nothing. Like the Modernists, Lawrence believed that the writer was whole, possessing a clarity of vision in opposition to his fragmented age, and that his word could be law or even religion. Like Eliot, he believed that

"The essential function of art is moral. Not aesthetic, not decorative, not pastime or recreation." Unlike most Modernists, however, Lawrence was more committed to expressing the flow of experience and extraliterary ideas than to the creation of a sovereign object of art. He prophesied the new shape of things, called for new symbols, like the Modernists, but didn't believe that man was central to the new age. He abhorred self-consciousness and humanism.

◆ Related Titles ◆

Lawrence considered all of his work to be "thought adventures"; each title was a further attempt to clarify his vision and to represent the quality of lived experience. There is a constant struggle between light and darkness in his work, although darkness is sometimes necessary to growth and lightness a superficial rationalism. That is, he sometimes turns conventional symbolism on its head, and all of his work is part of a continuing dialectic on "the relation between men and women."

The Rainbow and *Women in Love*, the two novels which immediately followed *Sons and Lovers*, continue to develop the themes, if not the characters, first formulated in the earlier book. "One sheds one's sicknesses in books," Lawrence wrote of *Sons and Lovers*; *The Rainbow*, like the earlier book, is a family chronicle, but it covers three generations instead of one, and it dissects the disintegration of modern life. *Women in Love* continues such a dissection with its savage satire; it also continues to suggest, especially through Birkin, the Lawrentian spokesman, that man must be moved by a power greater than himself and must never sacrifice his sensual being to his spiritual being or vice versa. It also expands the dialectic, however; Birkin marries Ursula by the novel's end, but he is not satisfied. He tells his wife that he needs two kinds of love: an inviolable and sacred marriage to a woman, and a deathless love with a man. Later novels — *Aaron's Rod* (1922), *Kangaroo* (1923), and *The Plumed Serpent* (1926) — assert this male principle and attempt to place woman into such a male-dominated world, while *Lady Chatterley's Lover* (1928), his last full-length book, renounces such ideas of societal reform and offers, instead, a tender relationship between a man and a woman.

Lawrence's short stories and poems work out the same ideas that he expressed more expansively in his novels and criticism. His earliest stories, such as "Odour of Chrysanthemums," deal with the deathly separation of consciousness between man and woman; they are set in the coal-mining region of Lawrence's youth. Later stories, such as "The Rocking-Horse Winner," dramatize the destructiveness of the money-world. To please a mother who is money-mad the boy in "The Rocking-Horse Winner" subverts his deepest nature and sexuality — he rides a rocking-horse to predict winners at the track until the falseness of his obsession kills him.

Even his latest fables continue to restate the themes developed in his earliest fiction. *The Man Who Died* (1931), one of his last works, has a Christ-figure return from death, not to ascend to heaven but to travel the world in search of a woman who might be his equal. He finally finds Isis, the Egyptian goddess, and mates with her; that is, Christianity and pagan religion merge. Characteristically, however, the conclusion is open-ended: Christ de-

cides to leave under cover of darkness, his wandering unfinished. The ending is apt, for Lawrence died in France, of tuberculosis, still a wanderer and a pilgrim.

Alan R. Davis
Moorhead State University

SOPHIE'S CHOICE

Novel

1979

Author: William Styron

◆ Characters ◆

*S*ophie's Choice focuses on the interrelationships between three characters: Sophie Zawistowska, a Polish Catholic and survivor of Auschwitz; Nathan Landau, her manic-depressive and drug-addicted lover; and Stingo, a young American would-be writer starting out on his career in the Brooklyn of 1947. Stingo overhears the passionate lovemaking between Sophie and Nathan in the room he occupies beneath theirs and becomes fascinated with the mercurial Nathan and the gaunt but sensual Sophie.

Sophie's revelations, carefully spaced throughout the novel, provide its essential plot, while she relies on Stingo as a kind of brother-confessor. The lies she uses to camouflage her participation in many of the past events, which she first presents in a sanitized and romanticized manner, also help support her own fragile equilibrium. In each of her revelations a choice is made or evaded, whether it involves her father's anti-Semitism, her failed attempt to seduce Rudolf Hess at Auschwitz, her participation in the resistance movement in Cracow and Auschwitz, or her various sexual rela-

tionships and strategies. In each of these she reveals the complicated roles she is forced or chooses to play, whether as victim or victimizer.

The tremendous guilt and self-hatred which haunt her, the legacy of her complicity in the Nazi death camp, her betrayal of both herself and her friends, and the shocking "choice" at her arrival in Auschwitz when she must surrender one of her children to the gas chambers, cannot be overcome. She tries to smother such memories in her self-destructive and sexually voracious relationship with Nathan, but his constant goading and accusations about her past and her survival finally take their toll. She has reconstructed a past that parallels the same sexual and suicidal patterns of her present and, thus consumed by guilt and despair, commits suicide.

Nathan is both Sophie's redeemer and destroyer. He rescues her from her bleak and lonely existence in New York but also uses her to satisfy his own sexual needs and play audience to his rampages and role-playing. Sophie's deferral to her father, her husband, the Nazi industrialist Walter Durrfeld, and the Nazi boss at Auschwitz, Rudolf Hess, is therefore repeated yet again in her relationship with Nathan. Nathan's paranoia and drug addiction fuel his many roles from virulent anti-Nazi to romantic seducer, from sexual demon to brilliant biologist, from literary critic to dazzling entertainer. He seduces Stingo as completely as he has seduced Sophie, but he is found out to be clinically mad and schizophrenic. His Jewishness may account for his fascination with the Holocaust and with Sophie's surviving it, but his complete mesmerization of both Sophie and Stingo does seem hard to believe at times. His suicide pact with Sophie completes their tortuous journey of self-discovery together.

Stingo is another of Styron's "innocents." He is morbidly drawn to the death of beautiful women as a theme for his first novel (a theme that fascinated Edgar Allan Poe) and to the possibility of an ultimate sexual encounter. His own point of view resonates with extravagant rhetoric and Gothic forebodings. In the end he thinks that he can rescue Sophie from Nathan, despite his infatuation with her lover, and wrestles with his own guilt about the South's racist past and his mother's horrible death. Slowly his obsession with Sophie develops into a kind of demonic possession, and when at the end of the novel they flee southward, he at last sexually possesses her. What he fails to realize is that Sophie has been doomed from the start, and she flees back to New York to complete the suicide pact with Nathan. Stingo, haunted by dreams and images of sex and death, pursues her and discovers the bodies. He eventually decides that he has matured and awakened as a writer.

The fourth character in the novel is the older Stingo who constantly upbraids his younger self and undercuts his earlier romantic flights of fancy. At the same time he tries to understand the Nazi rise to power and discusses several theories suggested by George Steiner, Richard L. Rubenstein, Hannah Arendt, Simone Weil, and others in his grappling with the constant presence of pure evil in the world and in history. He more or less decides that the master-slave paradigm lies at the heart of western civilization whether in racial slavery or in Jewish obliteration. His soberer thoughts place Stingo's shocks of recognition in a more ironic perspective and leave the problem of evil forever enigmatic and eternally present.

◆ Social Concerns ◆

The Nazi Holocaust in the twentieth century has been so overwhelmingly documented and discussed that it is difficult to grapple with the infernal and lasting effects of so incredible an historical event. For Styron it seems a natural outgrowth of his fascination with the individual self and the systems of domination and destruction that threaten to obliterate him. The ineradicable evil of the Holocaust still haunts western society today, and the shivers of disbelief and horror which still attend it — despite or because of the knowledge and ultimate proof of its happening — continue to occupy the imaginations of writers, survivors, and others.

Styron is also still fascinated with the process of growing up in the more insulated and isolated, at times "innocent" world of the America that he had known. Such isolation can lead to a tragic misunderstanding of the way the western world works. The novel not only explores and exposes the effects of the Holocaust on the Polish survivor,

Sophie Zawistowska, but also on the American outlook of the budding writer Stingo, a semiautobiographical character based on Styron's own youth. Stingo's apprehension of what has happened to Sophie, his recognition of his own complicity in her survival, guilt, and self-destruction, and his burgeoning sense of the violent and tragic dimensions to life lived in the twentieth century parallels in Styron's novel America's own recognition of the tragedy of human life, a knowledge most Americans would just as soon avoid. Stingo's South, Sophie's Poland, and Nathan's New York, where most of the novel takes place in 1947, all share a degree of guilt and complicity with the Holocaust itself.

◆ Themes ◆

The power of history to destroy and annihilate the individual self emerges in *Sophie's Choice*. As a result of Sophie's victimization at the hands of and complicity with the Nazi occupiers of her country, she commits suicide. Nathan Landau, her savior but also her victimizer and executioner, deriding her for her complicity in the Holocaust and at the same time drawn to her beauty and desperate sensuality, commits suicide with her. The novel is strewn with history's victims, a series of deaths from Stingo's mother to Maria Hunt, the doomed woman from his Virginia youth.

In order to survive as she has, Sophie has had to lie, steal, and cooperate with the Nazi authorities. Her very survival is based upon her cooperation with the enemy, and the guilt and terror that remain as the legacy of such involvement necessarily lead to her self-destruction. Sophie is no mere victim of history. She has also participated in it, if only to survive. Such personal complicity complicates her role as victim and adds to the tragic burdens and fate of Styron's novel.

As a product of the sexually repressed American era of the puritanical 1940s, Stingo is obsessed with sex and spends much of his time fantasizing about and plotting to possess Sophie. His own thirst for such a conquest suggests his own "Nazi-like" propensities, the need of the western man to dominate and devalue the woman. Such a master-slave relationship, however sexually expressed, parallels the other relationships in the novel between men and women in Polish, German, and American cultures and reveals an intimate connection between western sexuality, western dominance, and western imperialistic drives.

Styron's assessment of the American avoidance of tragedy and the lessons of history, with America basking in its own post-World-War-II victorious powers and seemingly triumphant optimism, is explored by the narrator, the older Stingo, who looks back on his loss of innocence, his own incredible complicity in the tragic events that have engulfed him, and at the same time tries to explain the seeming inevitability of the Nazi ascendancy. This constant quest in search of the ultimate meaning of Auschwitz propels both the narrator, Styron, and the younger Stingo, but in the end only the fact of evil remains, an enigmatic catastrophe that Americans must constantly try to understand in order never to repeat it. That awareness comes as the culmination in Styron's fiction so far of his persistent need to keep the tragic and horrifying events of history and the individual's complicity with them forever in the forefront of our minds.

Throughout the novel Styron also explores the process of interpretation and understanding and views them as acts of penetration and violation. Such acts infect the use of language as well, so that the interrelationships between sexual conquest, self-destruction, and murder, along with linguistic interpretation, reflect and eerily parallel one another. No one remains innocent. Both Stingos try to possess Sophie whether through interpretation or sexual conquest, and both lose her. Perhaps Styron is trying to suggest that to possess Sophie, sexually and spiritually, is to lose her, just as in trying to possess the ultimate implications about Auschwitz, the best we can possess is the ultimately inexplicable.

◆ Techniques ◆

As usual Styron structures his novel by re-arranging the time sequences within it to provide the most shocking and dramatic events which are gradually revealed and lead up to Sophie's "final choice" concerning the life and death of her children at Auschwitz. The older Stingo recalls the Stingo starting out in 1947. The younger Stingo plays brother-confessor to Sophie's narrative revelations which continually shift and change the closer she gets to the complex truth of her nature and of her way of surviving the Holocaust. Thus the reader must penetrate a nest of narratives beginning with the older Stingo, progressing to the younger, and then leading on to Sophie's revelations. The effect of this sequence of withholding information increases the necessity of its bursting forth, a kind of return of the repressed that, in being repressed, must all the more come forward and be finally expressed as violently and truthfully as possible. Such a consciously dramatic strategy parallels the use of similar patterns in Gothic novels and mysteries.

The elaborate labyrinth of Styron's technique implicates everyone and everything in various power plays and darker mysteries. Sex, death, language, and even Nazism reflect and partake of one another in so carefully orchestrated a structure that they, therefore, like the narratives themselves, seem intimately and inextricably bound up with one another. Styron's narrative techniques clearly implicate the reader in the process of self-discovery as well and intimate at some broader darker design that generates the master-slave patterns of western society of which we are all a part.

◆ Literary Precedents ◆

The second paragraph of Styron's novel mimics the opening of Melville's *Moby Dick* (1851): "Call me Stingo." In doing so Styron points to the confessional character of the novel and of his fiction in general and directs the reader toward a psychic journey and quest that propels so many great American novels such as Faulkner's *Absalom, Absalom!* (1936), Hawthorne's *The Blithedale Romance* (1852), and Fitzgerald's *The Great Gatsby* (1925).

◆ Related Titles ◆

Sophie's Choice distinctly parallels Styron's own journey as a writer. Stingo's fascination with the death of a youthful friend, Maria Hunt, suggests Styron's own when he wrote about the doomed Peyton Loftis in *Lie Down in Darkness* (1951). Similarly Stingo has been able to come to New York with the money from the sale of a slave, Artiste, back in Virginia in his family years ago. His fascination with Artiste and the resulting complicity with the system of slavery suggest Styron's own in writing *The Confessions of Nat Turner* (1967).

◆ Adaptations ◆

Sophie's Choice became a successful film directed by Alan Pakula in 1982. Meryl Streep as the doomed Sophie won an Academy Award in 1983 for Best Actress.

◆ Ideas for Group Discussions ◆

The Holocaust like racial slavery remains a monumental and troubled issue. Some writers have suggested that even trying to write about it only cheapens and "romanticizes" it. Styron's oblique connection with it — he never really takes us into the concentration camps — suggests that he is more interested in the effects of the Holocaust than in actually reproducing and re-creating it. All the characters in the novel are in some way affected by it, and this might be the broadest and deepest issue with which to begin an in-depth discussion about the novel.

1. Is there an unresolvable confrontation between the redemptive conclusions of Styron's novels and the landscape of depression and despair which they create? What do you feel about Stingo's "recovery" at the end of the novel?

2. What do you make of Dr. Jemand von Niemand in *Sophie's Choice*? Styron suggests that he forces the impossible choice on Sophie, to choose which of her children she will save and which she will send to her death, in order to commit such a great sin that his non-belief in God will self-destruct and return him to a sense of religious vision. He will play God in order to restore his own belief in God. What is the role of religion here? In such a place do religious values even matter?

3. Do Styron's characters in *Sophie's Choice* have free will, or are their "choices" predetermined by the historical context within which they find themselves? Could Sophie, for instance, have come from the American South with her values and attitudes? Are the characters so "trapped" in the fate of their cultures and their histories that no choices are really possible at all? Is there one specific choice that you think best represents the title of the novel?

4. Styron compares the American South to Poland. How similar do you think these two realms are? Is he trying to involve each with the other in the way of E. M. Forster's famous advice, "Only connect"? Do you think the connection is made? And if so, what are the results of it?

5. Is the choice that Sophie makes for suicide inevitable?

6. If Styron's view of human nature is so dark and if he believes that evil is forever loose in the world, how can we think of taking any political or social position to better the general lot of humanity? Styron is himself a political liberal and supports many liberal causes. Does this strike you as a contradiction? Or are there instances in *Sophie's Choice* where direct and per-

sonal social action definitely makes a difference?

7. From Styron's assessment of it, do you think the Holocaust is the logical extension of a master-slave vision of domination and submission that exists within the very fabric of western culture? Are there distinct differences here between the Polish, German, and American "outlooks" that would undercut that notion? Does Nazism finally seem the predetermined outgrowth of tendencies in western thought and culture? And if so, what does that bode for the future?

8. Stingo obviously undergoes a personal quest toward knowledge both of the horror in the world and in himself. Can these two be linked in any way? Is his role as a man comparable to Hess and Nathan and others in the novel? And if so, is Sophie's role as a woman "universally" true, or is she a product of her particular historical era? Does the relationship between men and women in this novel seem to be one more example of the master-slave ethos?

9. The novel concludes with Stingo's assertion that "someday I will understand Auschwitz." That is superseded by the older Stingo's idea that "someday I will write about Sophie's life and death, and thereby help to demonstrate how absolute evil is never extinguished from the world." Why is there a distinction made between these two points of view? Does the older Stingo think he knows something that the younger Stingo cannot? And if so, what?

10. Why do you think both Sophie and Stingo are so infatuated with Nathan? How does his role bring about the tragedy of the novel? Or is he more of a catalyst than a participant? Why do you think Styron has made him Jewish? Is Styron making a statement about the historical accuracy of Polish anti-Semitism?

11. Consider some of the other minor characters. What does Leslie Lapidus have to do with the scope and vision of the novel? Why is so much made of her sharp and obscene tongue? Why are there so many deaths from so many different sources in the book? And why is there so much sexual activity and fantasizing going on? Does this connect with the Holocaust in any way? Or is this just Stingo's obsession exacerbated by the mores of 1947?

Samuel Coale
Wheaton College

THE SOT–WEED FACTOR

Novel

1960

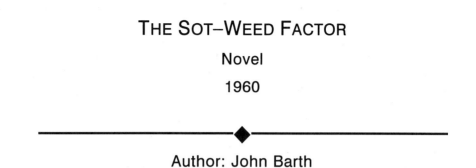

Author: John Barth

◆ **Characters** ◆

Ebenezer Cooke, the protagonist of *The Sot–Weed Factor*, is the son of a Maryland sot–weed factor or tobacco planter, although he is raised as an orphan in England together with his twin sister, Anna. After an education at home supervised by the family's tutor, Henry Burlingame, Ebenezer goes off to Cambridge where his wild imagination and inability to take the world seriously make him an indifferent student at best. Ebenezer's disposition here recalls the problems of Todd Andrews in *The Floating Opera* (1956) and is the source of many of his future difficulties. After Cambridge, Ebenezer embarks on a career as a poet in London. Hopelessly naive, he takes his own innocence and virginity as a sign of his calling, and he obtains a commission as the poet laureate of Maryland before he is sent to the colony to oversee his father's estate. Cooke's career as a poet is historically accurate and significant; there was an historical Ebenezer Cooke who wrote well-known satires upon life in colonial Maryland, including one which shares the title that Barth employs for his own novel, and parts of these poems are included in this narrative.

Cooke and his scheming servant are intercepted by pirates while crossing the Atlantic, and after being taken prisoner they are forced to walk the plank. They swim to shore and make their way to Malden, the site of Cooke's father's estate. Ebenezer, however, loses his estate in a bizarre afternoon of impromptu colonial justice. He regains it with great difficulty, largely with the help of Burlingame, his former tutor, who is embroiled in dark political intrigues in America involving Lord Baltimore, William Penn, the French, and the Indians. These political schemes and Burlingame's myriad disguises are an expression of Barth's concern with the absence of any sure knowledge of the world and with the often obscure effects of any single human action.

Ebenezer's sister, Anna, follows him to America, largely to pursue her passion for Burlingame, and these three are reunited at Malden after Ebenezer reclaims his estate from those who had turned it into a brothel and opium den. Joan Toast, a former London prostitute and Ebenezer's first near–mistress, uses her good graces and legal authority to help him. Although syphilitic and dying, she marries Ebenezer, and it is his consummation of the marriage that allows him to regain legal title to his inheritance. At the end of the narrative, Burlingame disappears into the machinations of colonial political life, and Joan Toast dies along with her infant son. But Anna's son, Andrew, lives, and is raised by Ebenezer and his sister at Malden.

With the publication of his satire upon Maryland, Ebenezer's laureateship is withdrawn, but he is offered it again later in life. However, Ebenezer declines this offer, and dies with little recognition. This mixture of disappointment and good fortune at the end of the novel restates Barth's assertion of the ambivalent effects of almost any human action.

◆ Social Concerns/Themes ◆

The Sot-Weed Factor returns to Barth's earlier exploration of the existentialist notions of action, choice, and value. Whereas his earlier fiction considered these questions in a contemporary context, Barth's third novel introduces an existential perspective into late–seventeenth–century colonial America. Throughout the novel, he suggests that the absence of any absolute order and the necessity of confronting the imperative to act is a persistent human dilemma; in addition, he suggests that early America was a lawless and perilous place, filled with murky political conspiracies and a thorough disregard for any sense of fair play.

Barth is also concerned with the difficulty in establishing a coherent sense of self and the assumptions that underlie any notion of the self. In part, this is accomplished through his use of twins in the novel to suggest opposition and the merging of contraries.

◆ Techniques/Literary Precedents ◆

The Sot-Weed Factor is a flamboyant imitation of an eighteenth-century novel. The narrator adopts the tone and locutions of period narrators, and his descriptions of early colonial life in Maryland and life in London are designed to recall descriptions from the literature of the time. However, the importance of this narrative strategy is twofold and distinctly contemporary: On the one hand, this parodic imitation of an earlier novelistic style draws the reader's attention to the conventional nature of narrative; on the other hand, the density of authentic historical detail suggests to the reader that Barth is recreating a plausible, although wildly humorous, colonial milieu. By exploiting the tension between these competing claims, Barth suggests the absence of any but a fictional order and at the same time the compelling necessity for choice and action as suggested by the realistic aspects of the novel.

One of the most conspicuous features of The Sot-Weed Factor is its immensely complicated plot, and in this respect Barth's novel resembles most closely its eighteenth–century models, particularly the intricate narrative of Henry Fielding's Tom Jones (1749). Another important literary antecedent is the work of Captain John Smith, whose account of the early exploration of Virginia and the Chesapeake area is hilariously parodied in Barth's novel. Consistent with the use of parody throughout The Sot-Weed Factor, this satiric imitation of John Smith's accounts calls into question much of early American history.

The Sot-Weed Factor continues the existential themes of Barth's first two novels. In its concern with value and action, it recalls the dilemma of Todd Andrews in *The Floating Opera*. In its preoccupation with the construction of individual identity and spiritual paralysis, however, *The Sot-Weed Factor* is a sequel to *The End of the Road* (1958). Since, in fact, Barth has described these three novels as a "nihilistic trilogy," they might well be read as complementary texts. In its treatment of the quest of an innocent figure, *The Sot-Weed Factor* also looks forward to the adventures of George in *Giles Goat-Boy* (1966) and ultimately to Barth's preoccupation with myth, found in much of his later writing. Descendants of the Burlingame-Cooke connection also return in *LETTERS* (1979) to continue their shady and equally inconclusive intrigues.

◆ Ideas for Group Discussions ◆

1. Does this novel express or imply a yearning for the past? What are some of the crucial similarities and differences between the America of Cooke's time and the America of ours?

2. What does Cooke's life story suggest about the desirability of innocence?

3. Are there any real people in the world like the character Henry Burlingame? Does this fictional portrait seem intended to teach us something about human nature? Is it exaggerated in order to point up important themes in the work? Is it designed for maximum comic effect?

4. What is likely to be the average reader's response to the sexual behavior of these characters? Can one generalize about the presentation of sexual matters in *The Sot-Weed Factor*? Are the more outrageous scenes mainly humorous? Disgusting? Thematically significant?

5. What does this novel imply about the nature and roles of women in late seventeenth and early eighteenth century British and American society? What does it imply about the nature and roles of women today?

Thomas Carmichael
University of Western Ontario
[Ideas for Group Discussions by Ron Smith,
St. Christopher's School]

SOUTH MOON UNDER

Novel

1933

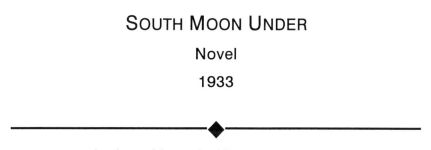

Author: Marjorie Kinnan Rawlings

◆ Characters ◆

Prior to starting *South Moon Under*, Rawlings lived in the Ocala Scrub for two and a half months, with an elderly woman named Piety Fiddia and her moonshining son, Leonard. The chief characters in the novel, Piety Lantry and her son Lant Jacklin, are very closely modeled on their real-life counterparts. Rawlings had not only helped Piety with her daily chores, but had joined Leonard in illegal deer hunting, in shooting and eating a limpkin ("if you haven't eaten roast limpkin, you just haven't eaten, but you can go to county, state and federal jails for shooting them" she wrote), and in running his moonshine still. Although not all of the other characters are as closely modeled after specific prototypes, they are very much drawn from various people Rawlings knew. One of Rawlings's chief stated goals in her Florida writings was to show her readers what sort of people the crackers really were — not grubby bumpkins or idealized woodsmen — but people confronting a beautiful but demanding environment with remarkable courage and good will.

◆ Social Concerns ◆

Rawlings had come to know and greatly admire the Florida "crackers" who inhabited the great scrub country of northern Florida — the area roughly identical with the present Ocala National Forest. In *South Moon Under* as much as any of her writing, Rawlings tried to show these people as they really were. She saw them as honest, living close to their environment and surviving often by the thinnest of margins, but with a remarkably resilient and positive outlook on life. Although some of her earlier tales of crackers had brought a protest from the editor of the Ocala newspaper that such people had never existed, it is clear that she had simply paid more attention to his region than he had; her works are now accepted as very accurate pictures of the time and place, and have served as documentary evidence for scholarly studies on cracker dialect and folklore.

Rawlings was struck by the fact that the inhabitants of the scrub were candid, trustworthy people, but nevertheless, as she wrote in a letter to her editor Maxwell Perkins, "almost everything they do is illegal. And everything they do is necessary to sustain life in that place." Certainly one of the implied thematic fulcrums of the novel is the distinction between what is legal (defined by society outside the scrub) and what is right (as determined by those who live in the scrub).

♦ Themes ♦

Although Rawlings's chief motive in writing *South Moon Under* seems to have been to show what the scrub crackers were like, and especially to celebrate the qualities for which she deeply admired them, and a secondary motive may well have been to depict the landscape itself, she was after all writing a novel, not a travelogue. The title *South Moon Under* suggests what is the most carefully and explicitly articulated theme of the book. As one of the characters explains, south-moon-under is one of the four daily cardinal positions of the moon. Deer tend to feed or sleep, readers are told, in harmony with the lunar movements. If animals are controlled by forces they cannot understand or influence or even be aware of, so too it may be with men. As the character Lantry says, "You got the say so fur, and then you got no say at all." At the climax of the novel (which occurs at south-moon-under) the protagonist, Lantry's grandson Lant (who was born under a full moon), thinks, "Forces beyond his control, beyond his sight and hearing, took him in their vast senseless hands when they were ready. The whole earth must move as the sun and moon and an obscure law directed — even the earth, planet-ridden and tormented." Rawlings's characters do what they do because of where they live, because of ancestral fears, and because of nameless, unknown urgings symbolized by the moon.

♦ Techniques ♦

The novel, following chronological order, embraces three generations of a family. Lantry comes to Florida from outside, establishes himself without ever really becoming a part of the land or the people, and dies fairly early in the novel, leaving to his descendants his name and his nameless fear. His daughter Piety and her son Lant are the two major figures in the book, which encompasses Piety's entire life but ends with Lant still a young man. The story takes place entirely in or very near the Big Scrub; character, plot and theme are all intimately bound up with the setting. The setting is shown in considerable, very accurate detail and is so unusual as to seem attractively exotic.

Rawlings took great pains to have her characters act and speak like the real inhabitants of the Big Scrub; as mentioned above, she lived with the prototypes of her main characters, and she took copious notes on them and their way of life. The dialect (although much of it is "eye-dialect": "ketch" for catch) is quite accurate and was one of the more striking and controversial features when the book was first published.

Certainly then, in *South Moon Under* as in all of Rawlings's important work, the setting — the place and its people — is paramount. Rawlings is thus unquestionably a regional writer — as a rule, the less connection a given piece of her work has with that part of north central Florida she came to know intimately and love, the less successful it is.

◆ Literary Precedents ◆

In her depiction of Florida as a "frontier eden," Rawlings has been compared by Gordon Bigelow to James Fenimore Cooper, with Lant Jacklin (among other Rawlings characters) resembling Cooper's Natty Bumppo — tough, honorable, little educated, self-reliant, a woodsman. Although her style is a bit uneven in *South Moon Under*, it probably owes something (as does the style of so many twentieth-century writers) to Hemingway.

In its central deterministic theme, as well as its carefully recorded details of the life of some of the least affluent members of society, *South Moon Under* seems squarely in the tradition of literary Naturalists — Zola and more immediately Frank Norris and Theodore Dreiser. Where Rawlings differs is in depicting things less grittily and in always giving her characters the courage, the strength, the skill, the cheerfulness, to confront their world gracefully.

◆ Related Titles ◆

All of Rawlings's Florida writings, which include all of her important works, are related in one way or another, most obviously in her careful and loving depiction of the land and people of north central Florida. These include *The Yearling* (1938) and *Cross Creek* (1942), the short stories "Gal Young Un," "Jacobs Ladder," and "Cocks Must Crow," and even the cookbook *Cross Creek Cookery* (1947).

C. Herbert Gilliland
U.S. Naval Academy

SPARTACUS

Novel

1951

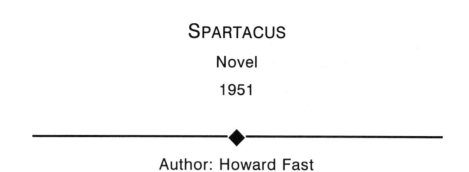

Author: Howard Fast

◆ Social Concerns ◆

Written when Fast was a victim of the blacklist and America itself in the grips of what David Caute has called the "Great Fear" of McCarthyism and the Cold War, this historical elegy uses Roman history to reflect contemporary social concerns. As in all his historical writing, Fast explores the contradiction between republican ideals and repressive institutions, using the Servile Wars, the uprising of Spartacus, his gladiators, and their slave followers against their Roman overlords, as a model for resistance to oppression throughout history.

The sight of over six thousand slaves crucified along the Appian Way becomes a motif for human suffering in the struggle for freedom, and as the author's epilogue to the self-published first edition: "It is a story of brave men and women who lived long ago, and whose names have never been forgotten. The heroes of this story cherished freedom and human dignity, and lived nobly and well. I wrote it so that those who read it, my children and others, may take strength for our own troubled future and that they may struggle against oppression and wrong — so

that the dream of Spartacus may come to be in our own time."

The slavery which is the dominant concern is the result not only of subjugating conquered countries, but also of a society's victimization of its own people. Roman freeholders and small farmers, evicted from their lands, are sold to make way for a plantation system peopled not by citizens, but by masters and slaves. Positive action and commitment to communal goals are necessary to defend individual liberty and pursue freedom, as Spartacus and his band of gladiators evolve — from killers pitted against one another for their owners' pleasure — to brothers acting together as an historical force and with a sense of their own destiny.

On the other hand, a corrupt and dehumanized Roman upper class, made callous and frivolous by privilege and power, regards others not as humans but as tools, a metaphor for a developed world and a ruling class impervious to the humanity and aspirations of others. Although seemingly omnipotent, this group plants the seeds for its own downfall, exhibiting a cultural death wish which makes it fascinated with crucifixions and gladiatorial combat and unable to understand human yearnings for affirmation. Winning the battle through sheer technological and state power, the Romans have clearly lost the war by sacrificing their own humanity.

◆ Themes ◆

The parallel between imperialistic technological cultures, Rome and America, is apparent in *Spartacus*. Resisting oppression and committing oneself to action for others, even self-sacrifice, is diametrically opposed to the self-centered, solipsistic Roman attitudes. Against the Roman slave system, rebellion brings not only unity, but also equality between people, races, and even sexes. Spartacus's gladiators, dispossessed from all corners of the Empire: Thracians, Jews, Gauls, Egyptians, Spaniards, and black Ethiopians, work together equally, women alongside the men.

The promise of redemption and transformation exists not only for groups but also for individuals, illustrating the primacy of individual responsibility, moral revelation through action, and people's capacity for change. Not only the embittered, alienated gladiators but also some Romans are transformed by the example of loving sacrifice and human endurance. The decrepit, fat, corrupt politician Gracchus, recognizing the moral superiority of Spartacus and Varinia and the bankruptcy of his own life and the system he serves, frees Varinia, the rest of his slaves, and taking his own life, liberates himself from a corrupt society which demands total submission from Romans and slaves alike.

Another of Fast's themes is the relationship of present events to the future. The final outcome of the slave rebellion, put down with great cruelty, will not be apparent until the future, as the community of resistance is solidified through the example of Spartacus and his band and the Roman system rendered even more bankrupt. In history, the human spirit will endure and ultimately prevail, as the descendants of Spartacus and Varinia continue their resistance among peasant villagers in the Alps. The themes of martyrdom, rebellion, conflict between opposing historical forces, and continuing human struggle against oppression help transmute social concerns into archetypal themes recurrent throughout all history.

◆ Characters ◆

Spartacus, the Thracian slave whose personal commitment and charisma unifies and leads the rebellion, is a prototype of the leader-martyr whose example illustrates humanity's timeless yearning for freedom. Varinia, his female counterpart, matches him in heroism and strength of commitment. Compared to Christ in his emphasis on love and brotherhood, his power to secure belief and renew hope, his suffering and death, Spartacus also demonstrates a childlike pure-heartedness and innocence. His personal warmth, loyalty, and patience are reflected in his rebellion, undertaken in the name of love rather than hatred or revenge. The qualities Spartacus and his slave followers exhibit are those of common humanity itself in its persistence and endurance in struggle. Although Spartacus is a leader, he is not the traditional "great man." The protagonists of *Spartacus* are the people themselves, shaping history in their persistent movement toward a more meaningful existence.

The slaves' antagonists are represented by the shallow, effete, mean-spirited young nobleman Caius and the class he represents. Unlike Spartacus, Caius is a twisted, small-minded neurotic, with no real role in history and no real purpose in his life at all, except to live in an unconscious, self-indulgent way upon the spoils of the slave system and Roman might. Instead of the tender sexuality and true affection between Spartacus and Varinia and the frank brotherhood between Spartacus and his comrades, human relations among the Romans are marked by distortion (Caius is a homosexual), betrayal, and contempt for others. Cicero, who observes the proceedings, is a principal spokesperson for repressive Roman ideology, a political "new man," amoral, opportunistic, cold, and hollow, not unlike those Fast observed on the prosecutorial bench during the McCarthy hearings.

◆ Techniques ◆

Fast's historical novels are always parables in which historical meaning is invoked by dramatizing moments in history which have special significance, recurring in a spiral which leads to some teleological or transcendent goal. The conflict of opposing forces and synthesis pointing to the future in *Spartacus* shows how an historical writer may unite narrative technique with historical theme, using action to create meaning. Character is the result of confrontation and choice, as individuals are moved to action which changes or forwards history, illustrating the innate goodness and capacity for positive change fundamental to the human personality or, on the other hand, the

capacity of repressive institutions to resist change and the future. In Fast, meaning is always the result of observable action, never simply passive subjectivity of observation, as Fast uses his talent for the story, for dramatic narrative, as a means of creating development.

The plotting of *Spartacus* ironically juxtaposes Roman speakers' own views of the events and the reader's impression. Since history is always the view of the victors, neither Spartacus or any of the gladiators ever speaks himself, as the entire story is told from the perspective of Romans involved in putting down the rebellion, as they observe the "tokens of punishment," the crucified slaves, during a holiday excursion to the seacoast. Narrative irony is accomplished chiefly in the character of Batiatus, the repulsive, morally bankrupt gladiatorial promoter in whose arena the rebellion began, and Crassus, the Roman general who put down the rebellion. These characters seek to explain how the rebellion began and what caused it. Conflicting narrative perspectives and different ways listeners comprehend or do not comprehend character and motivation are key ironic points.

In addition, Fast's mixture of violent action and intense feeling to shock and move the reader contributes to his narrative success. Some of his descriptive settings, such as the Nubian gold mine from which Spartacus comes, the gladiatorial combats and the crucifixions themselves, are justly famous. He is able to portray the feelings and aspirations of large groups and movements through panoramic description of material culture, settings and milieus, using objective reality to create historical meaning.

◆ Literary Precedents ◆

The tale of Spartacus has long played a role in popular culture; "Spartacus' Last Address to His Men" was a forensic recitation heard at many a high school declamation. In fiction, the narrative as parable and history as a moral tale was frequent in popular writing, as evident in the works of B. Traven, a radical writer who, like Fast, wrote parables which became block-buster entertainments, like *Treasure of the Sierra Madre,* a successful film in 1948. Bertolt Brecht, another defendant at the McCarthy trials, used parables for dramatic purposes, as did Arthur Miller, whose *Crucible* (1953) uses American sources to comment upon the trials. Classical historical settings had been popularized by Edith Hamilton in her books on mythology, and by Robert Graves, in *I, Claudius* (1934).

Roman themes were taken as commentaries upon the decline of Western civilization before the fascist onslaught, and many continental writers created parallels between mid-century political upheavals and ancient precedents. Rome became a metaphor for Western democratic culture. Anti-Fascist writers such as Feuchtwanger, in *Der falsehe Nero,* (translated title is *The Pretender,* 1936), mined the Roman matter for political purposes, and Lukacs speaks of a popular literature illustrating people's yearning for liberty in positive characters as part of the struggle against fascism, currents in progressive literary criticism which Fast echoes in *Literature and Reality,* published in 1950.

◆ Related Titles ◆

Spartacus brings together concerns

which had marked Fast's historical writing from the beginning. Both *The Last Frontier* (1941) and *Freedom Road* (1944) share the theme of slavery or subjugation, and the struggle against oppression in a Jewish context appears in *My Glorious Brothers* (1948). The crucifixion of a Jewish gladiator named David, one of Spartacus' most devoted companions, is depicted in great detail in one of the novel's most striking scenes. The shape-up of slaves at the gold mine and their lives in the galleys recurs in cyclical fashion as longshoremen line up on the Embarcadero and Dan Lavette's ships go down with all hands.

◆ Adaptations ◆

Spartacus filled the bill for an epic spectacular with thoughtful overtones, and in 1960 became a phenomenally successful film, with a screenplay written by Fast and Dalton Trumbo, produced by Kirk Douglas, who played Spartacus, and directed by Stanley Kubrick. The star-studded cast included Laurence Olivier, Jean Simmons, Charles Laughton, and Peter Ustinov, who won an Academy Award for his portrayal of the repellant gladiatorial manager Batiatus, Spartacus' owner. The violence, romance, and spectacle of the action fulfilled a taste for heroic good guys and vile villains, perhaps filling as well a national need to atone for McCarthyist excesses. However, it seems that much of Fast's historical "message" may have been lost in the spectacle.

Janet Polansky
University of Wisconsin-Stout

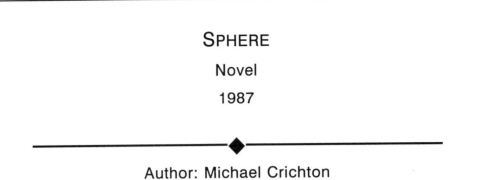

SPHERE

Novel

1987

◆

Author: Michael Crichton

◆ Social Concerns ◆

Two levels of social concerns are depicted in *Sphere*. At the core of the novel's plot is the question of how to approach an artifact of unknown origin that may have come from another planet. Crichton develops the various conflicts — military versus scientific interests, and cultural versus humanitarian ideals — that surround this issue. The struggle to protect individual rights comes up against the desire of special interest groups to psychologically manipulate individuals for their own ends. At stake is the future of the human race. During the debate over these matters, other, more basic social concerns surface, leading to questions about race relations and sexual discrimination. These conflicts are acted out in the backgrounds, attitudes, and actions of Harry Adams and Beth Halpern as they respond to the other members of the investigative team and to developing events.

◆ Themes ◆

The novel's many themes are psychologically interrelated. Besides examining the power of the mind to create reality (which has a literary correspondence as well), Crichton explores the possible application of Jungian psychology to group dynamics, especially as represented in the release of man's dark inner side. Crichton explores the theme that humankind is its own worst enemy, carrying the seeds of its destruction. The divisions within society (professional, racial, sexual) that block humankind's ability to function efficiently and effectively for its own good, the identification of the distinguishing characteristic in defining a human being as the imagination, the failure of the discipline of psychology to produce accurate guidelines for analyzing individuals, and the existentialist emphasis on human choice — all revolve around and reinforce one another throughout the course of *Sphere*.

Ultimately, it is implied by Beth's contrivance at the end of the book that all of these systems, procedures, philosophies, and cultural components can be undermined by one willful individual who places self-interest above everything else. Whereas in *The Andromeda Strain* Crichton celebrated the ideal of scientific teamwork, here he implies that when a group of individuals is incapable of operating as a team, all is lost.

◆ Characters ◆

A typical Crichton novel, *Sphere* is filled with a number of minor characters who are portrayed with a few deft touches that make them identifiable. However, these characters appear only briefly and remain undeveloped. Others, such as Hal Barnes, Alice Fletcher, Tina Chan, Jane Edmunds, and Rose Levy, become personalities, although they primarily function as character types.

Five characters are represented with enough depth to take on the semblance of real people: Ted Fielding, Harry Adams, Beth Halpern, Norman Johnson, and Jerry. Fielding, a forty-year-old astrophysicist at the Jet Propulsion Laboratory is inquisitive and vulnerable. In spite of his profession he functions on an openly emotional level and serves as a contrast to the seemingly more intellectual characters. Adams, a Princeton mathematician, is a black man whose exposure to racial bias has traumatized him so deeply that a reverse prejudice colors his perceptions and is the underlying motivation of all that he does. Thirty-six-year-old zoologist Halpern is Adams's female counterpart; her status as a victim of sexual discrimination has affected her similarly. In a sense society has created these damaged characters, and it seems almost apropos that they are the source of the destruction of their society, whether it is the temporary collection of people on the mission or, as suggested by Beth's actions at the close of the novel, the culture of the entire planet Earth.

The protagonist in *Sphere* — Johnson, the fifty-three-year-old professor of psychology from the University of California at San Diego — is also a father figure. Because he has insight but is limited in his knowledge, the reader attains understanding at the same rate that he does. A humanist, his insufficiencies partially blind him to reality and prevent him from saving humanity. The final character is an amalgam. "Jerry" existentially becomes the essence of whomever enters the sphere; its identity is a power — and the possessor of the power has the capacity to control reality and consequently the world.

◆ Techniques ◆

As in his other novels, in *Sphere* Crichton relies heavily on visual images, myriads of specific details, and scientific facts to provide a backdrop for constant action. To generate suspense he places a personable, intelligent, and competent main character in a deadly situation. Technical details (for example, the elaborate description and explanation of the habitat design) are juxtaposed with the excitement of personal, physical danger and the unknown. However, at times the reader is overburdened with unnatural sounding dialogue that provides too much information, such as naming all of the islands in sight or supplying both the common and the scientific names of shrimp and squid. As in his other works, although, Crichton is generally successful in his application of the formula developed in *The Andromeda Strain* (1969). One major technical innovation in *Sphere* is Crichton's plot twist, whereby appearance becomes reality and his characters' worst nightmares are realized.

The most obvious literary precursor for *Sphere* is Jules Verne's 1870 novel *Twenty Thousand Leagues Under the Sea*, not only in the setting but also in the battle with a giant squid. Peter Benchley's *Jaws* (1974) and *The Deep* (1976), along with innumerable science fiction tales of encounters with aliens and explorations of strange worlds, such as Arthur C. Clarke's tale of underwater life in the future, *The Deep Range* (1957), as well as those concerning time travel, the transformation of something imagined into something real, and mind over matter, might be cited too. There is an echo of George Orwell's *1984* (1949) in the concept that terror is peculiar to each individual and derives its full power from the individual's mind.

The close reader can also find parallels with Alfred Bester's *The Demolished Man* (1953) and *The Stars My Destinations* (1957) or with Robert Louis Stevenson's *The Strange Case of Dr. Jekyll and Mr. Hyde* (1886), particularly in relation to the creative power of the human mind and the release of man's dark inner side in a physical manifestation.

Crichton's personal experience often figures prominently in his storytelling. In *Travels* (1988) he relates some of his adventures during his travels around the world. The influence of several of the images conjured up by these experiences is evident in *Sphere*. Crichton is a scuba diver, for example, a fact that is evident in his descriptions of the underwater excursions and the unseen yet menacing presence of sharks in the travel volume. In the novel he comments on the difference between a fearful reaction to imaginary beasts and a blissful lack of awareness of their actual presence. In *Travels* he tells, too, of an encounter with an elephant in the African bush; the description of the elephant's eye peering through the window of his hut is remarkably similar to the depiction in the novel of the giant squid's eye as seen through the habitat's porthole.

◆ Related Titles ◆

Sphere is clearly related to Crichton's previous novels in style, plot structure, and handling of character. Stylistically, his works tend to be fairly straightforward and relatively simple, although cinematic in nature, that is, visual and full of action. The plot structure is similar throughout his fiction, and there are explicit parallels between *Sphere* and *The Andromeda Strain*. In both a scientific team is brought together by the military to deal with a life-threatening problem that may have originated in outer space. Furthermore, the patterns of bringing the characters together, the presentation of the problem, the approach to solving the problem, and the interactions of the characters within the context of the plot, are essentially the same. Style and plot come together in the semidocumentary devices of identifying locales, time settings, and major events through typographical techniques or division of the book into sections, titled chapters, and so forth. Lastly, while the numerous other characters are identifiably drawn, only the protagonist's character is fully developed.

Steven H. Gale
Kentucky State University

THE SPIRE

Novel

1964

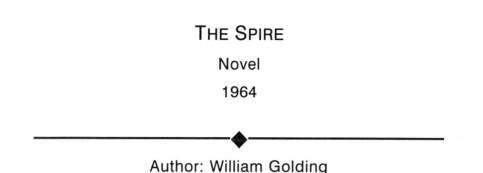

Author: William Golding

◆ Social Concerns/Themes ◆

Golding once declared himself "by nature an optimist, by observation and deduction a pessimist," and while much of his work concentrates on the blackness in man's soul, in *The Spire* he presents a more holistic view. In fact, *The Spire* affords Golding's clearest statement of the theme that man is a synthesis of good and evil. The impulses behind the building of the spire in the novel are both religious vision and personal pride; the drive to complete it is both admirable and repulsive; the finished edifice raises men's minds to God, but the human price paid reduces men to their basest natures. In this novel, man is an example of the unity that can exist in paradox. Because it acknowledges the simultaneous existence of good and evil in man, *The Spire* is Golding's most affirmative work.

Another important theme in this novel is self-knowledge. Jocelin, like every person, can come to self-awareness only by acknowledging both good and evil impulses within. Jocelin is blind to his true self as the spire is rising. But through a series of confrontations with characters he has exploited, or ironically been exploited by, he learns about himself and, by extension, others.

◆ Characters ◆

Dean Jocelin is the human force behind the building of the spire. He is a study in contradictions, and as such he reflects the theme. The idea of building the spire comes to him in a vision, so he believes he has been chosen to do God's work. But soon, religious fervor is replaced by pride and will as Jocelin exploits all those around him to achieve his aims. He simply shuts out from his awareness the damage he is doing, until in the end of the novel, he is forced to see the evil in himself.

Roger Mason, the master builder, is the representative of reason which opposes Jocelin's spiritual impetus. He calculates that the foundations are not adequate for the spire but is overruled and overrun by Jocelin.

Pangall and his wife Goody are two other victims of Jocelin's monomania. Their fate and that of the master builder demonstrates the degree of corruption that is part and parcel of raising the spire.

◆ Techniques ◆

Golding's most distinctive technique in this novel is linking symbols to develop his themes. Throughout the novel the spire represents the idealism or vision that enables man to do what seemingly cannot be done. The spire stands despite inadequate foundations and lifts men's hearts and minds. But opposing the spire is what Golding terms the cellarage, a pit dug at the center of the nave. It represents the evil that was also necessary to build the spire — the murders and exploitation. The apple tree, with its associations with the Fall, is an apt symbol for the nature of man.

Linking these three symbols, particularly at Jocelin's moment of self-awareness, Golding reiterates the theme of the simultaneous existence of opposites in man. When Jocelin on his deathbed sees the spire through his window, he says, "It's like the apple tree!" "It" can be both man and the spire. Root and blossom, cellarage and spire, evil and highest aspiration, the opposites are inseparable in tree, tower, and man.

◆ Literary Precedents ◆

Bernard S. Oldsey and Stanley Weintraub, in *The Art of William Golding* have posited two literary precedents for *The Spire*. T. S. Eliot's play *The Rock* (1934) and Henrik Ibsen's play *The Master Builder* (1892) both concern church-building. Both Eliot and Golding point out that the cost of creating the visible structure that reminds man of an invisible power can be extremely high. *The Spire* is similar to Ibsen's play in its exploration of physical and spiritual obsessions, and in its examination of the way characters see completion of the structure as expiation for the sins involved in building it.

◆ Related Titles ◆

Several other novels in Golding's canon deal with the theme of self-knowledge and the imposing of one's own will. In *Pincher Martin* (1956), the dead seaman pits his will against God's, refusing to give up. He learns that his will is no match. Sammy Mountjoy, in *Free Fall* (1959), looks back on his life to see where he lost his freedom. He finds that it was the moment he imposed his will on another and ruined her life. Like Sammy, Oliver, the protagonist in *The Pyramid* (1967), learns about himself in the course of the novel; but where Sammy wishes to overcome his dark side, Oliver is willing to live with it because the price to change is too great. An enigmatic combination of Sammy and Oliver, Edmund Talbot in *Rites of Passage* (1980) recognizes his failings and his role in another man's demise, but critics debate the degree of change that may result.

Rebecca Kelly
Southern College of Technology

SPRING MOON

Novel

1981

Author: Bette Bao Lord

◆ Characters ◆

Among the strengths of *Spring Moon* are the incredibly distinctive men and women who animate its pages and whose lives embroider the rich tapestry of the novel. Embodied in the Chang family and in its servants and friends are the people of twentieth-century China, the architects and victims of a changing culture. Lord has created incisively drawn, unsentimental yet sympathetic portraits: the elderly clan patriarch; the devoted Golden Virtue who retreats into total seclusion at the death of her husband; the gentle armchair revolutionary Bold Talent and Noble Talent, his soldier brother; the loyal family retainers; the idealistic young couple who endure the Long March with Mao Zedong; the shrewd August Winds — poor relation turned businessman — who can prosper in any political climate through his judicious use of bribery; the desperate slave girl who chooses death rather than becoming an elderly scholar's concubine. Each of these characters is so fully realized, so thoroughly human, so appealingly portrayed that even in the ideological conflicts between them the reader is often unable to decide who is right and who is wrong.

At the center of the novel, providing the narrative with its major thread, is its title character, a woman in whom the public forces of history and the private life of an individual become intertwined. Spring Moon, an intriguing addition to the growing ranks of strongly-realized literary heroines, is both the embodiment of traditional Chinese female virtue and a representative of Chinese womanhood in transition. During Spring Moon's long and eventful life, she watches as her world is destroyed, but she remains apolitical, committed only to the old ways, yielding and enduring while many of those whose lives intersect with hers are ruined by their confrontations with the implacable forces of change. Her two children become symbols of the new Chinese: Lustrous Jade, the humorless party member and teacher of the masses, who is eventually driven to suicide by the betrayal of her beloved Party; and Enduring Promise, the expatriate who prospers in his new life in exile in America. Strengthened by a prophecy made at her birth, that she will live to see five generations of Changs gathered together, Spring Moon endures until the prophecy is fulfilled when Enduring Promise, visiting China on official business for the American government, helps her to gather the scattered family members together at the ancestral graveyard.

◆ Social Concerns ◆

As one might expect from a novel based on the collapse of the Chinese feudal system and the subsequent Communist takeover, *Spring Moon* successfully presents the inevitable clash between two value systems, in this case the old Confucian ideals symbolized by the ancient philosophy of yielding and the modern ideals born of Western thought and communism and epitomized by confrontation. As an aid to the average reader (who is more likely than not to have little knowledge of Chinese history) Bette Bao Lord provides in an appendix a useful chronology of significant events in China from around 1990 B.C. to A.D. 1981.

Through the drama of the rising and falling fortunes of the House of Chang, a mandarin clan of landowning scholars, Lord chronicles the crucial period of the evolution of China through the long chaotic years of political turmoil and social unrest, beginning with the dissolution of the Manchu Empire and the unsuccessful revolutionary attempts to found a Chinese republic, through the two wars with the Japanese, to the Kuomintang's doomed struggle with the Communist forces. The author is particularly adept as delineating the problems encountered by Western-educated Chinese who, in their attempts to reconcile their traditional Chinese upbringing with their training (often in America), discover that not only has their education destroyed in them the ability to bend and

yield to circumstances and thus to endure, but they also are beset with inner contradictions and confusions. A particularly noteworthy element of *Spring Moon* is the diversity of political orientations displayed by its several protagonists, all in some way connected with the House of Chang, either by blood or by the ancient ties of loyalty. In the inevitable ideological conflicts — between mother and daughter, uncle and nephew, ward and protector, aristocrat and peasant, young and old — Lord creates a compelling portrait of an evolving society that by its changing threatens the very stability of its most basic unit — the family — which has long been responsible for its strength.

In this account of the violent demise of the ancient Chinese feudal society, many of the key players are forced to question their roles in the unstable emerging social order. Raised and educated within a familial structure — one that recognized patriarchal authority as supreme, that acknowledged the importance of good women even while relegating them to the inner courts to do needlework and gossip, that regularly observed filial rituals honoring long-dead ancestors — these traditional Chinese are suddenly thrust into a society built upon the needs of the masses, a society that advocates the education and military training of women, that raises to prominence the unlettered scions of peasant families, that recognizes no authority save that of the state and its appointed leaders, that denigrates family ties and reverence for ancestors and substitutes only loyalties to political ideologies.

These crucial dichotomies are reiterated in the "Author's Afterword" that ends the novel. Speaking of the trip to China that inspired her to write *Spring*

Moon, Lord remarks that her long absence and her maturity enabled her to experience her homecoming from dual perspectives, ". . . as mother and daughter, as Chinese and American, as younger and elder, as one person and a member of a clan . . ." In these dualities are outlined the social conflicts that inform Lord's book, that provide its universality and timelessness, that appeal to readers of different cultures.

◆ Themes ◆

Clearly the clash between the old way of life and the new is the dominant theme of *Spring Moon*. At the heart of the conflict is the ancient patriarchal way of life that takes its cues from the Confucian ideals of filial piety, humility and submissiveness in women, the pursuit of knowledge for its own sake, the virtue of yielding gracefully rather than breaking, the importance of preserving the family's good name at whatever cost to its individual members. Spring Moon, the central character, who has grown up sheltered and pampered in the richly appointed Chang courts, epitomizes the old China. Although educated like a man by a doting uncle, she nevertheless subscribes wholeheartedly to the tenets of Confucian conformity and to the importance of upholding familial honor even at the expense of personal needs and desires. In one of the most compelling ironies of the novel, Lustrous Jade, Spring Moon's only daughter, represents new China with its spirit of confrontation and revolution. Trained by Western missionaries who have instilled in her an idealism at odds with her practical Chinese heritage, Lustrous Jade enthusiastically embraces the doctrines of communism in her

belief that it offers the solution to China's social and political problems. The most painful rift in the novel — and certainly the most emblematic of its theme — is that between Spring Moon and Lustrous Jade, between mother and daughter, between old and new.

Related to and illuminating the novel's most pervasive theme are a number of secondary concerns: the toll taken by the revolution on China's scholarly class, the importance of a sense of honor, the many forms of loyalty and obligation, nostalgia for a vanished way of life. At the end when the ninety-year-old Spring Moon is discovered (by her illegitimate son who believes he is her brother) living forgotten in a hovel where the old Chang compound once stood, she is still the indomitable woman whose life story forms the framework of the novel; and when she gathers the scattered members of the clan together at the ancestral graveyard to honor their departed kin, it is clear that the old Chinese ways are not dead — they have yielded with the changing times, altered in form perhaps, but they have survived.

◆ Techniques ◆

Lord has recreated the feeling of the traditional Chinese novel through her understated style, by her use of poetic titles for each section, and by her incorporation of clan tales and passages from Chinese history or poetry as introductions to the chapters. Spanning eight decades and five generations of the House of Chang, the novel is built on the framework of Spring Moon's life from her pampered girlhood to her anonymous and impoverished old age.

Another technique that imbues the

novel with its strongly Chinese ambiance is Lord's use of symbols to tie together the multiple strands of her narrative. One example — the game of chess — should illustrate. The Chang chess set, bestowed on the founding ancestor by a grateful emperor, first appears as Bold Talent is packing his possessions to leave Yale and return to China to succeed his dead father as clan patriarch. As events conspire to make life difficult for the Changs, the chess set — safe in its cloisonné box — serves as a constant reminder to Bold Talent of his father's words, ". . . do not become too enamored of the process; remember the goal," words which he hears in his head later as he is dying from an assassin's bullet, having participated only in the process leading to his goal of a unified China. Ultimately, the set is buried in the ancestral courtyards, never to be reclaimed, even by the gathered clan members at the end. For Spring Moon, the game of chess has special significance: when her husband leaves to join the revolution he says farewell to her by setting up their chess set and moving his soldier into battle. He never returns, and thereafter, Spring Moon treasures the ivory soldier along with his Yale ring as reminders of a life past.

Readers who devour historical novels for their lurid depictions of love and death will discover in *Spring Moon* an elegiac restraint instead. Certainly there is simple material for sensationalism, but Lord never ruins her story by succumbing to the popular taste for sex and gore. When Spring Moon's slave girl hangs herself, the tragic deed is recorded with concentrated economy in two sentences. Only hinted at are Bold Talent's covert machinations to save Spring Moon from an unwanted marriage. Even more restrained is the revelation of the incestuous affair between Bold Talent and Spring Moon — uncle and niece — a relationship poetically outlined with distance and reticence, evoking compassion for two people, fated by circumstances and their strong sense of honor to give up the one happiness they have left in a life already marred by loss and separation.

◆ Literary Precedents ◆

A novel chronicling the fortunes of a Chinese family inevitably invites comparison with Pearl Buck's *The Good Earth* (1931); and to the extent that Lord's novel deals with generational conflict and relationships, the two books are similar. They differ in that Buck's characters are peasants whose troubles are mainly brought on by natural catastrophes, whereas Lord depicts aristocrats displaced by social cataclysm.

There are echoes also of Chinese writer Pa Chin who, in the 1930s, wrote of the demise of the patriarchal Chinese family system along with the Confucian ideals on which that system had been built. Unlike Pa Chin, however, whose chronicles of the end of an era reveal a deep-rooted disapproval of the old ways, Lord is more ambivalent in her sympathetic portrayal of the two ways of life, and of the very human characters caught in the conflict. Underlying *Spring Moon* is an unvoiced lament for the old gracious way of life, nostalgia made bittersweet by the novel's unvarnished account of life for those not privileged to be of the mandarin class.

Readers may discern in *Spring Moon* a decided parallel to two other historical novels — Margaret Mitchell's *Gone With the Wind* (1936) and Boris Pasternak's *Dr. Zhivago* (1958) — both dealing with civil strife and political unrest and their effects on the aristocracy. In all three novels the narrative follows the fortunes of members of the privileged classes, who grow up in luxury and reach adulthood only to watch a social cataclysm destroy the very society in which their upbringings have prepared them to live; in all three the characters are tested in extreme circumstances involving the conflict between tradition and change — circumstances that reveal in the lives of these people the amazing resilience of the human spirit under duress.

◆ Related Titles ◆

Although not a sequel to *Spring Moon, The Middle Heart* (1996) is strikingly similar in its vivid portrayal of Chinese history. The novel opens in 1932, when the Japanese have captured Manchuria. Three children united in their antagonism for the Japanese begin a lifelong friendship. As the loyalty, love and patriotism of the three friends are tested, the play of history on their loves is made clear.

◆ Ideas for Group Discussions ◆

Spring Moon is a novel about clashes. It deals with the clash of different generations, with the clash of different ideologies, with clash of different religions and with the clash of different cultures. It has a timeless quality because it deals with these larger than life themes. It invites readers to compare their own lives to the lives of the characters in the book. It invites readers to learn more about a different culture and by examining that "other"

culture, to learn more about their own.

1. Why does the suicide of Plum Blossom bring dishonor on the house of Chang? What does it foreshadow?

2. When he explains about Plum Blossom, the grandfather tells Spring Moon that "only the gods can alter fate" and she must "simply yield." What does he mean? Does Spring Moon agree? How can you tell?

3. On the journey back to China from America, Bold Talent tries to become Chinese as soon as possible. He separates himself from the rest of the passengers, puts on robes, and eats rice. Although he thinks he is successful, when he returns home, people point at him because he has no *quene*. Although he has let his hair grow, it is still not long enough. He thinks he needs a haircut and the Chinese think his hair is too short. What does this say about Bold Talent? Can he ever really be the same man who left China for America?

4. Bold Talent puts on mourning garb for his father. What color is the cloth? Colors have different significance for different cultures. Discuss the meaning of different colors.

5. When Bold Talent begins to teach Spring Moon to read and write, the family is opposed because it is dangerous for a girl and spoils her chances for a good marriage. They believe that the educated females are the malcontents who disturb the virtuous harmony of the household. Why do they feel this way? Are they correct? What happens to women who learn to read in this novel?

6. When Bold Talent tries to make a difference, he gives money to build a hospital, repairs a pump, and tries to make people less superstitious. Initially good things happen and then things sour. What happens and how does Bold Talent react? What do you think Lord is saying?

7. Different cultures have different wedding and marriage customs. Describe Spring Moon's wedding. What do the symbols mean? Can you think of some from other cultures?

8. Spring Moon feels that her husband and her father were very different and yet they surrendered to the same fatal sickness. What does she mean?

9. Spring Moon experiences many different things. If you had been Spring Moon how would you have reacted to learning how to read? To being married? To a mother-in-law?

10. Lustrous Jade becomes a revolutionary after rejecting Christianity. Other revolutionaries admit that they do not "love" the people — the people are often stupid, dull, or dirty and yet they continue their revolutionary activity. Lord presents portraits of revolutionaries that are not always complimentary. Is this a realistic portrait of revolutionaries? What makes a person a revolutionary?

Edelma de Leon Huntley
Appalachian State University
[Ideas for Group Discussions
by Elizabeth Ann Helmer,
University of Southern Mississippi]

SPY LINE

Novel

1989

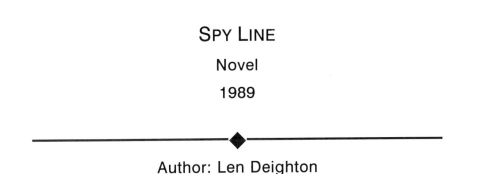

Author: Len Deighton

◆ Characters ◆

There are three main characters in *Spy Line*. Bernard Samson is a well-built, quiet man about forty years of age. He is of respectable middle-class origin — his father was a Secret Service agent as was his Uncle Silas Gaunt — who grew up in Berlin and speaks fluent German as well as English and Russian. An English citizen, he has a small home in a London suburb. He was a field agent — one of the best — for a number of years before being made a senior staff member of the German Station; although he is a non-college man, he has educated himself to a respectable degree.

He is married to Fiona, the daughter of an industrialist whose callous greed makes him a latter-day Bounderby of Coketown. She is Oxford-trained, a hardcore, independent woman who is also a Secret Service agent. They have two children. As the novel begins, however, he had previously, as related in *Spy Hook* (1988), been assigned the mission of discovering a mole in SIS and had more or less stumbled upon "Operation Hook." This discovery had resulted in the revelation that his own wife, Fiona, apparently is the KGB double agent, and she defects to East Berlin. Consequently, he himself is in disgrace because his superiors in the Department are suspicious of his loyalty as a possible collaborator with his treasonous wife. In fact, they have issued a warrant for his arrest. Therefore, he is on the run and hiding out in Berlin near the Wall in Kreuzberg.

Since Samson's wife had fled to East Berlin from London, where she worked at London Central (the H.Q. of SIS), the children abandoned at his home are left motherless. Samson therefore obtains the services of London Central employee Gloria Kent to care for the children. Gloria is a Hungarian refugee, the daughter of a dentist, also a Hungarian refugee. She is an attractive blonde and settles nicely into the Samson family. She falls in love with Samson despite the age difference, and he is likewise fond of her. Of course, one gathers that he does not expect to see Fiona again. However, because of the age difference between Gloria and Samson, some people question Samson's competence as a husband and father. But there are always people of this kind.

The story in *Spy Line* is essentially the story of these three people and how events affect their lives, and they do affect them with severity. Near the end of the novel Samson participates in a fire fight that allows Fiona to escape to the West through the Department's sacrifice of her sister's Tess's life. Her sister's corpse is fixed in such a way that the remains will be identified as Fiona's. Samson and Fiona are flown to the United States and domiciled in southern California for extensive debriefing. Samson learns that his wife's defection had been an elaborate cover story carefully orchestrated by the Department and that she had been in "deep cover" since her Oxford days. He had been a mere pawn in the "Great Game" in which Fiona was the Queen. But if the Department had gained something worthwhile — a result which seems problematical — the result has been tragic for the three principals. He was denied the promotion he deserved and his career is ruined, even though his reputation for loyalty and integrity may be restored. He has not really regained his wife, for it is clear that her mental and emotional life has suffered a severe blow from which she seems unlikely to recover. Finally, his relationship with Gloria would seem to be broken and the future of his children seems decidedly vague.

In the last volume of the trilogy, *Spy Sinker* (1990), Deighton tells the story mostly from Fiona's point of view, a technique which does not work well at all. Although she is called a "surrogate male" she is shown having crying jags and fits of self-recrimination and remorse.

◆ Social Concerns ◆

Deighton has completed two trilo-gies and has begun a third in which he develops the character and social relations of his veteran field agent Bernard Samson, of Her Majesty's Secret Service, whose name suggests his double personality. St. Bernard of Claivaux was a monk who, on the one hand, devoted himself to solitude and contemplation, and on the other hand, was a man of action, who organized, for instance, the Second Crusade. Also, the Biblical Samson was, on the one hand, a reflective judge, and on the other hand, a fierce warrior, who killed a thousand Philistines with the jawbone of an ass. The first and second volumes of Deighton's third trilogy, *Faith* (1994) and *Hope* (1995) have surprises that contradict previous assumptions. For instance, rumors are circulating that Tess is still alive in East Germany. What is to be made of such factual contradictions?

Deighton's psychodynamic studies of Bernard Samson in the trilogies go beyond his realistic spy novels such as *Funeral in Berlin* (1965). These studies move in the realm of the serious novel of character, psychological analysis, and sociological exploration. Samson becomes a fully developed character. His is a sharply delineated portrait of a self-educated, highly competent professional agent, who has married an Oxford-trained upper-class woman who is also an intelligence agent. They have two children. In *Berlin Game* (1983), Samson's task is to ferret out and unmask a Soviet mole. To his shock the traitor turns out to be his wife, who defects to East Berlin. Like the Biblical Samson, he has been betrayed by a woman. His wife's defection undermines his credibility with his superiors in the Department. Throughout the rest of the Tennis trilogy and into the second volume of the Fishing trilogy, Samson is desperately trying to regain his lost reputation.

◆ Themes ◆

Although an English citizen, Samson grew up in Berlin. Since his wife's defection, he has been suspected of treason and a warrant has been issued for his arrest. Hence he is hiding in Berlin in a "pad" located against the Berlin Wall in the sleazy part of the Kreuzberg district, where the counterculture flourishes and young Turk immigrants may molest a loner. In fact, some such hoodlums do molest Samson and he pulls a gun on them.

Perhaps the most important theme in *Spy Line* is that a secret service agent can become involved in an operation that the agency may pragmatically decide depends on his death or imprisonment. In Samson's case the Department's open doubting of his integrity and loyalty is not merely a gross assumption based on the stupid notion of guilt by association, but the Department *knows* all the time that there is no reason at all to doubt Samson. The doubt is a mere ploy and nothing but misinformation to lull the Soviets into considering Fiona a legitimate defector. Although Samson's life is preserved, Fiona's sister Tess is cold-bloodedly murdered and fixed to be taken as Fiona to preserve the secrecy of the operation.

Another theme is that secret intelligence is inevitably linked to politics. A nation's foreign policy decisions depend on adequate knowledge, some of which may have to be supplied by secret intelligence, because politicians have to decide courses of action in regard to the capabilities and intentions of foreign nations whether they are adversaries or allies. Without politics, intelligence collection by governments would not be necessary.

A third theme is that it is more or less natural that experienced field intelligence agents become somewhat paranoid, but they do not become paranoid to the extent that they feel that no one can be trusted. Samson explains: "I am not paranoid. That is to say, I am not paranoid to the extent of distrusting everyone around me. Only some of them."

Lastly, there is the theme that the privileged class, or those whose origins are aristocratic and who are mainly Oxbridgians, are no longer morally or intellectually capable of governing Great Britain. Moral responsibility, know-how, and talent must take precedence over inheritance. Samson's superiors tacitly acknowledge his meritocracy, despite knowing that his origins are middle-class and that he is a non-college man, when they consistently rely on his services because they feel confident that he can get the job done.

◆ Techniques ◆

The first two novels of the trilogy are told in the first person by the protagonist, a quiet, unpoetic, stubborn man not given to wit, sarcasm, or colorful display. His narration is plain, staid, and straightforward. It is occasionally sprinkled with some English slang or some German words, phrases, and sometimes a sentence — usually a quotation. The third novel *Spy Sinker* is told mostly from the point of view of Fiona, but this technique is predominately a failure. Critic Franz G. Blaha tells us why: The previous two novels are narratives that set forth Samson's quest to find the truth and to recover his lost reputation for loyalty and integrity. However, because Fiona did not share in this quest "her perspective," asserts Blaha, "is alien to the reader" of the quest volumes. Therefore, in Blaha's eyes, her attempt to tell what she had not experienced "is not very successful."

Deighton is masterly in constructing and sustaining intricate and complicated plots while concealing their import and impact until nearly the end of a novel. Sometimes the development of the action and its motivation will disappear into discussions that appear mere trivia only to surface when the reader is about to give up. Then the reader is carried by suspense until the actual motivations of the characters are made clear by the revelation of a completely different story from the one that had been entertained. Sometimes the protagonist, as in *Spy Line*, learns that he has been manipulated during the development of the action in ways he never thought possible by his own intelligence organization, without any regard for his welfare. He finds that his superiors, supported by their class status and motivated by personal ambition rather than by patriotism, have done him harm through irresponsible jockeying for promotion or the award of a knighthood.

Although Deighton wisely restrains himself in representing scenes of violence, his descriptions of violent action amount to masterly paintings of sharp and detailed imagery. For instance, in *Funeral in Berlin* his description of the terrible contest between the anonymous agent and aka Jonnie Vulkan in the garage is astonishing in its details, with Johnnie's death taking place by accident rather than at the hands of his anonymous agent. Also, in the same novel there occurs the masterly account of the accidental conflagration death of the villainous Hallam during the fireworks display. And in *Spy Line* there is the masterly depiction of the night fire fight on the East German Autobahn between the members of the Ford Transit van: Teacher in a gorilla suit firing a 9mm. Browning semi-automatic; the frantic Tess; and Samson firing his Webly Mark VI 455" revolver; opposing the members of the East German Wartburg: two Germans armed with pistols; Stinnes, armed; and Fiona; plus the loner Thurkettle, the mercenary assassin hired by the Department, who had come on a motorcycle and was armed with a pistol with a long silencer. "Bang. Bang. Bang. Bang. Bang." People dead. Blood. Samson wounded. Samson and Fiona reunited.

◆ Literary Precedents ◆

Deighton's Tennis trilogy, begun in 1983, preceded his Fishing trilogy, begun in 1988. In these lengthy and subtle character studies of one man in terms of his profession, we are reminded of French author Romain Rolland's ten volume study of a German-born musician in *Jean-Christophe* (1906-1912). But apart from the study of a man relative to his profession, Deighton's underlying purpose is not only to lash the "old boy network" in the SIS but also to flay the entire British upper-middle and aristocratic classes whose Victorian world view of Empire he thinks anachronistic in modern times. Deighton appears to believe that the present "governors" of Great Britain are morally irresponsible — if not amoral altogether — as well as being intellectually incompetent to cope with the social decadence and disorder currently ravaging the Western World.

What trilogies or longer studies of fiction Deighton may have modeled his work on — if any — is uncertain at best. The most likely, however, might have been John Galsworthy's two trilogies, *The Forsyte Saga* (1906-1921) and *A Modern Comedy* (1924-1928), both of which satirize the British upper-middle class relative to a particular man, Sommes Forsyte. Another likely influence might have been Evelyn Waugh's trilogy about Great Britain during World War II, *Men at Arms* (1952-1962). There is also the bitter fictional trilogy by Wyndham Lewis called *The Human Age* (1955-1956). Like Deighton, Lewis was also an artist and was the father of the movement in painting called *vorticism*. Another trilogy that might have interested Deighton is that of the American John Dos Passos, titled *U.S.A.* (1938), a study of the industrial United States from 1898 to 1929. At any rate, it is clear that following the success of his early "spy novels," which although realistic are still "thrillers," Deighton became more interested in the lengthy exploration of human character. Clearly, he means to pursue this task since he has already issued two volumes of another trilogy concerning Bernard Samson called *Faith* (1994) and *Hope* (1995) with the final volume no doubt being titled *Charity* in which further surprises will be forthcoming.

◆ Related Titles ◆

Deighton's *Winter: A Novel of a Berlin Family* (1987), gives the "historical" background for many of the characters who appear in the Samson trilogies, especially the Winters and the Renasselaers.

Deighton's latest trilogy designed to tie up the loose ends in the spy career of Bernard Sampson, according to Deighton himself, now consists of *Faith* and *Hope*), with *Charity* in the offing.

Faith is set in Berlin in 1987, where Sampson is trying to cope with the unexpected return of his wife Fiona, also a spy, who had supposedly been unmasked as a double agent and had consequently defected to East Germany. Now in *Faith* she has unexpectedly "redefected" as part of a lengthy and carefully devised plan by London Central to cause political unrest in East Germany. However, this novel has been criticized as too involuted and lacking in action to be strongly effective, but such a view may depend on a reader choice between interest in action as opposed to characterization.

In *Hope* Sampson is forced to deal with further complications which have arisen from Fiona's redefection. Rumors are circulating that Fiona's sister Tessa, who was thought to have been shot and killed in a firefight on the Autobahn when Fiona's returned from East Germany, is now alive and well in East Germany. Furthermore, Tessa's wealthy businessman husband, George Kosinski, has mysteriously disappeared from his Zurich mansion. And finally, Gloria, the young woman who had lived with Sampson to care for his children in the absence of his wife, and with whom Sampson had fallen in love, has also re-appeared, adding a further complication. Whether Deighton will clear things up in satisfactory fashion in the final volume of the trilogy, *Charity*, remains to be seen.

◆ Adaptations ◆

Deighton's *Spy Hook* was issued as an audio cassette by Chivers Audio Book in 1993, and *Spy Sinker* was issued in 1995. Both of these cassettes were considered unsatisfactory in the quality of their voice presentation by critic John Hiett.

◆ Ideas for Group Discussions ◆

In his Bernard Samson trilogies Deighton seeks to transcend the traditional spy novel by avoiding conventional stereotypes and moving toward the serious novel of character with its subtle analysis of motive and moral choice combined with dramatic action and a sense of style, as one sees in the novels of such artists as Stendhal, Proust, Conrad, and Henry James. This is not to say that Deighton's work is worthy to be compared with these authors; it is merely to indicate the direction in which Deighton has chosen to go in order to expand the narrow scope of the traditional popular spy novel.

Fruitful discussion therefore can be developed by attempting to judge Deighton's success in committing himself to the goal he evidently set for himself. But comparisons can be invidious, inappropriate, or illogical. One critic sees Deighton's presentation of seemingly unrelated events and characters which turn out later to be related as typical soap opera. But soap operas feature stock domestic situations, melodramatic love conflicts, and sentimental treatment, with the capital sin being adultery. Such is not the case with the "givens" of the spy story, which are national defense espionage and counter-espionage, intelligence agents and double agents employed by a national defense organization, and secret operations, with the capital sin being treason. At any rate, such legitimate questions as the following may fruitfully be discussed: How near or how far do Deighton's studies of Bernard Samson come to such realistic novels which combine action with the examination of character, motivation, and moral responsibility as Joseph Conrad's *Lord Jim* (1900), Henry James's *The Ambassadors* (1903), Stendhal's *The Red and the Black* (1831), or some other novel of like character and worth? Or, apart from characterization and plotting, how worthy of respect is Deighton's literary style? Or, do you think Bernard Samson an interesting enough person to attract new readers in the future? Or, do you think Deighton should give up his ambitious goal and do something else?

1. Might one say that although Deighton has succeeded in "deglamorizing" the spy story, he has not succeeded in wholly "demythologizing it"? Do you think it ought to be wholly demythologized, or might that be the secret of its power?

2. Halfway through Chapter 18 of *Spy Line* a masquerade party is held at the Lisl Henning-Werner Volkmann hotel to celebrate the new refurbishing. The outdoor aspect of the party is rained on and indoors the large crowd becomes quite wild until the affair takes on the character of a Mardi Gras carnival. This fervor comes to a climax at the end when Teacher, Samson, and Tessa are taking off in their Ford van to meet Fiona's party on the East German Autobahn, where a fire fight ensues and several people are killed, including Teacher and Tess. Do you think that the Mardi Gras type of carnival scene is symbolically related in any way to the fire fight and death scene on the Autobahn? If so, in what specific way?

3. In her ambition to pursue a patriotic quest, do you think Fiona denies her wifehood and motherhood by abandoning, perhaps forever, her husband and children? Although her quest was successful from an intelligence point of view, she herself paid a heavy price by suffering a mental and emotional breakdown from which she might never recover. Further, by her action, her sister Tessa met her death, and she caused her husband and children much harm and suffering. Do you think her successful patriotic quest was worth it?

4. While Fiona is on her patriotic quest, Bernard is on a quest to find out the truth behind her disappearance. Was she kidnapped by foreign agents as a hostage to be exchanged for some KGB spy who has been arrested in the West? Or, was she actually a double agent for the KGB and a traitor to her country and family? Might one say that Bernard is on a quest for spiritual truth in a moral wasteland? How do you see this matter?

5. When Fiona and Bernard are returning in the Ford van after the fire fight in which Teacher and Tessa were killed, she, at the wheel, asks him, "Are you all right?" But Bernard reports, "There was no tenderness in her voice. It was . . . the voice of a schoolteacher herding a class of busy kids across a busy street." He replies, "I'm all right." But he reports, "We should have been talking and embracing and laughing and loving. We were together again and she was coming home to me and the children. But it wasn't like that . . ." Although Bernard loves Fiona, does she really love him? Might it be that she is incapable of loving anyone but herself?

THE SPY WHO CAME IN FROM THE COLD

Novel

1963

◆

Author: John le Carré

◆ Characters ◆

Le Carré is distinctive in his type of spy, an anti-James Bond type, no longer the super-spy. Alec Leamus, the hero of *The Spy Who Came in from the Cold*, is a fifty-year-old professional, grown stale in espionage. He has just lost his final contact in East Germany as the novel opens, and he is not really sure of his reasons for remaining in the service. He has lost confidence in the machine in which he is operating. Consequently he lives through many roles, convincingly. He "goes to seed, [becomes] a resentful, drunken wreck"; goes to prison; and, most dangerous of all, falls in love. He eventually receives an opportunity to denounce the East German Mundt, and discovers the inhumanity and ruthlessness of the espionage world. Leamus is a series of roles, of masks, suffering from the tension of contemporary society, uncommitted and disillusioned.

One of the few charming feminine characters in le Carré's world is Liz Gold, who "had large components which seemed to hesitate between plainness and beauty." Naively enrolled in the Communist party, she commits herself wholeheartedly to Leamus. Indirectly betrayed in both her allegiances, she suffers the irony of a world in which truth is hard to find. Like her, the East German Fiedler, punished for being a Jew, places his confidence in communism. He has the material to prove the guilt of Mundt, but there is no place for clear-cut moral values in today's inhuman world.

On the whole, characterization is not le Carré's strongest point. The people he creates are too abstract, too much identified with their ideas to emerge as truly human. They have no past, no families, no history. They are shadowy, yet they represent well the contemporary person, tired, confused, and uncommitted.

◆ Social Concerns/Themes ◆

The fact that le Carré is sensitive to political fashion and is able to anticipate a timely issue is considered his most important achievement. Ostensibly, *The Spy Who Came in from the Cold* addresses the tensions in the 1960s between East and West Germany, and in general between the East and the West. The construction of the Berlin Wall became a symbol of this ideological conflict, and le Carré at the beginning of his career and thereafter was able to seize upon a timely situation, well-documented because of his own personal experience in Germany, and convincingly presented.

There is, however, a deeper concern in *The Spy Who Came in from the Cold*, and in basically all of le Carré's espionage novels. Le Carré addresses the moral ambiguities facing everyone in contemporary society. There are no absolutes, neither in one's private nor one's political life. World War II evoked patriotism; there were clear-cut issues, divisions of enemies and allies. Since the Vietnam War, in particular, these distinctions have become obscured; good is no longer justifiable, and evil is accepted as a part of life. Le Carré's creation of the double agent exemplifies this blurring of values, as does the image of mist so prevalent in his novels.

◆ Techniques ◆

As an espionage story, this work reveals all the labyrinthine intricacies of the profession of the spy. In developing the plot, le Carré is able to withhold information from his readers and keep them in suspense. *The Spy Who Came in from the Cold* has a remarkably simple plot, is not overburdened with characters, and develops in a linear fashion. Le Carré is sparing of description, although his own familiarity with Germany is evident. The Wall, which begins and ends the novel, is presented with starkness and strength, and becomes almost a person.

Le Carré is a master of language. He is particularly gifted in the use of dialogue, often presented like an overheard conversation. It is by dialogue more than by description that the characters reveal themselves. Le Carré is able to capture the naive questioning and unquestionable dedication of Liz, the cynical disgust of Leamus, and the cunning of Mundt through the words they speak. His sentences are crisp and terse; his vocabulary exact and creative.

The greatest asset of this novel is the change it brought to the typical espionage story. In contrast to the nineteenth-century figures, dedicated to the service of their country, le Carré has created a shadowy type, a profoundly unhappy person with doubts about his profession. He shows espionage as a cruel, cold, and bitter business. He evokes the political climate in the 1960s and the great postwar malaise with surprising clarity and intuition.

◆ Literary Precedents ◆

As an espionage story, *The Spy Who Came in from the Cold*, and all of le Carré's works, with the possible exception of *The Naive and Sentimental Lover* (1971), belong to the tradition of Somerset Maugham, Authur Conan Doyle, and especially Graham Greene; although he has created a more restless, ambiguous hero. In the literary world, he has echoes of Balzac, Stendhal, Dickens (especially *Bleak House*), and Henry James. Joseph Conrad is also one of his masters, especially in his later works.

◆ Adaptations ◆

The Spy Who Came in from the Cold was successfully filmed by Paramount in 1965, starring Richard Burton, who was nominated for an Academy Award for his brilliant portrayal. Le Carré has not participated in the filming of any of his works, and remains generally detached from them.

Sister Irma M. Kashuba, S.S.J.
Chestnut Hill College

THE SQUARE

Novel

1955

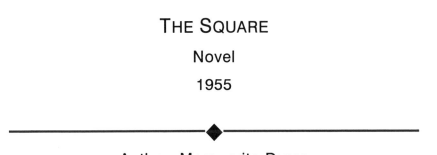

Author: Marguerite Duras

◆ Social Concerns/Themes ◆

French literature of the 1950s and 1960s is marked by a sense of estrangement and alienation. Writers more outspoken than Duras, such as Camus and Sartre, spoke of the absurd, and felt that human beings were trapped in life with no escape. *The Square* treats the same theme, but with more subtle undertones. The two protagonists, a young domestic servant in her early twenties and a travelling salesman, have no property, no social prestige, and seemingly no hope of improving their situation. The man in particular seems to have lost all ambition, and accepts his work as the sum total of his existence. He has little interest in society and its values.

The young woman, on the other hand, lives a monotonous and meaningless life, minding a child and caring for a senile woman, but hopes one day to escape this situation through marriage. Therefore, she goes to a local dance every Saturday in order to meet prospective suitors. So far no one has come along, but she trusts that "he" eventually will. One critic comments, "Conditions have annihilated her sense of identity. If she is somehow to be recreated as a person, if life is at least to start for her, she must be chosen by someone; this explains the importance of the theme of marriage in the book, the real theme of creation or re-creation."

Duras also addresses the question of the lower social classes. The young girl is a domestic servant, sent off to work at the age of sixteen without much hope of education or social advancement. One detects a note of sympathy for these people, as seen elsewhere in Duras's work, possibly because of the author's own poverty-stricken childhood. The young girl accepts her condition, yet her descriptions of service in the household and attention to the senile woman evoke compassion. In addition, during this period Duras was interested in communism, which is evident in the novel's emphasis on the working class.

The role of women in society has always interested Duras. One critic quotes Duras and comments: "Marguerite Duras's writing is a woman's writing, in this sense: 'For thousands of years, silence has been synonymous with women. Therefore, literature *is* women. It's women whether it speaks of women or is created by women.'"

Thus the young girl in *The Square* shows a passion in which she loses her own identity.

◆ Characters ◆

In keeping with the "new novel," this brief story has only three characters, one of whom, the child, appears only at the beginning of each part. He speaks only of his physical needs: he is hungry, thirsty, tired. In the second part, his name, Jacques, is revealed. He is evidently a charming child, for he elicits a sympathetic smile from the gentleman. The child is the catalyst that engages the man and the woman in conversation.

The other two characters have no names; they address each other only as "Sir" (*Monsieur*) and "Miss" (*Mademoiselle*). The young girl is in her early twenties, but the age of the gentleman is not revealed, although it is assumed that he is older. The scene takes place in Paris, but the origin of these two people is unknown as well. There is no physical or psychological description. They reveal themselves only through their conversation. In effect, the reader must get to know them only from the words they say. Thus they are more than just a representation of their respective social classes; they are distinct individuals. The girl is a victim of a social structure in which some people are destined to be the servants of others, but she is also a young woman who sees relief from her fate through marriage. The gentleman is representative of the rootless and hopeless, who see no escape from their monotonous existence.

◆ Techniques/Literary Precedents ◆

Many novelists of the latter part of the twentieth century tend to write what has been termed the "abstract" novel. As Robbe-Grillet explains, there is no omniscient narrator, such as that used by Balzac in the nineteenth-century, who like a god controls his characters and the events that happen to them. Instead, the characters are free to create their own existence, and a certain distance is established between the author and the reader. This enables the reader, in collaboration with the author, to create the story. It also creates a distance between the reader and the characters, thus appealing to the reader's intellect rather than emotions. The absence of place and personal names, of concrete descriptions, and of roots in the past characterize this abstract novel.

In *The Square*, Duras relies almost exclusively on relatively simple dialogue with no profound thoughts, no great discoveries. The two people use the formal "vous" (you), colloquial language, and uncomplicated syntax. Despite the simple vocabulary and syntax, however, it is evident that Duras has excellent control of language and style.

Finally, in *The Square* as in most of Duras's novels, there is no real denouement, no final conclusion. One may suspect that the two people will meet again and the gentleman may become the relief sought by the young girl. But on the other hand, it is possible that they will never meet again and his refusal to accompany her home is their farewell. There is no action in the novel; it is merely a glimpse of a moment in time, which may lead nowhere.

Duras can be placed in the feminine tradition of French literature, which, dating from Marie de France in the Middle Ages, flourished in the seventeenth century with such authors as Mme de Lafayette and Mme de Sévigné, and was especially strong in the post-war years of the twentieth century with Simone de Beauvoir, Natalie Sarraute, and Françoise Sagan, among others. She was also influenced by Ernest Hemingway and his so-called "American novel," especially in the years preceding *The Square*. The theme of alienation suggests her contemporaries Albert Camus and Jean Paul Sartre and the subjective quality is reminiscent of Marcel Proust. Her use of dialogue and concentration on the present suggests Alain Robbe-Grillet, in particular the scenario for the film *Last Year at Marienbad* by Alain Resnais. Duras's work also shows echoes of Gustave Flaubert, especially in the absence of denouement and the strong control of language.

◆ Related Titles ◆

Duras's previous works were in the tradition of classical and romantic French literature, with characters, names, places, and plot, although her characteristic style was beginning to emerge. It is interesting to note that these earlier works met with little success, except *The Sea Wall* (1950), which Duras would later rework as *The Lover* (1984). With *The Square*, she moved into an entirely new phase, that of the abstract novel. This is a style that Duras later developed and perfected.

◆ Adaptations ◆

The Square was adapted for the stage by Duras and successfully performed in Paris. It appeared in her book of plays, *Théâtre I*, published in 1965.

Sister Mary Helen Kashuba
Chestnut Hill College

STALLION GATE

Novel

1986

---◆---

Author: Martin Cruz Smith

◆ Social Concerns/Themes ◆

Although the narrative of *Stallion Gate* can be admired for its technique — for the clarity with which Smith develops a number of intersecting plot lines and the ingenuity with which he blends the actions of his fictional and historical characters — the novel's high ambitions are most evident in its treatment of its principal theme: the conflict between two visions of man's place in the world, that of the European scientific mind and that of the Native American mind, a conflict set at a crucial time, 1943 to 1945 and in a crucial place, Los Alamos and Trinity ("Stallion Gate" is a local name for the spot which J. Robert Oppenheimer renamed "Trinity" when he selected it as the site of the first test of a nuclear device.)

The first vision is that of such well-known scientists as Oppenheimer, Edward Teller, Enrico Fermi, and others; the second is that of the Pueblo Indians. Both visions are creative, but the scientists use their speculations and their technology to split the atom and produce a fission bomb; the Indians, inheriting a radically different world-view, use a quite different technology — dreams, dances, magic wands, pottery — for quite different ends. A secondary conflict emerges within the European-American community, as the visionary scientists find themselves increasingly at odds with the security-minded military authorities who sponsor the project.

The novel's protagonist, Sgt. Joe Peña, finds himself at the center of these conflicts. He is a Pueblo Indian who has been partially, but not entirely, alienated from his family and his people by his cosmopolitan experiences as a professional boxer and jazz musician and by his service as a soldier. Joe finds himself in sympathy with both the scientists and the Indians. As Oppenheimer's driver/bodyguard (selected in part because he had known Oppenheimer as a boy in New Mexico), he develops a personal relationship with Oppy (and in a subplot, he falls in love with a refugee mathematician, Anna Weiss). Joe becomes involved in the process of inventing the bomb — selecting the Trinity site, transporting radioactive materials, even climbing the tower at Trinity to free the prototype as it is raised to its final position. But Joe also rediscovers his inalienable links to his Indian heritage — to the home of his dead mother, to the ceremonial dancing and clowning of his people. He responds to the New Mexican landscape itself — the deserts and mesas, the villages and ruins.

Joe's ambivalent position is epitomized in his relations with his uncle, Ben, and Ben's blind companion, Roberto. At one point the blind Roberto holds the scientist (and traitor) Klaus Fuchs captive at gunpoint. As a security officer, Joe's duty requires him to apprehend the pair; as an Indian and a man, he must prevent their apprehension. Inspired by images of the destructiveness that will be unleashed at Trinity, Ben and Roberto wander through the novel's action, warning Joe that the project must be stopped. They use the "lightning wands" to invoke conflagrations that will disrupt the experimentation. Although he will not betray Oppenheimer and bomb, Joe also refuses to betray Ben and Roberto, finally arranging for them to escape to Mexico.

The second challenge to Joe's loyalty to Oppenheimer comes from Captain Augustino, the head of security (a character based upon the actual Captain Peer de Silva). Augustino assumes that the Europeans who work under his protection at Los Alamos are Communist subversives, and his suspicions focus upon Anna Weiss and upon Oppenheimer himself (ironically, he dismisses Joe's evidence that Fuchs is the actual traitor). Joe thus finds himself caught between the political paranoia of military security and the apolitical innocence of the scientists.

◆ Characters ◆

Sgt. Joe Peña is the central character;

indeed, he is the novel's only center. He connects episodes of science and romance, jazz and boxing, mysticism and technology, humor and melodrama; he connects the fiction and the history. As such, he is, as reviewers noted, overburdened. He is too excellent: He was an eighth-ranked heavyweight; he played piano with the jazz greats; he was in the Philippines with MacArthur, and escaped. On July 15, 1945, he outboxes an opponent, uses $50,000 to buy a jazz club, ensures that Ben and Roberto escape to Mexico, and then, as the scientists count down to the first explosion of an atomic bomb at 5:30 am on July 16, Joe wrestles with and kills his nemesis, Capt. Augustino, atop the tower at Trinity. And yet, despite the serendipity of his encounters, Joe emerges as a credible character, capable of carrying the thematic burden which Smith has placed upon him.

The remaining characters are defined in vignettes. Although they, too, are burdened with thematic significance — Scientists, Indians, and Soldiers — they emerge as engaging persons. Characters such as Oppenheimer, General Groves, and Klaus Fuchs seem to accord with their historical counterparts. (The same may be said of the quasi-historical Capt. Augustino.) And the Native American characters seem to be authentic in their beliefs and behaviors.

◆ Techniques ◆

The mixing of historical and fictional characters and historical and fictional events has enjoyed a recent vogue in American fiction. It is one well-suited to Smith's style: His novels have always displayed a thorough knowledge of more or less esoteric matters —

Gypsy lore, bats and Indians, life in Moscow. *Stallion Gate* applies this research method to recreating a historical context. Selecting a crucial moment in history, Smith has crafted an intelligent novel which becomes neither a sophomoric melodrama nor a thinly fictionalized lecture on bomb-makers and bomb-making (nor a simplistic sermon on evil scientists and good Indians). There is, instead, enough drama (enough character, setting, and plot) and enough lecture. The thematic conflicts, while not subtle, emerge concretely and organically within the drama.

The structure of the narrative also merits comment. Simple chronology governs the overall shape. The action begins in November 1943, when Capt. Augustino recruits Joe, and ends on the morning of July 16, 1945, when Joe kills Augustino and the bomb explodes. But within this linear development, Smith plays his different themes artfully. The novel pauses several times to describe the techniques of different arts — the art of jazz, the art of boxing, the art of pottery, the art of dance, the art of constructing atomic bombs. The art of *Stallion Gate* is perhaps most like that of jazz, with Smith skillfully introducing and recalling his themes. Although flawed by the excellence of the hero and the neatness of the timing, *Stallion Gate* is a very fine and thoughtful novel.

Coming as it does between two major novels featuring the Russian detective, Arkady Renko, *Stallion Gate* occupies an interesting position in Smith's development. Having begun as a pulp writer, Smith moved into what might be called increasingly ambitious pulps in the Gypsy novels and in *Nightwing* (1977). (In a sense, *Stallion Gate* returns at a higher level to some of the the-matic concerns of *Nightwing*, with a Pueblo army sergeant replacing the Hopi deputy sheriff.) Then, in *Gorky Park* (1981), he used the formula of a subgenre of the detective story as the basis for an ambitious novel which presented and criticized a complex social reality. *Stallion Gate* takes a further step away from popular conventions. The operative formula here — that of espionage fiction — provides only an intermittent, minor plot line. In the end, neither Capt. Augustino nor the reader cares much when Joe exposes Klaus Fuchs as the actual threat to the security of the project; the interest of the novel lies elsewhere. The issue of subversion is the central one, but the real subversives prove to be Oppenheimer and his team, and Ben and Roberto, and even Capt. Augustino. The jazz variations on the conventional formula are what really matter in the novel.

◆ Literary Precedents ◆

Although *Stallion Gate* is a serious novel, there are certainly precedents for several aspects in popular fiction. Espionage novels have, of course, a long history. The work of writers such as le Carré and Deighton is perhaps most relevant in the care with which they research the action and environments of their novels. Although they are written to a slightly different standard, the Matt Helm novels of Donald Hamilton may also be cited, especially as Hamilton and his hero are both avowed westerners, and several of the novels are set in Arizona and New Mexico. The Joe Leaphorn and Jim Chee novels of Tony Hillerman are detective stories rather than spy stories, but they share Smith's fascination with the Indian cultures of the Southwest. Finally, Smith's vision of Native American experience can be compared with that of such Native American authors as N. Scott Momaday and Leslie Marmon Silko.

◆ Related Titles ◆

The protagonist of *Nightwing* is Youngman Duran, a Hopi Indian deputy sheriff on a Southwestern reservation who is torn between the white and native worlds. With one foot in each camp and his fundamental allegiances in neither, Duran's cultural ambivalence makes him a uniquely sensitive instrument for recording the conflicts between traditional and technological forces that recur throughout *Nightwing's* account of an invasion by bloodthirsty vampire bats.

◆ Ideas for Group Discussions ◆

Despite its affiliations with popular literary genres, *Stallion Gate* should be approached as a deliberate work of fiction; formally as well as thematically, it is an ambitious novel. Significantly, it is Smith's one novel which does not belong to a series. There has been no sequel. Liberated by the success of *Gorky Park*, Smith composed a novel intended to stand alone as a literary achievement. It should be read as his claim to be taken seriously as a novelist. It surely justifies that claim.

Smith exploits a number of established fictional forms — the detective novel, the spy novel, the western novel, even the historical novel — to construct his narrative. The conventions of any of these forms can be the starting point for discussion of his achieve-

ment. How has he, for example, stretched the formulas of the spy novel to make his points? Some of the characters and plot elements clearly derive from espionage stereotypes, but equally clearly the novel presses them beyond their stereotypical functions. Is *Stallion Gate* limited by Smith's decision to begin with formulas? Do the characters and plot elements succeed in expanding convincingly beyond their conventional roles? Or do his formulaic premises allow him an unusual opportunity to develop his themes?

1. How does landscape — the terrain, the seasons, the human alterations — affect Smith's description of the struggles of his characters?

2. How does Smith contrast the scientific and the Native American ways of attempting to exercise control over nature?

3. How does Smith contrast the various ways his characters attempt to control one another?

4. How successful is Smith's grafting of a fictional melodrama onto the historical record of the creation of the atomic bomb?

5. Compare Smith's presentation of Native American culture with that of Tony Hillerman or Leslie Marmon Silko.

J. K. Van Dover
Lincoln University

STANLEY ELKIN'S THE MAGIC KINGDOM

Novel

1986

◆

Author: Stanley Elkin

◆ Social Concerns ◆

Although Elkin determined, after completing *George Mills* (1982), to give up writing because he felt that he had put everything he had into that novel, a fortuitous event inspired the book that will prove to be his masterpiece. While in London he saw on the BBC a long report about the departure of an airplane carrying terminally ill children to America for a dream vacation in Disney World. The writer's conflicting emotions were overpowering, and this conflict led him to compose a new novel. On the one hand, he felt overwhelming sorrow and compassion for children doomed to die and forced on public display with the disfigurations from their maladies in plain view. On the other hand, the artist in Elkin was repelled by the exhibitionistic spectacle of dragging these children to an amusement park and rubbing their faces in their mortality. Thus the odd, recent practice of providing a dream vacation for terminally ill children becomes a central question of this very distressing novel.

It is an issue Elkin treats with divided sympathy. The venture is well-intended. As he said in an interview, it is a "very grotesque good" intention, but one that raises the thematically central issue of how can we not try to do something, however hopeless, about the vicious fate these innocent children have inherited. As human beings what choices have we but to try to do something about the raw deal others, especially innocent others, get? But in our desire to do good, should we descend to the bizarre, the exhibitionistic? As Elkin portrayed cultural morbidity and sentimentality in the accounts of Jerry Lewis telethons and Meals-On-Wheels in *George Mills*, at what point does our compassion and determination to help others cross over to the grotesque?

Theme parks and amusement centers are relatively new phenomena in the American landscape, and these concepts have recently been exported to Europe and Japan. Elkin, who has longingly chronicled what he calls the "crap of our culture," found in Disney World a level of mendacity and hucksterism that put off even his cosmopolitan sympathies. The ironic element of the title of this book (to some degree modeled on the parodic *Stanley Elkin's Greatest Hits*, 1980) is that the "magic" occurs not in the rides or the illusions, which the children find banal, but in the privacy and shared affection they have been denied because of their illness. The kids are disappointed by the rides and exhibits at Disney World, but each find his or her magic in privacy, in shared mortality, and for two of the dying children, in love.

◆ Themes ◆

The key theme of *Stanley Elkin's The Magic Kingdom* engages a philosophical and ethical paradox. Because we share mortality, we feel some obligation to help those less fortunate than we, and especially those on whom life has played a cruel joke. There can be no more sympathetic figures than dying children, and no more powerful reminder of our powerlessness in the face of fate or inevitability. What, then, are our obligations to one another? At what point do these obligations become self-serving?

Elkin does not answer these questions, but the dignity with which these children face their mortality supports his theme of compassion and obligation. No one could refuse to try to help. Yet what can anyone do? His hero, Eddy Bale (among the first Elkin protagonists not identified by his vocation) throws all his energies into planning this expedition to compensate for his loss of his terminally ill son and the subsequent failure of his marriage. In the several conversations Eddy has with his dead son, Elkin suggests that this effort is psychologically self-serving. In fact, although most of the characters who accompany Bale on his adventure are motivated by altruistic desires, many have secret or suppressed agendas. At what point do our altruism and our self-interest

intersect?

A related theme is the dignity and fragility of life, however flawed. Quite deliberately, Elkin portrays human existence as flawed and even grotesque. His portrait of the Disney World parade emphasizes the thin line dividing the grotesque appearance of the terminally ill children from those of other parade viewers. Seeing how mis-formed everyone else is gives the children — and the reader — a new perspective on their shared condition. One of the boys describes this epiphany eloquently: "Jesus . . . weeps for all the potty, pig-ignorant prats off their chumps, for all the . . . dead-from-the-neck-up dimbos, . . . for all his chuckle-headed, loopy muggins and passengers past praying for." With this epiphany, the reader and children realize that the difference between these fated children and the rest of us is a matter of degree, not of kind. We're all mortal; we will all suffer and die sooner or later. We're all "passengers past praying for."

This is not a morbidly somber thought for the kids or for the reader. They learn, briefly (see the truly beautiful scene in which they hijack boats and find privacy from the crowd's stares at the aptly named Shipwreck Marsh), to accept their mortality and to savor the moments they have before they die — moments best invested in the company of people about whom we care.

Finally, the novel integrates this ambivalent, postmodernist version of the traditional *carpe diem* with a concern with the strategy of avoidance. Many of the characters who nurture the dying children have learned to avoid emotional vulnerability. Some of them learn to take risks, even if the consequences are likely to be catastrophic. Eddy Bale has practiced celibacy since losing his son and his wife, while "gray lady" Mary Cottle has avoided sexual contact because her previous, terminated pregnancies have resulted in deformed fetuses. Eddy has become a monk, tied to an ideal of public service, and Mary has become dependent on masturbation. When the expedition unravels with the death of one of the children, they unite in profoundly procreative copulation, "to make a troll, a goblin, . . . gorgon, cyclopes, Calibans, God's ugly, punished customers, his obscene and frail and lubberly . . ." With their resolve to create an imperfect future, Elkin powerfully reminds us that we are all dying children, and that only in accepting risks and finding love can we make our lives worth living.

◆ Characters ◆

Unlike many of Elkin's novels, characterization is the special strength of *The Magic Kingdom*. All the characters are individuated and each deserves special attention, from the zany physician Mr. Morehead, to the nurses Colin Bible and Mary Cottle (both are flawed, but both share love and concern for the children and each is in some ways an effective care-giver). Bale, England's greatest beggar, is a complex combination of humanistic, serious person seeking to do good, and frustrated, unhappy man who cannot face his present situation without a compensating illusion. Cottle, a nervous, unstable woman, is portrayed sympathetically as someone who can give authentic love, whereas nanny Nedra Carp, whose vocation would lead us to believe she is an able care-giver, proves to be parochial in her preferences and

to invite factionalism among the children. She is not, significantly, a factor in any therapeutic experience the children have in the book. Colin Bible, in some ways the book's real hero, engages in one nasty liaison, and gets the children's consent to be memorialized in a wax museum — but he does it out of love for his partner, a wax artist; and he brings many of the dying children, including Eddy's late son, close to peaceful self-acceptance.

The refusal to see character as simple or as uniform persists as well in the children. Some are nasty, others heroic, in their response to their diseases. Some have developed elaborate strategies for coping, but others have not come to terms with their condition. Several learn profound lessons from their experience in Disney World; a few learn practically nothing. The power and art of this novel depend on the fact that each child is represented, not as a type, but as an individual. Thematically, Elkin's point is that each deserves to be treated as a person who is dying, not as a member of the class "dying children." He drives this point home powerfully by representing the children, and their care-givers, as ranging along a broad spectrum from truly noble to mendacious — pretty much the range of human personality in the real magic kingdom, the world in which we live.

◆ Techniques ◆

The Magic Kingdom is among Elkin's less technically innovative novels, but it is brilliantly constructed around the paradox of a commercial enterprise called a "magic kingdom" in which little that we can call magic really happens, and in which the real magic is finally something we need to travel inward, not outward, to discover. Unlike his typical books, however, this is divided among the narratives concerning many of the care-givers as well as the eight dying children.

He does, moreover, interpose two distinctive narrative techniques in a book rich in purple passages, Whitmanian catalogues, and powerful metaphors. As the group rides to America, what appears to be a collective dream occurs, in which the dream of one character merges with those of another. The narrative offers the somewhat facile explanation that smoke from Cottle's cigarette causes each to dream a shared experience. In fact the episode foreshadows Elkin's theme of shared human experiences and the children's need for love and shared experiences. Moreover, there are recurring episodes in which Eddy Bale talks with, and asks approval from, his dead son. These episodes ground Eddy's obsession with helping the children in a reasonable psychological state — an unresolved grief — and remind us that children who die are not the sole victims of childhood illnesses.

Perhaps the funniest episode in all of Elkin occurs when Eddy gets an audience with Queen Elizabeth to support his quest. It is a perfect example of Elkin's offbeat, zany humor, while approaching a serious subject.

◆ Literary Precedents ◆

An interviewer once asked Elkin what other writers were doing the kind of thing he was doing, and Elkin answered that, as far as he knew, none was; he continued, "I hope nobody else is doing what I'm doing. I hope *I'm* doing what I'm doing." *The Magic King-*

dom is like that. Although it resembles other traditional and modern novels in minor ways, it is a thoroughly original and unique work of fiction.

The hard fates of children was a popular subject in Victorian fiction, and Dickens portrayed child victims sentimentally, as, to a lesser degree, did Hardy. Elkin's child victims are presented with compassion, but not sentimentally. In fact, some of them are quite nasty and hostile because of their condition.

Cultural icons have been the fictional stock of such contemporary novelists as Max Apple (*The Propheteers* [1987] studies the creation of Disney World) or E. L. Doctorow (*Ragtime* [1975] looks back on the Morgan Library, and *The Waterworks* [1994], is formed around a cultural signifier). Again, *The Magic Kingdom* is really a study in the phoniness of the cultural landmark, and a compelling analysis of our mortal condition.

◆ Ideas for Group Discussions ◆

Reading groups might find sharing their responses to Elkin's version of Disney World valuable, especially in that most of us have experience of that or other theme parks. How just is his portrait of this cultural icon? Are entertainment centers like Disney World apt metaphors for a culture many perceive as in decline? Several characters' behavior is worth discussing, and, even more than in most Elkin novels, the intense rhetoric of individual pages or sections may be profitably read and shared.

1. Is Eddy Bale's role as "England's foremost beggar" believable? Can you think of other philanthropic organiza-

tions whose leaders assume deferential roles to attract investment? Could such behavior become obsessive?

2. Is Colin Bible's treatment of Matthew Gale justified? Is Gale's revenge responsible for Rena's death?

3. Examine the long collective dream the children share. To what extent is each character's individual contribution to the dream a compensation for his or her illness?

4. Does Nedra Carp grow spiritually (early, Elkin calls her "a patriot of the propinquitous") as a result of the trip and Rena's disaster?

5. What are we to make of Colin Bible's assuming practical responsibility for the end of the dream vacation? Is this a result of Mr. Morehead's and Bale's weakness, or of Bible's growth?

6. Does Mr. Morehead's reason for making the trip, to validate a bizarre theory of genetics, undermine or qualify our sense of the high moral purpose of the trip?

7. Does Rena's death undermine the altruistic purpose of the whole enterprise?

David Dougherty
Loyola College in Maryland

STAR GATE

Novel

1958

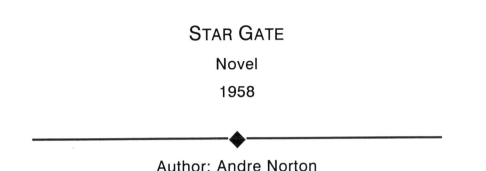

Author: Andre Norton

◆ Social Concerns/Themes ◆

Star Gate, the story of a world called Gorth, contains a strong folk epic flavor in the tradition of *Beowulf* (10th century). The struggle between good and evil is a continuing theme represented in the adventures of her hero, Kincar. He must leave his world to avoid seeing his followers slaughtered by those who are determined to rule Gorth. By chance he comes upon a fight between bandits and a group of men called Star Lords. He is accepted by them and joins their adventure, passing through a "gate" into a "parallel world." As Kincar leaves Gorth he is given a mysterious stone by the dying old chief, Wurd. The stone glows at certain moments and can become quite hot. While he does not understand its mysterious powers, it seems to serve as a protecting force for Kincar. Those who dare to touch the stone while he wears it end up with a hand reduced to a cinder. With the Star Lords, Kincar activates space ships that had been grounded and built onto a fortress of stone, and sends the enemy — gathered in one ship — hurtling into space. Kincar and the Star Lords free slaves being transported to the fortress

and befriend others who had been forced to live underground. The sense of justice and the determined battle against evil never slacken, and in the end good prevails.

Before she devoted full time to science fiction and fantasy, Norton's themes were varied but generally incorporated the good struggling against the evil, and her young protagonist would eventually overcome great obstacles to achieve a goal even though he would start out uncertain, if not bewildered by the abruptness of events. In her science fiction writing, certain themes run through many of her stories. These themes address subjects such as a relationship between men and animals (usually a direct mind-to-mind communication); one or more galactic empires in a "space-opera" setting; an ancient race or culture with mysterious power; time travel; the nature of existence after an atomic war; parallel universes and the occult.

In *Star Gate* the dominant issues are parallel universes, an ancient race, the mysterious powers of a strange stone that glows and is called a "Tie," and the exploits of a young protagonist who sets out on an adventure with no clear cut purpose only to gain confidence and skills as he proceeds to join forces with a group of men and becomes deeply involved in fighting evil.

◆ Characters ◆

Norton's characters are clearly perceived in the reader's imagination, and not as a result of detailed descriptions and exposition by the author. The characters become lifelike through their actions, through their approaches to problem-solving, and through brief physical description. Kincar, for example, is introduced in the third paragraph and is described as dressed in "soft suard fur"; he is not a giant but "well muscled" and endowed with six-fingered hands. From there on his personality, the quickness of his mind, emerges through his actions and his words.

Norton also deftly handles the characterization of Jord, Kincar's rival for stewardship of the "Holding"; Wurd, the ruler who is near death; and people whom Kincar meets on his journey such as Lord Dillan, Jonathal s'Kinston, and Vulth s'Marc. The believability of the characters facilitates the reader's acceptance of the strange names and languages invented by the author.

◆ Techniques ◆

Many of Norton's plots set the protagonist out on his own with little or no clear mission. In *Star Gate*, Kincar is asked to leave his homeland and rightful inheritance to avoid the useless bloodshed his stay would surely cause. There is no clear alternative goal for him to achieve. Where his path will take him is almost fortuitous; he might find a new world and a new adventure,

or come full circle to regain his inheritance.

In Norton's science fiction stories, the hero possesses some mysterious object of ancient lore, as the "Tie" stone which Kincar carries. Although it glows when danger threatens, he does not readily understand its powers. In *Star Gate*, as well as in other of Norton's stories, the protagonist is capable of communication with animals who prove useful in warning him of danger as well as in helping to combat evil forces. Norton's ability to make the characters of other worlds believable is an aspect of her technique that is not so easily assessed. Perhaps some of her success in this regard is due to the fact that, although nothing is outside the bounds of possibility in her other-worldly settings, a thread of traditional values can always be discerned in Norton's most imaginative works.

◆ Literary Precedents ◆

The influences that Norton acknowledges — *Beowulf* and books on folklore, legends, archaeology, anthropology, and the occult — are evident in most of her science fiction works. Also, one cannot be unmindful of the material Norton culled through her extensive reading of history. The times when people believed in witches, fairies, elves and trolls are significant to the substance of her writing. One critic contends that Norton is "re-enchanting" readers with her creations, and that her literary precedents are folk tales and legends as they were told around campfires by traveling storytellers.

The influence of specific legends and works may be seen, as well, in some of Norton's writing. For instance, the story of the Roman Emperor who ordered a legion to march to the end of the earth is a partial model for her Star Rangers. *Warlock of the Witch World* (1967) is strongly influenced by Robert Browning's poem, "Childe Roland to the Dark Tower Came." The folk tale "Beauty and the Beast" is the origin of *The Year of the Unicorn* (1965). Certainly her *Dark Piper* (1968) has its precedent in the tale of the Pied Piper. William Hope Hodgson's *The Night Land* is a viable precedent for *Night of the Masks* (1964).

◆ Related Titles ◆

Many of Norton's science fiction novels deal with strange planets, and are related to one another by other elements as well. *Operation Time Search* (1967) concerns breaking into an alternate world and bears a certain relationship to *Star Gate. The Zero Stone* (1968), to some degree, is related to the "Tie" stone in *Star Gate.* Their respective powers are different but the mystery behind these strange objects is an element Norton finds worthy of repeating. A prolific writer, since 1963 many of her books have dealt with the occult and parallel universes.

Robert A. Gates
St. John's University

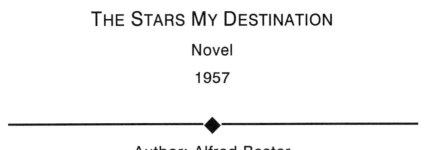

THE STARS MY DESTINATION

Novel

1957

◆

Author: Alfred Bester

◆ Social Concerns/Themes ◆

Where the main characters in *The Demolished Man* (1953) largely were from the upper strata of society, many of those in *The Stars My Destination* are the opposite, representing the lower social classes. Gulliver Foyle, the protagonist, is an uneducated, unskilled Mechanic's Mate 3rd Class on the twenty-fourth-century spaceship, *Nomad*. As in the earlier novel, events are put into motion in a business context, and they result in an overpowering desire for revenge. The outcome is that an individual again is goaded into a special awareness of himself and forced to develop supranormal powers in order to survive. The character's social awareness begins to develop next, and through extraordinary events the individual makes an evolutionary leap.

Gully begins as an insensitive egoist and ends up as a representative of the next development in the human race. He has become a superman in the sense that the characters in George Bernard Shaw's dramas become supermen. Essentially common people, Shaw's characters become animated by a life-force that compels them to seek others of a like constitution in order to advance the race. What for Gully started out as a mad, antisocial drive for revenge becomes a movement toward social responsibility that encompasses his entire culture.

The plot device that initiates the action in the novel is a simple one. During World War II, German submarines occasionally set traps by placing shipwreck survivors where they could be found; when another ship went to the rescue, it became easy prey for the submarine. As a consequence, survivors were sometimes left to die. Bester's story begins *in medias res*. That is, Gully already has been shipwrecked. He is the sole survivor of an attack by forces of the Outer Planets, and he has been marooned in space for 170 days. Suddenly, a ship appears that can rescue him — but inexplicably it leaves him stranded. Enraged, Gully focuses his whole being on finding the ship and its crew so that he can destroy them for having abandoned him.

There are two items that block Gully's act of revenge, though, and these complicating elements are what the novel is really about. First, humanity has discovered a mental process called *jaunting* that is a limited form of teleportation. Trained practitioners can move instantaneously from one jaunte stage to another up to 1,000 miles distant. Second, there was a secret cargo aboard the *Nomad*, a twenty-pound load of PyrE, a tremendously explosive compound that can be triggered by "will and idea." In other words, anyone can detonate the material merely by thinking about doing so. The explosive clearly would be the decisive weapon in the impending interplanetary civil war.

Through his adventures and narrow escapes, Gully is forced to control his mind to the point that he can jaunt through time as well as space. The stereotyped Common Man has risen above society and can now show humankind how to rise to his level. Moreover, Gully recognizes that mankind can be free to evolve only if everyone is part of the process as opposed to being controlled by a powerful few in the government (Y'ang-Yeovil) or big business (Presteign). Thus, he gives the secret of PyrE to the world in the calm assurance that if everyone has the power to destroy the universe, everyone will act with a sense of social responsibility to save the universe (a kind of futuristic Mutually Assured Destruction policy). Instead of seeing this as giving a loaded weapon to a child, Gully perceives his actions as being a means of impelling society to mature, as he has when responsibility is thrust upon him. The novel concludes with Gully in a meditational dream state. It is implied that when he awakens he will lead humanity as it awakens to its vast potential.

◆ Characters ◆

There are a variety of interesting characters in this novel, most of whom are willing to exploit or betray anyone or even to commit murder in order to achieve their goals: Saul Dagenham, the radioactive superpatriot; Robin Wednesbury, the telepath who broadcasts her own thoughts but cannot receive the thoughts of others; Presteign, a stereotypical ruthless businessman who has no sentiments for anyone other than his daughter and who is extremely manipulative; Olivia Presteign, who sees only in the infrared spectrum and is more bloodthirsty than her father; and Capt. Peter Y'ang-Yeovil, a racially mixed detective who communicates through body language. Nonetheless, the main character is Gully Foyle, and the rest of the cast of characters functions primarily to advance the plot or to expose one of the facets of Gully's nature. Gully is a common man with intellectual potential that has been stunted by his lack of ambition and who is awakened to realize that potential by an unexpected shock, a consistent theme in Bester's canon.

◆ Techniques ◆

Stylistically, *The Stars My Destination* is even more ambitious than *The Demolished Man*, although the devices that Bester employs in his second novel are the same as or an extension of those that he used in his first novel.

The most obvious, and initially the most striking, element is again typography, the utilization of different fonts (type faces) and patterns to replicate as closely as possible on the printed page the sensory effect of synaesthesia that Gully experiences. Synaesthesia is "that rare condition in which perception receives messages from the objective world and relays these messages to the brain, but there in the brain the sensory perceptions are confused with another" (*The Stars My Destination*). Thus, Gully sees sounds and hears shadows, and words with different sized letters undulate across the page to represent physically a sensory phenomenon.

Less superficially evident, but more effective in conveying the essence of Bester's message, are his utilization of dialogue and imagery. At the beginning of the story Gully speaks a language that the writer has invented to illustrate his protagonist's social status. This is an important creation for it establishes a benchmark against which Gully can be compared later in the novel so that the amount of change that takes place in his character is quite evident. The standard English that Gully speaks after being tutored in logic and the social graces by Jisbella contrasts dramatically with the harsh sounding dialect of the lower class. Bester reinforces this by developing a new grammatical pattern to demonstrate the subtle use of logic or the lack of logic that underlies the two distinctive dialects.

Likewise, the image of the hideous tiger mask that is tattooed on Gully's face captures the intense emotions that control him and set him apart from the rest of humanity (and vividly illustrates his survival drive) and at the same time provides a standard against which his progress can be compared as he learns to overcome his emotions and rely upon his intellect. The image of The Burning Man that reappears throughout the book serves a similar purpose. When taken together, these two images become even more significant, for they merge with the opening quatrain of William Blake's "The Tiger" that is quoted at the beginning of the

novel. These famous lines are from a poem in Blake's *Songs of Experience* (1794) collection, a group of poems that reverse conventional attitudes to show that true innocence can only be achieved through experience because true innocence must be chosen and a choice can only be made if the options are known (as in the parable of the prodigal son in the Bible). Again, Bester is working with various techniques to wed form and content in this tale about maturation. The fire, the emotional power, and the sense of control that forge Gully and open up a new universe for humanity are implied in the intertwining of these images and the literary allusion to Blake's poem. The full significance of Bester's conscious craftsmanship is underscored by the fact that the novel was originally published under the title *Tiger! Tiger!*

Finally, the repetition of the novel's opening paragraph at the conclusion of the tale serves as a frame that implies that the social concerns explored and evolutionary process manifested in Gully (and by extension the human race) are not just ongoing but eternal as well.

◆ Literary Precedents ◆

As was the case with *The Demolished Man*, elements in *The Stars My Destination* can be traced back to numerous examples in the science fiction genre (space and time travel and teleportation are obvious examples). There are also stylistic resonances with James Joyce, typographical connections with Laurence Sterne's *Tristram Shandy* (1759-1767), and the aforementioned thematic links with William Blake's poetry.

Bester's fiction is filled with literary

allusions, and one of the most interesting literary precedents for this novel is the incorporation of the plot line from Alexandre Dumas's *The Count of Monte Cristo* (1844). In "My Affair with Science Fiction" Bester admits that he had been "toying with the notion of using the Count of Monte Cristo pattern for a story. The reason is simple; I'd always preferred the antihero, and I'd always found high drama in compulsive types." He then goes on to relate how a story in an old *National Geographic* about the survival of a torpedoed sailor at sea who had been sighted by passing ships that refused to rescue him merged in his mind with the Monte Cristo pattern and thereby led him into the story that developed into *The Stars My Destination*.

◆ Related Titles ◆

While Bester is best known for, and has made his most important literary contributions through, his novels, he has also written numerous science fiction short stories that are extremely popular and considered classics of the genre. *Starlight* (1976) is a useful anthology of his short fiction because it brings together many of his best and best-known stories and because the contents of the collection span a considerable segment of his career, since it contains pieces published as early as 1941 ("Adam and No Eve") and as recently as 1974 ("The Four-Hour Fugue"). More importantly, a representative sampling from *Starlight* (which is actually a bringing together of two previously published collections — *The Light Fantastic* (1976) and *Star Light, Star Bright* (1976) — and includes the revealing autobiographical essay "My Affair with Science Fiction") shows that both the themes that control Bester's novels and the techniques that he uses to express them appear throughout his entire oeuvre and even in some cases were experimented with in short stories that preceded the longer works. Of additional interest are the brief introductions to each tale in which the writer explains how he came to write that particular story.

"Adam and Eve" arose out of Bester's impatience with what had become a science fiction cliché — a story in which it is revealed at the conclusion that the last two people left alive on Earth are Adam and Eve. In this telling, Steven Krane is a scientist whose experiment goes awry and literally destroys all life on Earth except him. Ultimately, the protagonist manages to crawl to a sea where his disintegrating body will start a new evolutionary cycle that will lead to today's world.

"Oddy and Id" (1950) is a Freudian tale in which the world discovers that no matter how well educated a person is, unconscious selfish drives will overpower all altruistic motives. In "Time Is the Traitor" (1953), Bester explores the Freudian consequences when a man tries to replace his dead girlfriend. When she is finally cloned, he has changed so much she no longer interests him and she is not in love with the man whom he has become. The moral of the story is: "The mind goes back. but time goes on, and farewells should be forever." "Fondly Fahrenheit" (1954) traces the interlocking psyches of a murderous android and his owner. The result of their mutual psychological projection is disastrous. When the android, who has taken on his master's subconscious maniacal personality, is destroyed, the master demonstrates the characteristics that the android had developed.

Richard Armour's comic and somewhat skewed observations on history are recalled by "The Men Who Murdered Mohammed" (1958). With a story line that can be traced back to H. G. Wells's *The Time Machine* (1895), this tale suggests that time travel in any meaningful sense is impossible because every person lives in an individual reality and there is no way, therefore, to affect anyone else's reality by traveling back in time since the lines are parallel but do not actually connect.

Bester's "obsession with patterns and dynamics" is found in an extrapolation of a "logically possible exaggeration of environment on a contemporary man," as he explains in his introduction to "The Pi Man" (1959). The typographical patterns that appear on the printed page are one of his stylistic trademarks.

An intriguing variation on extrasensory perception serves as the basis for "The Four-Hour Fugue." A Dr. Jekyll and Mr. Hyde dual personality inhabits the body of Dr. Blaise Skiaki, a research chemist for a perfume maker. Among Skiaki's talents is the ability, while in an advanced state of somnambulism, to identify a pheromone exuded by someone who has a death wish. Ironically, what Skiaki does while sleepwalking is discovered by Gretchen Nunn, who is an esper who is blind but does not realize it because she sees through other people's eyes. Neither can be cured, but their awareness of their situations means that together they can adjust and cope.

Steven H. Gale
Kentucky State University

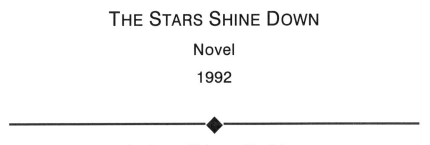

THE STARS SHINE DOWN

Novel

1992

◆

Author: Sidney Sheldon

◆ Characters ◆

In *The Stars Shine Down,* Sheldon resumes his usual practice of making a beautiful, intelligent woman his chief protagonist. As the novel opens, Lara Cameron is on her way to a birthday party in her honor where her guests will include dignitaries from both the political world and the business world. Her building projects have been highly successful, and she has tried to make her past as glamorous as the social position she currently occupies. Actually, she was poverty stricken, the daughter of an abusive alcoholic father. She has recently bought a castle in Scotland and buried him there. Unloved as a child, she has created a myth that her father was from a great family and was devoted to her. She is determined that her name, already on many buildings throughout the country, will soon be on the world's tallest Skyscraper. She is known as the "Iron Maiden," someone who gets what she wants, regardless of how she has to do it. But the Iron Maiden is also so beautiful and sexually appealing that no man can resist her. "No one really knows her" is a frequent appraisal of her character.

In Chicago after her successful career in Glace Bay, Lara forms an alliance with a young banker named Howard Keller. He became her chief assistant in the business enterprise she created in Chicago. Keller, although a genius in finance, has become a businessman only because circumstances forced him to abandon his dream of becoming a major league baseball star. His talent was there as all the coaches assured him, but his father deserted the family and his mother suffered a stroke that made it necessary for him to support the family by working in a bank. He, like most males who meet her, falls in love with Lara, but to her he is merely her trusted employee. His expertise enables her to realize her dreams, and she never realizes how much he loves her.

Lara, having conquered the world of real estate developers in Chicago, decides that she must challenge New York. Labor troubles force her to consult a noted attorney, Paul Martin, who at first refuses to help her. He is soon having a torrid affair with Lara, who is unaware of his underworld connections. Sheldon is fond of introducing Mafia figures into his novels and Martin differs little from the ones he put in his earlier novels, except for his genuine love for the heroine.

A concert pianist is Lara Cameron's unlikely choice for the love of her life. Philip Adler is considered by many critics to be the premier concert pianist of his era. The world of music provides some heightened glamour in the last part of the novel. Adler, against his will, falls in love with Lara Cameron. Sheldon is concerned with setting up a love affair between two very different people, using their differences to heighten the romance of the novel.

◆ Social Concerns ◆

In *The Doomsday Conspiracy* (1990), Sheldon showed concern about what unscrupulous businessmen were doing to the environment. No such concern is mentioned in *The Stars Shine Down*, although real estate developers are potentially as destructive as the villains of the earlier novel. Lara Cameron would be quite capable of erecting one of her office buildings or apartment houses in a pristine forest or on the site of a national monument. Sheldon presents how real estate developers operate, for he has studied the business with his customary thoroughness. Lara leads a glamorous life, but Sheldon does not try to make her lovable or even particularly likable. Rather, she survives by being more ruthless than any of her competitors.

◆ Themes ◆

The methods of real estate developers are explained as Lara learns the ropes of her demanding profession. She learns the importance of OPM — "Other people's money" as the devel-

oper borrows money for his projects. The government permits deductions on interest and depreciation while the developer's assets keep growing. Location is of primary importance too. A building in a strategic location can make a developer richer. Lara proves an apt pupil, and she becomes a developer with a flair for successful deals.

Lara is from Glace Bay, Nova Scotia, a predominately Scots city, so Sheldon gives his readers an introduction to Scottish history and customs. Lara's is a rags-to-riches story, a common theme in Sheldon's best sellers, and a significant part of the American Dream. After a miserable childhood, Lara becomes a powerful force in the world of land developers. Paul Martin's family also rose to prominence, but in a different kind of business venture. They are kingpins in the Mafia. Sheldon traces the family back to its origins in Sicily where they were poor tenant farmers on the estate of the local Don, who brutally mutilated and killed Martin's grandfather.

◆ Techniques ◆

The plot of *The Stars Shine Down* is circular in that the novel concludes where it begins, in the Cameron Plaza in New York City, where a birthday party for Lara with two-hundred distinguished guests is scheduled to take place. The great ballroom is deserted when she arrives and she, believing her career is over, relives her past from her beginnings in Glace Bay, Nova Scotia. Each important character in her life is given a series of flashbacks which explain how his or her character was formed. Gibellina, Sicily, 1879, is the farthest point in the past in the novel; it is where Paul Martin's Mafia origins are described. Lara's career takes her successively from her native Grace Bay, to Chicago, and finally to New York. Such shifts in locale are common in Sheldon's fiction.

Mystery, violence, and sex are always part of the package in a Sheldon novel. A would-be blackmailer, Bill Whitman knows that Lara lied to the chairwoman of a community board in order to get permission to build in that neighborhood. He is killed when the bucket of a crane slips its chain and falls on him. Later her husband Philip Adler is mugged and the tendons of his right hand severed by the assailant. The police trace the orders for both attacks to Lara's company. Adler believes his wife hired the thug because his concerts took him away too often. Paul Martin, her former lover and a known Mafia member is under suspicion, too. The association with Martin puts Lara under investigation because of a Nevada casino he helped her to build. Predictably, it is Lara's most trusted assistant, Paul Keller, who hired the thug responsible for both incidents. Lara is cleared of illegal dealings when Martin refuses to testify against her.

Sheldon continues his practice of ending most of his chapters with an exciting event in the lives of his protagonists. The concluding chapter of Book Three ends with the slashing of Philip Adler's right hand. As readers of romances would expect, the lovers Lara and Philip are reconciled in the novel's conclusion, and both of their careers continue, he as a teacher at Juilliard and she as a real estate developer.

◆ Literary Precedents ◆

A number of books have music and musicians as their subjects, and some are structured like musical compositions. Thomas Mann's *Doctor Faustus* (1947), for example, is the life of Adrian Leverkuhn, a fictional German composer of the twentieth century. His compositions are described in great detail. The novel also deals in length with philosophy and politics, especially those of the Nazi era. Marcel Proust's *Swan's Way* (1913), also deals extensively with music. It begins with an "Overture" rather than an introduction. One of its characters is Monsieur Venteuil, a church organist and composer, and Proust uses the theme from his "Little Sonata" in one of the climactic scenes. The problem with these novels might be their sheer complexity, which makes them more difficult to read than *The Stars Shine Down*. Readers may, however, want to see, for the sake of comparison, how other writers have used music in their works.

◆ Related Titles ◆

Most of Sheldon's books have characters similar to Lara Cameron, although she is much less vulnerable than earlier heroines. Sheldon's heroines seem to find Mafia leaders irresistible. His Jennifer Parker, in *Rage of Angels* (1980), first opposes but later has an affair with Michael Moretti, a New York racketeer. In *The Sands of Time* (1988), Lucia Carmine, whose family in Sicily has strong Mafia ties, hides in a convent in Spain after avenging the murder.

◆ Ideas for Group Discussions ◆

Sheldon's preference for women as his protagonists might be a subject for debate. As Lisa See points out in an interview published in *Publishers Weekly* (November 25, 1988): "What other popular novelist in the last two decades has so empowered his women characters? (Since *I Dream of Jeannie*, every Sheldon tale presents a woman in distress who rescues herself.)" However, these beautiful, successful women may not seem much more than the hapless victims of nineteenth-century melodramas to other readers. Is Sheldon actually furthering the feminist cause? In *The Stars Shine Down*, Lara Cameron is rescued from her predicament by the police and by the generosity of her former lover, Paul Martin. How does she differ from Sheldon's other heroines?

In his column "The Professional Response" in the January 1995 edition of *The Writer*, Sheldon says: "My characters come to life in my novel as I dictate the story." The characters are defined by the situations he invents. How effective is this method? Are the resulting characters believable?

1. Sheldon opposes censorship in any form. His novels have come under attack on several occasions, by the Reverend Jerry Falwell, for example, in the late 1970s when Falwell headed the Moral Majority. The Christian Coalition has come to the forefront since as the guardians of morality in this country. What might they find objectionable in *The Stars Shine Down*?

2. Which would readers of this novel understand better after they have finished reading, the world of real estate developers or the lives of great performers of classical music?

3. Lara Cameron seems to alternate between the role of martinet who fires people on the slightest pretext, and the romantic lady still looking for her Young Lochinvar to "come out of the West." In which role is she more believable?

4. Sheldon provides some historical background for a decade as his heroine continues her triumphant career. How useful is this information?

5. To what extent does Sheldon use techniques he learned as a writer of screenplays and television scripts?

6. Despite his success as a writer and producer of several successful situation comedies, Sheldon rarely, if ever, puts anything comic in his novels. Why is this? Would the novel be improved by such material?

7. Lara Cameron insists that she really works for people, not for money or prestige. "I dream," she says several times when explaining her motivations. How sincere are these ideals which she professes?

8. Since most of Sheldon's novels involve violent crimes and mystery, the police play prominent roles. Is his handling of police procedures comparable to that of writers such as Ed McBain or Joseph Wambaugh, both of whom are noted in this skill? How does Lieutenant Mancini in *The Stars Shine Down* compare to other fictional detectives?

9. Readers are often fascinated by our society's capacity for evil. Does Sheldon have a sound understanding of human depravity?

10. How does *The Stars Shine Down* compare to earlier novels by Sheldon? Has he changed his basic formula?

Karl Avery

THE NOVELS OF DANIELLE STEEL

Novels

1980-1996

◆

Author: Danielle Steel

◆ Themes ◆

Most of Steel's books follow a young woman's journey from youth to maturity, from ignorance in the art of loving, through a series of relationships with men, to self knowledge and a mature, balanced relationship.

The central concern of her novels is the search for a lasting love relationship. While the characters are uniformly wealthy, beautiful and involved in exciting occupations, events or experiences, beneath the surface level of plot and character description are the real key to Steel's phenomenal popularity. She uses all of the traditions of the formula, but they are secondary to the real focus, which are the uncertainties, conflicts, choices and mistakes that anyone could and most people do experience. Readers are treated to extraordinary, exciting and exotic events which provide escape from the daily grind of ordinary existence, and also ordinary, familiar and recognizable problems, which are not easily solved but which fail to destroy or defeat the love at the center of the story. Readers can make direct application of the choices and triumphs of the fictional characters to their own lives.

◆ Characters ◆

The key to Steel's success is in creating appealing characters. They are uniformly attractive and usually wealthy and successful, but on closer examination she reveals flaws which mark them as little different from the ordinary reader. All the wealth and beauty is little help in dealing with the most important aspects of life: the relationships between men, women, and their children.

Faye, in *Family Album* (1984) is a good example. She is a strong woman who makes choices and then lives with the results of her choices, admirable in her determination and endurance, and frightening in the force of her personality. She fights to keep the family together, observes the mistakes she makes. She demands a great deal from others as well as from herself, and loves as best she can. In this character Steel has created a complex, flawed and yet heroic woman. One understands why her children fight her influence and seek her approval. Externally, she is a figure from fantasy: beautiful, intelligent, the first major female director in Hollywood. But at home, she is just a mother, doing the best she can in the complex and imperfect relationships which are part of ordinary and real life.

◆ Social Concerns ◆

Loving

In *Loving* (1980) the first significant man in Bettina's life is her father, a celebrated and egotistical author. Although Bettina's life appears to be all that is glamorous and desirable, it is in fact hollow and destructive, a perfect example of the seductive quality of fame and wealth. Bettina lives in a jeweled cage, pampered and protected, but also used, as her entire life is geared towards pleasing her father at the expense of her own personality.

Bettina's father dies, and she is comforted by her father's friend Ivo Stewart, and then unfolds another fantasy story in the Cinderella mode. This cultured and much older man offers Bettina a more generous love than her father did, but it is still paternalism. Ivo allows her to explore her love of theater while maintaining the gilded cage of wealth and nurturing. For example, Bettina gets a job in an experimental theater but is picked up every night after the show by her husband's limousine.

The best thing Ivo does for Bettina is force her to leave him, again like a father who observes that the beloved young woman has grown up and is ready to fly the cage. Bettina precipitates this by falling into an affair with a very attractive actor, Anthony Pierce, but even before Bettina realizes it, Steel signals to the reader that this young man spouts the dangerous and egotistical charm of Bettina's father. So Bettina falls into the pattern of subjugating herself to the needs of others, as with Anthony, who dumps Bettina as fast as possible when she finds herself pregnant.

This appears to be the lowest point this still young heroine can experience. She loses the child and attempts suicide, but in the hospital another romantic fantasy appears to be unfolding. The handsome young doctor attending her reveals that he, too, is lonely and eager for someone to love, and Bettina finds herself ensconced in an urban gilded cage. John Fields is supportive of her emotional and physical needs, but tries to squeeze Bettina into the mold of wife and mother to which he ascribes. Bettina is forced to hide her play writing attempts, a clear sign of the destructive qualities of this superficially attractive relationship. But it is at the birth of her first child that the husband's true nature is revealed. All of the needs of the woman are ignored in pursuit of the perfect delivery from the obstetrician's point of view, and John, a doctor, sides with his medical colleague instead of his wife.

Bettina's growth as an individual is signaled by her ability to think through the faults of the situation and leave it of her own accord, as opposed to all of the previous relationships, which were ended by the man. She finds herself in New York, having received a rather implausible "lucky break" in finding a producer for her first play. She also meets one of the breed of new men, gentle, loving, and as giving to Bettina's needs as she had always been to men around her. In fact, he is willing to put his career as a successful theater critic in second place behind Bettina's growing success as a playwright.

This appears to be the perfect relationship, but Steel suggests otherwise. There is no spark, no fire, no tension between two equally vivid and dynamic individuals. Bettina needs a man as powerful and successful and special as she is, a man like her father as she is now a woman like her father, and Steel contrives that she be free and ready to fall in love when this ideal mate appears in the final chapter of the book.

Loving is a compendium of traditional female fantasy relations, celebrated so often in romance, and Steel takes each one and shows how it is potentially a trap for a woman, particularly one who has not learned much about her own needs, her own personality. Yet the book is not anti-male. There is never any suggestion that the entire system is geared by men to exploit women. Rather, women are responsible to learn about themselves, to grow up, and if need be, to experiment with relationships until they are capable of loving as fully and maturely as possible.

In this book, as in several others, Steel explores relationships which, traditionally, have been frowned upon. In this case, Bettina is a much divorced woman, yet her experiences are shown in a sympathetic light, so that the reader understands how such things might come about, without either judging harshly or glorifying unduly.

Crossings

Crossings (1982) is set during World War II, and although relationships between men and women remain Steel's dominant concern, the social and political realities of the period are also explored. Liane is happily married to her French husband Armand de Villers at the beginning of the novel, so that when she first meets Nick Burnham, unhappily married to the spoiled Hilary, she offers him sensitive sympathy only. Nick realizes that this is the sort of woman he considers ideal: a good mother, a loyal wife, and gently, purely beautiful as opposed to his own wife's flaunted sexuality. Nick's marriage is held together only by his concern for his son, but Liane's much stronger relationship is torn apart by external pressures. Armand is returned to France at the beginning of the war and then, at the fall of France, is forced to choose between his love of his wife and children and his love for his country. He chooses to send his family back to America and remain in Nazi-occupied France, apparently cooperating with the Germans but secretly assisting the underground. Liane, in turn, remains loyal to her husband despite the public knowledge of his collaboration and the cruel prejudice of her old friends. Even her family attempts to force her into a divorce, but she remains married to Armand. Besides the external pressure, there is a private conflict; Liane and Nick have met again, fallen in love, and now struggle to suppress their passion in loyalty to her husband and in hopes of saving his son from a messy divorce.

Steel presents a tortured love affair, where neither of the lovers is wicked, where both try to do the best they can, and yet where people are still hurt, where tragedy cannot be avoided. The novel suggests that actions should not be judged unless one knows all the facts; an apparent traitor may be a loyal citizen sacrificing all, and an errant wife may be caught between loyalty and passion and be simply trying to hurt the fewest number of people.

Changes

Changes (1983) explores the problems of a working woman juggling children and a challenging career. Melanie Adams seems to have it all: a high-profile and high-paying job as anchor of a national news broadcast, and attractive and well-adjusted teen-age twin daughters. But at what price? She has not allowed herself to risk deep involvement with a man since the father of the twins walked out on her years before the story begins. When she does meet a special man, all sorts of questions are raised which she and her lover must answer.

Peter Hallman has an equally successful and glamorous career; he is a heart surgeon, and he, too, is leery of falling in love as he is still recovering from the death of his wife. But despite their uncertainty and a lengthy courtship, they finally must admit that they are in love. And now the trouble begins. Melanie and Peter explore the sorts of compromises which make a mature relationship survive. This story doesn't end with the marriage ceremony, for Steel is very interested in just how one lives happily ever after. She shows the tensions which exist between husband and wife, no matter how loving they might be. The situation for Melanie and Peter is complicated by the new extended family; Melanie's two girls must share their mother with Peter and his three children.

Steel explores some of the problems parents must face. The youngest boy is lost in the mountains over night. Then Peter's son and Melanie's daughter begin a relationship, and a pregnancy results. Neither Melanie nor Peter deal with these problems perfectly, which endears them to the reader. In fact, there is no perfect solution, because the daily tensions, large and small, cannot be eliminated except in fantasy.

Underlying all the tensions, though, is a single problem which is finally addressed and solved, giving hope for a smoother life ahead. Both Peter and Melanie are afraid of change, but Melanie conquers her fears and commits herself to a new life. Peter, however, is less willing to change, to compromise, to adjust his life to accommodate his new partner. Finally Melanie leaves him for a time, and he realizes not only what she means to him but also how limited he has been in his growth. Life demands constant change, and rigidity can only destroy the positive aspects of living and loving.

Melanie and Peter are both, on the surface, stereotypes of contemporary fantasy characters. Melanie is the new superwoman, a success as mother, in her career, respected, financially secure as a result of her own hard work, and also beautiful, warm, loving and loved. Yet readers see the flaws in her otherwise perfect life, the emptiness at the center. And when she chooses change and chance over secure success, they applaud her growth. Peter first appears as the attractive doctor of romance, dedicated to work, but also lonely and longing for love. Beneath this surface lies the truth that the very things that make him a good doctor make him a poor husband; he is rigid, unwilling to change, and he cares so much for his patients that his family suffers. As his character unfolds, the reader likes him more, for his fears and weaknesses make him a more believable and approachable character.

Family Album

At first glance *Family Album* (1984)

appears to be set in the familiar mode of Hollywood saga of stardom, scandal and secrets. But Hollywood is merely the background for the relationships of family members. In this case, the tension between parents and children is even more central than the working out of the love between husband and wife.

Faye and Ward Thayer have their ups and down as a couple, but their children experience some of the problems which worry parents from California to New Jersey and beyond. Lionel, their oldest son, is a homosexual, and Steel presents his search for identity and love sympathetically. Faye and Ward, particularly Ward, are horrified by the discovery, but Steel asks her readers not to judge but to understand. She also presents tasteful sexual scenes and a homosexual marriage situation, a first in her writing and perhaps a surprise to many of her readers. Steel avoids stereotypes in Lionel, and places no blame for his sexual preference. Rather, it is presented as simply an aspect of his character, and he, like everyone else in the novel, is searching only for love and security.

Greg, the second son, is an all-American hero but, for all his success with women and on the football field, is a less appealing young man than his brother. With his character Steel explores another shared family experience, the loss of a son and brother in Vietnam. Both Lionel and Greg serve in Vietnam; Lionel volunteers after a lover is tragically killed and Greg is drafted when he flunks out of college. He dies when he steps on a land mine two weeks after being sent overseas. The cruelty of the loss, in the irony of the statistics, is brought home in this sudden and unexpected death.

Ward and Faye have twin daughters, Valerie and Vanessa, and with these two girls Steel explores various options in relationships and life choices for young women. Vanessa is the wild one, battling with her mother, sexually promiscuous, but finally fulfilling her promise and emerging as an outstanding actress. Valerie opts for college, where she finds a compatible, if not perfect, lover. In contrasting the two girls, Steel avoids judgments, but suggests that, despite their different avenues, both were seeking the same thing: fulfillment of their talents and energies as individuals, and only then a lasting, loving relationship.

The youngest child, Anne, presents the most problems for her parents, but Steel lays the blame firmly at Faye's door. When the other children were little, the Thayers had plenty of money, and Faye was able to devote herself to nurturing her family. But just after Anne's birth, it becomes apparent that Ward has squandered the family fortune, and Faye becomes the sole supporter of the family. Suddenly, she is just too busy to pay any attention to her youngest child. Anne grows up in the shadows, and makes the most spectacular and sensational mistakes of the children. She runs off to Haight Ashbury and joins a cult which indulges in multiple drug and sex orgies. Her family rescues her, but she is pregnant, and Faye forces her to give the child up for adoption. Only near the end of the novel is Faye able to admit that she was wrong in this, although she did it for the best, and Anne is able to agree. By this time Anne has followed a completely different route in her search for love and security. She has formed a relationship with the father of one of her friends, and this unconventional marriage turns out to be a suitable one for her.

Full Circle

In *Full Circle* (1984) Steel presents another young woman living and growing and learning about herself and the nature of love between men and women. Tana observes and judges harshly her mother, caught in a long term affair with her boss who fails to offer marriage even after his wife has died. Tana's first encounter with sex is also negative: She is raped by this same boss's son, and her mother refuses to believe her. Tana slowly overcomes the scars of these early experiences, but in the course of her life makes her own mistakes. She maintains a close platonic relationship with one man, has a brief, passionate and ultimately untimely affair with that friend's father, and then finds herself in a situation which mirrors her mother's. She meets an attractive, compatible man with just one problem: He has just separated from his wife. Tana's mother warns her that he might not be emotionally separated, and sure enough, Tana becomes the other woman, left alone at Christmas, always waiting for the phone to ring. Tana, and the reader, must reevaluate the harsh judgment placed on the first mistress, and to understand how such things come about. Tana is able to summon the courage to end the relationship, and begin another based entirely on compatibility. This, too, is finally revealed to be a dead end, and in the final chapters of the book Tana has the good fortune of meeting and marrying a suitable man.

Tana's life raises another social issue, for she is a very successful lawyer, and a great deal of her conflict with her mother and with the men in her life centers on her enjoyment in her work and the traditional view of the role of women. Tana's mother wants her to marry for wealth, security and a place in society. Tana argues that she has achieved all these on her own. Her compatible lover is offended when Tana's career is more successful than his own, and subtly and overtly presents blocks to her advancement. It is only in her final relationship, and only marriage, that Tana makes the important discovery, with her husband's help, that she can have it all, a happy marriage, an exciting career, and a family, too.

Steel spans two full generations in this novel, showing the early years for Tana's mother during and after World War II, in an attempt to explain the older woman's options and choices. This provides a contrast with Tana's life, and heightens the irony of Tana ending up in the same compromise relationship that her mother chose. Steel also touches on contemporary political issues by having Tana attend a southern girls' college and be roomed with its first black student. Tana finds herself drawn into the civil rights movement, and tragedy occurs when both her roommate's brother and the young girl herself are killed. But this is just a brief interlude in Tana's life, and she does not remain involved in the civil rights movement.

Similarly, the war in Vietnam makes itself felt, as Tana's platonic friend allows himself to be drafted, to Tana's horror, and returns paralyzed from war wounds. But this too is a personal rather than political issue for Tana, and she marshals her considerable energies getting her friend interested in life again rather than fighting against the war. She has a brief sexual relationship with a student radical, but refuses to become involved in his activities, which is just as well because he is caught trying to blow up the governor's house.

These political and historical events ground the novel in American history, and thus lend the story credibility, but remain secondary to the main concern, which is Tana's growing understanding of the complexities of love.

Five Days In Paris

In *Five Days In Paris* (1995), Steel returns to a romantic situation whose social commentary is based on the "duty" versus "passion" theme exploited so well in Robert James Waller's *The Bridges of Madison County* (1992).

As president of a major pharmaceutical empire, Peter Haskell has everything: power, position, a career and a family, which mean everything to him, and for which he has sacrificed a great deal. Compromise has been key in Peter's life, but integrity is the basis on which he lives. Olivia Thatcher is the wife of a famous senator who has given to her husband's ambitions and career until her soul is bone dry. She is trapped in a web of duty and obligation, married to a man she once loved and no longer even knows. When her son died, there was no bond left.

On the night of a bomb threat, these protagonists meet in Paris and their lives converge as Olivia carefully steps out of her life. In a café in Montmartre, their hearts are laid bare. Peter, once so sure of his path, so certain of his marriage and success, is suddenly faced with placing his professional future in jeopardy if he takes Olivia into his life. Olivia is no longer sure of anything except that she can't go on anymore.

At home again, they both must pursue their lives, despite challenges, compromise, and betrayal, holding to their memories of Paris.

Lightning

Lightning (1995) unfolds the story of a woman whose life is changed by one swift, unexpected stroke of fate. As a partner at one of New York's most prestigious law firms, Alexandra Parker barely manages to juggle husband, career, and the three-year-old child she gave birth to at forty. But Alex feels blessed with her life and happy marriage — until lightning strikes her. Suddenly a routine medical check-up turns her world upside down when tests reveal shattering news.

Sam Parker is a star venture capitalist, a Wall Street whiz kid, and is as proud of his longtime marriage to Alex as he is of his successful career. As a major player in New York's financial world, Sam is used to being in control — until he is caught off guard by Alex's illness. Terrified of losing his wife and family, and haunted by ghosts from his past, Sam is unable to provide any kind of emotional support to Alex.

Unable to cope with her needs, Sam takes his distance from Alex, and almost overnight she and Sam become strangers. As lightning strikes them yet again, Sam's promising career suddenly explodes in disaster, and his life and identity are challenged. With their entire future hanging in the balance, Alex must decide what she feels for Sam, if life will ever be the same for them again, or if she must move on without him, now knowing the uncertainty of the bonds of love and marriage.

Days of Shame

Days of Shame (1996) portrays families divided, lives shattered and a nation torn apart by prejudice during a shameful episode in American history.

A man ahead of his time, Japanese college professor Masao Takashimaya of Kyoto had a passion for modern ideas that was as strong as his wife's belief in ancient traditions. It was the early 1920s and Masao had dreams for the future — and a fascination with the politics and opportunities of a world that was changing every day. Twenty years later, his eighteen-year-old daughter Hiroko, torn between her mother's traditions and her father's wishes, boarded the SS *Nagoya Maru* to come to California for an education and to make her father proud. It was August 1941.

From the ship, she went directly to the Palo Alto home of her uncle, Takeo, and his family. To Hiroko, California was a different world — a world of barbeques, station wagons and college. Her cousins in California had become more American than Japanese. And much to Hiroko's surprise, Peter Jenkins, her uncle's assistant at Stanford, became an unexpected link between her old world and her new. But in spite of him, and all her promises to her father, Hiroko longs to go home. At college in Berkeley, her world is rapidly and unexpectedly filled with prejudice and fear.

Within hours of the bombing of Pearl Harbor by the Japanese, war is declared, and suddenly Hiroko has become an enemy in a foreign land. Terrified, begging to go home, she is nonetheless ordered by her father to stay. He is positive she will be safer in California than at home, and for a brief time she is — until her entire world caves in

On February 19, Executive Order 9066 is signed by President Roosevelt, giving the military the power to remove the Japanese from their communities at will. Takeo and his family are given ten days to sell their home, give up their jobs, and report to a relocation center, along with thousands of other Japanese and Japanese Americans, to face their destinies there. Families are divided, people are forced to abandon their homes, their businesses, their freedom, and their lives. Hiroko and her uncle's family go first to Tanforan, and from there to the detention center at Tule Lake. Steel's message is contained in the portrait of human tragedy and strength, divided loyalties and love. Set against the backdrop of war and change, the novel dramatizes the now-well told story of the betrayal of Americans by their own government and the triumph of a woman caught between cultures and determined to survive.

◆ Adaptations ◆

The following is a list of the television movies that have been produced based on Steel's novels. Generally, the miniseries format has been faithful to the plot and emotions of the novels, and has done a great deal to further enhance Steel's popular reputation.

Changes
April 1991

Crossings
ABC, 1986

Daddy
October 1991

Family Album
October 1994

Fine Things
October 1990

Full Circle
Fall of 1996

Heartbeat
February 1993

Jewels
October 1992

Kaleidoscope
October 1990

Message From Nam
October 1993

Mixed Blessings
December 1995

No Greater Love
January 1996

Now and Forever
Australia, 1983

Once In a Lifetime
February 1994

Palomino
October 1991

A Perfect Stranger
September 1994

Remembrance
Fall of 1996

The Ring
September 1996

Secrets
April 1992

Star
September 1993

Vanished
April 1995

Zoya
September 1995

Leslie O'Dell
Wilfrid Laurier University

STEEP ASCENT

Novella

1944

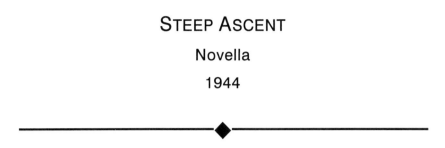

Author: Anne Morrow Lindbergh

◆ Themes/Characters ◆

Using the metaphor of flight, Lindbergh achieves a powerful story of spiritual adventure in *Steep Ascent*. A semi-autobiographical work, it enjoys an inherent authenticity and provides an insightful narrative. Lindbergh's portrayal of her protagonist's, Eve's, journey is both sensitive and provocative. She presents Eve as an astute observer, possessing a foreigner's eye for detail. Eve, an American, has been living in England for ten years as the wife of a British airman. She decides to accompany her husband Gerald on a flight over the Alps to Italy, despite apprehensions about leaving her son Peter behind, and concern for the health of the baby she is carrying. Initially Lindbergh draws the reader into the story with the bustle of activity and good-byes surrounding the preparations for the flight. No sooner has the plane taken off, however, than the metaphor permits the transformation of this seemingly simple story into an adventure of mind and spirit. No longer bound by temporal values of space and time, the flight allows Eve a period of meditation for reverie and reflection.

Eve experiences a series of revelations during the flight. She seems driven by a sense of urgency she does not fully understand. In the beginning she is preoccupied with time and with the fear of the dangers that might lie ahead. She observes the disappearing earth below with great longing, wishing somehow to possess it, feeling herself bound to its security; her own longing leads her to question Gerald's obsession with flying. She reflects upon the closeness the two share in the single engine plane in which they rely on their understanding of one another and a nonverbal communication composed of limited contact and gestures. Eve considers her motives for making the journey. She concedes that she is not seeking physical adventure, resolving that she is an "earth person." But she is not satisfied, not wanting to waste life she seems anxious to appreciate it on all levels. Eve analyzes life's texture as having three levels — a "top crust," a "middle everyday layer," and a rarely attained "inner core." Her anxiety leads her to the realization that the emotional fear which is plaguing her mind and body denies life, and that allowing this fear to take control is tantamount to a decision against life.

This realization allows her to understand her motive for making the journey: She wants to break through the middle layer of life, to reach the more fulfilling inner core. This knowledge allows Eve the freedom to defeat her fear and participate in the joy of living.

At the moment of Eve's epiphany, she experiences an exaltation that is paralleled by the plane's ascent over the Alps. As they break through the clouds, Eve reaches an understanding of Gerald's love of flying in her new awareness of life and the sense of freedom that her spirit achieves in its release from fear. Eve's decision to live, the decision to make the steep ascent despite the danger or the fear of the unknown permits her a sense of ecstasy, a momentary glimpse beyond life's middle layer. Flying then becomes a metaphor for letting go of the earth and a vehicle for reaching the inner core of life.

This elation is followed, however, by a period of great danger as the plane is caught in fog and is unable to locate a safe point at which to break through the cloud in order to prepare a safe landing. Eve's joy gives way to renewed fear and doubt. As she is reminded of her own mortality, she reflects on faith. She is reminded of a pilgrim's hymn, which lends the novella its title: "They climbed the steep ascent of heaven . . . through peril, toil, and pain . . . O God, to us may grace be given . . . to follow in their train. . ." The turning point comes as Gerald decides to make a "blind" descent risking the possibility of crashing into the mountains hidden by the clouds. In this instant, this test of faith, Eve's fear of danger and death dissolves. The final revelation, the revelation that brings her spiritual fulfillment comes with the acceptance that life is a gift, not a possession, and that to serve the gift, to participate in life is to remain open, aware and vulnerable. Eve's ability to transcend the fear of death comes from the selflessness she achieves as a server of life rather than a possessor. As a server of life, her decision to live becomes a decision not for herself but for others.

Although the crisis of nonparticipation experienced by Eve is not exclusively a women's problem, Lindbergh chooses to emphasize women's role as the "watchers and waiters" and the ordeal they face as they search for a sense of being. The apparent limitlessness attained in flight becomes the metaphor for the freedom that Eve's spiritual adventure affords. Eve's pilgrimage gives her the courage and fortitude to approach life with a new sense of awareness and to overcome the stagnation of nonparticipation.

◆ Techniques ◆

The "confessional" style of *Steep Ascent* weds itself strongly to the literary form of the diary, a form Lindbergh works with in much of her fiction. The most striking feature of this allegorical novella is the significant absence of dialogue — but for some dialogue in the opening pages, the narrative relies almost entirely on interior monologue. In part autobiographical, Lindbergh's work is convincing without becoming self-indulgent. Her use of evocative imagery and the cadence of her poetic style transform the story from a physical adventure to an adventure of the spirit. She emphasizes the spiritual elements of the journey or pilgrimage by alluding to religious themes. Merging idealized images with realistic elements, Lindbergh communicates a philosophy that asserts an optimistic belief in the participation of life. Despite her own apologies for not including a more passionate expression of the World War II politics in which the story takes place, her strong affirmation of life and the tenacity of the human spirit provides a subtle yet powerful argument against the destructive forces of warfare.

◆ Literary Precedents ◆

Lindbergh's ideology draws on a variety of artistic, literary, and philosophical sources. Her diaries and letters specify the influence of Joseph Albers, D. H. Lawrence, Rilke, and T. S. Eliot. In her review of Antoine de Saint Exupéry's *Wind, Sand and Stars* (1939), Lindbergh takes a quotation from Alfred North Whitehead's *Adventure of Ideas* (1933). "Adventure," he writes, "is nothing if it is not translated through the mind, through the spirit." There is no doubt that Lindbergh's theme embodies this concept of adventure. Her choice of metaphor and her literary style also owe much to the work of her contemporary, Saint Exupéry.

Amanda Mott

STEPS

Novel

1968

◆

Author: Jerzy Kosinski

◆ Social Concerns/Themes ◆

*S*teps involves the quest of a man shaped by the oppressive, brutal, and anarchic modern world to define himself as an individual. Once again, society and its institutions are seen more as threats than supports sustaining the individual. In his essay "The Art of the Self," Kosinski comments that "these formerly protective agencies like society and religion" now work to keep "the self from functioning freely." Some of the incidents recounted by the narrator bring out this grave malfunctioning, such as his account of finding a demented woman kept in a cage in a barn, where she had been sexually abused by the local farmers over several years. Even the local priest, obviously aware of the situation, had done nothing to rescue the woman. The priest only protested that the stranger did not understand the peasants.

The stringent pressures upon the individual person to conform in a collectivist society are emphasized in other episodes, such as the account of a university student, called the "Philosopher," who found that clean lavatories provided the one safe refuge where he could think in solitude; eventually he committed suicide in one of them. Kosinski also suggests the extreme depersonalization of which society is capable in the description of the architect who could design very functional concentration camps without any qualms by thinking of the purpose in terms of the extermination of rats rathrather than the murder of human beings. Moreover, as Ivan Sanders has stressed, the protagonist's escape from a war-scarred European country under a totalitarian system of government to the United States does not bring him into a brave new world. "In his new environment he is suddenly exposed to the casual barbarity of an impersonal, technological civilization." Throughout *Steps* Kosinski emphasizes the darker side of human nature that all too readily finds expression in society and in personal relationships.

In many ways, the protagonist proves to be a reflection of the world that he finds oppressive and restrictive, even while he seeks the freedom to realize himself most fully. As in *The Painted Bird* (1965), Kosinski shows that in this predatory world those like the narrator, who have been victims, strive to transform themselves into oppressors. Freedom comes to be associated with power; the protagonist of *Steps* seeks to assert the power of the self consistently and remorselessly, such as in his commitment to exacting revenge for wrongs done to him.

Moreover, the narrator brings the concepts of power and dominance into his personal relationships. He carries out to an extreme the Sartrean concept that the self is the subject that preserves its integrity by converting everything else into an object. The narrator transforms the love relationship into a power play in which the other person is regarded solely as an object. As Kosinski's comments in *The Art of the Self* make clear, the narrator considers the only satisfactory relationship "one of growing domination, one in which his experience — a certain form of the past — be projected into the other person. Until he has gained that dominance and the other is aware of it, his 'prey' is a rival." At the end, his departure from his mistress shows the lack of real commitment to or involvement with the other.

Nothing in the narrator's account indicates that he recognizes any deficiency in his personal relationships, but in *The Art of the Self* Kosinski describes love as "the attempt to be simultaneously subject and object, . . . the willing relinquishment of a single subject to a new subject created from two single selves, a subject enhanced into one heightened self."

♦ Characters ♦

The nameless I of *Steps* is a metamorphic figure who appears in a variety of roles, including vagrant boy in the villages, university student, photographer, ski instructor, soldier, and alien in a new country. The protean nature of the self is suggested in the representation. His varied movements through the chaos and barbarism of the modern world have been characterized by Jack Hicks as "the individual's deepest attempt to escape the encumbrances of fate and social control," as well as "the attempt to shore up a constantly eroding self that is sliding toward history and that is possessed in time by the consciousness of others." He is also a metamorphosing figure, invading and transforming other lives for his own self-satisfaction. He can seduce a laundry girl with the magic of a credit card and half transform her into a woman of the world or wonder how giving drugs to another woman will affect her. His ready victimization of others shows how deeply he has absorbed the oppressor's mentality in his own metamorphosis from victim.

Karl has emphasized the essential loneliness of the protagonist, who seeks dominance rather than love and friendship with equals, so that every act of reaching out to another becomes a contest. The protagonist does react against the oppressive forces in the society and rebels against the values of a collective society in his quest for personal freedom. Some of his turning toward the darker impulses of his nature has been seen as negative gestures expressing this rebellion. The protagonist's cruelty and aggressiveness, his constant manipulation of others, and his lack of any display of human warmth make him an extremely unattractive figure. Kosinski's own comment on the narrator suggests how fully the author envisions him as a product of a brutal modern world he is "always in step with the culture, unable to walk any other staircase."

◆ Techniques ◆

Steps represents Kosinski's most radical experimentation with the form of the novel. Here he dispenses with any kind of plot in the Aristotelian sense, as well as any chronological sequence. Kosinski links this approach with the modern artists' desire "to show time as we perceive it, experience as we absorb it. The shaping mind is at the center of the work and guides the work as it evolves." *Steps* consists of thirty-five seemingly disconnected episodes related by the narrator as observing participant. He has been compared to a camera eye ranging over scenes of cruelty and brutality that he has witnessed or dispassionately recollecting his own activities. The author has interspersed among these episodes fourteen italicized dialogues between the narrator and the young woman currently his lover. In their discussion of matters involving their relationship, the two explore the problem of how the self relates to others while preserving its own individuality. Thus their conversations pick up a major theme involved in the episodes described, which portray a range of activities, including victimization of various kinds, revenge, murder, and various sexual encounters.

Kosinski's pattern of sharply etched but separate incidents in *Steps* has been linked to his perception of his own life "as a series of emotionally charged incidents." He has told Gail Sheehy "to intensify life, one must not only recognize each moment as an incident full of drama, but, above all, oneself as its chief protagonist" Norman Lavers believes that Kosinski's episodic technique in this novel is his way of involving the readers by making them attend as fully to each episode as to events in their own lives. Kosinski himself saw this as enabling each reader to make his own individual journey through *Steps*, "automatically filling in its intentionally loose construction with his own formulated experience and fantasies"; he should leave each episode "with a hint of recognition."

Although no clearly discernible pattern connects the episodes, Kosinski has spoken of them as forming into a montage. Certainly the combined effect is a chilling representation of an anonymous, brutal, and amoral universe provided by a narrator who inhabits that wasteland. Occasionally, smaller connections linking episodes can be seen; the narrator may recall several incidents from a particular period in his life. At other times, the juxtaposition of incidents may have a thematic connection; for example, the narrator's obsession with revenge is emphasized when he tells how he killed the villagers' children and follows that with an account of how he ruined the career of a man at the university who had wronged him.

Kosinski's novel contains no tacit moral judgments against the brutal world it depicts; in fact, Kosinski has stated that he made each incident "morally ambiguous," thereby compelling the readers to resolve for themselves the moral issues involved.

◆ Literary Precedents ◆

With the writing of *Steps*, Kosinski joins the company of postmodernist experimental novelists, like the French writer Alain Robbe-Grillet, theoretician and practitioner of the "new novel" and American writers like John Hawkes, Donald Barthelme, and John Barth. Such writers rejected the traditional novel and sought to evolve forms that they judged more appropriate to the contemporary consciousness and its views of reality. For example, the influential Robbe-Grillet, with whom Kosinski is familiar, believes that conventional plots are distortions of reality and that the writer should not pretend to be able to explain the psychology or motivation of someone else. One of his key tenets is that the natural world must not be interpreted in human terms but simply presented as it is, in its "thereness" visually and sensually — "a smooth surface without signification, without soul, within vision, on which we no longer have any purchase." Characters are identified solely with the visual actions they perform or the events in which they appear. The "new novel" provides a scrupulously accurate report of observed reality that the reader can interpret in terms of his own experience and intelligence. In rendering this reality, the writer must focus on structures, since form gives a literary work its meaning. John W. Aldridge gives a very good assessment of Kosinski's place among such novelists. This critic finds Kosinski "energized by the post-avant-garde iconoclasm" of the experimental writers and influenced by New Novel theories and the black humor of modern satirists. Yet he maintains that Kosinski's vision is "primarily philosophical" rather than "attempting to explore in the French manner the various possible ways of dramatizing individual consciousness"; satire is a secondary feature of his work. Aldridge sees Kosinski as "concerned rather with understanding the nature and meaning of the human condition, the relation, quite simply, of human values to the terms of existence in an essentially amoral and surely anarchistic universe." He puts Kosinski among those like Kafka, Sartre, and Camus concerned with giving dramatic force to ideas in their fiction. Although Aldridge's view of Kosinski as "primarily philosophical" is controversial, he does correctly suggest that Kosinski adopted the experimental forms to fit his serious thematic concerns.

◆ Related Titles ◆

The Art of the Self à Propos "Steps" is a critical essay setting forth some of the philosophical concepts of the self that Kosinski drew upon in the novel. Kosinski also discusses the aesthetic principles that he sought to apply in his experimental techniques.

Norman Lavers provides a good analysis of the resemblances between *Steps* and *The Devil Tree* (1973). The latter portrays Jonathan Whalen's quest to find his identity through a number of short episodes arranged achronologically, as in *Steps*; it also depicts a number of scenes throughout the world in which people are seeking dominance over others through violence and cruelty; Whalen's relationship with Karen provides a recurrent focus in the novel, even as the protagonist's conversations with the young woman did in *Steps*. Although Whalen, the wealthy young heir to an industrial fortune, has a far different background from the nameless protagonist of *Steps*, he also has several different selves, struggles for dominance in his relationships, and cannot give himself over to a commitment to Karen. (Please see separate entry on *The Painted Bird* for the relation of *Steps* to that novel.)

The protagonist in *Steps* has also been compared to Tarden in *Cockpit*. Both are wanderers and adventurers with no fixed roots; both seek control over others and are manipulative and aggressive in their relationships with women; both follow a code of personal vengeance, although they also seek retribution for wrongs done to others. Levanter, in *Blind Date* (1977), resembles them in many ways. However, there are some important differences, as Lavers emphasizes: Levanter is less successful in maintaining control than the other protagonists, and he is more fully involved in self-appointed missions seeking revenge for grave wrongs done to others. Levanter is also portrayed as more human and vulnerable than his predecessors; he is also the first one to commit himself to marriage.

Gertrude K. Hamilton
Marymount College, Tarrytown

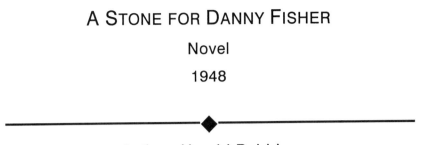

A STONE FOR DANNY FISHER

Novel

1948

Author: Harold Robbins

◆ Characters ◆

Danny Fisher IS a "jerk" in search of a picaresque adventure in which he might have been a rogue. Danny has the reader's full sympathy throughout the novel, *A Stone for Danny Fisher*, because of the point of view, but by any objective standard he misses his chance again and again simply because he fails to consider his options. He agrees to throw the Golden Gloves championship fight to enable his father to start his own business again, but he fails to realize that losing the fight will end the professional boxing career that was to be his ticket out of the slums. To make matters worse, his father throws him out of the house on the night of the fight for wasting his life in pursuit of a danger-ous boxing career, but it never occurs to Danny to explain that this amateur fight is to be his last. Then he allows his boxing skill to overwhelm the logic of the bad deal he has made and goes on to win the fight, leaving himself hunted for years by the gambler with whom he had made his dirty deal and a disappointment to the high school coach who had invested thousands of dollars in his potential as a fighter.

When he returns to New York, he takes no precautions to avoid his old ene-mies. Danny is totally lacking in intro-spection, and he does not change in the course of the work. This fact is not a flaw in the book's characterization but a necessary condition of the theme that fate is beyond man's control and un-derstanding.

There are a large number of minor characters, all etched with an almost Dickensian eye for the significant char-acterizing detail. Nellie Petito is the good girl Danny marries. She domesti-cates him. She also has an irrational premonition that Danny is in danger on the day they are moving back to his childhood home. With no good reason for her fears, she nevertheless turns out to be right, for Robbins is using her to illustrate his fatalistic theme. Sarah Dorfman (professional name Ronnie) is the whore with a heart of gold who saves Danny when he fails to throw the fight and barters away her own chance for happiness to support her disabled brother. Sam Gottkin (later Gordon) is a person from this world who makes it — for a while. He is already a high school coach at the beginning of the book, but he becomes a summer entre-preneur and then a major businessman.

But he too is a product and a victim of the urban scene, and he never really adopts middle class values. As a coach, he lets, indeed requires, squabbling boys to fight out their antagonisms. He is also carrying on an adulterous affair. And as a businessman he makes deals with gangsters on their own level and cuts what corners can be cut. Mimi, Danny's sister, sells herself into a loveless marriage with Sam as her way out of the slums.

Perhaps the most interesting characters in the book are Danny's parents, who strike the appropriate postures for lower middle class domesticity and fail to see when and how their dreams slip away from them. Danny's father is cold and rejecting and unwilling to listen to reason, but Danny never recognizes that he has adopted the very same stereotypic male attitudes, not only when he slugs the welfare investigator but even when, especially when, he is blaming his father for the death of his dog or for the loss of their home in the paradise that is Brooklyn.

◆ Social Concerns ◆

When Danny returns to New York after failing to throw a fight for bookie Maxie Fields, Robbins saves him from the consequences of his earlier action quite arbitrarily. In much the same way, Robbins later kills off Danny's daughter — and with the same purpose — to show that it is an unreasoning fate that guides "life among the lowly" (as Harriet Beecher Stowe subtitled *Uncle Tom's Cabin*). Of course, Danny is just a teen-ager at the time of the fight and only about twenty when his daughter dies; however, Robbins's portrait of Danny's world is effective and realistic just because the character

of Danny can tell the whole of his own life story without pausing for one moment of serious self-reflection. His shady dealings escalate from shoplifting, mugging, agreeing to fix a fight, and cheating the Department of Welfare to blackmail, black marketeering, and arranging to have his brother-in-law killed by a hit man, but he never considers the moral or even the practical implications of what he is doing. The hit goes wrong in the same way that the fixed fight does. Danny learns too late that he does not have the facts straight. This time the mistake kills him.

At another level the book illustrates lower-middle-class striving for the security and protection of a home of one's own. Danny's anger at his father begins when the family home is lost, and he finally resolves this anger on the day when he moves back into the house but can do so only because his father reaches out to him saying, "We've all come home again."

◆ Themes ◆

The social issue of the effect of fate on the aspirations of the lower middle class and the reciprocal concern for the security of a home are important thematic motifs in the book, but from Danny's point of the view, the theme of his life is probably "Without a buck, you're nothin' but crap." Although the novel is autobiographical, for Robbins the theme of the book as a whole is not so simple, but it is perhaps summed up in this observation of Danny's: "Someone you know all your life tries to kick your teeth in, and a man you never saw before and will never see again comes along and saves your life." Logically enough the book ends with a hymn to the "ordinary man."

♦ Techniques ♦

Danny Fisher narrates his own story in the first person, but by the ingenious device of a prologue spoken by Danny from the grave to the son he never knew, Robbins is able not only to maintain the verisimilitude of a first-person narration but even to describe plausibly incidents Danny had not witnessed in his life, for example the reactions of his mother on the morning she discovers that the milk service has been stopped for non-payment. Such passages are clearly marked with "I WASN'T THERE WHEN," making the shifts of focus easy to follow and helping to maintain overall consistency of mood.

Although Robbins is more a writer of incident than image, he can be wonderfully effective at important turning points in the story by presenting a minor detail of life in a way that suggests the whole direction of the story. For example, when Danny's mother does learn that milk service will be discontinued, she sits down in front of the open icebox. "Whatever cold was left in it would escape," Robbins writes, "but somehow it didn't matter. She didn't have the strength to get up and close the door. . . . She stared into the almost empty icebox until it seemed to grow larger and larger and she was lost in its half-empty, half-cold world."

To use Phyllis Bentley's terms, *A Stone for Danny Fisher* is almost all scene and no summary; that is to say, numerous episodes from Danny's life are presented to the reader, but there are no narrative links connecting these episodes. This technique gives a graphic urgency to the story and allows a long book to move very rapidly. The character Danny is also able to give the impression that he is neither self-centered nor self-justifying (although he is both) because he never comments on what he was doing but merely describes what he said and did. Thus the book avoids a possible sentimentality, and the technique helps the reader to focus on the theme that the evils of urban life and of the Depression have conspired to destroy what chance there might have been for happiness in the lower middle class.

Although liberally seasoned with explicit violence, *A Stone for Danny Fisher* stops the sex scenes just short of the graphic. In doing so in this book Robbins shows himself to be a remarkably astute judge of the threshold of reader arousal. This technique also suits the material well because Danny lives so naturally in a world of eroticism (and violence). The image of the girl next door purposely walking around naked in her bedroom to tease him is an emblem for the life he leads when he grows up — the pleasures of life are always just within sight — daring him to risk the disappointment of actually reaching for them.

A Stone for Danny Fisher is written in a racy, colloquial style, but it is written with such a sure control of the idiomatic that the father's occasional Yiddishisms seem a bit jarring; however, this fact may have increased the book's appeal by making the milieu seem only superficially and accidentally Jewish. The problems of Danny are, after all, the problems of all working class ethnics during the Depression.

♦ Literary Precedents ♦

A Stone for Danny Fisher is a *Bildungs-*

roman (or novel of growing up) in the picaresque tradition that goes back at least to *Don Quixote* (1605) by Miguel de Cervantes. More immediate ancestors include the nineteenth-century moral tales of Horatio Alger, turn-of-the-century muckraking novels of low life like *The Jungle* (1906) by Upton Sinclair, and proletarian novels of the 1930s like *Studs Lonigan* (1932-1935) by James T. Farrell. James Lane has also suggested a specific relationship between *A Stone for Danny Fisher* and *A Tree Grows in Brooklyn* (1943) by Betty Smith and *Knock on Any Door* (1947) by Willard Motley. In particular, Smith's Francie Nolan symbolizes the aspirations of those determined to overcome the dehumanizing effects of the modern urban experience through hard work. Danny Fisher illustrates how easy it is to be destroyed by this world.

◆ Related Titles ◆

After he had written the three novels *Never Love a Stranger* (1948), *A Stone for Danny Fisher*, and *79 Park Avenue* (1955), Robbins came to see them as forming a trilogy which he calls *The Depression in New York*. These are parallel stories involving different characters but all illustrating the struggle for survival of the lower middle classes during the Depression.

Never Love a Stranger is, with regard to incident and characterization, an intensely autobiographical novel. Even the name of the hero is Frankie Kane, the name Robbins received when he was, like his hero, a foundling, but Robbins imposes his fine sense of plot closure on the materials of his life up to this time (many of them reused, of course, in *A Stone for Danny Fisher*). The point of view of this novel is of interest because it has the same advantages for storytelling as the point of view adopted in *A Stone for Danny Fisher*. Frankie Kane narrates most of his own story in the first person, but the main narration is interrupted in places for first-person reminiscences by his friends. This allows Robbins to include the death of his hero — or anti-hero, for Frankie Kane is a stoic victim of social conditions just like Danny Fisher. *Never Love a Stranger* puts considerable emphasis on sex in a way that alienated reviewers, but Robbins was praised for his handling of religious misunderstandings and for his characterization. Some reviewers complained that the hero lacked introspection, leaving readers uncertain of his motivation; however, as in the case of Danny Fisher, this lack of introspection is the key to the social theme of the book.

79 Park Avenue is a rare use by Robbins of a female central character (*The Lonely Lady* [1976] is another). It is essentially the same story as *A Stone for Danny Fisher* and *Never Love a Stranger*, but Marja Fuldicki survives by turning to prostitution rather than gangsterism. The book was an early use by Robbins of the *roman à clef* since it is based in part on the Jelke trial.

◆ Adaptations ◆

Michael Curtis directed a movie version of *A Stone for Danny Fisher* called *King Creole* (1958). In order to tailor the material to star Elvis Presley, the locale was changed from New York to New Orleans, and the hero was made a Cajun rather than a Jew and given a talent for singing rather than boxing. Despite these major changes, the movie is faithful to the seedy atmosphere of the book and leaves many important character relationships intact. It shows an imaginative integration of the musical numbers into the dramatic story and includes what is probably Presley's best film performance. The supporting cast includes Walter Matthau, Vic Morrow, Carolyn Jones, Dean Jagger, Jan Shepherd, Paul Stewart, and Dolores Hart.

Never Love a Stranger was filmed in 1958 from a screenplay written by Robbins in collaboration with Richard Day. The director was Robert Stevens, and the movie stars John Drew Barrymore and Steve McQueen. In 1977, *79 Park Avenue* was a six-hour television movie directed by Paul Wendkos. It starred Lesley Ann Warren (fatally miscast), Marc Singer, and David Dukes and featured a huge supporting cast of name players. This movie was cut to four hours for rebroadcast. Neither of these adaptations was a critical or a popular success.

Edmund Miller
Long Island University
C. W. Post Campus

STORY OF MY LIFE

Novel

1988

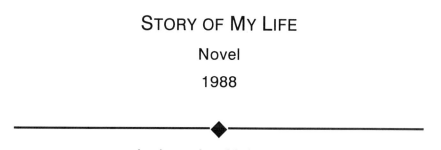

Author: Jay McInerney

◆ Characters ◆

Alison Poole is the novel's narrator and most-important character. Twenty "going on 40,000," she feels she has seen everything and done everything, and her jaded response to most of what she sees points out the emptiness of a life lived only from one thrill to the next. Her acting is the only thing that seems to give her life focus, and praise from her teacher seems to mean more to her than anything else. Her family and friends, for the most part, are hindrances; her sister Rebecca is an exaggerated version of what Alison might become, manipulating men for financial security, while their father is too busy pursuing girls Alison's age to make sure her financial arrangements are in order. Alison truly loves only her grandparents and her youngest sister, none of whom appears in the novel.

Dean Chasen, a thirty-two-year-old stockbroker who wants to be a writer, captures Alison's eye, and they circle warily into a short-lived relationship. Dean has just broken up with his girlfriend, and Alison later concludes that he only wanted someone to spend time with, but the desolation she feels after she betrays him with his friend Skip Pendleton suggests that their relationship had possibilities.

Didi is the ultimate party girl, attractive, sexy, and always carrying cocaine. Alison's feelings about her are mixed; on the one hand she recognizes Didi's sex appeal and feels inferior to her in some ways; yet she knows that Didi is often overbearing and manipulative, and that her drug use has gotten out of control. While Alison helps Didi get treatment, she does not entirely approve of the results, since Didi then criticizes her drug-using friends with the same vigor she once used to get them to snort cocaine with her.

None of the members of Alison's circle are satisfied with what they have, and all of them seek more — more money, more sex, more thrills. Only Alison's relationship with Alex, her first love, demonstrates the potential happiness that people can have together. Alison and Alex no longer have sex, but their friendship is one of the few stable areas in Alison's life, and consequently, in the novel.

◆ Social Concerns ◆

Like *Bright Lights, Big City* (1984),

Story of My Life is narrated by an observant, witty, and jaded member of Manhattan's party elite. Alison Poole's descriptions of drug use and casual sex reflect a slice of life in the present, which the novel's epigraph describes as an age of anarchy.

Drug use constitutes one of the major pastimes of Alison's crowd, and although she knows rationally that it is dangerous, she generally gets swept along with the crowd, willing to temporarily lose herself and her problems in a line of cocaine. A recurring plot element is a card with the emergency number of a drug treatment center which is transferred from character to character. At the end of the novel when Alison comes to her senses, she finally uses the card to call for help.

According to the characters in *Story of My Life*, love and sex in the modern world are hardly distinguishable; the continuous use of the phrase "in lust" blurs the distinction by blending the two. Sex serves many purposes in the novel: like drugs, it helps people to forget; it can create a momentary illusion of love and security; and it can be used to hurt. But the modern dangers of casual sex are also expressed through references to AIDS, as well as Alison's accidental pregnancy. None of the characters in the novel seems capable of a long-term relationship, and new liaisons are created almost from page to page. For Alison, much of her confusion about love and sex stems from her father's incestuous advances, which she says, almost soured her on sex forever.

◆ Themes ◆

Despite her other faults, Alison claims to believe in honesty, sometimes even taking it to an extreme. Although her behavior is not always consistent with her belief, the conflict between acting and being is a central one in the novel, expressed through the continual games of "Truth or Dare" and, paradoxically, through Alison's acting lessons. Although she is learning to act out roles, Alison's acting teacher encourages his students to draw from themselves to fill out the part. His highest praise, that someone is "inhabiting the role," comes only when he feels that the performance, and the emotions, are honest ones. Ironically, the money for Alison's acting lessons often comes through dishonesty, as when she tricks Skip into giving her money for an abortion she does not need, or when her father, who seems to be involved in some unsavory business dealings, sends money for her school.

Like McInerney's other novels, *Story of My Life* may be read as a *bildungsroman*, a novel that chronicles a character's coming-of-age and awareness of who he or she is. Alison faces many challenges, some sexual, some financial, all of which must be conquered if she is to become a complete person. At the end of the novel, Alison reaches some understanding about herself and who she is; even though she has not solved all her problems, her growing self-awareness and newfound acceptance of her own life must be read as a positive step.

◆ Techniques/Literary Precedents ◆

The first-person narration of *Story of My Life* allows interior views of the main character and captures the intelligence of a likable character living on the edge. Alison's narration is more casual than the unnamed narrator's in

Bright Lights, Big City, with many digressions and casual interpolations, and the erratic nature of her storytelling reveals her manic energy and the lack of coherence in her life.

The narrative technique evokes works like *The Adventures of Huckleberry Finn* (1884) and *The Great Gatsby* (1925), but a more important link to these works is McInerney's realistic approach to fiction. Like these two earlier novels, *Story of My Life* is a novel of manners, presenting the reader with an accurate picture of a certain time and place. The reader knows what the characters drink, where they eat, what drugs they take, what Broadway shows they see. This realism also has an artistic value: the shows Alison mentions, for example, are *Fences*, about the difficult relationship between a father and child, and *Les Liaisons Dangereuses*, a story of sexual misadventures and deceptions similar to Alison's own story. McInerney manipulates the concrete details so that they also illuminate character, plot, and theme.

◆ Related Titles ◆

With *Story of My Life*, McInerney continues to chronicle a frenetic world of alienation and frustration, but this work is the farthest outside himself. Using Alison Poole as a narrator, McInerney gives the reader a feminine outlook on society that did not exist in *Bright Lights, Big City*, or *Ransom* (1985). Although Alison is a typical McInerney character in search of meaning for her life, her outlook on men, sex, music, and fashions differs radically from the masculine viewpoint expressed in the author's earlier work.

◆ Ideas for Group Discussions ◆

1. Does McInerney's characterization of Alison seem realistic? Why or why not?

2. Why does the phrase "in lust," recur throughout the novel? What thematic purpose does it serve?

3. What comments does McInerney seem to be making about relationships in the modern world? Why are the family members Alison loves most absent from the novel?

4. As a work of literary realism, *Story of My Life* may be read as a cultural document as well as a literary work. What significant details do we learn about the world McInerney writes about?

5. In what ways does acting serve as a thematic device in *Story of My Life*?

6. What minor characters seem to be important in the novel? Why?

7. Many of the characters in the novel seem to be dysfunctional in some way or another. Does McInerney suggest that all people are scarred psychologically, or does he present some models of sanity?

8. In what ways can the novel be read as a coming-of-age story?

9. How does McInerney use abortion as a plot, thematic, and character-revealing device?

Greg Garrett
Baylor University

STRAIGHT

Novel

1989

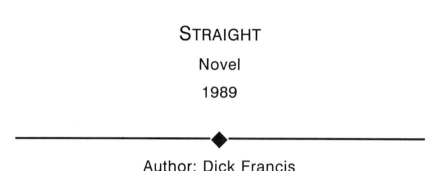

Author: Dick Francis

◆ Characters ◆

When asked by an interviewer to define the strong sense of morality underlying his books, Francis replied: "What it comes to, is that I never ask my main character to do anything I wouldn't do myself." Derek Franklin, who shares the initials of his name with the author, is a thirty-four year old loner who has suffered many emotional and physical injuries. Children of divorced parents, Derek and Greville had little contact over the years and scarcely knew each other, but a strong fraternal bond nevertheless existed. When Greville suddenly dies, Derek inherits "his business, his gadgets, his enemies, his horses and his mistress," a legacy, he says, that "nearly killed me." Through the course of the novel, Derek experiences a series of initiations. By the end, he has proved to be a quick learner of business and managerial skills; but however wiser he may be, he has not materially changed, remaining an upright and steady presence who moves easily between his worlds of racing and gem dealing.

As protagonist and narrator, Derek is the major figure of *Straight* with the other characters distinctly minor and functioning only in terms of how they interact with or affect him. The Saxony Franklin staff, on whom Derek — knowing nothing about gemstones — is completely dependent, is stereotypical. The main ones are Annette, Greville's fortyish personal assistant, who is loyal, hard-working, knowledgeable, but also timid and unimaginative; younger June, an alert blonde whose ability and initiative quickly lead Derek to realize "that without her the save-the-firm enterprise would be a non-starter"; and Jason, stockroom worker, all-around muscles of the firm, a sullen young fellow with spiky orange hair who proves to be disloyal.

The characters from the racing world similarly are predictable types, not unlike their counterparts in previous Francis novels. Trainer Milo Shandy is honest, frank, and "a perpetual optimist in the face of world evidence of corruption, greed, and lies." Nicholas Loder is another trainer, whose successes "attracted as owners serious gamblers whose satisfaction was more in winning money than in winning races," and his drug addiction leads him to betray his sport. Harley and Martha Ostermeyer, American horse owners, are as naive as they are wealthy. Finally, Thomas Rollway, also a racehorse owner, is a drug baron who feeds cocaine to horses as well as to people.

Two other members of the supporting cast stand above the rest as psychologically complex and ethically ambiguous figures. One is Prospero Jenks, an amoral Knightsbridge jeweller with a "young-old Peter Pan face." He specializes in one-of-a-kind display pieces emblazoned with gems and is a prime customer and friend of Greville, but nevertheless deceives him by switching part of a diamond consignment for cubic zirconia. Thanks to Greville's electronic Wizard, Derek learns of the theft and confronts Jenks, who admits to it, but says that his ethic is staying "ahead of the game" and that everyone steals. "Sure," he says, "I get a buzz when what I've made is brilliant, but I wouldn't starve in a garret for art's sake." Although he regrets the theft now that Greville is dead, his remorse is only skin deep, and, Derek thinks, "nowhere had it altered his soul."

Equally complex is Greville's lover, Clarissa Williams, forty-year-old wife of seventy-year-old Lord Knightwood. Not at all delicate, she is decisive and powerful, but also troubled: "It hasn't been a bad life, but before Greville, incomplete." After a brief romantic interlude with Derek, she decides that what she "had with Greville was unforgettable and unrepeatable," but before returning home to "do [her] best there," she saves Derek from likely death in the climactic episode of the novel.

◆ Social Concerns ◆

Francis portrays a materialistic soci-ety in the wide-ranging milieus of this novel, with a cast of characters that includes racehorse owners and trainers, drug dealers, gamblers, and diamond merchants. Pitted against them is narrator-hero Derek Franklin, a steeplechase jockey recovering from his latest injury and a man of self-effacing honesty. When he unexpectedly inherits Saxony Franklin, the gemstone business of his elder brother Greville, who was accidentally killed, Derek is thrust into an unfamiliar world of international trade. He also finds himself the putative victim of unknown enemies, for he unwittingly threatens their pursuit of profit and wealth.

Francis's plot also focuses upon the dubious tendency of people to rely increasingly upon gadgets, electronic and otherwise. Intended to simplify personal and professional lives, these mechanical wizards, Francis demonstrates, often become gimmickry obsessions that clutter and distort normal activities. Derek, his taciturn driver Brad, most of the employees of Saxony Franklin, and a wealthy American couple are the innocents: not only personally honest, but also unaware of most of the unethical and evil activities that surround them.

◆ Themes ◆

In the novel, greed and ambition beget evil, overshadowing people's good qualities, distorting reality, and initiating chain reactions that lead to death. Derek comes across this note by his dead brother: "The bad scorn the good, and the crooked despise the straight," an appropriate philosophical legacy to add to his material inheritance. As in earlier works, Francis here again deals with the racing scene, showing how the desire to capitalize on a horse's abilities inspires talented professionals to betray a trust that others have placed in them. An added dimension in the novel is the presence of drugs, with their destructive effects on men's morality and on animals' performances. The story lines involving the gemstone importing business and the attempts of a shady character to get a local gaming license emphasize the pervasive destructiveness of greed and evil.

Straddling these worlds of sport and commerce, admirable Derek Franklin and those like him ultimately overcome those who would destroy that which is good. Brute force may seem ready to overwhelm everything ranged against it, but by the conclusion, the meek — sustained by old-fashioned ideals and a stoic determination to endure — are triumphant, at least temporarily. Although Derek Franklin is a babe in the woods as new owner of his brother's firm, he possesses the physical and psychological wherewithal to succeed. In British racing parlance, the finishing straight — or homestretch — is the point at which a horse finally wins or loses an event. With Derek Franklin in *Straight*, Francis gives a new meaning to the term.

◆ Techniques ◆

By using the first person narrative technique, Francis makes Derek Franklin the focal point and achieves an immediacy of reader involvement with the hero's problems that would not otherwise occur. Further, there is a minimum of introductory exposition: *Straight* opens with Franklin caught up in a major crisis that involves not only his brother's death but also a threat to his own life. As a result of Greville's death, Derek finds himself in an unfamiliar milieu: a steeplechase jockey who has inherited a wholesale gemstone marketing business. He moves between these two worlds — old and new, familiar and unfamiliar — with ease, confidence, and courage, although he must confront physical, moral, and ethical challenges in both. By the end of the novel, he has broadened the range of his experiences, has learned about gemstones and how to engage in international commerce, and has suffered more injuries to his already battered body. He remains fundamentally the same person he was at the start, a moral paragon and a loner, but he is not at all too good to be true, for Francis's realistic delineation of background and character assure verisimilitude.

◆ Literary Precedents ◆

There may remain in later Francis novels some element of Nat Gould and Edgar Wallace, early writers of racing thrillers, but a more direct precedent may be the work of John Welcome, a friend and sometime collaborator. Another influence may be John Buchan, author of *The Thirty-Nine Steps* (1915); like him, Francis creates heroes who struggle against time and have a keen ability to escape from difficult situations. Francis himself has acknowledged a debt to Ian Fleming and also has expressed his admiration for such contemporaries as Desmond Bagley and Alistair Maclean.

◆ Related Titles ◆

Straight has many echoes of earlier

Dick Francis novels, including the first person narrative point of view and thoroughly admirable hero-detective who is a steeplechase jockey. In addition to providing insight into the racing game (including its seamy underside), Francis continues a practice that he began many novels ago: to feature another field alongside racing, in this case gemstones; and, again, he has done his homework, displaying a remarkable degree of knowledge about the specialty. The obligatory physical testing of the hero is present, as in the past, but there is less sadistic violence in *Straight* than in previous books, and the novel covers a shorter time span than its immediate predecessors.

Critics for many years have commented about Francis's failure to develop substantive and distinctive female characters. Clarissa Williams is somewhat more complex than her counterparts in previous works, and although she appears in only a few scenes, in the climactic episode she saves Derek from likely death.

Whip Hand

In *Whip Hand* (1979), Sid Halley, former steeplechase jockey and a sought-after private detective, deals with four cases simultaneously: he wants to clear his former wife's name as a result of her unwitting involvement in a phony charity; he tries to uncover suspected corruption in the ranks of the Jockey Club; he agrees to see if someone is indeed fixing the way horses in a syndicate run; and he attempts to learn why crippling and fatal ailments have been afflicting a wealthy horse owner's stable. The common motivation for all of these crimes is greed, and Francis pits Halley — selfless, warm-hearted, thoroughly honorable — against the forces of corruption. The common aim of the criminals is to enrich themselves at the expense of others, and this desire for money becomes so all-consuming that it leads to violence, thus begetting even greater crimes. In contrast, the erstwhile jockey's desire to succeed has nothing to do with financial gain or social status; rather, he simply aims to right wrongs, to purge the evils that are sullying a sport he loves and endangering the woman he has loved. As it must in a morality tale, good ultimately prevails over evil, at least temporarily.

As a result of a serious racing accident, Halley has a bionic hand and a new career as private eye. In addition to suffering continuing trauma from the physically maiming injury, he also has not recovered from the shock of his failed marriage. In this respect he is similar to most other Francis heroes, for a painful emotional shock in the past — such as the death of a loved one — haunts them as definitively as any physical wound. There thus is a pervasive sadness about Halley and the other Francis heroes, whose suffering and pain make them more sensitive and caring than most men, but rather than turning them inward, the stressful situations have led them to look beyond themselves and to become concerned with others' problems, sometimes as a means of escaping their own, but primarily to satisfy a sense of social responsibility that the suffering has spawned.

Halley is the only character in the novel who is fully realized; the others are merely types or two-dimensional, including his former wife Jenny, whose inability to make a go of marriage to a risk-taking jockey has left her bitter toward him and vulnerable to the advances of undesirable men; her father, retired Admiral Charles Roland, the one stable element in her life, who retains a brotherly relationship with Halley; Chico Barnes, a judo instructor whose brute strength (boyish and slender, he "could throw a two-hundred-fifty-pound man over his shoulder with the greatest ease") complements Halley's intelligence and compensates for his lameness; Rosemary, neurotic and frightened wife of George Caspar, one of the world's top horse trainers, whose leading two-year-olds inexplicably lose their touch as three-year-olds; Commander Lucas Wainright, patrician Director of Security to the Jockey Club, who unofficially asks Halley to look into alleged wrong-doing within his operation; aristocratic Trevor Deansgate (born Trevor Shummuck in a Manchester slum), "urbane, a man of the world, seeking top company, becoming a name in the City, the sycophant of earls," who owns one of the country's major bookmaking firms; Peter Rammileese, a farmer "who's made a packet of crooked dealings in horses"; and balloonist John Viking, who gives Halley the ride of his life. These and sundry minor figures, mostly from the racing world, are mere functionaries: helping or hindering Halley's progress, advancing or complicating the action.

Sid narrates the novel and is its central consciousness, and Francis's first order of business — a common practice for him in his books — is to provide insight into the character by means of a reflective prologue. In this instance, Halley's musings are interrupted by the arrival of a visitor who offers him a job. In rapid succession three more people ask him to look into matters for them. The rest of the book is devoted largely to his alternately directing his attention to one or another of the cases, three of which involve race horses, and

thus there is some overlapping of venue and characters. Halley's only distraction along the way is a romantic interlude (a recurring motif in Francis novels) with Louise McInnes, Jenny's roommate, who is only tangentially linked to one of the cases, but is a means by which Halley's emotional rehabilitation is fostered. Another recurring element is the physical violence, for at least once in a Francis book the hero is forced to confront danger directly and then to endure a vicious beating, in this case at the hands of men with pitchfork and chains: "I moved my head a bit . . . and simply lay where I was, feeling shapeless, feeling pulped, and stupid, and defeated . . . Jelly. A living jelly. Red. On fire. Burning, in a furnace."

Banker

Francis has said, "My heroes ... are the sort of chaps I'd like to meet . . . I do like to write about good types." Tim Ekaterin in *Banker* (1982) is such a man, an unheroic type who copes with the unsought and unwanted challenges — emotional, physical, and professional — that he confronts and somehow remains unstained by the corruption all around him in both business and sport. Whereas in traditional mysteries the amateur detective's insight and perception outpace his or her accumulation of facts and proof, Ekaterin is a novice whose progress toward the resolution is even more tentative than the reader's. He is as self-effacing a character as any who has served as a whodunit protagonist, and that he succeeds is as much a surprise to himself as to the reader. For most of the novel, in fact, he is learning — about investment banking, chemical compounding, thoroughbred breeding. He also is a young man in search of himself and his place in the world, not unlike Ross Macdonald's Lew Archer, albeit younger and not at all world weary.

The other characters come from the three worlds of the novel: Gordon Michaels, Tim's mentor in banking, takes Tim to the Royal Ascot, where he meets Dissdale Smith and Calder Jackson, the former a heavy better, the latter a veterinarian who apparently cures horses with odd medications and a mystical laying on of hands. Michaels's attention to Tim leads to the development of a relationship between Tim and Judith, Gordon's young wife. Through Gordon and Judith, Tim meets Penelope Warren, a pharmacist friend of theirs, who at first seems to have been introduced as an appropriate alternative to Judith, but Francis focuses upon her pharmaceutical knowledge rather than her romantic availability, and Tim soon realizes the usefulness of that professional expertise. When he does, the plot of *Banker* moves forward.

Not until the midpoint of *Banker* does the novel become a full-scale mystery, but the first half of the book is not merely preamble for the subsequent "whodunit"; it has a life of its own. At first the focus is upon a venerable investment banking firm in London; once a junior executive loans a stud farm owner five million pounds to purchase a thoroughbred, the action predictably shifts to the racing world. In both venues there is a seamy underside, with a variety of people involved in unethical and illegal activities that eventually destroy them. It is Francis's modern morality tale, an imaginatively crafted portrait of social climbers. Counterpointing them is the virtuous protagonist, apprentice investment banker Tim Ekaterin, whose insistent

pursuit of truth and justice — analogous to a ritual purgation — enables him to overcome the stigma of profligate parents and to assert his own identity. He is a strong moral force working against the immorality that pervades the social strata through which he moves. Ambition and greed are the corrupting social forces in the world of this book, but according to Francis's old-fashioned verities, virtue finally prevails and always is rewarded.

The action of the novel spans three years, an unusually long period for a detective novel. In the first year, Tim (who is the narrator) moves through his apprenticeship in investment banking, which is the means by which he comes to know Sandcastle, a five-million-pound thoroughbred, and his milieu. In the next section of the book, devoted to the second year, the focus shifts more clearly to the stud farm and broodmares, stallions, and breeding sheds; but the seemingly casual and dilatory pace continues. Such slowness is necessary to Francis's design, for enough time must elapse so that mares which Sandcastle has serviced can foal. In the third section, set two years after the opening scenes of the novel, the stallion's first progeny are born, and the birth of these deformed foals quickens the pace of the action. But before Tim solves the puzzle, he must pass another test, the obligatory ordeal through which Francis places his heroes. Knocked unconscious, Tim regains consciousness in a horse box at a stable. The person who carried him there makes a final appearance and then leaves Tim to contemplate both his enlightenment and likely fate in the company of a horse who goes berserk. The "rearing, bucking, kicking, rocketing nightmare" breaks one of Tim's arms, crunches an ankle, gives him "a swiping punch in the chest," and lands a "crushing thud" on a shoulder. Tim concludes: "This is death . . . dreadful, pulverizing extinction." Unprepared although he is for "the onslaught of so much pain all at once, and also not quite sure how to deal with it," Tim manages to endure and at the same time belatedly reach some firm conclusions about the case.

Gerald H. Strauss
Bloomsburg University

THE STRANGE CASE OF DR. JEKYLL AND MR. HYDE

Novella

1886

◆

Author: Robert Louis Stevenson

◆ Social Concerns ◆

It is difficult for a modern reader, surely familiar with the Jekyll/Hyde dual identity, to imagine the shock of those in Stevenson's time who had no notion of the phenomenon and who believed, until near the close of the text, that there are really two people involved. The social class of the main characters is significant. They are all "gentlemen," the only exception being Jekyll's servant Poole. This fact makes it possible for Hyde, who dresses like an upper-class person and who has adequate funds, to be as independent and free in his dire actions as he is.

The gentility of Mr. Utterson, Dr. Lanyon, Mr. Enfield, and Jekyll himself sets the tone of the novella: Only the highest moral behavior should be expected of people in this class of society. Thus, the disgrace that Jekyll works to avoid is all the more devastating and motivates his suicide at the end of the plot. Also, the class of the main characters emphasizes the degradation of Hyde when he enters the lower-class regions to perpetrate his foul actions.

◆ Themes ◆

As critic Jenni Calder points out, by the time Stevenson wrote this novella, he was deeply concerned with sending "a message about individual moral responsibility." Certainly, the author intended the tale to suggest the folly of toying with nature (as innumerable later works and motion pictures have done — and, especially as was to be done in Wilde's *The Picture of Dorian Gray*, five years later) and the grim consequences of doing so.

In the present day, when so much is known (and dramatized) about multiple personalities, the allegorical aspects of *Dr. Jekyll and Mr. Hyde* are obvious. Stevenson believed in the likelihood that there exists in even the most virtuous of persons a dark side. When he wrote the first draft of the text and was soon persuaded by his wife to make it a more allegorical work, he quickly agreed — the result turned what could have been a slender piece of science fiction into a classic. Some readers have gone so far as to find allegorical, symbolic significances in the names: Je=*je* in French; kyll could indicate kill (suggesting "I kill"); Hyde suggests concealment, as of one's identity. In any event, Stevenson was surely setting forth the notion that every person can be two persons. Freudian psychologists might well agree that the "dark" person is the one that people often encounter in their dreams.

The fact that the outline for the plot came to Stevenson in a dream is not only relevant but, in a way, extraordinarily striking. The psychiatrist who introduced the first organized study of dreams and their meaning, Sigmund Freud, did not publish his *Interpretation of Dreams* until 1901; and, his theories about the tripartite aspect of the human personality were not advanced until the 1920s — yet, in the definition of the "id" can be found a character study of Edward Hyde: "The mass of unbound energies, both libidinal and aggressive, which constitute part of the unconscious and influence conscious action by seeking discharge and immediate gratification. . . ." This passage, from the *Dictionary of Behavioral Science,* could be something written by Dr. Lanyon about the fearsome Hyde. Today, when multiple personalities are a popular field of study, such an early insight as Stevenson's must be regarded as almost amazing.

Following Freud, Carl Jung, with his emphasis on extraversion and introversion, was keenly aware of the duality often found in the human personality (a phenomenon that many of his adherents believed to be universal, especially in terms of the private versus the public persona of the individual). Later psychologists, influenced by these early leaders in the study of the unconscious, persons such as Karen Horney and Ernest Jones, tend to rely on some sense of the now obsolete term "split personality" (the word "dissociation" often taking its place, denoting "processes [that] function independently of

the rest of the personality") in their studies of aberrant behavior — professional analysts may analyze the phenomenon more thoroughly, but Stevenson dramatized it better than anyone else could.

◆ Characters ◆

The principal character is Dr. Jekyll (Stevenson pronounced it JEE•kil), although Hyde could be seen as a separate and perhaps equally important character. A vital aspect of the story that dramatizations usually overlook (as well as the fact that there is very little sexual material in the text) is that Jekyll knows that he is unleashing the immoral element of his personality — he is not simply experimenting in order to advance science: He is attempting, with success, to find a way to enjoy unwholesome urges without his identity being recognized. So, tramping down a child and even committing a murder (two of Hyde's more violent acts) are not completely unconscious deeds performed by some other "person."

Mr. Utterson, a lawyer who figures prominently in most of the tale, is typically upright (the setting is Victorian London) and loyal as a friend and companion. This virtue helps to cause the horror of the later discovery of Jekyll's demonic experiment to be more intense. The reader tends to share Utterson's revulsion and sympathy. The other characters, most notably Dr. Lanyon, are tangential and yet help to advance the relatively linear plot.

In the end, however, it is probably Hyde that the reader recalls most vividly. Although he is seen only on occasion in the text, his frightful appearance (well described by the author), his awful crimes, and his unexpectedly literate language (emanating, of course, from Jekyll) create a truly memorable image of a doomed soul.

◆ Techniques ◆

The story is told from several perspectives. It opens in the third person, with the focus largely on the perceptions of Mr. Utterson. There are several important letters that help to reveal the horrible truth about Mr. Hyde, one of great importance by Dr. Lanyon; and the last thirty or so pages are Jekyll's "Full Statement of the Case." In this fashion, the author manages, in a quite credible manner, to conceal the dual identity from the reader until near the end of the plot.

Another vital feature of *Dr. Jekyll and Mr. Hyde* is the style. While Stevenson is renowned for an elegant writing mode in almost all of his works, in this story it is of particular significance, most notably in the passages of description, such as this early picture of Hyde: "Mr. Hyde was pale and dwarfish, he gave the impression of deformity without any nameable malformation, he had a displeasing smile, he had borne himself to the lawyer with a sort of murderous mixture of timidity and boldness, and he spoke with a husky, whispering, and somewhat broken voice." Style is also essential in the creation of cold, damp London nights and, indeed the entire atmosphere of gloom and evil. Establishing the appropriate tone is of the essence for a narrative of this sort: An air of realism must be maintained to countervail the fictive aspects of the plot.

◆ Literary Precedents ◆

Probably the most relevant influence was Edgar Allan Poe, whose story "William Wilson" deals with dual identity. However, the direct origin of *Dr. Jekyll and Mr. Hyde*, as Stevenson claimed, was a dream, in which the basic outline of the plot developed. The same type of grim narrative can be found in the excellent short stories "Markheim," in which the central character has a sort of alter ego, and "Thrawn Janet," a tale of demonic possession. Also, perhaps the *Faust* legend, which Stevenson knew, was something of an influence. Of course, the folk tales and weird myths told to the young Stevenson by Alison Cunningham to entertain the ill child played a large part in the development of such phenomena in the author's unconscious mind — being released in impressive literary form many years later.

◆ Adaptations ◆

This novella has invited more adaptations than anything else that Stevenson (or almost anyone else wrote). The semi-Faustian aspect of the work seems to have "charmed" a number of producers. There is even a musical version, staged in 1995, which has achieved moderate success. An early stage version was written by T. R. Sullivan and was used by several film producers as a basis for later cinema versions. The first of these was the Vitagraph silent production, in 1908, directed by Sidney Olcott, who also wrote the screenplay. Four years later, Independent turned out another silent version, with James Cruze as director and in the leading role. Perhaps the best silent interpretation was the 1920 film starring John Barrymore, directed by John S. Robertson and produced by Famous Players-Lasky. Twelve years later, the version that many critics believe to be the finest was created by Paramount. It won Fredric March an Oscar for the leading role and cast two female parts for Miriam Hopkins and Rose Hobart, who contributed a more sexual aspect to the film than had appeared earlier. Rouben Mamoulian directed and produced the movie for Paramount. In 1941, Metro-Goldwyn-Mayer released another highly praised rendition, directed by Victor Fleming and starring Spencer Tracy, Ingrid Bergman, and Lana Turner. A British version appeared in 1959, entitled *The Two Faces of Dr. Jekyll* (also titled *House of Fright*). It was produced by Hammer and was directed by Terence Fisher. In a television film of 1972, Jack Palance starred as Jekyll/Hyde, Anthony Perkins took the role in a 1989 version entitled *Edge of Sanity*. The 1996 cinema rendering places much more emphasis on a female character; it stars Julia Roberts and John Malkovich — its title is *Mary Reilly*.

◆ Ideas for Group Discussions ◆

Since there are so many parallel narratives, in a variety of forms (print, cinema, television, stage), it might be interesting to compare some of these treatments of dual identity with Stevenson's work.

1. Is there any justification at all for Jekyll's undertaking the daring experiment?

2. Several prominent readers, Henry James, for example, found the device of the drugs confounding and somewhat difficult to accept. Does this aspect of the plot seem unacceptable? Is there another way in which Stevenson could have solved the problem of transformation?

3. Although Hyde actually commits only one murder, does the author successfully create a sense of pervasive evil in this character?

4. Did the fact that you knew the basic outline of the plot before reading the text in any way lessen the effect of the climax on you?

5. Apart from the transformation itself, clearly in the vein of science fiction, is there any other aspect of the narrative that seems to strain credulity? For example, are the behaviors of all the characters realistic?

6. Is the tone of the story maintained satisfactorily all the way through the text? Could more have been done to intensify it?

Fred B. McEwen
Waynesburg College

THE STRANGER

Novel

1942

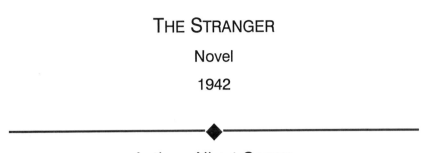

Author: Albert Camus

◆ Social Concerns ◆

The Stranger was the first great novel to emerge from French Algeria. The Arab presence figures prominently in the story, and stresses kinship, rivalry, and bloodshed. The violence expressed in the murder of the Arab by Meursault brings out the violence in Arab-European relations. The Arabs, however, were not natural enemies to the French, and the one who is killed in the story represents his race as a model of silence and contemplation. The fact that Meursault murders him needlessly shows that murder is not the solution to the Arab-European conflict, which was to erupt into warfare in the 1950s, and in which Camus took a side opposed to native independence.

Camus also addresses the question of justice in Meursault's trial. Actually, it is a parody of justice, for he is tried, not for killing a man, but for not having wept at his mother's funeral. Throughout his trial, he is robbed of his own identity, never really allowed to speak, and his lawyer uses the first person in his place. Meursault represents the person persecuted by society because he refuses its falseness and hypocrisy. He will have no part of its artificiality, and will not become involved in its game. In the end, he is convicted on a technicality, showing that the trial is a meaningless formality.

◆ Themes ◆

The Stranger, with the *Myth of Sisyphus* (1955; *Le Mythe de Sisyphe*, 1942), is Camus's great apology for the absurd. Camus himself described it as an "exercise in objectivity, the impersonal working out of the logical results of the philosophy of the absurd." According to Camus's philosophy at this time, life has no meaning; there is no hope for it ever to have meaning. There is no eternity; therefore, all must be done in this life. Indeed, this very thought brings happiness to Meursault at the end of his trial. Passive and indifferent to the forces of life, Meursault exemplifies a life without meaning, an idea that was to attract a world at war, and especially the French people, victims of a humiliating Occupation.

In the midst of this hopeless universe, Camus nevertheless shows a poetic appreciation of the Mediterranean atmosphere in which he grew up. Camus's evocation of the sun at the moment of the murder is lyrical, although it has been judged by some critics as a contradiction to the absurd and indifferent universe created up until this moment. The sea likewise appears in all its sensuality as Meursault and Marie bathe, the symbol also of life, and of evasion. Camus ends the book on a lyrical note, as Meursault, facing a starry night, would be willing to begin life again, and finally feels happiness in his acceptance of the absurd, like Sisyphus, whom, says Camus, one must imagine as happy in the futility of rolling his rock endlessly uphill.

♦ Characters ♦

Meursault, the protagonist, is a character who is ostensibly without awareness, except for immediate physical sensations. He is an "outsider," as the title sometimes appears in English, who refuses to play the game of society. There is a gap between what he feels and what goes on around him, and he constantly vacillates between total comprehension and total skepticism. Although he does not understand the people around him, he keeps on trying. He is unable to create a real relationship with other people. His attraction to Marie is purely physical; when she wants to marry him, he replies with his usual "It doesn't matter." His neighbor Raymond Sintès requests his help; he writes the requested letter mechanically. However, one has the impression that he keeps trying to enter into the world around him, but that he is too much of an "outsider" to succeed. His name suggests "*mer*," the

sea, and "*soleil*," the sun, which summarizes his contact with primitive physical sensations only.

Other characters are represented through Meursault's eyes, since the story is narrated in the first person. Marie appears as any woman, physically attractive, described often through her hair, her clothing, her body. One might doubt her commitment to Meursault, until she comes to visit him in prison, and is still interested in marrying him. Meursault's two neighbors, Salamano, and Raymond Sintès, are described humorously. Salamano looks like his dog, whom he constantly insults. Yet when the dog disappears, he is inconsolable. Raymond Sintès has a doubtful profession, a cluttered room, and a mistress on whom he wants revenge. Meursault is amused by them, but not overly involved. On the other hand, the judge of instruction, the lawyer, and the chaplain are presented ironically, in keeping with the parody of justice, the depersonalization of Meursault, and his refusal to believe in a future life.

♦ Techniques ♦

The Stranger is probably the most original of all of Camus's works. A narrative rather than a novel, it was really executed in the spirit of a "new novel," that writers of the 1960s, influenced by Camus, were to discover. Actually the story is the fragment of a tale, with many pieces left to the reader's imagination. The very fragmentation suggests the lack of coherence in the world of the absurd. The choice of language and style conveys Meursault's indifference and apathy. The absence of the passe simple, the past tense traditionally used in literature and present, is here replaced by the passe compose, or conversational past. The author makes free use of indirect speech, and thus accentuates the gulf between what is happening and what Meursault is thinking.

The novel is divided into two parts, with parallel structure. Critics generally consider the first part as superior and more original. It is here that Meursault describes the lack of relationship between the world and himself. The second part deals with his trial, and contains more irony and lyricism, with particular emphasis on solar imagery and poetry. In both parts, however, Camus shows his skill in narration as well as in lyricism.

◆ Literary Precedents ◆

Camus has often been compared to Pascal in his existential questioning and anguish, although Pascal was a firm believer in immortality. Among his nineteenth-century predecessors are the skeptical Vigny, and Stendhal, whose *The Red and the Black* (*Le Rouge et le noir*, 1830) also contains a mistrial and a condemnation on technicalities. Victor Hugo's *The Last Day of a Man Condemned to Death* (*Le Dernier jour d'un condamné*, 1829) also contains the reflections of a man in prison. Meursault's crime is similar to that in Samuel T. Coleridge's *The Rime of the Ancient Mariner* (1798). Germaine Brée sees in Meursault an echo of Fyodor Dostoevsky's Dmitri Karamazov, "whose real crime was not the one that he is tried for, but one which will lead him to a new level of awareness" (*The Brothers Karamazov* [*Bratya Karamazov*], 1879-1880). Finally, the short, unconnected sentences of the entire narration are most like Hemingway, who was a great

influence on many mid-century French authors.

◆ Adaptations ◆

The only one of Camus's novels to have been adapted for the cinema is *The Stranger*, produced by Paramount in 1967 and directed by Luchino Visconti. Emmanuel Roblès, a friend of Camus's, also shared in the screenplay, which was quite faithful to Camus's text. There is a short film, *Albert Camus: A Self-Portrait*, produced by Fred Orjain, which shows Camus talking about the theater, and which also gives some views of Algeria. There are a number of sound recordings of Camus's voice, where he reads selections from *The Fall* (1956), *The Plague* (1947), and *The Stranger*. The 1950 film *Panic in the Streets*, directed by Elia Kazan, although not directly inspired by Camus, treats the same theme of the plague as in Camus's *The Plague*.

Sister Irma M. Kashuba, S.S.J.
Chestnut Hill College

STRANGER IN A STRANGE LAND

Novel

1961

◆

Author: Robert A. Heinlein

◆ Social Concerns ◆

A critic has suggested that *Stranger in a Strange Land* helped to launch the 1960s, that tumultuous decade of protest and social upheaval, and certainly this controversial novel typifies in many ways the widespread rejection of established values characteristic of the period. *Stranger in a Strange Land* challenges the accepted wisdom of American society on religion, morality, sex, politics, and art. It was read approvingly by members of the Merry Pranksters, one of the original "hippie" groups, and its messianic hero was emulated by numerous self-proclaimed gurus — including, tragically, mass-murderer Charles Manson. The novel satirizes Western religions, proclaims an ethic of brotherhood and sexual freedom, and scoffs at the provincial and hypocritical values of American society.

Despite its cult popularity, however, Heinlein's novel is scarcely an expression of the egalitarian and democratic values preached by the hippies and other radicals. The novel's ideal community of "water brothers" is an exclusive and elite society. Only a select few are deemed capable of enlightenment,

and they expect the elite to inherit the earth through a rigorous natural selection that recalls the Social Darwinism preached by nineteenth century capitalists. *Stranger in a Strange Land* certainly rejects the nonviolent ethic proclaimed by most (although not all) of the decade's rebels; in fact the hero, Michael Smith, cheerfully "discorporates" his enemies and others of whom he disapproves — that is, he murders them by causing them (quite literally) to disappear. While Heinlein seems to share the discontent with American life and values voiced by radical youth, the solutions he offers differ drastically from those espoused by the youth movement and its supporters.

◆ Themes ◆

Stranger in a Strange Land is an overtly philosophical work, the first of Heinlein's novels to be so explicitly and unremittingly didactic. It is also the first of his novels to be seemingly obsessed with sexuality, a concern which has marked nearly all of his subsequent fiction. But Heinlein is by no means pornographic; indeed physical descriptions of the sex act and even of human bodies are infrequent and notably sketchy. His concern is instead with the morality and psychology of sex, which are discussed at exhaustive length in *Stranger in a Strange Land*. Western sexual morality, the novel argues, is rooted in jealousy, fear, and narrow prejudices, and the novel celebrates a new ethic of sexual freedom in which intercourse becomes virtually a sacrament.

Another dominant theme is religion. Heinlein can perhaps be described as an agnostic with mystical yearnings; he is not satisfied with merely materialistic explanations of life, but he appears to find traditional religious explanations an appalling compound of ignorance and bigotry. *Stranger in a Strange Land* features a good deal of pointed satire of established religions — especially American fundamentalism, rather thinly disguised in the novel — as well as straightforward attacks on Judaism and Christianity by the author's spokesmen. Yet Heinlein, for all his depiction of religious leaders as crass buffoons, does not dismiss the religious urge to explore ultimate questions about life and meaning. In fact, this novel begins his explicit probing of such questions, a search that is at the heart of most of his recent novels. Here, the title character and protagonist, Michael Smith, creates his own religion, which the novel suggests does answer those ultimate questions, and, after his martyrdom, Michael ascends to a comically bureaucratic heaven to resume his old position as the Archangel Michael. Almost certainly Heinlein has his tongue in cheek; yet some characteristics of the religion — especially its Calvinistic notion of a small group of the elite who alone will be saved — seem central to his thinking throughout his career.

◆ Characters ◆

Heinlein is not adept at creating vivid, three-dimensional characters. In essence he has one basic character (which most readers and critics suspect to be an idealized self-portrait of the author), the self-reliant, supremely competent man (or woman) who can survive and indeed dominate virtually any situation. Heinlein depicts this character at different chronological stages: the precocious young genius, just beginning to sense his enormous potential; the mature adult, master of many skills and survivor of many trials; and the wise old mentor, who knows both how and why things are as they are. Secondary characters tend to be either sketchier versions of the hero or stock figures of one kind or other.

Stranger in a Strange Land is in this regard a typical Heinlein performance. It is filled with stereotypes (the inquisitive journalist, the powerful politician dominated by his wife, the goodhearted stripper) and caricatures (several nasty portraits of sleazy religious con men and fascist cops). To a great extent this level of characterization is quite appropriate for the novel's satiric purposes; characters need not be fully realized human beings — they merely need to typify some belief or position which the novel wants to ridicule. Two characters, however, are more vividly presented, Valentine Michael Smith and his protector and mentor, Jubal Harshaw.

Michael and Jubal can both be profitably viewed as typical Heinlein heroes — at different stages of their development. Michael, the man from Mars, begins as a naif, innocent of human language and customs. Jubal, a doctor, lawyer, and successful writer, is his teacher. Jubal is a thoroughly entertaining character, one of Heinlein's best wise old men. Shrewd, cynical, witty, he sees through pretense and hypocrisy and has little patience with knaves and less with fools. He instructs Michael in the ways of the world and watches over his astonishing maturation into a kind of superman. Michael becomes virtually omniscient and omnipotent — telepathy and teleportation are only two of his tricks. But the more powerful Michael becomes, the less interesting and appealing a character he is. Since he can do everything, the novel is robbed of much of its dramatic tension. And since the novel's two principal characters are usually of one mind, *Stranger in a Strange Land* is also robbed of the tension that results from the opposition of powerful or appealing characters. A character, to be interesting, must face some problem — a dangerous enemy, a threatening environment, a moral dilemma. For Michael, the problems are nonexistent or too easily solved.

◆ Techniques ◆

Part of the novel's unity springs from its consistent parody of the Christian scriptures. Michael is the product of an anomalous birth (which the novel pointedly calls his "Maculate Conception") — his mother is impregnated by her lover, she dies in childbirth, then her husband kills the lover and himself, leaving Michael an orphan with three legal parents. After this grotesque inversion of the Virgin Birth, Michael endures a period of trial and temptation; he enters upon a public ministry complete with miracles, sermons, and a growing number of disciples; he offends and is persecuted by the state and the organized churches;

he has a final supper with his disciples and then accepts martyrdom at the hands of a mob; and he returns, more or less, from the dead, to inspire his followers. The similarity with Christ's life tends to underscore the differences in their messages.

The novel is flawed, in the eyes of most readers, by its talkiness. Many scenes feature one or more characters talking at great length, frequently in thinly disguised authorial lectures. It is redeemed, at least in part, by some wickedly funny satire of television, political leaders, and religious hucksters — a good deal of which remains quite pertinent today. Michael's death, for instance, is carried on live television, complete with sponsors and frequent commercial breaks.

◆ Literary Precedents ◆

In addition to the Christian Gospel, *Stranger in a Strange Land* is much indebted to a literary form that dates back at least to the eighteenth century. The key satiric device of the novel is Michael's innocence of earth language and customs. Since his first twenty years were spent on Mars (after his explorer parents die, he is adopted by aliens), Michael must learn everything, and his naive questions challenge many basic assumptions. This pattern can be traced back to figures like Montesquieu (*Persian Letters*, 1721) and Goldsmith (*Citizen of the World*, 1762) who invented oriental visitors whose comments exposed the foibles of contemporary society. Heinlein effectively adapts a classic satiric device for use in a science fictional setting.

Kevin P. Mulcahy
Rutgers University

THE STREET

Novel

1946

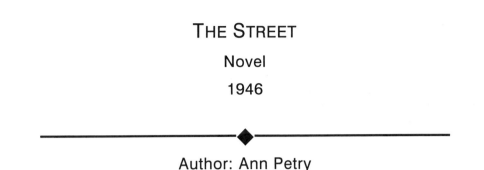

Author: Ann Petry

◆ Social Concerns/Themes ◆

The Street, Petry's best-known work, is often compared to Richard Wright's *Native Son* (1940). While there are similarities between the two novels, particularly in the portrayal of the economic plight of African Americans in northern cities, *The Street* moves in different directions. Both in its thematic concerns and its depiction of a black female protagonist, the novel is unique and significant.

Petry was ahead of her time in focusing on what are considered contemporary social concerns: latchkey children, single parenting, and the way the politics of sex establishes an unending maze of oppression. *The Street* examines the unique role of the African-American woman in maintaining sanity amid the triple threat of classism, sexism, and racism.

The novel presents the black woman as the center of the family and the community, as the person who shoulders the moral and ethical responsibilities of a race, and discusses how her relations with whites shapes the nature of interracial dynamics.

◆ Characters ◆

The Street presents a relatively small number of characters. These include Lutie Johnson's deceased grandmother, Granny, who was a major influence on Lutie and a source of kindness and comfort, and her grandfather, Pop, a bootlegger and ne'er-do-well. Lutie, the main character of the novel, marries Jim Johnson right after high school. They live in a frame house in Jamaica, New York, and at first Jim is the model husband and father. But when Jim loses his job, he begins to bring other women home while his wife is at work.

Eventually, Lutie leaves Jim and moves to Harlem. There Lutie and her eight-year-old son, Bub, move into an apartment building in which Mrs. Hedges, an important presence on the "street" of the novel's title, operates a whorehouse. William Jones is the perverted building superintendent who lusts after Lutie. When Lutie's rejects him, he tricks her son and gets him in trouble.

The remaining characters are Junto, a white man who owns Harlem real estate, whorehouses, and bars, and is a partner of Mrs. Hedges. He, too, tries to seduce Lutie. Boots Smith, who works as a musician in Junto's bars, traps Lutie in his apartment and is killed by her after an attempted rape.

The real protagonist of the novel is the street on which Lutie lives and, by extension, the seedy and downtrodden residents of Harlem. Lutie Johnson is at the heart of the novel and represents one of the "walking wounded" of the ghetto. She believes the American Dream of a comfortable life is attainable if she works hard enough. In the end Lutie sees she is not included in the American Dream, and when she realizes that no amount of sacrifice and work will save her or Bub, she deserts her son and runs away to Chicago. Lutie is a victim of economic racism and the bias of sexism, evils which prevent African-American men from earning a living and turn black women into virtual slaves and beggars.

◆ Techniques/Literary Precedents ◆

The Street is often described as a female version of Richard Wright's *Native Son,* and Lutie Johnson has been called a female Bigger Thomas. Petry's first novel is also seen as an example of the naturalism characteristic of twentieth-century African-American fiction. But to see Petry as a lesser Richard Wright is to slight her achievement.

The Street protests the racism and sexism in the urban North. Zora Neale Hurston's *Their Eyes Were Watching God* (1937) is another novel of womanist protest that has an African-American female protagonist. But Hurston's protagonist, Janie Crawford, is rural and southern and transcends her condition through self-discovery and self-definition. *The Street* presents a poor northern urban protagonist and does not go beyond protest. While Janie protests

her condition as black and female and eventually transcends her status, Lutie's story is one of protest and defeat, and she eventually flees the life on 116th Street. Lutie is sexually pursued by both black and white men, and it is this lust based on the conception of African-American females as fair sexual game which ultimately destroys Lutie. Indeed *The Street* is the first novel written by an African-American woman that details the triple oppression of African-American women — race, gender, and class. The novel is a pioneering rather than a derivative work.

◆ Related Titles ◆

Often seen as a single-work author or a children's writer, Petry published six short stories prior to *The Street.* "Marie of the Cabin Club" appeared in the Baltimore *Afro-American* newspaper in 1939; in 1943 "On Saturday the Siren Sounds at Noon" appeared in *Crisis.* Other stories preceding *The Street* were published in so-called "Negro Journals." These were written during Petry's stint as journalist. In 1944 "Doby's Gone" was published in *Phylon,* the scholarly journal associated with W. E. B. DuBois and Atlanta University. In 1945 "Olaf and His Girlfriend" and "Like a Winding Sheet" appeared in *Crisis.* In each of these stories female characters figure prominently.

The Narrows

As in Petry's first novel, female characters are prominent in her last novel, *The Narrows* (1953). African-American women are both major and minor characters, and they move the plot and shape the themes. Abigail Crunch is very much a New Englander, and strives to uphold that image. The major difference between Abbie and other New Englanders is her race: she is an African American. However, Abigail is out of touch with the real world, and lives vicariously through the men in her life: her late husband, the Major, and her adopted son Link Williams.

Link, a focal character, is killed at the end of the novel because of his involvement with Camilla Treadway, the white heiress of a gun factory. A boarder in Abbie's house, Malcolm Powther, is a butler to the Treadways and is indirectly responsible for Link's murder. Powther is almost as stiff as Abigail Crunch, and they both feel distant from the blacks who live in "the Narrows" section of the town. Malcolm Powther is the opposite of saloon keeper, Bill Hod, who is having an affair with Powther's wife, Mamie.

Mamie Powther is a sensual being in love with life. She is almost a stereotype of the whorish black female. Nevertheless, she is arguably the most interesting character of the novel. When Mamie is compared to Camilla Treadway, who is also involved in an extramarital affair, one can see the role of history and racial politics in the shaping of images of the African-American female. Also evident is the significant element of race when gender oppression is at issue. A minor character, F. K. Jackson feels herself an anomaly for being female and black.

The Narrows explores the intersection of race and class, and its destructive effects on a New England community. A subplot concerns an affair between a black man and a white woman which bears some resemblance to the tragic story of Romeo and Juliet. The novel also develops themes of violence and materialism in American culture.

Country Place

Petry's second novel, *Country Place* (1947) is almost a direct opposite of *The Street* in its setting, characters, and themes. The novel is set in Lennox, Connecticut, a place similar to the town in which Petry grew up. The narrator is a white male druggist and the major characters are all white; a housekeeper is the only character of color. Petry's major themes are the prevalence of provincialism and materialism and how these societal ills destroy the town's moral fiber. This seemingly idyllic village contains many of the same problems as urban areas. Human frailties in Lennox are fueled by the townspeople's search for happiness in materialism and their spiritual poverty. It is a time of the collapse of traditional values following World War II and of a stifling routine existence with little room for creativity. The inhabitants, especially those women and few men who remained during the war, are trapped in a tortuous and empty life.

The novel opens with the return of Johnny Roane, an army veteran, and ends with his departure to study art. Although the story traces Johnny's relationship with his wife Glory, Lil, Johnny's mother-in-law, and Glory, mother and daughter, are the central characters. Both women have affairs with Ed Barrell. Lil marries Mearns Gramby, the son of the wealthiest woman in Lennox, but does not find fulfillment with him or the things he can give her. Mearns controls and manipulates his wife, for he knows she does not love him and that she thinks she will be rich after his mother dies.

The single character of color is Neola, the housekeeper and maid, who is loyal to Mearns' mother. Neola is contrasted with Glory and Lil early in the novel. Lil, although from humble beginnings, scoffs at Neola and feels superior to her not because Neola is a maid, but because she is black. She makes derisive comments about Neola's getting a divorce, asking whoever heard of "a nigger divorce." The irony is that Lil remains trapped in a loveless marriage and Neola is freed from hers. In the contrasts between Neola and the white women, Petry shows that although women experience sexual oppression, gender discrimination is not necessarily a unifying factor for all women; race is a stronger source of conflict.

It is Neola and Portulacca, "Portugee," the Gramby gardener, who represent hope and moral justice in Lennox. The two plan to marry and are willed the Gramby mansion and a lifelong maintenance allowance.

Described by some as a "race free" novel, plot as well as character are often secondary to descriptions of the "country place" of Lennox. The town is presented as a commonplace town with calm and commonplace citizens. Petry summons the violence of nature to reveal the reality of the town. The hurricane that whips the water, thrashes the vegetation, and damages the buildings, also rips the veneer from the violent, greedy, and immoral lives of the major characters. Petry focuses on the physical details of the damage done by the storm.

Muriel W. Brailey
Wilberforce University

STRONG MEDICINE

Novel

1984

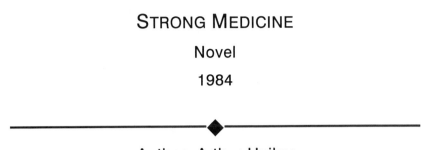

Author: Arthur Hailey

◆ Social Concerns/Themes ◆

Strong Medicine offers a close look at the functioning of a huge pharmaceutical industry. The author presents precise information about how drugs are developed, tested, approved, and promoted and about how public opinion and the industry itself react to its mistakes and its successes. Although he stresses the drug industry's humanitarian contributions, he also explores a range of abuses, as when the lure of vast profits sometimes obscures a concern for public safety. In the course of the story, the employees of Felding-Roth Pharmaceuticals face a series of problems and crises which are taken as typical of the industry. In particular, they must worry about the testing, release and recall of the drug Montayne, developed to alleviate morning sickness in pregnant women but found to be, like Thalidomide, deadly for unborn children.

The novel also deals with several issues of topical interest. Primary among these are the ethics of laboratory experimentation involving live animals, the ethics of marketing the same drug under many different names, the question of how much the general population should be told about the potential side effects of prescription and over-the-counter drugs and the problem of drug abuse among physicians. Occasional mention of world events, such as the assassination of President Kennedy, serves only to mark the passage of time since the characters' personal lives are not touched by politics in any significant way.

◆ Characters ◆

In each of his best-selling novels, Hailey assembles a cast of instantly-recognizable heroes, heroines and villains, summarizes their backgrounds, ambitions, fears and weaknesses, and puts them in situations in which they act in a predictable manner. Although frequently faced with major crises, these characters are rarely self-questioning or introspective and never escape from their stereotypical roles.

The only significant change Hailey makes in his standard method of characterization in *Strong Medicine* is to place a woman at the center of the story. Celia de Grey Jordan begins her career as a drug salesperson, the first woman ever to hold such a position at

Felding-Roth, and she rises through the ranks to become president and chief executive. As the story develops, she demonstrates superior courage, integrity, and foresightedness, never losing faith in herself or her will to fight for what she believes. In 1960, she convinces her superiors not to test Thalidomide on pregnant women, and with the same infallible instinct and sense of ethics, over the next three decades she struggles with the release and recall of Montayne, the hostility of some of her coworkers and her increasing responsibilities as an executive. She also preserves a near-perfect relationship with her children and her husband, Dr. Andrew Jordan.

Two other important characters represent the dangers and the triumphs of the pharmaceutical industry. Dr. Vincent Lord is an unscrupulous and bitter scientist who dreams of fame as the inventor of a substance that can counteract the negative side effects of all drugs. By falsifying the results of his research, he manages to place his dangerous invention on the market. In contrast, Dr. Martin Peat-Smith, a biochemist from Cambridge University who is the quintessence of scientific integrity, develops a drug to treat Alzheimer's disease that may have surprising powers as an aphrodisiac.

◆ Techniques ◆

The plot and structure of *Strong Medicine* are more linear than in Hailey's prior novels which all feature a medley of stories involving different characters related in various ways to the institution under examination. This novel, in fact, has a definite central character and plot and its few subplots are eventually resolved in decisions Celia makes about the policies and concerns of Felding-Roth. As in other novels by Hailey, the action unfolds in brief episodes filled with melodrama and suspense. When appropriate, the characters discuss the background and procedures of the drug industry, thereby introducing medical and pharmaceutical matters in a believable manner. The author sometimes seems to ask the reader to assume a skeptical stance toward the drug industry. His overall view, however, is conventionally optimistic, supporting reassuring assumptions about the methods adopted by the industry and showing how its contributions outweigh its abuses. At the end, as Celia prepares for a new battle, this time against critics of an experimental wonder drug, Hailey concludes that, everything considered, the drug industry has been "a benefaction for mankind."

◆ Literary Precedents ◆

Like Hailey's *Airport* (1968), *Strong Medicine* has some affinities with the muckraking tradition exemplified by Upton Sinclair, whose best-selling novel *The Jungle* (1906) was a well-documented attack on the meat-packing industry in Chicago. Also, Sinclair Lewis relied on careful and detailed research to satirize the medical profession in *Arrowsmith* (1925) and subsequently wrote penetrating fictional analyses of such fields as organized religion, big business, social welfare and hotel management. More recently, Joseph Wambaugh has drawn on personal experience to create gripping stories about police work in the modern city in novels such as *The New Centurions* (1971). Unlike these writers, however, Hailey is less interested in presenting thought-provoking and realistic images of American society than in offering his readers a few hours of entertainment and information.

made available?

Winifred Farrant Bevilacqua
Università Degli Studi di Torino
Turin, Italy

◆ Ideas for Group Discussions ◆

The pharmaceutical industry has come under significant criticism for making certain drugs available to consumers, for withholding other drugs that could benefit society, and for greatly overcharging for some products. Hailey develops some ideas about misguided or corrupt practices in the industry, and the group discussion could raise others and comment on the current appropriateness of Hailey's criticism.

1. What little-known aspects of the pharmaceutical industry does Hailey explain in this book?

2. What personal and professional characteristics make Celia de Grey Jordan an appropriate heroine for this story? Is she believable as an executive?

3. How does the subplot that involves Celia's husband Dr. Andrew Jordan in a battle against drug abuse among physicians complement the main story?

4. Does Hailey take a clear position on the ethics of experimentation on live animals?

5. In what ways does the novel emphasize how the desire for fast profit or for fame can sometimes create risks for the health and safety of the general public? When should the results of experimentation with new drugs be

THE STUDS LONIGAN TRILOGY

Novel

1932

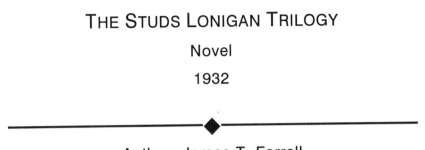

Author: James T. Farrell

◆ Characters ◆

Studs Lonigan, of all Farrell's characters, is perhaps the most fully alive, the most fully realized, primarily because he is a character built on internal contradictions. From the first, he demonstrates the conflict between his desire to be tough and his attraction toward the softer side of his nature. As a thirteen-year-old, hiding in the bathroom to smoke and feel tough, he thinks of Lucy Scanlon, who is already, and will remain, both his ideal of womanhood and a symbol of his aspirations. All his dreams of success include her, and many of them absolutely depend on her. But early in *Young Lonigan* (1932), Studs thinks of her, of a time when he had walked her home from school, and his reaction illustrates the inner war he fights, and loses: "He wanted to stand there, and think about Lucy, wondering if he would ever have days with her like that one . . . And he goddamned himself, because he was getting soft. He was Studs Lonigan, a guy who didn't have mushy feelings!" Well, Studs does have mushy feelings, but he denies them, just as he forsook his given name, William, for the tougher-sounding Studs. Thus, even as the novel begins, Studs has already made his choice, already set his direction. In his struggle to maintain that direction, however, he reveals his basic good nature and his human weaknesses, qualities which make him a powerfully appealing creation.

Farrell uses Weary Reilly as a kind of double for Studs. Weary really is the kind of tough guy Studs tries so hard to be, and Weary is an important measure of Studs's progress. Very early in *Young Lonigan*, Studs and Weary square off in a verbal sparring match that is only a prelude to the fight they have the following summer. Studs loses the sparring match, but he wins the fight, establishing himself as a tough guy on the rise. From that point on, Weary is always in the background, waiting for another chance. Meanwhile, he and Studs follow similar paths through *Young Lonigan*, Weary with one gang and Studs with another. But in *The Young Manhood of Studs Lonigan* (1934), Weary becomes the embodiment of the worst that this urban culture can produce. His toughness and his defiance lead him into a life of actual crime. He takes the tough-guy impulse to the extreme, thus providing a low end to the scale on which the reader measures

Studs's downward progress.

By the same token, Danny O'Neill and Lucy Scanlon represent the upper end of the scale. Lucy, in particular, offers a vision of what might have been. Studs imagines constantly, and with increasing regret, what life would have been like had he and Lucy gotten together. From the first chapter of *Young Lonigan,* when Studs dreams of walking Lucy home, to the end of *Judgment Day* (1935), when Studs hallucinates that Lucy kneels at his bedside, she acts as an ideal for him. As he propels himself downward, Lucy recedes farther and farther out of reach, finishing high school, attending college, becoming part of a different world — a world Studs need not have excluded himself from — but one where, as events turned out, he is clearly out of place. As an additional measure of Studs's failure, Danny O'Neill acts as a double for Studs on the positive side, just as Weary Reilly had on the negative. From the same neighborhood, with the same background, Danny turns his back on the old gang. Instead, he stays in school, attends the University of Chicago and becomes a writer. He opens himself to the very possibilities Studs had denied, thus Danny provides a further measure of what might have been.

◆ Social Concerns ◆

The saga of Studs Lonigan, if it does nothing else, demonstrates the closed nature of the supposedly open American system. Studs has dreams that are like everyone else's: He wants money, property, fame, respect, all the ingredients of the ever-elusive American dream. But Farrell writes of a world in which failure is far more likely than success. Literally every institution in Stud's life acts to bring him down: His family cannot combat the negative values he acquires in the streets, his religion is unable to provide any real hope or even any real energy in his life, romance is reduced by his environment to a series of animal-like ruttings, and the economy seems to be constructed so that a working man like Studs's father can rise just so far, but no further. Instead of acting to help people achieve their ambitions, or even remaining neutral, the socioeconomic environment resists those dreams, and whenever the Lonigans or any of the other principal characters try to get rich by making the same investments or getting into the same types of businesses as the rich people, these lower- and lower-middle-class people find that the system won't work for them as it does for their idols.

Farrell demonstrates this fault most clearly, of course, in the person of Studs Lonigan, whom readers first meet on the eve of his graduation from the eighth grade, hiding in the family's bathroom, smoking a cigarette. Studs has a great deal of energy, but no direction. He has been conned into believing that the things he wants should come easily to him. All he has to do is wait and the system will reward him. So he waits, and in the meantime he is dragged down into dissipation and disappointment by the values he finds in force on the street. The adolescent Studs wants to be a man, and with the right vision, the right perspective, he has the raw ability to achieve much. But he can see no farther than his own neighborhood, knows no values other than those of the tough-talking Irish immigrant culture to which he is confined by social standing, economic standing, and religion. So he tries to become a man in the only way he knows how, by being a fighter, by being a hard drinker, by cutting school, and by going to work for his father, Patrick, a painting contractor.

All these actions — one can hardly call them choices, or even decisions — lead Studs downward instead of upward. His desire to be the toughest guy in the neighborhood leads to a fight with Weary Reilly, a fight Studs wins. But his reaction demonstrates what he had come to believe was necessary for success: "Studs told himself he had been waiting for things like this to happen a long time; now they were happening, and life was going to be a whole lot more . . . more fun . . . and he was going to be an important guy . . . and he would be . . . well, in the limelight. Maybe it would set things happening as he always knew they would; and he would keep on getting more and more important." Studs had not tried to make anything happen; instead, he "had been waiting" for them to happen, and he felt that this event, this fight, would "set things happening." In other words, Studs was waiting, being acted upon, not acting. This method, if one can call it that, is characteristic of the way Studs approaches his future. Instead of acting to improve his lot by attending high school, Studs tries to keep up his image in the neighborhood, and being tough was inconsistent with being educated. So Studs went along with his pals and cut school, biding his time until the inevitable happened and he was expelled. In the meantime, he has begun to study the kinds of achievements that are applauded in the pool hall. He practices his smoking so that he will look tough and natural when he does it, and he begins to drink so that he can be a regular guy. And when his poor attendance at school results in his failing, he tosses the event off lightly, feeling that he can cut a better figure by working for his father and earning a paycheck.

Studs's desire for immediate gratification, in other words, leads him to throw away his chance for an education, one way off the streets, in favor of the pursuits that ultimately result in his death. Smoking and lead-based paint damage Studs's lungs so that, at age twenty-seven, beaten to a pulp in a long-awaited rematch with Weary Reilly, Studs collapses, drunk, in the gutter on New Year's Eve, contracting a case of pneumonia from which he never fully recovers.

Farrell uses Studs to show how brutal life can be. The environment determines Studs's fate, and there seems to be little Studs or most of his doomed friends (Studs is not the first to die) can do to change their destinies. Thus, Farrell demonstrates the awesome power of the world around Studs, the way it dominates his life, the way it robs an individual of choice, of opportunity. Studs is doomed from the first moment, and throughout the three novels of this trilogy, his movement is always downward. The greatest moment of his life occurs in the summer after his graduation from the eighth grade, and his life, for all intents and purposes, stops there. He grows older, but no more mature, for nothing in his environment challenges him to grow up. Yet there are many weaknesses for an aging adolescent to fall heir to, and Studs Lonigan's life comprises a litany of them all.

◆ Themes ◆

Perhaps the most compelling theme

in the saga of Studs Lonigan is that of self-destruction, and in this theme both Studs and his culture are at fault. Studs wills himself into his tough-guy act, but it is a much-desired and much-admired role in the Prairie Avenue gang he adheres to. In making this choice, Studs must deny the softer, more sympathetic aspects of his nature, and once he chooses this general direction, the world around him ensures that he cannot turn back. He defeats Weary Reilly, and in seeking the further applause of the people who admire him for that victory, he sets his destructive course in motion.

The city serves as a subtheme underscoring the basic theme of self-destruction. Studs's field of action lies between the University of Chicago and Lake Michigan, and he is constantly struggling against the forces those two places represent. He must belittle education, turning away from the genteel world he identifies with the intellectual in favor of what he sees as the tough, manly life of the pool hall and the gin joint. He also denies the responsiveness he feels toward nature, as demonstrated in the passages when he is in the parks or near the lake. He responds to these influences, showing that he is capable of appreciating natural beauty for its own sake, but then he retreats from such feelings, labeling them "sappy" or "goofy." In this sense, Studs personifies an industrial society's struggle against nature, as if the natural world were a new frontier to be conquered and ruthlessly subdued.

Thus, Studs's world is best represented by a bleak city landscape. It is an artificial world, a manmade world, and as such it has little sympathy for the individual, little patience with those whose lives take the wrong direction. They, like Studs, are expendable, for in the city there are always many others ready to take the place of those who step out of line.

Farrell also makes it clear that he does not see the world as totally evil or totally without possibilities. He has simply chosen to portray this side of the world in this trilogy. Thus, while Studs seeks his own destruction, and other main characters — Weary Reilly and Davey Cohen, for example — end up in a condition similar to Studs, other characters manage to advance, to preserve and even to build upon their potential. Danny O'Neill, Helen Shires, Lucy, Muggsy McCarthy, and others are examples of enlightened individuals, people who stayed on course and have advanced. But these characters exist on the fringes of Studs's world, and the reader sees them briefly and infrequently. Farrell uses them to measure Studs's downward progress, for most of them started out with the same possibilities Studs had, and as they improve, Studs's downfall becomes more and more obvious, even to Studs. Farrell uses Studs to show how bleak and empty a modern urban existence can be, but he also points out that it does not have to be that way. There are ways out of the streets, but finding them requires energy and persistence, and while Studs has energy, he lacks the persistence which allows Danny to overcome the same influences that affected Studs.

◆ Techniques ◆

Farrell's most striking technique is an almost photographic realism. Having grown up in the milieu he describes, he knows the characters and the setting intimately, and he renders them with a realism and an objectivity that is so close to case study that the Studs Lonigan trilogy is today more often studied in sociology classes than in literature courses. This realistic approach, a characteristic of Farrell's writings, led him to develop a different sense of imagery, an urban imagery replete with patterns of light and dark, of openness and confinement, an imagery that takes advantage of the man-made structures, from the sidewalks and vacant lots to the architectural side of the city. His prose style is therefore markedly nonlyrical, in places even ugly, but it conveys the reality he is trying to recreate. Farrell consistently refuses to romanticize his characters. They may romanticize themselves and their own lives, but Farrell refuses to grant that their dreams are anything but idle and, for the most part, futile musings.

Their dreams are futile because of Farrell's heavy use of determinism. These characters, however they may dream about change, lack control over their lives. They may, as Danny, Helen, Studs, and Weary do, choose — or, more appropriately, drift into — a general direction, but for the most part they are acted upon, passive. They react to events in the world around them, rather than shaping those events. As a result, the overall atmosphere of Studs Lonigan is gloomy, for the main character and most of his friends are doomed, if not to failures of the magnitude of Studs's and Weary's, then at least to mediocrity.

◆ Literary Precedents ◆

Farrell himself claimed two principal literary forebears, Proust and Joyce. Proust, whose *Remembrance of Things Past* (1913-1927) inspired Farrell's de-

sire to write twenty-five novels, each a "panel of one work," provided an example of the attention to detail which Farrell evinces. Proust wrote endlessly about small events, demonstrating basically that there are no insignificant events, that each act has its impact on the individual. That realization fit in very well with Farrell's strong sense of determinism and with his penchant for filling his stories with detail, showing not just the major events in a main character's life, but seemingly every event in his characters' environment.

Joyce, on the other hand, provided a model for exploring the sub- and unconscious minds of characters, as well as an example of an author who works within an urban landscape. Joyce's imagery, his Dublin, and his Irish background all had an impact on Farrell, who attributed Studs Lonigan's dream sequence in *Judgment Day* to the influence of *Ulysses* (1922). But perhaps more important is the example Joyce sets in the area of urban imagery. Joyce, in *Ulysses* (and Farrell in *The Young Manhood of Studs Lonigan* and *Judgment Day*), employs an urban imagery that, in Joyce's case, is lyrical, setting a mood of unreality for Stephen and Bloom's wanderings through the streets of the city, particularly at night. But Farrell adapts that imagery to his own ends, creating from it a heightened sense of reality, a tactile sense of the environment his characters struggle against.

◆ Related Titles ◆

The Studs Lonigan Trilogy includes *Young Lonigan, The Young Manhood of Studs Lonigan,* and *Judgment Day.*

◆ Adaptations ◆

There have been two adaptations of the Studs Lonigan saga, one in 1960 for the screen and one in 1978 as an NBC miniseries. The film version is notable only for the fact that the money from the film rights saved Farrell from bankruptcy in the early 1960s. The cast was weak, and the story almost mercilessly truncated, to the point that the sense of realism is lost, and the film romanticizes Studs in a way that Farrell refused to do.

The television miniseries, some six hours long, could more closely recreate the books, and a much stronger cast was able to create characters that were real, not romanticized caricatures. Even so, the miniseries of necessity had to select which portion of Studs's life to focus on, for to produce a literal rendering of the novels would require more broadcasting time than any network would be willing to devote. As a result, the adaptation focuses on Studs's family, and Charles Durning's strong portrayal of Patrick Lonigan is one of the brightest points of the miniseries. Colleen Dewhurst was also impressive as Mary, Studs's mother, particularly in the climactic scenes when she and Catherine, Studs's fiancée, sit by Studs's bedside, watching him die.

William Condon
Arkansas Tech University

A SUMMONS TO MEMPHIS

Novel

1986

Author: Peter Taylor

◆ Social Concerns/Themes ◆

A Summons to Memphis, Taylor's last novel, is an extended study of his principal theme, well represented in his other work: the familial strife that arises in the face of change.

The change in this family is caused by a move that the family makes early in the narrator's life from the old southern town of Nashville to the modern southern city of Memphis. This changes the lives of the narrator's sisters, severely limiting their chances of making good marriages, eventually leaving them unmarried and dissatisfied. The stress that ensues after the move drives the eldest son to enlist, fight in the war, and die. And it compels the narrator to partially alienate himself from the family and move to New York and adopt a non-Southern lifestyle.

◆ Characters ◆

In *A Summons to Memphis* the characters represent a family and the friends of that family. The father is forced to leave his home in Nashville because of a business disagreement that haunts the family even decades after the incident.

The family is brought together again when the children are middle-aged. Their widower father has decided to marry again and the two middle-aged but liberal-minded sisters have summoned their brother to return to Memphis to try and prevent the marriage. What ensues is a lengthy reminiscence about the family's move, the father's attempts to manipulate the lives of his children, and finally the children's attempts to tell an aged father how to live the few remaining years of his life.

◆ Techniques ◆

Taylor's major technique is the nonchronological revelation of the complexity of family relations. There is much irony and much humor in the situations, but the narrator recognizes the humor and irony only in hindsight and conveys it ambiguously. Throughout his literary career, Taylor's technique has remained basically the same, as have his themes, giving the reader the feeling that he is seeing pieces of a life collected in random order and put together much like a large, complicated jigsaw puzzle.

◆ Literary Precedents ◆

Taylor combines several traditions in his stories. His place in the southern tradition is obvious with his introversion, concentration on tradition, and scrutiny of private behavior. His preoccupation with psychology places him in the tradition of Henry James and others, although Taylor's style is quite dissimilar.

His short stories and novels are private rather than public, quiet rather than boisterous, contemplative rather than active. Readers more than likely will perceive the works as autobiographical in nature. However, this quality may be as much the effect Taylor's stories have upon the reader's identifying with events as it is the writer's personal story.

◆ Related Titles ◆

In most of Taylor's work, his major concern is with change and the contrast that it produces between parents or grandparents and their children or grandchildren. Two of his short story collections, *In Miro District* (1974) and *The Old Forest* (1985) continue this theme.

In the title story, "In Miro District," the contrast is between a grandfather, who remembers Nashville by its ancient Spanish name, the Miro District, and his sometimes-wild grandson. In "The Captain's Son" the contrast is that of attitudes and lifestyles. The contrast and differing views often result in conflict. The conflict in families and between friends provides a poignant comment on life in an ever-changing South.

All of the narrators of these stories are males representative of the younger generation. In "The Captain's Son," the narrator tells the story of his sister's marriage to a man reared in Memphis, a city of the modern world. Lila, the sister, is soon corrupted by her aimless husband. "Brother," as the narrator is called, recognizes this fact first, commenting that alcohol is the culprit. Lila and her husband soon retreat to Memphis and to silence, while the narrator goes on with his life facing a less-than-bright future.

"In Miro District" is about a young man's exploits, mostly sexual, and his grandfather's tyranny. The grandfather actually is not a tyrant but an understanding old man who is less stern than most adults would be, given the circumstances. However, the gap between the grandfather and the grandson only widens as the young man grows older. The story ends with the young man's feelings of alienation and separation, revealing his lack of understanding of the character of his grandfather, the relative whom he probably most resembles.

Like *In Miro District*, *The Old Forest* concentrates on family relationships and conflicts. "The Old Forest" is the story of social perceptions and the strong will that one must have not to allow those perceptions to shape events. The conflict between parents and children is explored in "The Gift of the Prodigal," a conflict that provides an old man with a purpose — to be a confidante to a son whose problems give the old man a sense of being needed. "Two Ladies in Retirement" shows the contrast between the way of living in an older town and a new way of life in a modern city.

In "Two Ladies in Retirement," three

generations engage in a genteel battle of wills. The oldest group is represented by two aging women, Miss Betty Pettigru and her companion and cousin, Mrs. Florence Blalock. Because they are alone, they must move from Nashville to St. Louis, where they live with Miss Betty's relatives, the James Tollivers, representing the next younger group. The youngest group consists of the Tolliver children: Jimmy, Vance, and Landon. The old ladies worship the children and try to maintain their Nashville lifestyle in this extended family.

Conflict soon arises, though. The servants' lives are disrupted when the old ladies move in; the order of the house changes; the boys change; and a showdown finally happens. The resolution is the realization that life cannot remain the same. All must change.

Lesa Dill
Western Kentucky University

THE SUN ALSO RISES

Novel

1926

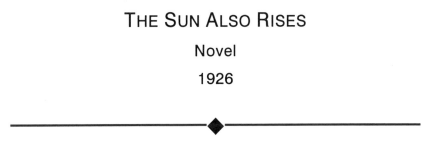

Author: Ernest Hemingway

◆ Characters ◆

Hemingway's characters are often viewed in terms of three general categories: exemplars, apprentices, and anti-exemplars. While careless application of this scheme may result in oversimplification, it is a useful way of approaching his fiction. The exemplars are the characters who have attained to some code of conduct which is, in Hemingway's view, exemplary. Often the exemplar may be a minor character making a cameo appearance, or a somewhat static character illustrating certain principles of skill, professionalism, courage, honor, achieved knowledge and equilibrium.

It is in the nature of things, and perhaps essential to successful fiction, that the major characters must be more apprentice than exemplar, for they are the ones who have room to grow and to change in the course of the action. Their growth is often imaged in terms of their recognition of the stature and knowledge of the exemplars. Anti-exemplars, quite clearly, represent what some would call the negative path, the patterns of behavior that the apprentice must avoid. Hemingway's disposition of characters, then, provides a moral paradigm (not a moralistic homily); he disavowed the word didactic as a description of the thrust of his work, but he accepted the word instructive.

In *The Sun Also Rises* there are several exemplars, each embodying certain aspects of Hemingway's scheme of values. Count Mippipopolous, a minor character, is a straightforward exemplar: he has lived and suffered a great deal, he has been in seven wars and four revolutions, he has been wounded and he has endured with style. He has excellent taste in wine and champagne and a ritualized sense of enjoyment. He is polite and generous. He is, he says, "always in love." It is precisely because he has lived and suffered a great deal, although he does not talk about it much, that he is able to live his life "all the way up." Jake is the apprentice who observes and approves the Count's behavior, who sees that the Count knows the secret: "You must get to know the values."

Another important minor character, the Spanish innkeeper Montoya, exemplifies other aspects of moral behavior, embodies similar values in a more formalized code — that of the aficionado — the man engaged by the world of *toreo*. Montoya clearly stands for dignity and decorum, for the courage, passion and ritual sense of things bodied forth in the bullring. Finally, there is Pedro Romero, the young matador who exemplifies, in his art, skill, and courage in the bullring (and out), all of the categories of grace under pressure with which Hemingway is here concerned.

Since it is Jake who grows through observation and interpretation of the conduct of these exemplars, the familiar character-schematic would suggest that Jake is the apprentice. Yet it could be argued that Jake, by the end of the book, is the principal exemplar. Both arguments are probably legitimate since, by definition, all true apprentices are working toward the achieved values which the exemplars incarnate, and the job of the fiction is to show them approaching that condition. Some readers would say that Brett is an apprentice who fails some of the lessons and passes others, who demonstrates moral confusion and bad behavior on some points and moral fineness on others, such as her renunciation of Romero at the end of the novel. The important thing in a discussion of characters under the exemplar-apprentice heading is a sense of delicacy.

As for anti-exemplars, the major instance in *The Sun Also Rises* is Robert Cohn, who is seen to be immature, a kind of adolescent dreamer (aged 34) who gets all of his ideas from romantic books. He precisely embodies other anti-exemplary traits such as self-pity, self-absorption, boredom, sentimentality, and the kind of pseudo-toughness and macho-aggressiveness which seeks to solve all differences with fisticuffs. (The Hemingway hero, contrary to some muddled impressions, never does this.) Two concrete indications of Cohn's anti-exemplary state of being

are found in his boredom at the bullfights and in his sleeping through the most beautiful landscapes of their passage through the mountains. Thus, he is shown to be unengaged by the novel's two primary expressions of the code, of a sacramental connection.

◆ Social Concerns ◆

For many readers in the 1920s, *The Sun Also Rises* seemed to be the story of their time, the vivid record of a "lost generation" shattered in various ways by the experience of World War I and its aftermath, a generation profoundly skeptical of the bankrupt values of a botched civilization. Many readers identified with the work in this fashion, perhaps reading into it too much of their own disillusionment and the fashionable nihilism of the 1920s. Some saw the novel as a veritable textbook, illustrating the premise stated in the famous epigraph to the novel, taken from Gertrude Stein: "You are all a lost generation." In fact, however, Hemingway's intent was quite different: the work was built around a refutation of that epigraph, which Hemingway regarded as "splendid bombast." He did not feel lost, some of his characters were not at all lost; they were, he said, "a very solid generation" and, in any case, "there was no such thing as a lost generation."

The novel was also read as a *roman à clef* which brilliantly depicted the fashionable bohemian and expatriate life of the Parisian Left Bank, following the movements of certain well-known prototypes from cafe to cafe in Paris and then south to Spain for a grand drunken fiesta. In part, the book had the kind of *succes de scandale* which is based on gossip and guessing-games as to the identity of the characters. However, the concerns which make the novel one of the very few classics of modern American fiction have more to do with the necessity of seeking a code to live by, in the face of the multiple wounds of war, violence, deracination, and the accompanying dislocation of values.

◆ Themes ◆

Hemingway said that *The Sun Also Rises* was not intended as "a hollow or bitter satire, but a damn tragedy with the earth abiding forever as the hero." Certainly the earth does abide and is celebrated in this novel, especially in the Burguete-Roncevaux fishing scenes in the Pyrenees, where Jake Barnes and his friend Bill Gorton find telluric serenity and strength through hiking and fishing in the high country. Far from being a mere pastoral interlude in an otherwise frenzied novel, the fishing scenes serve to reinforce the primary theme of quest or pilgrimage which informs the work.

Against the countertheme of the "lost generation," Hemingway constructs a pattern of quest for "grace under pressure." The war has indeed shattered the lives of some of the characters. Although the war is there as implicit backdrop and is mentioned only briefly in conversational asides — "Oh, that dirty war" — it is Jake's war wound, resulting in his sexual incapacitation, which provides the central dramatic dilemma: Jake's impossible love for Brett Ashley, another character who has suffered from the war. Put simply, the book is about the successful efforts of Jake, one who might be "lost" because of the war, to find himself. It is also closely concerned with the behavior of others, especially Brett

and Robert Cohn, who are seen in various phases of finding and losing themselves. Those who are not lost possess some sense of "grace under pressure."

The grace in Hemingway's celebrated phrase is a physical, aesthetic, moral, and spiritual matter; the pressure includes the press of events and decisions, the complexity of moral choices, the chaos and violence of the times, and, above all, the presence of death leaning over, gnawing at every human being. The primary incarnation of grace under pressure in this novel is the ritual of *toreo*, the bullfight, which is meant to convey an emblem of exemplary moral behavior, rooted in courage, honor, and passion. It is also an analogue, Hemingway maintains, of religious ecstasy and it provides a triumph over death. Fishing, then, yet another ritualized activity with symbolic overtones of renewal and redemption, provides secondary confirmation of the novel's primary theme. The wounded hero, in his quest for wholeness, undertakes a pilgrimage across the face of the "abiding earth," into the sacral mountains where he fishes (very much a wounded Fisher King-figure of myth). There he finds rejuvenation and continues his journey to the fiesta of San Fermin, the profoundly religious festival of Pamplona, centered around the bullfight.

Hemingway remarked that *The Sun Also Rises* was the most moral book he had ever written, that it was a kind of "tract against promiscuity." It is precisely that, although many readers have missed the point. The sexual promiscuity in the book is only the most obvious form of promiscuity, literally, a lack of standards of selection. The novel, then, is concerned to discover — or recover — the values, the standards of selection that one might live by in a violent, promiscuous age. Those values are summed up in the infinite ramifications and the intricate gradations of the complex rubric-grace under pressure.

◆ Techniques ◆

Hemingway is most conventional in his more or less straightforward chronological ordering of his narratives, told through first-person point-of-view (*The Sun Also Rises* ; *A Farewell to Arms*, 1929) and third-person point-of-view (*For Whom the Bell Tolls*, 1940; *The Old Man and the Sea*, 1952). He is most unique in the intense imagistic and poetic concentration of his style, the seamless fashion in which the thing that is said or made and the manner of saying it or making it are one. He eliminates all ornamentation and employs the most rigorous standards of selectivity in his effort to render "the real thing, the sequence of motion and fact which made the emotion."

His style is often said to be conspicuously American, colloquial and natural, eschewing all pedantic, latinate and abstract words. However, his style is far from being colloquial in the sense, say, of Mark Twain's use of the vernacular, of folk-speech. Hemingway's voices depend upon an elaborate aesthetic which distrusts adjectives and adverbs; relies on nouns because they are the closest to things; modulates sentence rhythms carefully through skillful use of repetition, parallelism and counterpoint; and builds upon the doctrine of the Imagist poets which requires that the writer render things precisely and convey "an intellectual and emotional complex in an instant of time."

Another finely honed Hemingway technique is his masterful use of dialogue to reveal character, to carry the movement of a story, and to generate almost unbearable tension without the use of intervening commentary or dialogue tags. Some critics have maintained that he had one of the best ears ever employed in the creation of dialogue, while others have maintained that no one ever spoke the way his characters do. Both assertions may be true and both may miss the point. The fact is that his dialogue is highly stylized, contributes immensely to the success of his fiction, and is one of the unique technical legacies he left to the modern novel.

Another device frequently employed with unrivaled brilliance is the symbolic landscape. Hemingway said that he learned to write from studying Cezanne's paintings; as an apprentice writer in the early 1920s he declared that he was "trying to do the country like Cezanne." It is as difficult to say as it is easy to see what Hemingway meant if one examines his use of color, plane, form; Wright Morris notes Hemingway's "Cezanne-like simplicity of scene. . . built up with the touches of a master"; "great effects are achieved with a sublime economy" and "style and substance are of one piece, each growing from the other." Along with this, there is the skillful deployment of landscape as *paysage moralise,* landscape suffused with history, numinous landscape nodding to and mirroring the soul of the character who moves through it. Landscape, according to Octavio Paz, is a "metaphysic, a religion, an idea of man and the cosmos," and it "always points to something else, to something beyond itself." In Hemingway, landscape points to the deepest significations of his work.

For the most part, Hemingway's techniques, narrative strategies, style, and devices remain more or less constant throughout his career, although the later novels show a certain relaxation of the tautness and restraint of the early work.

◆ Literary Precedents ◆

There is a tendency among some readers of Hemingway to see him as such an unprecedented force in fiction that his careful apprenticeship, his disciplined assimilation of the best of his forebears and contemporaries may be overlooked. Hemingway himself had much to say about the matter, including his well-known declaration: "All modern American literature comes from one book by Mark Twain called Huckleberry Finn." Aside from Twain, Hemingway dismissed most nine-teen-th-century American writing and located his literary precedents in the work of such European masters as Flaubert and Turgenev. Hemingway also acknowledged his debt to Joseph Conrad, whose influence was perhaps more a matter of reinforcing Hemingway's subject matter and thematic approach than it was a matter of style. Certainly Conrad's persistent plumbing of the mysterious depths of human experience, clothed in the framework of tales of adventure and travel, is reflected in Hemingway's characteristic fictional mode.

Among his near-contemporaries most often cited as influences, four figures stand out: Ring Lardner, Sherwood Anderson, Ezra Pound, and Gertrude Stein. From Lardner, Hemingway learned early how to write tough, ironic prose that disciplined and held just below the surface his outrage and in-dignation. From Sherwood Anderson he may have taken a sense of open and episodic structure and colloquial speech rhythms. Both of these precedents, however, were very early influences, visible in his apprentice work, and a major step in Hemingway's prose mastery is made when he sees, with devastating clarity, the weaknesses and limitations of these writers. (See especially his parody of Anderson's manner and matter in *The Torrents of Spring,*. 1964)

Far more important as influences were Pound and Stein. Hemingway said: "Nobody taught me as much about writing as Ezra." Pound guided him through a survey of French fiction and transmitted the principles of Imagist poetry which Hemingway, more successfully than any other writer of prose, translated into his fiction. The avoidance of what Pound called "emotional slither" and the drive to — in Hemingway's words — "strip language clean, to lay it bare to the bone" are at the heart of Hemingway's work. From Stein, Hemingway learned "many truths about rhythms and the uses of words in repetition that were valid and valuable," as well as the necessity of clarity "so the reader will see it too . . . and have the same feeling that you had." Hemingway quickly assimilated the lessons of Pound and Stein and forged his own style on the foundations they had laid.

When asked late in life about influences and "literary forebears," Hemingway mentioned, along with Pound, Stein and his friend James Joyce, the following names: Twain, Flaubert, Stendhal, Bach, Turgenev, Tolstoy, Dostoevski, Chekhov, Marvell, Donne, Maupassant, Kipling, Thoreau, Captain Marryat, Shakespeare, Mozart, Quevedo, Dante, Virgil, Tintoretto, Bosch,

Breughel, Patinier, Goya, Giotto, Cezanne, Van Gogh, Gauguin, San Juan de la Cruz, Gongora — and there he broke off his list, saying that it would take a day to remember everyone. The careful student of Hemingway's career will take seriously his list of forebears which includes not only writers but musicians, mystics and painters, all of whom played a crucial role in the formation of Hemingway's art of looking, listening and creating. Contrary to the popular impression, few writers have read and absorbed so many diverse influences as did Hemingway. His sense of commitment to his craft and to art was intense (an "almost holy" sense of vocation), and it is only in the light of the complex relationship of the individual talent to tradition that one may understand his memorable Nobel Prize statement: "How simple the writing of literature would be if it were only necessary to write in another way what has been well written. It is because we have had such great writers in the past that a writer is driven far out past where he can go, out to where no one can help him."

◆ Related Titles ◆

The reader who wishes to understand Hemingway's notion of "grace under pressure," and his love for Spain is referred to his classic nonfiction study of Spain and the bullfight, *Death in the Afternoon* (1932). Many of the short stories provide variations on the themes of the major novels as well as economically rendered core images and controlling metaphors which reappear in those novels. Two of Hemingway's best-known short stories set in Spain are "A Clean Well-Lighted Place" and "Hills Like White Elephants."

◆ Adaptations ◆

There have been many attempts to translate — perhaps transpose is the more accurate term — Hemingway's work into film. *The Sun Also Rises* was first made into a disappointing film in 1957; it has been a disastrous television miniseries (1985). Neither version captured the spirit of the work or displayed any comprehension of the novel's themes. Many other Hemingway works, including a number of the stories, have been adapted to film. The general verdict has been that, at best, the films fail to capture the subtlety and complexity of the work and, at worst, they are travesties of Hemingway's world.

H. R. Stoneback
SUNY-New Paltz

SUTTREE

Novel

1979

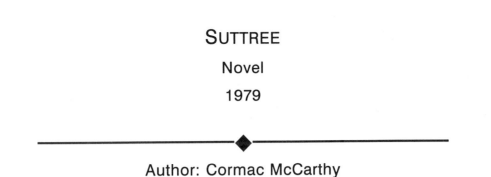

Author: Cormac McCarthy

◆ Social Concerns ◆

*S*uttree is a novel that takes a long, hard, detailed look at the basic concepts of society and what we call "civilization." The assumption that civilization represents a positive advance for the human race is questioned and challenged by the very fabric of the narrative.

The main character, Cornelius Suttree, despite his intelligence, education, and middle-class background, decides to live on a houseboat on the Tennessee River on the outskirts of Knoxville. He is a fisherman by profession. His lifestyle of voluntary poverty forces him to engage in a vigorous struggle to survive on a day-to-day basis. He not only *sees* poverty; he *lives* it. His friends form the very lowest class of society: They are sympathetically portrayed street bums, criminals, perverts, and other societal outcasts. Like Suttree, readers see the "benefits" of civilization up close and firsthand.

Just as the entire city of Knoxville is described as being precariously perched on top of a honeycomb of tunnels and caverns, the novel subtly insinuates that our entire system of civilization is undermined by its inherent flaws. The social ills dramatized include poverty, alcoholism, pollution, perversion, racism, police brutality, and crime. In the face of these problems, Suttree and his friends form a caring community and achieve an attractive and meaningful brotherhood, wherein perhaps lies their salvation.

◆ Themes ◆

Suttree is a large novel, epic in some ways, and it is densely and richly thematic. One of the novel's most significant thematic clusters concerns Suttree's quest for personal spiritual growth. His search for God makes this a deeply religious novel, one which delves into the profoundest questions of existence on both philosophical and psychological levels. Suttree's estrangement from his mother, aptly named Grace, symbolizes his personal crisis of faith. He is a lapsed Catholic, and the questions he ponders are basic ones: What is reality? Is there a God? If so, is the nature of God malevolent? Suttree primarily turns inward for the answers to these questions so that from one perspective the novel assumes the form of an interior journey. Although the point has been debated, Suttree does seem to achieve a degree of spiritual progress by the end of the novel. Various epiphanies reveal to him such insights as "all souls are one and all souls lonely" and "[God] is not a thing. Nothing ever stops moving." Ultimately, Suttree overcomes his sense of duality and his obsessive fear of death.

Critics have also pointed out that the novel explores a number of existential themes. Suttree's repeated flirtation with suicide shows him to be wondering why he should continue to live in an absurd world. Suttree also rejects one form of authority after another, thereby increasing his freedom and his chances of living an authentic existence. The novel seems to endorse William James's view that the beginning of wisdom is to embrace a tragic vision of life, one which unshrinkingly recognizes the inevitability of suffering, loss, and death. On the streets of Knoxville, Suttree lives authentically because he sees the tragedy of life on a daily basis. It is only when he is temporarily seduced into an affluent, comfortable lifestyle with the prostitute Joyce that he becomes alienated from his true self.

On a sociological level, the novel combines Marxist, Thoreauvian, and Christian thought to attempt to invert the usual bourgeois pyramid of values. To the casual observer, Suttree may seem little more than a street bum, an unhappy man at the bottom of the hierarchy of success. But according to Christian paradox, "the last shall be first"; according to Marx, the proletariat is exalted over the aristocracy; and according to Thoreau, "a man is rich in proportion to the things which he can afford to let alone." Following Thoreau's standards, Suttree is truly rich and truly successful.

◆ Characters ◆

The cast of characters in *Suttree* is impressively large. It includes some of Suttree's family members, but mostly they are his acquaintances and friends. An often-quoted passage near the end of the novel accurately describes Suttree's usual companions as "thieves, derelicts, miscreants, pariahs, poltroons, spalpeens, curmudgeons, clotpolls, murderers, gamblers, bawds, whores, trulls, brigands, topers, tosspots, sots and archsots, lobcocks, smellsmocks, runagates, rakes and other assorted and felonious debauchees."

At the center of this web of outcasts is Cornelius Suttree, affectionately known to his friends as Old Suttree, Sut, Youngblood, and Buddy. What separates him from his poor, often handicapped, companions is that his poverty is deliberately chosen despite the hardships that it entails. He is not without his character flaws as his alcoholism, his unhealthy relationships with women, and his alienation from his son attest. Suttree rejects his father's middle-class value system and the authority of the religion he has been taught, but then he must struggle to fill the void created by those rejections. It is through this struggle that Suttree proves himself to be heroic. In fact, McCarthy takes pains to characterize his protagonist as an epic hero, frontier hero, and modern existential hero, all rolled into one.

Of all of McCarthy's protagonists, Suttree is by far the one that readers are allowed to know most intimately. He is the only one who ever speaks directly to the reader, and he is the one whose consciousness we are admitted into most deeply. He may also be McCarthy's most likable protagonist. He has a good sense of humor, a friendly personality, and a deeply compassionate nature, as he demonstrates when he checks on Daddy Watson, takes a catfish to the ragpicker, donates four pennies to blind Walter, or spends days in the caverns under Knoxville searching for Harrogate, who has nearly blown himself up.

The character next in importance to Suttree is his sidekick, Gene Harrogate, whom he meets in a correctional facility after Harrogate has been convicted of practicing an unusual perversion. Harrogate is the most humorous character that McCarthy has yet created. His hare-brained, get-rich-quick schemes (such as poisoning bats for the bounty and building a boat out of automobile hoods) land him in one predicament after another. He is known at first as the country mouse and later as the city rat, and these animalistic comparisons are continued when he makes his home in a burrow-like hollow at the foot of a bridge spanning the Tennessee River. Although at times he has a certain innocent charm, he is reckless and has little self-awareness. Despite his limitations, however, he usually has a laughably swaggering and pretentious self-confidence. By depicting Suttree's loyalty to this ne'er-do-well, McCarthy emphasizes his main character's heroic compassion and humanity.

◆ Techniques ◆

What readers of Cormac McCarthy are usually most impressed with is the overpowering style he achieves through his virtuoso command of language. Through this style, McCarthy is able to render scenes that would ordinarily be merely disgusting or grotesque or repulsively violent in a some-how beautiful way. In *Suttree*, McCarthy may be at the very height of his verbal powers.

McCarthy's narrative point of view is almost always third person, but *Suttree* is unique. Most of the novel does have an outside narrator, but at certain points Suttree addresses readers directly. These lapses into first-person narration provide the novel with a more personal and intimate tone. This seems to be McCarthy's most autobiographical novel, so perhaps the materials were too personal to handle as objectively as he typically does. Or perhaps because McCarthy wanted to emphasize Suttree's *inward* journey, he realized that a more intimate point of view was required.

Some readers might feel that the novel has *no* structure or resolution, but because the story is primarily an unconventional, internal story, the author employs some unconventional structures. Marking Suttree's spiritual progress are many scenes in which he experiences some altered state of consciousness, such as dreams, semiconsciousness resulting from head trauma, hypnosis-like memories, and hallucinations. Of particular importance on Suttree's path to enlightenment are three episodes of visions and hallucinations: the first, brought on by his weeks of deprivation in the Smokies; the second, induced by the drug Mother She gives him; and the third, the result of his near-death experience from typhoid fever. By focusing on these mystical experiences, McCarthy is able to dramatize Suttree's inner, spiritual journey.

◆ Literary Precedents ◆

Because a river is central to this

novel and because Suttree lives on a houseboat, readers may naturally be reminded of *The Adventures of Huckleberry Finn* (1884). Suttree indeed participates in the same kind of basic, multiracial community that Huck and Jim achieve on their raft.

Suttree is also reminiscent of *Walden* (1854). Like Thoreau, Suttree chooses to live in natural environs, but on the edge of civilization. Neither repudiates society, and both occupy a middle ground from which they can observe nature *and* humanity.

With its emphasis on traveling, on altered states of consciousness, and on resistance to the establishment, this novel is also in the tradition of such Beat Generation literature as Jack Kerouac's *On the Road* (1957).

◆ Related Titles ◆

Suttree is a larger, funnier, more ambitious, more personal book than the three McCarthy novels published before it, but it does include some of the same types of outcast characters that appeared in the earlier novels.

Jimmy Blevins as described in Part I of *All the Pretty Horses* (1992) seems to have been cast from the same mold as Gene Harrogate. Both are pitiable but comic troublemakers who test the compassion and loyalty of their companions to their very limits.

◆ Ideas for Group Discussions ◆

There is much to discuss in this novel. There are scores of interesting characters and many complex psychological, philosophical, sociological, and religious issues to explore. It is a very rewarding novel to study, and it de-serves much more attention than it has so far received.

1. What are the humorous elements in this novel, and what are the functions and effects of this humor?

2. In what ways is Suttree heroic?

3. How exactly does Suttree progress spiritually in the course of the novel?

4. Do you admire Suttree for voluntarily choosing a life of rugged poverty?

5. What do Suttree's dreams reveal about him?

6. What does Suttree's relationship to the Indian Michael reveal?

7. Examine how Suttree rebels against parental, governmental, and societal authority without rejecting community.

8. To what extent is Gene Harrogate fated by forces beyond his control and to what extent is he responsible for bringing about his own doom?

9. What are the several symbolic implications of the Tennessee River?

10. What is the significance of all the scatological materials?

William C. Spencer
Delta State University

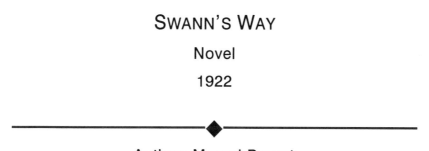

SWANN'S WAY

Novel

1922

Author: Marcel Proust

◆ Characters ◆

One of Proust's greatest writing achievements is his character portrayal. Each of the major characters is a synthesis of people whom Proust knew in his own life, or portraits of his contemporaries. The narrator is one side of Proust himself, modest and unassuming, without Proust's maternal Jewish heritage and without his own brother Robert. Swann is another side of Proust, a society figure who frequents all the famous salons, modeled also on Charles Haas and Louis Weil. Bergotte, the famous author, is a composite of Anatole France, Henri Bergson, Maurice Barrès, and Ernest Renan. The parents and aunt of the narrator are based on Proust's own family. Françoise the family servant, is a composite of many of the Prousts' domestics.

Proust presents his characters with exactness and often with humor, allowing them to reveal themselves by their words and concrete actions. One meets Bloch, the Jewish friend of the narrator, who always hums biblical songs; the snobbish Legrandin, who speaks like a book; Aunt Léonie, the invalid who remains in bed, talks to herself, never sleeps, and who tells herself she must remember she hasn't slept. There are also tragic figures: Swann in his frantic pursuit of Odette; Mlle. Vinteuil, the lesbian who mocks her father's portrait. Proust allows his characters to reappear as his fantasy and inspiration dictate. Sometimes the reader simply receives a glimpse of them, as the narrator's first meeting with Gilberte, or Odette, the lady in pink at Uncle Adolphe's house. At other times, they play a major role, especially in the long ruminations of the narrator regarding dreams, his need for his mother's goodnight kiss, his desire to overcome time. As Fowlie states, "While drawing upon a very real subject, [Proust] so transforms it as to make it a fresh creation, unique, and at the same time soundly based upon historical reality."

◆ Social Concerns ◆

Primarily interested in the world of art, symbolism, and memory, Proust nevertheless considers the social aspects of his society in the many volumes of his work. He writes of the prewar years (1900-1914) and the striking social mobility that characterizes this period. At this point, the old aristocracy was collapsing, to be replaced by the bourgeoisie and several Jewish and American families. The glimpse into Mme. Verdurin's salon at the beginning of the "Swann in Love" shows a bourgeois salon, replacing the old aristocracy so popular in French history. Odette de Crécy, the object of Swann's love, is a member of this circle, and her daughter Gilberte will follow the same evolution in the society of her times. Painter states that Proust wrote the great obituary of the French nobility whom he had loved all his life.

Proust writes of a very circumscribed society during the prewar years, yet he gives vivid portraits of French society at the time, perhaps the best that exist. The provincial bourgeoisie come to life in the portraits of Combray, especially of his Aunt Leonie and her curiosity about her village and all that happens there. The servant class is ably portrayed in Françoise, the faithful family servant who is in reality a composite of many figures, with her devotion to duty and to the family, her peasant good sense and ruse, and her cruelty and intolerance. As Wallace Fowlie states, "Out of a detailed analysis of French traits in two social classes and a few portraits of servants and members of the lower classes, Proust created a recognizable humanity with the abiding features of goodness and wickedness."

◆ Themes ◆

Proust forever will be known as the poet of memory, "the whole universe in a cup of tea." Early in the first volume of *Remembrance of Things Past*, the author dips a little cake called a madeleine into a cup of tea, and with the familiar taste of his childhood, recalls his days in Combray. The experience of involuntary memory will return about eight times in the course of the novel, and represents for Proust the conquest of time and the attainment of a certain kind of eternity through memory. In this way Proust joins his contemporaries Freud and Jung in their discovery of the world of the subconscious and of esoteric myths and symbols.

The problem of the oversensitive child, extremely attached to his mother and frightened by his father, appears in the opening pages and throughout "Combray," the first major section of *Swann's Way*. With delicate humor and graphic symbols of death, the author describes his compelling need to kiss his mother good-night, even when she is engaged in a dinner party. Both mother and father give in to the nervous whim of their son, and he realizes that he will never be free of dependence during his lifetime.

Swann's Way is dominated by the themes of love and sensuality. Proust traces the entire gamut of this emotion, and evokes all of its excesses and inversions. In a beautiful May-time scene, the author first sees little Gilberte Swann against a hawthorn bush, and she will forever remain as he first saw her, a love idealized. On the other hand, the voyeuristic author observes the lesbian actions of Mlle. Vinteuil and her friend in front of her father's portrait, and thereby makes the acquaintance of the world of evil. Proust, himself a homosexual, although the narrator of the story is not, places great emphasis on this type of love. He describes it overtly with sadistic overtones, usually expressing it tragically and painfully, unlike Gide's triumphant confessions.

The second major part of Volume I, "Swann in Love," is totally devoted to the theme of passion and jealousy. Swann is hopelessly enamored of the unfaithful and coquettish Odette de Crécy, and soon recognizes her inability to maintain a commitment. With ruthless jealousy and suspicion he pursues her every move. Unable to live with her, he cannot exist without her, and pursues her with morbid curiosity and passionate desire. He also shows the tenderness of a lover, evoking a musical phrase (*la petite phrase de Vinteuil*) that is the symbol of their love, and the cattleyas, flowers that evoke their first night together. Swann eventually marries Odette, realizing a certain self-destruction, but at the same time the redeeming force of memory and art.

Proust the artist dominates the entire work, particularly the first section, "Combray." Delicate nature imagery evokes lilacs, hawthorns, and water lilies, in which he sees both the beauty of the Virgin Mary and the gates of hell. The church at Combray, not a masterpiece of cathedral architecture, nevertheless becomes a memorial to history and to Proust's own ancestry. Literature as a form of art also occupies a prominent role in the novel. The author's idol and inspiration, Bergotte, recreates the past in his work and brings the author and the reader into immediate contact with his innermost and otherwise inaccessible self.

◆ Techniques ◆

Although Proust uses a great many psychological elements in his work, particularly in regard to the role of memory and dreams, his greatest originality lies not in his psychology nor in his observations on art, but in his form and style. His sentences and paragraphs, lengthy and complex, are musical, leading the reader where memory and inspiration freely carry the author. His details are exhaustive, yet his elaborate use of metaphors and symbols suggests another reality. His descriptions of people and places are so exact that they come alive. Illiers-Combray appears in the distance as the train approaches it, and the reader sees every detail as the narrator saw it some hundred years ago. The jeweled stained glass windows of the parish church sparkle as precious gems through the pages of the narrative.

In Proust's work, nothing really happens, but for him the most important events in life are those that one has forgotten, that will return one day through involuntary memory. It is not plot that is important; there is in fact hardly any sense of intrigue. It is rather the internal mirror of the author's spirit, and by extension, that of every person. Valéry calls Proust's style "prismatic," and states that Proust believed that only metaphor could give eternity to his style. Completely narrated in the first person, except for "Swann in Love," Proust makes the world of the artist and the inner world of sensibility a reality for the reader, far better than his equally famous contemporaries Valéry, Gide, and Claudel. Another of his successful techniques as a novelist is his ability to present several themes at the same time, without losing the thread of any. He is able, better than Balzac or Stendhal, to weave imperceptibly the drama both of the individual and of society.

◆ Literary Precedents ◆

Although Proust's novel was a new

form of literature, analogous to James Joyce's "stream of consciousness," he is a true product of his times. In the tradition of Baudelaire, whom, with Vigny, he considered the greatest poet of the nineteenth century, his work abounds in symbols and correspondences between the senses, and between objects and ideas. Endowed like Baudelaire with deeper powers of perceptiveness, he is able to express greater insights into the mysterious inner world of the spirit. There are also literary echoes of Mallarmé and of Nerval, particularly in the role of dreams, which Nerval sees as a second life, and whose opening of *Sylvie* (1853) recalls the beginning of "Combray." The idea of a *"roman-fleuve,"* popular at the turn of the century, recalls Balzac's *Human Comedy* (1895-1896, 1911), and the techniques of Balzac in portraying the individual and society are apparent in Proust. The philosophical ideas pertaining to time are most closely allied to Bergson, and the artistic theories are those of John Ruskin, to whom Proust was particularly attracted.

◆ Related Titles ◆

Remembrance of Things Past is composed of seven volumes, all related and depending on the initial idea of the search for remembrance and revitalization of things past. With the exception of the last volume, *The Past Recaptured* (1931; *Le Temps retrouvé*, 1927), they are less known and read than the first volume, *Swann's Way*. The theme of the two ways, Swann's way, and Guermantés' way, which appeared in the first volume, represented in the child's imagination the two roads leading from the family home, as irreconcilable as east and west, and will be repeated in the succeeding volumes. The two ways will finally be reconciled in the last volume, when Gilberte Swann marries Robert de Saint-Loup.

Within a Budding Grove, (1919; 1924), Part II of the novel, which Proust reworked for six years after the publication of *Swann's Way*, is longer and more complex, and corresponds roughly to the narrator's adolescence. In the first part, "Madame Swann at Home," Marcel is introduced to Swann's Paris apartment. He has left Combray and the security of the family home, and he finds himself in the world of Paris society. The second part, entitled "Place-Names: The Place," finds the narrator at Balbec, a place which is mentioned in passing in *Swann's Way*. Here he meets three members of the Guermantes clan: Mlle. de Villeparisis, Robert de Saint-Loup, and the baron de Charlus. The highlights of the first part are Marcel's meeting with Gilberte, his transitory and intense love for her, and the acquaintance of his literary idol, Bergotte. Yet both loves are tinged with reality; neither is the idealized person of his dreams. His growing independence, yet difficulty in finding his inner self characterize this volume. The second part, with Balbec, its trees, and the ocean, as a background, contains many intricate developments. Among the most significant is the meeting and subsequent attraction to Albertine, and his association with the painter Elstir, and thus his initiation into the world of art. Proust addresses the question of incommunicability and misunderstanding throughout this complex volume, as well as the need of solitude for literary and artistic creation.

Part III, *The Guermantes Way* (1925; *Les Côté des Guermantes*, 1920-1921), is also divided into two parts, one at the

Paris home of Mme. de Villeparisis, and the second at a dinner party in Paris at Mme. de Guermantes' residence. This selection is a study of society's forms, and false perceptions of it that individuals cultivate. The duchess of Guermantes, Oriane, is one of Proust's best developed characters. At the same time, the end of the Guermantes line marks the dissolution of the French aristocracy. As Marcel dispels the illusions he has had about the Guermantes in the first volume of the novel, he analyzes the limitations that isolate human beings from one another, and make them mysteries even to themselves. In presenting the characters as they meet in the Paris salon of Mme. de Guermantes, Proust inserts comic and ironic overtones in his portrait of ambition in high society.

In contrast, the second part opens on a note of sadness with the death of Marcel's beloved grandmother. Along with scenes of love and sensuality, Proust explores delicately the theme of friendship, especially that of Marcel and Robert de Saint-Loup. The death of Swann at the end of the volume explores the whole mystery of life and its ending, along with the end of friendship. The introduction of the puzzling Charlus opens the way for succeeding volumes, especially Part IV, *Cities of the Plain* (1927; *Sodome et Gomorrhe*, 1922), where Proust will treat in a somewhat tragic although overt manner the question of homosexuality, an important subject of his novel. Not handled in a moralistic sense, sexual inversion is nevertheless allied for Proust to the suffering and social ostracism it entails.

After The Captive (1929; *La Prisonnière*, 1925) and T*he Sweet Cheat Gone* (1930; *Albertine disparue*, 1925), volumes which discuss the disintegration of love, Proust completes the lengthy novel with *The Past Recaptured*. This final volume, implicitly based on France during and right after the war, is the triumph of Swann's way over Guermantes, or a new bourgeois society over the old aristocracy. Many characters return: Gilberte, unhappily married to Robert de Saint-Loup, who has died in the war; Françoise, the aging servant, a mixture of gentleness and cruelty, morality and ignorance; Charlus, degraded yet with a patriotic sense of justice and a vast culture; Jupien in his hotel or male brothel.

More than anything, this final volume is the victory of art, and Proust's acceptance of his literary vocation. On his way to the matinee at the Princesse de Guermantes, Marcel has three experiences similar to the madeleine in Part I. He strikes his foot against some uneven flagstones, and the flagstones of Venice return to his consciousness. In the library of the Guermantes' residence, a servant strikes a spoon against a plate, and he relives the hammer of a train wheel at Combray. Finally, a starched napkin brings him back to the hotel at Balbec. Marcel now sees the role of the artist, the effective communication of such moments of ecstasy. He has realized the true essence of time, the ability to resurrect the past into a kind of eternity through involuntary memory. With this realization come the constraints imposed upon the artist: solitude, and subject matter which he cannot choose, but which will be imposed on him through his own life and vocation. He will become a great writer, and Part I, *Swann's Way*, is about to begin.

◆ Adaptations ◆

In 1962, Producer Nicole Stéphane

acquired all film rights to the novel from Proust's niece. After several abortive attempts, including the cooperation of Harold Pinter who wrote a brilliant screenplay which was never to be filmed, Stéphane turned to Peter Brooks. He did not complete the task, which was finally assumed by Volker Schlöndorff. The film was produced in Paris in 1984, with Jeremy Irons, an Englishman, as Swann, and Ornella Muti, an Italian, as Odette. Entitled *Swann in Love*, and based primarily on the material in the "Swann in Love" section of *Swann's Way*, the film attempts to show twenty-four hours in the life of Swann. To many viewers, Irons proved disappointing. Odette was slightly more convincing. Although Schlöndorff did not attempt to recreate Proust, but rather to create a new genre for film, the final result is vastly inferior to Proust's panorama of the end of an age and of a tormented and jealous love.

Sister Irma M. Kashuba, S.S.J.
Chestnut Hill College

TALES OF THE SOUTH PACIFIC

Related Short Stories

1947

◆

Author: James Michener

◆ Social Concerns/Themes ◆

In *Tales of the South Pacific,* Michener explores themes common to most of his works: racism and bigotry; the brotherhood of humankind; the effects of war, violence, exploitation, and authoritarianism on the human psyche; and man's destruction of his environment. Michener has stated that the book was written "under extremely difficult circumstances. I was in the Navy on Espiritu Santo in the South Seas . . . I was sure the people who were bitching so much about the Islands would not remember them that way. I try to anticipate history."

◆ Characters ◆

Lieutenant Tony Fry, who appears in nine of the nineteen tales, is one of the most anti–authoritarian of the American characters in *Tales of the South Pacific.* Readers meet Fry in the first tale, "The South Pacific," when Admiral Millard Kester orders Fry to remove from the side of his old TBF the twelve painted beer bottles illustrating Fry's twelve "heroic" beer–ferrying missions. In the tale "Mutiny," which takes place on Norfolk Island, Fry becomes involved with a descendant of one of history's best known mutineers, Fletcher Christian. The old woman Teta Christian and her family object to the navy's building an airstrip on their island because the most strategic place for the airstrip is in the middle of a stand of pine trees planted by their ancestors. Siding with the mutineers, Fry dynamites a bulldozer in protest against the desecration of that "living cathedral." In "The Cave," Fry lives comfortably in a cave on Tulagi while he receives transmissions from the "Remittance Man," a British trader who risks death by sending reports of weather and troop movements to the U.S. Navy. Although Fry continues to laugh at military protocol, he succeeds in confessing his own fear of death and learns to respect the Remittance Man's courage. The Remittance Man's death leads Fry to question the nature of a courage that enables human beings to risk their own lives for a cause. In the story "The Landing on Kuralei," Fry gives his own life when he chooses to move inland with the Marines, thus becoming one of the legendary heroes whom the narrator describes as always being "somewhere further up the line."

Through the evolution of Fry's character, Michener's readers learn the realities of war — and death.

In the third story, "An Officer and a Gentleman," Michener introduces Ensign Bill Harbison, Tony Fry's foil. Although Harbison is a man who begins his navy career with both intellectual and athletic promise, he should have enlisted in the army, where his abilities would have earned him quick promotions. Unfortunately, the snobbish Harbison believes that officers in the army are little better than enlisted men. Slowly rotting on Efate Island in his less-than-demanding role as recreation officer, Harbison exercises his body playing various sports and his mind playing with the emotions of navy nurses. However, none of the plebeian nurses are serious competition for Harbison's Vassar-educated wife, to whom he writes creatively passionate and melodramatic letters describing his "heroic" four-day adventure on a raft. Harbison, who spends much of his time trying to persuade his commanding officer to transfer him to active duty, finally receives his much desired transfer to combat before the climactic battle in "The Landing on Kuralei." When Tony Fry dies on Kuralei beach, Harbison, who has used his father-in-law's influence to obtain a rest and rehabilitation leave, is alive and well in New Mexico.

One of the navy nurses whom "gentleman" Bill Harbison sets out to seduce is Nellie Forbush, a romantic young woman from Arkansas who wants to experience life. Because navy nurses are officers, Forbush is forbidden to fraternize with the enlisted men of her own class, who might love her for herself. On Efate, Nellie Forbush is an officer's prize catch, a pretty white "rarity" among all the brown faces. A naive target for Harbison's wiles, Forbush is rejected when her marriage proposal shocks Harbison into seeing her as a woman he "wouldn't look twice at in the States."

To add to her disillusionment with love, Ensign Nellie Forbush is exposed to the unromantic reality of duty in the South Pacific. Having left Arkansas with a hunger for "new thoughts and deeper perceptions," Forbush recognizes the irony in the clipping from a Little Rock newspaper which declares her "Our Heroine." Nevertheless, Forbush's heart and her romantic idealism are soon captured by Emile De Becque, a wealthy and courageous plantation owner who fled his native France after knifing a bully. Although Forbush loves De Becque, who proposes honorable marriage, she refuses to marry him. As Harbison rejected Nellie Forbush because of class snobbery, so Forbush rejects De Becque because of racial bigotry. De Becque, who has lived in the South Pacific for twenty-six years, has fathered eight illegitimate daughters, two of whom are half Polynesian. Although rejecting a lifetime of bigotry takes a quieter kind of courage than storming a beach, it is courage which finally enables Nellie Forbush to be a "heroine" who can accept De Becque as a "man" and his dark skinned daughters as human beings.

The most memorable character in *Tales of the South Pacific* is the old Tonkinese woman Bloody Mary, whom Michener introduces in the story "Fo' Dolla'." A source of entertainment for the bored marines, who amuse themselves by teaching her obscenities and buying her souvenirs, Bloody Mary is named for her betel stained mouth, which looks as if it has been "gashed by a rusty razor." Although Mary is one of many women from Tonkin China (Vietnam) who have indentured themselves to wealthy French planters like Emile De Becque and Jacques Benoit, she clearly subverts their exploitation of her talents. In one month, Mary earns more money selling grass skirts to Americans than she can earn in a year under the colonial system of indenture; thus, Benoit forces through laws which prohibit Mary and her cronies from selling the skirts. While officers are forced to uphold local laws, the enlisted marines see Mary as a rebel, a "symbol of ageold defiance of unjust laws."

Bloody Mary is the mother of lovely Liat, who lives on Michener's mythical Bali-ha'i, where wise Frenchmen have sequestered all their virgin daughters, no matter what race they are. Through Bloody Mary and Liat, Michener introduces a male/female relationship which is doomed because of racial bigotry. "Very fine" is the way Bloody Mary describes Marine Lieutenant Joe Cable, who is the scion of an old Philadelphia family and a Princeton graduate, and very fine is the life which Bloody Mary dreams of for her daughter. Although Cable feels that no self-respecting officer would make love to a "native" girl, he is obsessed by the delicate Tonkinese girl from the moment her mother introduces them. Yet, when Bloody Mary insists that Cable marry his young lover, he refuses; for no matter how much he loves Liat, he cannot introduce a Tonkinese wife to his Philadelphia parents. Lacking the courage that Nellie Forbush shows in a similar situation, Cable watches as Bloody Mary gives Liat to Jacques Benoit, a lascivious exploiter of young girls, and ironically, the same planter who is responsible for the laws which forbade Mary to better her economic

standard. Disgusted by his own behavior and angry at his peers who plague him about his relationship with Liat, Joe Cable proves his bravery in the battle at Kuralei and dies a "man" at last.

Another unusual figure in *Tales of the South Pacific* is Luther Billis, whom Michener describes as a "big dealer." A modern Long John Silver with his sagging belly, bare chest, numerous tattoos, long hair, and gold earring, Billis manipulates officers and enlisted men alike to get what he wants. When he wants to visit Vanicoro Island, Billis interests Lieutenant Tony Fry in the religion of that island, the worship of pigs. Vanicoro's sacred boars are staked out for seven years so that their tusks grow back into their jawbone, making a complete circle through the roots. Michener uses these boars and the agony they endure as a metaphor to explain the pain, suffering, and death experienced by the men and women serving in the South Pacific.

In the last of the tales, "A Cemetery at Hoga Point," the first-person narrator of the story visits the grave of the dead hero Lieutenant Joe Cable. Lying close to Cable's grave is the grave of Commander Hoag of the Sea Bees, who miraculously constructed a landing strip in fifteen days and died in performance of his duty. Not far from both these men is the grave of a man whose death was the result of his own negligence: He drunkenly drove his jeep off a cliff. Heroes or cowards, rich or poor, black or white, officer or enlisted men — in a cemetery, there are no classes: "There are only men."

◆ Techniques ◆

Always extremely meticulous in his

research, Michener wrote *Tales of the South Pacific* from his personal experience during World War II. A. Grove Days states that Michener thought of his South Pacific stories as a novel unified by "strong" themes, by a "changing but limited setting around the Pacific islands," and by a number of "recurring figures." The nineteen stories, which climax in the tale "The Landing on Kuralei," have three narrators: a first-person officer-narrator who tells thirteen of the stories; Lieutenant Bus Adams, who narrates two stories; and an omniscient narrator, who relates four tales.

◆ Literary Precedents ◆

Novels describing the adventures of white men in the tropics have fascinated western readers since the publication of Daniel Defoe's *Robinson Crusoe* in 1719. Herman Melville romanticizes his account of the Marquesans in *Typee* (1846). Robert Louis Stevenson's *Treasure Island* (1883) describes the adventures of the boy Jim and the pirate Long John Silver. Joseph Conrad, who explores the concept of courage in *Lord Jim* (1900), treats both racial and economic exploitation in *Heart of Darkness* (1902). Nordoff and Hall's *Mutiny on the Bounty* (1932) describes the life of sailors in the South Pacific as well as the famous eighteenth-century mutiny led by Fletcher Christian.

Novels stressing the futility of war also abound in western literature. These include Leo Tolstoy's *War and Peace* (1865-1869), which discusses Napoleon's invasion of Russia; Stephen Crane's *The Red Badge of Courage* (1895), which describes a young Union soldier's first battle experience in the American Civil War; and Erich Marie Remarque's *All Quiet on the Western Front* (1929), which explores World War I through the eyes of a German soldier.

◆ Adaptations ◆

In 1949, Rogers and Hammerstein were inspired by the tales "Our Heroine" and "Fo' Dolla'" to write one of Broadway's most successful musicals, *South Pacific*, starring Mary Martin as Nellie Forbush and Ezio Pinza as Emile De Becque. Michener himself fought to keep "You Have to Be Taught," a song about racial bigotry, in the show. A film of *South Pacific* starring Mitzi Gaynor and Rosanno Brazzi was produced in 1958.

◆ Ideas for Group Discussions ◆

Tales of the South Pacific evolved out of Michener's own wartime experiences, which may account for its tone of authenticity. Knowledge of the war in the South Pacific, especially the United States Navy's actions, would enhance discussion of the book, so it may be a good idea to have someone research the subject or have someone who was there speak to the group about what life was like in the region and era. If the book is to be the focus of a major discussion, it might prove helpful to have individual discussion group members study individual stories and present brief reports on them. They could explain historical events, symbolism, and themes, which vary from story to story. A broad discussion of the book might successfully focus on Michener's concern with telling the truth about the war in South Pacific, and whether he exaggerates his account by focusing on figures like Fry, Harbison, and Bloody Mary, who seem to be character types rather than individualized people.

1. Rarely does a literary work offer the opportunity to see the foundations of an author's style, technique, and point of view as plainly as *Tales of the South Pacific* does. The interrelated short stories of this book evolve into the complexly intertwined plots of *Hawaii* and later novels. Ask readers well versed in Michener's work to explain to other discussion group members how the structure of *Tales of the South Pacific* is echoed in Michener's later work. What themes become more fully developed later on? What concerns in this book become universal ones for Michener?

2. *Tales of the South Pacific* can be read as separate short stories or as a single work. Which approach comes closest to what Michener seems to intend? Can the book be better understood one story at a time or only when thinking about all the episodes at once?

3. "I try to anticipate history," declares Michener. How well does he anticipate history in *Tales of the South Pacific*, published in 1947? Did he predict any events or social changes? Did he manage to convey the life and times of the South Pacific well enough that later events make sense in light of what Michener says?

4. Lieutenant Tony Fry appears in nine of the stories in *Tales of the South Pacific*. Does he serve to tie any themes or events together? Is he a stock figure — the rebellious individualist common to much American fiction — who lacks individualized character traits? How

well does he compare to Yossarian of Heller's *Catch-22* (1961)?

5. How well does Michener handle racial issues in *Tales of the South Pacific*? Does he anticipate the future importance of any racial or ethnic issues?

6. Of the book's figures, which is the most fully developed, well-rounded character? Who do you get to know well enough to understand how he or she thinks?

7. What does the account of Cable tell about life in the South Pacific and the mixing or clash of cultures?

8. How do the Americans react to the exploitation of people such as Bloody Mary and Liat?

9. Is there any way to separate real-life incidents from the imaginary ones in *Tales of the South Pacific*? What is history? What is Michener's creation?

10. This may require some research, but the results could be interesting. Look back to 1947 and explain what about American readers in that era made *Tales of the South Pacific* particularly appealing to them. Why did the book retain its interest for many years? Why was it adapted to stage and to motion picture screen?

11. Does the musical adaptation of *Tales of the South Pacific* capture the essence of the book? What did the adapters choose to emphasize? Why?

Diana Wells Barrow
University of Tennessee at Chattanooga
[Ideas for Group Discussions
by Kirk H. Beetz]

TALKING GOD

Novel

1989

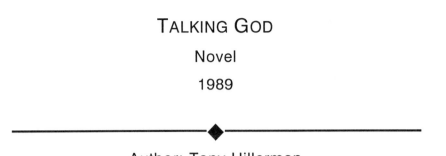

Author: Tony Hillerman

◆ Social Concerns/Themes ◆

Named for the ceremonial mask depicting one of the powerful Navajo *yeibichai* or principal gods, *Talking God* focuses in a number of ways on the conflict between the European-based white culture and traditional Native American tribal customs and metaphysics. The mystery is structured around two separate and yet oddly interrelated instances of a native people's attempts to repossess certain religious and ancestral artifacts housed in the vast collections of the venerable Smithsonian Institution. The novel underscores the clash of cultures by sending Joe Leaphorn and Jim Chee — separately — to Washington, D.C., the former in search of clues to the identity of an anonymous murder victim, the latter in response to a friend's request for help in a case involving a museum conservator who wants to become a member of a Navajo clan.

Talking God examines an increasingly significant ethical question: At what point should the quest for knowledge and truth give way to the demands of cultural traditions and taboos? Henry Highhawk uses his position as an employee of the Smithsonian to publicize

the fact that the thousands of Indian skeletons in the museum's collection are, in fact, the products of archaeological plundering of ancient burial grounds and that these skeletons are the ancestors of a living people and should be returned to the tribes for reburial. Also in question is the museum's possession of artifacts that are important to the practice of active religions.

◆ Characters ◆

Although the setting has moved from the desert country of Hillerman's other novels to the concrete and pavement of Washington, D.C., Lt. Joe Leaphorn and Officer Jim Chee are once again the somewhat uneasily-paired protagonists, both drawn to the city unofficially in pursuit of information about two seemingly unrelated incidents. Both men's personalities are exemplified by the ways in which they adapt to the new environment: Leaphorn dons the three-piece suit and dress shoes that serve as the Washington uniform; Chee continues to wear his comfortable boots.

Janet Pete, who has moved to Washington at the behest of her former law professor and current lover John Mc-Dermott, is beginning to question the rightness of the move and the validity of her feelings for McDermott. The first signs of her discontent are her telephone call to Jim Chee and delight at deal with the renegade Highhawk who is her client.

Hillerman has provided *Talking God* with his most psychologically fascinating antagonists. Henry Highhawk, clearly on the wrong side of the law in many of his actions, is a likeable man who claims Navajo roots through a grandmother born to the Bitter Water Clan. Strongly attracted to the customs and traditions of the Navajo and desirous of becoming an official member of a Navajo clan, Highhawk has appointed himself the spokesman of all Native American tribes whose ancestral and religious relics are stored in the Smithsonian warehouses. Displaying a real flair for attracting media attention, Highhawk not only focuses the publicity spotlight on himself through his digging up of the skeletons of prominent New England pioneers, but also threatens an even more spectacular "crime" for which he wants Janet Pete to act as defense attorney.

Leroy Fleck—the genuine villain of the piece and the assassin whose actions tie the elements of the plot together—is a study in psychosis. Raised by a mother who clearly favors an older son, Fleck has spent most of his life vainly attempting to earn his mother's approval, even as a teenager taking the blame and serving a prison sentence for a crime committed by his brother. The brother has long since disclaimed any connection with the family, but Fleck continues to care for his now senile mother, paying for a series of rest homes by hiring himself out as a hit man, a trade he learned in prison.

◆ Techniques ◆

Hillerman's training and experience in journalism taught him that there are stories to be found everywhere. The plot of *Talking God* grew from a piece in the *Washington Post* about a group of militant Indian activists who demanded that the Smithsonian surrender to them certain of the Native American bones in their possession.

Hillerman uses three distinct points of view — Leaphorn's, Chee's, and Leroy Fleck's — cutting from one to another with cinematic rapidity, allowing the reader to follow events and actions from the vantage of their plan and execution. This use of parallel narration is particularly effective at the finale of the novel when Hillerman finally connects all of the subplots into one denouement.

The contrapuntal structure of the novel is enhanced by Hillerman's deftly compact and accurate descriptions, which allow the reader to visualize the Smithsonian storage system, a desolate murder site by the railroad tracks, Henry Highhawk's cluttered study and office, the drabness of Chee's hotel, the spare furnishings of Fleck's apartment, and a streetside public telephone booth — all locations that contain clues to the puzzling events that form the plot.

◆ Literary Precedents ◆

Indebted to the police procedural, *Talking God* also borrows from the political thriller and the psychological crime novel. In this intricately plotted novel, Hillerman creates a tangled web involving Chilean politics, Navajo tradition, the Washington bureaucracy, and the lives of individual people. He provides detailed excursions into the warped psyche of Leroy Fleck, the once skinny runt now turned trained hit man thanks to the federal prison system. With the subplot involving a political vendetta, the plot moves into the realm of international intrigue and diplomacy.

♦ Ideas for Group Discussions ♦

Talking God offers many avenues for discussion. The most popular avenue is likely to be the issue of archaeological study of human remains, especially those belonging to existing peoples. To avoid having the discussion becoming a simplistic good-guy-bad-guy argument, a discussion group might look into actual archaeological practices. For instance, some readers might be surprised to discover that archaeologists do in fact dig up the remains of early New England settlers; the cultural conflict might not be one of insensitive archaeologists versus native peoples, but a more profound disagreement over how human remains of any sort should be treated.

1. Chee's romantic life is complicated. What does it add to the novel?

2. What does the title signify?

3. The issue of plundered Native American remains is a real one. Some remains were returned to Native American tribes. When did this happen? How was it done? Were the remains given to the appropriate tribes? How well does *Talking God*'s account compare to the real-life events? Are the issues accurately depicted?

4. How significant is the problem with museums holding sacred artifacts? Does Hillerman present the differing views on the matter fairly? Are there other issues that are more important to Native Americans?

5. Is Highhawk truly dedicated to helping Native Americans, or is he just a headline-grabber? Is he a complex character or a simple one?

6. Should we readers feel any sympathy for Fleck?

7. *Talking God* deals with other social issues than just what should be done about Native American remains held by museums. What are they? How do they fit into the plot?

8. Chee and Leaphorn have sadness in their lives. Does this humanize them? Does it affect how they do their work?

9. Who provides more suspense, Highhawk or Fleck?

E. D. Huntley
Appalachian State University
[Ideas for Group Discussions
by Kirk H. Beetz]

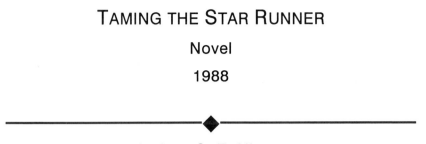

TAMING THE STAR RUNNER

Novel

1988

◆

Author: S. E. Hinton

◆ Social Concerns/Themes ◆

Many of the social concerns and themes that characterize *Taming the Star Runner* closely resemble those in other Hinton novels: adolescent loneliness and the need to belong (which find outlets in gangs); the inevitability of change and the loss of innocence as the protagonist grows up; and Oedipal conflicts, worked out both in actual and in surrogate families. Travis Harris, age fifteen, has gone to live with his uncle in Oklahoma rather than go to juvenile hall as punishment for assaulting his stepfather with a poker. Although he misses his inner-city friends and occasionally feels frustrated by his loneliness in his new school, he is a stubborn loner. He usually prefers the company of his cat, and tells himself he is grateful for his uncle Ken's seeming lack of interest in him. Gradually, however, Travis comes to appreciate the family ties that Ken represents and accepts his own need to grow up.

As with earlier Hinton books, drugs and sex remain on the periphery of the story, although Travis knows he is attractive to girls and is himself attracted to Casey, an eighteen-year-old horse trainer who works for Ken. When his friend Joe arrives unexpectedly, running away from involvement with a drug pusher and the murder of two of his friends, Travis summons the courage to get Ken's help and to send Joe back to face his punishment. Teenage drinking is treated as a fact, however; Travis sometimes longs for a drink at his uncle's, and once goes on a bender from which Ken must rescue him.

Unlike Hinton's earlier novels, *Taming the Star Runner* has distinctly autobiographical elements. Travis has written a novel and sent it off to a publisher. An editor contacts him, comes to visit, and tells him his book, after a little revision, will be published. Hinton has obviously drawn on her own experience here, having published her first novel when she was in her teens. Hinton is also a lover of horses, and her knowledge of riding is evident in her descriptions of riding classes, a horse show, and Casey's activities. The language in the novel is generally rougher than in Hinton's previous work, and is a more accurate representation of teen-age speech.

Awareness of social class, especially as adolescents experience it in school, has been a hallmark of Hinton's fiction.

In *Taming the Star Runner* Hinton contrasts Casey's social class with that of the girls she teaches riding. Travis finds these girls unbearably silly, with their giggles, their piano and ballet lessons, and their clothes-consciousness. Casey works hard to support herself, and Travis respects and admires her for that. But the clear class distinctions that characterized *The Outsiders* (1967) are subdued in this book and are more suggested than described.

Also unlike Hinton's other novels, the world of *Taming the Star Runner* is not populated solely by teenagers. Travis interacts with his uncle Ken (who at thirty-seven seems very old to Travis), with the editor of his book, and with eighteen-year-old but very independent Casey. The immediacy and sense of living completely in the present that characterizes *The Outsiders* are considerably tempered in this novel by a sense of the past and of the future, represented by these older characters and by Travis's sense of his own future as a writer.

◆ Characters ◆

The novel is told from the point of view of Travis Harris; as he tells the story, his conflicting feelings about family, friends, and himself emerge, but the reader also watches him grow into acceptance of his complex situation. Ken, Travis's uncle, is undergoing a divorce as well as financial troubles, but he gradually makes room in his life for Travis and for their relationship, as he helps Travis gain a new perspective on their family. Teresa, Ken's wife, and their young son Christopher are minor characters but their presence in the book broadens it to include other kinds of life and other points of view besides that of the teen-age male.

Casey Kincaide is skilled, tough, demanding, and determined to tame the wild stallion, Star Runner. Travis admires her grit, and eventually confesses to her that he loves her. Although she refuses him, his admiration continues and their friendship deepens. Casey is one of Hinton's best-drawn female characters, suggesting dimensions and depths that are not fully explored in this novel. Eleanor Carmichael, the editor, is also distinctly individual. The richness of these two characters shows that Hinton's skill at depicting women has grown.

Joe, Travis's friend from back home, shows what Travis might have become had he stayed there. Star Runner, the huge and powerful horse, represents the part of Travis that cannot be tamed.

◆ Techniques/Literary Precedents ◆

The most striking change in Hinton's technique is that *Taming the Star Runner* uses third person, rather than first person narration. Although the novel is firmly anchored in Travis's perceptions and actions, this shift suggests a new perspective on Hinton's teen-age narrators.

The autobiographical elements in the novel also herald a shift in Hinton's approach, offering a certain playfulness, a hint that she is more comfortable with her own identity. They are not inserted gratuitously, however, but are an essential part of Travis's character and of the plot.

Hinton's editor has said that she submitted the story outline for this novel to him nine years before she wrote the book, and that the outline changed very little. Hinton herself, however, has changed in the interim; she said in a recent interview, "I'm older and I'm a parent. My writing is changing."

The Adventures of Huckleberry Finn (1884) and *The Catcher in the Rye* (1951) are still classic literary precedents for Hinton's work, but this novel, with its third person narration and its emphasis on Travis's growth into a writer, also suggests James Joyce's *Portrait of the Artist as a Young Man* (1916).

◆ Related Titles ◆

Taming the Star Runner shares some surface details with Hinton's *Tex* (1979), such as the rural setting and the emphasis on horses. It also shares many of the same themes which mark Hinton's work and make her popular with young adult readers. However, *Taming the Star Runner*, with its larger world and its more interrelated concerns, is subtler than her earlier novels. The autobiographical elements suggest Hinton's more mature self-consciousness as a writer, and the more fully realized female figures demonstrate her growing confidence in her powers of characterization.

Lucy Rollin
Clemson University

TANGO CHARLIE AND FOXTROT ROMEO

Novel

1986

◆

Author: John Varley

◆ Social Concerns ◆

In *Tango Charlie and Foxtrot Romeo* civil servants and politicians cynically debate the fate of a child discovered living in a quarantined space station. They are driven more by fear of popular opinion than by any desire to do what is morally right. This common portrait of public servants can be found in numerous works of fiction. Of more topical interest is the disease Neuro-X, which resembles AIDS in the fear that it generates in people. One character, Doctor Blume, even suggests that "Neuro-X destroyed her immune system," a characteristic of AIDS. In the novel, Neuro-X is a virulent disease that is transmitted in mysterious ways. No safeguard seems effective. Even physicians dressed in airtight suits catch the disease and die within days.

The disease is confined to a space station and a space ship, both of which have been quarantined, and the space station left to orbit the moon. Thirty years later observers learn that a living girl who appears to be about seven years old is on board. Her presence on the station opens a vigorous debate among people on Luna (the Moon) about whether the child's life or the safety of the public is more important. Should the child be saved, even though she may be a carrier of the deadliest disease known to humanity? Should the station be destroyed and the girl killed in order to safeguard against the possibility of Neuro-X being transmitted to the general population?

These matters echo some of the debate about AIDS, particularly when there was doubt about how the disease was transmitted. Just how much risk should the general public be expected to accept? When does discrimination against those with the disease exceed justification and become cruel prejudice?

◆ Themes ◆

Tango Charlie and Foxtrot Romeo is a moving story of the struggle to save a stranded child. The mere fact that a child is in danger moves some characters to want to save her. When the "child" turns out actually to be over thirty years old, the decision to save her or not becomes more complicated, as if an adult's life were less valuable than that of a child. Still, the girl looks very young, and in many ways she is mentally a child. Her confusion about what is happening endears her to Corporal Anna-Louise Bach, and Megan Galloway, who decides to help her regardless of her real age. This theme of mortality is emphasized by the initial reaction to the discovery of the girl's real age: Could she hold the secret of immortality, freedom from death? Then the harsh reality of the girl's situation dashes the observers' hopes, and debate focuses on whether the girl can be saved. The theme of mortality is enriched by the question of whether anyone would be eager to save the child if she were a mature woman. Varley offers no answers, and the question remains unresolved and troubling.

◆ Characters ◆

Corporal Anna-Louise Bach is the point-of-view character for most of *Tango Charlie and Foxtrot Romeo*. She is too acid-tongued for her own good and has been placed in a dead-end job because she failed to show respect to incompetent superiors. She supervises the crew of the New Dresden Police Department's monitoring room. When the presence of a living person on the space station Tango Charlie is suspected, this crew activates the station's few functioning cameras and observes the girl. Bach is a sad, lonely figure. She is attracted to vacuous, muscular men and drifts from one unfulfilling love affair to another. She empathizes with the isolation of the girl and acts out of morality and emotion, rather than regard for public opinion.

The little girl calls herself Charlie. Why she has remained a child for more than thirty years is a mystery, although the disease Neuro-X might be a factor. She is Tango Charlie's only human survivor, kept company by the descendants of Shetland Sheepdogs that survived the Neuro-X plague, as well as by Tik-Tok, the space station's computer. Her time is spent maintaining the space station and raising Shetland Sheepdogs to exacting dog-show competition standards. Tik-Tok makes sure that Charlie follows a busy daily schedule of chores, sees to it that she eats nutritious meals, and encourages her to bathe and groom herself. She is lonely but does not know it. When first seen on camera, she presents a startling picture; with makeup smeared on her face like war paint, she seems surrounded by a sea of flowing dogs wherever she goes. Her courage in the face of isolation and her childlike innocence help make *Tango Charlie and Foxtrot Romeo* one of Varley's most passionate and moving works.

The news reporter Megan Galloway is an unusual character. Once paralyzed from the neck down, she became famous as a mechanized being who moved with the aid of a golden exoskeleton. She became famous because of her ability to exploit the glamorous and erotic possibilities her extraordinarily beautiful exoskeleton offered. Medical science eventually advanced enough to restore most of her natural mobility, although she walks with a cane. Now a glamorous reporter, she wears ornaments that resemble parts of her discarded exoskeleton. When she learns through informants of Charlie's plight, she takes an immediate interest in the child's welfare. Beneath her cynical shell, there is a responsible and caring person who tempers her desire for a good story with compassion. Like Charlie, she is something of a freak; she empathizes strongly with the little girl's loneliness and creates a plan to save the child. She is a bizarre, other-worldly figure, yet with a core of humanity that makes her a believable, sympathetic character.

◆ Techniques ◆

Tango Charlie and Foxtrot Romeo resembles a tragic drama in which the plot leads inevitably to catastrophe (usually death) for the main character. Although Bach does not die, her efforts end in disaster. Like a tragedy, Varley's novel is plotted in movements in which certain elements dominate. *Tango Charlie and Foxtrot Romeo* is first a mystery story in which Bach and others try to learn the truth about who is on the space station; then a moral story in which characters are ethically tested by the plight of the girl; and finally a suspense story in which the protagonists struggle to save Charlie from certain death. Each movement reveals different aspects of the characters. For instance, in the mystery movement, Bach demonstrates her quick mind; in the moral movement, she reveals a depth of emotions that have not been expressed through her shallow love life; and in the suspense movement, she shows the courage of her convictions.

By shifting scenes back and forth from Bach to Charlie, Varley gives the reader a rounded view of the little girl. At first, she greets the mystery of her discovery with irritation — she is a busy person with no time to waste talking with outsiders. As she warms to Bach, Charlie feels the loneliness of her isolation and expresses despair at losing her loved ones. First she cries for a dead puppy; later she faces up to the pain caused by her mother's death. Her courage in these situations seems natural. Varley includes character touches, such as her literal-mindedness when asked questions, that make her believable. When she finally puts her trust in Bach, she reaches a level of maturity that exceeds that of the adults who are trying to help her. She confronts the universal human problem of mortality and overcomes her fear of death.

A tragedy touches on matters of universal human importance, and as the plot unfolds it humanizes and explores these themes. *Tango Charlie and Foxtrot Romeo* does this, making it a remarkable literary work. If there is a false note, it is Bach's seeming failure to grow. Her grief yields to the passage of time and yet another brawny man. On the other hand, this woman, who was resigned to her fate as the oldest recruit in the police force, has discovered in herself the capacity to do what is right in spite of powerful opposition and the courage to risk her future for someone who cannot defend herself.

◆ Literary Precedents ◆

Perhaps the most famous science fiction book to deal with an attempt to control a virulent disease is *The Andromeda Strain* by Michael Crichton (1969). Although that novel features people sealed in a research laboratory for somewhat the same reasons Charlie is sealed in her space station, its themes are very different. The motion picture *Silent Running* (1971) features a man isolated on a space station that contains some of the last examples of earth's natural world. He kills others and eventually kills himself to protect the wildlife on the station, leaving one lonely little robot to care for the living things. Like *Tango Charlie and Foxtrot Romeo*, the movie evokes strong emotions, although it lacks the thoughtfulness of Varley's novella. The conflict between incompetent civil servants and compassionate ones is an old idea, featured in many works of fiction. *Tango Charlie and Foxtrot Romeo* is exceptional for its presentation of the problems of mortality through a character who is at once a little girl and a woman, as well as for its well-paced plot and genuine emotional content.

◆ Related Titles ◆

The imaginary future of *Tango Charlie and Foxtrot Romeo* appears in at least one other of Varley's works, the short story collection, *Blue Champagne* (1986). There, the character Megan Galloway also appears. She is paralyzed from the neck down but moves with the aid of an elaborate golden exoskeleton. In *Tango Charlie and Foxtrot Romeo*, recent medical advances have given her back much of her natural mobility, although she uses a cane to help her walk.

◆ Ideas for Group Discussions ◆

Tango Charlie and Foxtrot Romeo touches on at least two matters that are worthy of further discussion. One is the theme of human mortality and the relative values our culture places on the lives of children as opposed to grownups. Why should Charlie's age matter at all? The other matter is that of a deadly disease and how society reacts to it. The parallels between Neuro-X and AIDS are plain enough, somewhat less plain are the parallels with other diseases such as tuberculosis, polio, ebola, legionnaires' disease, and other frightful and virulent diseases. Which is more important, the welfare of the possibly diseased individual human being or the welfare of society at large? Bach and Galloway make their choice: They favor the individual person. Others, more in the background of the narrative, favor the security of society. Did Bach and Galloway make the moral choice? Were they wrong in letting their emotions overrule their minds? How should we, the novella's readers, make our choices regarding deadly diseases and the diseased? These are truly tough issues to decide.

1. Imagine that you are the person who must decide what to do about the space station and Charlie. What do you do? No cheating — you must stick to the level of technology Varley portrays in *Tango Charlie and Foxtrot Romeo*.

2. Does Bach do what is right?

3. Varley leaves some questions unanswered, such as why Charlie has not aged. How does this affect your appreciation of the story?

4. Why is Bach, a seemingly intelligent woman, attracted to empty-headed men?

5. Why would it make a difference about whether she should live or die if Charlie is thirty-seven years old instead of seven? Are the lives of thirty-seven-year-olds of no value?

6. How would a happy ending change *Tango Charlie and Foxtrot Romeo*? Say that Charlie lives: Would *Tango Charlie and Foxtrot Romeo* be better or worse? What else would have to be changed to suit the new ending?

7. Most great literary works touch on

universals in the human condition; that is, they explore issues that nearly all people have in common. To be great, a work of literature must offer profound insights into such issues. What universals of the human condition does *Tango Charlie and Foxtrot Romeo* explore? How well does it explore them?

8. In what ways does *Tango Charlie and Foxtrot Romeo* echo the debate about AIDS? Does Varley offer any suggestions for how to treat people with the disease?

9. How accurate is Varley's depiction of how public officials behave when faced with a moral crisis?

10. Analyze the characterization of Charlie. Varley has set himself the task of making her both a believable seven-year-old child and a believable thirty-seven-year-old. What techniques does he use to accomplish this? How well does he succeed?

11. Is *Tango Charlie and Foxtrot Romeo* a tragedy?

Kirk H. Beetz

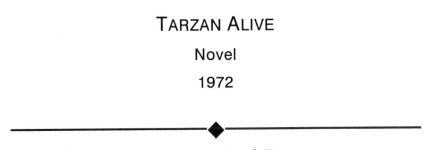

TARZAN ALIVE

Novel

1972

◆

Author: Philip José Farmer

◆ Characters ◆

In order to write the "true" story of Tarzan, Farmer had to condense Edgar Rice Burroughs's twenty-four Tarzan novels into one volume of manageable length. This need to condense and eliminate may explain why Tarzan is the only well-developed character in *Tarzan Alive*, and why not even Jane among the secondary characters seems either complex or interesting. However, by focusing on just one character, Farmer did allow himself the opportunity to create a multifaceted personality for his hero. To Farmer, Tarzan represents an ideal. His ancestors were exposed to radiation which improved their genetic structure, making him a superior mutation of normal human beings. In training, he is an animal, cunning in survival lore and free of the decadent inhibitions of civilization. Once Tarzan leaves the real jungle of Africa, he is equally masterful in the jungle of international law and finance, managing to take control of his family fortune without revealing his true identity. Moreover, like the gods, he is immortal, having taken an elixir given to him by a witch doctor.

The narrator also reminds us, more often than necessary, that Tarzan is an archetypal Trickster, that mythic figure who resents the strictures and vexations of civilization and who enjoys a good joke at civilization's expense. As a Trickster, Tarzan is also a potential savior, and as his life progresses, providential appearances become his main activity. When he is not saving others, usually arriving at the last moment and back from being thought dead, he often behaves like a jealous god, as when he slaughters the cannibals who murdered his foster-mother. Also like a jealous god, and like Farmer, Tarzan is hard on "false" religions, defrocking or killing witch-doctors and exposing them to their enslaved multitudes. In the aftermaths, Tarzan is usually given the chance to become a high priest or even a god, but like Odysseus returning to his wife, Penelope, Tarzan always returns to Jane.

Along with Tarzan's symbolism as the incarnation of Natural Man, his undying love for Jane may be his most important quality for Farmer, as it probably was for Burroughs. Burroughs's ambivalent fascination with eroticism was always a strong element of his appeal. Sexual situations abound in his writing; nothing is ever explicit, but white women are frequently carried off by villains and are always being saved by Tarzan, who is, of course, above such behavior, although his superhuman strength implies an equally superhuman sexuality. To Burroughs, it appears to have been obvious that Natural Man came equipped with Victorian morals, almost as if they were built into his genes. In contrast, Farmer has always acted out in his writing a romantic rebellion against such morality, so it is intriguing that his own version of Tarzan (at least, in *Tarzan Alive*), also keeps his sexuality decently in check until appropriate moments. Perhaps Burroughs's description of Tarzan's relationship with Jane represents an ideal so potent to Farmer that he does not wish to alter it: Tarzan discovers that he is not the beast of the apes or the god of the cannibals, but the man of Jane Porter. More than anything else, his loving relationship with Jane signals irrefutable proof of his essential humanity.

◆ Social Concerns ◆

In grade five, Farmer first began reading Edgar Rice Burroughs's Tarzan novels, a discovery which so impressed him that his school friends were soon calling him "Tarzan" because of his fondness for climbing trees and swinging from branch to branch. As well, Farmer also has a large collection of pulp fiction dating back to the 1920s, including original editions of Burroughs's novels. Clearly, then, *Tarzan Alive* was written as the result of a lifelong fascination with a figure Farmer describes as "Nature's last creation of a Golden Age man," and not as a direct response to specific social conditions.

Nevertheless, the fact that Farmer found a receptive audience for the nine Tarzan-related titles he published from 1969-1976 is no coincidence. The late 1960s and early 1970s were a period of social history during which many people, particularly young people, were intensely distrustful of the "establishment," as represented by the government, the military, and industry. If people felt neither powerful nor free, so the argument went, the culprit could only be "civilization." Tarzan, in contrast, is popular culture's most famous embodiment of the idea that people in their natural state are powerful and free creatures. Burroughs's novels imply that if we would simply return to our natural element, we would regain the power and freedom that are our natural birthright. Tarzan, therefore, represents a universal fantasy of the Natural Man: savage at times, but innocent of civilization's decadence and corruption. He is Burroughs's dream of ourselves, a dream that exerted a powerful appeal in society at just the same time that Farmer was writing his own series of Tarzan novels.

◆ Themes ◆

Burroughs (1875-1950) wrote serviceable prose at best, but what he lacked in style, he more than compensated for in sheer invention. He possessed a powerful and vivid imagination, and with it, he created the fantasy of a primitive being concealed inside ourselves: an absolutely good hero dominating a world of savagery and beauty. Moreover, Burroughs also had a coherent vision of life. Like most mythic literature, his Tarzan books are about what a thing man is, how like an ape and how like an angel.

Burroughs's world view, as revealed in the Tarzan novels, coincides closely enough with Farmer's to account for two of the three major themes of *Tarzan Alive*. First, like Burroughs's Tarzan, Farmer's Tarzan must discover that he is more than an ape. He has a survival ethic unrestrained by sentimentality or a feeling of community and a capacity for violence uninhabited by conventional morality. He also has a libido to match his great strength, a sexuality free of the repression and hypocrisy of civilization. Burroughs "tames" this potentially uncontrollable Natural Man by creating Jane Porter to be his mate and save him from complete primitivism. Furthermore, in case we miss the point, Burroughs repeats this process in Tarzan's son, Korak, who, like his father, is redeemed by the love of a woman, a small girl he adopts, protects, and learns to love as she grows to womanhood. This double demonstration of, in effect, the transcendental power of the feminine principle must have appealed to Farmer, whose writing often elevates female characters to the status of divinities. His own version of Jane is not only "strikingly beautiful," but "tough and self-controlled." Inevitably, after Tarzan first meets her, he acts out the best qualities of his character by giving her his hunting knife before they spend their first night together in the jungle. Farmer's narrator compares this gesture to "that of the medieval knight who placed a sword between himself and his chaste lady love."

Tarzan is no mere knight, however, for acting like a god is for him, as for Odysseus, Hercules, or Beowulf, his other temptation — other, that is, than reverting to a beast. Both Burroughs's and Farmer's stories of Tarzan correspond exactly to the structure of all classical hero myths. Like Romulus and Remus, Tarzan is raised by animals, and like King Arthur, he is unpromising as a child. Like the sword bequeathed to Theseus by Aegeus, the books from which Tarzan learns to read are the magical gift left by a departed parent. Later, like Hercules and Perseus, Tarzan slays the beast and rescues the fair maiden, before discovering that like Oedipus and Moses, he is the lost heir to a "throne." In Burroughs's case, these parallels with classical myth indicate not sophistication, but rather, the instinctive level at which myths communicate and from which Burroughs's fantasies originated. In Farmer's case, however, these parallels were consciously understood, developed in elaborate detail, and enriched and transformed. Farmer's creative reworking of the Tarzan myth becomes the basis for an assertion of faith in the heroic, an expression of disappointment in the modern world, and a challenge to the reader to maintain some sort of heroic ideal.

Farmer created his own version of Tarzan from a wide variety of fictional, historical, and anthropological sources, and in the process, blurred the boundaries between fantasy and reality. In the biography, the narrator assumes that Burroughs based Tarzan on a real person and fictionalized Tarzan's life in order to protect the "real" Tarzan's privacy. The narrator, then, claims to be writing Tarzan's "true" biography by supplying crucial facts which Burroughs deliberately withheld, altered, or distorted. The final results demonstrate a mammoth task of research and also a parody of academic scholarship. Farmer reconceptualizes and renarrates the Tarzan novels, luring us into a world of fiction only to confront us with the world of history, thus asking us to rethink the categories by which we would normally distinguish "fantasy" from "reality."

◆ Techniques ◆

After the spectacular success of the first Tarzan novel in 1914, Burroughs wrote and published steadily for the next thirty years. He could produce a novel a month, working five or six hours a day, dictating to a secretary. He seldom revised his first draft, did not mind interruptions, and could work anywhere, even among his children. In view of his writing methods and the fact that he never actually went to Africa, the Tarzan novels are unavoidably full of gross improbabilities and striking inconsistencies, including talking apes, lost civilizations, and a race of men eighteen inches tall.

Farmer's most significant strategy in reworking Burroughs's fantastic material into a "true" biography was the use of a naive persona as his researcher/biographer/narrator. This narrator believes that Burroughs knowingly created inconsistencies and impossibilities because he was under the orders from "Lord Greystoke" (Tarzan) to conceal the true identify of his subject; that is, Burroughs was only pretending to be writing fiction and deliberately violated credibility. Farmer's narrator often goes to extraordinary lengths to excuse Burroughs's absurdities before providing his own "factual" version of events. For example, he admits that Tarzan's journey to "Pellucidar" at the center of the Earth could not have happened in reality, but argues that Burroughs accurately recorded Tarzan's dream vision of visiting such a place. Noting that Burroughs has Tarzan's son being born in 1912 and fight-

ing in World War I in 1918, the narrator claims that Tarzan actually had two sons and that Burroughs concealed the existence of one in order to protect Tarzan's identity. The narrator also supplements his discoveries and revisions with all the trappings of serious academic scholarship. *Tarzan Alive* has an elaborate genealogy of Tarzan's ancestors, "Acknowledgments," a "Forword," no less than five "addendums" totaling eighty-six pages, and a detailed bibliography and index. All this scholarly paraphernalia creates a strong sense of imaginative play for its own sake while simultaneously raising serious questions about the relation between fiction and reality. In fact, Farmer succeeded so well in creating the illusion of a "real" biography that some public libraries stock *Tarzan Alive* in their "B," or "Biography," section.

◆ Literary Precedents ◆

The precedents of *Tarzan Alive* fall into two categories: previous fictional biographies, autobiographies, and memoirs, and postmodernist experiments in metafiction. First, Farmer has often acknowledged the influence of W. S. Baring-Gould's *Sherlock Holmes of Baker Street* (1962) on his own versions of fictional biography. As well, in his introduction to "An Exclusive Interview with Lord Greystoke," he refers to a series of "splendid examples" of this subgenre, including Cyril Northcote Parkinson's *The Life and Times of Horatio Hornblower* (1970) and George MacDonald Fraser's better known Flashman novels, supposedly the memoirs of a character in Thomas Hughes's *Tom Brown's School Days* (1856). These and other fictional biographies have in common an attempt to remain faithful to the letter and spirit of the original while "correcting" discrepancies, filling in gaps, and generating new theories. Farmer describes this process as "a lot of fun and hard work," and he clearly enjoys playing the kind of very sophisticated literary games that a fictional biography requires.

Fictional biographies can be considered part of a larger, widespread movement in the arts called "postmodernism," which (Trickster-like) enjoys blurring conventional boundaries and confounding audience expectations. In literature, this impulse often results in "metafiction," or fiction that goes beyond the usual concerns of fiction to consider the nature of fiction itself. For postmodernist writers like John Fowles, John Barth, Robert Coover, and Kurt Vonnegut, Jr., the real subject of fiction is fiction: the double process by which a story or novel is written by an author and then "decoded" by a reader. *Tarzan Alive* is very much in this tradition. Farmer's narrator often takes the reader into his confidence, explaining the difficulties he had in discovering the "facts" and the criteria he used to evaluate them. By using a famous figure from a popular culture as his point of departure, Farmer avoids the dry, abstract quality of some metafiction and succeeds in maintaining the reader's interest in a well-known hero.

◆ Related Titles ◆

Farmer has published two other works dealing with the same version of Tarzan who appears in *Tarzan Alive*: "An Exclusive Interview with Lord Greystoke" and "Extracts from the Memoirs of 'Lord Greystoke.'" The "interview," first published in the April 1972 issue of *Esquire* and repub-

lished in *The Book of Philip José Farmer* (1973), brilliantly demonstrates Farmer's ability to make a fictional character seem real. Farmer prefaces the interview with an explanation of how he tracked down his subject to a hotel on the coast of West Africa and was granted a fifteen-minute conversation. During the interview, Tarzan, who is now eighty-five years old but looks thirty-five because of his immortality treatment, speaks with quiet dignity of his life and main concerns. He explains some of the inconsistencies in Burroughs's novels, reveals something of his philosophy of life, and remarks that like Mark Twain, he has only one prejudice: "That is against the human race." As he speaks, the reader can almost share the interviewer's awe at being in the company of this legendary figure. Greystoke's memoirs complement the interview and appear in *Mother Was a Lovely Beast* (1974), an anthology Farmer edited about "feral humans," or humans raised by animals. Tarzan seems a bit pedantic and dull in these memoirs, which devote a great deal of space to his rather dry account of the language and customs of the humanoid creatures (not apes) who raised him in the jungle. In retrospect, Tarzan was wise originally to allow the story of his life to be written by Burroughs.

Tarzan Alive is also directly related to the eight other Tarzan titles Farmer published: *A Feast Unknown* (1969), *Lord Tyger* (1970), *Lord of the Trees* and *The Mad Goblin* (1970), *Hadon of Ancient Opar* (1974), *Mother Was a Lovely Beast* (1974), and *Flight to Opar* (1976). Collectively, these works present at least three very distinct versions of Tarzan, ranging from *A Feast Unknown's* "phallic superman," who can achieve an orgasm only when killing an enemy, to

Tarzan Alive's familiar gentleman of the jungle, who would rather die than offend Jane Porter. *Lord Tyger*, with its more socialized version of the phallic hero, is often singled out as one of Farmer's best novels.

Finally, *Tarzan Alive* is also part of what Farmer calls "the Wold Newton Family," a series of works based on the premise that in the eighteenth century, a meteorite landed near Wold Newton in Yorkshire, irradiating a number of pregnant women, who subsequently gave birth to supermen. From this event, all of the world's superheroes are descended, including Doc Savage, Sherlock Holmes, the Shadow, and, of course, Tarzan. Farmer has written several further adventures of these and other related characters. The most significant are his fictional biography *Doc Savage: His Apocalyptic Life* (1973) and his two novels *The Other Log of Phileas Fogg* (1973) and *The Adventures of the Peerless Peer* (1974). Probably not even Farmer could provide a complete explanation of the incredibly intricate and ingenious network of connections existing between *Tarzan Alive* and the rest of his many stories and novels.

♦ Ideas for Group Discussions ♦

Tarzan Alive will be appreciated most by those readers already familiar with Burroughs's Tarzan novels, so reading at least one or two of them is advisable. Discussions can then consider what use Farmer has made of his primary source material in creating his own version of such a well-known figure. Readers should also focus on the ways that Tarzan serves as a vehicle for social criticism, particularly of environmental issues, and how as an Outsider, he is well suited to provide an objective commentary on the follies and cruelties of civilization. Finally, given Jane's importance in Tarzan's life and to the biography's themes, readers might want to question Farmer's apparent decision to leave her undeveloped as a character. How convincing is the supposedly larger-than-life love affair between Tarzan and Jane?

1. Popular culture's superheroes, such as Tarzan and Doc Savage, have generally been ignored by literary critics and scholars. What does *Tarzan Alive* illustrate or imply about how popular culture can be used by "serious" writers?

2. Compare the imaginative scope of *Tarzan Alive* to that of Burroughs's Tarzan novels. How does Farmer create a much larger mythic figure than Burroughs was able to imagine?

3. The task of a mythmaker is to consolidate and rationalize a number of loosely connected stories into a coherent pattern. With this in mind, consider the use Farmer has made of his many sources, as itemized in his bibliography. For example, what is the function or effect of all the references to natural history and anthropology?

4. How is Farmer's explanation of the true identity of the creatures who raised Tarzan central to *Tarzan Alive's* credibility? More generally, what function do language and linguistics have in the biography?

5. Consider the personality of Farmer's narrator. What can we reasonably conclude about him from what information he provides and how he provides it? In general, what is his attitude toward his source material?

6. Also prepare a personality profile of Tarzan. As the narrator presents him, what are the main reasons for his appeal? Is he effective as a "real" person, or does he remain on the level of a symbol of natural forces?

7. Paying particular attention to Chapter Twenty-Five, "The Rest Is Silence," consider *Tarzan Alive* as an elegy for nature and for natural and primitive values.

8. Is the biography's presentation of technology and the other tools of civilization entirely negative? For example, what enables the young Tarzan to transcend the primitive condition of the humanoids who raise him? In general, what is Farmer's attitude towards the relationship between technology and nature?

Peter Klovan
Grant MacEwen Community College

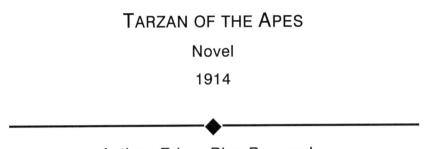

TARZAN OF THE APES

Novel

1914

◆

Author: Edgar Rice Burroughs

◆ Characters ◆

Nearly all of Burroughs's characters are recognizable stereotypes, from the unfortunately comic Negro servants and brutal villains to the supremely beautiful women, good-hearted but weak-willed men, and noble heroes, natives, and even beasts. Tarzan, though, goes beyond stereotype to archetype of the heroic masculine figure. Jane Porter sees a face of "extraordinary beauty, . . . a perfect type of the strongly masculine, unmarred by dissipation, or brutal or degrading passions." The entire Chapter 20, titled "Heredity," stresses Tarzan's perfection. He kisses the locket where her hand had rested in "a stately and gallant little compliment performed with the grace and dignity of utter unconsciousness of self. It was the hallmark of his aristocratic birth, the natural outcropping of many generations of fine breeding, an hereditary instinct of graciousness which a lifetime of uncouth and savage training and environment could not eradicate." Throughout the book and the series, descriptions stress Tarzan's godlike qualities and character, and his actions — primarily of rescue and protection — reinforce

the divine nature of his being. Burroughs normally tends to ignore psychological possibilities, but Tarzan does occasionally reflect on his situation as a man of two worlds, not completely at home in either. He rarely laughs, choosing to smile instead, and his perverse practical jokes as an ape-man gradually give way to a grim humor about the "civilized" world. While given to occasional fits of rage, when his world and family are threatened, or subject to plot-necessitated bouts of accidental amnesia, Tarzan nevertheless rarely descends to the merely human.

Jane Porter, too, typifies the Burroughs heroine with her extraordinary beauty described in the vague, sentimental, and suggestive vocabulary of the pulp magazine: age 19, with waist-length blonde hair and a "lithe, young form," her hands often press "tight against her rising and falling bosom." Yet as fit mate for the jungle god she loves, Jane has enough strength and composure to endure the abductions, near-deaths, and "fate[s] a thousand times worse than death" which she faces throughout the series. In the first novel she shoots a lioness, remains conscious when carried off by a great ape, and retains her wits alone in the jungle at the mercy of a wild white man. She rarely faints or shows the weakness of the typical persecuted heroine, remaining instead clear-headed and committed to the same practice exhibited by the heroes: action rather than passivity. Other characters follow the stereotypical patterns of evil villains, noble friends, weak good men, wise (or absent-minded) elders, broadly comic or satirical portraits of servants, businessmen, natives, royalty, and whatever else the plot may require. Many minor characters literally recur in various novels, but they seem nearly interchangeable anyway.

♦ Social Concerns ♦

Society and societies lie at the heart of almost all Burroughs's books; indeed, one of his chief strengths derives from his ability to imagine in considerable detail social worlds removed from but parallel to the real world. Whether these societies derive from history, as in the African lost cities founded by ancient Romans or by stranded medieval Crusaders, or from his fertile imagination, as in the wild cities and creatures of Barsoom (Mars), they become convincing through enormous detail of language, social behavior, and tradition. Throughout the Tarzan series, and probably one of the bases of its appeal, runs the constant contrast between the "civilized" world of men and the "uncivilized" world of the jungle. *Tarzan of the Apes* begins with the worst of society: victims of violent mutineers provoked by a brutal ship's captain, the young Lord and Lady Greystoke become marooned on the coast of West Africa where they survive for eighteen months, after which

the she-ape Kala takes their year-old son to replace her own dead baby. So the boy grows up in the society of apes, with its rudimentary language (including names for animals and people — "Tar-zan" means "white skin"), strong sense of family, and clear political structure based on the kingship of the strongest member.

In an extended fable of evolution, Tarzan learns to overcome the physical strength of the apes through, first, his superior speed and reasoning power, then through his discovery of weapons — ropes, his father's knife, and, finally, spears, bows, and arrows taken from a native village. Teaching himself to read and write from books found in his father's cabin, Tarzan yearns for the life of man, not apes. When the beautiful, young Jane Porter, her absent-minded father, and William Clayton, Tarzan's cousin and the Greystoke heir, become similarly abandoned by mutineers at the site of the cabin, the ape-man sees his own kind, again introduced by brutality and murder, and falls in love. Rescuing Jane from Terkoz, his foster father, Tarzan carries her into the jungle, but reveals his innate human breeding in comparing his intentions with those of Terkoz: "[It] was the order of the jungle for the male to take his mate by force; but could Tarzan be guided by the laws of the beasts? Was not Tarzan a Man? But how did men do? He was puzzled; for he did not know." Chivalry is an ideal human characteristic, presumably bred into the best of the species. Later, Tarzan learns the ways of the world from a Frenchman, d'Arnot, whom he has saved; d'Arnot takes Tarzan to civilization and, through fingerprints, proves Tarzan's ancestry. At the novel's end, however, having rescued Jane from a forest fire in Wisconsin, Tarzan refuses to press his claim to the title, since she had become engaged to Clayton, and reaffirms his jungle birth in a remarkable Victorian renunciation; remarkable, indeed, in a man only three months out of the jungle. Throughout the novel, Burroughs stresses the contrast of the worlds, as when Tarzan "wiped his greasy fingers upon his naked thighs and took up the trail of Kulonga . . . ; while in far-off London another Lord Greystoke . . . sent back his chops to the club's chef because they were underdone."

Despite Tarzan's evolutionary progress, however, the jungle generally contrasts favorably with the more effete and far more ruthless, greedy, and corrupt modern civilization. Tarzan's reflection on the murderous mutineers burying a treasure chest — "Men were indeed more foolish and more cruel than the beasts of the jungle! How fortunate was he who lived in the peace and security of the great forest!" — remains a fairly consistent ideal throughout the entire series. In *The Return of Tarzan* (1915), d'Arnot introduces "Monsieur Jean C. Tarzan" to Paris society where the ape-man "smoked too many cigarettes and drank too much absinth . . . because he took civilization as he found it, and did the things that he found his civilized brothers doing." After escaping assassination and fighting a duel — "Your Paris is more dangerous than my savage jungles," he tells d'Arnot — Tarzan returns to the jungle, saves Jane, again shipwrecked near the old cabin, and eventually marries her, settling on a Kenyan estate. The jungle world is far safer, for both Tarzan and Burroughs, who had difficulty depicting the real world.

In addition to suggesting the general superiority of the jungle world, Burroughs also deals with religious and political issues. He wrote his son, "I am a very religious man, but I do not subscribe to any of the narrow, childish superstitions of any creed." Tarzan, like his author, conceives of God as Creator and force of Nature, and in many books he, like John Carter on Barsoom, exposes and destroys the hypocritical and self-serving religions which control their followers by superstition. In the initial book, when Tarzan actually eats offerings set out to appease a jungle god, "the awe-struck savages . . . were filled with consternation and awe, for it was one thing to put food out to propitiate a god or a devil, but quite another thing to have the spirit really come into the village and eat it." In the delightful series of stories dealing with Tarzan's youth, *The Jungle Tales of Tarzan* (1919) the ape-boy learns of religion among other things, reasoning that "the flowers and trees were good and beautiful. God had made them. He made the other creatures, too, that each might have food upon which to live"; but even the untutored savage discovers the essential religious question when he asks, "Who made Histah the snake?"

Politically, Burroughs's views reflected the conservative ideas of his time. He distrusted communism, and his early villains were often Russians, even though his books later became extremely popular in the Soviet Union. His attitude appeared most dearly in an unsuccessful story, "Under the Red Flag," which depicted America under a Communist government; believing that the publishers were afraid to print the story, Burroughs reworked the tale into a futuristic novel, *The Moon Maid* (1926), one of his most interesting nonseries books. The two world wars during which he wrote also brought out jingoistic ideas in which German soldiers become disgustingly sadistic and inhuman beasts (*Tarzan the Untamed*, 1920), horribly and mercilessly destroyed by Tarzan who believes they have killed Jane; in Tarzan and *The Foreign Legion* (1947), the World War II Japanese soldiers also reflect the propagandistic views of wartime America. In the 1930s, his controversial anti-German sentiments hurt his foreign sales, and Burroughs attempted to tone down his consistent use of foreign villains. As he grew older, too, Burroughs came to emphasize the brutality and waste of war for war's sake, deploring this instance of "civilized" man's inhumanity to his fellows: In *Tarzan and the Ant Men* (1924), he shows how the tiny Minunians go to war because of patriotic ideas, not the "chicanery of politics" or the "thinly veiled ambition of some potential tyrant," or the "captains of the outer world who send unwilling men to battle for they know not what, deceived by lying propaganda, enraged by false tales of the barbarity of the foe." In *Tarzan of the Apes*, Burroughs comments how the ape-man "killed for food most often, but, being a man, he sometimes killed for pleasure, a thing which no other animal does; for it has remained for man alone among all creatures to kill senselessly and wantonly for the mere pleasure of inflicting suffering and death."

◆ Themes ◆

While Burroughs reiterates the ideas of the "noble savage" — the possibility of natural goodness, strength, and superiority inherent in mankind even though brought up in violent Nature — and the evolutionary progress of civilization, including its less praiseworthy

manifestations, he also comments upon "the rise of civilization, during which mankind gained much in its never-ending search for luxury; but not without the sacrifice of many desirable characteristics, as well as the greater part of its liberty." The Burroughs books are escapist literature in many senses, for not only do they provide a means of escape from the harsh, real world (of a Depression and two world wars — the pulp magazines, after all, were a mass entertainment medium equivalent to modern television), but they also celebrate, like American writers such as James Fenimore Cooper, Mark Twain, and Ernest Hemingway, an escape from the world of conventional and superficial restriction into a world of freedom and action, where an heroic figure can triumph over the perils of man and nature. Tarzan finds in the jungle a world of danger where he depends solely on his own physical and mental powers. In a jungle outpost on the outskirts of civilization with d'Arnot, Tarzan accepts a wager to kill a lion with knife and rope, and returns gratefully to the jungle: "it was with a feeling of exultant freedom that he swung once more through the forest branches. This was life! ah, how he loved it! Civilization held nothing like this in its narrow and circumscribed sphere, hemmed in by restrictions and conventionalities. Even clothes were a hinderance and a nuisance. At last he was free. He had not realized what a prisoner he had been."

The conception of Tarzan thus functions as both theme and character in the novels. In exercising his abilities, Tarzan serves as a model of the ideal man. His supreme confidence in his physical and mental abilities, assures his remaining triumphant, invincible, lord of the jungle, untamed, terrible,

---

and magnificent, as the titles of the later books suggest. His grace, speed, strength, and skill match his cunning, reasoning, resourcefulness, and adaptability to produce a super-man able to function effectively in any situation, indeed any world (as a later trip to the Earth's Core suggests). To a query about his reasons for writing, Burroughs replied:

Of course the primary motive of a story like *Tarzan of the Apes* is to entertain, yet in writing this and other stories I have been considerably influenced by the hope that they might carry a beneficial suggestion of the value of physical perfection and morality. Because Tarzan led a clean, active, outdoor life he was able to accomplish mental as well as physical feats that are so beyond the average man that he cannot believe in their possibility, and if that idea takes root in the mind of but a single young man, to the end that he endeavors through similar means to rise above his environment, then Tarzan of the Apes will not have lived in vain.

Other equally simple themes recur throughout Burroughs's works. Foremost among these is the power of love, as depicted in the perfect physical and mental union of Tarzan and Jane Porter. His love for her tames his savagery (and releases his romantic chivalry and self-sacrifice) — while her love for him releases some of the natural instincts repressed by society; after Tarzan kills Terkoz, "it was a primeval woman who sprang forward with outstretched arms toward the primeval man who had fought for her and won her." And later, after being rescued from the forest fire, Jane reflects that her attraction "seemed to her only attributable to a temporary mental reversion to type on her part — to the psychological appeal of the primeval man to the primeval woman in her nature." The love theme also motivates the constant search and rescue sequences that serve for plot in most of the books. In addition, Burroughs comments on the despoiling of nature by man, the barbarity of hunting, and the sexist superiority of the male. (In *Tarzan and the Ant Men* he teaches the effete young men of a matriarchal tribe how to use weapons to regain their power.) On a more personal level, Burroughs inveighs against lawyers and the ineptitude of the motion picture industry: in *Tarzan and the Lion Man* (1934), Lord Greystoke himself auditions for the role as Tarzan but is rejected as "not the type."

◆ Techniques ◆

As the characters recur, so do the plots. Burroughs wrote quickly, with a firm knowledge of what his readers wanted. In 1913, his peak year, he wrote over 400,000 words; he usually spent from one to three months on a novel, rarely rewriting except to accede to an editor's request. According to Lupoff, "His speed record for a full novel was set on *Carson of Venus* (1939), produced in twenty-six days," while the good *Warlord of Mars* (1919) took thirty days. Writing at such speed meant the use of episodic plots in which coincidences abound and logic usually disappears. Mutinies, shipwrecks, menacing beasts, sojourns in lost cities (usually paired and at war), kidnappings, rescues, chases, and wars provide all the incidents needed to keep Tarzan (and John Carter, Carson

Napier, and David Innes) extremely busy. Burroughs also became adept at the cliffhanger ending — as evidenced by the conclusion of the first Tarzan novel — which called for a sequel. Since the novels were originally serialized in magazines and newspapers, most seem to break naturally into novelette-length episodes even when originally conceived of as unified wholes. Yet this haste also produces a certain breathlessness in Burroughs's writing that carries the reader uncritically along. Even his strongest critics admit his ability to tell a fast-paced story. Burroughs often understates even big action scenes, focusing instead on telling details that stimulate the reader's imagination into filling in missing descriptions; some fights take mere paragraphs, and the next threatening situation builds immediately. New thrills and strange new creatures engage the reader before he can even contemplate the coincidences.

A final recurring technique involves Burroughs's use of a frame story to establish the reality of the tale. Usually this situation concerns a character, often identified as "Burroughs," receiving a manuscript or message carrying the story. So *Tarzan of the Apes* begins, "I had this story from one who had no business to tell it to me, or to any other," and the narrator pieces together the account from various sources, including the nameless storyteller and the actual diary of John Clayton. The frame story of *The Eternal Lover* (1925), a nonseries adventure set in both modern and prehistoric times, takes place at the Greystoke estate, "my having chanced to be a guest of Tarzan's, making it possible for me to give you a story that otherwise might never have been told." These frames provide the most reality to tales weak in plotting, dialogue, and character development.

◆ Literary Precedents ◆

Tracing specific literary sources may not be particularly valuable, for Burroughs was not a literary man — according to Porges, Burroughs thought that Owen Wister's *The Virginian* (1902) was among the greatest American novels. While some literary works, such as *Gulliver's Travels* (Jonathan Swift, 1726) as a source for the Ant Men, seem fairly obvious, and Lupoff's book finds some interesting parallels in long-forgotten science-fiction works, it seems more likely that his ideas came from common myths and from popular fiction itself. In commenting on the origins of Tarzan, Burroughs mentioned having read Kipling's Mowgli stories, but most often he referred to ancient legends such as Romulus and Remus for examples of children raised by animals (and becoming mythical). The popular fiction of Burroughs's early life, however, included such models as the dime novels for action entertainment; the tales of Jules Verne, including *Journey to the Center of the Earth* (1864) and *From the Earth to the Moon* (1865), and, later, of H. G. Wells and Sir Arthur Conan Doyle, including *The First Men in the Moon* (1901) and *The Lost World* (1912), for imaginative science fiction; and the romances of H. Rider Haggard for African lost empires. Burroughs wrote a British newspaper in 1931: "To Mr. Kipling and Mr. Haggard I owe a debt of gratitude for having stimulated my youthful imagination." For notions about the subconscious primitive nature of man, Burroughs would also have been familiar with the work of naturalists such as Frank Norris and Jack London — he considered writing a biography of the latter, the author of *The Sea Wolf* (1904) and *Before Adam* (1906). Burroughs, however, reverses the naturalist creed: Where they saw men reverting to the bestial, Burroughs showed the best elements of humanity — honor, chivalry, justice, heroism, love — inherent in the savage, along with the best, not worst, qualities of the primitive.

◆ Related Titles ◆

Direct sequels to *Tarzan of the Apes* include *The Return of Tarzan* and *The Beasts of Tarzan* (1916). Twenty-one other adult Tarzan books appeared, the most interesting of which include *Jungle Tales of Tarzan* (stories); *Tarzan and the Ant Men*; and *Tarzan and The Foreign Legion*. Probably the last Tarzan book is *Tarzan: The Lost Adventure* (1996) compiled from notes that Burroughs left by Joe R. Lansdale. This Tarzan is in the dark spirit of the Burroughs sequels. Here Tarzan is aided by Jad-bal-ja the lion and Nkima the chimp in defending a party of American archaeologists in search of the Lost City of Ur. He combats brigands, the savage inhabitants or Ur, and a mantis-like monster from the Earth's core — a reminder that Burroughs' Tarzan novels were as much science fiction as jungle adventure.

◆ Adaptations ◆

Tarzan's extraordinary popularity derives as much from his appearances in media other than Burroughs's books. Nearly fifty authorized Tarzan movies have appeared, with some twenty actors portraying the ape-man, beginning with Elmo Lincoln in the 1918 silent classic, one of the first films to gross over a million dollars. The twelve movies from 1932 to 1948 starring Olympic swimmer Johnny Weissmuller and, originally, Maureen O'Sullivan as Jane, became the most popular. Burroughs disliked the films, primarily because of the portrayal of the ape-man as semi-articulate and uncultured, but the Weissmuller image has continued to dominate the public perception. Burroughs mocked the films in *Tarzan and the Lion Man,* and, later, in *Tarzan and "The Foreign Legion"*: when Col. John Clayton reveals his famous identity to the R.A.F. crew with whom he has been serving, the incredulous gunner from Chicago comments, "Is dat Johnny Weis[s]muller?" Burroughs was more fortunate in his book illustrators which included the American artist N. C. Wyeth, J. Allen St. John, and, finally, his own son, John Coleman Burroughs; more recently, Frank Frazetta gained much of his fame by illustrating the early paperback reissues.

Under the direction of Edgar Rice Burroughs, Inc., Tarzan came to radio in 1931, with the author's daughter and son-in-law playing the leading roles in what was the first prerecorded, syndicated radio series; over 350 fifteen-minute shows were sold to stations in every state, in Europe and in South America. In 1932, a syndicated comic strip began appearing in newspapers, a strip which continues to this day; the original artist was Hal Foster, whose powerful drawings and imaginative placing of text (which continued to develop in "Prince Valiant") had immediate appeal. Later, the intensely physical drawings of Burne Hogarth increased the popularity, and these early strips have become collectors' items. In 1936, Tarzan appeared in comic books, receiving his own comic in 1947, a series which also still continues. Burroughs also licensed his registered trademark to manufacturers of clothing, watches, masks, candy, toys, records and numerous other articles; Gabe Essoe even reports that in 1943 over three million loaves of Tarzan bread were sold. Tarzan came to television in 1966 in the person of Ron Ely for a three-year run of popular and well-produced hour-long episodes which attracted generally good reviews; some episodes became feature films shown abroad. It has been estimated that a Tarzan movie is being shown somewhere in the world at any given moment. In all these efforts, Burroughs or Burroughs, Inc., had some hand, and it is little wonder that the literary character has become so engrained in the public consciousness.

In 1984 director Hugh Hudson released one of the few Tarzan movies that remained faithful to the original character created by Burroughs. *Greystoke: The Legend of Tarzan, Lord of the Apes* (1984) opens with the shipwreck and Tarzan's ultimate adoption by the animals. After just enough footage in the jungle to establish Tarzan's credibility as an apeman, the film takes a dramatic leap from West Africa back to Scotland, where Tarzan, the seventh Earl of Greystoke, claims his title. In one of the best films to reexamine the man vs. nature theme, this story places the purity of Tarzan, who has been uncorrupted by other people, against the hypocrisy of Victorian society and the ultimate dark end of Tarzan's attempt to be more man than ape.

Nelson C. Smith
University of Victoria

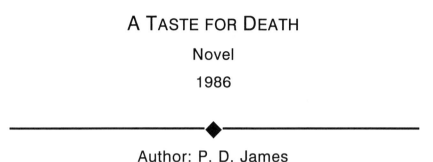

A TASTE FOR DEATH

Novel

1986

◆

Author: P. D. James

◆ Social Concerns/Themes ◆

In *A Taste for Death*, James portrays the conflict of a fatherless child with an alcoholic and promiscuous mother. Young Darren, who accompanies the elderly Miss Wharton to St. Matthew's Church, seems to have some clue to a murder. Because of this, the policeman Massingham insists upon seeing his home, which is a wretched hovel in a poor section of the city. The mother is oblivious to the problems of her son, who collects stolen objects on which he manages to survive. Once saved by welfare, he is sickly, and was spared by the murderer. The problem of juvenile crime is delicately probed by James, who has had personal experience in dealing with young people and their social difficulties.

James's preoccupation with the issue of abortion is reflected in the spurious medical practices of Dr. Lampart, who has gained his popularity by violating the law and performing abortions when the parents are dissatisfied with the sex of the child. In addition, Theresa Nolan commits suicide after an abortion because of guilt. Her grandparents, traditional Irish Catholics, have mixed emotions: her grandfather condemns her as a sinner; her grandmother takes a more merciful and humanitarian attitude. Although there is no resolution of the problem, the issue is important to this novel.

The women's issue, of relative unimportance in James's previous novels, acquires more prominence here, especially in the attitudes of Adam Dalgliesh's new assistant, Kate Miskin. She has chosen her present career to demonstrate her equality with males, and she occasionally resents Dalgliesh's air of masculine superiority. Barbara Berowne, on the other hand, described by her mother-in-law as "third rate," shows the traditional pride of the nobility, as well as the traditional view of woman-as-mother.

The depiction of espionage movements and a possible connection with the IRA, reflect contemporary political concerns. But a Marxist revolutionary "cell," established by Ivor Garrod, is actually a vehicle for personal vengeance. Inspector Duxbury characterizes the Workers Revolutionary Campaign as "little more than a front," because "Garrod prefers to run his own show." A young woman, Diana Travers, who allegedly dies in an accidental drowning, was a sort of double agent for Garrod and for the Special Branch, and was used to spy on Berowne's political career as Minister of the Crown.

Religion always plays a major role in James's novels. Here, the murder takes place in a church sometime after the victim has had a "religious experience." This religious experience changes his entire life, and he is now prepared to sell the ancestral home, abandon his mistress, and resign his post in the government. James contrasts this unexplained conversion with the progressive de-Christianization evident in the members of the Church of England. Many of the major characters confess disbelief in traditional church doctrines and are mystified by Berowne's sudden change of heart. James never fully explains Berowne's religious experience, leaving much of it shrouded in mystery.

◆ Characters ◆

James is especially noted for the character delineation in her novels. Her detective character, Commander Adam Dalgliesh, who appears in other James novels, has been described by one critic as "a catalyst who allows people to show themselves." Here he is more intimately involved since the victim came to him before the murder to show him a poison pen letter. In fact, throughout the investigation, Dalgliesh occasionally betrays his personal connection to the victim. He remains the cool, dispassionate detective, however, who questions suspects calmly and objectively, with a maximum of consideration. He is also the clever investigator, who manages to see connections that escape others. He is respected by his associates, feared by suspects, and

acknowledged by all as an expert in his field.

A Taste for Death presents Dalgliesh with a new associate, the young Kate Miskin. Having no family except for an aged grandmother who raised her, she is vaguely in search of her identity and is anxious to prove herself in a masculine world. When urged by her teachers to seek a profession more "socially significant," she replies that she could not "think of anything more basic than helping to make sure that people can walk safely in their own city." She has a mild infatuation with Dalgliesh, who feels the same toward her, but he shows extreme discretion in this regard. In the end she proves her valor and intelligence during an unexpected encounter with the murderer, thus gaining the respect of the reader, if not the police force.

The Berowne family is from the petty aristocracy, a departure from James's usual portrayal of the middle class. Although they cling to their ancestral home, their wealth is not proportionate to their social claims. Lady Ursula, an eighty-two-year-old matron, who was attractive to men in her day, maintains a household with servants and schedules, and upholds the integrity of the family until the very end. Lady Barbara, Sir Paul's second wife and the widow of his brother, is, according to Lady Ursula, "third rate." Her beauty is her main asset, and she has used it to attract two husbands, as well as her current lover, Stephen Lampart.

Sir Paul Berowne, the victim, is a baronet, a Minister of the Crown, and a government minister with higher aspirations. He is a man who, according to his estranged daughter Sarah, "wanted to be good." The reader learns about him progressively as the police investigation reveals his past. One day, after a religious experience, he resigns his office, plans to sell his home, and requests to spend a night in St. Matthew's Church.

The murder investigation reveals that he had a mistress who was totally devoted to him, that he had enemies among his household, and that he was strangely linked to two other deaths, that of Theresa Nolan, one of his mother's nurses, and of Diana Travers, a member of the housekeeping staff. He is also linked to a derelict, Harry Mack, who is found dead beside him. In life, he aspired to truth and sincerity, but his death leaves many mysteries.

James introduces a range of suspects. Father Barnes, the rector of St. Matthew's, is a poorly-clad, unimpressive priest, and an improbable spiritual advisor for Sir Paul. Miss Wharton, who brings flowers each day to the church and acts as caretaker, befriends the waif Darren. After accepting the kindness of the murderer, she almost brings destruction to little Darren, the abandoned child who must survive by his own resources.

Ivor Garrod, a self-styled revolutionary who seeks his own advantage; Stephen Lampart, an obstetrician who attains wealth and reputation in defiance of the law and who gains the beautiful Barbara Berowne as his mistress; and Massingham, a devoted but rather chauvinistic policeman, are all woven convincingly into the plot, united by a link to the murderer or the victim.

◆ Literary Precedents ◆

James's great talent is in her portrayal of characters. According to one critic: "The people in her books are anything but paper figures; all but the most peripheral are three-dimensional, their backgrounds finely drawn, and their actions the inevitable result of the interaction between their personalities and the circumstances that confront them." The same critic notes that James has continued to improve her characterization with each succeeding novel. Although the criticism was written before this novel, it was indeed a good prediction, for the characters in *A Taste for Death* are even more complex and believable than those in previous novels. Adam Dalgliesh evolves with each novel, developing the maturity that comes with age and experience.

The mystery aficionado seeks a plausible plot that is not obvious until the very end and yet provides adequate clues to clarify events when the mystery is revealed. James moves quickly from one character or situation to another, holding the reader's interest, often giving false clues, but never false information.

One also finds a sense of place in James's novels. She describes her locales well, and the homes fit perfectly into the London landscape. Her interest in architecture leads her to describe buildings in detail: St. Matthew's with "the green copper cupola of the soaring campanile of Arthur Blomfield's extraordinary Romanesque basilica"; the Berowne home, 62 Campden Hill Square, "an urban oasis of greenery and Georgian elegance . . . one of the rare examples of Sir John Soane's domestic architecture . . . its neo-classical façade in Portland stone and brick dominated the terrace and the whole square, inalienably a part of them, yet looking almost arrogantly unique."

James's natural descriptions are also arresting. For example, in Holland Park "the beds had been richly patterned with the summer display of geraniums, fuschias, heliotropes and begonias. But now the time had come for the autumn stripping. Half the beds were already bare — expanses of soft loam littered with broken stems, petals like blobs of blood and a scatter of drying leaves."

James writes in the tradition of Agatha Christie, Dorothy Sayers, Ngaio Marsh, and Margery Allingham. Siebenheller remarks that although these authors are all female, English, and mystery writers, James departs from that tradition. "Her concern is with reality, not make-believe. The worlds she creates are peopled with varied and interesting characters whose actions spring from believable motivations and whose reactions are true to their complex personalities. And her victims, as she has often remarked, are truly dead."

James claims Jane Austen as her favorite author. Her novels reflect the order, sanity, and gentility of Austen's world. Critics have compared her to Dickens and Balzac in her ability to create characters. In *A Taste for Death*, young Darren has overtones of Dickens's David Copperfield and Victor Hugo's Gavroche, and James's use of popular language is accurate and true to life. Although she is normally more at home with the proper language of the English middle class, James shows great insight into other levels of society.

◆ Related Titles ◆

A Taste for Death, James's tenth novel, is her longest and most ambitious. Her large and varied cast of characters ranges in social class from poor waif to minister of the Crown. Characters also display a greater psychological scope, ranging from religious ecstasy to revolutionary zeal. In its range of issues, the novel seems less of an English period piece and more of a contemporary novel.

The character of Adam Dalgliesh has also matured. Dalgliesh is a rounded character who has grown older and wiser, as well as more compassionate and understanding, with each new novel.

A Taste for Death seems a much more modern novel than its predecessors. James's themes are contemporary and portray the disintegration of society through broken marriages, extramarital affairs (and sexual infidelity. The characters obviously belong to the end of the twentieth century); those in previous novels often harkened back to the nineteenth century. James seems more attuned to current issues, more sensitive to feminism, and more overt in presenting related questions.

◆ Adaptations ◆

A Taste for Death was presented on the television series "Mystery," which has featured many of James's works. The interpretation was faithful to the novel, although it did not follow the same chronology. The novel begins with the murder, and the television performance, done in five parts, showed some events which were later uncovered during the investigation before presenting the murder. It is done convincingly with excellent actors.

Sister Irma M. Kashuba, S.S.J.
Chestnut Hill College

THE TELL-TALE HEART

Short Story

1843

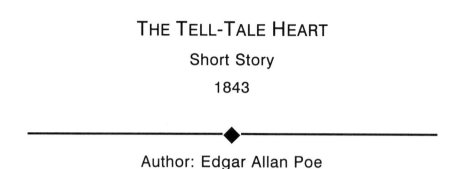

Author: Edgar Allan Poe

◆ Social Concerns ◆

Poe is unconcerned with the broad social issues of his time. His protagonists are, by and large, not social figures. Instead, they seem to live cut off from society, detached from the large world around them and either content to, or doomed to, live alone. It may be that the short story form itself, which Poe is most credited with creating in America, is a form that is less suited to dealing with social issues than it is with solitary people. The novel, which is able to place characters within a realistic external world, is more open to the depiction of social issues than the short story, which usually focuses on one or two characters confronting psychological and metaphysical issues.

◆ Themes/Characters ◆

Although there are two characters involved in the story — an old man and the younger man who lives with him — it is really about a single character. An examination of the nature of the narrator's obsession shows how Poe sets up this story about a split psyche.

The narrator insists that he loves the old man, has no personal animosity toward him, does not want his money, and has not been injured by him. Instead, he says he wishes to kill the old man because of his eye! Although there is no way to understand this obsession, the reader must determine the method and meaning of the madness. For Poe, there is no such thing as meaningless madness in fiction.

To understand what the old man's eye means to the narrator, it is necessary to examine the relevance of other themes and ideas. Besides the theme of the "eye," there are two primary motifs: the idea of time and the identification of the narrator with the old man. The narrator says at various points in the story that he knows what the old man is feeling as he lies alone in bed, for he himself has felt the same things. He says the moan the old man makes does not come from pain or grief, but from mortal terror that arises from the bottom of the soul overcharged with awe. "Many a night, just at midnight, when all the world slept, it has welled up from my own bosom, deepening with its dreadful echo, the terror that distracted me."

The narrator's own terror and awe is

related to his obsession with time. He associates the central image of the beating of the heart with the beating of a clock; he says the old man listens, just as he has done, to the death watches (a kind of beetle that makes a ticking sound) in the wall: He emphasizes how time slows down and almost stops as he sticks his head into the old man's room. To comprehend the meaning of time for the narrator, we must consider the significance of the title and ask: What tale does the heart tell? Although at the end of the story, the beating heart beneath the floor gives the murderer away, more generally, every heart tells the tale of passing time — each beat bringing one closer to inevitable death.

The narrator's strong identification with the old man and his obsession with the eye, suggests that the narrator really wishes to destroy the "I," that is, himself. The only way to defeat time is to destroy that which time would inevitability destroy, that is, the self. But to save the self by destroying the self is a paradox that the narrator cannot overcome. Indeed, by destroying the old man's eye, the narrator indirectly destroys himself in the end by exposing himself as the murderer.

◆ Techniques ◆

"The Tell-Tale Heart" is one of a number of Poe stories that focus on an obsessed protagonist/narrator. Indeed, what holds the story together and holds the attention of the reader is the single-minded voice of the madman who, even as he denies his madness, tells a story that confirms it. Poe's use of a first-person narrator obsessively recounting a past event is an important element in his contribution to the short story form as a highly unified aesthetic entity.

Poe's theory that every element in a short prose story should contribute to its overall effect is exemplified by the fact that the protagonist/narrator is obsessively concerned with his irrational desire to kill the old man because of the old man's eye and by his rational method of proceeding. Poe's stories are often characterized by a psychological mania held in check by the rational control of the narrative structure of the story itself. The narrator insists that his logical plot to kill the old man and the calm way he tells the story are evidence of his sanity. This reflects Poe's primary narrative method.

As is usually the case with first-person narratives, there are multiple settings to the story. The action of the recounted tale takes place in the house the narrator shares with the old man. At the same time, the narrator is telling the story from either a prison or an insane asylum where he has been incarcerated. But even more importantly, the setting is actually inside the obsessed mind of the narrator himself, for the crucial climactic event of the story — his hearing the beating of the dead man's heart — take place solely within his own tortured imagination.

◆ Related Titles ◆

"The Tell-Tale Heart" is one of a group of Poe stories that deal with obsession and madness. The central and most explicit of these stories is "The Imp of the Perverse" (1845), a combination of story and essay in which a Poe narrator discusses and illustrates how humans often persist in some act or behavior for the very fact that they should not. Although the story notes such examples as procrastination in action and digression in speech, the central example is murder and a compulsion to confess.

Even more closely related to "The Tell-Tale Heart" is the story "The Black Cat" (1843), in which Poe once again uses the notion of the "Imp of the Perverse," some primitive force in the human mind that drives one to commit an act for the very reason that one should not. Once again, the story focuses on a protagonist who murders someone and then gives himself away by a final act of bravado, much like the narrator in "The Tell-Tale Heart."

Other Poe stories that deal with an obsession or an unmotivated compulsion to murder are "The Premature Burial" (1844), and "The Cask of Amontillado" (1846). Stories which focus on a central character who seems obsessed and thus whose sanity is in question are "The Fall of the House of Usher" (1839), and "Berenice" (1835).

♦ Adaptations ♦

"The Tell-Tale Heart" has been the subject of more than one film treatment, but the best version is a short animated film narrated by James Mason. The surrealistic animated images reflect the distorted psychological perspective of the narrator and visually reflect the principle elements of his obsession.

The Tell-tale Heart, a 1961 motion picture version of the story, was directed by Ernest Morris. Its cast includes Laurence Payne, Adrienne Corri, and Dermot Walsh. In it, a shy man becomes a murderer when he sees a ladyfriend bedding down with another man.

♦ Ideas for Group Discussions ♦

"The Tell-Tale Heart," like many of Poe's stories, is deceptively simple at first reading. One might easily dismiss it as a story about a crazy murderer who kills without motivation. However, this would underestimate both Poe's idea of artistic control and his concern with the deepest urges of the human heart. To read "The Tell-Tale Heart" meaningfully, one must take Poe's fictional theory seriously and attempt to understand the relevance of all the details of the story. This transforms the temporal narrative flow of the story into a meaningful pattern which makes sense of what at first seems to make no sense.

Reading "The Tell-Tale Heart" is like trying to solve a mystery story; in this case, the mystery is the motivation of the killer. The key to motivation in a Poe story is his use of a central idea or effect to hold the story together. As a result, everything coheres around this effect and radiates from it. The core of the story is like an obsession that can be identified by the principle of repetition, since those obsessed return again and again to the core of their obsession. Thus, the reader must be alert to repetitions in the story, references to single-minded motifs or themes. These repeated details are the "clues" to the mystery; repetition is the principle by which the reader makes a distinction between relevant and irrelevant details. "The Tell-Tale Heart" is a classic example of Poe's method.

1. The narrator insists from the very beginning of the story that he is not insane. What characteristics does he say prove his sanity? What characteristics suggest his madness instead?

2. Look carefully at the narrator's discussion of his motivation for the crime. Why does he assure the reader that he loves the old man and has no reasonable cause to kill him?

3. Notice how cautiously the narrator sets up the murder of the old man. How does he do this? Why does he take so long before killing him?

4. Notice all those places in the story when the narrator identifies with the old man. Discuss the nature of this identification.

5. Discuss all the references to time in the story — watches, clocks, time passing. Why is the narrator so concerned with time?

6. Notice the narrator's insistence that what is mistaken for madness is actually an overacuteness of the senses. What sense is particularly acute? What relevance does this have in the story?

7. When the police call to investigate, why does the narrator invite them in and ask them to stay for a while? What does this reveal about his personality?

8. If this is not a supernatural story which actually presents the beating of a dead man's heart, then what makes the narrator finally confess?

9. Although this is a story of madness, for Poe there is no such thing as "meaningless madness." What is the nature of madness in the story?

10. Poe insisted that every detail in a short story should relate to its central effect and thus contribute to a unified story. What unifies this story? What central effect holds it together? How can you tell the difference between those details that are meaningful and those that are not?

11. Poe is often concerned with the theme of time and mortality, that is, how human beings are trapped in time and thus doomed to death. Explain how this story reflects this common Poe theme.

12. Look at other Poe stories which focus on an obsessed, seemingly mad, narrator, such as "The Black Cat," "The Imp of the Perverse," and "The Cask of Amontillado." What characteristics do the narrators in these stories share?

Charles E. May
California State University
Long Beach

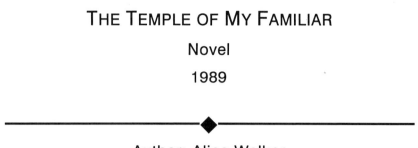

THE TEMPLE OF MY FAMILIAR

Novel

1989

◆

Author: Alice Walker

◆ Characters ◆

The Temple of My Familiar contains more characters than all of Walker's other novels combined, including several that reappear from *The Color Purple* (1982). Drawn from various continents, the number and diversity of these characters are appropriate to the theme of the connectedness of each and all. The concept of the unity of all people is further reinforced by having the central characters, who live continents apart physically and mentally, cross paths and develop intimate relationships during the course of the novel.

Lissie and Zede are the two characters who most clearly carry the novel's message of the need for a new vision. Zede, like Lissie, has "dream memories" of her ancestors who trace their lineage from Latin America back to Africa. In her many incarnations, Lissie has been both animal and human, male and female, white and black. Although she has more often been exploited than the exploiter, she has been and done all. Both characters (especially Lissie), function primarily as symbols rather than realistic characters.

The other female characters, Fanny and Carlotta, struggle to achieve the self-realization Lissie and Zede have already won. They chafe within the narrow roles defined by the dominate culture. Fanny is unhappy with her subordinate role in both her marriage and a racist society. She has a hatred of oppressors that she fears she cannot control. To develop her sense of selfhood she travels to Africa to observe and learn from female relatives. Carlotta, a much different type of woman, faces essentially the same problem. Abandoned by her husband, she becomes the submissive woman for Fanny's husband that Fanny refused to be. She acts and dresses the part but ultimately, like Fanny, remains unsatisfied. Her search for identity also takes her through new age approaches such as massage and yoga. However, she only discovers her identity through community with other womanists, in particular, through her relationship with Fanny.

If female characters in Walker's novel have to learn to reject the marginalized roles assigned them, Walker's male characters have to learn to accept the side of themselves that they have marginalized — the feminine side. Two of the three male characters have a developed feminine side. Hal, Lissie's husband, is so sensitive to the birth of his wife's first child that he gives up sex to avoid causing such pain, yet he loves delivering his wife's babies (who are fathered by other men). He is effective as a symbol, but as a character he borders on the absurd. Arveyda, the other sensitive black male character, is a new age music star, but with a domestic side. He bakes whole-wheat bread and after reading some womanist tracts his wife brings home, he recognizes their author, Shug, as his spiritual mother. Suwelo is the male character most intent on learning to develop his feminine side. Through Lissie's tutelage, he learns to give up his love of pornography, a fetish that symbolizes his desire to continue the oppression of women, and is brought to see women as equals.

By the novel's conclusion, Walker's main characters have all reached the same philosophical viewpoint: nothing is to be excluded from the circle of life except that which oppresses. In *The Color Purple*, Celie says that if God listened to black women, life would sure be different. *The Temple of My Familiar* illustrates the efforts of black womanists to transform the world by reviewing the past and countering divisive forces in the present.

◆ Social Concerns ◆

In *The Temple of My Familiar*, Walker tries something almost destined to fail. She challenges the West's Eurocentric vision of the world — its myths of human origins, its concepts of history, its ideas on political relationships, its attitudes toward the environment, its views on male/female relationships. The male-dominated white culture has written the script and cast the players for thousands of years. In *The Temple of My Familiar* Walker recasts the roles and rewrites the script. Formerly marginalized people (principally African American females) take center stage — a much broader one than just Europe and North America — and play the heroic roles. Walker undoubtedly chose this approach because she knows, as does every chronicler of a people, that a people's concept of themselves and their prospects for the future are influenced by the accepted stories of their past. Those whose pages of history are cast in a dim light or worse, no light at all, must often struggle with an imposed, unacceptable identity or none at all. So, by rescripting history, Walker hopes to better the prospects of people marginalized by the hegemony of the white male.

A central social concern of the novel is the importance of a new vision of human interaction that emphasizes inclusion rather than exclusion. An old saying goes: "There are two kinds of people in the world — the kind who divide the world into two kinds of people, and the kind who don't." Walker — who has been accused of seeing the world in terms of black and white, female and male, right and wrong — celebrates in *The Temple of My Familiar* the connectedness of all things. Certainly racism and sexism are concerns in the novel, but Walker has a larger concern here which has not been central to her fiction previously. Walker is still concerned with race and sexism; she still views the world from the perspective of a black womanist. But with her focus on cosmic consciousness, the label "black womanist" seems too narrow to define her new approach. Although some critics have expanded the label to "new age black womanist,"

Walker has supplied her own description: "My full title that I've given myself at this juncture is pagan agnostic ecstatic."

Since Walker has always expressed a strong concern for the rights of the excluded and exploited, it is not surprising that she would extend that concern to animal rights and the protection of the environment. The "familiar" of the title, in fact, refers to animals, principally the lion, which have long suffered in their relationship with humanity. According to one of Walker's characters, Lissie, familiars were once treated by women as companions and equals, but that relationship threatened male egos and they were driven away. In other stories in the book, Walker describes with equal indignation the wanton destruction of South American rain forests, African complicity with Western powers who dump radioactive wastes in Africa, and the destruction of the ozone layer. In the face of these assaults on the defenseless, Walker contends that "it is fatal to see yourself as separate." For her, healthy change will come only when society learns to see itself from a holistic perspective and with the understanding that all are one.

♦ Themes ♦

A central theme in the novel is the challenge marginalized people face everywhere in creating an identity. Fanny, for example, faces two unacceptable roles — either as a victim of racism and sexism or as a possible perpetrator of retaliatory violence. She, like many characters in the novel, seeks a new role. The source of new ideas does not seem to be from traditional books. Witness Suwelo, the college history teacher, and Carlotta and Fanny, college literature teachers who are spiritually lost. The sources seem to come from other places, principally women's lives — specifically from women with past lives in the case of Lissie and Zede, or from dreams which hold archetypal memories as Franny's dreams do. These sources are better guides to achieving a viable identity. Walker puts the importance of these sources of knowledge this way: "a people's dreams, imaginings, rituals, legends . . . are known to contain the accumulated collective reality of the people themselves." In *The Temple of My Familiar* the wisdom that comes from these founts directs the characters to seek their identities in the connectedness of all things rather than in opposition to anything.

In Walker's novels, a new identity cannot be achieved without support. There are no lone heroes. Those who struggle up from oppression, those who are lost and find themselves, succeed within a community of support. The first place to look for support is the family. Fanny travels back to Africa to consult her father. She seeks out her mother for advice and makes alliances with her sister. She also tries reading books by little-known women writers, joins consciousness-raising groups, and enters therapy. Carlotta reconciles with her mother, and in an act that demonstrates that she has stopped competing with women for the attentions of men, she befriends Fanny. It is Fanny who, through her massage sessions, puts Carlotta in touch with her body, which she became alienated from in her drive to attract men. Suwelo, who lost his parents in a car accident, finds his support from surrogate parents, Lissie and Hal, who help him undergo values realignment. Arveyda, who lost his mother early in life, falls in love with his wife's mother, who renews his passion. He also discovers a new "spiritual mother," as he calls her, in Shug. The novel ends with the four central characters living communally.

It is no surprise that in a novel with a central theme about the necessity of recreating the world, that the importance of artistic vision would also be a theme. Artists, after all, create worlds. All the major characters in the novel practice some creative art on the way to building a new vision of themselves and their relationships with others. Hal and Lissie, both painters, paint portraits of each other, an act which symbolizes their re-creation of each other in their relationship. Arveyda sings his wife, Carlotta, "into understanding her mother." Carlotta, a costume designer, like her mother, takes up painting and eventually becomes a musician, a bell chimist, in order to play with her husband. Fanny takes up playwriting after her father, and with her sister writes a play of her father's life. With her husband, Suwelo, who has taken up carpentry, Fanny designs their house, a symbol of their finally reconstructed relationship. No less important is the fact that all the characters are storytellers — an art which Walker sees as the central art in re-creating the world.

In all of Walker's novels the protagonists undergo spiritual transformation from depression and ignorance to hope and understanding. Grange Copeland transforms from self-centered to caring; Meridian Hill, from sickness to physical and spiritual health; Celie, from poor and degraded to financially independent and respected; Tashi, from victim to martyr. The theme of spiritual transformation is central to *The Temple of My Familiar* as well. Each of the characters search for wholeness.

They are split by a world in conflict, by a world that is divided into sides — by race, by sex, by religion, by political system, and so on. The novel suggests that by the will to find identity, by community, and by artistic vision people can transform into whole human beings.

◆ Techniques ◆

Walker's principal technique in *The Temple of My Familiar* is to revise the Western representation of reality, which depicts itself as separate from and superior to other cultures, by telling stories that stress connection and equality. In her own words, Walker has said: "What I'm doing is literally trying to reconnect us to our ancestors. All of us. I'm really trying to do that because I see that ancient past as the future, that the connection that was original is a connection; if we can affirm it in the present, it will make a different future." Fanny unearths stories of black contributions to American history that have been neglected or suppressed. Lissie presents reinterpretations of ancient myths. Zede recounts horrors and heroism that would have been left in the jungle and out of recorded history. This deconstructive technique might well have been acquired from the feminist movement or from modern critical theory; however, Walker was most probably influenced by the Black Aesthetic of the 1960s. As critic Elliot Butler-Evan explains the goals of that movement: "The major thrust of Black Aesthetic narratives as oppositional or alternative texts was the production of alternative representations of black life, positing significant self-reconstruction and definition, and the deconstruction of the ideological assumptions underpinning Western constructions of reality."

As critic and novelist J. M. Coetzee points out about Walker's rewriting of history, however: ". . . history is not just storytelling. There are certain brute realities that cannot be willfully ignored. Africa has a past that neither the white male historian nor Ms. Walker can simply invent."

Walker employs the same deconstructive technique not only on broad cultural topics but also on the characters' personal relationships. In *The Temple of My Familiar* the traditional institution of marriage is a failure. Exclusive pairs fail because one of the partners is always privileged. To achieve sexual egalitarianism, paired relationships must open into triangular ones. Triangles are, after all, a woman's sign of peace throughout the novel. Hal and Lissie's relationship is troubled until it opens to include Rafe. Fanny and Suwelo's relationship is exploitative until Arveyda enters in. Arveyda and Carlotta's relationship is marred by jealousy until she is to accept her mother as having been Arveyda's lover. Paired relationships are broken and eventually characters are healed by the love triangle, which in traditional Western literature invariably spelled disaster. In Walker's novels, however, the destructive triangle is transformed into a symbol of cooperation and equality.

◆ Literary Precedents ◆

The Temple of My Familiar is a unique novel, with few literary precedents. Much like Lissie's dream familiar, it is not recognizably bird, fish, or reptile. Nevertheless, Walker would claim to owe a debt to Zora Neale Hurston to whom she has often referred as her literary foremother. Hurston's novel *Their Eyes Were Watching God* (1937) is also concerned with the search for identity in an oppressive and exploitative world.

While both novels are concerned with the same struggle, however, the solutions are different. Hurston's character achieves her identity by adhering to her individual artistic vision, while Walker's characters achieve whole, healthy identities through participation in a community of people with a holistic vision of life.

The Temple of My Familiar has perhaps been most influenced by Virginia Woolf's *Orlando* (1928). Walker quotes from the opening of Woolf's novel in an epigraph. Woolf's central character, Orlando, experiences life as a male and later as a female over a period of three centuries. Most importantly, Woolf uses this fantastic technique to expose cultural biases and illustrate the essential equality of the sexes. Walker quotes a passage in *Orlando* in which the young man is batting at the shrunken and suspended head of a Moor. It could be that Walker, while acknowledging her predecessor, is also calling attention to Woolf's selective view of equality.

◆ Related Titles ◆

Walker's last three novels share a number of characters. Shug, Celie, Nettie, Olivia, Adam, and Tashi from *The Color Purple* appear briefly in *The Temple of My Familiar*. Olivia, Adam, and Tashi are central characters in *Possessing the Secret of Joy* (1992). Fanny, who only appears in *The Temple of My Familiar* is the daughter of Olivia and the granddaughter of Celie. Walker has said that the novels are not intended to be seen as sequels, and indeed no character who has a major role in one book has anything but a minor one in the others. The characters reappear because as Walker said, she had a hard time leaving some of them or in the case of Tashi she did not have the space at the time to tell her story.

◆ Ideas for Group Discussions ◆

Inasmuch as *The Temple of My Familiar* can be classified, it resembles a novel of ideas and perhaps it is best approached in that way. A place to start might be with the controversy over a premise influenced by the Black Aesthetic Movement that the history of oppressed peoples can and should be rewritten imaginatively in order to deconstruct "the ideological assumptions underpinning Western constructions of reality." Was Walker successful anywhere in the novel with this technique?

A second thrust of the novel is in advancing ideas about where the world should be headed in areas such as the institution of marriage, directions for social change, attitudes toward racism, mankind's relationship toward animals, and so forth. Walker's ideas should stimulate an interesting discussion.

1. All the central characters seem to evolve to a higher consciousness. What social responsibilities, if any, are part of their new consciousness?

2. Does it seem to be true that Walker's homogenized view of the sexes and races through Lissie dilutes moral responsibility for sexism and racism?

3. What various roles do love trian-gles play in *The Temple of My Familiar*?

4. In Walker's novels the central female characters often make a big to-do over their discovery of masturbation. In what ways is masturbation used symbolically in this novel?

5. Does Fanny's experience show the way one can combat racism without becoming a racist?

6. Walker took much criticism for her depiction of black males in *The Color Purple*. How do the black male characters appear in this novel?

7. Suwelo obviously has much to learn about how to treat women. Does Arveyda share any of his oppressive tendencies?

8. Why does Lissie write to Suwelo in disappearing ink?

9. What relationship does Lissie's story of the familiar have to do with the stories involving the central characters in the novel? What do they need to set free?

10. Is modern African society as it is depicted in the novel any better or any worse than Western Society?

11. Can you identify where the source of all trouble comes from in *The Temple of My Familiar*?

12. What link does there seem to be between memory and imagination in the novel?

Dennis Baeyen
Cuesta College

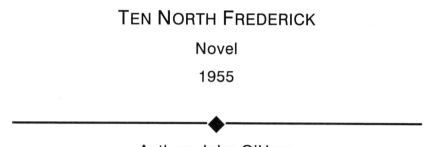

TEN NORTH FREDERICK

Novel

1955

Author: John O'Hara

◆ Characters ◆

Many of the characters introduced or mentioned in *Appointment in Samarra* (1934) appear in *Ten North Frederick*. The novel begins in 1945, just after Joe Chapin's death, but its action spans the decades since 1880, when Chapin's father first moves to the house in Gibbsville whose address is the title. Dr. English, his son Julian, Whit Hofman, and others are minor characters in the drama of the Chapin family, while Arthur McHenry, Joe's law partner, and Mike Slattery, the Gibbsville political leader, assume more central roles — the latter as a counterpoint to Chapin's impractical ambitions. The female characters in *Ten North Frederick* are particularly strong, not only in their complexity, but also in their ability to manipulate life to their own advantage. Chapin's mother, Charlotte, and his wife, Edith, nurture and direct his ambition so that they can benefit from its anticipated rewards. Both are women for whom love means power and ownership; on her wedding night, in fact, Edith Chapin says to the sleeping Joe, "I own you." Yet these women are not malicious; O'Hara portrays women who, because they are denied most masculine forms of power, participate vicariously by requiring their men to succeed in their stead. As in *Appointment in Samarra*, the central characters are presented from multiple perspectives, a device that underscores the variety of roles each person plays in a community.

◆ Social Concerns ◆

Ten North Frederick, O'Hara's fifth novel, is the first after *Appointment in Samarra* to be set in Gibbsville, and it enlarges upon several of the concerns of that early novel. Joe Chapin is a more single-mindedly ambitious person than is Julian English in *Appointment in Samarra*: He wants nothing less than to leave each of his children a million dollars and to become President of the United States. Although Chapin is not presented as a power-hungry schemer, he has been raised by his mother to believe that his own potential is limitless. The American dream of wealth and political influence, however, eludes Chapin, as happiness eludes Julian English; both men substitute social forms for human responses and end by being bewildered by the emptiness of their lives. *Ten North Frederick* explores the mechanics of party politics, including the power of local political leaders such as Mike Slattery, but O'Hara is less concerned with political corruption than with the ability of ambition to blunt or even eradicate one's essential humanity. To maintain what he believes to be the proper image for an aspiring politician, Chapin manipulates the lives of others, even forcing his daughter to divorce the dance-band musician with whom she has eloped and to end her pregnancy by abortion.

◆ Themes ◆

As is often the case in O'Hara's novels, a major theme in *Ten North Frederick* is human isolation. At Joe Chapin's funeral, which occurs at the beginning of the novel, one of his cousins remarks, "I could never figure Joe out," and as the novel continues the reader becomes aware that there is very little to "figure out" about Chapin: his life has consisted of surfaces; its reality has been identical with its façade. Even with his wife, Edith, Joe Chapin has a formal, almost businesslike relationship, and it is only when he falls in love with his daughter's friend Kate toward the end of the novel that he is willing to acknowledge his own vulnerability and understand the feelings and needs of another person. Chapin's isolation is created by his ambitions, and a corollary theme in the novel is the illusory and ultimately temporary nature of personal power. Mike Slattery, the Irish politician, understands this, and his realistic appraisal of what he can and cannot do contrasts with Chapin's impractical dreams. Nor can Joe Chapin change as he might like to

toward the end of his life; as O'Hara notes at the beginning of Part Two, "Only death itself causes that overnight change, but then of course there is no morning."

◆ Techniques ◆

By beginning *Ten North Frederick* with the funeral of its major character, O'Hara essentially starts at the conclusion of the story and then traces the events that have led to this point. The comments of the people gathered for the funeral become the threads that have been the tapestry of Joe Chapin's life and also the life of Gibbsville over a period of sixty-five years. The narrative voice several times refers to the story as a "biography," but although there are some superficial resemblances between the life of Joe Chapin and that of Franklin Delano Roosevelt, this is not the biography of an actual person. Instead, O'Hara uses the concept of biography as a device to step away from Chapin and view him as a figure in a larger drama. *Ten North Frederick* consists of two parts. Part One, by far the majority of the novel, tells the story of Joe Chapin until the point at which he begins drinking himself to death. The last fifteen pages form Part Two, a coda that summarizes Chapin's last years and his withdrawal from the life of Gibbsville: "When Joe Chapin had begun to cease to feel . . . the story became not Joe Chapin's but the stories of other people, and with Joe's part in the stories one of diminishing importance."

◆ Literary Precedents ◆

The elusive nature of the American

Dream of wealth and social prominence — and its detrimental effect on those who pursue it — has been a frequent concern of American writers since the late nineteenth century. William Dean Howells's *The Rise of Silas Lapham* (1885), F. Scott Fitzgerald's *The Great Gatsby* (1925), and John Dos Passos' *U.S.A.* (1937) are just a few of the novels preceding *Ten North Frederick* that deal with this theme. Like these other writers, O'Hara is deeply sympathetic with those whose dreams are thwarted; from his perspective, the fault lies not with the individual people who pursue the promise of American success, but with the emptiness of the promises themselves. Jay Gatsby and Joe Chapin both "create" themselves in accordance with what the culture seems to demand of the successful individual. O'Hara's novel differs from Fitzgerald's, however, in its far more detailed delineation of the social matrix from which his character comes: Gatsby is a mythic, symbolic figure, whereas Chapin, like Howells's Silas Lapham, is an ordinary person caught up in the economic and social forces of his era.

◆ Related Titles ◆

Anyone who reads more than one of O'Hara's novels set in the Gibbsville area comes to understand the geography, the social strata, and the values of the region and its inhabitants. The fictions do not proceed chronologically, as do the novels in John Updike's "Rabbit" trilogy, but familiar characters, such as Dr. English and Mike Slattery, and places, such as Lantenengo Street and the nearby town of Lyons, link the novels and stories and give the reader a sense of continuity. Together, O'Hara's Pennsylvania fic- tions provide a social history of the region during the first half of the twentieth century.

◆ Adaptations ◆

A film version of *Ten North Frederick* was made by Twentieth-Century Fox in 1958. Directed by Philip Dunne and starring Gary Cooper and Geraldine Fitzgerald, the motion picture was not successful.

Nancy Walker
Vanderbilt University

TENDER IS THE NIGHT

Novel

1934

Author: F. Scott Fitzgerald

◆ Themes/Characters ◆

Tender Is the Night is the story of a man's gradual deterioration and collapse. Dick Diver is a brilliant young psychiatrist when the novel opens, married to a woman who was one of his patients. Their relationship resembles Fitzgerald's and Zelda's, as Diver is both lover and protector to Nicole Warren. Diver is also trapped by the Warren wealth, using their resources to become a partner in a Swiss clinic and unable to avoid the temptations of an extravagant social calendar which is forcing him to neglect his research. He is eventually driven out of his position at the clinic when he loses interest in his profession and turns to alcohol for diversion and surcease. When Nicole leaves Diver for a glamorous European soldier of fortune, he tries to resume his career in America but fades into oblivion as a small-town doctor.

Although Fitzgerald several times protested that the novel should not be judged simply a picture of "Americans abroad," the characters do represent recognizable American "types." Nicole and Dick (while surely based somewhat on the Murphys, with what An-

drew Turnbull calls "their organized sensuousness, their fine gradations of charm") clearly represent the author and Zelda — the mention of which, implying a weakness of imagination causing an excessive dependence on simply observed behavior, pained Fitzgerald considerably. Yet, these two essentially idle persons could well stand for a number of American expatriates in Europe in the 1920s and 1930s.

Even secondary and tertiary characters, such as the actress Rosemary Hoyt, the professional soldier Tommy Barban, and the crude businessman Albert McKisko, can be viewed as standing for such real persons who almost infested certain areas of the Riviera and similar tourist havens. Much of the essential conflict in the novel stems from the presence of such surrounding characters, who tend to excessively admire the Divers or to criticize and misunderstand them and their eccentric lifestyle.

While Dick's descent into unhappy obscurity (in contrast to Nicole's satisfactory relationship with Tommy) at the close of the book is the essential focus of the novel, the development of Nicole from a spoiled, rich, insecure, even neurotic woman takes an important place in the thematic thrust of the text. Expatriates fascinated Fitzgerald, and he understood the type of person who became such an "uprooted" visitor in a foreign land. Thus, the realization of the alien settings is of great importance in the revelation of the reaction of the various characters to such an influence and to the advancement of the themes of waste and loss, so grimly developed that Marjorie Kinnan Rawlings found the book "disturbing, bitter, and beautiful."

Much of the beauty lies in the symmetrical plot, which, though not nearly so tightly woven as that of *The Great Gatsby* (1925), never strays from Nicole and Dick or the friends and acquaintances (such as the vulgar composer Abe North, whose death upsets the Divers greatly) that affect their lives, including Nicole's sister Baby. The emphasis always remains on the lives of the rising Nicole and the falling Dr. Diver.

Diver's loss of self is presented as a manifestation of the weaknesses that are the shadow side of personal charm and talent. As Matthew Bruccoli astutely observes, "The spectacle of Dick Diver's collapse is harrowing because he is destroyed by the same elements in his character that might have made him a great figure. His heroic aspirations dwindle into a fatal pleasingness." Fitzgerald himself classified *Tender Is the Night* as a philosophical or psychological novel and was pleased when a medical journal touted it as a contribution to an understanding of the psychobiological sources of human behavior. The novel is much less concentrated than *The Great Gatsby*, but its expansiveness permits Fitzgerald to achieve insights by accumulation and by what he called "lingering after-ef-

fects." A mood of sadness and regret pervades the novel, echoing Fitzgerald's own sense of his career at that time of his life.

◆ Adaptations ◆

The 1962 film version of the novel (enhanced by a superb background musical score, which was nominated for an Academy Award) starred Jennifer Jones as Nicole, Jason Robards as Dick Diver, and Paul Lukas as the Swiss psychologist who tries to "save" Dick. The movie was directed by Henry King, who achieved some fine visual effects (especially scenes on the Riviera); but, the general critical judgment was that the story moved too slowly, despite several striking episodes, but supplies a seemingly realistic image of Europe in the 1920s.

◆ Ideas for Group Discussions ◆

While many critics and general readers believe that *Gatsby* takes the palm as Fitzgerald's greatest literary achievement, many others view *Tender Is the Night* (a title taken from Keats's "Ode to a Nightingale," a fact that invites discussion) as the more insightful and fully developed novel. Consideration might be given to a careful comparison of these works, with an eye toward deciding which is indeed the more penetrating vision of the human condition. Also, the novel was published in a revised version in 1948; in this text, the antecedent information is taken from its interjected position and presented entirely, along with the rest of the plot, in chronological order. Readers might find it instructive to compare these texts, to determine whether the device of antecedent information "works" better than a linear presentation of the plot, or whether the revision was an improvement on the original publication.

1. If Amory Blaine's life can be seen as a striving for "selfhood," might Dick Diver's be viewed as a loss of that quality?

2. Does the European setting for much of the novel contribute to the effect of the book — for example, the clash with the Italian that Dick experiences?

3. One theme of *Tender Is the Night* is said to be "the tyranny of the weak." Does the relationship between Dick and Nicole really support this claim?

4. In view of modern attitudes, does the "psychology" found in the novel seem genuine and believable? What symptoms appear to be the most realistic?

5. Does the parallel, found by some readers, between Dick's "fall" and Fitzgerald's "failures" emerge as valid? Are there "holes" in the theory?

6. Apart from the discord between Dick and Nicole, what is the principal conflict in the novel? Does it enhance the thematic impact of the text?

Leon Lewis
Appalachian State University
[Adaptations and
Ideas for Group Discussions
by Fred B. McEwen,
Waynesburg College]

TERMS OF ENDEARMENT

Novel

1975

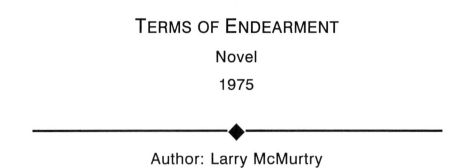

Author: Larry McMurtry

◆ Social Concerns/Themes ◆

Terms of Endearment is the sequel to *Moving On* (1970) and *All My Friends Are Going to Be Strangers* (1972). The fourth in McMurtry's "urban tetralogy" is *Evening Star* (1992). The first two novels are examinations of the various ways in which men and women fail each other. McMurtry's original intent was to have continued that examination, but this novel focuses on a parent-child relationship: the bond between a mother and daughter, with its failures, betrayals and its absolute loyalty.

◆ Characters ◆

Aurora Greenway, mother of Emma, dominates the novel. She is a profoundly eccentric woman, who charms men but is essentially uninterested in them. Her emotions are reserved for her daughter, whom she manipulates, torments, protects and loves fiercely. The other major character, Emma, is less strong and not in the least a comic creation. She chooses a traditional marriage to a man who fails her. Although she loves her own children, her mother remains the most important person in her life.

◆ Techniques ◆

The novel is divided into two unequal sections. The first and longest part is Aurora's story. It is a comic *tour de force*. Aurora is drawn against a moneyed Houston setting; her only friend is her maid; her days are filled with adventures that at times approach slapstick. McMurtry's skill at creating believable women characters is displayed to its advantage; while comic, Aurora is always believably human, never grotesque. The second part of the novel, Emma's story, is dramatically different from the first section; McMurtry returns to realist narrative, serious and without irony, as he tells of Emma's short, unhappy life. The two parts of the novel are vastly different: one, discursive, comic, satiric; the other, short, sad, elegiac. Although this has bothered some critics, it is clear that McMurtry has succeeded in creating two strong women characters and has defined, with skill and tenderness, the mysterious blood tie between mother and daughter.

◆ Literary Precedents ◆

Terms of Endearment is in the tradition of the modern regional novel. It defines the twentieth-century Texas urban setting in a way that recalls Dreiser's Chicago setting of *Sister Carrie* (1900); Edna Ferber's *Giant* (1950) is also a precursor that is specifically Texan.

Another literary precedent can be identified as those novels whose action revolves around the relationship between a parent and child. McMurtry examines the traditional elements of conflict between mother and daughter as well as the strong love and loyalty that transcends all other bonds that people form.

Finally, the novel's great delight in its characters' eccentricity derives from both British and American traditions. Aurora Greenway's roots are simultaneously in the "humours" character of British literature and in the western, larger-than-life tradition of American literature.

◆ Related Titles ◆

The earlier two novels share theme and characters with *Terms of Endearment*. *Moving On* is the story of Patsy Carpenter, Emma's best friend. In this novel, Emma and her husband Flap are seen in a relatively happy time. As Patsy's marriage fails, Emma's is seen as flawed but stable. Emma is depicted as unfailingly kind, a devoted mother and friend. Emma appears briefly in *All My Friends Are Going to Be Strangers* as the friend and one-time lover of the hero, Danny Deck. This novel also concerns a failed marriage; Emma, again, is seen as a good friend. In *Terms of Endearment*, Patsy appears briefly, and Emma, dying, escapes pain and the demands of the living into dreams of Danny Deck.

The novel returns to both characters and themes of McMurtry's earlier works. The most marked change is the pervasiveness of a sense of the inexorability of time. Although this, too, has always been present in McMurtry's fiction, it assumes a new centrality in this novel. *Some Can Whistle* (1989) also provides a sense of closure to many of the unresolved questions of the earlier novels; it removes the mystery about Danny's fate and allows him to grow old and approach death in a realistic way rather than in the romantic and mysterious darkness of the swirling waters of the Rio Grande. This revisionist ending is more fitting and more disturbing than its rehearsal.

The novel's central character and narrator is Danny Deck, the hero of an earlier novel, *All My Friends Are Going to Be Strangers*. That novel ended with Danny, his marriage over and his parental rights denied, destroying his novel and walking into the Rio Grande. In *Moving On* and *Terms of Endearment*, Danny's friends assume that he is dead. *Some Can Whistle* depends upon McMurtry's little joke: Rather than being literally dead in the waters of a river, Danny, a successful Hollywood writer, is figuratively dead as he uses his Hollywood wealth to isolate himself from friends, love and living. Into this living death bursts T. R., the grown-up child that Danny has never seen. Danny is a wonderful McMurtry character — eccentric, bewildered by almost everything, living alone with a housekeeper and keeping in contact with the outside world by telephone. But McMurtry's great triumph is T. R., who locates and invades Danny's protected half-life, demanding that he love her, save her and her two children, help her break her boyfriend out of jail, give her plenty of money to spend on junk, protect her, and now, when it is too late, be her father. Poor Danny, bewildered but full of good will, tries to oblige, and the collision between the aging, reclusive, sophisticated father and the disaster-prone, redneck young daughter provides the novel with its plot and its central theme. That the two learn to love each other is amazing; that they lose each other violently is heartbreaking. Surrounding the central characters of Danny and T. R. are a host of marvelous McMurtry creations: T. R.'s lover, Muddy, a failed burglar; her children, Bo and Jesse; and the man who kills her, Earl Dee.

Set in the present, *Some Can Whistle* deals with a number of themes, the most important of which is the relationship between parent and child. This is a familiar theme in McMurtry's work, and he is both eloquent and convincing in his analysis of the dynamics of the relationship between an absentee father and his neglected and abused daughter, grown to adulthood surrounded by violence, fanaticism, and unnecessary sorrow. McMurtry examines this issue with delicacy and restraint. The novel also deals with the issue of aging — the tendency to withdraw from active participation in the business of living; the pain of learning to live a life that encompasses violence, murder, loss, and great love.

Some Can Whistle is a traditional realistic novel. It is a richly detailed account of modern life; set in Texas, it is less grounded in regional concerns than McMurtry's earlier works. It is also traditional in its use of the first person narrator. Danny Deck's voice is richly individual — elegiac, regretful, gentle, and detached, even in loss and

sorrow. One is made aware of his loss of power through aging, his regret at that loss of power, and his mild gladness that the storms of youth are forever behind him. The first person narrative allows McMurtry to approximate the process of letting go that is a part of growing old. It is delicately and poignantly achieved.

◆ Adaptations ◆

Terms of Endearment was made into an enormously successful motion picture in 1983. It won five academy awards, including Best Picture, Best Actress (Shirley MacLaine as Aurora), and Best Supporting Actor (Jack Nicholson as Aurora's lover, Garrett Breedlove). Debra Winger, who played Emma, was nominated for Best Actress. Although the film is substantially different from the novel, it is true to McMurtry's intent to define the relationship between a mother and daughter.

Elizabeth Buckmaster
Pennsylvania State University

THE TERRORISTS

Novel

1975

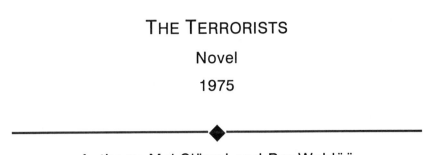

Authors: Maj Sjöwal and Per Wahlöö

◆ Social Concerns ◆

To consider any one of the Sjöwal and Wahlöö novels out of its canonical context is unthinkable. While *The Terrorists* has been chosen here for its timeliness and its critical status as one of the two best of the series featuring policeman Martin Beck, it can only be considered as the last thirty chapters of a major novel that began 270 chapters earlier. Maj Sjöwal and Per Wahlöö entered their collaboration — the literary one and the social one are utterly intertwined — because of their mutual ambition to analyze Swedish society through the crime novel and their mutual revulsion at what they saw happening to their nation. The first of the novels, *Rosanna* (1965), was written shortly after Sweden had nationalized its police force and shortly after Swedish policemen were first required to carry weapons. From that beginning through to *The Terrorists*, these two social issues were dominant in the saga. The authors repeatedly demonstrate the folly of relinquishing an effective decentralized law enforcement system for a centralized bureaucracy. While the continuing characters manage to function effectively because they are well trained and concerned policemen, younger members of the force are often preempted by the system.

Almost as important in the series as the ineffectuality of bureaucracy headed by ambitious politicians is the question of the correct place for firearms among the policeman's tools. In *The Terrorists*, for example, most crime prevention is accomplished through skill, intelligence, and occasionally an uncanny ability of one of the characters to lock into the mind of his adversary. Only in a spectacular arrest of two of the terrorists must the heroes resort to firearms — and then only to dismantle a bomb — not to hurt people. The subject of arrest had strapped to his body a bomb intended to blow up his assailant, himself, and any incidental bystanders. A detective, whose record in target practice had been adequate at best, manages miraculously to disarm the bomb with his gun just before it detonates. In this novel, the bureaucracy is thwarted when three very nearly insubordinate policemen eschew the Swedish "S.W.A.T. Team" mentality of their superiors and apprehend the terrorists on their own. From the text, it is clear that, had the central police system had its way, many would have died or been injured in unsuccessful attempts to bring criminals to justice.

Another social concern which runs through the series is the relative helplessness of the individual — policeman, victim, and criminal — in the face of a government more concerned with publicity than people. Here the individual is represented, not only by the continuing characters who do their jobs in spite of a hostile system, but by an eighteen-year-old mother whose only concern is to raise her child in a healthy environment outside the system. When her independence fails, this young woman turns to the welfare state for help only to find herself thwarted at every turn and finally becomes a criminal out of desperation — an example of bureaucracy's failure to serve the individual.

And, of course, the rising tide of terrorism in the western world becomes a major concern in this book. Here the reader is treated to an analysis of how terrorists manage to wreak their havoc often undetected and certainly undaunted. More than any other novel in the series, *The Terrorists* shifts point of view away from the continuing characters, and the readers come to know intimately several men who have chosen terrorism as a career.

◆ Themes ◆

The major theme in all the Sjöwal and Wahlöö novels is the individual's struggle for survival in a society that would thwart individuality. In *The Terrorists*, as in all its precedents, a hardy group of capable policemen attempt to solve and prevent crimes in the only effective way: intelligent analysis of the problem and tireless following up on even the most apparently insignificant clue. They are constantly badgered to make premature arrests, abandon apparently hopeless cases, and show off law enforcement hardware — all in the name of appeasing the public — never to create a safer society. And Rebecka Lind struggles, in a "free" society," to live a life meaningful to her only to discover that to receive society largesse, one must conform to meaningless expectations.

A second and almost as important theme is the growing violence in a culture which has functioned very well for centuries without it. In Sjöwal and Wahlöö's Sweden, violence among those outside the law increases in direct proportion to the violence espoused by law enforcement agencies. The novels are sprinkled with contrasts (and later comparisons) between Sweden and the relatively violent United States. Everyone is aware of how things are done in America, and everyone except the power structure has no desire to see the situation emulated in Sweden. In Martin Beck's Stockholm, terrorism is thwarted by brains not by arms — and then only by using the same brainpower to outwit the bureaucracy. And the violent crime that is committed is done, not by a highly organized international terrorist organization with diabolically clever equipment, but by a desperate, childlike woman with an antique pistol.

Rebecka Lind, who in an uncanny prophecy assassinated the Swedish prime minister, is typical of the "criminals" who people the Martin Beck novels. A social outcast with nowhere to turn, she might have been saved and she might have contributed to the quality of life had the Swedish welfare state been a genuinely caring society.

In *The Terrorists* as in the other series novels, criminals are often victims and victims are equally often criminal — the reader learns in no uncertain terms that both the target of the terrorists and Rebecka's powerful victim are not worthy human beings whatever recognition society has accorded them and that society itself is badly in need of restructuring. Even so, in the book's final sentence, when Martin Beck's best friend mentions "Marx" as if to imply that Karl Marx might have an answer to Sweden's ills, readers have already been shown that the problems cannot be so simply solved as to exchange one ideology for another.

◆ Characters ◆

Perhaps the strongest element in a strong series of books is Sjöwal and Wahlöö's characterization. Personages in these novels fall into two broad categories: characters and non-characters. Characters, even those who make cameo appearances, are finely drawn and usually win the audience's sympathy in one way or another, and the best appear repeatedly.

The non-character category is reserved for generic losers without whom no society is complete, and high level officials who exemplify the Peter Principle, whom readers never get to know personally. Kristiansson and Kvastmo (Kvant, in earlier books) exemplify the losers in *The Terrorists.* These two men in a patrol car represent the poorly trained and even more poorly motivated policemen who replaced the earlier "flatfoot" on the beat. Unlike their predecessors, they have no personal contact with the people they supposedly protect and no sense that their purpose is to serve the public. They do, however, provide black comic relief. They exemplify what happens when law enforcement becomes a job and officers are screened only for their skills and not for finer qualities. They are either lazy or blind followers of rules; they treasure their firearms which they are likely to use without provocation; and their ineptitude complicates the tasks of their more conscientious colleagues. Other non-characters in *The Terrorists* are a right-wing U.S. senator with no sense that he should comply with the mores of the country he is visiting — the target of the terrorists — and Sweden's unnamed prime minister whose chief concerns are ceremonial and for whom government is a matter of appearing at the right place at the right time.

The characters, however, are much more interesting. Martin Beck, of course, is never without the sympathy of the audience. Like the other characters, he grows with each appearance. In Beck's case the growth is both in rank and in ability to manage his private life. In *Rosanna* (1965), he is a First Detective Inspector attached to the Homicide Division of the Swedish national police organization — an entity similar to the FBI with much further ranging responsibility. In *The Terrorists*, he has become Chief of the National Homicide Squad. His rise has been steady and consistent. He knows he is one of the best Swedish police, but he puzzles throughout the ten books about precisely why. Readers know it is because of his commitment to the job, his ability to see the individuality of everyone he comes in contact with, and his dedication to doing his part to make the world, if not better, then certainly less uncomfortable. His career success in the early books is contrasted with his personal unhappiness. His marriage is a disaster for him and, one presumes, for his unloved wife, and yet he has not the strength to make a change. By the final books, he has divorced his wife, sampled a few promising relationships which he has found not quite right and settled down with the consistent companionship of an ideal, independent woman — neither of them ready to relinquish autonomy for a formal commitment. In *The Terrorists* then, his personal life is satisfying while his career has become exceedingly unsatisfying because the bureaucracy demands near hypocrisy and hinders skillful police work.

Another reason for Beck's job dissatisfaction in the last books is that his best friend and another continuing character, Lennart Kollberg, has left the force to avoid compliance with a system he considers inane. Kollberg's blissful late-life marriage provides balance for Beck's early personal unhappiness, and his refusal to carry firearms even when ordered to do so provides the authors opportunity to include continued dialogue on the advisability of an armed police force. Interestingly, in *The Terrorists*, Kollberg, who had been a crack shot on the police range has been employed part time by a museum because his analytical powers are ideal to classify a bequest of antique firearms. Apparently, both the character and the authors find museums the proper place for storing weapons.

Kollberg and Beck are joined on the Homicide Squad by other equally well drawn, if less visible, detectives. There is the computer minded Melander whose limited analytical powers are offset by the fact that he forgets nothing. And there is Einer Ronn, conscientious and slow witted, junior detective with a nose continually inflamed by allergies who grows from inept in the early books to capable and trustworthy in *The Terrorists*. The Squad is supplemented by a succession of eager, young and inexperienced detectives: Stenholm in the early books before he is killed in *The Laughing Policeman* (1970) and Skacke who becomes Beck's partner after Kollberg's resignation. Both of them begin as hopeless kids, and, through their own ambition and association with the dedicated and successful Homicide Squad, become first class policemen. These supporting characters are dwarfed in *The Terrorists* by the fifth member of the Homicide Squad, Gunwald Larsson. Larsson, who in previous books was a supporting character, is always fearless, intelligent and good to have around when daring feats are required. In the earlier books, however, he is an overdressed, sports car-driving, antisocial oaf with a private income whose presence when there is no crisis is an irritation at best. He grows throughout the saga, and by the conclusion of *The Terrorists*, when he is fifty and his inheritance has been spent, readers know that he has become a fine policeman — it is primarily his contributions that enable Beck's team to save the country from a terrorist attack and ignominy — and will become a congenial colleague for Martin Beck.

The place of women in the Sjöwal and Wahlöö microcosm is a fascinating subject for examination. Women move into strong positions in the canon as Western consciousness is raised in regard to sex discrimination and the contribution women make to society. In the first books, from the mid-1960s, women occupy the space they did in real life. Beck's wife is an unsympathetic nag; Kollberg's wife-to-be is sexy, a good cook, and a cheerful companion. Other women are murdered or they get questioned — they are appendages. In *The Laughing Policeman,* Ase Torrell is introduced as the broken hearted "roommate" of the murdered policeman and the first woman worthy of complete characterization. She joins the force and becomes a continuing character, and in *Cop Killer* (1968), her skill in questioning more sensitive witnesses has made her a valuable member of the squad. In *The Terrorists,* Torrell is ready to take her place among the elite of Beck's crime solving circle and Kollberg's wife has grown to where she is a fully realized character and the main breadwinner of their family.

Throughout the canon, the Stockholm police are supplemented with continuing law enforcers from the provinces who demonstrate advantages of decentralization no longer possible for the Stockholm agency. Mansson, for example, head of the Malmo police, can be relied on to carry out any of Beck's requests in a manner consistent with good police work and without the constant haranguing of a political National Police Commissioner. And Allright, provincial chief of the Anderslov police, cheerful, astute, and skilled, but mostly happy that he lives away from the high crime regions around Stockholm, recalls halcyon days when murder was exceptional in Sweden.

A consideration of characterization in Sjöwal and Wahlöö would not be complete without mention of the myriad witnesses and criminals, each of whom comes to life under Beck's astute questioning and the authors' limitless supply of detail. Most of these peripheral characters are victims of the system in one way or another. While readers are forced to agree that Rebecka Lind, for instance, is guilty beyond a doubt, that the murderer-rapist in *Rosanna* must pay for his crime, and that the almost juvenile delinquent in *Cop Killer* has made disastrous mistakes, they also see every one of them as prisoners of the system. Even the wealthy, middle-class murderer in *The Laughing Policeman,* whom everyone rejoices to see arrested, is in his own way merely a victim trying to protect himself. While criminals are victims, victims are often criminals. In most cases, those who are murdered, robbed or otherwise wronged are not themselves innocent although they may never have broken a law.

◆ Techniques ◆

To construct their plots and make their points, Sjöwal and Wahlöö use a chronological narrative with frequent alternations between one place and another. In the early chapters of *The Terrorists,* the narration jumps from Stockholm's police headquarters where preparations are being made for an unpopular state visit, to an unnamed South American country where Gunwald Larsson is observing antiterrorist precautions, to the farcical trial of Rebecka Lind for bank robbery.

In each setting, and in each of the other novels, the themes are developed through the thoughts of Martin Beck and through conversations between him and his colleagues. The plot, on the other hand, depends on the thorough plodding of dedicated detectives following every clue. Every effort is made to show successful police work as the product of long hours with few immediate rewards. Perhaps the most typical situations the authors use to develop these ideas — and the ones which most distinguish the Beck series from other police procedurals — are the "think tank" sessions in which the Homicide Squad brainstorms about seemingly solutionless crimes until the germ of an idea evolves from their combined minds.

Finally, however, the solution in some way depends on coincidence or "hunch." In *Cop Killer*, while the police know whom they want and why, they are saved more weeks of slow sifting work because a car turns up by chance at the right place at the right time. And the last of the terrorists is caught in part because Gunwald Larsson "feels" that he will try to escape Sweden in the Christmas rush.

◆ Literary Precedents ◆

Writers from Daniel Defoe and Samuel Pepys through Charles Dickens and Arthur Conan Doyle to Bernard Malamud and Dashiell Hammett have used urban crime to examine social ills. To this tradition must also be added Sjöwal and Wahlöö, but today's police procedural novel owes less to literary tradition than to cross fertilization between roughly contemporary writers. Sjöwal and Wahlöö have been aptly compared to Georges Simenon, Ross Macdonald, and Raymond Chandler, at least in Chandler's *The Long Goodbye* (1954). Each of these authors of detective fiction has, like the writers of the Martin Beck series, made the personal life of the continuing detective character integral to his professional accomplishments, and in each case the character has matured as he has grown older in succeeding books. Each of these authors has been recognized as transcending the detective fiction medium and writing "novels" in the truest sense, and each has achieved at least some mainstream critical recognition. Sjöwal and Wahlöö have added to these qualities a large group of perpetual characters and a story that continues from one novel to another.

◆ Related Titles ◆

One of the aims in the Martin Beck series is to present a different element of police homicide work in each of the novels. For example, in *Rosanna* the Swedish Homicide Squad must deal with mindless and almost motiveless murder by a deranged killer. In *The Man on the Balcony* (1967), they confront child sexual abuse; in *The Fire Engine that Disappeared* (1969) increasing drug traffic in the welfare state; and in *The Abominable Man* (1971) a heavily armed sniper on an apparently impregnable perch. In *The Man Who Went Up in Smoke* (1966) Martin Beck is called upon to work outside his usual jurisdiction to solve a possible crime with potential political implications in Eastern Europe, and *The Locked Room* (1972) converts the traditional "locked room mystery" into a novel of crime in the city.

Several of the novels call upon Beck and his colleagues to solve crimes new to Sweden. While *The Terrorists* introduces Sweden to the international problem of terrorism, in *The Laughing Policeman*, the Homicide Squad is confronted with the first Swedish mass murder. Because *The Laughing Policeman* vies with *The Terrorists* for identity as the best of the series, special mention should be made of it here. Perhaps what brings this novel to life and exceptional praise is the search for motive. Apparently fruitless investigations into the private lives of each of the murder victims to see if any one of them inspired the gunman acquaints the audience with a range of fascinating characters and slices of Swedish life worth savoring. One of these investigations, for instance, which puts the police no nearer to a solution of the killing, results in the incidental breakup of a drug ring. The plot of *The Laughing Policeman* is taut, the crime relevant and terrifying, and the conclusion satisfyingly ironic. One notable subplot to this novel is worth mentioning. In it, the Swedish Christmas holiday is revealed as a commercial carnival comparable to that in the U.S. and both Beck and the authors seem to be cynical toward it. In *The Terrorists*, six years later in Beck's and the author's lives, Martin Beck can sympathize with colleagues who must be away from their families at Christmas. As Beck grows happier and the authors' children grow older, apparently, the observance of Christmas takes on meaning beyond its surface materialism.

◆ Adaptations ◆

Two film adaptations of Sjöwal and Wahlöö works have been made. Film rights to *The Man on the Balcony* were sold to Universal Studios in 1969 but apparently were never used. In 1974, however, Twentieth Century Fox released its motion picture version of *The Laughing Policeman*, starring Walter Matthau. While the film itself was well received by those unfamiliar with the books, much of the spirit was lost when the setting was changed to San Francisco, the Swedish Homicide Squad became American bachelor policemen and "action" was added to please an American audience. A faithful and excellent Swedish version of

The Abominable Man called *The Man on the Roof* was released in 1979. Alert Americans can occasionally catch that movie, sometimes with subtitles, other times dubbed, on public television or in the art houses that feature old classics.

Sue Bridwell Beckham
University of Wisconsin-Stout

TEX

Novel

1979

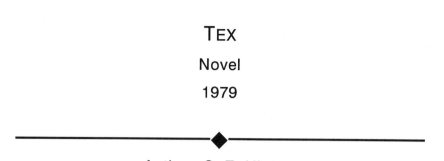

Author: S. E. Hinton

◆ Social Concerns ◆

Tex is unusual in the writings of Hinton in that it leaves the area of urban peer-group gangs and situates itself in the rural part of America. Tex is more concerned with school, with motorcycles, and with his horse, Negrito, than with gang life. The notion of social class does come up obliquely through run-ins with Cole Collins, the father of a girl Tex likes, who does not think that Tex and his brother fit the model he envisions for those who should associate with his daughter. Lem, an older character, is a drug dealer so that he may maintain a middle-class lifestyle rather than a lower-class one.

Illegal drugs are a major theme in this novel because Lem, the drug dealer, involves Tex in his machinations when Tex runs away from home. Unwanted pregnancy is also given a special poignancy as Tex learns that he is the product of an illicit union between his mother and a rodeo rider that took place while his father was in prison; this realization is one of the high points of the novel as Tex attempts to come to a fuller understanding of himself and of his family.

Tex also tries to have a much more "normal" relationship with a girlfriend than Hinton narrators usually do. Tex notes with a growing awareness that he is beginning to like Jamie Collins in more ways than merely as a friend, and he keeps up this liking for her even when her father severely disapproves. In a rural setting outside the world of gangs these relationships are not so clearly and completely controlled by the peer-group pressure of a gang.

Sexual relations outside of marriage and illegitimacy are, however, made more intense and poignant in this novel; in a climactic moment Tex learns that his father is not his true biological father. This wedding of social concern to the plot is done expertly in *Tex*, and it demonstrates how carefully Hinton can use social concerns in a story line.

◆ Themes ◆

Hinton again uses the theme of the teen-age youth maturing as expressed in the central character of *Tex*. In fact, *Tex* as a novel is again the story of a narrator who (like Ponyboy in *The Outsiders*, 1967) is made to undergo some of the most intensive weeks of his life. At the end the reader again sees the character come to a new realization about himself and his world, though this new insight is achieved subtly.

The theme of alienation again appears in *Tex*, as it does in all Hinton novels. Tex feels apart from his world, a world that seems to be beyond his control most of the time; for example, he loses his treasured horse, Negrito, who is sold by Tex's brother to get food for them. The scene of loss is part of the high drama in the book. Cole Collins, the father of Jamie, does not approve of Tex and his brother for reasons Tex cannot completely understand. Finally, Tex feels intensely alienated from his father — he is not his father's child. The interview Tex has with his father after learning this startling fact is among the very best scenes in the novel; it is also a mark of Tex's growth toward maturity.

◆ Characters ◆

Texas McCormick (Tex) is the narrator of the novel; through his experience the story is developed and told to the reader. He is young, given to pranks, and loves his horse, Negrito, who must be sold in the course of the novel. Mason McCormick (Mace) is Tex's older brother and father substitute when their father is on the rodeo circuit; he is a well-liked basketball star and his schoolmates often model themselves after him. He sees his ability in basketball as a way to get a college scholarship and escape from a lifestyle in which he feels entrapped. Pop is the biological father of Mace and the supposed father of Tex. His early life included a prison term during which his wife had an affair with a rodeo rider

which produced Tex. Johnny Collins is a good friend to Tex and sometimes plays pranks with him. Jamie, Johnny's sister, is also a friend to Tex; she becomes the object of his budding desire more as the novel progresses. Cole Collins is the father of Johnny and Jamie; a stern disciplinarian, he does not approve of Tex and Mace and does not want his children to associate with them. He does, however, assist in saving Tex's life when he is wounded. Lem is an older friend of Tex and Mace who is now married and lives in an apartment in "the city." He sells drugs to maintain his lifestyle and allows Tex to accompany him after Tex runs away from home. Tex is wounded during a drug sale with Lem.

◆ Techniques ◆

The world of *Tex* is a rural one, and love of the outdoors and horses pervades it. His regret over Negrito's loss seems deeply felt. The visit to the city with its attendant evils is used as a contrast to the more idyllic country life.

Tex does not use the enveloping technique of *The Outsiders*, although some critics praised it for the fuller character development of Tex, for the solidly constructed story, and for the restraint and humor of the narrative. The ending of *Tex* is not as startling as the conclusion of *The Outsiders*, but it is not as obtrusive either. Hinton brings the story of Tex and his eventual insight into his relationships with others to a closure at the end of the novel, but here she does it with a subtle touch and allusive grace. A brief discussion between Mason and Tex ends the novel, a discussion that takes into account much of what has gone before: Mason's desire to escape and a sense of helplessness in his responsibility, their relationship with "Pop," and the love-hate affinity they have shared while trying to make their lives together. The novel ends as the two boys plan a fishing trip for the next morning, but it also indicates the cleansing quality (Tex is symbolically cleaning his gun) of self-realization and deeper understanding of others that Tex has found in himself as the narrated story line completes itself in a moment of hope for the future and its possibilities.

◆Adaptations◆

Tex was filmed as a Buena Vista release by Walt Disney Productions in 1982. It was directed by Tim Hunter, and it starred Matt Dillon, Jim Metzler, Meg Tilly, Bill McKinney, Ben Johnson, Jack Thibeau, Emilio Estevez, and Frances Lee McCain. It was produced by Tim Zinneman with music by Pino Donaggio. The screenplay was by Charlie Haas and Tim Hunter.

Charles M. Kovich
Rockhurst College

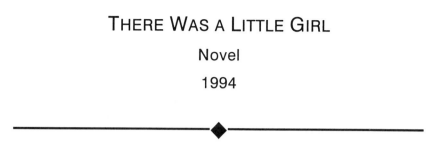

THERE WAS A LITTLE GIRL

Novel

1994

◆

Author: Evan Hunter/Ed McBain

◆ Characters ◆

Matthew Hope is the focus of this series and the novels revolve largely around his activities and are filtered largely through his consciousness. Matthew is a divorced, middle-aged lawyer who lives alone in the middle-sized city of Calusa, Florida. His daughter, with whom he tries valiantly to maintain a close relationship, is now attending boarding school in Connecticut. The distance between father and daughter frustrates Matthew to no end. Susan, Matthew's former wife, with whom he briefly entertained a renewed relationship and currently is on friendly speaking terms, lives nearby.

Matthew's professional life revolves around his law practice, which has undergone something of a change as he gradually has shifted over his emphasis from real estate to criminal law. In the process he has become involved, often unwillingly, in a number of criminal investigations which he has solved or helped to solve. Currently he has two private operatives working for him: Warren Chambers, a black man who as a character allows McBain to raise questions about racism, and the

tough but sexy Toots Kiley, whose presence in the novels introduces much of the gender material. Also present in the novels is the overly weary local cop, Morris Bloom, who provides Matthew with whatever official backup he needs. Morris also supplies a bit of avuncular advice now and then when Matthew extends himself a bit too far out into the dangerous world of crime. In the past he has also quite unsuccessfully tried to get Matthew into some sort of physical shape. Now he seems to have given up.

Currently, Patricia is the woman in Matthew Hope's life, and although there have been lots of women in Matthew's life in the past, he seems to be having the most serious relationship with her than any woman since his wife. In this novel McBain seems to enjoy playing Patricia and Susan off against one another as they jockey for position at the hospital while waiting for Hope to come out of his coma.

There Was a Little Girl also features a rather large cast of characters, both living and dead, who are developed along with the circus material in the plot. Unlike most of the secondary figures in the Matthew Hope novels, this circus lot is rather strange and includes an alluring female midget, a narcissistic lion tamer, a sexually strange juvenile trapeze artist, and a couple of old-time circus entrepreneurs. McBain weaves the generations together and traces the sins of the parents which are most certainly visited upon their children.

◆ Social Concerns ◆

Evan Hunter, once again writing under the Ed McBain pen name, began a second series in 1978 with the publication of *Goldilocks*. Unlike the 87th Precinct novels the new series was set in Florida and featured a local real estate attorney, Matthew Hope, who gradually converts his practice to criminal law, and as the series has progressed, he has spent more time solving crimes than litigating them. Each title in the series is taken from a fairy tale or nursery rhyme.

The Matthew Hope novels have allowed McBain to branch out in his crime fiction. As he readily admits, Matthew is more upscale than the characters in the 87th Precinct series and the narratives tend to be more graphically violent and sexual. Strange as it may seem McBain has kept the violence and sex fairly muted in the police novels in spite of the urban realism and grittiness of their milieu. The Florida setting figures prominently in these mysteries but it is not as important as the city in the 87th Precinct series. Unlike John D. MacDonald or Carl Hiaasan, McBain does not push environmental issues very hard, although he does mention the gradual decay of this once Edenic natural world, a motif which everyone who writes about Florida seems to use.

As with his previous series the personal details about Matthew Hope's failed marriage, his daughter and former wife, and his ongoing search for another woman to love, provide leavening to the murder and greed that make up the crime plots. These novels focus more closely and at greater depth on single crimes and criminals. And while there are a couple of private detectives and secretary who work for Hope, there is not the ensemble of characters as in the 87th Precinct.

◆ Themes ◆

There do not seem to be any overriding themes, like the decline of the city in the 87th Precinct series, which threads through the Matthew Hope books. More of the focus is on the personal desires and human failures of a few characters set against the background of the palmy Florida landscape. With the tighter focus, however, McBain is able to probe more fully the psychology of his characters and to push more heavily on motivation. Also, he is able to explore more fully such things as family connections and local history and the interconnection between the two.

There Was a Little Girl begins with Hope lying in a coma as a result of being shot by someone who had set up an appointment with him in connection with a real estate deal Matthew is working on for a small local circus. As he is examining the particulars of the transaction, he uncovers the mysterious death of a circus performer which has wide-ranging ramifications, possibly even for the deal he is about to close. The effects of the past on the present quickly take hold of the narrative and Hope's curiosity leads him into a major investigation which has far-ranging consequences. While he lies in the hospital, he thinks about the case he has been pursuing but also about his life, his divorce and relationship with his former wife, and his daughter. It becomes a very reflective novel, one in which Matthew takes stock of his life and examines the successes and failures of his career, thus raising all sorts of issues surrounding marriage, commitment, family, and relationships between the sexes.

Before the story is finished, the reader learns that Matthew has uncovered all manner of sexual perversions, child abuse, drug trafficking, and blackmail. The novel provides a cornucopia of crimes within a very constricted stylistic framework.

◆ Techniques ◆

McBain uses the Matthew Hope novels to extend his fictional range, both thematically and stylistically. He has done this with many of his other non-87th Precinct McBain novels as well, but not in such an extended fashion.

The narrative task McBain sets for himself in *There Was a Little Girl* is to construct a story told through the consciousness of a man in a coma. The plot unfolds piecemeal as Matthew mentally wanders back and forth from the past to the present in a kind of literary collage of images, vignettes, and backstories. It is a very interesting literary experiment, and the technique works especially well in this novel, which deals so heavily with the past. The concentration on Matthew's consciousness and mental shifting it goes through allows McBain to run the stories of Matthew's past parallel with the history of the characters he is investi-

gating. Interspersed among Matthew's foggy recollections is the present time story of the investigation into his shooting which Bloom, officially, and Toots Kiley and Warren Chambers, unofficially, are conducting. The narrative shifts McBain achieves make for fascinating reading.

As with his other crime novels, McBain's prose flows smoothly and economically. It is precise in its rendering of the details of place and the nuances of character. As in all of his fiction, McBain/Hunter's writing in this novel proves him once again a consummate professional.

◆ Literary Precedents ◆

There are echoes of many other crime writers in the Matthew Hope books. Especially in this novel, one gets a taste of the family saga as history which Ross Macdonald perfected in his California-based novels of the 1950s with Lew Archer. No one can write crime novels about Florida without calling to mind the long-running series by John D. MacDonald or the current series of books by the Miami-based journalist Carl Hiaasen. Matthew Hope's position as the reluctant lawyer/sleuth also brings to mind William Tapply's Boston lawyer Brady Coyne. The idea of a professional in one field straying over into the business of solving crimes has a long history, and the problems inherent in such a cross-over plague Matthew in many of the same ways they have plagued protagonists in other crime series.

However, this McBain series is not derivative. He has fashioned a world and a set of characters which owe more to his own previous novels than to any other writer working in the genre.

There Was a Little Girl

Since *There Was a Little Girl* is part of a series, the most clearly related titles are also part of the series and the ongoing story of Matthew Hope and his adventures. While each novel can be read separately there is a gradual unfolding of his life in the collective set. Like the 87th Precinct novels, this is a timeless world but one in which both the characters and the details of the locale and its history do change episode by episode.

In the current novel Matthew is left in his coma at the story's end. As with any good serial the reader is left hanging, not knowing his fate. This is complicated further by the presence of both Patricia and Susan and by Matthew's memories about the two women. Will he try to get back together with his former wife or commit to his current female friend? Tune in tomorrow.

The Matthew Hope series comprises: *Goldilocks*, 1978; *Rumpelstiltskin*, 1981; *Beauty and the Beast*, 1982; *Jack and the Beanstalk*, 1984; *Snow White and Rose Red*, 1985; *Cinderella*, 1986; *Puss in Boots*, 1987; *The House That Jack Built*, 1988; *Three Blind Mice*, 1990; *Mary, Mary*, 1993; *There Was a Little Girl*, 1994.

◆ Ideas for Group Discussions ◆

The Matthew Hope series provides an opportunity for discussion as both individual titles and as a group. Since McBain always writes about topical issues, there is plenty to talk about in his books. Especially relevant are various environmental issues as well as the personal concerns faced by his protagonist.

1. In what ways are the Matthew Hope books the same and different from McBain's other works? Compare and contrast such issues as environment, characters, and style.

2. How does this novel transcend the conventions of the mystery genre? In what ways is *There Was a Little Girl* more like a conventional contemporary novel?

3. Notice how cleverly McBain works the title into the story as more than merely suggestive of the nursery rhyme from which it was taken. Is there a connection of fairy tale and myth to the narrative of the novel?

4. What social issues are raised by the novel? How are they raised and what questions arise from their presence?

5. Discuss the literary style, its mixture of effects, and the ways the style shapes our reading of the story.

6. How does McBain use the circus grotesques to shape the story he is telling? How does the novel relate them to those outside the circus world?

7. What is the importance of "the past" to this novel? McBain does much to link together the actions from the past with the events of the present. How does all of this work to develop the story?

8. Why did McBain make Matthew Hope, initially at least, a real estate lawyer? What narrative possibilities does that give him?

9. The reading group might look at another one or two of the Matthew Hope series and do some comparative

readings with this one. Is the series changing over time? Does the group notice any patterns to the novels?

10. Think about how this novel, although legitimately within the crime genre, plays with the conventions of the "murder mystery," narrowly defined, and without breaking the boundaries expands them.

Charles L. P. Silet
Iowa State University

THEY WHISPER

Novel

1994

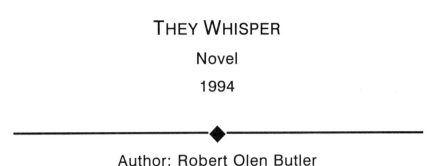

Author: Robert Olen Butler

◆ Social Concerns ◆

More sensual than Butler's prior novels, *They Whisper* gives a male protagonist's world view, focused almost wholly on his attraction to women, his few experiences of intimacy without sexual involvement, his lavish sexual involvements, and his frequent fantasies of involvement. Ira Holloway marries Fiona, a lapsed Catholic who eventually discloses that, as a child, she was molested by her father. She turns to a rigid, fixated practice of her faith, linking the efficacy of the rite of confession to Ira's ability to perform sexually on demand. Thus, Butler presents the reader with a man who perceives the world primarily in terms of his own sexual satisfaction — without any consequences such as AIDS, herpes, chlamydia, or any of a hundred other realities which actually confront the erotically athletic person in everyday life.

Through Fiona, Ira sees contrasts to his own schedule of desire as irrational demands or outbursts of a woman who is mentally ill. The women who serviced him in the sex shops of Saigon when he was a young GI, the women he dallies with during his marriage to Fiona, all seem readily attracted to him because he has "soft eyes" and is somehow irresistible to them. The women are able to come into his life and leave without major consequences for either of them, and Ira stays with Fiona essentially to protect their son, assuring him that they conform to many of her religious practices and weather her vicious rages because she was abused as a child and needs to be protected as an injured adult.

Butler, while taking the reader into very detailed experiences with Ira, Fiona and various secondary characters, presents a situation in which women's desires for sex are rendered via a male's perspective, while the intricacies of women's expectations in a relationship are either enacted in Fiona's jealousy that runs beyond reason, or in the here-today-gone-tomorrow lives of Ira's short-term lovers.

The function of religion in Ira's life is little more than accession to ritual as a means of containing the mental illness of an abused child grown into an adult professional victim. While Butler as a novelist expresses more concern for a reader's ability to share the experience of the story's characters than for a reader's ability to abstract ideas or morals from the story, he has woven an effective video-age tale which would allow a thoughtful reader of either gender to step back a moment and consider the consequences of living with the warps and blindnesses which Ira and Fiona display. Their world is fundamentally organized by competition between male sex drive and insane rage of an abused and abusive female. Religion is not a source of solace or strength for change, but another weapon in the battle of the sexes.

◆ Themes ◆

Ira's purity of desire for intimacy outstrips whatever sense he may have of traditional notions of morality, or even recognition that a "liberated woman" in his modern times might not wish to be viewed constantly as a sexual object. For Ira, any female who comes into view — physically or via memory — is a subject for detailed sexual fantasies and seduction: Good sex is true worship; bad sex is distorting and distorted religion. And somehow, although he claims to be an equal opportunity admirer, a reader never finds Ira in bed with a decidedly homely or overweight paramour.

Father-son bonding arises as Ira moves to protect John from Fiona's fixations and rages. When John is old enough to have a fascination for trains, Ira and he spend Saturdays riding the trains in and around New York — even though Ira commutes to and from work by train five days a week. Ira is not beyond including a day with a lover in the father-son train schedule, and he frequently assures John that going to Mass with mother is simply a means to help counter her fits of insanity. Thus, while Ira expresses great love and

concern for his son, the vision of life and of relationships with women that he can convey to the boy is simply his own — nothing broader or more balanced than what he himself lives out.

Fiona enacts the wounded woman cycle in the story. Abused as a child and recalling the scenes of abuse as an adult, she alternates between feeling incapacitated by the early exploitation and being a domineering, manipulative, raging emotional abuser herself. Although she never cites the phrase directly, she lives out the Old Testament maxim that "The sins of the fathers are visited upon the children to the third and fourth generation."

◆ Characters ◆

Ira Holloway's desire for intimacy comes early. He establishes a special emotional tie to Karen Granger when he is ten years old, because he looked at her feet in the X-ray machine in his uncle's shoe store. His need for attention prompts him, in high school, to sneak into the girls' rest room and scribble praise of his supposed sexual prowess on the walls of toilet stalls.

In Vietnam, because he was fluent in Vietnamese, he recognized that while another American serviceman assumed the prostitute with him was exclaiming in ecstasy at appropriate times in their conjugal moments, the woman was actually calling out "You pig!" and other, even less complimentary epithets. Ira Holloway's name presents a challenge to native speakers of Vietnamese, so the women at the sex shop or steam bath he frequents call him Mr. "Ai" which, with a rising tone, means "love" in Vietnamese. Since he himself is received so readily by the women he approaches, it never occurs to him that the curses directed at another might ever apply to him. He blithely describes in graphic detail the mechanics of lovemaking the women use with him, and the procedures he uses with them.

Should one speculate on other significance in the name "Ira Holloway," there was an American military installation in South Vietnam named "Holloway." Also, when considering the protagonist's erotic fixations and wanderings, some could well consider his life, in the long term, a "hollow" existence, or could say he repeatedly sought Freudian enclosure in the female.

Fiona, as she settles into the roles of wife and mother, moves from being apparently carefree, teasing, and passionate to being a driven, compulsive lover, almost sadistic in her angers. While she works for a time in an art gallery, she refuses to manage an exhibit of paintings based on a motif she reads as too suggestive of female labia, and quits. Growing steadily more compulsive about the rite of confession, Fiona begins to demand that Ira prove she has stimulated him immediately after they have been to Mass or confession: "I want to make love with you for the first time without guilt." As is common with persons victimized as children, Fiona carries a sense of sin and guilt which she truly should not own. Seven years of psychiatric sessions, though, have not pried the problem from her self-image: They have only pried the fees from her pocketbook. She becomes progressively more ritualistic in her demands and likely to fly into a rage of self-deprecation and jealousy if Ira cannot physically respond to her within a minute or two. She equates orgasmic pleasure with divine grace, and any failure to achieve ecstasy on her own terms she sees as a mark of personal failure due to unforgiven sin.

Although Jewish and Christian traditions have included various interpretations of sexuality over the millennia, and the sex act in a variety of relationships has been condemned, sexual relations within the context of marriage have long been revered as a sacred gift. Fiona's legalistic patterns for acceptable intercourse with Ira and her irrational outbursts at the least lapse from her timetable portray her blindness to the principles of grace and forgiveness in the very rites she compulsively pursues. The doctrine of incarnation, interpreted through Fiona's tortured life, reduces to the streetwise philosophy of the alienated: Religion is just so much bad sex.

Several other women and girls Ira has seen or known, some casually, some very intimately — populate his reveries throughout the novel. Miss Hue, Miss Chien, Miss Trang, Blossom, Sam, Miss Xau, Amanda, Tran Thi Hoa, Rebecca Meuller, Kesree, and others appear and disappear as he contemplates the waxing and waning of his love for Fiona and his efforts to shield their son John from the worst of her behaviors. Other men figure only slightly in Ira's pastiche of sensual experience.

◆ Techniques ◆

Related as a first person narrative by Ira Holloway, the novel moves through its 333 pages in the hardback edition with modest breaks at the end of a section, and with a single enlarged capital letter opening the next passage. Other novels by Butler show clear chapter identities: Each chapter is numbered and begins fresh on a page. *They Whisper*, however, has no clear "book chapter" divisions; rather, less intrusive breaks between sections parallel the scene divisions in a play or film script, and the reduced blank space interrupting the flow of words allows the mind to hold the novel as more nearly stream-of-consciousness in form.

In *They Whisper*, as in his other work Butler uses the blends of past and present to create the sense of Ira's reverie flowing forth and back in the stream of consciousness. Sentence structures vary from short grammatical statements to occasional fragments within standard dialogue, to rambling run-ons.

Sections varying in length from a paragraph or two to several pages are rendered in italics to mark the feminine voice Ira hears whispering to him in his reverie. Such passages may display a fine sense of descriptive detail, and may carry a reader's thoughts toward "female perspectives," but still, they are reported by a male persona, and still they reflect what the male ego wants or needs to hear whispered, not necessarily what the woman in focus might actually think or say.

Erotic passages appear more frequently in *They Whisper* than in *The Alleys of Eden* (1981). The vocabulary in erotic scenes varies from clinically precise to back-alley blunt. A reader first encountering Butler's writing in the short story collection *A Good Scent from a Strange Mountain* (1992) will recognize that the literary art that garnered the Pulitzer Prize is usually quite genteel in its vocabulary, while the novels include harsher exchanges, and *They Whisper* is at times quite generous with terminology of the street and the locker room.

◆ Literary Precedents ◆

In naming biblical books as literary precedents, Butler did not specify that canonical embarrassment to the pious known as The Song of Solomon or The Canticle of Canticles, but the Old Testament does contain it, nevertheless, and its imagery shows a lover's graphic attention to the neck, breasts, and skin tones of the beloved. To explain the presence of such erotica in the sacred writings, theologians must see it as an image of the love of God for Israel, or the love of Christ for the church. Down through western literary tradition, there have been recurrent connections between the intensity of human-to-human sexual love and the divine love for the human being. Always, whether in the writings of mystics such as St. Theresa of Avila, the bawdy of Chaucer's Wife of Bath, the comic portrayals of lovers in Shakespeare's *Midsummer Night's Dream* (c.1600), or Butler's *They Whisper*, the writer risks the charge of impiety or outright blasphemy when the erotic, and especially the pagan erotic, is brought near traditionally sacred rites and images.

Without declaring specific connections to prior works, Butler has produced a novel which returns to the premise that human sexuality offers an intense way to perceive the divine — a premise ancient in both Western and Eastern traditions. In Ira's discussion of love with Nguyen Thi Hoa, the Buddhist premise that human unhappiness results from uncontrolled desire is overtly explored.

The plaint that a traditional crucifix should show Christ completely naked on the cross if a true perspective on incarnation is intended appears in Butler's *Sun Dogs* (1982) as well as in *They Whisper*, and certain approaches to lovemaking found in *They Whisper* will also seem familiar to readers of Butler's earlier novels.

Although *They Whisper* is not plotted as a novel about Vietnam, but about a man's attempts to interpret his world through Eros, the main character is posed as a person who took full advantage of most every opportunity for sexual contact during his tour of duty with a military intelligence unit in Vietnam. Thus, *They Whisper* has passages that parallel portions of *The Alleys of Eden, Sun Dogs, On Distant Ground* (1985), and *The Deuce* (1989). In addition, the use of reverie and flashbacks in the mind of the narrator connect Butler's novels.

In the latter decades of the twentieth century, television shows, radio talk shows, movies, books, and magazines have steadily included more erotic topics, more clinical detail in the management of such topics, and freer use in public of terminology once restricted to locker rooms, boudoirs, and the streets. Writers more often include terminology which, in the early days of television broadcasting, would have been consistently censored. In the last years of the century, certain items of the old taboo vocabulary are permissible, while others are still banned or beeped from a broadcast.

As mentioned in the discussion of precedents, in *They Whisper*, Butler falls in line with an ancient pattern of a character in some way associating human erotic experience with an un-

derstanding of the supernatural. Although he states that he writes in order for his work to share sensory experience rather than provoke ideological debate, the experiences presented in *They Whisper* certainly are ripe for discussion of male and female perspectives on erotic experience, for discussion of the relative success of Fiona's interpreting divine grace and the doctrine of confession and absolution through personal erotic experience, and for discussion of Ira's apparent ability to float through multiple sexual contacts with "no strings attached," no surprise pregnancies, and no surprise maladies.

1. While Ira Holloway frequently tells of the religious background of his women in Vietnam and repeatedly conveys Fiona's perspectives on Catholic rites and doctrines, he seems to find no enduring personal guilt when moving from lover to lover either before or during his marriage. Is Ira a man without morals? Is he a man without religion? If he finds religion of no consequence for himself, why does he agree to go to Mass and confession with Fiona?

2. While Ira remembers his opportunities for sex and passion in Vietnam and seems to have scant regrets for lovemaking there, certain events do arouse guilt in him. What events does he regret, and why?

3. Declaring intense need to be close to women and to share various intimacies with women, Ira Holloway sometimes relates his close study of a woman seen in passing, detailing how he imagines her body parts, almost millimeter by millimeter. The "women's voices" in his head tend to ex-

press similar passion for him. How realistic are Ira's portrayals of women's interest in him? Would the average woman feel comfortable having either a stranger or a friend gaze at her intently, as though he were undressing her with his thoughts? Would the average woman realistically dream so frequently and so intensely about male anatomy as Ira dreams about female anatomy?

4. Ira's erotic experiences and fantasies are usually graphically detailed. Could Butler achieve the same or better effects by using the "less is more" principle and reducing the overt sexual descriptions? Does the reading public now tolerate explicit erotica or demand it?

5. What is Ira Holloway's occupation? Where does he work? Where does he live once he has a family? Why does he settle in a town so far from work? How does his commuting affect the family?

6. What was Fiona's line of work? How long does she work outside the home? When does she quit her job, and why? How does she expect Ira to respond to her resignation? Does he react as she predicts?

7. Fiona becomes pregnant and bears a son. How does she respond to being pregnant? How does she respond to the expectation that she nurse the baby? How long does she nurse? How do the pregnancy and birth experiences affect Fiona's marital relations with Ira? How does Ira feel about the physical and emotional changes he sees in Fiona?

8. What connections does Ira draw between the Catholic tradition of con-

fession and the practice of psychiatry? What value does Ira see in either approach to discovering self and gaining wholeness? Does Ira himself feel a need for either confession or psychoanalysis? Does he avail himself of either approach in a sincere manner?

9. How does Ira seem to identify or define jealousy? Does he experience jealousy himself, or is it — in his view — a woman's weapon for irrational argument?

10. How does Ira perceive Fiona's intensifying religious activity? Do her contacts with the parish priest help Fiona hold her anxieties in balance? Does Fiona seem to understand the Catholic perspectives on the grace of God and the premises of confession of sin, absolution from sin, penance, and resolution to amend one's life?

11. In relating the joys and sorrows of Ira and Fiona, has Butler drawn the reader to a serious consideration of the relationship between wholesome human love and the love of the divine for the human, or has he simply produced one more lurid novel for an increasingly voyeuristic reading public?

12. Literary critics long have warned against "the intentional fallacy," which is assuming that an author is always directly reporting his or her own beliefs, feelings or experiences. Allowing Butler the freedom to create characters who are not drawn exactly from his own experience, how many factors in *They Whisper* appear to parallel or be drawn from Butler's personal history?

Ralph S. Carlson
Azusa Pacific University

THE THIEF WHO COULDN'T SLEEP

Novel

1966

◆

Author: Lawrence Block

◆ Characters ◆

Evan Tanner is another of Block's individualists. He is a quasi-unofficial spy who works when he feels like it on his own terms for a government agency so secret that the CIA does not know what the unnamed agency does. Tanner's belonging to lost causes gives him allies and potential friends in places all over the world, friends who need to hear just the password or the names of other members to accept him instantly. Block has written that Tanner is the archetypal outsider; his joining fringe groups is the other side of his opposition to the establishment. Tanner's inability to sleep gives him time to read and to gather unusual information and to learn many arcane languages, knowledge that allows him access to people in far-away places and strange cultures. His knowledge of languages also lets him hear and understand secret information that others do not think he can interpret.

One group of characters in the series consists of Tanner's romantic interests, and a function of his charm is the number of attractive young women who go to bed with him with no trouble, no explanations, no time to get to know him, and no complications or recriminations afterwards. The women kiss him hello and kiss him goodbye, providing available sex with no strings attached. This easy sex is part of the mystique of the super spy like James Bond. One love interest, Annalya Prolov, whom Tanner revisits in *Tanner's Twelve Swingers* (1967), is not jealous when Tanner tells her that he makes love to other women when he reassures her that he has babies with only her.

Villains in the series are not usually very formidable. Often the men working against him are motivated by understandable self-interest and greed, and Tanner can outwit and foil them with his greater forethought, perspicuity or luck. There are no arch-villains like Bond's Goldfinger or Dr. No. Tanner becomes violent only as the series goes along, finally killing a despicable old Nazi and a British supplier of girls for white slavery. Block resists crudely categorizing everyone who is against Tanner's objectives as fiendishly evil.

◆ Social Concerns/Themes ◆

A major theme is that of the wanderer, of the hero with the ability to travel through the world and be at home. Allied with this wandering is the idea of freedom. The Irish girl Nora tells Tanner that she has only dreamed of taking the bus to Dublin from the village outside Limerick where she keeps house for her father and brother. Tanner's mobility attests to his freedom, as does his lack of ties to a humdrum, workaday world. He can go and do as he pleases with few hostages to fortune.

Later, themes of friendship and family seem to emerge with Tanner going on his travels to rescue friends: a virgin sold into white slavery and a woman musician who disappeared on a Far East tour. Tanner's trip to Latvia is originally to bring out his American friend's fiancée, a journey for friendship and romance. One method of creating family ties for Tanner is his fathering children on Annalya in Macedonia, a good place to which he can return, a sanctuary from modern tensions and complexities. Tanner partly establishes a family for himself by rescuing and unofficially adopting a little girl, the rightful princess of Lithuania. The girl, Minna, is precocious and, like Tanna, gifted at languages, a child in his own image.

◆ Techniques ◆

The Thief Who Couldn't Sleep begins *in medias res,* in the middle of the action with Tanner shut up in a Turkish jail, a technique Block recommends in his column on fiction. The main line of action is a treasure hunt, a hunt for the American gold in Smyrna. Complicating the treasure hunt are Tanner's allegiances to lost causes, his reputation as an oddball, and the presumption of many that he must be a CIA operative or some other kind of spy. Like earlier classic spy novels, when the amateur becomes enmeshed in spying, he has to see the adventure through.

At the end of the treasure hunt, Tanner gives himself up to the U.S. Embassy and the CIA in order to go home. The result involves the serendipity that is also part of the Tanner adventures. When Tanner falls into good fortune, he knows enough to accept it. Tanner invokes a secret service without even a proper name, and the nameless Chief sends two men to rescue Tanner. Without the Chief, the novel would go in a circle from Turkey to America, jail to jail. If there are secret agents (like the CIA) who are team-oriented, there could also be agents so secret that they work as individuals. The world has proved to be so absurd that the exaggerations of Tanner's world could also exist with only a little suspension of disbelief, or so the reader is asked to believe.

◆ Literary Precedents ◆

Perhaps the ultimate model for the Tanner Series is *The Odyssey* (c.1050-850 B.C.) with the hero traveling through the world, meeting adventures, some of which threaten to keep him from getting home. In *Tanner's Twelve Swingers,* Tanner keeps picking up *impedimenta,* people who want him to rescue them, making each new stage of the journey more difficult.

The first Tanner adventure refers repeatedly to James Bond, distinguishing Tanner from the glamorous super spy. Tanner can be seen as an anti-Bond. Tanner has no license to kill and he often chooses guile rather than brutality in the series. He does not have the sophisticated technology of Bond's tricky concealed weapons. Technology requires the backing of the system, and Tanner is on his own. In the Tanner books the world is not divided into two camps with the angels on the side of the superspy and with the devils all who oppose him. Tanner starts out at least as an alternative to Bond, the violent professional who divides the world into "them" and "us."

◆ Related Titles ◆

Other Evan Tanner adventure novels include *The Canceled Czech*, 1967; *Tanner's Twelve Swingers*, 1967; *Two for Tanner*, 1967; *Tanner's Tiger*, 1968; *Here Comes a Hero*, 1968; *Me Tanner, You Jane*, 1970.

Kate Begnal
Utah State University

THIN AIR

Novel

1995

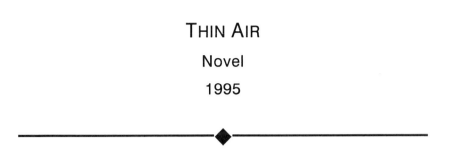

Author: Robert B. Parker

◆ Characters ◆

Most of the characters in Parker's recent Spenser novels are pretty familiar to anyone who has been following the series. Spenser, himself, continues to mature in his sensitivity to his own shortcomings and in his relations with others. Nevertheless, he must maintain a certain protective distance at times in order to deal effectively with the forces of evil. There are still times when he must be hard and unyielding in order to survive and to do his job. The dialectic between openness and sensitivity and control and professionalism Parker developed early on in the series continues in this book. While he changes he also remains largely the same.

Lisa Belson is also reminiscent of other women Spenser is hired to find or rescue. Plagued by an unsavory or at least hidden past, she must help the detective uncover her dark side in order to resolve the narrative and to also become healthy again. The heavies are largely Hispanic but retain a tangential relationship to the criminal elements from the other books. The fact that Spenser hires a Chicano shooter from an L.A. gang to replace the miss-ing Hawk provides only a minor difference. Both Hawk and Spenser's current backup function in the same way, watching Spenser's rear and providing a contrast to his basic humanity. The police remain on the periphery, if still on Spenser's side. The detective still walks a thin line between the forces of good and evil.

◆ Social Concerns ◆

Many of the social concerns in the Spenser novels are those of crime fiction in general: decay of urban life, growing levels of violence in American life, increasing lack of community, decreasing sense of safety, and the usual human failings of betrayal, lust, greed, jealousy, and murderous rage. Parker puts his particular spin on these themes by having them filtered through the consciousness of his P.I., Spenser, who has a special view of the world, part humorous detachment, part passionate engagement, which helps to balance out the world Parker explores in the series.

Thin Air is a fairly typical, late Spenser novel with the exception that Hawk, Spenser's dark alter ego, is missing, but his role is taken by a hard-nosed Chicano enforcer Spenser borrows from an underworld acquaintance in L.A. who owes him a favor from years back. The plot is fairly simple as is often the case with the series: Spenser is hired to find a missing woman and that investigation plunges him into a larger, darker criminal world and provides the occasion for him to right some other wrongs. It is questionable how much Spenser is one of those knights of the streets critics like to write about so much, but he does seem to have a tendency to poke his nose into trouble in order to help his friends and clients out of trouble.

As has been true from the very start of the series, the books deal in part at least with raising Spenser's consciousness about gender issues, and by the time of *Thin Air* he has come a long way, thanks largely to the continuing tutelage of his longtime, and often long-suffering, female companion, Susan Silverman, who manages to keep him aware of his sexist leanings. Frank Belson, Spenser's old friend from the Boston Police Department, comes to him to report that his new, and much younger wife, has gone missing, and he asks the private investigator to look into the case because Spenser can go where the officials cannot by using contacts and methods denied the police force. The search for Lisa Belson turns out to be far from a straightforward missing person's investigation, however, because Lisa has largely hidden her past from her husband. What Spenser uncovers about her and how he goes about rescuing her from her abductor forms the basis for the broadening of the plot and plunges Spenser into the scary world of the Hispanic-controlled drug trade in a middle-sized, economically-depressed Massa-

chusetts town now run by two rival gangs.

The search for Lisa is also about the crime of stalking, and the need some men have to control the women in their lives, exploiting them for their own ego gratification. The stalking issue also brings to the surface of the novel the issue of relationships, a persistent theme of all of the Spenser books. This time the relationships are multiple and unusually complicated by Lisa's dark history and an affair she had with a Chicano just before meeting Frank and her recent marriage. In Parker's world a character's past usually comes to haunt his or her present.

Thin Air also explores the consequences of the breakdown of social norms caused by the money and extra-legal power generated by the enormously lucrative drug trade that allows underworld thugs to wrest political control from the legal authorities. The economic decline of the community produces poverty and hopelessness which provides the background against which the criminals are able to flourish. In this story two drug lords are fighting over turf and Spenser and Lisa get caught in the middle. As is often the case in the Spenser series the conclusion of the narrative does not resolve the larger social issues but merely provides a momentary stay against the destruction of the central characters. In the end, one of the drug kingpins is destroyed leaving the territory firmly in the hands of the other. And Spenser is unable to control the larger world in any reasonable way. He just rescues Frank's wife and helps to restore the status quo while the organized forces of crime remain in power. It is true that he does help to eliminate the worse and most unpredictable of the evil men, but he is unable to restore innocence to this most flawed of worlds.

◆ Themes ◆

The concurrent themes of official and individual corruption form the grounding of the plot. The drug lords have seized control of the local environment and established compounds from which they operate their illegal activities. The corporate nastiness spreads beyond the confines of their covert operations and when one of the drug dealers kidnaps Belson's wife, it brings together the two themes. Lisa becomes involved because in her past she for a short period was the lover of one of her abductors. In the course of his investigation Spenser discovers that at one time she was also a prostitute. Before she can be successfully reunited with her husband and presumably restored to her present conventional life, her past must be brought to light just as the hidden drug world must be exposed. This is a plot trajectory characteristic of many of the other novels in the series.

Just as it is necessary to expose the truth of Lisa's past before she can hope to develop a lasting relationship with her husband, it is also necessary for the community of the small town to acknowledge the presence of the corruption created by the secret drug operations before it can hope to achieve some measure of corporate health. Although by the end of the novel it is implied that Lisa and Belson may be able to resolve their problems, it is more problematic for the body politic. Most of the underworld remains intact and capable of continuing its corrupting activities.

Spenser once again proves to be capable of rescuing the woman in distress, which allows Parker to explore such issues as stalking and other feminist questions about woman's empowerment, or lack thereof, but the narrative does not allow him to do more than raise these issues. As one of his continuing themes, the questions about women's powerlessness remain largely unanswered. One could read such a dilemma in two ways: either Spenser represents traditional patriarchal attitudes about women's need to be rescued and therefore provides a limiting view or he provides a more liberating attitude by uncovering the plight of women and exposing the injustices meted out against the sex. The critics have discovered both readings in the series.

◆ Techniques ◆

If anything, Parker's prose has become smoother and faster-paced in the later novels, and they now provide one of the quickest reads in contemporary crime writing. It is an achievement hardly equaled in the hard-boiled tradition. The quality of the prose, however, is deceptive and often leads critics to misperceive the larger qualities of the books. It is only on repeated readings that the accomplishments of Parker's writing become really evident. Spare, concise, tightly descriptive, these novels nevertheless provide one of the most carefully sustained and developed series going. His prose style has allowed Parker to explore the maladies of the contemporary world in both depth and clarity, and by keeping the narrative firmly focused on Spenser's consciousness, Parker has also been able to provide his readers with tales both surprising and satisfying, consistent and yet full of innovation.

Thin Air

Literary Precedents

No one can read the Spenser novels without recalling the Hammett/Chandler/Ross Macdonald tradition out of which he works. But, like so many other contemporary crime novelists, Parker plays with the particulars of the form. Spenser, while retaining many of the characteristics of Sam Spade, Philip Marlowe, and Lew Archer, does exhibit personal traits at odds with his predecessors. Parker has expanded and updated what was becoming an all-too predictable genre. In Spenser's relationship with Susan and his friendships within the police force Parker has made him much less of an outsider, more fully an individual. These changes are consistent with the achievements of many modern mystery writers, but Parker must be credited with being among the first to create a character so well rounded. Spenser is still a series figure who maintains a fairly consistent persona, but he is just less programmatically so.

Related Titles

Spenser of *Thin Air* can be fairly easily related to the character appearing in the previous Parker books. He also can be compared to such series as those of Michael Z. Lewin's featuring Albert Sampson or Ed McBain's Matthew Hope books, both of which contain a flawed, often very human protagonist of the soft-boiled type. William Tapply and George V. Higgins have mined the Boston environment and helped to establish a real tradition of crime fiction set in the area. But the Spenser of the novels has evolved in quite different ways, and his on and off relationship with Susan is quite unique

in both the prominence it receives in the books and in the importance it has on the developing character of the detective.

Ideas for Group Discussions

Because of the varying topical nature of the subjects dealt with in the Spenser series and because of the changing nature of the central figure, Parker's crime novels offer a particularly rich subject for discussion.

1. *Thin Air* offers an especially good starting point for discussing the entire run of books. An evocative way to begin might be to compare the character of Spenser in the first book *The Godwulf Manuscript* (1974) with his portrayal in a middle novel like *Early Autumn* (1981), to his appearance in this book of the series.

2. One could also trace the development of other characters like Susan Silverman or Hawk throughout the series.

3. Since Parker obsessively returns to the same themes, tracing their development would also prove interesting, especially since the books have evolved over time.

4. What about the use of setting through the books? Parker no longer confines himself to the Boston area and has had Spenser travel to other parts of the country in pursuit of his cases. How does he use these other locales? Are there similarities in the sense of place?

5. The Spenser books play with the idea of gender — what it means to be a

man or a woman. Is there a pattern in Parker's use of such a theme? If so, how so?

6. The group might read a classic hard-boiled detective novel like Hammett's *The Maltese Falcon* (1930) or Raymond Chandler's *The Big Sleep* (1939) and compare how these writers create character or use place or develop plot with how the same elements work in *Thin Air*.

7. Since Hawk functions as Spenser's alter ego, it has allowed Parker to explore sides of the detective and in ways unavailable to other writers in the mystery tradition. How has Parker worked this element of his fiction?

8. How does the presence of the Hispanic drug gang affect the novel? What ethnic questions does it raise?

9. How does the fact that both Hawk and Susan Silverman are largely missing from this Spenser book affect our reading of it in light of their importance in the other books in the series?

10. Through his connection with Frank Belson, Spenser seems to be more closely associated with the official forces of law and order in this book. Does that affect how we view his actions as a dispenser of justice?

Charles L. P. Silet
Iowa State University

THINGS FALL APART

Novel

1958

Author: Chinua Achebe

◆ Social Concerns ◆

As the title, taken from W. B. Yeats's poem "The Second Coming," implies, the chief social concern of *Things Fall Apart* is the undermining of traditional Igbo society as it is dominated and misunderstood by British colonizers bringing with them the Anglican Christian religion. Although the hero, Okonkwo, is a deeply flawed man, cruel to his wives and children, whose major tragic flaw is his fear of failure and an accompanying inflexibility, his ill-fated progress through the novel is as much the result of errors in judgment and inflexibility on the side of the British as his own. Consequently, rather than presenting Igbo society as a pristine one, and the British as totally evil, Achebe acknowledges faults on both sides and therefore creates a credible view of his own Igbo society.

While the Igbo have practices that are rigid and cruel, such as that of invariably throwing away twins and occasionally killing innocent hostages — the death of Ikemefuna inflicted in part by Okonkwo's own hand is the subject of much critical debate — they also have clan meetings to resolve disputes and a fair-minded flexibility in their encounters with the British and their religion. Furthermore, when the Igbo openness and flexibility are greeted by double crossing, as when the tribal elders are imprisoned, brutalized, and humiliated after they seek to make peace after the burning down of a church, the reader is encouraged to be sympathetic.

No matter what social forces are seen to be at play at any given moment in the novel, individual responsibility is never discounted. Things get worse when Mr. Brown, the flexible Anglican preacher, is supplanted by Mr. Smith, a fanatic. Likewise, the decision to kill Ikemefuma, prompted supposedly by Oracle of the Hills and the Caves, has severe repercussions, especially for Okonkwo. The fanaticism of Enoch, a Christian convert who unmasks an *egugwu* (a sacred impersonator of an ancestral spirit) is likewise condemned as it leads to the burning down of the church. Furthermore, the novel authenticates the spirituality of both Christian and Igbo religions, as transgressions of either belief by the fanatics of the other lead to dire consequences.

◆ Themes ◆

The novel was written in reaction to European assessments of African culture as found in Joseph Conrad's *Heart of Darkness* (1902) and Joyce Cary's *Mister Johnson* (1939) and some critics have seen in it an effort to reverse the European view, presenting Igbo society as enlightened and the European/British colonizers as in the dark. Rather, it is an attempt to present accurately Igbo society and what its people endured in the clash of their culture with that of the British. With so much apparently determined by British occupation and rule, one major theme is that of fate vs. free will. Much of the interest in the book lies in Achebe's subtle handling of these forces as the characters both British and Igbo are in turn manipulated by or appear to steer successfully around forces beyond their control.

Okonkwo can be seen as psychologically determined by his weak father to avoid the appearance of weakness at all costs, hence his killing of Ikemefuna. Yet his own tribesmen have exonerated him from having to take a hand in the killing so that his choice is not externally determined. Misunderstanding and rigidity by chiefly male characters on both sides exacerbate already strained conditions of the colonial system. Achebe is careful to point out elsewhere that the British did not export democracy to the colonies; rather they undermined it and tried to govern the Igbo, who had a form of democracy in place, by a hierarchical, totalitarian system.

The testing of conventional wisdom on both sides by experience is also a common theme that is carried out by Achebe's use of both Christian and Igbo beliefs, proverbs and stories. Thus the fanatical Mr. Smith relies on biblical stories "of sheep and goats," "wheat and tares," and of "slaying the prophets of Baal." Ironically, it is his extremism that in part leads to the burning down of the church. On the other hand, the Igbo allot part of the Evil Forest, a demonic location where twin babies are thrown away, for the building of the church. When the church then prospers and no parishioners are harmed, the Igbo religion is dealt a severe blow. Likewise, the Church finds a ready convert in Okonkwo's abused son, Nwoye, who is attracted by the "poetry of the new religion," having been ridiculed for liking the traditional Igbo tales told by women. Furthermore, pariahs called *osu*, people who as part of a priest caste are not given a place in the clan and are buried in the evil forest, are also drawn to the new religion, presaging the Igbo society's downfall through its own arbitrary social exclusions.

The arbitrary quality of traditional tribal custom is signaled also by the symmetrical blood crimes of Okonkwo, the killing of Ikemefuna, presumably a choice, and the accidental killing of a dead man's sixteen-year-old son at the man's funeral. Although he suffers severe remorse over his complicity in the first killing, the second one has been an accident. Yet the tribe punishes Okonkwo with banishment for the second killing and not at all for the first. Obierika, who has befriended Okonkwo both times, is totally puzzled, and the episode leads him to speculate about his own "throwing away" of his twins, also decreed by the Earth Goddess. The chapter ends with the poor man consoling himself with the proverb about collective guilt: "If one finger brought oil, it soiled the others."

The often unavoidable unfairness of

life apart from the ravages of colonialism is elsewhere also a prominent theme. Ekwefi, Okonkwo's second wife, has had ten children and nine have died before age three. She then gives birth to a daughter, Ezinma, who, because of the deaths of all her prior siblings, is assumed to be an *ogbanje,* a child who repeatedly dies and returns to its mother to be born. The recurrent deaths have happened despite all prayers and namings intended to avert the tragedy, and the fear, of course, is that Ezinma will die also. Although frequently sick, she does not, and her health is partly owing to the efforts of her father, who enlists medicine men, tends her when sick, and even follows Ekwefi when Ezinma is spirited away in the night by the Priestess Chielo. The episode is a validation of the marriage and human nurturing and in some sense of the power allotted to women in the seemingly sexist polygamal society.

Despite his magnanimity toward some British characters and his objectivity about the shortcomings of the Igbo, Achebe is justifiably engaged in a severe indictment of colonialism and its brutality. And his indictment is not without the irony that the British could have ruled more completely and efficiently, with less retaliatory bloodshed and arson on the part of the Igbo, had they ruled more intelligently. Frequently, it is blunders, not real rule, that ruffle the surfaces in Igbo land, the humiliation of the men called in peace to speak with the British, the fanaticism of Smith. The British district commissioner whose idea for a book, *The Pacification of the Primitive Tribes of the Lower Niger,* ends the novel, merely underscores the narrow point of view that Achebe has spent his whole novel trying to dispel.

◆ Characters ◆

The chief protagonist is Okonkwo, whose flawed but fascinating nature displayed against the backdrop of the encounter of the Igbo with the white man and his religion, has brought comparisons to Greek tragic heroes. Although his father has been poor — the Earth Goddess had never given him decent crops — Okonkwo is respected by the community in spite of that because of his character and his prowess at wrestling. Ironically then, it is his own psychological problem with his father's poverty, not some arbitrary limitation dictated by the gods, that leads to many of his other shortcomings, not the least of which is his constant desire to prove his virility. His narrow definition of what is masculine causes him to despise stories (and consequently the wisdom imparted in them) and words as the domain of women. He has a tender side, but squelches most tender impulses. Thus he is fond of his hostage "son" Ikemefuna, yet participates in his killing even after he is exonerated from having to do so. He maltreats his own son as too womanish, yet dotes on his daughter, the only surviving child of his second wife.

Okonkwo spends much of his early manhood building up wealth and position only to be banished when he accidentally shoots a boy at a funeral. Forced to flee to his mother's kinsmen in Mbanta, he is unable to consolidate his gains, although his friend Obierika brings him money and keeps him informed. In his absence, the Christian church makes inroads in Umuofia, and the nearby people of Abame have been slaughtered in retaliation for their killing of one white man. Soon the Christians find their way to Mbanta, where Okonkwo dismisses them as a joke, ironically just when his own son is being drawn to the faith. The exile period foreshadows tensions that will erupt into conflict once Okonkwo returns to Umuofia. In Mbanta, a Christian convert kills the sacred python, but as the perpetrator dies in his sleep, retaliation against the Christians is deemed unnecessary.

Upon returning to Umuofia after seven years banishment, Okonkwo discovers that many have converted to Christianity and that a more direct form of colonial rule has taken root, completely uprooting tribal justice and destroying families by imprisoning young men for long periods. When the good Anglican priest, Mr. Brown, tries to pay a visit, Okonkwo spurns him, still angry that his first son Nwoye has converted. When the fanatical Mr. Smith takes over, bad turns to worse as the fanatical Christian Enoch is unchecked and profanes the tribal religion by unmasking an *egwugwu*. Retaliation by the tribe takes the form of a church burning, which is in turn avenged by the ambush, beating, head-shaving, and other humiliation of the tribal delegation, including Okonkwo. He never recovers from the humiliation, and the first chance he gets, he murders a British messenger. Rather than die at the hands of the British, he commits suicide.

Other characters in the book are minor compared to Okonkwo. Of male characters, his best friend Obierika is the most fully drawn. It is Obierika who advises him early on that he does not need to take a hand in the death of Ikemefuna, and who saves what money he can for him during the seven years banishment. Obierika is a sort of neutral male character who often sees things a bit more clearly than his friend because he is less driven to prove himself. Yet at the novel's crisis points, Obierika too is confused and troubled, as when he muses about the gods' insistence on sacrifice of innocent life after Okonkwo is banished.

Okonkwo's father, Unoka, is sketched at the beginning of the book as a decided contrast to the son. He is a musician who spends money and never pays back what he borrows and is a coward in war — all this added to his poor luck with agriculture. Other male African characters who figure importantly in the plot as foils for Okonkwo are his son, Nwoye, whose lack of virility, love of stories, and defection to Christianity pain his father, and Enoch, the fanatic Christian who attacks the masqueraders of the spirits of the dead, incurring the burning of the church in retaliation.

British male characters include the two Anglican ministers, Mr. Brown and Mr. Smith, and the District Commissioner, whose bigoted idea for a book ends the novel. By far the most sympathetic of the three is the wise and tolerant Mr. Brown, who realizes that true success in converting the African depends on respect for the traditional Igbo religion. Mr. Smith, the fanatical Anglican with his either/or agenda, and the District Commissioner, with his utter lack of understanding and sympathy, are more typical of Europeans presented in Achebe's work.

Important female characters are Okonkwo's second wife, Ekwefi, and her only surviving child, Ezinma. Ekwefi was to have been the first wife, but he was too poor to marry her; after two years, she left her husband for him. As her babies die one after another, and she has to come to terms with the knowledge that she is the victim of an *ogbanje*, she not only gains stature through her suffering but is important because she is the only other character in the book besides Ikemefuna who brings out the gentle side in Okonkwo's nature. As the mother of the magical Ezinma, she is also a sort of heiress to the spiritual life of the tribe, which while apparently male-dominated is utterly dependent on the female Earth Goddess. She, along with her daughter, is the prototype for later, more complexly drawn and central female characters, like Beatrice in *Anthills of the Savannah* (1987).

◆ Techniques ◆

Achebe uses the traditions, narrative and otherwise, of two cultures in a highly allusive work that fully exploits their proverbs, tales, religious rituals, and customs. Narrative structure is only apparently simple in this novel. Okonkwo's life is evaluated in the light of both Igbo and Christian traditional values — values that often intersect. His fear of being thought of as weak causes him to negate the importance Igbo culture places on peaceful settlement of conflict and diplomacy. When telling stories to his children, he tells only tales of violence and bloodshed. Indeed, as critics have pointed out, his rigidity makes him resemble Old Testament figures from the Bible more than New. The sacrifice of Isaac is evoked both in his actual murder of Ikemefuna and his psychic murder of his own son Nwoye, who takes the name Isaac upon his conversion. (His accidental killing of a third male child causes his banishment.) The more rigid British characters, such as Mr. Smith and the District Commander then appear like his white counterparts. Achebe is able at the same time to use Christian values to expose what is arbitrary and cruel about the Igbo religion, such as the existence of the pariah *osu*, and the throwing away of twins, and the Igbo custom and belief to expose the absurdities and contradictions in the Christian/European perspective. The efforts of the missionaries in Mbanta (the place where Okonkwo is exiled) to explain the trinity right after telling the crowd that there is only one God are met with hilarious rejoinders.

References to the white prelates as albinos and officials wearing beige shorts as "ashy buttocks" have even led some critics to see the book as a reversal of Conrad's *Heart of Darkness* (1902) — the novel is presenting the white man as other and absurd, a sort of horror. Yet the existence of even one sympathetic Christian cleric in Mr. Brown seems to undercut this reading. Achebe is aware that the interplay between the two cultures has gone too far to be reversed, and the most optimistic moments in the book are those that point to the preservation of human values and productive lives despite the trauma of change. That Nwoye gains a productive life that he could not have had with his father is a blessing, as is the saving of his sister from the plight of the changeling.

The manipulation of proverbs, both Igbo and biblical, and the testing of them against experience is also a common technique. Mr. Smith fails because, unlike Mr. Brown, he wants to make Christianity more selective. "Narrow is the way and few the number," he argues, doubtless buttressed by scripture, and he is appalled by the pockets of ignorance of common doctrines. Sometimes, the experience the proverb is meant to contain is too large and unfathomable, and the proverb seems pasted on, as if the character is clutching at straws, as when Obierika tries to rationalize his throwing away of his twin children: "The Earth had decreed that they were an offense on the land and must be destroyed," and "If one finger brought oil it soiled the others."

A corollary to his concern with truths of two intersecting cultures is Achebe's problematical (at least for Western, more scientifically-minded cultures) substantiation of spiritual realities. The Ekwefi/Ezinma story is often cited in evidence of this aspect of his work. For not only are the Christians seen to err when they blatantly disregard Igbo beliefs, the spiritual is validated in both cultures and, among other things, provides a long view for lives and struggles of the characters. Okonkwo and Ezinma secure their daughter's chances for life and avert the fate of the *ogbanje* by careful vigilance and ritual, not by denying its reality or thwarting the belief irreverently.

Indeed, the hubris that denies belief and tradition appears to be the chief tragic flaw on both sides. At times the narrator will enter the point of view of Okonkwo in order to expose it ironically, as in the following passage:

> Nwoye knew that it was right to be masculine and to be violent, but somehow he still preferred the stories that his mother used to tell . . . stories of the tortoise and his wily ways . . . of the quarrel between Earth and Sky long ago.

The stories of the new faith, stories that Okonkwo has no use for along with the Igbo ones, draw Nwoye to it. This is but one of the opportunities for irony that Achebe makes use of throughout the book.

The novel follows a more or less sequential narrative line, although it is sometimes disrupted by flashbacks, as when the courtship of Ekwefi and Okonkwo is remembered after their vigil over Ezinma. Later novels, especially *Anthills of the Savannah*, are to exploit distortions of chronological sequence even more fully.

Other hallmarks of Achebe's style are his ability to intersperse Igbo and pidgin expressions where appropriate for context sketching characters, and to adapt English to the rhythm of his African language. His numerous translations of Igbo proverbs reflect this ability, and as he uses them he builds a serious respect for a culture little understood previously by Westerners.

◆ Literary Precedents ◆

Achebe wrote his first and most famous novel partly in response to two works by European writers whom he had found wanting in their view of Africa: Joseph Conrad's *Heart of Darkness* and Joyce Cary's *Mister Johnson* (1951). To quote his own famous essay on Conrad, "An Image of Africa: Racism in Conrad's *Heart of Darkness*," the European sets "Africa up as a foil to Europe, as a place of negations at once remote and vaguely familiar, in comparison with which Europe's own state of spiritual grace will be manifest." Africa's "triumphant bestiality" mocks European "intelligence and refinement"; it is projected as "the other world." Metaphors of silence and frenzy characterize Africa as a whole, and the people are treated as subhuman creatures lacking any real speech (they have only "a violent babble of uncouth sounds"). Conrad is "a purveyor of comforting myths," and only F. R.

Leavis was astute enough to complain about "Conrad's adjectival insistence on inexpressible and incomprehensible mystery." The falsification reaches its nadir in his caricatures of Africans as dancing dogs; Achebe notes especially the fire stoker on the boat. Achebe admits that it is the narrator, Marlowe, and a secondary narrator, who tell the story, but lacking an alternative frame of reference, he finds Conrad very close to Marlowe. That Conrad's racism was not picked up by white critics, argues Achebe, is owing to the in-grained nature of racism in our culture. Although Conrad saw the evils of im-perialism, his view was flawed because he did not connect it with racism. Al-though some critics have accused Achebe of being Conrad in reverse, his negative views of the British (often communicated through characters) are invariably qualified and balanced by his inclusion of many flawed African characters, and at least a sprinkling of wise British ones.

The case of Cary's *Mr. Johnson* (which Achebe considers "appalling") is dif-ferent and regarded by some critics as a step in the right direction that falls short of the mark. The novel centers on the building of a road — a task justi-fied as an incentive to commerce but one that finally makes unanticipated inroads into the African culture threat-ening it with dissolution. The breakup, however, is callously witnessed through the eyes of chief characters who are British. Achebe, as Christo-pher Wren has pointed out, shares the central proposition that colonialism destroyed African culture and does not posit anything in its place, and that events set in motion by colonialism have unpredictable results. Yet Achebe's vision of Africa, as evidenced by his fictional place Umuofia (op-posed to Cary's Fada), is one of a com-plex culture, and consequently the reader's view of it is more fully experi-enced. Achebe's novel has the advan-tage of the inside African view, and a more modern view, and a generous artistic vision that make it in many ways the larger and more important work.

◆ Related Titles ◆

As this is Achebe's first novel, there really are not any earlier related titles. *No Longer at Ease* (1960) can be consid-ered a sequel, as it tells the story of Okonkwo's grandson, who by being educated in England rises to a good position as a colonial civil servant only to meet his downfall when he takes a bribe. The book is narrated as a flash-back, and is less about the hero's moral culpability as it is about his being caught in the complex web of circum-stances and contradictions which colo-nialism has woven since the time of his grandfather. Like his grandfather, Obi Okonkwo has serious flaws, yet unlike his grandfather, his flaw is basically his indecisiveness, which ironically prompts him to leave the twenty pounds in marked bills on his desk as he ponders his predicament. His per-sonal life suffers from the same indeci-siveness and falls apart as well when he neglects his girlfriend Clara and she undergoes a botched abortion.

◆ Ideas for Group Discussions ◆

Achebe's *Things Fall Apart* is a ground-breaking novel, specifically African in vision, yet universal in themes and scope. The fictional time for the novel is around 1920, and although his locations are fictional, they are based on his actual experiences of life in an African village. Provocative areas for group discussion lie in comparisons of Igbo life and values to the European Christian culture that sought to supplant them, comparison of the African "hero" Okonkwo to predecessors in Western literature — he has been compared in his stature and flawed nature to the heroes of Greek tragedy, and the question of the problem of colonialism. Comparisons to his literary predecessor Joseph Conrad, and the question of whether Conrad was racist in his portrayal of Africa, especially when his novel is set against Achebe's fuller picture, will also stimulate debate. The charge some critics aim at Achebe — that his portrayals of Europeans make him a Conrad in reverse, may be evaluated.

The political situation in present day Nigeria is so alarming that many of Achebe's writings, this one included, have appeared prophetic. Bringing the values expressed in Achebe's novel to bear on the behavior of the present regime, and the West's reaction to it, may also be useful.

1. Okonkwo kills three people in the course of the novel. Look carefully at each of these episodes. Is he to be exonerated for any of the deaths? Is the killing of Ikemefuna premeditated, spontaneous, or done in obeisance to the Earth goddess? Do you believe Okonkwo's participation was necessary? The act has been compared to the biblical sacrifice of Isaac; do you see any parallels?

2. Mr. Smith can be called a fanatic compared to the more circumspect Mr. Brown; some have compared Smith's narrow views to the rigidity of Okon-kwo. Does such a comparison hold up?

3. Look carefully at Chapter 11 where Ekwefi and Okonkwo keep an all night vigil over their only daughter, Ezinma, and at the flashback in Chapter 12. How does this chapter qualify your view of Okonkwo? Is this a break in his character, or are there other places in the novel that work in a similar way?

4. Evaluate the relationship between Okonkwo and his son, Nwoye. Is Okonkwo's view of the masculine idiosyncratic or does he reflect the mores of his culture?

5. Umuofia benefits materially when the British and the Christians gain a foothold there. What is the author's attitude to this gain?

6. Evaluate the Igbo judicial system and compare it to that of the British.

7. How ingrained are Igbo customs? Are they sometimes changed?

8. Evaluate the position of women in Igbo society. Is the predominant deity a god or a goddess? Is storytelling primarily a male or a female activity? How does Okonkwo treat his three wives? Which wife suffers the most at his hands?

9. Compare Okonkwo to his father Unoka. How is the father used to explain the son's shortcomings? What shortcomings and strengths does the father have?

10. How does Achebe use proverbs, both Igbo and Christian, to comment on or assess the actions of the characters?

11. What appears to be the author's attitude about the Igbo custom of throwing away twins? How does this custom figure in the sacrifice of Ikemefuna? Note especially Nwoye's reaction.

12. Who is Okonkwo's favorite child? Why?

Elizabeth Q. Sullivan
State University of New York
Farmingdale

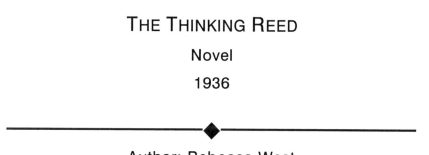

THE THINKING REED

Novel

1936

◆

Author: Rebecca West

◆ Social Concerns/Themes ◆

The most praised of West's novels, *The Thinking Reed* expands upon themes first set forth in *The Return of the Soldier* (1918). West's concern here is the malaise of Europeans after the First World War, a malaise created in fact by the war. The world through which Isabelle, the novel's main character, moves is a world without order, and the disorder which eventually results, symbolically, in the Stock Market Crash of 1929, looms near the novel's end. Through Isabelle's American perspective and her affairs with several European men, West critiques French and English, as well as American, culture after the war, finding culture without the order it had before the Great War.

Isabelle, an American from St. Louis, lives in France and in the course of the novel becomes involved with four different men: Laurence Vernon, an American whom she nearly marries; André de Verniers, a French aristocrat who is completely corrupt and decadent; Marc Sallafranque, an automobile manufacturer as corrupt as de Verviers; and Alan Fielding, an English painter who befriends her when her marriage

to Marc breaks up after she miscarries her child. These men represent certain aspects of society in decline, and Isabelle has only one lasting relationship (with Marc) with any of them.

These relationships have much to say about European society — conspicuous wealth, lack of real love, and shallow, materialistic thinking — but they also say much about Isabelle. West continually moves from a critique of society to a rather harsh critique of her main character. Isabelle cannot resolve what she knows with what she feels. Her intellect conflicts with her sexual and emotional needs, thus her marriage to Marc. Isabelle does not see the contradictions which surround her: She readily blames society for many others' problems but finds her own problems personal and individual. West heightens this conflict between self and society at the novel's end when Isabelle misunderstands her Uncle Honoré's dire warnings about the Stock Market. Marc and Isabelle have reconciled, and Isabelle refuses to allow society's problems to impinge on her personal happiness. West's society at the end of the novel is still disordered and on the brink of economic collapse. Isabelle's critiques of society ring ironically hollow as she does not heed her uncle's warning but is content, like those she often criticizes, to be concerned only with herself.

◆ Characters ◆

Isabelle is one of Rebecca West's most fully drawn characters, fraught with complex human contradictions and problems. Unlike the other characters in the novel who seem to stand for society in decline, Isabelle is a fully drawn modern woman for whom previously prescribed roles often do not apply. Her first husband, Roy, is killed before the novel's present time, providing Isabelle with freedom and money to go to France. Moreover, it is her American background and values she shared with her husband that provide a sense of loss, as well as the point of view necessary for her to look at European society. From this detachment, Isabelle tries to examine what she finds in Europe.

But Isabelle is more than a spokeswoman for West's condemnation of post-World War I Europe. Isabelle's emotions entangle her, in a very real way, in what she knows is wrong because Isabelle is also impulsive. Her reconciliation with Marc at the novel's conclusion is the result of her impulsive behavior. Yet one wonders at the novel's end if Isabelle can resolve the contradictions within herself to live happily with Marc as she promises him in their reconciliation scene when she says she will have his child.

◆ Techniques ◆

The novel is narrated by an omniscient, third-person narrator. West uses this technique for two reasons. One, she is able to use Isabelle as an instrument to critique European society, and, two, by creating narrative distance with Isabelle, West can also more forcefully point to the complexities in Isabelle's character. Thus West gains more with a third person narrator than with a first person narrator such as Jenny in *The Return of the Soldier*. West also uses the "off-stage" voice of Isabelle's Uncle Honoré, who communicates from America with Isabelle in Paris about financial matters. His letters to Isabelle provide a common sense, American counterpoint to the instability and turmoil of Isabelle's public and private worlds. West found Americans honestly straightforward when she visited America in the 1920s; certainly Uncle Honoré (and to an extent Isabelle) is modeled on her perceptions of Americans.

Again *The Thinking Reed*, like *The Return of the Soldier*, is controlled by West's use of irony. The contrasts between Isabelle's views of European society and her inability to act upon her critique is ironic. And Isabelle's refusal to act on Uncle Honoré's warnings about world economics in 1929 is an historical irony West plays with as Marc and Isabelle happily reconcile what the reader has seen is a bad marriage. In *The Thinking Reed*, West illustrates why many have called her a superb ironist.

◆ Literary Precedents ◆

Many novels contemporary to West's elaborate the social and cultural malaise of the 1920s caused by the First World War. In America, F. Scott Fitzgerald's *The Great Gatsby* (1925) illustrates the shallowness of the rich in the

Jazz Age. In England, Ford Madox Ford, D. H. Lawrence, and Virginia Woolf, in various modes, critiqued a valueless modern society. Behind all these writers lies T. S. Eliot's central critique of postwar modern society, the poem *The Waste Land* (1922). Many waste land motifs run through West's novel. And West's harsh condemnations of modern economics has precedent in the novels of Charles Dickens, such as *Bleak House* (1852-1853). Although these precedents provide a context for understanding West's novel, *The Thinking Reed* remains one of West's most original and innovative novels. And therein rests it popularity and value for the contemporary reader.

Stephen Mathewson
University of New Mexico

THIRST FOR LOVE

Novel

1950

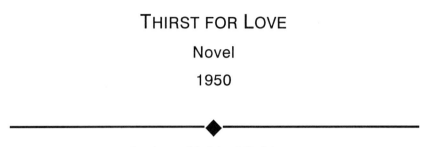

Author: Yukio Mishima

◆ Characters ◆

Thirst for Love is the story of a young widow, Etsuko Sugimoto, who becomes the mistress of her father-in-law, Yakichi Sugimoto. While living at his estate, Etsuko becomes infatuated with a young farmhand, Saburo, whom she kills when he tries to make the advances to her she seemed to be inviting. The work is complicated by a long flashback to the last illness of her husband, with typhoid fever from drinking polluted water, and her tireless efforts to keep Ryosuke Sugimoto alive so that he could continue to suffer the unassuageable thirsts of that ailment. That was her revenge for the torments his infidelities had caused her in the earlier years of their marriage. She, like the hero of *Confessions of a Mask* (1949), is a person twisted by her past who glimpses for a time, under the influence of sexual desire, something that seems like a way out of confusion. In the earlier work, readers are not told whether that young hero will find out that his way out is an illusion; there is no doubt that the heroine of *Thirst for Love* was happier with the illusion of loving her young farm hand than with the actuality of his amorous approach.

Minor characters include Saburo, the hired man; Miyo, the hired girl, pregnant with Saburo's child; Kensuke and Chieko Sugimoto, Etsuko's brother-in-law and sister-in-law, who live in the same dwelling with the rest of the characters and have their own interpretations of what is going on.

◆ Social Concerns/Themes ◆

In spite of the fact that Mishima associated with Japan's wealthy and titled people, particularly when he was a student, he seems to have held them in contempt. His presentation of the old man in this book — a company president now retired as a farmer — shines with that contempt. To some extent his attitude toward Japanese women was similarly unfriendly. In this work, therefore, he indulges in some sharp social satire of the men and women of station in Japanese society. The rather ignorant young man in the story, with his wholesome, earthbound values, seems to come off much better, particularly when he takes part in a wild country festival, an event in Japanese culture that Mishima always treated with reverence.

The principal theme of the novel is expressed in the ironic title. The love the woman endures from her father-in-law is like water to a person dying of typhoid fever: He longs for it, but it does him no good — perhaps even aggravates his torment, just as it was the cause of it at the beginning. Her love for the young farmer is the same thing in a twisted way: She longs for it but rejects it violently when it is offered to her.

◆ Techniques ◆

The use of symbolism in the title, with its relation to typhoid fever, is deft and unobtrusive. The technique by which the book begins (with Etsuko purchasing a pomelo to place on her husband's grave in the busy Osaka terminal) permits the reader to observe Etsuko carefully before he is apprised of her predicament. The exciting festival scenes, lighted by blazing bamboo trunks, underscore the fury of Etsuko's passion for Saburo.

◆ Related Titles ◆

Confessions of a Mask

Mishima rejected conventional morality and the precept that literature should serve a redeeming social purpose. Even so it is difficult for any of the Japanese to ignore the deep Confucian indoctrination their society exerts. On the surface the theme of *Confessions of a Mask* (1949), a somewhat autobiographical novel, is self-centered and rebellious. Underneath that surface there is a note of censure of the protagonist for his inability to marry and raise a family as his parents expect and, above all, for the lies that permitted him to dodge the draft and his opportunity to die for his country. Before he died Mishima himself would, however tardily, marry, father a family, and die shouting the name of the Emperor.

Confessions of a Mask is written in first person presenting the childhood and adolescence of a man with a history like the author's: brought up by a doting grandmother who did not allow him to play with boys his age, who seemed to be attempting to shut his mother out of his life, who surrounded him with adult female company and, when he was old enough, introduced him to the world of classical Japanese theater — the *Noh*, the *Bunraku*, and, most important, the *Kabuki*, all of them with male actors and reciters portraying female roles. *Confessions of a Mask* is engrossed with the problems of that child when he grows to manhood and tries to play a male role with women and in the war going on at that time. He seems to resolve his confusions in an infatuation with men: young, athletic, muscled, rank with the odors of exertion and even excrement.

The principal characters are: first, the unnamed first-person narrator, a young man filled with sado-homosexual desires attempting to will himself into normal heterosexuality; Sonoko, the vivacious girl who is attracted to him and whom he would like to bring himself to love and marry; Omi, the muscular older boy whom the protagonist loves from afar; several muscular, also unnamed, young men whom the narrator mentally undresses and dismembers with much blood and gore; and an unnamed prostitute whose failure to arouse the narrator sexually convinces him that his homosexuality is innate and incurable.

The book begins with an epigraph quoting Dostoevski on the beauty of sodomy. Its first chapter attempts to reconstruct the young narrator's life practically from the moment of his birth, spending several pages quibbling on whether he can remember his first hours out of the womb. The successive chapters continue with the reporting of adventures involving the narrator's sadomasochistic impulses and his efforts to stifle them and channel them elsewhere even though they bring him great joy.

The most ingenious technique lies in the disguising of the autobiographical connections in the novel. It is not necessarily a confession; it is at best a masked confession, whatever that is. Although it tells the story of a young man very much like Mishima, there are some glaring differences which Japanese scholars — schooled in autobiographical criticism — would mark. The title is used in a second sense in its implication that the narrator is playing a false part in society, which would disapprove of his real self if he showed it to them completely or even confessed all.

Japanese literature has a long tradition of confessional writing, ranging from the diaries of court ladies written a millennium ago to the I-novels of the late nineteenth and early twentieth centuries, and even the bowel-movement analyses of Mishima's beloved Junichiro Tanizaki (1886-1965). Mishima was also drawn to the writings of André Gide, Raymond Radiguet, Oscar Wilde, and Thomas Mann, which, with Guido Reni's painting of San Sebastian, would have given him many models for his developing book. Rousseau's *Confessions* (1782) and various of the works of De Sade come

most readily to mind when one thinks of Western titles possibly related to this work. Mishima seems also to have learned much about how to present the problems of young men in Goethe's works, notably *The Sorrows of Young Werther* (1774) and *Wilhelm Meister* (1777-1829). In Japanese literature, works of Ihara Saikaku (1642-1693) such as *The Life of an Amorous Woman* and particularly *The Life of an Amorous Man* show strong sexual-confession precedence at work even in the seventeenth century.

Forbidden Colors

In 1951 and 1952, Mishima published the two parts of *Forbidden Colors*, which is a frank and, in some ways, scholarly sequel to *Confessions of a Mask*. The author took notes for it while visiting gay bars in Tokyo, always accompanied by a representative of his publisher. It is the story of a young man with homosexual inclinations who, urged by an ailing mother, is about to enter what he fears will be a disastrous marriage. He tells his troubles to a rich old author, who pays him to marry the girl and wreak revenge on certain coy women friends by leading them on sexually and disappointing them. The novel continues with narration of the progress of the marriage, including a graphic description of the birth of the couple's child; with several disastrous heterosexual encounters, as planned; and with a number of homosexual adventures, presented at times with wonder, at times with disgust, and frequently with humor. Throughout, the reader is given a running commentary on the ruses, the lore, the joys, the sadness, and the explosive bitterness of the homosexual world.

Because of the arrangements Mishima made for studying the world of the Japanese homosexual, he was able to present his material in this work at times with a degree of detachment. At times it is almost reportage. The reader is informed about how the denizens of the gay bar seek sexual partners, how restlessly they move from one lover to another, how they suffer when favored relationships go sour. Readers become guests at a gay party, witnesses to an attack by a huge American on a small Japanese. Readers are told what it means when a rich bachelor takes a handsome young man into his household or as his guest on a trip abroad, what it means when a bachelor is said to have forsworn marriage because a girl he loved died when they were young. Beneath all the exclamations about beauty and ecstatic unions, there is a note of dissatisfaction and despair over the fragility of homosexual love affairs.

The principal character may be a handsome young man named Yuichi, with a body "like the Apollo molded in bronze by an artist of the Peloponnesus school." Rivaling him for domination of the novel is Shunsuke Hinoki, an old author suffering from various ills of old age who counsels the young man on his marriage and, at the beginning, even on the homosexual adventures which he, the old author, has never known. Another character is Yuichi's suffering and invisible wife, Yasuko. Then there is Mrs. Kaburagi, a flashy, immoral woman whom Shunsuke has tried unsuccessfully to seduce and Yuichi successfully attracts and frustrates. Another woman, named Kyoko, whose principal fault seems to be that she is empty-headed, is similarly treated. There are also the many homosexual lovers of Yuichi, one of whom is a

captain of industry, another of whom is Mrs. Kaburagi's husband — a nobleman, in fact — Count Kaburagi.

The most striking technique lies in the presentation of the complex relationship binding the young author Yukio Mishima — still in his twenties at this time — the old author Shunsuke Hinoki, and the young man Yuichi Minami (note the initials). The confessional complexity of *Confessions of a Mask* seems to be at work again. It seems possible that the old author represents "Mishima the detached reporter" or perhaps "Mishima the man of experience," who is giving the young man so close to being the author himself advice on his life — which is, after all, bound closely to the novel being written — as well as the connection between his sexuality and art. The book was described in *Time* as portraying "posh lust."

♦ Adaptations ♦

Thirst for Love was produced by Kazu Otsuka in 1967 and directed by Izen Kurahara. The film does not follow the plot of the novel very closely, but the essentials are there: the brooding sexual frustration of the heroine, the prying of the relatives around her, the virile strength of the young man she is fascinated by.

The Temple of the Golden Pavilion (1959) was made into the film *The Conflagration (Enjo)* in 1958, directed by Kon Ichikawa. It emphasizes the protagonist's disgust at his father's weakness and his mother's sexual infidelities as the root causes of his deviation. Ichikawa has considered it the film he enjoyed most.

The story "Patriotism" was made into the film *Rite of Love and Death* in

1965. It was directed by Mishima himself, with the assistance of Masaki Domoto. First shown in Paris with French subtitles in September of 1965, it was runner-up for the Grand Prix at the Tours Film Festival held in January of 1966. It established box office records when it started appearing in Japan in April of the same year. The plot follows the story all too closely. The story is a shocker; the film is worse.

Alfred H. Marks
SUNY at New Paltz

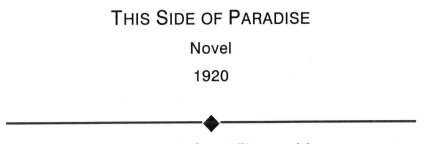

THIS SIDE OF PARADISE

Novel

1920

♦

Author: F. Scott Fitzgerald

◆ Characters/Techniques ◆

Amory Blaine is Fitzgerald's conception of what he would like to have been in his first two decades. He is full of idealistic innocence with naive ideas about courage, honor, and duty. He sees himself as a natural aristocrat who has an exalted if nebulous destiny surely to be realized. The Monsignor, based on a very admired older friend Sigourney Fay, represents wisdom and spiritual enlightenment. He is a guide to Catholic morality and social values. Rosalind Connage is a New York debutante, wealthy and desirable, a version of the modern American woman in rebellion against the strictures of family and social expectations. Eleanor Savage is a kind of "reckless romantic" whose self-destructive tendencies are both exciting and disturbing for Blaine, who is too conventional to really become involved with her. Rosalind is patterned after Fitzgerald's wife Zelda, and the young poet Thomas Parke D'Inviliers is based on his friend at Princeton John Peale Bishop. Fitzgerald worked with a method he called "transmuted autobiography," and the innovative aspects of the narrative, including plays and verse, are deviations from strict autobiographical chronology caused by Fitzgerald's inability to handle the two narrative voices, Blaine's and the novelist's.

◆ Social Concerns/Themes ◆

Like many first novels, *This Side of Paradise* is largely autobiographical. Amory Blaine, the protagonist, is drawn from Fitzgerald's adolescence and young manhood. The narrative follows Blaine from his relatively pampered childhood, where he had a very close relationship to his mother, through the difficulties of adjusting to the outside world in prep school and then on through his development as a "romantic egoist" at Princeton. The years at Princeton represent the first genuinely realistic depiction of American college life, and suggest that life on the campus is exciting and intellectually stimulating. For aspiring collegians, the first part of *This Side of Paradise* was like a guidebook, offering suggestions about how to behave socially, and some sense of the curriculum, mentioning sixty-four titles and ninety-eight writers. Fitzgerald later called the book "A Romance and a Reading List," and the romantic element included Blaine's unsuccessful courtship of Isabelle Borge.

The second part of the book follows Blaine's attempt to realize his destiny through a commitment to a religious vision of morality. Monsignor Darcy, the most sympathetic character in the book, encourages Blaine's search for religious meaning; and, although he is not able to convince Blaine to go to Rome, he is able to give him a firm sense of good and evil. This moral sense is tested by two romantic interludes. Blaine is unnerved when he loses Rosalind Connage because of his meager financial resources but turns to spiritual matters for some consolation. When he has a brief affair with Eleanor Savage, who is alluring but too wild for him, he finds similar comfort in justifying his behavior in terms of the nature of sin. His attempts to develop "personagehood" to compensate for his romantic disappointments is a kind of quest in which he hopes to fulfill his destiny by becoming a "leader" who serves humanity by his wisdom and moral guidance.

◆ Ideas for Group Discussions ◆

Many readers have found in this youthful performance by Fitzgerald a sense of the author's testing his talent, trying to determine which narrative strategies "work" and which fail. Discussion could focus on the ways in which the author seems to be attempting various approaches to the task of creating a worthy text: for example, a quote from "Casey Jones," the use of subheads (as with "The Philosophy of the Slicker"), and the inclusion of "poetic" passages at the close of chapters (in italics).

Since the book is clearly "experimental," some thought could be given to the question of its length. Given the tightness of a The Gatsby (1925), readers, when considering This Side of Paradise, might consider whether the novel is too long (more than twice the length of Gatsby) and, if so, what parts could be excised, without damage to the thematic effects.

When thinking of characterization, readers often try to judge whether a given personage in a novel is truly "round" or simply "flat," in E. M. Forster's terms. For instance, are the female characters truly "developed" or simply convenient devices in the creation of Amory's personality and experience?

1. Is Amory's attempt to achieve "personage" comparable to the efforts, sometimes seen today, of many people to attain "self-actualization," or a similar advanced state of personality development?

2. Is the book a genuine *bildungsroman*? Is the "quest" theme adequately developed?

3. Are the digressive "asides" of verse and drama too distracting to allow a clear grasp of the text? Is the plot excessively episodic?

4. Is the picture of college life in the 1920s too idealized? Is the notion of a true "liberal education" so outmoded that Fitzgerald's vision seems like ancient history — or, is it still relevant today?

5. How might Amory's relationships with Rosalind and with Eleanor be contrasted? Do the surnames Connage

and Savage suggest any symbolic intent by the author, such as "to connote, or mean" and "untamed"?

6. Does the element of Catholicism in the novel seem fully sincere (especially in view of Fitzgerald's own lapse of commitment to his faith)? Does the element provide an added dimension of moral significance to the book?

Leon Lewis
Appalachian State University
[Ideas for Group Discussions
by Fred B. McEwen,
Waynesburg Collge]

THE THORN BIRDS

Novel

1977

Author: Colleen McCullough

◆ Characters ◆

Although the priest, Ralph de Bricassart, occupies fewer pages in *The Thorn Birds* than the protagonist Meggie, his character has occasioned the most comment. Extremely good looking, compared by some critics to Rhett Butler, he never takes advantage of his looks to accept the many sexual opportunities afforded him, except for his brief lapse with Meggie. However, his ambition helps him connive to inherit a fortune which would have gone to Meggie's family, the Clearys. Ralph is a man destined to power, and one who wields it well and effectively, largely for the good of others. We see him, a bishop in the Curia in Rome in 1943, standing up to the German General Kesselring, and almost immediately later showing pity and compassion to a frightened, bewildered, yet intelligent and determined young German soldier who has become locked in St. Peter's basilica after coming there to pray.

The three Cleary women include Fiona (mother of Meggie and seven sons), a woman disillusioned and worn out by betrayal and overwork; Meggie, who seems to lose her love twice, when Ralph forsakes her in order to remain in the priesthood and when her son by Ralph joins the priesthood and dies young in a drowning accident; and Meggie's daughter, the willful and strangely unattractive Justine, who becomes an actress and attempts to have all the liberation and freedom her mother and grandmother missed.

Fiona, also known as Fee, loves her children, especially her oldest son, fiercely and unconditionally, but is unable to show the emotion that another woman might have felt naturally; work and hard life have crippled her ability to show her fierce love. That she loves her children is shown in the beginning of the novel when, although very poor, she nonetheless buys Meggie a doll for her birthday.

Meggie, the novel's central character, is buffeted by love and strives against her love for Ralph and her desire for a better life for herself and her family. Her fierce devotion to Drogheda, her ranch, keeps her going through many setbacks. When her son Dane dies, Meggie uses the fact that Dane is Ralph's son as well to try to get Ralph to use his influence to bring Dane home for burial.

Fiona's husband, Meggie's father,

Paddy Cleary is a hardworking, simple, good hearted, and perpetually bewildered man who dies early. A man who believes in old ways and in keeping in one's place, he cannot afford for his children to remain in school, needing them on the home place to work; he believes as well in the strict delineation between woman's work and man's work. Both policies are hard on Fee and her eldest son, Frank, and this creates a rift between father and son. He is a character who imbues in his children the capacity for hard work and love for the land; an Irishman, he fled to New Zealand, where the novel begins, after killing an Englishman.

Paddy's sister, Mary Carson, is a hardhearted, wealthy, evil woman, who is infatuated with Ralph de Bricassart and leaves most of her vast fortune to him and the church. She dies after throwing a grand party on her seventy-second birthday, announcing that she will die that night; she does.

◆ Social Concerns/Themes ◆

The author's most popular book is her most purely entertaining, with few overtly moral messages, as it traces three generations of an Australian family from 1915 to 1969. It does, however, show the subjugation and lack of freedom for the women who are dependent on men and have few options without them. They register some prefeminist protests, but only the woman of the third generation breaks away for a life of her own, and it is not satisfactory either until she marries, which is the last event in the novel.

The central character, Meggie, carries a lifelong love for an ambitious priest, Ralph de Bricassart. It is briefly consummated, resulting in an illegitimate son (who later becomes a priest); she also has a daughter by a man she marries (unhappily) mainly because he resembles Ralph. The forces that keep Meggie and Ralph apart dominate the story, including the priest's inevitable placing of his job (and his incredible and successful ambition) ahead of his love.

In the character of the priest, Ralph de Bricassart, the novel also touches on the demands of the religious life, the sacrifices required, the impossibility of achieving spiritual perfection. We see Ralph loving and desiring Meggie, but knowing that he is best suited to the high offices in the Church that he eventually holds.

◆ Techniques ◆

What keeps *The Thorn Birds* from being a potboiling soap opera is the author's gift for atmosphere and description. She details animals, plants, and city and country life of Australia through several generations and contrasting regions. She includes spectacular storms, fires, and a variety of landscapes, as well as several detailed battle and war scenes, which vividly evoke a time and place which are strange and exotic to most readers. Through McCullough, we see the desert of North Africa, the jungles of New Guinea, the labyrinthine corridors of the Vatican, and the broad sweep of the Australian plain.

In addition, and as noted by critics such as Walter Clemons, the novel's dialogue is very dramatic and even declamatory. While it can be said to be unrealistic, it can also be said that the relentless drama of the dialogue and the almost *deus ex machina* nature of events serve to keep the novel's pace moving through several hundred pages and fifty-four years of history.

◆ Literary Precedents ◆

The Thorn Birds was generally referred to as an Australian *Gone With the Wind* (1936), hence the frequent comparisons of Ralph to Rhett Butler. Meggie, however, bears no serious resemblance to Scarlett O'Hara — except perhaps that both women are survivors. Her family is only faintly reminiscent of the aristocratic Georgia families such as the Wilkses or O'Haras. Meggie has Drogheda, like Scarlett has Tara; both women bear a deep love for the land — their land.

In a situation reminiscent of the famous play and movie *The Hasty Heart*, and faintly recalling *One Flew Over the Cuckoo's Nest* (1962), a newcomer into the group stirs up conflicts, repressed sexual passions in both sexes, resulting in breakdowns, violence, and three deaths.

◆ Related Titles ◆

An Indecent Obsession (1981) combines several elements of *Tim* (1974) and *The Thorn Birds* but is more melodramatic and perhaps more unpleasant than either. It concerns a nurse, significantly named Honour, caring for six men who suffer various psychological and physical disorders in a tropical hospital ward at the end of World War II (and falling in love with, and having a brief love affair with, a newcomer to them). As in *Tim* there is much talk of brain and mental handicaps, and the central situation of a reserved woman who "thaws." As in *The Thorn Birds,* she (like Ralph de Bricassart) is torn between love and duty. In fact, she comes to feel that duty is "the most indecent obsession of all."

The Thorn Birds perhaps presages the Roman novels with its partial concentration upon the focus of one family caught up in the great sweep of world history. However, except for Ralph, and unlike most of the Roman characters, the Cleary family are not major actors in history, but instead are largely acted upon, whereas the Romans are largely causers and instruments of their own fates.

◆ Adaptations ◆

The 1983 ten-hour miniseries of *The Thorn Birds* was one of the top-rated television events of its year and one of the most popular miniseries yet made, with Richard Chamberlain, who had been popular in his miniseries role of John Blackthorne in the miniseries of James Clavell's *Shogun* a few years earlier, receiving much publicity for his portrayal of Ralph. Rachel Ward portrayed Meggie, Mare Winningham portrayed her daughter Justine, Philip Anglim played the role of Meggie and Ralph's son Dane, and Ken Howard played Rainer (the young German soldier Ralph meets and who, in a not-too surprising coincidence, meets and later marries Justine). Other characters, such as Fee, were de-emphasized, and McCullough's vivid settings were not fully utilized. The relatively short role of Mary Carson was built into a panting emotional showcase for veteran star Barbara Stanwyck, who won an Emmy award for her work.

The mini-series spanned the time between 1920 and 1962 but omitted the years around the time of World War II when Meggie was raising her children and Father Ralph was in Rome. The 1996 CBS four-hour film, *The Thornbirds: The Missing Years*, starring Chamberlain, Amanda Donohoe and Maximilan Schell, returns to the war years, when Meggie's estranged husband (Schell) returns to Drogheda to rekindle the passion and anger of their tormented marriage. Father Ralph is torn between his love for Meggie, his love for God, and his love for the glamour and power of the church.

♦ Ideas for Group Discussions ♦

The Thorn Birds contains much material on the ways that families deal with crises, especially large social crises like droughts, war, social class issues, and spiritual and personal subordination, but also more intimately related issues, such as emotional crippling, unplanned pregnancy, and death. As *The Thorn Birds* has been criticized as a "potboiler" type of book, a good discussion might begin by examining how realistic these issues are as they are presented in the novel, especially as they are presented in light of their chronological context.

1. Discuss the role of Fee and Paddy Cleary. Are they good parents? Could or should they have been better?

2. Is Mary Carson a completely evil or bad character, or does her desire for Ralph humanize her in any way?

3. Is Dane's death from drowning an expected event? Can you see it foreshadowed in the novel? Or is it simply a convenient plot device?

4. Why does Meggie tell Ralph that Dane is his son, and why does it have the effect on him that it does?

5. Ralph De Bricassart is a Catholic priest, and eventually a cardinal. Yet he breaks his vows and fathers a son with Meggie. Does this make him a bad person? Does it make him more human?

Robert D. Whipple, Jr.

Dudley Brown
Allegany Community College

THORNYHOLD

Novel

1988

Author: Mary Stewart

◆ Characters ◆

Gilly is the central character of *Thornyhold*, and her growth and maturing is the core of the novel. As she blossoms from a shy, sad girl into a lovely and loving young woman, we see the events through her eyes. All the other characters are minor and shadowy. The mischievous, seductive Mrs. Trapp, the handsome recluse writer Christopher John, and the retarded, brutish but somewhat pitiful Jessamy are almost stereotyped in their roles as the evil witch, the prince charming, and the monster. The fairy-tale parallels are prominent. Gillian is the sleeping beauty. When she arrives at Thornyhold, she is shy and insecure, and her personality and emotions have not been allowed to grow — she is truly in a sleep. It takes a fairy godmother to counteract the spell that her harsh and uncaring mother has thrown over Gilly's life. At the magical place of Thornyhold, she is awakened by her love for Christopher John. Since it is her story, she is the only character who grows and changes and reveals depth. The others remain flat personalities whose role is simply to promote Gilly's growth. Even Christopher John, her Prince Charming, is seen only through her eyes and is not a rounded character. This does not detract from the enjoyment of the novel, since the reader identifies and knows Gilly intimately, and thus is able to share her emotional flowering.

◆ Social Concerns ◆

A lonely, harsh childhood has left Gilly Ramsey with low self-esteem and a joyless life. The only special moments she has experienced are due to the occasional appearance of her Cousin Geillis who introduces Gilly to the beauty around her. Wherever cousin Geillis is, there is magic, and magic becomes intertwined with reality when she leaves Gilly her house at Thornyhold. The shy, timid young girl discovers powers and insights she never knew she had, but she also encounters a darker side of magic — witchcraft. Like Sleeping Beauty, she is awakened to the magic of life and eventually to love. Thus the novel traces the growth and personality of a young woman to the full flowering of love and self-esteem. The topic of maturing and growing up has always been of interest to readers, and the romantic fulfillment of love is a popular element of romance fiction. Mary Stewart has created a number of young, self-reliant heroines who reflect both the desire of independence, and a need for a close, personal relationship. In true romantic style, they achieve the best of both worlds. They are modern women, but "the knight on the white charger" still arrives to carry them off into the sunset of love.

◆ Themes ◆

Mary Stewart uses an almost fairy-tale-like setting and theme to illustrate the various elements of magic. There is the magic of beauty that Gilly discovers in the old house and gardens, a setting that is reminiscent of the castle of Sleeping Beauty with its surrounding hedge of thorn bushes, and as in Sleeping Beauty, there is also evil magic of the uninvited bad fairy. Here she is Mrs. Trapp, a neighbor, who dabbles in darker secrets, opiates and dream-inducing states. But her evil is not taken too seriously and has an almost comic side. Mrs. Trapp is a witch, but a fairly inept one who cannot always predict the outcome of her "spells," and in the end becomes a victim of her own sorcery. Gilly, on the other hand, seems to have some real powers that she does not understand, and her mysterious cousin Geillis was known to the neighbors as a witch, albeit a good one. Yet this is a light-hearted novel, and the conflict between good and evil magic takes on a humorous aspect as Gilly and Mrs. Trapp compete for the favors of an eligible man, the writer Christopher John. Like Shakespeare's early comedies, the forest world of *Thornyhold* is one of hu-

mor, sometimes bordering on the ridiculous. There are lovers' quarrels, misunderstandings, misplaced love potions, and the ending is in the true fairy tale style — "they lived happily ever after."

◆ Techniques ◆

From the beginning, there is a strong hint of the supernatural, starting with the mysterious Cousin Geillis. She appears and disappears unexpectedly, always bringing laughter, joy, and a sense of wonder to lonely Gilly. The mystery is strengthened with the seemingly uncanny prediction Geillis makes of her own death, and her promise that she would always be there for Gilly. When white doves bring Gilly messages from her dead relative, it seems as if Cousin Geillis was really a witch, although a benign one. Yet Stewart always provides a logical explanation for the miracles — the doves were really sent by Christopher John at the request of Cousin Geillis before her death, and the mysterious experiences of Gilly during her midnight journey to the gathering of the witches turns out to be an illusion created by Mrs. Trapp's potions. Stewart leads the reader deep into a fairy tale, and then returns him with a laugh to reality, but a very pleasant and romantic reality. And yet, in the final conclusion when all seems clear and logical, there is the comical result of a magic love potion, and we are left with the question, do Mrs. Trapp, Gilly, and her aunt really possess magic powers?

As in most of her novels, Stewart's strength lies in her ability to create a place and atmosphere, but unlike *My Brother Michael* (1959, which is set in modern Greece, and *Airs Above the*

Ground (1965), which takes place in Austria, *Thornyhold* does not have a geographically accurate setting. Instead, it is simply a green place in the English countryside, surrounded by thick woods and a huge thorn hedge. There are gothic elements, romance, suspense, and a pleasing and entertaining melange that is difficult to classify. Although quite different from Shakespeare's play, there is *A Midsummer Night's Dream* (c.1600) quality to the setting and the events. Magic is pervasive, although not always taken seriously, and in the end, magic and setting are one, when Gillian's granddaughter says: "I sometimes think that Grandmother could have been a witch if she had wanted to."

♦ Literary Precedents ♦

Unlike Stewart's earlier mystery/romance novels, *Thornyhold* does not have any references to contemporary places and events. It has the character of a modern fairy tale, an updated Sleeping Beauty. Many fairy tale stereotypes are used — the fairy godmother who mysteriously appears and always seems to know what Gillian is thinking, the animals that bring messages, even Gillian's bleak early childhood that echoes the trials of Cinderella and other suffering fairy tale heroines.

The woods and landscapes surrounding *Thornyhold* are romantic settings, peopled by benign rustic characters. The lovers, rustics and fairies of Shakespeare's *A Midsummer Night's Dream* (c.1591-1596) would have been right at home in the forest surrounding the old house of Thornyhold.

♦ Related Titles ♦

Although *Thornyhold* shares certain aspects of mystery and romance with Mary Stewart's earlier novels, it is an independent work. Unlike such novels as *My Brother Michael* or *Airs Above the Ground*, it lacks elements of realism, international intrigue, and reference to contemporary events.

♦ Ideas for Group Discussions ♦

Mary Stewart's *Thornyhold* is a romance. Romances and romantic ideas date, historically, to the Middle Ages where popular stories, told for a courtly audience, spun yarns of noble knights who saved damsels in distress and suffered incredibly for the sake of love. They dealt with a never-never world, and even during the Middle Ages were far removed from a harsh reality. Today, romances no longer tell about knights and supernatural adventures, but the basic elements are still there — the noble rescuer, the young woman in distress, and the "they lived happily ever after" ending. Often looked down upon as escapist literature, they form a very enduring type of writing. The reasons for their popularity, and the elements they embody, could serve as stimulating basis for discussions on the literary merit of the romances, the reasons why they have retained their popularity through the centuries, and the light they shed on the wishes and of modern society.

1. Mary Stewart deliberately creates mystery that hints at the supernatural, yet finds a perfectly rational explanation. How does she manage to make the reader believe?

2. Does Stewart say that there is magic? Does she say there is not? Does the reader know where she stands? If not, what effect is she creating?

3. There is some real evil in the events surrounding the intended sacrifice of the dog Rags. Yet Stewart turns it into a positive experience. Why? The true fairy tale does not shy away from villains and monsters and dark magic. Yet in this novel, these are only hinted at and turn out to be relatively harmless. Is this a weakness of the novel?

4. Gilly is much less of a modern independent heroine than the young women in other Stewart novels. Why? Does the reason have something to do with the romantic fairy tale character of this story? Are young, independent, self-assured women unsuitable for true romantic heroines? Does Stewart reach back for older female stereotypes?

5. What techniques does Stewart use to build up suspense? Does the rational solution of the seemingly magical events make the reader feel let down? Why or why not?

6. What is the true magic in this story?

Ingeborg Urcia
Eastern Washington University

A THOUSAND ACRES

Novel

1991

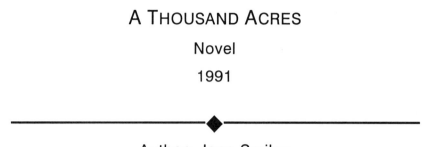

Author: Jane Smiley

◆ Characters ◆

A Thousand Acres, set on a farm in Iowa, has a large cast, but the primary character is Ginny Cook Smith. The reader experiences events through Ginny's eyes. Deeply immersed in the routines of marriage, housekeeping, and farming, Ginny has not actually examined herself, her family, or her neighbors critically. This passivity has served her well during what — until she reaches her mid-thirties — appears to have been an uneventful life

However, once her father decides to transfer ownership of the farm, Ginny must examine herself, her family, and her neighbors. She gradually realizes that under the placid surface lie agendas she has not recognized. Initially, she concentrates sympathetically on her father whose erratic, irrational, and drunken conduct baffles and eventually horrifies her. In her own eyes she has done nothing to justify "Daddy's" denunciations. In her concern, Ginny consults frequently with her sister Rose who reveals secrets about their father's incest which stagger Ginny but reawaken submerged memories. Her concept of Rose, too, undergoes change as Rose reveals the dynamics of her

marriage to Peter Lewis, a former musician who made an uneasy truce with farming to marry her.

Ginny herself discovers her own sexual confusion when she finds herself increasingly attracted to Jess Clark. Jess brings news of different lifestyles, including organic farming and vegetarianism. Fascinated by Jess, Ginny eventually commits adultery, but the affair quickly ends when events become frantic and Jess's romantic interest turns elsewhere, namely to Rose, whose husband Peter has committed suicide. Ty Smith does not learn of Ginny's affair, although he may suspect it, but the stress of managing the farm, especially after the death of Peter Lewis, cools his relationship with his wife.

Ginny's realization of the self-centeredness of those around her and their exploitation of her naivete drive her into flight. She returns only when Rose on her death bed asks her to look after her two daughters.

Besides the central family, Smiley provides a fairly large supporting cast. Of crucial importance is the Clark family, in which a similar transfer of power has created a similar crisis involving Jess, his brother Loren, and their father Harold, who toys with his two sons over which one will inherit the property. Other community members include Marv Carson, a banker whose eagerness to modernize the Cook farm with easy credit eventually plunges them into debt and bankruptcy, Henry Dodge, the ineffectual pastor of the local Lutheran church, and Mary Livingstone, an older woman who was a friend of Ginny's mother and who supplies crucial information about the dead woman.

◆ Social Concerns ◆

Through a crisis in the Cook family precipitated by Laurence Cook's seemingly impetuous decision to turn ownership and management of his Iowa farm over to two of his daughters, Rose and Ginny, and their respective husbands, Peter Lewis and Ty Smith, and to disinherit his third daughter, Caroline, Smiley explores the history of settlement, development, and dispersal of a Midwestern farm community. Besides indicating the courage, determination, and greed that motivated the founding pioneers, Smiley focuses on the price that succeeding generations paid for both material success and failure — the single-minded dominance of the men and the passive anonymity of the women. These characteristics lead to suicide and emotionally stunted lives, which are further injured physically by accidents and the long-term effects of pesticide pollution — cancer and infertility. Thus, as families break up under the never-ending pressures of weather, isolation, market fluctuations, and bank foreclosures, agribusinesses buy up the bankrupt farms, remove the houses, and establish massive industrial farms. Family survivors disperse to the metropolitan areas to become wage earners or, if they have the education, professionals.

◆ Themes ◆

Central to A Thousand Acres is the theme that the transfer of power from one generation to the next is fraught with tension, the older persons regretting the loss of power, the younger chaffing for responsibility. The consequences of the transfer are that buried secrets can resurface and that established relationships may collapse. Smiley uses an Iowa farm family to develop her King Lear-like situation.

Ginny Cook Smith, the point of view character, has led a seemingly placid life into her mid-thirties, the only significant disappointments being the death of her mother while she was a teenager and five miscarriages during her marriage. Otherwise, she expects to lead the routine life of a farmer's wife for the remainder of her days. The events following her father's decision to transfer ownership and management of the farm to Ginny, her sister Rose, and their husbands force her to examine her relationship with her parents, her siblings, and her spouse. Her father's decision to disinherit his third and youngest daughter Caroline, a lawyer, is the first sign that all will not go well.

As Laurence Cook's behavior becomes more erratic and vitriolic following the transfer, Ginny realizes that she has not understood him and his motives. As she tries to reconstruct her childhood and youth, she discovers that he has abused and thwarted her, especially after her mother died. Her sister Rose's revelation that their father's domination included incest dredges up submerged memories for Ginny. She is torn between anger against her father and a desire for a reconciliation based on his sense of remorse, a remorse that is impossible as he steadily slips into mental incompetence.

Ginny's relationship with her sisters becomes increasingly complex. Initially she sees Rose as her ally and confidant because they have lived and worked in close proximity for years. After the death of their mother, their father made them close because they had to keep house for him and Caroline. Later, Caroline complicates matters by joining their father in a suit to void the transfer of the farm, charging mismanagement. Further complicating Ginny's relationship with her sisters is that Ginny envies Rose her two daughters, Pam and Linda, whom Ginny often "mothers." To make matters worse, Ginny discovers that she and Rose are rivals for the affections of Jess Clark, the recently arrived prodigal son of a neighbor, who has returned to Iowa after a decade's absence. Ironically, both Rose and Ginny admire Caroline because she has escaped the farm and made a modern career for herself.

Ginny's marriage to Ty Smith is also tested by the crisis. Ty, the son of a relatively poor farmer, is disappointed by his wife's miscarriages and has given up hopes of having children. However, the transfer of the farm energizes him and his brother-in-law Peter Lewis into developing an ambitious plan to increase hog production. For both men it is their chance to prove their farming skill free of the domination of their father-in-law. However, Ginny begins to see that her husband's affection rests as much on his ambition to be a successful farmer as on his love for her. Further complicating her mari-

tal situation is her affair with Jess Clark, a deserter during the Vietnam War, whose ostensible welcome becomes soured when his father disinherits him. These experiences and realizations lead to the eventual dissolution of Ginny's marriage and her loss of any desire for Jess.

These personal catastrophes leave Ginny baffled, initially anxious to reconcile on the one hand, but increasingly aware that too much has happened for the family to reconstruct relationships. In exhaustion she flees her home and family for the anonymity of a waitressing job in the Twin Cities, only returning to aid her two nieces whose parents have both died. Her one hope is that by escaping the tyranny of the farm, the girls will establish meaningful, rewarding lives for themselves. Thus, by the conclusion Smiley has vividly described the collapse of a rural way of life.

◆ Techniques ◆

A Thousand Acres is written in the form of Ginny's plain-spoken memoir of the crisis in her life that led to the breakup of her family and marriage. Much of the novel reflects Ginny's appreciation of the commonplaces of rural, small-town Midwestern life — descriptions of the spacious terrain, the seasonal fluctuations in the fields from spring plowing and planting through autumn harvests, the bounty of picnics and church suppers, the details of house, garden, and field work, and the awesome weather. However, like the aquifers that underlie the prairie, the human lives regularly but unexpectedly erupt to reveal emotional intensities — violence, passion, hatred — that startle onlookers and participants.

These intense moments of revelation of darker, grimmer, greedier personalities prevent the novel from becoming a romantic paean to bucolic farm life. In fact, the contrast in moods is what gives the novel its power and universality. These are *King Lear*-like tragedies of ordinary, recognizable Americans whose very success in commercial farming has narrowed their understanding of the broader possibilities of life symbolized in Ginny's memories of the Ericson family, former neighbors, whose very commitment to enjoying life made their success at farming problematic.

◆ Literary Precedents ◆

Besides *King Lear* (1608), *A Thousand Acres* builds on precedents going back to the local color movement of the nineteenth century, in which writers like Hamlin Garland and Willa Cather chronicled the efforts of pioneers, often immigrants, to bring the midwestern prairies under cultivation, and the emotional, financial, and physical price many paid for developing this vast agricultural breadbasket. Later writers like Frank Norris, Theodore Dreiser, Sinclair Lewis, Sherwood Anderson, and Edgar Lee Masters showed how even after the farms and communities were established, frustrations arose among the descendants of the first generation. Business cycles, geographic isolation, weather fluctuations, and cultural narrowness limited full development.

Equally important is Smiley's larger theme of the transfer of power from one generation to another. Drawing upon Shakespeare's *King Lear* in which Lear, the father of three daughters, subdivides his kingdom, Smiley shows

the disastrous consequences for all involved when such a decision is based on selfish motives. Like Lear, Laurence Cook does not abdicate generously but uses his gift to test his daughters' and sons-in-law's loyalty and affection. Those who accept his impulsive gift he hates; she who refuses, he loves.

Precedents in American literature may be found in more recent works. Eugene O'Neill's *Desire under the Elms* (1925) and Tennessee Williams's *Cat on a Hot Tin Roof* (1955) each present domineering farmers whose pride in ownership and accomplishment plague their children with conflicts and tests as to who will inherit.

◆ Related Titles ◆

A Thousand Acres culminates a series of earlier works in which Smiley explored the relationships within families with domineering parents and the control of land. In *Barn Blind* (1980), Katherine Karlson removes her husband and children to rural Illinois where she single-mindedly pursues her dream of training a national and international equestrian champion through her four children and students. The consequences are emotionally calamitous for the husband and children and lead to the breakup of the family. The novel *At Paradise Gate* (1981), told from the point of view of Anna Robison, the mother of three adult daughters, recounts events occurring in the twenty-four hours before the death of Ike Robison, their husband and father, respectively. As Anna struggles to deal with the needs of her querulous invalid husband, she meditates on their earlier life in Wyoming where she and Ike struggled unsuccessfully to establish a ranch before giving up and heading to

Iowa with their children. In the novella *Good Will* (1989), Bob Miller pursues a monomaniacal dream of creating a subsistence farm in central Pennsylvania to make himself, his wife Elizabeth, and their son Thomas as independent of mainstream America as possible. His idyll collapses when their son, on attending school, rebels against his difference. His behavior eventually causes social welfare authorities to intervene.

In *Duplicate Keys* (1984), a different similarity emerges. Alice Ellis, a thirty-year-old divorcee librarian in New York, struggles to comprehend herself and her midwestern circle of acquaintances after the murder of two friends. In the investigation that follows she, like Ginny Cook, learns that her values have been based on false assumptions and that those considered close friends have, in fact, wittingly betrayed her. However, unlike Ginny, Alice is able to build a more mature emotional attachment with a less-than-perfect man who enthusiastically pursues a career in botany.

◆ Ideas for Group Discussions ◆

The very ordinariness of the people and situation make *A Thousand Acres* a rich source for discussion. Readers will often recognize similarities in their own lives — what to do with aging parents, how to face childlessness and infertility, how to run a family business, how to deal with betrayal by relatives and neighbors. Moreover, in a period when pundits publicize the necessity of dealing with economic and social change, *A Thousand Acres* shows the wrenching effect such forces can have on the people affected.

1. When do you first suspect that Ginny may not fully grasp the implications of the situation she experiences? Is she a naive narrator?

2. What symbolic and characterizing value does the game of *Monopoly*, which the Smith's, Lewis's, and Jess Clark play, have in predicting later events?

3. In what ways does the novel attack the impact of industrialized, scientific farming upon the prairie and its human inhabitants?

4. What changes in Ginny does her destruction of the canned sausage and sauerkraut at the end of the novel suggest?

5. In what ways does Smiley describe characters in terms of food?

6. How might Laurence Cook be considered the victim of his cultural environment? What qualities of personality needed by his progenitors to survive prevent him from adjusting to change in the culture?

7. How does Smiley satirize small-town professionals like bankers, lawyers, and clergy? What does their ineffectiveness imply?

8. Why is it impossible for Caroline to be reconciled with her sisters? Does the breakdown in communication arise through the fault of any one of the sisters?

9. Can Rose be considered the truly tragic sister both as a protagonist and victim? If she is not tragic, is she a villain?

10. How does the flatness of Ginny's

language reflect both her character and that of the community she writes about?

11. How does Smiley's depiction of rural midwestern culture build on the work of earlier writers like Cather, Rolvaag, or Lewis?

12. In what ways does Smiley place a feminist interpretation on the *King Lear* story line?

Lawrence B. Fuller
Bloomsburg University of Pennsylvania

THREE FARMERS ON THEIR WAY TO A DANCE

Novel

1985

◆

Author: Richard Powers

◆ Characters ◆

Richard Powers's novels are fundamentally novels of ideas rather than novels that depend heavily upon characterization. In this novel, readers learn the history of the three young men in the Sander photograph "Three Farmers on Their Way to a Dance, 1914" — Hubert, Adolphe, and Peter — but this information is incidental to the author's concern with the social and political crosscurrents that determine their lives and shape their societies.

The narration is autobiographical but only in the broadest terms. One will not learn dependably about Powers's personal life through analyzing the narrator, although the actual incident that generated this novel occurred at a crossroads in his life when, after completing the master of arts degree, he set out, jobless, for Boston. His search for information about August Sander actually did extend over his early months in Boston. The photograph and the implications of its title continued to haunt Powers.

In regular interchapters, Powers writes about historic figures who, in one way or another, helped to direct the course of history that lead the world toward twentieth-century Modernism. Prominent among these is Henry Ford, to whom several interchapters are devoted. Other such chapters are devoted to Sarah Bernhardt, Walter Benjamin, and others who, in their way, are related to the novel's main narrative frame.

Mrs. Schreck, a cleaning woman in Peter Mays's office building, takes a motherly interest in Peter, son of Peter in the Sander photograph, leaving him bonbons and generally showing a maternal interest in his welfare. As it turns out, she knows the Sander photograph and something about its subjects, who lived in the same part of Europe from which she came. She cannot, however, provide Peter with the information about them that he seeks.

◆ Social Concerns ◆

In his first-published novel, Powers deals with nothing smaller than the origins of twentieth-century Modernism. The book, spawned by a haunting August Sander picture of three young Westerwald peasants gussied up for a Saturday night on the town, begins in the Netherlands as Europe hovers on the brink of World War I. The story moves through the intervening years to 1980s Boston with the story of Peter Mays, a computer editor and son of the brightest of the three peasants, also named Peter, in the Sander picture.

Powers's chief concern is with the interconnectedness of human events. His novel seeks to demonstrate how every drop in the mainstream of history impinges on the other drops. His unnamed narrator, pausing between trains in Detroit, wanders into the Detroit Institute of Arts to pass the idle hours until his train for Boston departs. In the museum, he is transfixed by Sander's haunting photograph, *Three Farmers on Their Way to a Dance, 1914.* He becomes obsessed with trying to find out more about Sander, but, mistakenly thinking that this photographer's last name is "Zander" rather than "Sander," his quest for more information leads him nowhere until he accidentally unearths in Boston the information he has been pursuing.

Peter Mays has a similar experience: He stumbles upon a print of the Sander photograph among family items in his mother's attic. He begins a quest that leads to a panoply of historic information, all interrelated, that has meaning in his life.

The pursuits of both the narrator and Peter Mays are personal pursuits; each for his own reason feels the need for information about the artifact (the photograph) he has found. Powers's main social concern is with the interconnections, the convoluted webbings, that make personal history part of the broader march of the history of civilization, in this case Modernism.

◆ Themes ◆

Powers's themes are intimately con-nected with the social concerns mentioned above. His obvious quest in this novel is to understand the structure of human existence. As in all his other writing, Powers is concerned with ideas and with their conjoining parts, their necessary connections. His conflicts cannot be stated in simple terms — man against nature, man against man, man against himself. These terms imply divisions; Powers quests after connections.

In two of his characters, the narrator and Peter Mays, Powers focuses on the theme of obsession, not only as a means toward the end of achieving broad cultural understanding but of unlocking as well the secrets of human existence. This book is about the whys, whats, and hows of the world as we perceive it. The quest is more intellectually demanding than many contemporary authors have dared impose upon their readers.

Three Farmers on Their Way to a Dance marks the beginning of a quest that Powers continues in all of his subsequent novels. He desperately needs to know what life is about. His obsessive search is the underlying theme of all his writing.

◆ Techniques ◆

Three Farmers on Their Way to a Dance consists of multiple texts, all interconnected historically. Each set of three chapters is arranged so that the first chapter focuses on the main narrative frame, the story of the three farmers and eventually of Peter Mays. The second chapter is an historical or philosophical essay that reflects the broader social context within which the narrative occurs. The third chapter focuses on a significant historical figure who, like Henry Ford, had an effect on the development of twentieth-Modernism.

Powers approaches time with a simultaneity that helps unify the seemingly disparate elements of his narrative. Either explicitly or implicitly, the three farmers are present in each of the book's twenty-seven chapters; Powers appears to imply by his narrative structure that all things eventually touch, that all human involvement in life and in society exists within some all-encompassing structure. It is this structure and its meaning that Powers seeks to understand and, in this novel (as in most of his other writing), to mimic.

◆ Literary Precedents ◆

A literary precedent is not identical to a literary influence. Serious writers have universally wrestled with similar problems both thematically and in terms of how to control such matters as time and space. Having said this, one can then observe that James Joyce, particularly in *Ulysses* (1922), and T. S. Eliot, most notably in *The Waste Land* (1922), came to grips with the same structural dilemmas that faced Powers as he set out to write one of the most ambitious novels of the last half of the twentieth century.

Certainly Pynchonesque elements also can be detected in Powers's novel, particularly as it seeks to unify related but strongly disparate forces. William Vollmann has dealt with similar structural problems in most of his novels, as has Rolando Hinojosa in a work like *Becky and Her Friends* (1990), in which a protagonist is presented through the eyes of those who know her with no concern over contradictions in their perceptions of her.

◆ Related Titles ◆

All of Powers's books to date use regularly spaced interchapters to relate the basic narrative frame to its historical context. In *Operation Wandering Soul* (1993), these interchapters span millennia, whereas, in his earlier novels, they are more narrowly focused. Characters do not recur from novel to novel.

◆ Ideas for Group Discussions ◆

The philosophical and intellectual depth of Richard Powers's writing makes it suitable for group discussions among sophisticated readers. *Three Farmers on Their Way to a Dance* is filled with puns, subtle allusions, and several levels of meaning, all of which dictate that those who wish to derive the strongest insights from the book will discuss it with other knowledgeable readers.

It is a rare author who works so totally within the world of ideas as Powers does. Initially, this may discourage some readers who will not be able in his writing to identify easily the sorts of memorable characters that emerge from a Dickens novel or from the writings of such later writers as Willa Cather, Ernest Hemingway, F. Scott Fitzgerald, or Reynolds Price. Nevertheless, reading a novel like *Three Farmers on Their Way to a Dance* and subjecting it to the collective scrutiny of a discussion group will do a great deal to expand readers' minds, to nudge them into new areas of literary perception.

1. In a broadly social and philosophical sense, what does the title mean?

2. What specific contributions to twentieth-century Modernism did Henry Ford make according to Powers?

3. How does Powers relate the Sarah Bernhardt episodes to the novel's first and main narrative frames?

4. Are the physical and philosophical landscapes of *Three Farmers on Their Way to a Dance* interrelated? Elaborate.

5. Would the philosophical purposes of the novel have been attained had the novel's impetus been a work of sculpture, an oil painting, or a piece of classical music rather than a photograph?

6. How did Peter Mays get his last name? What are the implications of this bit of information?

7. Toward the end of the book the narrator says that the three subjects of the Sander picture "had led lives as verifiable, if not as well documented, as any of those Great Personalities I had poured over." Given what you know about Powers, what are the broad implications of this statement?

8. Aside from his obvious wish to shorten World War I, why did Henry Ford sail the *Oscar II* to Europe? What did the trip accomplish?

9. Henry Ford once said, "All history is bunk." Is *Three Farmers on Their Way to a Dance* the kind of history Ford had in mind?

10. What major narrative strands do you find in this novel? How does the author interconnect these? Making a diagram may help you.

11. Allusions to the Christmas party in Peter Mays's office recur through much of the novel. Is this a significant point of reference? If so, how?

R. Baird Shuman
University of Illinois
at Urbana-Champaign

THUNDER ROLLING IN THE MOUNTAINS

Novel

1989

◆

Author: Scott O'Dell

◆ Characters ◆

The narrator of *Thunder Rolling in the Mountains* is Sound of Running Feet, the daughter of Chief Joseph. In many ways she resembles O'Dell's earlier female protagonists, but her personality is less developed. She remains a chronicler of events, curiously distanced. Unlike Bright Morning, who has a complex but very deep relationship with her husband Tall Boy, Sound of Running Feet's love relationship remains in the background. Perhaps the reason is that all the events are overshadowed by the tragedy of Chief Joseph, and that the unhappy outcome is a foregone conclusion from the very first page.

The character of Chief Joseph is closely modeled on his historical counterpart. He is not a literary creation but rather a biographical product of known facts. Even his speech consists of recorded utterances, such as the famous "I will fight no more forever." O'Dell does not create personal relationships for him — even his relationship with his daughter Sound of Running Feet is not developed.

Swan Necklace, one of the few fictional characters in this novel, is proba-

bly the most developed. Although he plays a minor part as the intended husband of Sound of Running Feet, he undergoes growth and change. The reader sees him first as a peaceful artist — he paints blankets and is working on the wedding blanket for his own wedding — who is forced to accompany two of the main trouble-makers, Red Moccasin Tops and Wah-Lit-Its. Reluctant at first, he becomes a fierce fighter and advocate of resistance, representing the attitude of many of the young Nez Perce braves. His death is as purposeless as many of the tragic events; he is treacherously killed for a saddle by some Assiniboin Indians.

The remaining characters are mainly historical figures playing out their roles. There is Looking Glass, the renowned but not always prudent leader, Ollokott, Chief Joseph's brother, Too-hul-huol Sote, each a famous Indian warrior, and on the side of the U.S. Army, General Howard, determined to subjugate the Nez Perce, and Colonel Miles, who treacherously breaks the treaty with Chief Joseph. They are not developed as characters beyond their roles in the events.

In his earlier novels about Native Americans, O'Dell seems to offer a prospect of hope. His young protagonists endure suffering, but at the end they see a brighter future. In *Sing Down the Moon* (1970), this future is possible when the protagonist and her husband turn their backs on civilization and return to their old way of life. The same is true in *Zia* (1976), where Karana flees from the white society and returns to the natural environment she has known for most of her life. *Thunder Rolling in the Mountains* offers no such solution. It is dominated by the pessimism of Chief Joseph who declares that there is no refuge left for his people. He compares the white settlers to sand on the shore and predicts that they will wipe out all the Indians. Nevertheless, he agrees with the young leaders who counsel escape to Canada. The change from O'Dell's earlier novels is notable — there is a sense of futility here that did not appear before. No longer is it possible for the Nez Perce to find freedom and salvation in the solitude of nature and their old way of life. There is no place to hide.

In no other of O'Dell's novels dealing with native American themes has the conflict between the whites and the Indian been so tragic as in *Thunder Rolling in the Mountains*. This may be partly due to the historical events surrounding Chief Joseph and his people. Few Indian leaders were as careful about coexisting with the whites, and few were hounded as persistently by the U.S. Army as the Nez Perce. Ironically, their final defeat comes when they are almost within reach of freedom, only a short distance from the Canadian border, and it is brought on because of Chief Joseph's humanity, and his refusing to sacrifice the old and the children of his tribe to the rigors of escape.

◆ Themes ◆

Man's inhumanity to man might well be the title of the theme of this novel. Even though Joseph has tried to live in peace with the whites, and even though his people ask nothing more than to be left alone, they are driven from their homeland, deprived of their horses and cattle which represent their livelihood, and hunted like wild animals. The same settlers who are helped by the Indians, turn informers on them. Not one of the white people, from miners to homesteaders to various military leaders ever seems to have considered the Indians as human beings. Their behavior stands in direct contrast with Chief Joseph's actions. When the Indians capture some white women, they release them and even give them horses. When the army encounters a village of women and children, it butchers them as enemies. There is not the least consideration given to even their most reasonable request. They are ordered to evacuate their homeland in the Wallowa mountains in early spring. When their leaders point out the difficulty of crossing the rivers swollen by spring run-off, and ask for a later time, they are disregarded. As a result, they lose most of their cattle, and their old people and children are endangered.

Not all the Nez Perce agree with their leader, and many feel, as Joseph's own daughter Sound of Running Feet does, that it would be better to fight than to give in. Yet they are overruled by Joseph who feels that shedding blood is wrong, unless they are forced to defend themselves. Every time the Nez Perce take a stand and fight, they win, but their victories become hollow as the final confrontation approaches inevitably. If we stand and fight, Joseph admonishes, the end will only come more swiftly.

♦ Techniques ♦

O'Dell's books are characterized by their evocative and unique style. This, his last novel, offers fewer of the colorful and detailed descriptions that are found in his earlier works. This may be because the book was completed by his wife, based on notes he was developing before his death. Where the dialogue in his earlier books was descriptive and added a unique dimension to his characters, here it mostly chronicles events. One of the reviewers of the book, Margaret Bush, says of the novel: "Events and characters are sketched quickly, and the many short scenes of the trek and the fighting become a sort of awful travelogue." There is little room for descriptions of natural harmony between the people and their land, perhaps because such a harmony is no longer possible.

♦ Literary Precedents ♦

There are a number of accounts dealing with the actual story of Chief Joseph and his people. O'Dell draws heavily upon these sources and stays close to them. Essential to the book's existence are two eyewitness accounts compiled by Lucullus V. McWhorter: *Yellow Wolf: His Own Story* (the recollections of Chief Joseph's nephew) and *Hear Me, My Chiefs!* (based on eyewitness accounts on both sides) as well as

Chief Joseph's Own Story (1925), which he told on his trip to Washington D.C. in 1897.

The story of Chief Joseph is only one of many cases of fatal confrontations between the U.S. Army and the Indians. The prototype is probably Custer's Battle at the Little Bighorn, which has been the subject of several often conflicting accounts, including Evan S. Connell's *Son of the Morning Star* (1984), a highly colored retelling by his wife, and the massacre at Wounded Knee which has been covered in *Bury My Heart at Wounded Knee* (1970) by Dee Brown.

♦ Related Titles ♦

A number of O'Dell's own novels tell about fatal cultural clashes between Indians and whites in both North and South America, among them *The Captive* (1979), *The Feathered Serpent* (1981), and *The Amethyst Ring* (1983), which deal with the conquest of the Mayan empire by the Spanish.

♦ Ideas for Group Discussions ♦

The story of Chief Joseph is one of the most famous episodes in the history of the West. As in his earlier novels, O'Dell sees the whites as alien despoilers. The question arises whether O'Dell's descriptions of Indian life and the depiction of native American characters are perhaps too idealistic. How accurate is his portrayal? Is it influenced by the "noble savage" concept of the eighteenth century? Are the settlers overdrawn, since they are all morally corrupt? Do O'Dell's stories portray a historic period or a nostalgic memory? How do they compare with other famous Westerns such as Cooper's Leather Stocking Tales and McMurtry's *Lonesome Dove* (1985)? A discussion of the settling of the West may also lead to larger issues such as the doctrine of Manifest Destiny.

1. There is a strong sense of fate in this last novel of Scott O'Dell. From the very beginning, Chief Joseph states that the tragedy of his people is unavoidable and merely a matter of time. Why does he feel that way? Even as the Indians are winning battle after battle, there is a sense of doom hanging over them. Does this mean that Chief Joseph was an inept leader or merely a realist?

2. Sound of Running Feet is much less developed than O'Dell's earlier Indian heroines. What is her function in the novel? Why did O'Dell show us the story through the eyes of a young girl and not Joseph's or at least one of his warriors'? Would the story have presented itself in a different way through a different narrator?

3. The tragedy of the Nez Perce is the tragedy of Joseph, but Sound of Running feet and Swan Necklace survive the hardships and almost reach Canada. Swan Necklace dies at the hands of hostile Indians rather than white soldiers. What is the purpose of this episode in the novel? Why did O'Dell chose this fate? After all, his character Swan Necklace is not a historic figure, and the manner of his death is the author's invention. Why does he not allow the young people to make a new start as he did in *Sing Down the Moon*?

4. In earlier novels, one of O'Dell's themes is the harmony between man and nature. This is not an issue in *Thunder Rolling in the Mountains*. Does the author feel that there is no possibility of such a harmony any more? How has the situation changed since Karana made a life for herself on a deserted island, and Bright Morning returned to rebuilding her life at the canyon with one sheep and one lamb?

5. Like the heroes of classic tragedy, Chief Joseph sees his world crumble. What is his tragic flaw?

Ingeborg Urcia
Eastern Washington University

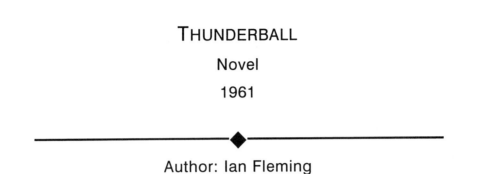

THUNDERBALL

Novel

1961

Author: Ian Fleming

◆ Characters ◆

*T*hunderball is a brighter novel than *Goldfinger* (1959) largely because Bond is a merrier character. In *Goldfinger*, he broods about the deaths of innocent people and the cruelty of his profession. He begins *Thunderball* depressed and sick, but a happy adventure with Pat Fearing at Shrublands perks him up, and through most of the novel he is in good humor, having fun with himself and the pretensions of those who work in the field of espionage.

Bond is surrounded by colorful characters. In addition to the brilliant M and the sexy Pat Fearing, there are the proprietor of Shrublands, Joshua Wain, who has "alot of bushy gray hair above an unlined brow, soft, clear brown eyes, and a sincere and Christian smile"; C.I.A. agent and old friend Felix Leiter, who had been Bond's "companion on some of the most thrilling cases in Bond's career" and has a steel hook for a right hand; and Dominetta Vitali, whose real last name is Petacchi, and who prefers to be called "Domino." She is a "girl of authority and character" who gives "the general impression" of being a "willful, high-

tempered, sensual girl." Courageous and determined, she turns out to be Bond's match and the cynical 007 ends up in love with her.

The villains are not as impressive in this novel as in *Goldfinger*, largely because the leader of SPECTRE, Ernst Stavro Blofeld, stays in the background for most of the novel. A Pole who betrayed his country to Nazi Germany, Blofeld has constructed a terrorist organization with former members of the Gestapo, SMERSH, and organized crime. "Blofeld's own eyes were deep black pools surrounded . . . by very clear whites," and his "gaze was a microscope, the window on the world of a superbly clear brain, with a focus that had been sharpened by thirty years of danger." Two hundred and eighty pounds, extraordinarily self-disciplined in all his habits, and coldly calculating, Blofeld has the potential to seize the imagination the way Goldfinger does, but M out-thinks him early on and he falls to the background.

His organization is felt throughout the novel. "SPECTRE" stands for "The Special Executive for Counterintelligence, Terrorism, Revenge, and Extortion." Its chief field operative is Emilio Largo. Large and handsome, Largo was an Olympic athlete: "the muscles bulged under the exquisitely cut shark-skin jacket." Furthermore, "Largo was an adventurer, a predator on the herd. Two hundred years before he would have been a pirate . . . like Blackbeard a blood-stained cutthroat who scythed his way through people toward gold." He has "a cool brain and an exquisite finesse behind his actions." All in all, he is a standard spy-story villain without distinctive traits. Bond and Leiter have little trouble outwitting him.

◆ Social Concerns/Themes ◆

Nuclear weapons often figure in the James Bond tales. In *Thunderball* (1961), nuclear blackmail is the focus of the story. SPECTRE, a terrorist organization, steals two nuclear bombs and demands that Great Britain and America pay it $100,000,000 or it will blow up first a valuable government installation and then a large city. This theme of terrorists struck a nerve in a public worried about the potential of nuclear war, and *Thunderball* was a spectacular best seller.

SPECTRE's scheme is intricately worked out. Bribes to a corrupt pilot in the Royal Air Force yield a stolen aircraft, a dead aircrew, and two nuclear bombs. Pretending to be treasure hunters, SPECTRE operatives hide the bombs at sea, off the Bahamas. A British rocket testing center in the Bahamas is their first target; Miami is the second. The narrative moves too fast for readers to worry much about the improbability of the plot, and the chosen targets are logical enough to give the terrorism a hard edge of menace.

Another social concern focuses on healthy and unhealthy living. The novel begins with James Bond having a "hangover, a bad one, with an aching head and stiff joints." Heavy drinking and smoking and fast living in general have left Bond in terrible physical condition. "There is no way to health except the natural way," declares M, the head of the British Secret Service. He sends Bond for mandatory treatment at a health club called Shrublands. The results are miraculous: "He had never felt so well in his life. His energy had doubled." In fact, "Bond awoke so early and full of beans that he had taken to arriving at his office early and leaving late, much to the irritation of his secretary." Bond even takes to drinking tea, which he had always regarded as a sissy's beverage. He and M take to discussing whole wheat bread, natural grains, and yogurt, as well as to decrying "dead" foods: "denaturized foods — white flour, white sugar, white rice, white salts, whites of egg." Even after he resumes some of his old bad habits, Bond is a healthier and more energetic foe for SPECTRE.

◆ Techniques ◆

Fleming uses the tease method of maintaining suspense. Early on, he reveals that Bond has "upset, if only in a minute fashion, the exactly timed machinery of a plot that was about to shake the governments of the Western world." By the end of chapter 5, the details of SPECTRE's plot against the Western world have been revealed, except for the targets of the bombs. Fleming repeatedly hints at thrills to come, even using Leiter's appearance in the Bahamas to point out that Leiter has been part of some of Bond's "most thrilling cases." The plot is intricate, the narrative is fast-paced, and the theme of nuclear blackmail can stir up enough emotions that the poor contest between Bond and Largo may not be noticed.

◆ Literary Precedents ◆

Criminal mastermind Blofeld is reminiscent of the coldly calculating crime lord Dr. Moriarty of Arthur Conan Doyle's Sherlock Holmes stories. Both regard murder as merely a tactic in their contests against the forces of good; both lead international criminal organizations; and both are terrorists.

Almost from the moment of the detonations of atomic bombs on Japan, nuclear weapons became an important theme in popular literature. Science fiction authors in particular made stories about the aftermath of nuclear war a commonplace of fiction in the 1950s. In 1957, English novelist Nevil Shute, then living in Australia, published *On the Beach* ; it was an international sensation. Like *Thunderball*, it capitalized on the public's fears about nuclear weapons — this time by speculating on the potential effects of nuclear war. However, the focus on the use of nuclear weapons by terrorists was unusual when *Thunderball* was published.

◆ Related Titles ◆

James Bond titles include: *Casino Royale*, 1953 (also published as *You Asked for It*); *Live and Let Die*, 1954; *Moonraker*, 1955 (also published as *Too Hot to Handle*); *Diamonds Are Forever*, 1956; *From Russia with Love*, 1957; *Doctor No*, 1958; *Goldfinger*, 1959; *For Your Eyes Only: Five Secret Exploits of James Bond*, 1960, short stories; *Thunderball*, 1961; *The Spy Who Loved Me*, 1962; *On Her Majesty's Secret Service*, 1963; *You Only Live Twice*, 1964; *The Man with the Golden Gun*, 1965; and *Octopussy: The Last Great Adventures of James Bond 007*, 1967, short stories.

◆ Adaptations ◆

On the copyright page of the novel *Thunderball* is this notice: "This story is based on a screen treatment by K. Mc-Clory, J. Whittingham, and the author." The 1965 motion picture *Thunderball* credits the screenplay to Richard Maibaum and John Hopkins, while declaring: "Based on the original story by Kevin McClory, Jack Whittingham, and Ian Fleming." As with *Goldfinger*, *Thunderball* was a United Artists release and was produced by Kevin McClory. The direction by Terence Young is sure-handed. The wonderful special effects of John Stears won him an Academy Award. Sean Connery plays James Bond; Claudine Auger plays Domino; Adolfo Celi plays Emilio Largo; Rik van Nutter plays Felix Leiter; and Bernard Lee plays M. The gadgetry of the film *Goldfinger* proved to be such a hit with audiences that gadgets became a regular part of the subsequent James Bond motion pictures. The technological wonders co-star with Connery in *Thunderball*.

For a discussion of other adaptations of James Bond novels, see the biographical entry on Ian Flemming.

Kirk H. Beetz

THY BROTHER'S WIFE

Novel

1982

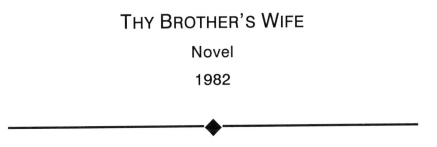

Author: Andrew M. Greeley

◆ Characters ◆

Thy Brother's Wife is more a novel of plot and ideas than of characters. The characters are essentially embodiments of ideas and instigators of plot. The dynastic father, Mike Cronin, is a hard-driving, self-made millionaire whose Irish charm aids his seductions of countless women. Paul Cronin, the son he has destined for the Presidency and for the husband of his beautiful foster child Nora, is the evil figure of the novel who is willing to lie, cheat, and even kill in order to succeed in the path his father has chosen for him. The most intimate knowledge the reader has of Paul comes at the end of the novel when he takes a suicidal boat ride on Lake Michigan.

Greeley manages to realistically convey the psychological conflict of a man torn between hope and despair, between a drive to survive and a terrible fear of exposure. Both Mike and Paul are larger-than-life characters who represent both social and moral ideas. They personify the historical upward mobility of the Irish Americans as well as the choice of evading moral responsibility and commitment. Paul's evil nature is the logical extension of his father's rise to the top.

Sean Cronin, the priest destined to become Cardinal Archbishop of Chicago, is more sensitively drawn. Although not an obviously autobiographical figure like Kevin Brennan in *The Cardinal Sins* (1981), Sean is a character who shares some of Greeley's most intense concerns, such as the role of celibacy in the priesthood, the Church's position on birth control, and the commitment to the priesthood. Sean's precipitous rise within the Church shares the larger-than-life aura of Paul and Mike Cronin, and the novel is told from his perspective. Greeley intends Sean to be read as a symbol of love and commitment, humanly flawed but faithful.

The most important character on the symbolic level is Nora: "a sturdy spring flower . . . with the lithe body of a woman athlete . . . Her flawless complexion was framed by rich auburn hair that fell halfway to a willowy waist." Idealized in her physical description, she also represents the ideals which Greeley extols in the novel: the ability to give in fully to her adulterous yet pure love for Sean and then to castigate him for feeling guilty about their love. She has a healthy attitude toward both commitments and lapses. It is she, at the end of the novel, who loves Sean and herself enough to push him into keeping his commitment to the Church. On the realistic level, she may seem too good to be true, but on the symbolic level, Nora represents the feminine, loving and forgiving side of God.

◆ Social Concerns ◆

Greeley's major focus is on social concerns within a Catholic framework, such as the responsibility of the church toward the urban poor and the suburban family. *Thy Brother's Wife* is especially concerned with the roles of women and sexuality in the context of Catholic morality. It focuses on the difficulties, particularly of Irish Catholics, in reconciling the sensual and material pleasures of this world with the spiritual purity and self-denial preached by the Church.

The novel is set nostalgically within the context of John F. Kennedy's years in the White House. In Greeley's eyes, that era marked a confluence of historical events productive of hope and glory for American Catholics. The Irish had been assimilated enough to send one of their own to the White House, and at the same time Vatican II was stimulating waves of renewed enthusiasm within the international Catholic Church. The worldly protagonist, Paul Cronin, politician son of a multimillionaire, works with Bobby Kennedy and sees him assassinated. Paul is an evil amalgam of all the character flaws imputed to the Kennedy men. Paul's brother, Sean, destined to rise parallel to Paul within the Church hierarchy, ends up on the papal birth control commission in Rome, meeting with Pope Paul VI and expressing Greeley's own well-known views on sexual morality within the Church. As a sociologist of religion, Greeley has argued that the papal encyclical against artificial birth control undermined all the positive aspects of Vatican II and ultimately led large numbers of Catholics away from the Church. The two brothers thus witness what Greeley sees as devastating blows to the hope and enthusiasm of the early 1960s. Greeley is frequently called a "romantic" in a derogatory sense, but in a more literary sense, his faith in redemptive imagination as an antidote to the failure of political reform resembles the ideology of the Romantic period. Despite his vows of celibacy, Sean's passionate love for Nora is meant to show a participation in God's love of which Paul is incapable.

◆ Themes ◆

The central theme seems to be the relationships between passionate sexual love, sterile and exploitative lust, and the all-encompassing love of God. Sean the priest spends his life in love with Paul's wife, Nora, while Paul is incapable of loving her. Greeley believes that the love of a woman offers a powerful and fruitful model for humans of God's love. Sean Cronin is a fallible human being who is yet faithful to his commitment to the priesthood. Nora is a sacrament, a powerful symbol of what God's love is like. Greeley seems to want to shake up his readers' preconceptions about faith and morality, and to open their hearts to the essence of Christianity, which is love.

◆ Techniques ◆

Except for some background in

Chapter 2, the narrative of *Thy Brother's Wife* proceeds rapidly, in clearly specified chronological order. The style is simple, almost terse, and the fictional characters are intertwined with the nonfiction setting and history.

The most literary aspect of the novel is its use of allusion to construct its role as "Holy Thursday," the first book of *The Passover Trilogy*. A note on the Jewish and Christian Passover, treating it as a springtime feast of liberation and renewal, precedes the narrative and explains the function of passages from St. John's Gospel which are used as epigraphs to major sections of *Thy Brother's Wife*. By emphasizing the links between Judaism and Christianity (and their links, in turn, with primitive fertility rituals), Greeley seems to broaden the boundary of his novel beyond the parameters of Irish Catholic Chicago. The first epigraph prays for community and for keeping people from evil. The narrative opens "after supper on Holy Thursday," 1951 and closes just before Mass on Holy Thursday, 1977. The protagonist, Sean Cronin, sings a hymn which expresses the main themes of *Thy Brother's Wife*: "Where charity and love prevail/here God is ever found" and "Our brotherhood embraces all/whose Father is the same."

◆ Literary Precedents ◆

Thy Brother's Wife can be seen as an historical novel in the tradition established by Sir Walter Scott. Even though the era is only two decades earlier than the publication date, the nostalgia for a lost period of hope and renovation is highly romantic. The book is ambiguous about its relation to history. On the one hand, fictitious characters interact with real people and events; on the other hand, a "Disclaimer" precedes the narrative in order to establish that it is not a *roman à clef*. The author's "Personal Afterword" claims for the novel a place in the tradition of religious parables. The texture of the book is a mixture of historical reality, myth, archetype, romance, and allegory and perhaps best lends itself to being read as the same blend of fact, legend and lore as Greeley's first novel, *The Magic Cup* (1979).

◆ Related Titles ◆

Thy Brother's Wife shares many features with Greeley's next two novels in *The Passover Trilogy*, which are set in approximately the same time frame and which continue to develop the same themes of sex, love and commitment, whether to God or another person. While the second book, *Ascent into Hell* (1983), follows very closely the format, chronological narrative and style of both *The Cardinal Sins* and *Thy Brother's Wife, Lord of the Dance* (1984), shows considerable advances in subtlety and artistic technique.

Whereas *Thy Brother's Wife* represents the community of the Last Passover Supper on Holy Thursday, *Ascent into Hell* represents the forgiveness of Good Friday. In the prefatory statement on Passover, Greeley maintains that three experiences define the Judaeo-Christian religion: "Community, Freedom, and New Life." Each of the three novels emphasizes one of these motifs. *Ascent into Hell* celebrates the freedom gained through forgiveness. Scriptural allusions to Jesus's seven last words on the cross serve as epigraphs for the six books into which the narrative divides. A "Personal Afterword" asserts that although the novel appears to be about a priest's conflicts over breaking his vows of celibacy, it is "primarily a story of God," not unlike Biblical tales of human vices.

Ascent into Hell pushes the concerns of *Thy Brother's Wife* to a new level. Rather than showing an interlude of incontinence in a life committed to priestly celibacy, the second novel depicts priests and nuns who reject their vows and marry. Rather than using an idealized female character to suggest the power of love, Greeley wants this novel to present through the character of Maria "a sacrament of God and a revelation of how God works." The novel received mixed critical reception.

The third novel of the trilogy, *Lord of the Dance*, met with improved critical response and marked two new departures in Greeley's fiction writing — moves into the genre of mystery and the subject matter of parapsychology. Instead of the liturgical and Biblical allusions used in the first two books of the trilogy, *Lord of the Dance* uses the image of dance as a symbol of the act of creation. Nietzsche provides one of the major epigraphs: "The only God worth believing in is a dancing God." The notions of God as avenger, rule maker and rational creator are replaced by images of God as joyous free play and life. Each part of the novel takes its name from a different dance form. Noele, the red-haired and green-eyed protagonist, both literally and symbolically represents Christmas and Easter, birth and rebirth. Noele's psychic powers represent Greeley's findings that parapsychology is for many people an important aspect of spirituality.

◆ Ideas for Group Discussions ◆

A reader needs to be neither Catholic nor Irish to form strong opinions concerning Andrew Greeley's novels. Discussions can center on both the manner of his storytelling and the content he presents. Because of this, they can serve as excellent exercises in how various and often opposing literary opinions can be formed, and whether or not they are supported by valid or invalid evidence.

And because so much of what he writes is drawn from his own research, Greeley can also serve as a springboard from fiction into other genres. The seeds of his novels can be found in many of his sociological and theological books as well as in his poetry and personal journals. In many cases, actual scenes from the novels can be traced quite directly to passages in his other writings. "Fiction is the best way of getting . . . insights through the secular barriers into general culture," he has said. Greeley's works can provoke an interesting debate about why a writer whose works are grounded in the empirical data he uncovers might be called unrealistic by critics.

1. When asked in an unpublished interview what he hoped would be the major topic of discussion among those who read his books, Andrew Greeley replied without hesitation: "That God loves them." Using *Thy Brother's Wife* or one of the related titles, discuss whether Greeley's intent comes through to a reader or whether there is truth in the assertion made by one reviewer who maintained that if this kind of epiphany is Greeley's intent, then he needs to rewrite.

Thy Brother's Wife

2. There is a cliché which asserts that "You can't tell a book by its cover." While many critics of Greeley believe he makes best-seller lists because of his suggestive covers, the cover photograph of *The Cardinal Sins* is actually part of a series by Rena Small entitled "Non-exploited Women's Bodies." How do you "read" the cover of *Thy Brother's Wife?* What expectations does the cover create for the story? Were these expectations fulfilled when you read the novel? Why or why not?

3. In several talks he has given and articles he has written, Andrew Greeley complains that no book reviewer can resist using the word *steamy* in reference to his works. Using *Thy Brother's Wife* or one of the related titles, find a sexual scene and examine the description closely. Compare what you read here with a passage from another popular fiction writer. How "steamy" is Greeley? Does the "steam" blur your vision of his message?

4. Read Andrew Greeley's *Faithful Attraction* (1991) or *Sex: The Catholic Experience* (1994), studies of marriage and sexuality based on extensive sociological data gathered by Gallup Polls and National Opinion Research Center surveys. How does *Thy Brother's Wife* or one of the related titles serve as a dramatization of the empirical data about marriage and sex uncovered by the survey? Discuss why you think Fr. Greeley may have taken up his third career as a novelist.

Eve Walsh Stoddard
St. Lawrence University
[Revised and expanded
by Madonna Coughlin Marsden]

A TICKET TO THE BONEYARD

Novel

1990

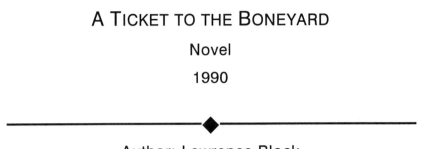

Author: Lawrence Block

◆ Social Concerns/Themes ◆

Social concerns seem to be minimal in the latest Matt Scudder novel, *A Ticket to the Boneyard*. Although prostitution (including transsexual prostitution) is part of the story, it is presented only as another way to make a living, one which has its own peculiar job-related problems. The theme of the insecurity of urban life — with the attendant need for locks and "security systems" — is less a social concern than a matter of individual terror. Matt lives out the law of the jungle — eat or be eaten; kill or be killed — mostly uncritically, and no separate narrative voice puts this extreme behavior into any social context.

The themes are mainly put forward in a negative form: actions subvert the stated moral positions. Matt says that one shouldn't play God after remembering how he framed James Leo Motley for assaulting a police officer. Motley was trying to take over as Elaine Mardell's pimp, hurting her physically during and after sex. But Matt then plays God in the ultimate act of killing someone, deliberately taking what cannot be restored — life. The theme of fatalism is introduced with Matt's read-

ing and thinking about Marcus Aurelius, a Roman Stoic, who counsels that everything happens the way it is supposed to, so human worry (and presumably effort) are unnecessary. But Matt continues to try to track down Motley and to eliminate him. At the end of the novel, Scudder says that it is a cold winter but that he just dresses warmly and walks through it. He refuses to admit that he does not walk through untouched.

◆ Characters ◆

James Leo Motley comes from nowhere to try to take over the prostitute Elaine Mardell's life. He is muscular and wiry, with eyes that display his hatred for women, and with a knowledge of pressure points by which to inflict pain on a human body. He preys on people because he can. Elaine Mardell tries not to let a life of prostitution grind her down, and she saves her money to buy real estate for a secure financial future. Matt Scudder considers her a friend although he has not seen her for years and at first fails to recognize her code name, Cousin Frances. None of Motley's other victims are close to Scudder and the reader gets to know none of them as individual beings: They exist in the novel to be killed. Scudder sends the women he feels close to out of town. He feels some closeness to Elaine only after she has been attacked by Motley. Mick Ballou reappears to supply Matt with a gun. At the end of the story Matt says that he feels the most kinship with a career criminal and a prostitute, Mick and Elaine.

◆ Techniques ◆

Block's narrative techniques in this novel constitute almost a change of genre. He is no longer writing the traditional hard-boiled detective novel in which the detective preserves some integrity and humanity in the midst of a savage world. The novel is closer to a revenge fantasy. If it were set in the future, it would be a dystopia; as it is, it is a vision of a nightmare world, in which everyone is a killer or a potential killer.

The novel returns to a character from the first Matt Scudder mystery, *In the Midst of Death* (1976): Elaine Mardell, a prostitute whom Matt patronized, protected, and treated as an informant. In the earlier mystery, Matt concluded that everyone is a little on the take, but that murdering someone is crossing the line into evil. *A Ticket to the Boneyard* erases that line. Matt tells a police lieutenant in Ohio that he does not have a client, and so presumably he is no longer a detective. The novel also includes graphic depictions of sadistic violence against women, and makes James Leo Motley into a monster who must be destroyed by the antihero Scudder.

◆ Literary Precedents ◆

The Adventures of Roderick Random (1748) by Tobias Smollett is a picaresque adventure in which the protagonist recounts his resentment of his enemies and his thirst for revenge, which is sometimes satisfied. However, closer to the methods of *A Ticket to the Boneyard* are modern crime novels that put the reader into the mind of the murderer and let him act out the murderer's crimes.

The seductive woman who tempts the detective to relinquish his integrity has been a staple of hard-boiled detective fiction. In Dashiell Hammett's *The Maltese Falcon* (1930), Sam Spade is sexually tempted by the murderous Brigit O'Shaunnessy, but instead turns her in to the police. Mickey Spillane's Mike Hammer practiced the ultimate rejection of the sexual temptress by cold-bloodedly shooting her. Dashiell Hammett's *Red Harvest* (1929) is an example of a hard-boiled detective novel in which corruption seems endemic and the integrity of the detective is shaken. Tales of murderous innkeepers are part of Gothic fiction. Albert Camus wrote *The Stranger* (1942), in which the rich stranger who was killed was the family's long lost son.

◆ Related Titles ◆

In *Out on the Cutting Edge* (1989), characters besides the grimy, hard-drinking ex-cop private eye Matt Scudder, include Mickey Ballou, who wears his father's bloody butcher's smock when he wants to intimidate his criminal associates, and Eddie Dunphy, an ex-convict who does odd jobs and sometimes attends the same Alcoholics Anonymous meetings as Matt. Willa

Rossiter, who identifies herself as the superintendent of Eddie's building and a former member of the Progressive Communist Party, becomes Matt's lover. Paula Hoeldtke, a would-be actress and waitress who steals for thrills, and her boyfriend Neil, one of Mickey's bartenders, are less well developed. Other characters include Paula's father, who hires Matt to find her, and some of Matt's AA associates.

In this novel Block focuses on the problems of the urban real estate market in which rent-controlled apartments coexist with high-rent uncontrolled apartments. Unable to find shelter, homeless people beg on the streets. Money-hungry landlords have more than a casual interest in their tenants dying, since that will make valuable living space available at much higher rents. Such owners keep apartments empty so that they can cast ballots for the building being converted to a co-operative — a process that can bring the owner millions of dollars in profit.

A recurring theme in Block's series is the brutality of the city, a savagery that contrasts with the ideal of the city as the jewel of a civilization. A traditional mark of a civilized people is hospitality — the welcome and safe passage accorded to travelers and strangers as well as neighbors and kin. In Greek and biblical cultures, the killing of strangers signals a savage and ignorant people, and the city is almost totally comprised of strangers, who need to turn to the good will of unknown people for shelter. Block also explores the theme of corruption and guilt and pictures the victims and bystanders as sharing the guilt with the criminals. Eddie Dunphy, whose death Matt investigates, was a small-time criminal, and Paula Hoeldtke, the subject of another of Matt's cases, is morally corrupt. Matt identifies subconsciously with the "Butcher Boy," Mickey Ballou, a criminal enforcer, more than he does with his former police friends. The only victims who are not lawbreakers are the elderly who are ready to die.

In the character of Willa, Matt's lover, Block creates a complex web of human traits influenced by alcohol, death, and seduction. The strong subconscious pull of this web is indicated by the fact that Matt has drinking dreams while he is sleeping with Willa. An awareness of the dangerous combination is doubled when Jan, a recovering alcoholic whom Matt dated previously, tells the story of Paul who was sober for many years until a pretty French woman in Paris asked him to have a glass of wine with her. Now, Jan says, Paul combines uncontrollable drinking bouts with hospital detoxification stays. His friends worry that this pattern will soon kill him. It is as if the seductive, but deadly alcohol is personified in Willa. Another element that underscores the play of irrational forces is Matt's developing friendship with the Butcher Boy, Mickey Ballou, in an association similar, Matt says, to what often happens with drinking buddies. They feel emotionally close to each other, telling each other stories, without developing any deep ties. Another dangerous Mickey is a Mickey Finn, the chloral hydrate that Willa gives to her victims to put them out before they are killed.

Kate Begnal
Utah State University

A TIDEWATER MORNING

Novel

1993

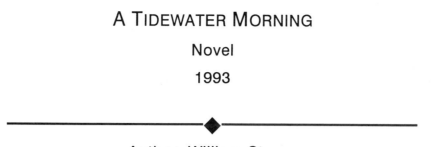

Author: William Styron

◆ Social Concerns ◆

Styron often explores in his fiction the loss of innocence and the discovery of knowledge, a psychological quest in the form of an overarching fable in which his main character discovers the intolerable certainties of life — death, loss, race, war, self-destruction — through a process of recollection and dramatically presented revelations. All of his major novels can be read essentially as fictionalized memoirs or meditations about the past, often beginning at the end of the story and unearthing it slowly, as in *Lie Down in Darkness* (1951) and *The Confessions of Nat Turner* (1967), or looking back on the past from a particular present moment in an effort to re-create and discover where things went wrong and how revelations of unbearable tragedy affect the writer and his characters, as in *Set This House on Fire* (1960) and *Sophie's Choice* (1979). In *A Tidewater Morning* Styron re-enacts this same process in three semi-autobiographical tales about the young man Paul Whitehurst that explore the palpable fascination with and horror of war in "Love Day," the death of an old black man in "Shadrach," and the

death of his mother in "A Tidewater Morning."

In the three tales Styron examines the segregated mores of the Tidewater world in which he and Paul Whitehurst grew up in the 1930s, the nostalgic memories of a bright, middle-class, white boy growing up in a friendly village filled with local characters, the virile if politically suspect hierarchy of men at war, and his own despondent moods and desolate emotions. He also presents the battle between Whitehurst's parents' backgrounds and attitudes as played out within the emotionally repressive household of genteel evasion and his mother's inevitable death from cancer.

Styron explores the racially charged arguments about color and class that existed at that time and the different perspectives from the point of view of a Pennsylvania Yankee and a Tidewater southerner. At the root of all these issues lie an ineradicable grief and suffering that cannot be transcended by the platitudes of organized Protestant religion, of regional racism, and of blustering Marine camaraderie.

Several themes parallel and reflect one another in this series of interconnected stories. The most obvious may be the one in which Styron's various social concerns affect his characters. World War II, the Great Depression, and the lingering racist legacy of slavery consistently reveal the power of historical circumstance to maim and victimize individual people. In "Love Day" on April Fool's Day, 1945, Paul Whitehurst on his troopship remembers witnessing a dogfight in the sky the day before, at the same time he learns that his Marine unit will be involved not in a real battle but in a mock amphibious attack in an attempt to draw the Japanese away from the authentic invasion. In "A Tidewater Morning" at the age of thirteen he reads the headlines in the local paper in 1938 about the approaching war. In both cases the war underscores the human discord and sense of anxious urgency that surround and envelop him.

The Tidewater of the 1930s that Styron re-creates is a veritable wasteland, having been played out by years of tobacco growing. Within this exhausted landscape the Great Depression has settled all too clearly, and his characters must do what they can in order to survive, whether it be through Paul's newspaper route, his father's job at the Newport News shipyard, or the Dabneys' making illicit whiskey at their illegal still.

In "Shadrach" an old black man returns to the Dabneys' land to die, a fugitive from slavery returning to the place from which he was sold years ago. His death ends an era in Paul's life as does the death of his mother and the interminable grief of his father. But it also reveals the clashing perspectives about color and class that persist in his parents. Adelaide Whitehurst is a Pennsylvania Yankee, a graduate of Bryn Mawr, who looks down on all the people of the Tidewater and views them from the perspective of higher and lower classes. Jeff Whitehurst maintains that the Southerners' perspective of the black is far more humane and caring than his wife's. The issue, ever present, is not so much resolved as exacerbated by their individual ways of looking at things, thus dividing them as man and wife, Yankee and Southerner, father and mother.

Within or beneath these more social concerns lies Styron's constant sense of dislocation and human discord, the never-ending and relentless pain that comes from the irrevocable feeling of loss, sorrow, homesickness, and despondency. On board the troopship Paul experiences this sense of homesickness and remembers an argument between his parents when he was eleven years old. He remembers all too well his cancer-ridden mother's stony rage and his father's sweeping sense of desolation that no amount of social concern can eradicate. Human suffering lies at the heart of Styron's vision in all its many facets, and the deaths of Adelaide Whitehurst and Shadrach only add to the continued awareness of the young Paul Whitehurst's suffering and the older narrator's years later.

Styron persists in tracing the landmark experiences of growing up — Paul's experience of war in 1945 and the memory of his parents' bickerings in 1936, his memory of the Dabneys and Shadrach's death in 1935, and his mother's death in 1938. These epiphanies mark the end of childhood innocence and reveal the continuing sense of depression and desolation that will not leave him. Growing up becomes a hazardous course which must deal with death, loss, war, and their irrevocable effects. At the same time Paul Whitehurst remains a solitary soul, an only child (as Styron was) left to cope with the horrors that life reveals to him and his own despondent introspection. The process of growing up uncovers a series of wounds and remembered events that will not heal.

◆ Characters ◆

Several of Styron's minor characters represent types more than they do individuals, although Styron does give them individual characteristics which humanize them. Lt. Col. Timothy ("Happy") Halloran is a professional Marine who sports a handlebar mustache, a nonsafety razor, a swagger, and a style that Paul Whitehurst can only envy. Paul realizes that Halloran is a political neanderthal and that he tells rambling, pointless tales about his life in the Marines, but he still remains infatuated by his virile presence. The Dabneys are the Whitehursts' social inferiors, "poor white trash" who cuss and fulminate, keep a slovenly house, make illicit whiskey, and have no desire to aspire to bourgeois gentility. And yet when Shadrach, the ancient slave, returns to Dabney's land to die, Dabney takes him in and sees to it that Shadrach's meager hopes are fulfilled. Likewise an autocrat like Mr. Quigley, who runs the local store and oversees the boys' paper routes, capitulates to Paul when the boy decides he wants to quit his route. All these minor characters flesh out the stories of Paul's remembered youth.

Paul Whitehurst is a sensitive, solitary soul, dogged by his memories of death and loss, which he cannot shake. He succumbs easily to homesickness aboard the troop ship, admires the dogged persistence of Shadrach who has come home to die and view the Dabneys' millpond one last time, and tries to avoid discord at all times, fleeing into the domain of his own troubled introspection. He devises ways to confront and avoid these darker memories and recognizes the loss of his own innocence in the process.

The Whitehursts provide the background of discord throughout these stories. Adelaide sings beautifully, but the ravages of cancer are slowly destroying her stamina and good will. Jeff believes in traditional values, but his wife's suffering drives him to condemn the palliatives of the Presbyterian minister and his wife, who come to comfort him, and gives rise to his lacerating sense of doubt in a godless universe.

◆ Techniques ◆

Styron's three interlocked tales re-enact the process of memory and its effects on Paul Whitehurst. In each story he seeks out a moment of epiphany or revelation which encapsulates the depth of his vision of human suffering and history's victimizing powers. In states of near-trance or reverie, Paul recalls scenes from his past in the meditative or confessional mode of many contemporary and traditional Southern novels. The first-person narrator relates his emotional state to the exhausted Tidewater landscape which surrounds him. Styron's style, a slow, lapidary, and mellifluous prose, in its rhetorical power suggests the influences of such Southern writers as William Faulkner and Thomas Wolfe, although these influences have receded in Styron's later work.

Styron's confessional mode of writing novels in the first person can be traced to such diverse American writers as Herman Melville in *Moby Dick*, (1851), J. D. Salinger in *Catcher in the Rye* (1951), and Saul Bellow in *The Adventures of Augie March* (1953). Many contemporary novels rely upon the first-person narrator, linking the story directly to historical, semiautobiographical, and cultural events. The blend of fact and fiction became popular in the 1960s when Styron was at work on *The Confessions of Nat Turner*.

◆ Related Titles ◆

In *Darkness Visible* (1990) Styron confronts many of the personal experiences he fictionalizes here. The underlying depression and sense of personal desolation underscore this book and *A Tidewater Morning* as they do his other major novels.

◆ Ideas for Group Discussions ◆

Because of the kinds of issues Styron has written about, his short stories and novels easily provoke group discussions of all kinds. The relationship between the individual and historical circumstance, his analysis of western civilization and its involvement with and creation of both Nazism and racial slavery, his treatment of men and women in different historical periods, his emotionally charged use of language to try to capture the effects of the monumental issues that confront him, his peeling away at the façades of memory and recollection, his need to both reveal and re-veil or conceal the depths and often tortuous paths of his subjects, his comments upon the creation of history and fiction and how they are intimately interrelated: All of these topics can lead to stimulating and provocative discussions.

1. Can you trace any development in terms of growth and self-knowledge in Paul Whitehurst from 1935 through 1936 and 1938 to 1945? What has he learned about himself and life? Are his parents' concerns about him valid in view of what he becomes?

2. What is Styron's approach to war? Does it seem similar to or different from the Depression? Are the two in any way linked here?

3. Styron makes the case for these three stories as representing the memories of a single place, the Virginia Tidewater of the 1930s. How does this sense of place affect his characters? Could they have come from anywhere else?

4. What can you discern about Styron's attitude toward blacks in these stories? Does it strike you as a contemporary attitude, or is it very much a product of the period about which he is writing?

5. Compare the lives and routines of the Whitehursts and the Dabneys. How does Styron play them off against one another? Why does Paul gravitate toward the chaos of the Dabneys' household? Is there some larger issue of social hierarchy being suggested here?

6. So many of the incidents in these stories focus on death and loss. Can you locate some positive aspects that are the result of these events? Do they add up in terms of some overall vision within Styron's fictional landscape?

7. Notice how carefully the style creates mood and detail. Each word seems particularly chosen and placed. How does this affect your reading of the stories? How does it direct you toward considering some issues as opposed to others?

8. The attitudes toward blacks as expressed by both Adelaide and Jeff Whitehurst are very different. Do these attitudes still exist today? Are each of the "combatants" fair in assessing the point of view of the other? Are such attitudes really products of geography?

9. How does the Whitehurst family function, or fail to function, here? Is this a product of the 1930s? Or do you see it as a universal dilemma?

10. Jeff Whitehurst attacks religion with a vengeance. Is his attack a valid one? Does Styron seem to agree or disagree with it? How can you square Jeff's outburst with his general belief in Christian and traditional values?

11. Styron writes about paper routes, country stores, the comfort of a country village. How does this insulate and/or support his characters? Is there too much nostalgia here in conjuring up memories of childhood and the small town? Are these characters merely products and/or victims of such a place?

Samuel Coale
Wheaton College

THE TIDEWATER TALES

Novel

1987

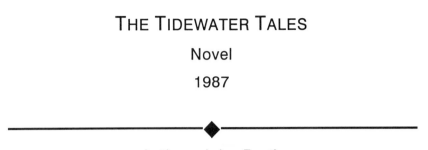

Author: John Barth

◆ Characters ◆

Peter Sagamore and Katherine Sherritt Sagamore, both thirty-nine years old, are the book's joint protagonists and narrators. Peter is a college professor and a moderately successful writer who began his writing career with a thick novel full of the abundance of life. But he has become "a writer's writer," which in his case means a painstaking minimalist whose meticulously pared down work reaches silence at the book's opening. His hugely pregnant wife (eight and a half months, with at least twins) immediately recognizes the dangerous urgency of this problem: Her husband's entire identity, his life, is dependent upon his being a writer. And the depth of their love means that her life is dependent upon his. Eventually the reader discovers that Peter has been silenced by his knowledge of the world: His ex-student and "CIA friend" Doug Townshend has been passing Peter information about his own and others' clandestine activities, most troublingly those of "the Doomsday Factors," agents who cavalierly trade in the possibility of planetary destruction. In flashback we see that Peter has shown courage in his increasingly complicated dealings with sinister CIA figures, but he is honor bound to keep certain confidences. This is one source of his writer's block, since he cannot use this material in his fiction. He is deeply distressed by what he has learned about his government and the perilous state of the world. Indeed, on the conscious level he and Katherine have both come to see the world's situation as hopeless. Hopeless people bring neither books nor children into the world. Or do they? Peter and Katherine, happily married and physically healthy, find their life together sweet and satisfying, but neither believes that the world they love and love in will endure. It is their irrational, instinctive impulses that have kept them productive and vital. Now, their visceral vitality is weakening.

Peter is from a lower middle class tidewater family of no ambitions and, except for his books, no distinguished accomplishments. Katherine is from the patrician Sherritt family of private schools, prestigious colleges, public service, historic land holdings, and hefty trust funds. The social synthesis of their blissful marriage, however, is not Barth's main interest. Peter represents one side of the writer's mind: the side devoted to exquisitely finished art, art beyond the contaminating arbitrariness of the world. Katherine, an oral historian who becomes an oral storyteller in her desperation to help her husband regain his voice, represents the writer's other side: the side that wants to include everything, to let artifice take a back seat to life and the joy of creating. "Share-it," her punning maiden name commands her husband, whose "more sagas," is an appellation that remains painfully potential until the book's closing pages. Just as Katherine's huge belly represents the bounty of biological life, her exuberant, often artless oral tale-spinning represents the bounty of the primitive narrative that Peter has lost touch with.

Katherine and Peter embody the novel's core question: How does one go on living (storytelling) in the face of present atrocities and future annihilation? The answer seems to be found in Peter's grim parable of the caged chickens who live obliviously on the back of a python destined to eat them. It takes Peter 655 pages to accept that the crucial difference between humans and these chickens is not so much that humans *know* their days are numbered, but that they can turn even such hopeless situations into enlightening and perhaps entertaining stories. As long as one lives, one will make stories, Peter learns. That is what human consciousness does, whether it writes them down or not. To live a life of health, one must find pleasure in necessity. Or, as Barth says in *Sabbatical* (1982), "If life's a journey and the grave its goal, getting there is *all* the fun."

Peter must re-learn a love of the perilous world through storytelling, must learn how to let the world into stories, rather than meticulously keeping it out; and he does so by sailing for fifteen days apparently aimlessly around the Upper Chesapeake Bay as he and his wife take turns telling the story of their lives to the unborn children in her womb. Peter is constantly in danger of losing heart and falling into a nihilistic silence. But stories keep coming to him, encouraging him. Katherine is their most important agent, since she is the one who, despite her impending delivery, recklessly proposes that they sail away from the mundane world of solicitous family and concerned friends, competent doctors and safe hospitals. She thus brings Peter into the realm of stories, which is what the varied objects and craft floating on the Bay stand for.

Barth uses a detailed knowledge of the Bay to move his characters and his reader gradually from the plausible world of identifiable contemporary experience (the year is 1980) to the world of adventure and wonder. In fact, by having the "realistic" characters tell one another tall and taller tales, Barth fuses the two worlds, thus overcoming the traditional barrier between the "realistic" and the "fantastic" in fiction. At crucial moments when despair threatens to overwhelm Peter and Katherine, chance floats a story to them, sometimes literally, as when they open a distress-flare canister to find a mysterious manuscript. At other times they encounter figures out of legend and literature: Odysseus and Nausicca from *The Odyssey* (1050-850 B.C., Theodoros and Diana Dmitrikakis are the names they go by now), Don Quixote turned mariner (Donald Quicksoat, these days). Everyone they encounter has a story. The characters in the main narrative frequently tell their stories over an elegant shipboard dinner and at-least satisfactory wine. The stories are filled with details and marvels, mixing past and present, fiction and fact in the way that Peter must learn to do again. Despite a psychologically unconvincing but dramatically necessary quarrel on days eight and nine, Peter and Katherine remain as close as a couple can be. In the course of the narrative, both have been sexually attracted to storytellers of the opposite sex — in particular "Odysseus and Nausicca" and Frank and Leah Talbott — but despite opportunities to act on these attractions, each has remained not only faithful but completely candid with his/her mate.

From time to time the protagonists make new friends on shore or boat to boat, new friends who sometimes turn out to have connections with the CIA and thus bring the specter of destruction and meaninglessness back into their story. Trips ashore for provisions bring Peter and Katherine into contact with family and old friends who believe the couple is behaving irresponsibly in sailing a motorless boat in all weathers with Katherine's due date so near. And family and friends also come to Peter/Katherine in their own boats, finally lashing an assortment of craft together into a motley flotilla whose rich community of diverse characters provides story after story of the wonders and trials of the "real world," as well those from the imaginations of these tale-intoxicated people.

By the end of the book, inevitable death has receded for a time. Through hubris or conspiracy the most sinister and loathsome characters have destroyed themselves, Katherine has delivered healthy twins, and Peter has begun the book we have just finished reading. Lest he be charged with sentimentalism (as he was by some reviewers of *Sabbatical*), Barth hints throughout *The Tidewater Tales* that perhaps the best storytellers are those in the CIA, whose fictions — like Peter Sagamore's, constituted of facts, half-lies, and outright falsehoods — lead to annihilation. Barth is engaged in a celebration, however; and those ugly stories, like the bloody corpses of all the virgins before Scheherazade, are not allowed center stage.

◆ Social Concerns ◆

Like *Sabbatical* (1982), the Barth novel that immediately preceded it, *The Tidewater Tales* is more topical than Barth's earlier works, which tend to view social and political activism in ironic ways. This novel deplores in uncharacteristically *un*ironic terms CIA "dirty tricks" and greedy business's toxic waste dumping, not to mention the U.S. government's nuclear brinkmanship that Barth implies is doomed to lose its balance eventually. Barth's setting is the Chesapeake Bay, only a few miles down the Potomac River from the nation's capital and site of CIA headquarters, numerous espionage "safe houses," a variety of military installations, and an increasing number of toxic "minidumps." From time to time the characters catch glimpses of chilling clandestine operations, most memorably symbolized by the floating corpse of J. A. Paisley, a CIA operative who has died under mysterious circumstances. The still-lovely Chesapeake Bay is the location of the characters' childhoods as well as their current waterside residences. It is also, as Barth makes clear, Ground Zero for perhaps inevitable nuclear war. Barth and his most sympathetic characters are angered, horrified, and saddened that this historical and ecologically significant estuary should be so corrupted and imperiled.

The female characters in *The Tidewater Tales*, like those in *Sabbatical*, represent another change in Barth's work from his earlier to his later career. Here is a new respect on the novelist's part for what are frequently called "women's issues." Barth's Katherine Sagamore is not only narrator but protagonist, and like *Tidewater Tales's* less-central characters, the robust May Jump and the clairvoyant Carla Silver, for example, she is intelligent and resourceful, a fuller and more dynamic figure than the passive women typical of earlier Barth fictions. Barth drives home his concern to represent female experience more completely by devoting a significant portion of the novel to matters of rape, abortion, and pregnancy, and to Frank Talbott's feminist TV drama entitled *Sex Education*. It is true that Barth treats Frank's clumsy play with some irony, but it is gentle irony that reveals sympathy for Frank's and his wife Leah's loss.

◆ Themes ◆

Although *The Tidewater Tales* and *Sabbatical* are more obviously conscious of current social issues than Barth's earlier novels, Barth's central theme remains constant throughout the fiction of his later career: the importance of narratives in our lives, how we use stories to make sense of ourselves and our world. *The Tidewater Tales* seems to approve of Katherine's and her lesbian friend May's good-hearted social activism, but it is not their arguable political logic that Barth endorses so much as their nurturing of the storytelling impulse. Katherine and May are members of HOSCA (Hands Off South and Central America), an activist organization dedicated to obstructing what they see as the American government's

imperialistic meddling in other nations' affairs. But it is the fact that they are founding members of ASPS (The American Society for the Preservation of Storytelling) which seems most significant to Barth, and during the course of the novel each validates her right to claim membership in that organization. Katherine saves her husband and her marriage with loving storytelling. May Jump, through Carla Silver, who acts as her mouthpiece, tells the story of "Scheherazade's First Second Menstruation" and of that legendary Arab storyteller's visit to the twentieth century, "tell-along" narratives that make explicit for the reader and for the characters the life-or-death nature of good-faith communication with one's fellow humans. And of course the novel before us, drafted, Barth's fiction has it, jointly by a loving couple and "now" to be finished by the rejuvenated writer Peter Sagamore, is testimony to the saving power of narrative. The characters live for us because we can read about them; and within the novel itself, Peter finishes a grateful Frank Talbott's *Sex Education* play, a work which itself concludes with happy male/female relations and which makes it possible for the beginning writer Talbott to continue to live a productive life, now that his vocation as a writer has been affirmed.

Barth is often described as a bawdy writer, and it's true that, especially in his earlier books, his high-spirited characters often engage in sexual adventure. But sex is never present in Barth's work for merely sensational or commercial reasons. Although it is abused by evil characters like Katherine's ex-husband, the sadistic rapist Pooney Baldwin, in *The Tidewater Tales* sexual intercourse is most significantly a Barth metaphor for the Self's tender communion with Another — which to Barth's novelistic mind means narrative. "Sex and stories, stories and sex. Teller and listener changing positions and coming together until they're unanimous," writes Barth. Katherine and Peter's decision to write a novel about their lives and sailing experiences is not less significant to them than their decision to bring children into a world constantly threatened with evil and death. In the course of their long fortnight of sailing, Barth has his protagonists discuss at length (and demonstrate) the parallels between composing and copulating and between giving literary and literal birth. It is a theme in American literature as old as Walt Whitman's *Leaves of Grass* (1855).

◆ Techniques ◆

From the very beginning of his career innovative techniques have been as important to Barth as action and character. Although some of Barth's techniques are almost excruciatingly obvious in *The Tidewater Tales* (such as naming Peter and Katherine's boat *Story*), in this novel Barth brings the self-conscious narrative to a new level of complexity at the same time he renders it less obscure and more pleasurable to the general reader. To such conventional suspense questions as Will the CIA harm Peter or his family? Barth adds such questions as How will Peter and Katherine create the suspense required to make the CIA plot properly chilling to the reader? As readers we move forward not only to find out, for example, who this "Odysseus" character is but also how Peter/Katherine are going to handle this violation of verisimilitude.

Barth uses practically every device imaginable to draw attention to the fact that Peter and Katherine are struggling to contrive the novel as we are reading it, and Barth ups the ante considerably by making us wonder how, if Peter has "writer's block," he can be doing any of this writing at all? From time to time Barth has Peter catch up with the narrative; that is, Peter reports that he has now written the notes in *Story*'s log that catch up to the "now" of the note-taking. That we continue to be pleasurably mystified as to how this "writing" is proceeding is part of Barth's strategy to dramatize the very action of selection and invention, to let us realize that planning a book is not writing it, that jotting notes about what one is going to write is not the same as writing the actual sentences. We witness, in other words, the continuous process of conceiving and drafting — but not finishing and polishing — a complex novel about contemporary issues and experiences and how the human consciousness registers, evaluates, and sorts those issues and experiences. The fluid nature of some of the novel's "facts" may well suggest a philosophical position about the indeterminate nature of truth — but it is first and foremost a demonstration of how writers change things as they go along. That Katherine's fetuses begin as several and end up as only two owes less to mysterious biological processes than it does to the fact of novelistic revision. The pattern of twos gradually becomes more insistent in the joint author's mind — or in Peter's after he has redrafted the work of the joint author. (We are never sure how many drafts stand between the words we are reading and the actual moment of "first draft.") Peter will flesh out the detailed written form of the mainly oral narrative of Peter/Katherine. The elaborate table of contents and bewildering array of chapter headings and subheadings turn out to be the notes Peter has jotted in their boat's log. The last page of Barth's book is the title page of Peter's, reading, apparently as Peter drafts it, "The Tidewater Tales: A Novel." That we encountered it as the first page when we began reading Barth's novel simply means that we have been through the drama of its composition, a drama of experiencing the world as well as of casting that experience into words. "Now" the official version of Peter's return to literary "maximalism" will be written.

Barth's technique in *Tidewater Tales* is designed to show that this novel is not only a book about love's endurance in an evil world and not only a primer on how to turn one's experience into a novel, but also a drama of how even the nonnovelist's mind works to receive, evaluate, and find words for the experiences and fantasies that we all have as we go about our daily business. Ultimately, writing is thinking, Barth relentlessly implies, and thinking is, in some fundamental sense, writing, since we all make narratives of our lives, if only in our heads.

◆ Literary Precedents ◆

The overarching structure of *The Tidewater Tales* takes its inspiration from the tradition of the sailing narrative, in Western literature most notably found in Homer's *Odyssey* and in American literature in Twain's *The Adventures of Huckleberry Finn* (1884), books referred to often in *The Tidewater Tales*. Barth's novel is an homage to these books as well as an addition to the venerable tradition of the sea adventure.

Probably the most striking aspect of The *Tidewater Tales'* structure, however, is its tale-within-a-tale motif, a device Barth borrows from his most constant muse, Scheherazade of *The Thousand and One Nights,* who had to tell her king story after interlocked story in order to save her life. Just as John Barth corresponds to the anonymous narrator of this Arab classic, Peter and Katherine Sagamore correspond to Scheherazade, warding off the death of Peter's art and of their marriage by telling under pressure the stories of their childhoods, their earlier sexual affairs, their first meeting, their courtship and marriage, Peter's encounter's with the CIA, and especially the unfinished story of their two-week sail on the Chesapeake Bay. Barth has elsewhere referred to the Scheherazade frame tale as "the primary tale" of *The Thousand and One Nights,* and has estimated that the book "contains 169 secondary tales . . . told by Scheherazade . . . 87 third-level tales told by the characters in Scheherazade's second-level tales, and 11 fourth-level tales told by the characters in those third-level tales told by the characters in the second-level tales told by Scheherazade, the heroine of the nameless author's primary tale: some 268 tales in all." (*The Friday Book,* 1984).

Barth's *Tidewater Tales* aims to exceed even this level of exuberant complexity as it gives us, for example, Barth's telling us of Peter and Katherine's telling their unborn children of Carla Silver's telling the assembled friends and family on the flotilla of May Jump's telling Carla of Scheherazade's telling May of John Barth's telling Scheherazade of Barth's writing a story about Scheherazade. The finest of *Tidewater Tales'* multitude of stories is perhaps the long "third-level" tale of

Odysseus's last voyage (told by Theodoros and Diana Dmitrikakis).

Barth's foregrounding of the process of composition — that is the dramatization of the writing and revision process itself as a part of the daily life of his characters — can also be seen in such works as Joyce's *Ulysses* (itself a reworking of Homer's *Odyssey*). In *Ulysses* (1922), like Barth in *Tidewater Tales*, Joyce gives us characters who are aspiring and practicing writers. Joyce's Leopold Bloom and Gerty McDowell, like Barth's Frank Talbott, are inexperienced writers seen planning and drafting literature of poor quality. Frank Talbott is working on the sophomoric television drama *Sex Education*; Bloom and Gerty work out some of the details of mildly pornographic fiction. The attempts by *Ulysses'* Stephen Dedalus to produce more refined literature can be seen to correspond to some of Peter Sagamore's more serious work.

♦ Related Titles ♦

Every book-length fiction in the Barth canon features writing about writing and tales within tales, and several employ time travel across the fiction/history barrier, a device Barth uses more thoroughgoingly in recent works. Of course, every writer repeats broad themes, certain character types, and basic plot patterns. Barth is unusually fond, though, of recycling not merely general features of his works, but details and devices of every kind. The corpse of J. A. Paisley made its first appearance in Barth's *LETTERS* (1979). Frank Talbott's *Sex Education* play, whose protagonist is an ovum, is a companion piece of and a feminist reply to Barth's "Night-Sea Journey" in *Lost in the Funhouse* (1968), where a

sperm cell is the narrator and protagonist.

But the Barth book *The Tidewater Tales* has the strongest connection to is *Sabbatical*. Indeed, some critics have said that in these books Barth has finally returned to the realistic settings of his first two books, *The Floating Opera* (1956) and *The End of the Road* (1958), this time, however, to describe in great detail the geography and customs of tidewater Maryland, thus implying that Barth is truly a Southern writer, one of those for whom "place" is essential.

While it is true that these books share an "un-Barthian" interest in local color, the similarities between them go far beyond affectionate reportage. *Sabbatical* and *The Tidewater Tales* are not only set on the Chesapeake Bay, they are set there during the summer of 1980. *Sabbatical* also has joint narrators who are also married and drafting before our eyes the story of their relationship and the present voyage.

Barth subtitles the books "A Romance" and "A Novel," respectively, following Nathaniel Hawthorne's famous distinction between works that present the "possible" (and even the "impossible") and those that confine themselves to the "probable." Hawthorne sees the Romance, his artistic preference, as offering the author more freedom to shape his material. These are rough designations of the popularly accepted categories of fantasy (or "imagination" or "art") and realism (or "fact" or "life"). *Sabbatical: A Romance* features preposterous coincidences (the miraculous return of a *boina*, a type of beret) and legendary creatures (Chessie, the Chesapeake Bay's version of the Loch Ness Monster); and *The Tidewater Tales: A Novel* tends to avoid these sorts of things, at least on its "primary" and "secondary" levels.

But the most astounding connection between these two Barth books can be found in the fact that the latter has, in effect, swallowed the former — that is, *Tidewater Tales'* Frank and Leah Talbott are the "real life" versions of *Sabbatical's* protagonists Fenn and Susan Turner, and their "real life" adventures related there are shown in *Tidewater Tales* to be the amalgam of fiction and fact that every novel creates. Frank spells out to Peter and Katherine precisely how and why he fictionalized his and Leah's lives in the book Barth's readers will have just finished, if they have read his books in the order of their publication. The abortion we saw dramatized in the earlier book is a trauma Frank and Leah Talbott continue to face in *The Tidewater Tales*. The miraculously returning *boina* and the appearance of Chessie the sea monster, on the other hand, are things Frank made up to give their lives structure, "magic," and a more conclusive meaning than they in fact have. Barth (creating the fictional version of the "real" version of *Sabbatical's* fictional characters) names their boat *Reprise* in *Tidewater Tales* (it was *Pokey* in *Sabbatical*) to signal the continuation of the action of the previous novel. It is one of Barth's especially delicious ironies that Leah Talbott's mother, Carla Silver, in *Tidewater Tales* is more colorful than her "fictionalized" portrait in *Sabbatical*. Frank Talbott is, after all, a beginning novelist.

Barth's inclusion of his "Romance" inside his "Novel" demonstrates that Hawthorne's traditionally accepted distinction is a false one, both in literature and in life. We fictionalize our real lives in our own heads, just as novelists turn "facts" into fiction in their books. The greatest writers, Barth has often said, aim for the marvelous *and* the real. Therefore, realism — the "Novel" — swallows fantasy — the "Romance" — and digests it into a book that is both, rendering its subtitle highly ironic.

♦ Ideas for Group Discussions ♦

1. What differences are implied in *The Tidewater Tales* between written and spoken stories? Between those who invent stories and those who merely tell them? Do these differences have any bearing on the novel's themes?

2. Is the quarrel between Peter and Katherine believable? How important is it that the reader feel that a serious rupture — perhaps even a breakup of the marriage — is possible?

3. How is the relationship of the Sagamores similar to and different from that of the Talbotts? Why does Barth create such similarities and differences?

4. Is Doug Townshend a force for good or for evil in the other characters' lives? To what extent can we determine the truth of his statements to Peter? What is the significance of Frank Talbott's *Kubark*, his nonfiction exposé of the CIA?

5. How are we to take the convenient helicopter crash that eliminates Pooney Baldwin and Willy Sherritt? Does Barth expect us to attribute this event to Peter's and Katherine's fiction-writing or to other forces and causes? Can such questions be asked about other crucial events?

Ron Smith
St. Christopher's School

TILL WE HAVE FACES

Novel

1956

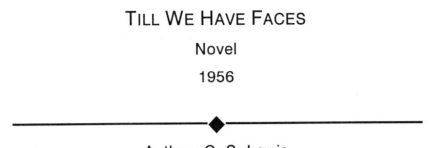

Author: C. S. Lewis

♦ Characters ♦

Readers meet the protagonist, Orual, as an old woman, preparing to die, stating that she will write down her accusations against the gods. As the book proceeds one becomes completely absorbed in her words and by her vision. Lewis convinces readers of her reality because of her consistency: she is the ugly little girl who grows up as an ugly woman; at the same time she is kinder than she knows and more selfish than she realizes. He traces her life through the approximately forty years which occupy her reminiscences as she accuses the gods in the first five-sixths of the book. Her courage, her hatred for the blood-thick Ungit, her rejection of Orual so that she could be more and more Queen of Glome, and her constant mourning for Psyche, the beloved sister whose doom she caused, elicit a sense of recognition of a troubled woman separated by time and culture from readers, but one with them in her humanity. Lewis has her speak directly to the reader about the many stories which may have grown up about her, telling the reader that most of them are false. Her candor in this matter adds to her verisimilitude and her ethos. It makes one view sympathetically her complaints against the gods which fill the first part.

Just as readers view Orual exclusively through her embittered eyes in the first part, so do they see the other characters. Her sister Redival is a golden-haired, younger, wanton, jealous agent of mischief whose bitterness toward, and hatred of, Psyche makes no sense to Orual. Psyche is not only beautiful; she is noble, courageous, loving, wise, and, at appropriate times, capable of anger. Indeed, Psyche's perfection is believable, in the main, because of Orual's being the source of one's impressions of Psyche and because Psyche is not the central character.

Other noble but more flawed characters include the Greek rationalist slave, the Fox (called Lysias just once in the novel) whose love for Psyche and Orual persists throughout the novel. This love as well as his rationalistic philosophy strongly contribute to Orual's persona, just as his comments in the first part give the perceptive reader clues about what the gods' answer will ultimately be. In his clearly motivated actions, Lewis constructs a character whose lack of belief in the other, the supernatural, does not prevent him from seeing ultimately the insufficiency of that stance and from accepting his responsibility for not having given Orual a larger vision. The second major sympathetic character is Bardia, the military and diplomatic counselor of the Queen. His valor and courage, his loyalty and simplicity, his sheer goodness aid Orual in her efforts. He is the unknowing object of her love, a love which is as total for him as it is for the Fox and for Psyche.

Orual's father, King Trom; her old nurse, Batta; the old Priest; and his successor, the young Priest, Arnom, are part of the barbarism of Glome. Each, as Orual sees him or her, is part of the mysterious world of Ungit. Trom and Batta are violent and instinctive; they are not seen by Orual as sources of light or peace or joy. The old Priest's unwavering faith in Ungit earns Orual's grudging respect; the young Priest's attempts to combine the Fox's Greek rationalism and the blood-thick mystery of Ungit ultimately do not satisfy Orual. But all four characters are carefully delineated, memorable, and more than mere symbols.

The final sixth of the novel, part two, contains the answer of the gods to Orual's charges. And here one's views of most of the characters change. Redival's pathos is made explicit, one which is convincing even as it is a surprise. The limits of the Fox are acknowledged by him and finally seen by Orual. Trom is not the terrible villain he has been viewed as being. Batta has some redeeming qualities. But most of all readers learn with Orual that her love has been suffocating, destructive, jealous. At the same time one is also made even more aware of her goodness, her growth in beauty, her lifetime of expiation for a crime which she

committed with more deliberateness than she would admit: her rejection of joy, joy in itself and joy for Psyche.

These characters are not symbols, nor are they allegorical; they are fully fleshed human beings with flaws and vices, hopes and fears, virtues and love. Through it all, however, Orual's centrality is unarguable.

◆ Social Concerns/Themes ◆

In an introductory note to the English edition of the novel not included in the American editions, Lewis presents four themes which "suddenly interlocked: the straight tale of barbarism, the mind of an ugly woman, dark idolatry and pale enlightenment at war with each other and with vision, and the havoc which a vocation, or even a faith, works on human life." Each of these themes is explored throughout the two-part retelling of the Psyche/Cupid narrative. The barbarism of Glome is personified in the king, Trom, with his arbitrary and thoughtless cruelty toward his daughters. Glome's goddess, Ungit, expresses the barbarism even as her worship has about it depths of significance which indicate that the opposing rationality of Fox, the Greek tutor of Orual, although more humane is not necessarily the correct alternative. Finally, in the character of Orual, the protagonist, what happens when a mission, even a noble one, absorbs a human being's whole person to the exclusion of love, is exposed in all its pathos.

Clearly, Lewis in this novel is not interested in social commentary or in satirizing contemporary trends and movements as he is in his space trilogy. Rather, he is dissecting a soul, describing its operations, its motions, its growth from self-delusion to truth through pain and love.

◆ Techniques ◆

Lewis employs a first-person central reminiscent point of view in the novel. Readers see what Orual sees, as she remembers it in the first part; as she learns it in the second. Her dreams and visions, vehicles for much of the archetypal subtext, are also used by Lewis to prefigure the revelations of the second part and to justify them. And the two-part structure itself is an original means of organizing the narrative. It enables Lewis to present this autobiography with an immediacy a more conventional ordering would not have. Moreover, by casting the account in the form of a deposition, a legalistic accusation of the gods for their abuse of humankind, Lewis strengthens his protagonist's characterization, for on her believability rests the plausibility of the novel.

◆ Literary Precedents ◆

In a "Note" appended to the novel, Lewis writes that "The story of Cupid and Psyche first occurs in one of the few surviving Latin novels, the *Metamorphoses* (sometimes called *The Golden Ass*) of Lucius Apuleius Platonicus, who was born about 125 A.D." After summarizing the original, Lewis says of Apuleius, "in relation to my work he is a 'source', not an 'influence' nor a 'model.'"

Carol Nevin Abromaitis
Loyola College at Baltimore

TILL WE MEET AGAIN

Novel

1988

◆

Author: Judith Krantz

◆ Social Concerns/Themes ◆

Till We Meet Again spans the period of the two world wars, and the issues surrounding the wars are a major thematic concern. Krantz portrays the folly of diplomats, as their maneuvering plunges Europe into a conflict that destroys the Edwardian world. As the singer Maddy, Eve Coudert also sees the monotony, futility, and horror of war, while entertaining the troops.

At the outset of World War II, Delphine illustrates the naiveté and pride of the French, refusing to acknowledge the menace of Hitler or the vulnerability of the Maginot Line. Bruno, Paul's son by his first marriage, displays a covert anti-Semitism and the greed of the speculating bankers. Although cynically aware that Chamberlain's concessions are dooming Europe to another great war, Bruno half-admires Hitler, and to gain money and status, he collaborates with the Nazis.

Like all of Judith Krantz's novels, *Till We Meet Again* offers a web of romantic alliances, but this novel is also a social history of the twentieth century. A major subject is the increasing importance of air travel. Early in the novel, Eve Coudert enjoys the diversion of a thrilling ride in a hot air balloon; a generation later her daughter Freddy becomes a stunt pilot for the movies; but, in both cases, air travel is considered a form of entertainment. A few years later, however, the airplane proves its military value in World War II; it soon also demonstrates its worth in transporting goods and, eventually, people.

Also important in the novel is the role of an established social order. Tradition can be a stabilizing force when, as in the case of Paul de Lancel, it leads an individual to increase his knowledge, preserve his land, and improve the lot of his employees; but an insistence upon tradition for its own sake destroys the character of Paul's son Bruno. In short, tradition must involve honor and loyalty to the highest principles; when it becomes haughty and autocratic, an aristocracy deserves only destruction.

A prime example of changing conventions is society's attitude toward show business and entertainers. When Eve Coudert runs away from her upper middle class home in Dijon and appears as a singer in a Paris music hall, she is immediately considered declassé by both the French aristocracy and her own social class; by marrying her, Paul de Lancel temporarily alienates his family and permanently damages his diplomatic career. When he is assigned to Los Angeles, however, he discovers his wife's career is accepted and admired there, and when his daughter, Delphine de Lancel, becomes a star of the French cinema, she is much in demand socially.

Another social issue is the increasing sexual openness of women. Accepting the Edwardian code of behavior, the Couderts equate a young woman's innocence with ignorance; thus, Eve — who is not permitted to go out without a chaperone — is easily seduced by the itinerant actor, Alain Marais. Even though Marais is her only lover before she meets Paul, society considers Eve a tramp. Later, in Los Angeles, the under-age Delphine drinks and smokes with the older men she dates, but she remains a virgin; her first lover is Nico Ambert, the director who discovers her and makes her a star. Unlike Eve, who genuinely cared for Marais, Delphine does not fall in love until she meets Armand Sadowski, the director she eventually marries. In contrast, Eve's younger daughter, Freddy (Marie-Frédérique), at seventeen, falls in love with her flight instructor, a man twice her age, and rebelliously leaves home to live with him. When she meets Tony Longbridge, she is attracted to him and immediately goes to bed with him. The situation is similar with David Weitz, the neurosurgeon who treats her after her plane crash.

Eve and her daughters have differing views of women's role in society. Eve is ambitious for recognition as a singer, but she sacrifices her career to become Paul's wife. Until Delphine meets Armand Sadowski, she considers men only a means of achieving the degree of sexual arousal that makes her an appealing actress. She devotes herself to pleasing Armand, however, and when he returns from the concentration camp at the end of the war, she becomes first his nurse, then his wife, and eventually the mother of his children. Yet she does not abandon her career as an actress; instead she continues to enjoy the adulation of French moviegoers.

Freddy is even less conventional. In high school she persuades the school authorities to allow her to take a course in shop instead of home economics; she secretly works to pay for flying lessons, hitchhiking to get to the airfield; and she refuses to attend college. After she leaves home, Freddy becomes a movie stunt pilot in order to buy the equipment she needs to compete in air races, and during World War II, she is a member of the Air Transport Auxiliary in Britain, ferrying new fighter planes from the factories to the air bases.

At the war's end, Freddy is bored with her role as the wife of a British squire; and, seeing the logic in Jock Hampton's dream of establishing an air freight company, she talks her husband into moving to California and beginning an air transport company, Eagles, named for his old squadron. Freddy is the partner who combines aggressive marketing, business logic, and feminine wiles to sign the first customers, and when the business appears to falter, she keeps it afloat by securing financing and management expertise from her former stunt boss, Swede Castelli. Her take-charge attitude eventually causes the breakup of her marriage to Tony Longbridge, but for Jock Hampton it is one of her most attractive qualities and the basis for a marriage of true equals.

Overall, the lives of Eve and her daughters illustrate the importance of independence and determination. Each of these women sets goals from which she refuses to be deterred. As a young girl, Eve challenges the Edwardian social code when she sneaks out to take a daring hot air balloon ride, and she thoroughly enjoys the sense of freedom that comes with flying. Later, similarly intrigued by the touring music hall show and infatuated with its star, she defies convention to attend the show, rendezvous secretly with the star, and follow him to Paris. The scandal of appearing in a music hall does not dissuade her from a career as Maddy, the celebrated singer, but she shows equal courage when she marries Paul and confronts the disapproval of his family and friends.

Eve bequeaths her love of show business to her daughter Delphine, for whom marriage does not preclude a movie career. Until she meets Armand, Delphine's only love is the motion picture camera, and she will not permit the initial opposition of her family to stand in the way of her becoming a cinema star. In Freddy, Eve's taste for the freedom of flying is intensified. Like Eve, Freddy faces some disapproval, however, from those who believe her independence is justified only by the exigencies of wartime; nevertheless, she appears also to have inherited management skills which Eve has no occasion to use until Paul's death forces her to assume management of the family vineyards.

◆ Characters ◆

Eve Coudert de Lancel, Delphine de Lancel Sadowski, and Marie-Frédérique de Lancel Longbridge Hampton are typical Judith Krantz heroines. Spectacularly beautiful and talented, larger than life, each in her own way rejects her background of affluence and privilege, overcomes social, financial, or physical obstacles, and achieves a position of power as part of an extremely glamorous lifestyle. In short, the de Lancel women live every woman's romantic fantasy, and at age thirteen, Freddy's daughter Annie, who manifests the same daring and independence of spirit, seems poised to repeat the family pattern.

Interestingly, Krantz's less important female characters, though sometimes foolish or weak, rarely seem to be truly evil; villainy appears the almost exclusive province of dissolute male characters, and the novel's one deceitful woman, Marquise de Saint-Fraycourt, could be said to have been corrupted by her husband. Insofar as they affect the plot, the minor female characters provide support for the heroines. Each of the de Lancel women has one close woman friend whose actions change the course of her life. In Paris, Eve meets Vivianne de Biron, a retired music hall performer who comes to her rescue at a desperate moment, arranging her audition at the Olympia Theater and initially managing her career. In Los Angeles, Margie Hall introduces Delphine to the older men who take the two of them to gambling establishments; and, although Margie actually proves to be the more conventional of the two, eliminating her influence is Paul's reason for sending his daughter to stay with her grandmother in Champagne.

Through the Honorable Jane Longbridge of Longbridge Grange, her roommate in the Air Transport Auxiliary, Freddy meets her first husband, Jane's brother Antony. Later, Jane's assertion that Jock Hampton has always been in love with Freddy is the catalyst for their reunion and subsequent marriage. Judith Krantz's significant male characters are unfailingly handsome and accomplished, and most also occupy positions of wealth or prestige. Invariably they are passionate and skillful lovers, but the degree of their concern for the feelings of their sexual partners is one reliable indicator of their nobility.

The shallowness and superficiality of Alain Marais are shown when he copies Harry Fragson's music hall act, and when he anticipates Eve's sexual initiation almost exclusively in terms of his own pleasure. Likewise, Bruno de Lancel, the novel's villain, is interested only in his own gratification; so it is not surprising when he betrays his family and his country for personal gain. As a young boy he prefers sex with older women who are more easily manipulated, and even his one great passion for Marie de Rochefoucauldt is actually an obsession to possess one whom he cannot easily control.

In contrast, Krantz's heroes immediately fall overwhelmingly and unselfishly in love. Vicomte Paul-Sebastian de Lancel loves Eve from the first moment he sees her in the bombed-out farmhouse, though his behavior at that time does not even suggest his love. As soon as World War I ends, however, he returns to Paris and proposes marriage. Likewise, Jock Hampton falls in love with Freddy when she lifts her wedding veil and he sees her face for the first time, but he is too honorable to declare his love until he believes she has had time to recover from her divorce.

Armand Sadowski too eventually acknowledges that he has loved Delphine since their first interview, but —

recognizing her need to be the pursuer in a romantic relationship — he initially feigns indifference. Even in the cases of Antony Longbridge and Terence McGuire, who cannot match the force of Freddy's personality, their immediate and overwhelming attraction to her indicates the sincerity of their passion, and each is to some degree unselfish in choosing to leave Freddy.

Also characteristic of Krantz's heroes is their need for adventure and their dedication to a cause; in fact, they are warriors first and lovers second. For example, not only does Paul de Lancel delay his courtship of Eve until he has completed his wartime duties, but at the beginning of the war, he feels obligated to enlist for military service even though his young wife, Laure de Saint-Fraycourt, is pregnant. Her death in childbirth moves him to postpone all other such commitments until the war's end; his enlistment is also the cause of lifelong hostility on the part of his son and his former in-laws. Armand Sadowski shows similar qualities of patriotism, choosing to remain in France and join first the French army and later the Resistance. Tony Longbridge and Jock Hampton are aces of the Eagle Squadron in World War II, while thirst for adventure leads Terence McGuire to volunteer for heroic service in Canadian units of the RAF, as a pilot in World War I and as an instructor in World War II.

◆ Techniques ◆

In *Till We Meet Again*, as in the earlier Krantz novels, the primary appeal is the fast-moving, romantic plot. With cinematic style, Krantz shifts from one subplot to the next, maintaining the flow of this complexly plotted novel. Famous for her detailed descriptions, she provides abundant sensory details, which enable the reader to visualize the clothes, landscapes, furnishings, and other surroundings, and thus to experience vicariously the adventures of the central characters. By focusing upon the sexual awakenings of the young women and by presenting the moments of sexual intimacy as they are contemplated by the participants, Krantz also increases the subtlety with which the passion is handled and reenforces the overall tone of romance.

Sometimes criticized for plot manipulation in which her characters meet famous people of the era, Krantz introduces relatively few well known people in this novel, and those who are present serve to establish the main characters against a specific background of time and place. The reader has no sense of obvious authorial contrivance.

♦ Related Titles ♦

While there is a kinship among all Krantz novels in terms of plot and characters, *Till We Meet Again* shows most similarity to *Princess Daisy* (1979) and *Mistral's Daughter* (1982). Freddy's business success is reminiscent of Daisy Valensky's, and Delphine's relationship with her manipulative half-brother Bruno approximates Daisy's relationship with Ram. In fact, Bruno strongly resembles Ram in the charm and physical attractiveness which initially conceal his ruthlessness and his need to control women, especially his sister. Likewise, the three generations of de Lancel women — Eve, her daughters Delphine and Freddy, and Freddy's daughter Annie — parallel Maggy, Teddy, and Fauve of *Mistral's Daughter*. Also present in both novels are the background issues of anti-Semitism, German occupation, and the French Resistance.

♦ Adaptations ♦

Till We Meet Again was adapted as a CBS miniseries directed by Charles Jarrott, and produced by Steve Krantz (Judith's husband) and Keith Richardson.

Charmaine Allmon Mosby
Western Kentucky University

TIME AND AGAIN

Novel

1970

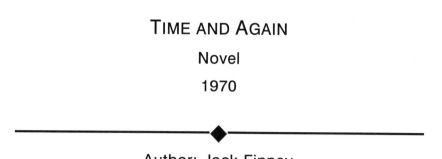

Author: Jack Finney

◆ Social Concerns ◆

Time and Again describes Si Morley's discovery that he can live in two different eras: contemporary New York City and the New York City of 1882. He must decide in which era he wishes to spend the rest of his life.

The context of the novel is the radicalism of the late 1960s. The novel reflects the worry about the dying city, the traditional urban centers threatened by white flight, black rioting, and resulting urban blight. It grows, too, out of crisis of authority prompted by the Vietnam War, the growing realization that citizens should not leave all important decisions to a central government. Finally, the novel discusses the relation between individuality and community, a debate strong in the era when alternate lifestyles, like the commune and the open marriage, competed with traditional social structures for the allegiance of the individual.

◆ Themes ◆

Si Morley chooses to live in the New York of 1882. He finds that old New York has a quality of life that modern New York cannot match. Although more primitive in technology, its citizens have a joyousness about life, a knowledge of why they are alive, that twentieth-century New Yorkers no longer possess. Two world wars and a current desultory military action in Vietnam, Si Morley discovers, have taken the spirit out of people and have left them confused about the purpose of living.

Nor is the problem just the people. The physical structure of New York City shows the differences. The New York City of 1882 is a rainbow of rural, suburban, and urban landscapes. Walking a few blocks in any direction will take Morley from commercial center to quiet residential neighborhood to active farmland, without ever leaving Manhattan island. Contemporary New York City, however, is all concrete and steel, unvarying canyons of high-rise apartment and office buildings.

The third theme of the novel is Finney's contribution to the ongoing debate among fantasy writers about time-travel. If someone from the present travels into the past, will their actions change the past and therefore the future known today as present? Si's visit to the past is made possible by a secret government experimental unit. Once time travel is proved possible, the project directors begin speculating upon the possibility of changing the past deliberately. Si chooses at this point to enter the past permanently, unwilling to see how government bureaucrats think the present should be improved.

◆ Characters ◆

Si Morley is a typical Finney protagonist. Allowed to speak in the first person, Si reveals himself to be a modest, sensitive, self-reliant individual who passionately cares that life should have meaning and purpose. Discontented in his repetitive job as a commercial artist and by a love affair which may or may not hold promise, Si is ripe to respond to a situation, person, or task that demands his full energy.

Julia Charbonneau proves that person for Si in the world of 1882. Helping her aunt run a boarding house, Julia is a beautiful and sensitive woman. She and Si are immediately attracted to one another: She can show him around pastoral New York while he can charm her with seemingly incredible predictions about the future. Julia needs, however, more than a friend. With no careers available to even a bright female in 1882, Julia faces a marriage of convenience just to survive.

Jake Pickering, another citizen of 1882, passionately loves Julia. Although she does not reciprocate, he offers the opportunity for a respectable marriage. Jake is a hard-drinker, given to fits of outrage and boorish behavior; he lives comfortably, but seems preoccupied. His preoccupation turns out to be a plot to blackmail Andrew Carm-ody, a New York financier, who benefited from the criminal activities of the infamous Boss Tweed gang. Jake becomes Si's competitor in two ways: for Julia's heart and for the key to Carmody's career. Jake is a marvelous antagonist: mean-spirited, overwrought, and clever. Happily Si combats him; a real villain is preferable to the faceless bureaucrats of the twentieth-century.

Ruben Prien and Dr. Danzinger direct the experiments to place people in the past. Not sharing Si's affection for the past, they look upon time travel as a problem in physics and an opportunity to effect changes in the present. Clever in certain ways, their intelligence and imaginations are limited by the need to follow the orders of superiors, watch budgets, and maintain secrecy. As foils, these characters enable Si to appreciate his own special reaction to the past; as Si learns that his interests are not the same, he increasingly realizes that he must take independent action.

◆ Techniques ◆

Time and Again is a skillfully constructed narrative. The double plot and quick-paced dialogue hurry the story forward. As the plots gradually interweave and Si is forced to become an active participant in Jake Pickering's plot as well as an observer of the past, Time and Again becomes a novel that cannot be put down until the last page.

The unusual feature of Time and Again is the fact that it is illustrated with pictures and sketches of nineteenth-century New York. Professedly testifying to the reality of Si's adventures, these black-and-white illustrations also create a nostalgic mood. Seeing the faces of the people Si meets and the places he visits helps the reader easily accept Si's decision to remain in the past. Through the photographs Finney conveys much factual information about New York City's history and architecture.

Illustrated novels are rare today, but once the common practice was to illustrate important works of fiction. The writings of nineteenth-century authors such as Charles Dickens, William Thackeray, and Mark Twain were often illustrated with drawings envisioning important scenes from the novel. Thus *Time and Again* is not only a novel about the nineteenth century, it also looks like a novel from the past.

◆ Literary Precedents ◆

Travel through time is an old fictional device, dating back to the mid-eighteenth century. Nineteenth-century novels of time travel such as Edward Bellamy's *Looking Backward* (1888) or Twain's *A Connecticut Yankee in King Arthur's Court* (1889) depended upon the hero falling asleep to change eras. H. G. Wells's *The Time Machine* (1895) introduced the notion of constructing a machine that would allow a voyager to travel forward or backward. Much popular science fiction about time-travel relies upon the device of a time-machine to generate the story. Finney provides an interesting twist by assuming that time-travel is a product of deliberate imaginative effort. Si Morley experiences time not as a stream, but as shadow of the present given substance by sensation. Si moves into the past by recreating the sights, sounds, touches, smells, and tastes of 1882.

◆ Related Titles ◆

A man living in two worlds is the premise of an earlier Finney novel, *The Woodrow Wilson Dime* (1968). In this novel, however, the worlds exist side-by-side rather than in sequence. Ben Bennell discovers that spending a Woodrow Wilson dime sends him into a parallel but different universe in which he is married to a different woman and holds a different job.

The Woodrow Wilson Dime, though, is comic while *Time and Again* is nostalgic. The longing for a better past appears in several stories included in Finney's second collection of stories, *I Love Galesburg in the Springtime* (1963). In the title story a town actively resists the inroads of the present: A trolley magically appears to scare off a factory builder, and a horse-drawn fire engine unexpectedly saves a burning Victorian mansion. In "Where the Cluetts Are," a modern couple build a house from nineteenth-century architectural plans and find themselves physically and mentally reconstructing an earlier era.

Robert M. Otten
Marymount University

THE TIME MACHINE

Novel

1895

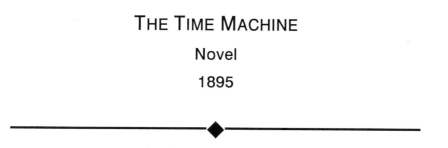

Author: H. G. Wells

◆ Characters ◆

The two most important characters in *The Time Machine* are the Time Traveller and the narrator. Both are complex men, each trying to make sense out of what he experiences. The Time Traveller is an "eminent scientist" and is accustomed to dispassionate scientific research. He is also an adventurer who makes a daring trip into the future. Although he is anonymous, which makes him easy to view as just a symbolic figure, he has a strong personality that matures during his days in the future. Confident in the inevitable triumph of science and secure in his political prejudices, he is at first delighted with the "Golden Age" of the Eloi. Sure, the Eloi are not very bright and their days are filled with frivolity, but the loss of human ambition seems to him to be compensated by the openness and sharing in the Eloi society. He even forms a friendship with an Eloi female, Weena.

The Morlocks are a terrible shock to his faith and prejudices. Technology's promise of a destiny beyond the sky has been denied. The Morlocks seem to lack the aesthetic sensibilities of the Eloi and have no ambition to direct their machines for a better future. This awful knowledge is compounded by the Morlocks' victimization of the Eloi. Weena helps the Time Traveller come to view the Eloi not as a decayed upper class but as people. With his faith in the proud ambitions of a technological society shattered by the knowledge that the technology of the future will be devoted to cruelty and the debasement of humanity, and with his confidence shaken that in a class war the good side and the bad side will be easy to identify, he must fall back on his own internal resources.

The Time Machine is a tragedy because there seems to be no way to alter an immutable future of the devolution and failed promise of humanity. As in great tragedies, the main character faces the truth in himself when his grief is greatest; when he discovers the Morlocks have murdered Weena, he is "almost moved to begin a massacre of the helpless abominations about me, but I contained myself." Daylight has come and the Morlocks are blinded on a hillock and at the Time Traveller's mercy. At this terrible moment, he controls his animal self, and the good in the individual man triumphs over cruelty and evil.

The narrator is not well drawn but is nonetheless important. It is he who relates the story to the reader. What he chooses to tell, what he finds significant, will color the Time Traveller's story. He is a skeptic and unwilling to take the Time Traveller's story at face value. Even so, he tries to be fair. Early in the novel, he and his fellows witness an experiment in which a "glittering metallic framework" disappears. Although the narrator calls what he sees "absolutely unaccountable," he tells exactly what he saw: "the little machine suddenly swung round, became indistinct, was seen as a ghost for a second perhaps, as an eddy of faintly glittering brass and ivory; and it was gone — vanished!" The narrator provides careful and detailed descriptions; his skepticism and honesty encourage belief in the reliability of his narrative.

The narrator is accompanied by men representative of society. For instance, there are the "Medical Man," the "Psychologist," and the "Provincial Mayor." These representatives of confident, successful modern man refuse to believe their eyes and find the Time Traveller's account ridiculous. They seem unlikely to change the bleak future that the Time Traveller has seen. Even so, the narrator comes to believe: "At last I understood." Three years later he still awaits the Time Traveller's return. That is a hopeful note.

◆ Social Concerns ◆

On one level, *The Time Machine* is a straightforward satire of the society of late Victorian England. In the future year 802,701, the "Time Traveller" encounters the seemingly ideal society of the Eloi. These peaceful and playful people live in a pastoral land without industry and pollution. They share everything with one another: food, shelter, and the land. "Communism," the Time Traveller says to himself. Victorian socialism seems to have triumphed in the far future, creating a happy and classless society. The weaknesses of the Eloi are that they are small, silly, and incapable of sophisticated abstract thought. Apparently, the comforts of their lives have shaped the evolution of the Eloi — they seem to have devolved, that is retrogressed in their physical and mental abilities.

Then, to his horror, the Time Traveller discovers the Morlocks, who live underground. They live in an industrialized world that provides some of the basic needs of the Eloi. Pale white and unable to tolerate even moonlight, at night they climb out of the ground to feed on the Eloi. The Time Traveller realizes now what has happened to humanity: "It seemed clear as daylight to me that the gradual widening of the present merely temporary and social difference between the Capitalist and the Labourer was the key to the whole position . . . There is a tendency to utilise underground space for the less ornamental purposes of civilization; there is the Metropolitan Railway in London, for instance . . . Even now, does not an Eastend worker live in such artificial conditions as practically to be cut off from the natural surface of the earth?" The Morlocks are the descendants of industrialized society's laborers. Furthermore, the upper classes try to shut out the lower classes from high society, making "intermarriage which at present retards the splitting of our species along lines of social stratification, less and less frequent." The "Haves" have become the Eloi, indolent and childlike, who are the descendants of those who fed off the labor of others. The "Have-nots" have become the Morlocks, who in a terrible twist of evolution feed on the helpless Eloi. The Morlocks and Eloi satirically represent the evils of a society in which wealth and goods are inequitably distributed. There is great anger in this satire; it comes from an author who at the time of writing thought he had little time to live and whose lower-class origins and lower-class accent had inhibited his advancement in spite of his intellectual promise.

Another social concern is implicit in *The Time Machine*: human evolution. The novel depicts a far future, thus allowing enough time for the slow working of natural selection as Charles Darwin had conceived it. Some critics have misinterpreted this theme of evolution, arguing that it contradicts Wells's faith in technological progress. This is unfair to Wells and is too simplistic. He believed progress was possible, but he believed evolution was inevitable. In *The Time Machine*, natural selection, which is only biological and thus indifferent to morality, has evolved humanity into two separate species. In later writings, such as *The Shape of Things to Come* (1933), Wells plainly shows that he believes a worldwide calamity that destroys modern society may be necessary before a more just and progressive one evolves. In any case, people have the power to shape their futures, but those futures may not necessarily be progressive; humanity may devolve into beasts.

The idea of social and biological devolution has influenced many twentieth-century writers. For instance, Pierre Boulle uses the concept for the premise of *Planet of the Apes* (1963), in which humanity has devolved while apes have evolved. Another use of the idea is exemplified by L. Sprague de Camp's *Rogue Queen* (1951), in which a society devolves, although the people in it do not biologically degenerate. In these, as well as in *The Time Machine*, the notion that "progress" is not inevitable is important.

◆ Themes ◆

In 1895, H. G. Wells was underweight and suffering from respiratory illness; believing that he had only a short time to make his mark as a writer and in need of money, he assembled ideas that he had developed in magazine articles and crafted *The Time Machine*. In order to make it a profitable novel, he made it into a sensational adventure. He also made it thematically complex. The social satire is plain enough, but Wells also developed themes of beauty, the divided self, and, at bottom, good and evil. In a well-known remark, author V. S. Pritchett declared, *"The Time Machine . . .* will take its place among the great stories of our language. Like all excellent works it has meanings within its meaning and no one who has read the story will forget the dramatic effect of the change of scene in the middle of the book, when the story alters its key, and the Time Traveller reveals the foundation of slime and horror on which the pretty life of his Arcadians [the Eloi] is precariously and fearfully resting."

The Time Traveller descends into the underground realm of the Morlocks. It is all "great shapes" and "grotesque black shadows" cast by the flames from his matches. Then: "The Morlocks at any rate were carnivorous! Even at the time, I remember wondering what large animal could have survived to furnish the red joint I saw." Slime and horror, indeed!

The land of the Eloi is lush with flowers and full of games and laughter. Wells borrows from the ancient pastoral tradition, which entertains weary urban dwellers with tales of a "Golden Age" when people were one with nature and the problems of civilization were undreamt of. The Time Traveller even calls his "communist" paradise the "Golden Age." But the beautiful Eloi are not pastoral shepherds; they are the sheep, and the Morlocks are the wolves. The beauty of the world of the Eloi masks hideous ugliness.

In the hearts of the descendants of humanity, the spirits have withered. "However helpless the little people in the presence of their mysterious Fear, I was differently constituted," observes the Time Traveller. "I came out of this age of ours, this ripe prime of the human race, when Fear does not paralyse and mystery has lost its terrors." In the Time Traveller, beauty and ugliness are still united in a whole man, and he can face both with courage. The Eloi refuse to even acknowledge the horror of the Morlocks; the Morlocks quail in the light. The symbolism in this implies that a life of only beauty and pleasure is a childish and empty one, even as the Eloi are like foolish children. To survive, humanity must face its ugliness.

The theme of the divided self was a common one in Victorian literature. Usually, an author would use it to contrast strait-laced morality with hidden sexual desires. In *The Time Machine*, the Eloi are seemingly free of animal desires. On the other hand, the Morlocks are rapaciously hungry, and they are animal-like — afraid of light, smelly, and without appreciation for beauty. Part of their ability to evoke horror may be the Morlocks' representation of the dark side of human nature.

A few critics have seen the portrayal of the evil of the Morlocks as a betrayal of *The Time Machine's* social themes. Some have expected Wells to present a "communist" future society as an unalloyed triumph because he was a Socialist. Wells was too complex a man for such simplicity. While a member of the Socialistic Fabian Society in the first decade of the twentieth century, he tried to usurp the dominance of the society by George Bernard Shaw and Sidney and Beatrice Webb in part because as someone born into the lower classes he resented the presumption of those from well-to-do backgrounds telling people like himself what was good for them. Not everyone who said he was a Socialist was an ally, and not every society that looked ideal was good. In this sense, *The Time Machine* is "dystopian" because it portrays a future society that should be "utopian" but is instead an abomination.

At bottom, the novel has deep emotional resonance because it is an examination of good and evil, and as in real life, the two are not simple and are not easy to recognize: They are complicated. The Morlocks and the Eloi are two parts of modern man. Long after he has seen the "red joint" in the caves of the Morlocks, the Time Traveller refuses to acknowledge to himself that what he saw was a butchered Eloi. Eventually, he comes to terms with the dark horror in himself and overcomes his political prejudice against the descendants of the "capitalist" exploiters of the working class. He recognizes evil in the Morlocks and realizes that some ethical values transcend politics. Therefore, he takes action against the Morlocks. As a fully integrated man, he knows that evil flourishes when the spirit is lazy, as when the Eloi simply refuse to face the horror in their lives. This knowledge motivates him to again ride his machine through time. Evil must be actively confronted.

◆ Techniques ◆

The Time Machine was written to make money as well as to make Wells's mark on literature. One technique he uses to hold the interest of readers is to have the Time Traveller relate his story as a marvelous adventure from which he has just returned. The atmosphere thus created gives the narrative the air of a fairy tale, as if he were Sinbad returned from sailing to enchanted lands, or Odysseus back home from his magical voyage through the lands of the cyclops, the sirens, and other mythical beings. Many critics refer to the tone thus created as "mythic," meaning it captures some of the basic beliefs of contemporary culture and gives them form and direction. The narrator serves the reader, asking the questions that sensible people would ask and focusing on the details that readers would want to know. Yet, the narrator is open-minded enough to allow himself a sense of wonder and therefore allows readers to marvel at the tale. In addition, *The Time Machine* is compact; its events are pressed close together. This gives the narrative a breathless speed, and the imaginative inventions of Wells rush one upon another, maintaining excitement.

◆ Literary Precedents ◆

The wondrous adventure tale is a fundamental part of the Western literary tradition. The earliest literary works known are tales of mythic magic and wondrous events. In the Sumerian *Epic of Gilgamesh* (c. 2000 B.C.), the adventures are part of a quest. In the *Odyssey* (c.1050-850 B.C.), they are part of a lost warrior's wanderings. *The Time Machine* presents a great traveler's journeys, from the 1890s all the way to the end of the world.

The Time Traveller is also for a time stranded in the land of the Eloi after the Morlocks take his time machine. This has been a popular convention of fiction since the publication of Daniel Defoe's *Robinson Crusoe* (1719). In *The Time Machine*, the convention forces the Time Traveller to make some difficult choices between Eloi and Morlock, between courage and cowardice.

The Time Machine is also an important "seminal" work. That is, it sets two important precedents that subsequent authors follow. The first precedent is that of the time machine. It enables someone to voyage back and forth to past and future. The time travel story has become commonplace in science fiction and a time-travel device is a staple of the genre.

The other significant precedent is the concept of "time" as the "fourth dimension": "'Clearly,' the Time Traveller proceeded, 'any real body must have extension in four directions: it must have Length, Breadth, Thickness and Duration.'" Wells's reasoning may not withstand close scrutiny, but Albert Einstein was later to characterize "time" as the fourth dimension. Wells's describing the universe in four terms — Length, Breadth, Thickness, and Duration — has inspired a multitude of fictional adventures through both time and space. The television show *Dr. Who's* Tardis, for instance, is a time machine that may wander through millions of years and millions of light-years in any single journey.

◆ Adaptations ◆

In 1960, George Pal produced and directed the motion picture *The Time Machine* for Galaxy Films and MGM. The screenplay was written by David Duncan, an author of popular novels as well as screenplays. The 103-minute color film stars Rod Taylor as George, the Time Traveller; Yvette Mimieux as Weena; and Sebastian Cabot as Dr. Philip Hillyer, the character thought by some critics to be the novel's narrator.

At the time of its release, critics generally thought the motion picture was too tame for 1960 audiences. In recent times, the motion picture has come to be regarded as an entertaining success for George Pal, although critics almost invariably are disappointed by the absence of Wells's most important themes and by the shallowness of the plot, which portrays the Eloi as slaves who with the help of Rod Taylor rebel against their Morlock masters. The special effects are much admired, and Gene Warren and Tim Barr won Academy awards for them. Wah Chang created the time-travel sequences. In the film, the Time Traveller still comes from the 1890s, and his gadgets and time machine look Victorian.

In 1979, *Time After Time*, a motion picture inspired by Wells's *The Time Machine*, was released. Produced by Herb Jaffe for Warner Brothers and Orion, it was scripted and directed by Nicholas Meyer. The story was created by Karl Alexander and Steve Hayes. The 112-minute color film stars Malcolm McDowell as H. G. Wells; David Warner as Dr. Jack Stevenson, the utterly evil Jack the Ripper; and Mary Steenburgen as Amy Robbins, a 1970s bank employee who eventually joins Wells in the 1890s as his second wife.

In *Time After Time*, H. G. Wells himself is the builder of the time machine. As does the Time Traveller in *The Time Machine*, he tells his visitors about his discovery of how to move through time. One of these visitors, Dr. Stevenson, steals the machine and journeys to 1979 San Francisco. He is delighted by the relaxed sexual habits of the time and sets about slaughtering women. Horrified at the thought of what Jack the Ripper might do to the ideal society of the future, Wells pursues him through time. He saves Amy Robbins, sends Dr. Stevenson off to a suitable doom, and returns to 1890s London with his ladylove. The motion picture is edge-of-the-seat suspenseful, and the actors deliver fine performances, but these qualities do not fully compensate for the ugliness of the film's premise and horrible butchery of innocent women.

◆ Ideas for Group Discussions ◆

The Time Machine is a short novel, yet the possibilities for its discussion seem endless. Every aspect of it offers opportunities for discussion, and the numerous commentaries on it suggest many avenues for approaching the inner workings of the novel. One way for generating discussion of the novel could be to have discussion group members research different aspects of the novel and then report his or her discoveries to the group. For instance, one group member might research the scientific reality behind the novel and report on how close Wells came to modern theories about time as a fourth dimension and whether scientists think time travel is a credible possibility. Another might investigate the wealth of science fiction tales about time travel and report to the group how other authors have handled the theme. Still another member might read Wells's early essays on time, published in popular magazines, and compare his ideas in the essays with what he does in his novel. Another might investigate the effect the novel had on the general public, and so on.

The Time Machine features a complex working out of ideas about society, evolution, technology, and science. Almost any discussion of the novel would do well to begin with what the ideas are and how they are expressed. In the novel, Wells suggests that modern class structure is cruel and will lead to future evils. He also suggests that evolution is not a matter of endless progress, but is a function of environment that can lead to changes that are not influenced by human concepts of ethics or social advancement. Further, technology is presented as something indifferent to human need and desires; it shapes people ruthlessly. He also seems to assert, as have writers before him, that science does not have all the answers to the mysteries of the universe. Implicit throughout is the social criticism that people in the industrialized world are too self-satisfied and could be mindlessly plunging into an awful future.

1. When Wells wrote *The Time Machine*, he was very sick and stood a good chance of dying. This makes the novel an effort to leave a unique mark on the world; Wells could not have known that the novel would make him the money he needed for medical treatment that would prolong his life. What seems to be the result of Wells's effort to make his mark, to show the world what he could do?

2. Wells had ample reason to resent the upper classes of England that looked down upon him because of his poverty and lower-class accent. Why is this not reflected in *The Time Machine*? Why is the Time Traveller forgiving and forbearing, when the situations of the novel offer him ample opportunities to bash those whom H. G. Wells would have had reason to most despise?

3. Many readers think the Time Traveller is none other than Wells, himself. Is the Time Traveller really Wells, or is he a literary creation like other similarly named characters in the novel — figures such as the Medical Man and the Provincial Mayor?

4. How accurate are the views on social and natural evolution in *The Time Machine*? The later *Outline of History* (1920) shows that Wells took his ideas on evolution seriously, and the *Time Machine* is his first significant presentation of his views on the subject. Does evolution really work the way he says it does? Does society somehow evolve, too?

5. *The Time Machine* was written more than a hundred years ago, and some of its ideas seem out of date. Certainly, the view of the aging sun has long been supplanted by other scientific theories. Why does the novel still have a strong hold on modern audiences?

6. How good are the characterizations in *The Time Machine*? Is the development of the Time Traveller from smug Victorian to open-minded observer credible? Do any of the other characters change or grow?

7. What is the value of the social

commentary? Does it do any good?

8. What in *The Time Machine* would have been new and innovative in 1895? Is it much imitated?

9. It can be fun to speculate on what happens to the Time Traveller after the end of the novel. A good evening's entertainment can be had by having group members read aloud their stories of what could be the Time Traveller's next adventure. Is he in the past? Does he return to the future to a time before Weena is killed and save her? What does he learn next about society and evolution?

10. Is *The Time Machine* a good story? What about it holds or loses your attention?

Kirk H. Beetz

A TIME TO KILL

Novel

1989

♦

Author: John Grisham

♦ Social Concerns ♦

A Time to Kill takes place in the town of Clanton, in Ford County, a fictionalized version of Grisham's home region, northern Mississippi. The area is rural, removed from the bustle of life in the city. The town's population is 8,000, 74% of them white, but the black presence is quite visible. This environment recalls the settings of a multitude of Southern novels, notably William Faulkner's Yoknapatawpha saga set in the same region.

A crime with profound racial overtones disrupts the region. Two rednecks kidnap, repeatedly rape, and leave for dead a ten-year-old black girl. Her father, Carl Lee Hailey, blows the attackers apart with an M-16 as they leave the courtroom after their bail hearing. Grisham claims that he created this plot in response to watching a similar girl agonizingly testify in a rape case. Most of Clanton's citizens agree that if a white father had committed such vigilantism against two black rapists, he would not suffer any legal penalties. But as a black man, Carl Lee faces capital murder charges and is eligible for the death penalty if he is convicted. Because Carl Lee clear-

ly planned and carried out the offense, his most obvious defense strategy is to plead not guilty by reason of temporary insanity.

As an account of Carl Lee's case, *A Time to Kill* provides one of fullest literary representations of the sequence of legal procedures in a murder case: preliminary hearing — bail hearing — grand jury deliberation — arraignment — hearing for motions — actual trial. The book further dramatizes the shattering impact of this case on the region; Grisham makes his book a portrait of the attitudes, lifeways, and nether side of the contemporary Deep South. The portrait, done with fine humorous touches and an appreciation for the region, is not always flattering; Grisham presents deeply-ingrained corruption, racism, and proclivities for violence.

Within a large cast, the book centers on Carl Lee's white attorney, Jake Brigance. Jake defines himself by contrast with Clanton's Sullivan firm: "They [the Sullivan lawyers] had the big farmers, the banks, the insurance companies, the railroads, everybody with money. The other fourteen lawyers in the county picked up the scraps and represented people — living, breathing human souls, most of whom had very little money. These were the 'street lawyers' — those in the trenches helping people in trouble. Jake was proud to be a street lawyer." Although he may have idealism for his job, he defends these people in trouble by whatever means possible. Grisham explains Jake's views on taking black clients who face assault charges: "Jake enjoyed the stabbings because acquittals were possible; just get an all-white jury full of rednecks who could care less if all niggers stabbed each other. They were just having a little fun down at the tonk, things got out of hand, one got stabbed, but didn't die. No harm, no conviction." These are hardly the thoughts of an idealist. Jake is quite willing to use discomforting, even morally dubious tactics to win his cases. Carl Lee's case provides significant incentives to win: Jake feels great empathy with Carl Lee, and Jake realizes that winning will make him the hottest lawyer in Ford County. So Jake will do what it takes to win.

Jake's attitudes toward his cases exemplify the American adversarial system of justice. Unlike some European systems in which trial participants sift evidence before a panel of judges, the trial procedure in America pits two sides against each other in a contest in which strategies often matter more than the unbiased presentation of evidence. The lawyers become advocates, champions, even servants of their respective sides rather than to the truth or to justice. Jake and his adversary, ambitious District Attorney Rufus Buckley (fictional prosecutors are always politically ambitious), may believe in the rightness of their positions, but they also relish the thrill of the contest and allow the trial to take on a momentum of its own.

As both lawyers desperately want to win, both readily use tactics that stretch taste and ethics. Both sides get early access to the list of potential jurors. Both sides employ psychiatrists who will say in court whatever the case demands regardless of the real mental condition of the defendant. Jake needles Rufus to upset him, embraces Carl Lee's family in a show of sympathy to impress the jury, and brutalizes the rapists' mothers during cross-examination — tactics which may not advance the cause of justice but which do win advantages for Jake's side.

As unsettling as Jake's actions may seem, he fights a larger, more malevolent evil. The revived Ku Klux Klan, galvanized by the racial aspects of the case, tries to bomb Jake's house, kills an officer who was guarding him, and intimidates potential jurors. This last act means that they have access to the jury list, and haunting the plot is the strong possibility that they got it from Rufus, that the D.A. is totally corrupted.

Grisham refuses to cast Jake as a noble, always-by-the-rules, idealistic attorney, but Grisham also renders Jake's enemies as far greater offenders than he; Jake cannot adequately defend Carl Lee unless he resorts to questionable tactics.

The book presents an overall atmosphere of deception. Black jurors, who tend to oppose the death penalty, know to lie and say they support it so that they can stay in the jury pool and thus maybe serve for Carl Lee's case. A black minister hoards money intended for the relief of the Hailey family and refuses to release it. Sheriff Ozzie Walls, a very appealing character, illegally coerces a confession from one of the rapists and then tortures a confession from a bomber. As repulsive as

Ozzie's victims are, he treats them with a cruelty that is disturbing. Jake's lawyer friends obtain for him forbidden information. Lucien Wilbanks, Jake's mentor and a longtime advocate of liberal causes, bribed a juror in an earlier case and wants to bribe one of Carl Lee's jurors. Almost no character is a knight-on-a-white-horse, a wholly good person. Grisham deftly keeps readers off-kilter. Readers may root for Jake and Carl Lee, but Grisham constantly remind readers how grubby, unpleasant, and morally dubious each man can be.

The contestants in the adversarial system seldom mention justice except as a means of grandstanding. Jake and Rufus, and the other lawyers as well, essentially want to win specific outcomes, which they call justice. They do operate under some basic principles. Jake does believe that Carl Lee should not suffer for killing the rapists, and arguing insanity — regardless of the facts — is the best means to achieve that result. No character expresses faith in the system. Law and trial procedures seem inadequate to deal with the social problems raised by the case. The jury, none of whom accepts the insanity defense, finally admits what everyone has felt all along, that if the races in the case were reversed, the white killer would win acquittal. And so the jurors decide to treat Carl Lee as they would treat a white defendant. The irony here is that as the jury affirms equality of the races in court, it then disregards society's murder laws. Moral absolutes about justice do not apply in this environment. Grisham's ribald portrayal of Jake's friend Harry Rex Vonner displays what success means in the legal community: He "was a huge slob of a lawyer who specialized in nasty divorce cases and perpetually kept some jerk in jail for back child support. He was vile and vicious, and his services were in great demand by divorcing parties in Ford County. He could get the children, the house, the farm, the VCR, the microwave, everything. One wealthy farmer kept him on retainer just so the current wife couldn't hire him for the next divorce." Harry Rex gets results; in his practice, results matter much more than appeals to higher standards. Harry Rex is the sort of lawyer people hire because he effectively serves the interests of his clients. He does not serve an idealized version of how lawyers should advance the cause of justice. Lucien Wilbanks admits the moral confusion that engulfs the Hailey case when he says to Jake, "Now, you can win the case, and if you do, justice will prevail. But if you lose it, justice will also prevail. Kind of a strange case, I guess. I just wish I had it." In a morally relative universe, Lucien's comments affirm, the contest is more important than the principle.

As the novel unsettles readers in its depiction of the "justice" system at work, it offers an equally challenging portrait of race relations in the supposedly enlightened South of the 1980s. (Some readers express surprise that novel has a contemporary setting. Grisham's *The Chamber* [1994] refers to the Hailey case and places it in 1985.) In Ford County the races intermingle peacefully; the three-quarters white population even elects a black sheriff, Ozzie Walls. Yet awareness of racial difference permeates this society; race matters in every decision. Ozzie's elections placate the federal Justice Department and forestall investigations of local voting practices. The setting of bail in criminal cases differs depending on the race of the accused. The grand jury votes along racial lines. Selection of the foreperson of the grand jury becomes an exercise in affirmative action. Judges and prosecutors consider how their actions in the Hailey case will affect their efforts to keep the black vote. In such a tense, hyper-aware environment, the Hailey case serves as a match to a powder keg and ignites violent racial confrontations. In 1963, Martin Luther King described Mississippi as "a desert state sweltering with the heat of injustice and oppression." The sobering question suggested by the novel is how much has Mississippi really changed.

Grisham daringly writes a two-page exposition of the thoughts of Lester, Carl Lee's brother, about race relations in Clanton; that is, a white author gets into the mind of a black character about the very issues that separate black and white. Having fled Mississippi for a better paying job up North, Lester feels depressed at returning to see anew the unchanging, almost unescapable poverty in which Southern blacks live. He takes the racism as a given: He is impressed by the high bails given the rapists, because people who kill or assault blacks seldom get high bails. Grisham places the racial epithet "nigger" into the speech and thoughts of many characters, white and black. The word seems to occur constantly and in all combinations: black speaking to black, white to white, black to white, and white to black. Ozzie uses it when he interrogates a white suspect, and Jake uses it when speaking to Ozzie. The redolence of the word, although potentially very disturbing for some readers, illuminates the race relations of the setting and gives the novel a sharp edge.

As Grisham takes on the issue of race relations, he likewise addresses the status of women in the New South.

Women are not yet equal; they have a circumscribed, lesser place. None of the local officials or lawyers is a woman; women instead take the traditional jobs of clerk and secretary. Jake's wife is a teacher, a respectable profession for an intelligent female in this setting. He shuttles her and their daughter away for safety when the case turns ugly. When the jailed Carl Lee hears his wife complain about needing money, he tells her bluntly that he will find a way to provide and that she should mind her place. Jake's final speech to the jury asserts that daughters are different, special, a difference that explains Carl Lee's rage over the rape of his little girl — by extension Jake argues that women remain on the traditional Southern pedestal. Grisham is not being an unthinking sexist; he deliberately points to the chauvinism in contemporary Mississippi, just as he points to the racism by the use of the epithet. And into this setting, onto this pedestal, he places Ellen Roark, a half-Southern, half-Northern liberal law student who wants to assist Jake on the case. She has impressive legal talents — she does masterful research for Jake — and an alluring body, alluring more so for her refusal to wear a bra unless she is going to court. She disturbs the men because she can match them in law, and because her presence keeps reminding them of sex. Clearly Jake, who cannot fathom having a woman for a friend or a law partner, feels tempted by her. But for all her banter, she does nothing untoward (although the scene of Ellen and Jake outside the restaurant deserves discussion). She says with arch irony, "I'm a woman, and I'm in the South. I know my place." Readers have various responses to her. Some find her admirable, even judge her to be the best legal mind in the book; others will dismiss her as coarse and flirtatious. However readers take her, Grisham presents her as a specimen of modern womanhood, very unlike what the Mississippi locals expect, and thus a challenge and maybe even a role model.

◆ Themes ◆

Jake certainly is a committed lawyer, yet the book sketches how this commitment exacts costs in his ethics, his family life, and his mental stability. In the novel's morally relative world, commitment may be the only idealism available: There are no standards except to fight relentlessly for one's cause. Grisham describes how other committed lawyers suffer for their embrace of their cause. Norman Reinfeld, the white NAACP lawyer who specializes in desperate capital cases and who almost seizes the Hailey case from Jake, is both an idealist and a tenacious fighter: "with each execution [of a client — he has seen four] he renewed his vow to break any law, violate any ethic, contempt any court, disrespect any judge, ignore any mandate, or do whatever to prevent a human from legally killing another human . . . He seldom slept more than three hours a night. Sleep was difficult with thirty-one clients on death row... He was thirty and looked forty-five." Reinfeld is both energized and worndown by his thankless duty. This passage again refers to the novel's premise that the judicial processes need to be stretched and even abused, as Reinfeld does. Lucien Wilbanks, during the heyday of his practice, felt zest for adopting the cause of civil rights, but his efforts exacerbated his already eccentric, abrasive personality and his alcoholic tendencies. As she is perhaps the novel's best legal mind, Ellen Roark is also the most openly idealistic character; she announces that her ambition is to be a radical lawyer and fight against capital punishment in the South and that she is ready to endure public scorn for her cause. She is enthusiastic and unspoiled, perhaps what Reinfeld was like when he was younger. The unanswered question is whether her commitment can withstand the trauma she experiences in Clanton.

◆ Characters ◆

Discussion of the novel could begin with how readers respond to Jake, if they feel he is a "good" lawyer, whatever "good" means. Jake is not a white knight. He is flawed and multifaceted: capable of honor, willing to challenge the rules, able to be ferocious in pursuit of his cause, tentative in response to temptations (from alcohol and from Ellen). He will not do anything to win, as he will not allow Lucien to bribe a juror. Jake wants to win the case himself through the use of his own tactics. Perhaps this pride in himself emerges as his dominant feature.

Any number of supporting characters merit discussion as Grisham lavishes on his creations full-bodied descriptions, backgrounds, and meaty scenes. Ellen, Harry Rex, Norman Reinfeld, Lester, and others exemplify Grisham's mastery of characterization. This willingness to spend time with the thoughts and histories of secondary players recalls the discursive techniques of fellow Mississippian William Faulkner; for both authors, the detailed character portrayals enhance the realistic sense of place, the appeals to history as an explanation of the present, and the thematic concerns. With two particular characters, Grisham twists stereotypes in unexpected ways to create unique individuals. Ozzie Walls seems to partake of the traits of the stereotypical tough white Southern sheriff. Ozzie uses violence as he hauls away offenders and lowlifes; he coerces a confession by reciting what happens to rapists in prison; he savagely beats a bomber outside Jake's house; he freely says "niggers" to refer to blacks when he talks to whites. Making the man who possesses these standard traits black disconcerts expectations. (A good contrast to Ozzie is black police chief Tucker Watts in *Chiefs* [1981] by Stuart Woods. In the early 1960s, Tucker Watts encounters considerable resistance when he takes command of the police in a white-majority Georgia town.) As the scion of Clanton's leading family, Lucien would be expected either to be aligned with business interests or to be wholesomely liberal (in the manner of Faulkner's do-gooding lawyer Gavin Stevens). Instead, Lucien divorces himself from his past and turns radical, pursuing every unpopular cause he can find and glorying in his status as a pariah. He tells the story that when he was little he unknowingly tried to get on the segregated school bus with his black playmates, thinking they would all go to school together. The story makes the common white Southern distinction that country playmates could be black but schoolmates could only be white. The story also recalls and inverts the famous scene in Faulkner's *Absalom, Absalom!* (1936) in which the young poor white Thomas Sutpen is turned away from the front door of a plantation house; both Sutpen and Lucien learn that they are different and that they have their

special, reserved places. Both resolve to remake themselves and to establish their own places where these affronts cannot occur again.

◆ Techniques ◆

A Time to Kill is not a streamlined novel, as are Grisham's later efforts in the thriller genre. In addition to vivid characterization, Grisham lingers over many specifics of place. A fine scene in which Jake takes Ellen to a restaurant leads to a humorous and succulent discussion of Southern food. All the details offer the reader a total immersion into a highly particularized place populated by extremely well-drawn characters.

For a first novel, the book reveals highly accomplished techniques. Grisham deftly juggles his large cast. He demonstrates the suspense that will fuel his later career as he sends trouble after trouble to beset Jake. As he does in other novels, he grabs readers with a tense, violent start: He describes the rape of the girl without being pathetic yet still conveying the horror and while making odd fun of the attackers (one complains that the little girl dripped her blood in the beer cooler). He adopts a flat, understating style that makes the events disturbing: As the men throw their beer cans at the girl, Grisham writes, "Willard had trouble with the target, but Cobb was fairly accurate." Grisham also shows his flair for dialog, another skill that will become a trademark. Especially when he narrates a courtroom exchange, the dialog snaps and seems authentic. The blistering cross-examinations Jake and Rufus inflict upon each other's experts show both Grisham's achievement at dialog and his adeptness at narrating technical legal processes.

Grisham employs a wry humor, unexpected with such downbeat material as rape, vigilantism, and capital murder. *A Time to Kill* is a surprisingly funny book. He throws in asides such as this description of Norman Reinfeld as he and Jake are about to meet: "Reinfeld was no pushover when it came to arrogance . . . He was arrogant and insolent by nature. Jake had to work at it." Ozzie threatens the white rapists, who endure the menacing stares of the black inmates in the nearby jail cells: "stay quiet, or he would integrate his jail." In scenes that could be unrelievedly horrible, Grisham finds a source of mirth. Having left the tortured bomber alone to dismantle his device, Ozzie, Jake, and another officer debate who should go check on the bomber. The officer suggests Jake, as, after all, it is Jake's house that is being threatened. When a cross burns on Jake's yard, the officers wonder what to do, as they had never seen a burning cross before, and ask whether it will flame itself out. After being intimidated by Jake in court, one of the rapists' mothers howls theatrically as she is led from the courtroom. *A Time to Kill* encourages sober reflection on the state of law and race relations and also encourages smiles and guffaws from readers. Perhaps this mix of techniques accounts for Grisham's success: swiftly-paced stories, thoughtful and complex treatments of issues, and a dry, satiric tone.

◆ Literary Precedents ◆

The plot skeleton of *A Time to Kill* recalls that of the legal classic *Anatomy of a Murder* (1958) by Robert Traver. Both novels concern cases of revenge killings that follow sexual assaults: In Traver's book, a military officer avenges an offense against his wife. In both cases the legal strategy is the same — argue not guilty by reason of insanity. The lawyers in both novels take the cases as a means to further their careers. And each lawyer gets valuable help from an often besotted older attorney. The machinations of the trials comprise the heart of both books. Yet Grisham approaches his material with much more ambition; Grisham's book is a deeply-thought-out social tapestry. For Grisham, the northern Mississippi setting is integral; for Traver the locale of the upper peninsula of Michigan is quaint.

Grisham's works are the most popular examples of the groundswell of fiction about the law that seemed to begin in 1987 with Scott Turow's *Presumed Innocent*. Both Grisham and Turow linger over the technicalities of trial procedures, and both portray how the network of relationships among those in the justice system — defense attorneys, prosecutors, and judges, all who know each other well previous to the cases at hand — impact on the trial. Grisham and Turow also both challenge the reader by presenting protagonists who are often not heroic, indeed, who cross moral lines. And both authors use the trials to expose a network of corruption. Turow's setting is a northern city, and the corruption infests the city's legal and political institutions. Turow writes a mystery, and so appeals to the dark urban world of hard-boiled fiction, reminiscent of Raymond Chandler. In this aspect, Turow and Grisham diverge. Grisham takes a broader approach, disclosing the faults embedded in the entire society, taking on issues of race, sex, class, and the pitfalls of the entire judicial process.

As a social commentary on the South, *A Time to Kill* bears comparison with the two recognized masterpieces of Southern writing about the law: *Sanctuary* (1931) by William Faulkner and *To Kill a Mockingbird* (1960) by Harper Lee. In addition to devoting considerable space to trial proceedings, these Southern novels address how the defense attorneys bond with their clients, and how the cases become for each lawyer a sacred duty. The three lawyers, however, contrast sharply. Faulkner's Horace Benbow and Lee's Atticus Finch are idealistic patricians who take difficult cases because their principles demand that they do so. In court, each is dignified and respectful of the rules. Jake, a product of the middle class, is ruthlessly practical in the conduct of his case. The trio of lawyers provides significant contrasts in views of law, opinions about their towns, resilience when faced with courtroom setbacks, and appeals to the jury. In each novel, the decision of the jury reflects profound, deeply-ingrained attitudes. Each book offers a probing and critical portrait of Southern society. Faulkner and Grisham both charge that their settings — both novels use northern Mississippi — suffer from vast corruption, from a network of evil that probably encompasses the district attorney. Pondering why the outcomes of the cases in the three novels differ opens up questions about how the South has changed over the fifty-eight years between the publications of *Sanctuary* and *A Time to Kill*.

◆ Related Titles ◆

Grisham's other novel set in Ford County is *The Chamber* (1994), an equal-ly hard-edged look at racial and legal attitudes in contemporary Mississippi. *The Chamber* follows the last month — a time punctuated by desperate, doomed appeals — leading up to the execution of an aged Klansman for murders committed in the 1960s bombing of a law office. Grisham lingers in his portrayals of the lawyers who devote their careers to death penalty appeals — they are idealists who use any means possible, including deceit, in seeking their seldom-achieved goals. Grisham continues to flesh out the observation that a legal proceeding is essentially a contest in which tactics matter and in which the truth is too often irrelevant. Both Ford County novels present grim and challenging views of capital punishment, remarkable because these are popular novels yet the American public strongly supports the death penalty.

A real case that occurred subsequent to the publication of *A Time to Kill* provides a significant touchstone for discussion. In April 1993, Ellie Nesler of Sonora, California, shot to death her son's alleged molester during a court proceeding. Her defense was, predictably, not guilty by reason of insanity, despite ample evidence that she carefully planned her attack. In August 1993, a jury found her guilty only of manslaughter; then in September the same jury, in a separate sanity proceeding, declared her sane, meaning that she faced the full weight of the law in regard to sentencing. She received ten years for the shooting and the included weapons charge. During the summer of 1993, the *Los Angeles Times* ran several articles covering the case that would make interesting contrasts to events in Grisham's book.

◆ Adaptations ◆

Grisham's open emotional attachment to his first novel rendered him shy about selling the film rights even as Hollywood's appetite for his books led in 1993 to the record-setting $3.75 million sale of the rights to a book he had not yet completed (*The Chamber*). Finally in August 1994, Grisham allowed purchase of the rights for *A Time to Kill* by the team that made a version of *The Client* which respected the text and which earned financial success. Grisham received a staggeringly $6 million, plus some approval over casting and the script, plus the role of co-producer (along with Arnon Milchan, whose New Regency Productions would make the film for Warner Bros.), Michael Nathan, and Hunt Lowry.

During summer 1995, director Joel Schumacher shot the film in a very cooperative Canton (obviously close in name to the fictional Clanton), Mississippi, using locals as extras. Canton happily boasted the Mississippi feature crucial to the plot: a distinctive-looking courthouse situated on a square that serves as a focal point of town life. The CBS news show *48 Hours* produced an hour-long program on the filming, highlighting the unsettling atmosphere of shooting scenes about contemporary Southern racial strife in a real Southern town.

The film premiered in July 1996 to great success, competing well for an audience amidst more special effects-driven summer fare. The film had been heralded by numerous articles about the production and many approving profiles of Matthew McConaughey, the 25-year old unknown who plays Jake. (The movie alerts non-Southerners that Jake's surname should be pronounced as "bri-GANCE," an example of the Southern tendency to accent second syllables.) Schumacher and Grisham reportedly clashed repeatedly over who should play the lead, finally agreeing on McConaughey, who had been cast in a supporting role and who looks a lot like Grisham. McConaughey seems to inhabit the role, and the strong acting by the entire cast is the film's greatest asset. The players include the versatile Samuel L. Jackson as Carl Lee; Sandra Bullock, who nicely underplays Ellen Roark even though she lacks the right hair color; and previous Academy Award winners Kevin Spacey (as Rufus Buckley) and Brenda Fricker (as Jake's secretary).

Yet Schumacher and screenwriter Akiva Goldsman vary significantly from the novel even as they respect the book's basic plot. A key change involves Jake: as occurred with the muting of Mitch McDeere's ethical lapses in the film of *The Firm*, this movie presents Jake as an earnest greenhorn instead of a wily, self-assured gladiator. The film's Jake takes the case out of guilt for not telling Ozzie about Carl Lee's implied threats; the Jake of the novel had told Ozzie and has lots of motives to take the case, including fellow-feeling for Carl Lee and not excluding lust for fame. The film's Jake seems over-matched in court. Carl Lee has to tell him what to ask Deputy Looney; in the book Jake rehearses the testimony with the Deputy. The film's Jake desperately needs Ellen to deliver information on how to demolish the state's psychiatrist; the Jake of the book already knows how, just desires some specific research from Ellen. In the film, Jake needs pep talks from four different characters (Ellen, Lucien, his wife, and Carl Lee) before he can deliver his summation. And in that summation he delivers an apology for his rookie performance followed by the story of the rape with the races reversed. In the novel, a juror tells this story at a pivotal point in deliberations, but having already described the attack at the book's opening, Grisham resists giving her full speech. He resisted being sentimental; the movie does not resist.

The movie seeks for a wholly emotional impact whereas the novel deftly avoids becoming maudlin The movie seeks more to satisfy than to unsettle. Thus the film eschews the book's odd humor, the pounding and constant use of "nigger" by almost everybody, the shading of the "good" characters. Gone are Ozzie's legally dubious extortion of the rapist's confession, Harry Rex's procurement of the jury list, Lucien's serious consideration of bribing a juror, Carl Lee's dismissive treatment of his wife when she asks about money. Instead the film offers good guys and bad guys, and the bad guys are very bad. The book's Klanners are self-important figures of dark comedy; Grisham describes the swearing-in: "Sweat dripped from their faces as they prayed fervently for the dragon to shut up with his nonsense and finish the ceremony." The film aggrandizes the Klan into a serious-minded, malevolent force. (In Delaware, local Klanners actually protested outside a theater that was showing the film.) As for the good guys, the film depicts them as hard-working and sincere. The film adds audience-pleasing scenes such as Jake's dog appearing safe amidst the ashes of Jake's house and the ending sequence of a racially-inclusive picnic By rendering Jake and his friends as near paragons of virtue, the filmmakers lull the audience into forgetting that this story is about vigilantism. Indeed, the film places at the final picnic the black youth who dropped the fire bomb that killed the Klan leader; this youth is a deliberate killer, but the film seems to give him approbation by finessing the whole issue of what constitutes a murder.

More than the expected alterations and compressions inherent in any screen translation, these changes seem to reflect the film industry's notorious timidity in presenting hard-edged material for mass consumption. The good acting and strong sense of place rescue the movie; it is a superior translation than, say, the amazingly wrong-headed effort to film Tom Wolfe's scathing satire *The Bonfire of the Vanities* (1984-1985). Yet nor is *A Time to Kill* in league with the film versions of *Dead Man Walking* or the obvious touchstone *To Kill a Mockingbird*, movies which retain the disturbing and challenging spirits of their sources movies which people talk about.

◆ Ideas for Group Discussions ◆

This novel fits comfortably in discussion groups and classes devoted to law and literature, crime and literature, and Southern writing. The book challenges readers to re-examine their overall trust in the justice system: in trials as mechanisms for finding truth, in prosecutors, in expert witnesses, in juries. Asking for reactions to this portrait of the system can initiate a lively debate, as will asking readers to evaluate Jake. Grisham endows the characters with such colorful traits that many of them can spark a good discussion: is Ozzie just in tormenting the bomber, is Ellen an admirable woman, would you hire Harry Rex to handle your divorce?

Atticus Finch of *To Kill a Mockingbird* offers a strong contrast to Jake, and invoking Harper Lee's novel relates not only to legal matters but to the Southern setting. Readers could discuss how the South of this novel matches the progressive reputation of the contemporary South. Many books that highlight race and violence in the South, especially those by William Faulkner, can be compared to *A Time to Kill* as a means of asking how the South has or has not changed.

1. This novel describes in detail the judicial proceedings of a capital murder case. How do the proceedings relate to the issue of justice? Do the proceedings produce justice? How does skill at law figure the accomplishment of justice? How does the book impact your beliefs in the American system of criminal justice?

2. What does "justice" mean in this novel? How often and in what contexts do the characters use the term?

3. Who are the "good" lawyers in the book? What does "good" mean in this context — adept at legal tactics, or morally upstanding, or both?

4. If you were in legal trouble, would you hire Jake Brigance? (If you needed a lawyer for a divorce proceeding, would you retain Harry Rex Vonner?)

5. How comfortable are you with the resolution of Carl Lee's case?

6. Why do so many lawyers want to defend Carl Lee? Jake turns down the chance to defend Pete Willard, but fights off others to keep Carl Lee as a client. Why?

7. If Jake did lose the case to Norman Reinfeld of the NAACP, would the basic defense strategy have been different? If Carl Lee is to insist upon his right of trial, what possible strategic options does an attorney have in defending him? (Here you might consider the Nesler case from California in 1993-1994 as a real-life analogue.)

8. What aspects of the book do you think you will recall when you read about or discuss other court cases?

9. Is Ozzie a good sheriff? Is his interrogation of the bomber just?

10. Consider the book as a portrait of the contemporary South, and look at Grisham's attention to matters of social class, race, the status of women, small town life, even food. How does the region seem alike and different compared to your own home place? How is book like or unlike other literary portraits of the South?

11. How would you define race relations in Clanton?

12. How do you react to the characters' frequent, even constant use of the racial epithet? What does its use mean to these characters?

13. What is the status of women in Clanton? What does Grisham accomplish by inserting Ellen Roark into this environment?

14. This book is not in the thriller genre, yet matched the sales of Grisham's thrillers. How can you explain this book's best-selling appeal? What is your reaction to Grisham's assessment that this is his best book?

John F. Jebb
University of Delaware

THE TIN DRUM

Novel

1959

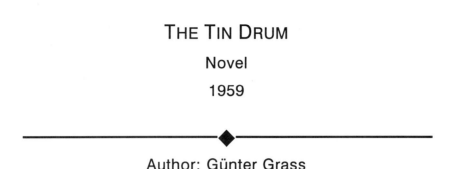

Author: Günter Grass

◆ Social Concerns ◆

Despite Grass's assertions that his novels have no specific meanings, it is obvious that his social concerns and themes are inextricably interwoven in all of his works. *The Tin Drum* covers the period from the 1920s through the 1950s and ranges from Danzig to Germany and France. Oskar Matzerath's odyssey through the nightmare of Nazism has been interpreted as a parable for the German experience, but it should not be seen as a precise allegory. As do many Postmodern stylists, Grass insists that there are no "meanings" in his works, that he is interested in language and style, not extraneous abstractions. He has said, "So many of them [critics] look for symbols and allegories and deeper meanings, but sometimes I write of potato peels and mean potato peels."

His denials to the contrary, all his work is rich with archetypal overtones, which are simultaneously universal and specific to the German people. Although readers certainly would not accept the events in *The Tin Drum* on a literal level, they have the resonance of mythology. Oskar has been compared to Apollo, for example, in that the sound of his drumming or his voice wreaks vengeance from afar. Incredibly, he traces his descent from a man hiding in a potato field under a woman's large skirts. Grass converts an historic period, still within the vivid memory of many people, into a period of legend. Supernatural feats occur. Complex interconnections are drawn between people and events that belie the frayed fabric of common reality. One sees similar thematic qualities in the great novels of Herman Melville, whom Grass acknowledges as an influence. Against the verifiable reality of whaling in *Moby Dick* (1851), a cosmic, archetypal game is played out. Magic mingles with realistic detail, creating a world far more evocative than a straightforward tale of whaling and obsession. In *The Tin Drum*, numerous hints of a larger meaning are sprinkled through the novel, although they are never allowed to form a simple crystal. Mystery is maintained in both novels and thereby each is enriched, yielding up varied meanings. The "power of blackness" that Melville sought is manifest also in Grass: His fictional world, apparently so clear, becomes more perplexing as one examines it. For example, *The Tin Drum* may be the fantasy of an unreliable, perhaps insane, narrator as in so many modern novels, or Oskar may be a Christ-child figure in a world gone mad. He simultaneously seems both, a strange combination of opposites. There are no easy answers in *The Tin Drum*, which is why it is one of those rare great novels that may be mined many times for its themes of guilt, national identity, and the artist's role, yet never become exhausted.

◆ Characters ◆

Oskar, the strange boy who refuses to grow and who has been called a fantasy figure in the tradition of German folk heroes, will remain one of the most unforgettable characters in world literature. Besides willing himself not to grow, Oskar has extraordinary powers over people around him, as well as the ability to shatter glass with his voice. Other critics have likened Oskar to the artist. His tin drum seems like a toy to the adults around him; yet, it has a powerful influence on events. In one major scene in the novel, Oskar disrupts a Nazi rally by hiding under the bandstand. By beating out the rhythm to "The Blue Danube" he confuses the band and annihilates the Nazi songs. When he shifts into a Charleston, the spectators begin dancing and the whole spectacle is ruined. The Nazis, however, set out to find leftist saboteurs and ignore little Oskar. Although many may believe art cannot affect anything important, Grass, to many critics, is pointing out its power. When Oskar becomes part of a traveling show, he falls under the influence of a dwarf, Bebra, who also considers himself an artist. Grass seems to be saying that artists, despite their being regarded as curious dwarfs, not only have power, but nearly supernatural power. Compared to Oskar, the other characters of *The Tin Drum* are secondary. They are always, however, vividly drawn and powerfully imagined, in a way reminiscent of Dickens's minor characters. Oskar's family, particularly his mother and grandmother, and the traveling players Bebra and Roswitha are among a panoply of characters who keep this lengthy work consistently lively.

◆ Techniques ◆

Although Grass is renowned for his linguistic playfulness and his careful avoidance of simplicities of theme, W. Gordon Cunliffe points out that Grass uses all the skills of a Realistic author. He can re-create the behavior of shopkeepers, peasants, policemen, and waiters. His sensitivity to dialects is extraordinary. His details make skat players, gypsies, party officials, and schoolmasters come vividly to life, even when they are the subject of satire or direct ridicule. Much of this derives from his specific interest in the locale of Danzig. Grass is thereby part of the tradition of modern authors like James Joyce, William Faulkner, and Cesare Pavese, whose works are intimately related to a particular place. He often uses the actual names of shops and people from Danzig. Much of the vividness of *The Tin Drum* derives from its careful, sometimes shocking, observations of such things as an eel-infested horse's head in the sea, a potato dumpling, or the inside of a toy shop. They create a solid background upon which the archetypal, supernatural elements can be played out.

Besides the previously mentioned affinities of the works of Melville, Joyce, Faulkner, and Pavese, critics have also pointed to the picaresque *Simplicissimus* (1669) by Johann Jakob Christoffel von Grimmelshausen. One of the most interesting comparisons, however, has been drawn with Laurence Sterne's *Tristram Shandy* (1759-1767). Grass admits admiring the great eighteenth-century novel and critics have pointed out several influences. First, much of *The Tin Drum*, despite the many real horrors it depicts, consists of humor. Many scenes are irreverent or silly or filled with slapstick. With the detachment and narrative distance of *Tristram Shandy*, Oskar watches the world around him go through its madness, and with the cold eye of a child, reveals it for all its ludicrousness. Like Sterne, Grass has a keen eye for absurdity, even in the midst of the ideas and events which most people take with great seriousness. Secondly, a great deal of the humor is linguistic. Puns, as well as unbelievable and inexplicable metaphors, are crucial parts of Grass's style. Like Sterne, he is interested in invention for its own sake, playing of word games, and imitating dialects. When asked about the peculiar form of his prenatal autobiography, Tristram Shandy says, "Ask my pen; it governs me; I govern not it." Grass, who denies the necessity of thematic abstractions to fiction, is arguing a similar view. The novel creates itself in its most suitable form. If the author attempts to force it to play philosophical parlor games, the integrity of the work is destroyed. Neither Uncle Toby nor Colonel Tim in Sterne's novel is the definitive symbol. Likewise, Oskar is not, and must not be, reduced to a single symbol.

Grass followed *The Tin Drum* with *Cat and Mouse* (1963; *Katz und Maus*, 1961), and *Dog Years* (1965; *Hundejahre*, 1963), and the three have been dubbed the "Danzig Trilogy," because they share many elements. *Cat and Mouse* features a deformed character, like Oskar, from Danzig. Joachim Mahlke's deformity is an extraordinarily large Adam's apple, and he is desperate for acceptance by his peers. His solution is to acquire an Iron Cross which will hide his bulging throat. Although a successful athlete, he does not achieve acceptance and comes to a mysterious end. As the "mouse," Mahlke has been called the most admirable person in Grass's fiction and the entire work a moral parable. Critics, however, have been somewhat bewildered by this novel. *The Tin Drum* was a long, complex novel. By comparison, *Cat and Mouse* seems tiny and obvious in its meanings. Limiting itself to the war years in Danzig is seen by some as an overcoming of the weakest parts of *The Tin Drum*, those episodes that take place outside Danzig. Others think the shortness a liability as it caused the allegorical structure to be too prominent.

A West German film production of *Cat and Mouse* was released in 1969, starring Lars and Peter Brandt, the sons of ex-chancellor Willy Brandt, for whom Grass tirelessly campaigned in the elections of 1965 and 1969. Directed by Hansjurgen Pohland, the film caused much outrage because of a masturbation scene, and was not notably successful. The West German/French co-production of *The Tin Drum* in 1979, however, was a tremendous success. Director Volker Schlondorff stuck closely to the novel and chose the perfect Oskar in David Bennent. The film also starred Angela Winkler, Mario Adorf, and Daniel Obrychski, and, among other awards, won an Academy Award for Best Foreign Language film.

J. Madison Davis
Pennsylvania State University
Behrend College

TO KILL A MOCKINGBIRD

Novel

1960

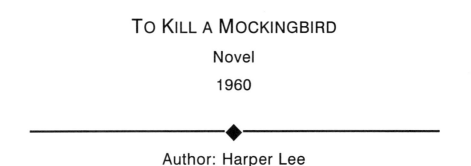

Author: Harper Lee

◆ Social Concerns ◆

The Civil Rights movement was at its height in the United States in the late 1950s and early 1960s. Many of the concerns of that movement are reflected in *To Kill a Mockingbird*. The novel is set in Alabama in the 1930s, but its picture of the relations between whites and blacks may be considered essentially accurate for the entire South and, in certain respects, the nation as a whole for much of the twentieth century. The racial tensions and prejudices portrayed in the novel correspond exactly to issues of national concern at the time the novel was published.

Lee's picture of racial prejudice is for the most part subtle: prejudice and inequity are elements of the social structure in Maycomb County (the novel's setting) rarely questioned by white or black and so ingrained and accepted that few even consciously notice their existence. The blacks live in a separate location, have their own church (which the white narrator, a young girl, once attends, to the dismay of her visiting aunt), and have occupations of lower pay and status. At the trial of the black man Tom Robinson, blacks wait patiently for white families to go into the courthouse before they enter, and once they are in they sit in a separate section, the "Colored balcony." Lee, usually subtly and by indirection, points to the irony of Maycomb's white citizens claiming to be Christians while treating their black neighbors as they do. In one of the novel's most powerfully ironic scenes, the children's schoolteacher tells them of Hitler's persecution of the Jews and claims that in America "we don't believe in persecuting anybody." One child asks why Hitler would pick on the Jews: "They're white, ain't they?" In another scene, readers are introduced to the women of the Missionary Society, most of whom, despite their professed concern for the Mrunas of Africa, seem unaware that they are participating in the oppression of blacks in their own city.

But Lee's portrayal of racial prejudice is not always subtle or indirect. The trial and conviction of Tom Robinson reveal Maycomb's racial tensions and inequities with unmistakable clarity. With Tom accused of rape, the trial hinges on the potentially explosive fear, widespread among Maycomb's whites, that black men are a danger to white women. An attempt to lynch

Tom before the trial is foiled. Despite the fact that Atticus Finch, a brilliant and popular lawyer, is appointed to defend him, most consider Tom doomed from the start. No one can remember a black accused by whites ever being exonerated. The prosecuting attorney uses accepted prejudices to make his case: He is indignant, for instance, when Tom, a black man and therefore inferior to any white, says he felt sorry for his white accuser. And although it becomes obvious that the case against Tom is so flawed as to be worthless, he is still convicted.

There are signs of hope and change, though, in the world portrayed by the novel. There is much that is good in the relations between whites and blacks in Maycomb. Some of the town's citizens quietly applaud the attempt to clear Tom Robinson. Atticus Finch and a few others work actively to promote justice. Atticus' children seem as yet uncorrupted by their society's ailments and respond naturally with fairness and compassion. One of the greatest signs of hope is the length of time — hours rather than minutes — it takes the jury to reach a decision. No one can remember it taking a jury so long to convict a black man.

Besides the racial concerns, *To Kill a Mockingbird* offers a fascinating picture of other aspects of life in the South in the 1930s: the various social groups (including city folk, country folk, and "white trash"); the economic problems of the Depression; religious life; new educational theories of questionable practical value (introduced by the schoolteacher from northern Alabama); and political issues and conflicts (New Deal reforms, hints of tension between the South and its critics in Washington, and so on).

◆ Themes ◆

Besides the theme of racial prejudice and injustice, the novel's other themes also have much to do with how people relate to each other. The conviction and death of Tom Robinson, for instance, is made analogous to the mistreatment of "Boo" (Arthur) Radley: Both are compared to "mockingbirds" who "sing their hearts out for us" and do no harm. It is a sin, readers are told, to mistreat or kill such harmless creatures, even when they do not fit the dominant norms. Related to this concept are the themes of empathy and compassion. Atticus Finch tries to teach his children empathy; he tells them they cannot really understand another person until they "consider things from his point of view," until they "climb into his skin and walk around in it." Atticus even tries to help them understand what is behind the worst misdeeds in the novel, such as those of the Ewells (Tom Robinson's accusers), by considering the wrongdoers' circumstances and way of looking at things. It is suggested that empathy and compassion of this kind are necessary for social harmony, especially among the many "sorts" who make up Maycomb society.

Another theme is human dignity and effort in the face of difficult circumstances. The blacks of Maycomb, for instance, form a highly religious, close-knit, and compassionate community, and, despite their mistreatment, they do not as a group succumb to despair or bitterness. Another example of dignity and struggle is that of the Cunninghams, poverty-stricken country people who maintain their self-respect and experience moral growth, even under very trying circumstances. Mayella Ewell, too, although yielding to prejudice, family pressure, and personal loneliness in her mistreatment of Tom Robinson, nevertheless struggles to rise above her circumstances: The geraniums she grows are her attempt to create something beautiful and worthwhile in ugly and abusive surroundings. Her loneliness, along with that of other characters, such as Boo Radley, is stressed enough to suggest another theme: that of loneliness itself, experienced to some extent by everyone and, for some, especially those neglected or excluded by others, a condition that comes close to being life's essence.

Perhaps the novel's most important theme is that of growing up. As in many other novels, children change and learn as they grow older. But in *To Kill a Mockingbird* the theme of growing up is particularly poignant since, along with the usual rigors of moving toward or into adolescence, the children experience a difficult, and to some degree disillusioning, awakening to the differences between themselves, including their sense of right and wrong, and the attitudes and practices of the place where they live. The great challenge the children face, the novel suggests, is to remain true to their sense of what is right and at the same time maintain their loyalty and love for the community to which they belong. To do both will require them to understand and appreciate people different from themselves and to struggle, without condescension or self-righteousness, to get along with people who violate their sense of what is right. Atticus Finch is the novel's great model for this ideal.

◆ Characters ◆

Despite the novel's essential simplicity, it is difficult to point to a single character as the most important. The narrator, "Scout" (Jean Louise Finch), is a natural focus of readers' interest. But she is much of the time an observer, while her older brother, Jem, is more actively involved in many of the novel's events and conflicts. In fact, much of what she learns comes as she watches Jem and his struggles to understand. In many ways, Atticus Finch is the novel's hero. Despite his quiet, reticent personality, he is the main source of moral understanding and the greatest example of courage in the novel. Boo Radley, too, is a sort of hero: He befriends and helps the children, even saves their lives, and does it almost invisibly. It is only at the end of the novel that the children realize what an important role he has played in their lives. Tom Robinson also earns readers' sympathy and admiration: He is strong, gentle, and guileless, but he despairs of white "justice" and is shot in a hopeless attempt to escape. There are many other memorable characters, effectively distinguished by action, appearance, and the novel's vigorous, believable dialogue: Dill (Charles Baker Harris), the children's bright, yarn-spinning playmate; Calpurnia, the stern, loving Negro cook and housekeeper; Bob and Mayella Ewell; and the Cunninghams.

But the Finches — Scout, Jem, and Atticus — are clearly at the center of the novel. As the novel begins, Scout is almost six years old, soon to start school. She is devoted to her father (her mother died when she was two). A tomboy who takes part in the games and adventures of Jem and Dill — when they will let her — she is at once naive, precocious, feisty, and kindhearted. She has learned to read before starting school, and she is unusually perceptive and curious. But there is much she does not understand, and her wisdom is intuitive rather than fully conscious. When, by shaming the men who have come to the jail bent on a lynching, she rescues her father and Tom Robinson, she does so unintentionally and without fully understanding what has happened: She meant only to be friendly to one of the would-be lynchers. Her curiosity about Boo Radley and her vivid fantasies about what he might be like show her, like the other children, to be uninformed and unconsciously insensitive. But, always inclined to be sympathetic, she achieves by the end of the novel an empathetic understanding of Boo, and showing him affection comes naturally for her. Especially early in the novel, Scout is pugnacious, getting into fights with her brother, schoolmates, and others; but she is instinctively kind. Although her process of learning and growing up is shown less directly than Jem's, it becomes clear by the end that she has grown in poise, strength, and understanding.

Jem (Jeremy Atticus Finch), Scout's older brother, experiences a more difficult process of growing up. He is entering adolescence. His attitude toward girls is beginning to change: At the start, he wants his sister to stop acting like a girl; later he criticizes her for not acting like one. He is highly idealistic. He genuinely believes justice will be done and Tom Robinson found innocent. He is bitterly disillusioned when the opposite happens. He is just beginning to understand some of the uglier facts of life, but at the same time he is learning greater empathy for other people. He is also acquiring a growing sense of independence. He demonstrates this most graphically when he defies his father, who is in front of the

jail surrounded by a mob, and refuses to go home.

Atticus Finch, a lawyer and Scout and Jem's father, is an elusive and complex character. Bookish and quiet, he is nevertheless impressive in the courtroom and is capable of great courage. He abhors violence and urges his children to find other solutions to problems, but he turns out to have a reputation, from past years, as an excellent marksman and is required to demonstrate his skill by shooting a mad dog. He can be firm, even hard-nosed, with the children, but is also tolerant, sympathetic, and understanding. He is their greatest teacher, both by example and by his wise and carefully measured words. He has a dry wit, self-control, and unshakable integrity. He is at odds with many of the values and practices of his community, but still feels great loyalty towards it and tries to understand the people he disagrees with. He is eager to avoid conflict, but when he believes it is his duty to pursue a course of action, he will do so without hesitation.

♦ Techniques ♦

To Kill a Mockingbird is beautifully shaped and is written in a graceful, evocative style. The setting and events are vividly and believably portrayed. And although the novel is written with careful artistry, the author and her techniques remain (with rare lapses) unobtrusive. One of the most effective techniques involves the use of a first-person narrator. Although the voice is that of a mature woman, the point of view is carefully restricted to that of a young girl. For the most part, readers see and hear only what Scout experienced as the events took place. Lee offers a fresh look at the world of adults by presenting it through the eyes of a child who is at once perceptive and naive. Scout is a keen observer of the world around her, but because she does not fully understand the events she observes, many of the novel's serious concerns are conveyed by implication. They are all the more absorbing for being so conveyed. Such evils as racism, injustice, and social conflict are heightened by their contrast with the naive idealism of Scout and the other children, who have an instinctive sense of fairness and compassion. Because the narrator keeps to a child's point of view, there is often a contrast between her perceptions and those of readers. Readers can see, for instance, dangers Scout is quite unaware of when she runs into the middle of a lynching mob. The narrator's naivete is a fiction — Scout's skill and vocabulary as narrator are not those of a child — but it is a fiction readers accept.

Another technique involves plot. Some readers have accused Lee of including episodes that do not contribute to the main plot structure. But every event and character can be justified as contributing in some way to the fictional world Lee has created or to the novel's main themes, and the episodes are effectively arranged and connected. The main events grow in tension until they reach powerful climaxes in the trial and in the attack on the Finch children. There are two main threads of plot: first, the children's relationship with Boo Radley; and second, Atticus Finch's defense of Tom Robinson and its consequences. The two threads converge when Boo saves the children from Bob Ewell's attempt at vengeance for Atticus' part in the trial. The two threads are also related

in other ways. Boo Radley and Tom Robinson are both victims, and both are compared to mockingbirds. Furthermore, the two threads of the plot are both parts of the children's process of growing up.

The novel's symbols are, with the possible exception of the mockingbird, unobtrusive but effective. The mockingbird symbol — the harmless potential victim — may be a bit obvious for some readers' tastes, but it memorably conveys some of the novel's central values. Other images that function as symbols arise more naturally from the literal events of the novel and work at a less conscious level. They include the gifts Boo Radley leaves for the children in the knothole of an oak tree; the pants sewn up, folded, and laid across the fence where Jem lost them; and the blanket Boo puts around Scout without her noticing it. Mayella's geraniums, growing in slop jars, effectively convey her attempts to rise above her ugly surroundings.

◆ Literary Precedents ◆

To Kill a Mockingbird is related to a variety of literary precedents. As an evocation of life in the South, especially as experienced by children, it is reminiscent of Mark Twain's *Tom Sawyer* (1876) and *Huckleberry Finn* (1884). Besides the superficial resemblances, Lee's work is like those of Twain in its humor, warmth, and humane social concern. Some critics have also seen a connection between *To Kill a Mockingbird* and Carson McCullers' *The Member of the Wedding* (1946): both tell of life in the South from the standpoint of a young girl growing up. In her concern with racial and social issues, Lee may also be seen as related to two other

Southern writers, William Faulkner and Flannery O'Connor. But although Lee, like Faulkner and O'Connor, sometimes writes about violent events and strange or grotesque characters, her approach to such subjects is different. Rather than emphasizing or exaggerating the violent and grotesque, Lee presents them with restraint and even understatement. Her style is normally quiet and graceful, and much of the power of the story is conveyed by implication.

Besides her Southern roots, Lee also draws on other elements of the literary tradition. In a general way, *To Kill a Mockingbird* is indebted to many novels about growing up. In her style and approach to her subject matter, Lee has roots in the eighteenth and nineteenth centuries. In particular, she points to Jane Austen, "writing, cameo-like, in that little corner of the world of hers and making it universal." Besides admiring Austen's concern with life in a "little corner of the world" and her skill in portraying diverse and sometimes eccentric characters, Lee is probably also drawn to Austen's careful craftsmanship and her graceful, witty style. Lee would like, she has said, to be "the Jane Austen of south Alabama."

Bruce W. Young
Brigham Young University

◆ Adaptations ◆

In 1962 *To Kill a Mockingbird* was adapted as a motion picture, with the screenplay written by Horton Foote. A winner of three Academy Awards, it was directed by Robert Mulligan and starred Gregory Peck as Atticus Finch. The motion picture is remarkably faithful to the book and has received both popular and critical acclaim.

To the Lighthouse

Novel

1927

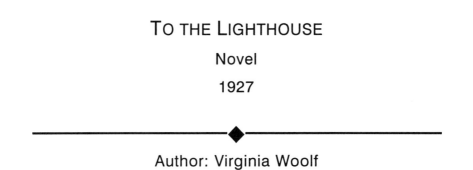

Author: Virginia Woolf

◆ Social Concerns/Themes ◆

To the Lighthouse is considered to be a semi-autobiographical text which recollects family holidays which Woolf took with her family at St. Ives, Cornwall, although the novel is set in the Hebrides.

"The Window" is the first of the novel's three sections. It is the longest and describes in detail a summer day on which Mr. and Mrs. Ramsay along with their eight children and several guests are on holiday. Among these favored guests are the poet Augustus Carmichael, the painter Lily Briscoe and the academic Charles Tansley. On this holiday, there is much family anxiety as James, the youngest child, wants to visit the lighthouse in spite of his father's desire to thwart his attempts to do so. This section of the text resolves around a dinner party as Mrs. Ramsay reflects on change.

"Time Passes" follows with the death of Mrs. Ramsay and of her son, Andrew, who is killed in the War. Woolf's lyricism flows throughout this section as the family home is abandoned and is ostensibly renewed during the postwar period with the arrival of Lily Briscoe and Mr. Carmichael. "The Lighthouse"

sees Lily Briscoe successfully complete a revelation of shape-in-chaos which she believes she owes to Mrs. Ramsay, and the pilgrimage of Mr. Ramsay, Camilla, and James to the lighthouse explores the rivalry and loss which torment them.

Woolf's concerns here are both personal and social: She represents in her novel the pain of grieving and the weight of the past, either real or imagined, and the effects of both on the individual. There is, through the comparisons and contrasts made through the central figures of Mrs. Ramsay and Lily Briscoe, a discussion of women's sexuality, creativity, and subjectivity which draws out Woolf's analysis if masculine and feminine texts and of the gendering of modes of perception.

◆ Characters ◆

Several characters come to life in this novel, from Charles Tansley, an unpleasant young academic, to Augustus Carmichael, an elderly friend of Mr. Ramsay, to the many children of the Ramsay's who have very different characters at the beginning of the story but emerge fully through Cam and

James at its close. A beautiful and loving woman, Mrs. Ramsay represents all that is good in the world. She is the perfect mother, the perfect wife, and she is the perfect hostess. She seems to create warmth and love through her courage and strength which bring a social coherence out of the chaos that threatens to engulf her family and guests. Most important, she is the embodiment of society's perfect woman: She embodies the feminine principle, the life force, which affirms both her and her family. Mrs. Ramsay becomes a type of muse and a heroine. She is both a doer of great deeds and an inspiration to others. Some critics consider her too perfect, yet for most readers, she is created by Woolf with such liveliness and vivacity that she radiates from the narrative. It is Virginia Woolf's — and Lily Briscoe, Charles Tansley, Mr. Ramsay, and James's — perspectives of Mrs. Ramsay that we are given. She becomes a multiperspectival and subjective portrait rather than an objective case history.

In opposition to Mrs. Ramsay, Mr. Ramsay is the embodiment of the masculine principle: self-centered, objective, melodramatic, and in constant need of support. He is ostensibly a famous philosopher, and the plot develops as his students and disciples follow him to his summer home. He constantly searches for his own reality in an attempt to understand and define for himself existence and life. Although he is initially an irritating figure, and perhaps even comic, at the end of the novel, we see Mr. Ramsay as a man who has been unable to live his life because of his intense search for what life is.

Woolf's Lily Briscoe is a friend and protégée of Mrs. Ramsay who is shy, sensitive and fears marriage or any type of emotional investment. Lily desires to keep herself purely dedicated to her art which she believes will immortalize both herself and the beautiful Mrs. Ramsay. It is the portrayal of Lily which shows Woolf's aesthetic belief that just as the artist must depend on the muse, the muse must depend on the artist.

◆ Techniques/Literary Precedents ◆

Woolf's technique of narrating through a stream-of-consciousness and imagery reached their full potential in *To the Lighthouse*. The narrative layers subjective perceptions and rapid transitions between multiple consciousnesses, and the novel is constructed in three sections which reflect this fluidity, ending with a narrative many years after the events described in the first section take place. These devices allow Woolf to further dramatize the devastations that follow in the wake of World War I. The novel explores questions of temporality and "objective" reality while placing its central concern on the obscurity of human relationships; here, Woolf's text dialogues extensively with Freudian psychoanalysis and, in particular, with Freud's Oedipal scenario.

In all of Woolf's novels, her conceptions of form and self owe a great deal to ideas that she had absorbed in her wide reading of both English Romantic poets and the *fin-de-siecle* French writers. Her readings show a fusion of novel and lyric that did not lead, as expected to the dilution of the novel; rather, it intensified the novelist's task. The interior monologue is created by mental associations which proceed independently of time or cause and facilitate the interweaving of motifs, figurative language, metaphor, simile, and intense symbolism. The significance of the stream-of-consciousness is not only that it is logical and planned, but that it creates the subjectivities of the characters.

To the Lighthouse is considered to be one of the exemplary texts of literary Modernism and its stream-of-consciousness technique is treated as the apotheosis of western Realism. For these reasons, Woolf's novel now occupies a central place in the critical debates surrounding the definitional parameters of literary Modernism and the role of women's writing in its definition.

Sarah E. Maier
University of Alberta

To Sail Beyond the Sunset

Novel

1987

◆

Author: Robert A. Heinlein

◆ Social Concerns/Themes ◆

*T*o Sail Beyond the Sunset, published on Heinlein's eightieth birthday, proved to be his final novel. While some critics have seen the novel, along with his other late works, as an expression of solipsistic despair, it seems more a defiant affirmation of life in the face of debilitating illness and approaching death. Indeed the title and the epigraph are taken from Tennyson's poem "Ulysses," in which the hero refuses to rest after his long journeys and instead sets out once more:

Come, my friends
'Tis not too late to seek a newer world.
Push off, and sitting well in order smite
The sounding furrows; for my purpose holds
To sail beyond the sunset, and the baths
Of all the western stars, until I die.

The heroine and narrator of her own story is Maureen Johnson, known to Heinlein's readers as the mother (and later lover) of his most famous charac-ter, Lazarus Long, hero of *Time Enough for Love* (1973). Maureen, who was rescued from death in the twentieth century and whisked to the forty-fourth century by Lazarus and his extended family in *The Number of the Beast* (1980), spends most of this novel in prison on a parallel earth, which allows her to tell us the story of her life. Maureen gets to do what Heinlein characters love most — talk.

Perhaps the central concern of Maureen's story is sex — a theme common to all of Heinlein's novels since *Stranger in a Strange Land* (1961), but increasingly important since *I Will Fear No Evil* (1970). More precisely, it is a celebration of sexuality and a scathing attack on prudishness, repression, and attempts to limit sexual expression to socially approved forms. In fact, at one point Maureen suggests that the only unnatural sexual practice is monogamy. Maureen is a devotee of sex — with a man, with a woman, alone, in couples, in groups, as often as possible. And when she is not having sex, she delights in talking about it. But while Maureen is in many ways attractive in her unabashed sexuality, the novel's treatment of sex is ultimately unsatisfying. Part of the problem lies in the book's length (over four hundred pages) and in the frequency of the sex scenes. While Heinlein is by no means pornographic and rarely even very explicit in his sexual descriptions, the coy sex scenes grow increasingly tedious.

A second and more serious difficulty is that Heinlein's ideas about sex are not complex enough to demand elaboration over several hundred pages. His ideas are in fact simple: Sex is good — perhaps the highest good. Anyone mature enough to have sex should be free to have sex with any consenting partners. The only rules of sexual morality inferable from the novel are the necessity for consent, the importance of good sexual hygiene, and the absolute need to make provision for any children.

Heinlein has always been a trenchant social critic, and there is good satire of the hypocrisy of American social norms for sexuality. But the model of sexual life proposed here — a large and constantly expanding group marriage that seems free of tensions or disputes — is not rendered in a convincing way. Aside from a few reservations, explained as holdovers of an obsolete moralism, none of the numerous husbands and wives experiences any difficulties. The greatest writers have always recognized the exhilarating and agonizing complexities of sexual love. While there is certainly justification for celebrating sexuality, a more complete vision would also recognize the darker side of sexual obsession, jealousy, manipulation, and betrayal, as well as the countless ways that people have used sex to control and hurt one another. Heinlein sees that darker side as a by-product of traditional morality, but he fails to make an effective case. His utopian

view seems too simple and unrealistic.

Fortunately, both Maureen and Heinlein have other things on their minds. The heart of the novel is a loving re-creation of life in late nineteenth- and early twentieth-century mid-America — especially Missouri, where Heinlein grew up. There is a pastoral, elegiac tone, a fondness for that time that is deeply moving. It is rather ironic to suggest that a great science fiction writer — a man who taught a whole generation to think about the future — wrote the best part of his final novel about the past. But then, it is only our past up to a certain point. What becomes increasingly clear is that Maureen inhabits an Earth, indeed a universe, that is a close parallel to ours — a world in which the Japanese attacked San Francisco, not Pearl Harbor, and in which Leslie LeCroix was the first human to land on the moon. Most importantly, it is a world in which the stories from Heinlein's well known Future History series are the reality.

This combination of fictive autobiography and a parallel universe allows Heinlein to retell twentieth-century history in his own way. He can use one time line to comment on the other, for example, to contrast the internment of Japanese-Americans in our time line with the riots that killed thousands of Japanese-Americans in Maureen's. Thus he can suggest that the policy of internment was not as cruel and unjustified as most Americans now believe. At other times, Maureen simply editorializes about what went wrong in the twentieth century — the decay of education, the disappearance of good manners (which Heinlein sees as a sure sign of disaster for a society), the loss of patriotism, and an obsession with rights to the neglect of responsibilities.

As always, Heinlein is hard to pigeonhole. While his characters are, like him, profoundly skeptical about democracy, they are intensely patriotic Americans. While Maureen seems at times a conservative's dream woman — deferential to her man, proud to call herself a "brood-mare" — she is also a woman who takes no guff from men, who earns degrees in science, law, and philosophy after raising seventeen children, who becomes an influential member of the board of directors of a major industrial concern, and who articulates stinging criticism of male sexism. Heinlein celebrates free love on one page and expounds on the need for strict disciplining of children on the next. Heinlein is his own most complex character, and the novel's structure allows him free reign to comment and complain about American society.

One other theme warrants at least brief mention — Heinlein's notion of "the world as myth," the idea that we create what is usually called reality. It is a sign of Heinlein's ability to surprise that in his last few novels he asks a question normally associated in science fiction with Philip K. Dick: What is "real"? To what extent is the world shaped or even created by our senses — our minds? Heinlein even appears to have fun with critics who have long identified solipsism as one of his central themes. Here (and in *The Number of the Beast*) Heinlein proposes — perhaps jokingly — Pantheistic Multiple-Ego Solipsism, the notion that all of the countless universes are just something we all got together and imagined. While Dick's explorations of the fragile nature of what we call reality are often disturbing and even terrifying, Heinlein seems mostly to be enjoying himself and offering a heartfelt tribute to the power of human imagination.

◆ Characters ◆

Heinlein's success with characterization has always been mixed. As critics have long noted, most of his protagonists conform to a basic pattern; they are highly competent individuals (men, women, or aliens) who have mastered the skills to survive and flourish in a hostile universe. Profoundly individualistic and skeptical of all authority, they are yet willing to sacrifice themselves for the good of their community. Cynical and cantankerous, they retain a deep, if selective, sentimentality. Heinlein is generally quite successful with his protagonists, who, gifted with something of his own voice, are witty, allusive, and prone to folksy, even corny humor. They generally share his remarkable gift for explaining how things work, of making what could be dry lectures into fascinating discourses. And he skillfully depicts a mentor relationship — the wise old man (or woman) explaining things to a gifted, but as yet naive, individual.

Those who dismiss Heinlein as fascist, racist, or sexist forget that for Heinlein, the characteristics of the competent individual have never been restricted to white males — or even to human beings — but to an elite of brains, talent, and courage. In his later novels, however, the characters are less likely to demonstrate competence or offer the wonderfully lucid explanations that grace such novels as *Have Space Suit Will Travel* (1958) or *The Moon Is a Harsh Mistress* (1966). They are more likely to indulge in long monologues and harangues — to the detriment of the story.

Heinlein has always had difficulty with secondary characters and antagonists. His villains tend to be caricatures and his secondary characters are either stock figures or clones of the protagonist. Heinlein never hesitated to identify himself with a woman, a black, an alien, or a sentient computer — so long as that character shared his own hardheaded skeptical intelligence. What he rarely did, at least successfully, was to sympathize imaginatively with characters whose ideas he disliked. Thus the basic conflict tends to be between fully realized characters and one-dimensional caricatures — with a subsequent loss of dramatic tension.

Such is the case in *To Sail Beyond the Sunset*. Maureen is a vividly drawn character and her father is effectively depicted as her mentor and hero. Even their similarities in speech and thinking are justifiable as reflections of their close relationship. Her first husband sounds a good deal like her father, but given her incestuous feelings toward her father, it is certainly plausible that she would have chosen such a man. But virtually all the other characters who are positively depicted sound like Maureen and her father. Even characters drafted from other Heinlein stories or novels, where they had their own distinctive voices and personalities, lose much of what originally made them memorable. Except perhaps for Lazarus Long, all seem but pale reflections of their former selves. The absence of a genuine antagonist for Maureen really harms the novel. There is no genuinely "other" mind and voice for her to test herself against, and thus all of her victories seem too easily won.

◆ Techniques/Literary Precedents ◆

The basic structure of the novel, a fictional autobiography, dates back to the earliest English novels, in particular those of Daniel Defoe. *To Sail Beyond the Sunset* could in fact be profitably compared with Defoe's *Moll Flanders* (1722), the story of another "irregular lady." Both Defoe and Heinlein came from Calvinist backgrounds; both were firm believers in commerce and exploration; both were fascinated with how things work; and both pioneered in forms of literature scoffed at by the "high culture." Their protagonists share a number of traits, especially a radical individualism. Moll and Maureen are survivors, women who seem to come out on top despite the dangers and difficulties they confront, and both are pleased with their ability to compile a fortune. Both ignore social customs and traditional morality whenever it suits them.

The differences between the writers and their novels are also instructive. While Defoe doubtless took some pleasure in depicting Moll's sexual irregularities and her life as a thief, he takes equal pleasure in subjecting her to the throes of a guilty conscience and an ultimate repentance and conversion experience. Heinlein, on the other hand, portrays Maureen as something of a moral exemplar in her forthright sexuality and her refusal to be dominated by repressive social norms. The tension that always exists in Defoe between the lover of adventure, intrigue, and wealth, and the believer trembling before God is lacking in Heinlein.

A number of critics have remarked on the strains of Calvinism in Heinlein, what one has perceptively called "Calvinism without theology." Heinlein was raised as a Methodist, and while he abandoned traditional religious beliefs at the age of thirteen, some marks of his early training persist in his exploration of free will and determinism, and especially in his belief in an elect group — an elite not of grace, but of superior intelligence, courage, and determination. Heinlein's elect, like that of Calvinist theology, is marked off by worldly success and riches.

Maureen is certainly one of the elect. She is smarter and more successful than the mass of humanity, and her eventual home on Boondock in the forty-fourth century is clearly Heinlein's equivalent of heaven, where she joins in a community of the saints, her extended family of husbands and co-wives, where, as the last line of the novel puts it: "we all lived happily ever after."

One other literary precedent or influence deserves mention. Samuel Clemens is represented in the novel as a hero of Maureen and her father, and Clemens himself even makes a brief appearance. Critics have often suggested a number of parallels between the two writers. At his best Heinlein's voice is similar to Twain's plainspoken, conversational, and graced with a pungent wit, and a knack for striking metaphors and tall tales. He also shares Twain's skepticism. Both writers spend a good deal of time satirizing their societies and lampooning sacred cows, and both reject their childhood religion and turn a jaundiced eye on the behavior of the faithful. And both produced their best work in what were ostensibly juvenile works — *The Adventures of Huckleberry Finn* (1884) and Heinlein's juvenile series.

to *Methuselah's Children,* 1941) and continued with *The Number of the Beast* and *The Cat Who Walks Through Walls* (1985). But one of the premises of these novels is the ability to travel not only through space and time, but to parallel universes, which allows Heinlein to incorporate most of the characters from his Future History series (a group of stories and novels later published as *The Past Through Tomorrow,* 1967), and nearly any of his other books. Characters from *Methuselah's Children, The Man Who Sold the Moon* (1950), *The Moon is a Harsh Mistress,* and *Stranger in a Strange Land,* all rub elbows. The effect is at times witty, but not nearly as successful as Heinlein or his fans would have hoped — perhaps because there is relatively little plot. Once Maureen gets to the forty-fourth century, beyond Lazarus, accumulating a larger and larger family from his past and from the present times of several universes, the characters have little to do but talk. Despite the uneven quality of the novel, however, it is unfortunate that we can no longer look forward to the next Heinlein novel.

Kevin P. Mulcahy
Rutgers University

◆ Related Titles ◆

To Sail Beyond the Sunset is related to a sizeable proportion of Heinlein's science fiction. It is the fourth novel in a sequence that began with *Time Enough for Love* (itself a sequel of sorts

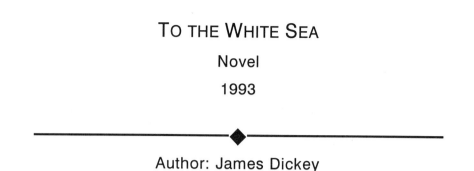

TO THE WHITE SEA

Novel

1993

◆

Author: James Dickey

◆ Characters ◆

Take Hemingway's most macho man multiplied to the fifth power and you begin to see the hero of *To the White Sea*, a hunter and survivor whose world has no place for women. Then place him in psychological territory reminiscent of Conrad's *Heart of Darkness* (1902), and you have tail-gunner Muldrow, shot down but not out over Tokyo, cutting a swath across Japan in his wartime adventures, part human, part wolverine, and part poet.

Muldrow is a loner, regarded by his Air Force colleagues with a mixture of awe and fear. He seems entirely detached from the events from the war, calmly going over the contents of his survival kit, shooting down planes with cool calculation, and measuring everything and everyone in terms of what he can "use."

Yet Muldrow also is exceptionally attuned to beauty, to grace, to small moments that others might not notice. For instance, he is enamored of the cold and his ability to thrive in it. He describes in poetic terms what it feels like to run without snowshoes after a long winter of wearing them, reveling in the capabilities of his body. He trea-sures his tools, particularly his knife, with its flexible blade and the shine it produces in moonlight. When he spends several days at a waterfall he draws strength from the beauty of the setting, wishing he never had to leave.

These aspects of Muldrow's personality make him a complex character who defies labeling. He seems in some senses a killing machine, but Dickey presses the reader to move beyond a stereotypical conception of a warrior. How can one person kill so efficiently and still remain a sympathetic character? That Dickey elicits empathy with this violent character is testament to his skill as a writer.

Other parts of Muldrow's character explore the boundaries between humans and animals. For example, he is obsessed with flying — not in a plane but as a bird. He can camouflage himself as well as any animal does. After doing what he can to ensure his safety, he sleeps easily and soundly, not burdened with the worry that most people would have in such a situation. This animal nature allows Muldrow to survive his experience.

By endowing Muldrow with a mixture of animal and human characteristics, Dickey has created a disturbing yet fascinating character. Muldrow embodies the best and worst of human behavior; he acts almost as a Rorschach blot upon which the reader can project internal values about violence and humankind's place in the natural world.

◆ Social Concerns ◆

In *To the White Sea* Dickey illuminates one man's metamorphosis into pure animal, operating on a survival level, killing instinctively, constantly searching for what he can use and discarding what he cannot. At the same time, this metamorphosis is marked by startling memories of color, speed, and cold; an elemental oneness with nature; and lyrical descriptions of the man's thoughts and actions as he makes his desperate journey. The novel operates on a primal level, bringing to life a character who pursues an essential quest, delivered in prose as tough and powerful as the man himself.

Muldrow, an American tail-gunner in World War II, is shot down during a bombing raid over Tokyo. Knowing he will be beheaded if captured, he decides to make his way north through Japan to the island of Hokkaido, where he hopes to find the cold and isolation reminiscent of his Alaskan boyhood. War, with its simultaneous chaos, bonding, isolation, and terror, is one of the emotional foundations of the book. Everything Muldrow does is set against the backdrop of war, and the novel itself is a meditation on the nature of war, a force as elemental as the glaciers Muldrow remembers from Alaska.

The violence that accompanies war, of course, constitutes a social concern. Dickey's presentation of the firebombing of Tokyo is sure to be a catalyst for

controversy. Equally disturbing, though, is Muldrow's enactment of violence. The massive violence of a bombing raid contrasts with Muldrow's one-man vendetta as he moves up north. Muldrow becomes a predator, killing without remorse to take what he needs, but he is not operating at an animal level. He imbues violence with thought: he kills for vengeance, he endows his victims with respect or dismissal, he ruminates on his tools for killing, and he gains energy from the lives he takes. Dickey's treatment of violence, therefore, illuminates not only its national manifestation (in war) but the more intimate violence which pervades modern society in the forms of murder, domestic violence, and serial killers.

◆ Themes ◆

A number of themes — war, violence, nature, sacrifice, and boundaries — are woven together in the overriding theme of the book, Muldrow's quest. His trip from a sewer pipe in Tokyo to a blood-and-feathered last stand on Hokkaido constitutes not only the framework for the book but a major theme, as Muldrow, in a long tradition of heroes from Odysseus to Don Quixote, must overcome obstacles to achieve his goal. Muldrow's quest is unique because it is extraordinary; he does not just want to survive, he wants to travel through his enemy's heartland and gain his freedom.

Like other heroes, Muldrow is transformed by his quest. The war propels him to dire circumstances, violence both aggrieves and sustains him, and his own nature shifts as quickly as the terrain under his feet, as he moves from instinctive behavior to thoughtful reflection to nostalgia.

The theme of nature manifests itself in several ways in the novel. First there is nature in the physical world which surrounds Muldrow, in the air above Tokyo, the terraces for farming, the lakes and streams and ocean. This nature is something to be traversed, acknowledged, and used. Then there is the physical world which Muldrow remembers from his childhood, a place of magic, evoked in lyrical terms, as in this description of seeing an iceberg calve:

> When the ice slid off the near side of it, the brightest blue I ever saw in my life came right at us, it seemed like, so deep and pale it could have been some new kind of scientific thing, a new kind of light that nobody had ever seen before. The ice just slid down off it, and it was there, a thing, a new color just invented, but one that had also been waiting in the ice for a long time, a real long time, just for two guys in a kayak to see it.

Muldrow's awe of nature includes a respect for life that is seemingly at odds with his remorseless killing. These opposing aspects of human nature are another theme of the book, as Dickey explores what it means to be human. Are we part of the animal world? Or apart from it? Muldrow, who reveres wild animals, particularly the wolverine, the marten, and the hawk, becomes a wild animal himself as he treks toward Hokkaido. His quest is to enter the natural world as fully as he can — to gather it into himself and to disappear into it. Many times, through killing, eating, or camouflaging himself, he achieves just that.

Yet he has human motivations and memories, as well as a sense of time and death, and these boundaries separate him from pure animal existence. He has a notion of death as sacrifice. He creates rituals peculiar to human beings. No matter how close he comes to transforming himself into a predator of the natural world, his human consciousness is never erased, not even at the end when he is "in it, and part of it" with only his voice remaining.

◆ Techniques ◆

The first-person narrator allows the reader to empathize with a character she or he would probably fear in person. Muldrow is not a person easily approached, and his actions are extraordinary. The only way for a reader to appreciate Muldrow, rather than be simply terrorized by him, is to feel the workings of his mind, share his memories, and absorb his awareness of the natural world.

Another technique which adds to the richness of the novel stems from Dickey's skill as a poet. Passages of *To the White Sea* are lyrical. The prose is poetic in its imagery and energy, as in this example, one of many when Muldrow describes light: "The sun on top of water is one thing, but sun *in* it — down somewhere under the surface where it makes a kind of a box shape, you could say, a box that changes, that goes in and out like it's breathing — that's something else again, I'll tell you." Sometimes images jump out of the ordinary prose in which they are embedded, as when Muldrow is in a boat on his way to Hokkaido: "The water rocked me; I rocked the water."

The intensity of the prose matches perfectly the events in the novel. Dickey maintains a taut suspense and gives the reader a heightened awareness of detail.

◆ Literary Precedents ◆

To the White Sea follows a long tradition of quest literature, beginning with Greek classics like the *Iliad* and *Odyssey* (c.1050-850 B.C.) and continuing to the present day in works as dissimilar as Joyce's *Portrait of the Artist as a Young Man* (1916) or Margaret Atwood's *Surfacing* (1972). The quest motif is common and its basis is simple: The hero searches for something and must overcome obstacles to attain his or her goal. In Muldrow's case, his quest is not only to survive (which would be the typical response of an ordinary person) but to march through enemy territory to a safe place. His quest is to find cold weather, which for him represents a benign environment and a return to his boyhood.

Cormac McCarthy's *All The Pretty Horses* (1992) offers an interesting juxtaposition to this novel. Both feature protagonists whose quests are fraught with violence.

◆ Related Titles ◆

Dickey's third novel shares some qualities of the first two. Like *Deliverance* (1970), *To the White Sea* describes a quest in an inhospitable landscape. Like *Alnilam* (1987), the backdrop is the military. But the main connection between *To the White Sea* and Dickey's other work is to be found in his poetry. In particular, "Firebombing," which shows the perspective of a World War II bomber, is easily linked with the novel. "Into the Stone" and "For the Last Wolverine" both connect to the animal theme of the book.

Dickey is still exploring themes which marked his early work: violence, death, and humankind's relationship to nature. Like Hemingway, Dickey creates male characters who are isolated and able to connect with others only in limited ways. Like Dostoevsky, Dickey probes the nature of violence and the psychology which allows it.

This novel, though, exemplifies a return to more accessible fiction. After the popular success of *Deliverance*, *Alnilam* was not well received. The title itself was indicative of the inaccessibility of the book, and readers were put off by the length of the novel. In *To the White Sea* Dickey returns to a shorter form, a tightly focused and controlled narrative, and a plot operating, literally and figuratively, at an elemental level.

◆ Ideas for Group Discussions ◆

To the White Sea is Dickey's third novel, following *Deliverance* and *Alnilam*. All three books revolve around male characters who are physically, emotionally, and mentally tested. *To the White Sea* is perhaps the most extreme of the three, with a single character thrust into desperate circumstances where he not only survives but seems to thrive. The novel is controversial, as much of Dickey's work has been over the course of his career, for its treatment of violence, war, and women. Below are some elements to consider when coming to your own appraisal of *To the White Sea*.

1. Does *To the White Sea* glorify violence? How is violence portrayed in various episodes in the book?

2. Compare perspectives on war (the Colonel in the opening, Major Sorbo, Muldrow, Japanese soldiers, the citizens of Tokyo). What overall view of war does Dickey offer?

3. Consider the main character. Is Muldrow a superhuman? A subhuman? Are his actions realistic? What motivates his actions?

4. What effect is achieved by having Muldrow narrate the book? How does this perspective affect our interpretation of events? How would our understanding of events differ if the book were narrated by, say, a Tokyo resident, a Japanese farmer, or a news reporter from the United States?

5. Dickey's work has been much criticized for its treatment of women. Discuss the female characters in the book (the old woman Muldrow beheads, the Japanese girl at the pool, the college girl in Alaska, the women in the village). How would you characterize those portrayals?

6. Nature is a pervasive force in *To the White Sea*. What view of nature does Dickey offer? Consider elements (fire, water, air, earth) as well as flora and fauna.

7. Images of flying, both natural and mechanical, are central to the book. What do you make of Muldrow's obsession with flying? Is this preoccupation common to humankind?

8. Fire also is a recurrent element, as in the firebombing, Muldrow's flint, the fire of bullets, and the heat Muldrow feels as he dies. Why is fire emphasized? To what aspect of human nature does fire appeal?

9. Dickey has achieved more fame as a poet than as a novelist. Which passages in *To the White Sea* strike you as particularly poetic?

10. Given the success of *Deliverance* in its film version, would *To the White Sea* make a good film? What aspects of it would most appeal to the moviegoing public? What aspects of the novel would be in danger of being lost?

Amber Dahlin
Metropolitan State College of Denver

TOO LATE THE PHALAROPE

Novel

1952

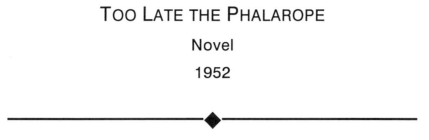

Author: Alan Paton

◆ Social Concerns ◆

The focus of attention in Alan Paton's fictional works pertains to South Africa and South African problems, to the social dilemmas brought about by apartheid as a political system. By so doing, Paton plans to expose apartheid, to show its effect socially and economically on the various ethnic groups and peoples of South Africa, and to awaken his readers' conscience with the belief that they will work to eliminate the system. The exposure of apartheid as a system in its very many facets has been well done. *Cry, the Beloved Country* (1948) is devoted specifically to the plight of the blacks in South Africa as they are caught in the web of laws and of frustrations of apartheid. In *Too Late the Phalarope* he concentrates on the agony of the Afrikaners (descendants of the original Dutch settlers) and then in the short stories — *Tales from a Troubled Land* (1961), especially "Life for Life" and "Debbie Go Home" — he examines the human condition of the Colored (mixed race) peoples of South Africa. Thus the various segments of the society undergo his scrutiny.

Alan Paton's typical preoccupation

with other social issues that continue to plague both the underprivileged and the privileged are again evident in *Too Late the Phalarope* as he addresses prostitution, morality and immorality (particularly in regard to human sexuality), illicit brewing of liquor, philanthropic activities, crime, poverty, hero-worship, village life versus city life.

◆ Themes ◆

Too Late the Phalarope, like all of Paton's fictional works, cuts across a wide canvas of thematic concerns. Restoration, repentance, mercy, the different faces of love, fear, pride and arrogance, hate, distrust, obedience, rigidity, Puritanism (what Paton himself calls Puritanical Christianity), pride of "pure race" are all subsumed by the quintessential theme, apartheid. A central aspect of the policy of apartheid, the infamous Immorality Act, is the main focus of Paton's second novel. Until very recently, the law forbade sexual relationships across the color line. The law itself was originally enacted as the Immorality Act Number 5 of 1927 and later intensified and expanded to the Prohibition of Mixed

Marriages Act of 1949 and the Immorality Amendment Act of 1950. Paton's use of the "iron law" has been stated categorically in the novel "that no White man might touch a Black woman, nor might my White woman be touched by a Black man." The consequences of such legislation are so serious that "to go against this law, of a people of rock and stone in a land of rock and stone, was to be broken and destroyed" (a quotation highly reminiscent of Alex La Guma's *The Stone Country*, 1974).

The theme of human sexuality in the novel can be approached from various angles. Some critics view the work as a tragedy of sex, for engaging in a sexual act with Stephanie (a black woman from the location of Maduna Country) Pieter brought disgrace upon himself and caused his father's death through grief. Pieter's predicament had always been psychological, the problem having developed from his childhood relationship with his uncompromising father. The problems unfortunately manifest themselves in his married life. His wife, Nella, having been raised in the Calvinistic tradition, believes that sex in marriage is only for procreation, and not for enjoyment. Pieter, on the other hand, believes sex should be for physical and emotional pleasure. When Nella withholds sex, he turns to Stephanie, who is an expert in such matters. Pieter yields to temptation and ruins himself and the van Vlaanderen family.

Another sexual level in the novel, again a direct consequence of the Immorality Act, is the Smiths' callousness in murdering their black maid whom Mr. Smith had impregnated. This sexual theme is directly connected to the theme of lack of restoration, lack of forgiveness, betrayal on the part of both Pieter and Sergeant Steyn, and the

sympathy and love that Pieter's mother continues to display despite his heinous sin. The sinning aspect of Pieter's act is one which is seen as being against the Church and against the Afrikaner race. In the words of Captain Massingham, the tragic element involved in Pieter's downfall pertains to the fact that the people cannot forgive or forget. "There is a hard law, Mejouffrou, that when a deep injury is done to us we never recover until we forgive." He tells Tante Sophie that "an offender must be punished, I don't argue about that. But to punish and not to restore, that is the greatest of all offences." Jakob cannot forgive and will never forget — he prefers death to forgiveness. Nella's father echoes Jakob's attitude, adding that he would shoot the transgressor of the law "like a dog." The only characters who support Pieter are Tante Sophie, Captain Massingham, Mathew Kaplan, and Pieter's mother.

◆ Characters ◆

The strength of characterization in this novel is supreme. Old Jakob, the Afrikaner patriarch is proud in the Afrikaner tradition and nationalism. Callan identifies these nationalistic tenets as *"volk, kerk, taal, land"* (people, church, language, soil). When Flip van Vuuren at Jakob's birthday party drunkenly demands to know "what's the point of living, what's the point of life?" Jakob pontifically reiterates this Afrikaner nationalistic philosophy: "The point of living is to serve the Lord your God, and to uphold the honour of your church and language and people . . ." Backed by the Dutch Reformed Church and coupled with the past history of Afrikanerdom (in which the Afrikaners see themselves as the chosen people and the conqueror of races), Jakob and his compatriots believe that the Afrikaner identity should be kept pure and separate. Having evolved from a family that traces its roots to the Voortrekkers of 1836, the van Vlaanderen family are of pioneer stock. Along with these beliefs, the importance of masculinity, obedience and subservience of son and wife is unquestionable. The white inhabitants of Venterspan all belong to this group and believe in this philosophy, except for Captain Massingham and the Kaplan Brothers.

Jakob is stern, proud, pious, intransigent. He is six foot three, with heavily lidded eyes and a lame leg. He is intolerant of the English, hating General Smuts for being too pro-English and reading only the Bible. Weekes describes him as "Boer to the bone." Because of these elements of his character, there is conflict between Jakob and his son: Jakob calls Pieter's D.S.O. and other war decorations "foreign trash," and when Pieter breaks the Immorality Law, Jakob curses him forever, reading from Psalm 109. He calls his lawyer, de Villiers, to disinherit Pieter. More seriously, Jakob crosses out Pieter's name from the 150-year-old family Bible and destroys traces of every gift his son had ever given him.

The father-son dilemma had been a psychological one since Pieter's childhood. The only connecting interests between them are stamps and the phalarope, but when the time came for them to learn more about the phalarope, it was already too late: Pieter had already committed his sin and was on the road to condemnation.

Pieter van Vlaanderen, the hero, is famous as a superb police officer, next-in-command to the Captain, an excellent rugby player and Captain of the Venterspan Rugby Football team, a splendid scholar and a soldier decorated for bravery, handsome and well built. He is the type of man in whose presence one cannot tell dirty jokes. In the Maduna Country location, the black children thought of him as a god because of his linguistic ability, his riding skills and his heroic wartime exploits. Pieter is respectably married to Nella and raises a respectable family. No one except Sophie is aware of Pieter's problems. He flirts with his cousin from the city and stoops to temptation, breaking the Immorality Act. Thus he brings upon himself the fateful consequences. In the tradition of the Greek tragedy, Pieter exhibits a tragic flaw: he cannot refrain from what he hates, "the mad sickness." Sergeant Steyn and Stephanie become the agents of Pieter's downfall. Steyn has an ulterior motive: by tricking Stephanie, he manages to trap Pieter and then reports Pieter to the police. Steyn betrays Pieter because of hatred — he has been promoted over Steyn even though Steyn has seniority in terms of police service.

Tante (Aunt) Sophie is a unique character in this novel. Her role is that of recorder of events that lead to the total ruination of the van Vlaanderen family. Being single and horribly disfigured, Sophie is more of an outsider in her brother's home, and for this reason, she makes use of the greatest opportunity to observe and record details of which other household members are unaware. She is the first to notice the marital problems of Pieter and Nella, and the first to become aware of Pieter's infidelity with Stephanie, the black woman. Again, Sophie is the first to notice the human qualities of her stonelike brother, Jakob. She sacrifices her security in Jakob's home by defying his injunction against visiting Pieter in prison. She is a credible narrator, not withholding her biases and her unqualified admiration for Pieter, constantly praising him. Sophie is very opinionated, immediately characterizing Elizabeth Wagenaar, who succeeded her sister-in-law as President of the Women's Welfare Committee as "surely one of the world's most stupid women." She laments the fact that people adored Pieter too much, like a god, but refuse to forgive or forget once he falls: "I pray we shall not walk arrogant, remembering Herod whom an Angel of the Lord struck down, for that he made himself a god." Mrs. Minna van Vlaanderen, Pieter's mother, is a good woman, subservient to Jakob in the real Calvinistic sense. But Minna, together with the Jewish Kaplan brothers, the social worker and the magistrate, are the only whites who care for the welfare of the blacks. Minna does a great deal of philanthropic work, especially as President of the Women's Welfare Committee. Tante Sophie testifies to Minna's love for her son even in time of trouble. "If ever a woman was all love, it was she . . ."

Stephanie, the black woman with whom Pieter becomes involved, has been a victim of circumstances, especially the circumstance of apartheid. Although she is classified as black, she is fair-skinned and her parentage is unknown. She has an illegitimate child and is a compassionate figure, taking care of Esther, an unrelated, aged black woman. To support herself, her child, and Esther, Stephanie brews liquor illicitly. This sends her to prison frequently and jeopardizes her chances of being the custodian of her own child. Having met a man as powerful as Pieter, who is obviously in a position to help her, she uses the only means at her disposal. Again, as a victim of circumstances, Stephanie is tricked by Sergeant Steyn into planting the evidence against Pieter, thereby destroying his life and his family forever. Like Matthew Kumalo and Johannes Pafuri, the police recruit someone who was once an ardent admirer of Pieter for his brilliance and unselfish assistance, and who then turns traitor.

The minister, Dominee Stander, is more interested in maintaining the status quo than in getting involved seriously in tragic family affairs. He is secure in his church.

◆ Techniques ◆

In terms of the mechanics of technique, *Too Late the Phalarope* is far superior to *Cry, the Beloved Country*. Ironically, however, *Cry, the Beloved Country* has enjoyed much more popularity. The language is still Biblical, as in *Cry, the Beloved Country*, with Biblical rhythms and tone. As in *Cry, the Beloved Country*, where Paton makes use of many Zulu terms, in *Too Late the Phalarope* he employs a multitude of Afrikaans words, phrases and idioms to lend local color and authenticity. The plot is simple, uniform and focuses mainly on one topic, without any of the elaborate digressions that *Cry, the Beloved Country* contains. The setting is confined to the geographical area of the small country town of Venterspan, an Afrikaner stronghold, and to the environs of Buitenverwagting ("Beyond Appreciation"), Nooitgedacht, Weltevreden ("Well Satisfied"), Dankbaarheid ("Thankfulness"), and Maduna's Country (the location and reserve for the black population). The characterization is focused on the protagonist, from beginning to end, with other characters coming into the story in order to shed more light on Pieter van Vlaanderen and his family. Narrative technique in *Too Late the Phalarope* differs slightly from *Cry, the Beloved Country*, yet resembles the latter in certain ways. The narrator is Sophie van Vlaanderen, the unmarried sister of Jakob, the patriarch of the van Vlaanderen family. She is an objective analyst of events, greatly credible on account of her long residence and intimate association with the van Vlaanderen family. However, Sophie is not an omniscient narrator, and for this reason, she uses Pieter's diary to fill in the gaps of detail in her knowledge. From the text diary, printed in italics, Sophie's intuitions and suspicions regarding Pieter's family and sexual problems, are proven to be very accurate. In this implementation of the diary technique, *Too Late the Phalarope* resembles *Cry, the Beloved Country*. Tante Sophie regrets that Minna van Vlaanderen, Pieter's mother, did not write the story "for maybe of the power of her love that never sought itself, men would have turned to the holy task of pardon, that the body of the Lord might not be wounded twice, and virtue come of our offences."

Too Late the Phalarope's tight construction makes it an easier and more enjoyable reading experience than *Cry, the Beloved Country*. Paton's chapter division brings to mind the division of books in the Bible. According to Edward Callan, chapters one through nineteen can be viewed as "The Book of Temptation" and chapters twenty through thirty-nine "The Book of Retribution." A "Book of Restoration, Reconstruction, Forgiveness" is totally absent. This is because, as Pieter explains to Dick early in the novel, to break the law "is a thing that's never

forgiven, never forgotten. The court may give you a year, two years. But outside it's a sentence for life." Pieter's situation is ironically and tragically similar to Arthur Jarvis's story.

Dialogue again is distinctly Patonian, following the pattern of *Cry, the Beloved Country*. The element of suspense is masterfully handled as Pieter is tortured by fear of discovery. His fear is unrelenting, but surfaces unexpectedly just when he begins to gain confidence.

◆ Literary Precedents ◆

Like *Cry, the Beloved Country*, *Too Late the Phalarope* is another protest novel against apartheid. *Too Late the Phalarope* is more immediate in its impact because it touches the Afrikaner character, the Afrikaner sense of decorum and uprightness, as well as the Afrikaner history. Some critics see a connection between *Too Late the Phalarope* and classical Greek tragedy, especially in terms of the tragic flaw of an otherwise unblemished hero. They refer specifically to Sophocles' *Oedipus Rex* (429 B.C.) and the parallels between Tante Sophie and Teiresias, both unwilling perceivers of imminent doom, and of the deaths of both Jakob and Laius, respectively. There are distinct echoes of Dostoevsky's *Crime and Punishment* (1866), as well.

The Immorality Act as a point of literary interest in South Africa has also been well documented by Athol Fugard in his play, *Statements after an Arrest under the Immorality Act*. The atrocious and destructive nature of the law in South Africa and Paton's excellent treatment of its effect in *Too Late the Phalarope* might have encouraged Fugard to reinforce the idea of the

stupidity of legislating against inter-
personal, interracial relationships.

◆ Adaptations ◆

Paton and Robert Yale Libatt adapted *Too Late the Phalarope* as a drama,
staged in New York in 1956, and in
1965 his short story entitled "Sponono"
was also adapted for the New York
stage with the help of Krishna Shah.

C. Lasker and K. Amoabeng
SUNY, Stony Brook

TOO MANY COOKS

Novel

1938

Author: Rex Stout

◆ **Characters** ◆

Too Many Cooks, like all Stout's Nero Wolfe books, has two fully realized characters, Nero Wolfe and Archie Goodwin, and a large supporting cast of deftly-sketched minor figures. Nero Wolfe dominates every scene in which he takes part with his sheer physical presence (Archie guesses his weight at 310 pounds), his matchless brain, and his overwhelming rhetoric. No one can ignore him; no one can intimidate him; no one can resist for long his combination of persuasiveness and stubbornness. He manages equally well whether he is lecturing European chefs on American contributions to *haute cuisine,* extracting information from suspicious black waiters and cooks, or defying the coercion of the authorities. While stirring from his chair as seldom as possible, he contrives to make the world come to him.

Stout keeps Wolfe from seeming insufferably superhuman by allowing Archie Goodwin to narrate. Partly to maintain his own self-respect and to assert his own unquenchable personality, Archie constantly sticks pins in his employer, both in direct conversation and in his descriptions as chronicler.

He gleefully points out Wolfe's morbid fear of moving vehicles, his inability to take off his own trousers on a train, his willingness to butter up Jerome Berin. When Wolfe seems inclined to neglect business, Archie lets him know about it. Archie is perhaps the one person Wolfe can never bully; Wolfe values him for that, as well as for his versatility, courage, and loyalty. Although he calls himself Wolfe's "secretary, bodyguard, office manager, assistant detective, and goat," Archie is no flunky: He is a formidable individual in his own right.

The other characters are too numerous to be fully developed. The most interesting minor figure is Dina Laszio — daughter of one of the chefs, ex-wife of another, widow of the murder victim, and catalyst of the mischief. As a siren who reduces otherwise civilized men to howling on hillsides, Dina Laszio incarnates all that Wolfe rejects in his quest for the Good Life.

◆ **Social Concerns** ◆

In *Too Many Cooks,* the fifth of the Nero Wolfe books, Stout says things about the treatment of blacks in this country that only became fashionable twenty-five years after the publication of this novel. During one of his rare excursions from his New York brownstone, Wolfe investigates a murder at a West Virginia spa. Although the local sheriff, who "knows how to deal with niggers," has learned nothing from them, Wolfe questions fourteen members of the kitchen staff as a group. He overcomes their understandable reluctance to get involved in a "white man's murder" by treating them precisely as he would any other group of men. His speech on their responsibilities to their society and their race — so unlike what they are accustomed to hearing from whites, neither bullying nor patronizing — moves the key witness to speak up. His patient follow-through elicits valuable supporting information from the others. Most importantly, Wolfe honors his bargain with them in full: He obliges the sheriff and district attorney to refrain from maltreating the witnesses, and the manager to refrain from firing them. The message is clear: These blacks are men like other men and deserve more respect than many of the whites in the book. Stout must have felt proud of this scene, for in 1964 he brought back Paul Whipple, the key witness, in *A Right to Die* (1964), even having him quote long passages from Wolfe's speech verbatim.

◆ Themes ◆

Nero Wolfe is the most truly philosophical of fictional detectives. His famous eccentricities, already well-established by the preceding novels in the series, stem from the same preoccupation that motivates him in *Too Many Cooks*: a quest for the Good Life. Having formed his opinions regarding how one ought to live, he defends them with ferocious integrity. His disagreements with Archie Goodwin, a man of equal integrity, arise from their differing views on what constitutes the Good Life and how one should go about seeking it. His clashes with others result from their moral, ethical, and aesthetic confusion, and their efforts to impose on Wolfe.

The novel opens with a journey by train, which Wolfe grimly endures because he is the guest of honor of Les Quinze Maîtres, a group of famous chefs who gather once every five years. He accepts on general philosophical grounds, out of reverence for "the greatest living masters of the subtlest and kindliest of the arts," but he has a more specific motive as well: to get a recipe. He offers the Catalan chef Jerome Berin five thousand dollars for the privilege of being able to enjoy *saucisse minuit* at his own table, musing, "I have only so long to live — so many books to read, so many ironies to contemplate, so many meals to eat." His single-minded pursuit of the recipe is sometimes comic, but is saved from absurdity by his conviction that "that sausage [is] high art." This is aesthetics, not greed.

Archie enjoys poking fun at Wolfe's obsession, but knows and respects his employer well enough to accept it. And Wolfe's quest has dignity when contrasted with the rapacity and vengefulness rampant among the others at the spa. As he gently reminds Paul Whipple, who has questioned the worth of a sauce-tasting competition: "each of us has his special set of values, and if you expect me to respect yours you must respect mine." He snaps at his oldest friend, Marko Vukcic, who has fallen once more under the sexual spell of his ex-wife: "You know very well what life consists of, it consists of the humanities, and among them is a decent and intelligent control of the appetites which we share with dogs. A man doesn't wolf a carcass or howl on a hillside from dark to dawn; he eats well-cooked food, when he can get it, in judicious quantities; and he suits his ardor to his wise convenience." He tells the siren exactly why he does not like her — because of how she has warped Marko: "It is not decent to induce the cocaine habit in a man, but it is monstrous to do so and then suddenly withdraw his supply of the drug."

Wolfe solves the murder, of course, and fulfills his function as a nemesis of crime and a restorer of order. But he does so not for his amusement, or for pay — although he gladly accepts his special fee. Ultimately, his work in *Too Many Cooks* is a defense of the humanities against those who have let their appetites take over.

◆ Techniques ◆

Already by this time Stout was making good use of the special advantages of the series. Reading *Too Many Cooks*, for the many who know the earlier novels, is a return to a well-loved context. The novel is self-contained, however. The references to established elements are self-explanatory or peripheral, and thus a first-time reader of Stout would not get lost. If one ignores the intertextuality of the Nero Wolfe saga and examines *Too Many Cooks* on its own, one finds a variation on the classic country house murder. Stout brings together a group of quirky characters in an isolated setting, strews the ground liberally with motives and clues and red herrings, and invites the reader to match wits with the detective. Although the characters do a great deal of eating and talking, there is enough conflict, suspense, and action (even Wolfe gets shot at) to keep the pages turning. The culprits are caught, and order is restored. There is even a romantic interest, since it is Wolfe who is a misogynist, not Stout.

◆ Literary Precedents ◆

No one can miss Stout's indebtedness to Sir Arthur Conan Doyle. He takes the basic concepts of the Great Detective and the sleuthing duo, and exploits the possibilities even more thoroughly than had his precursor. Thus, he portrays Wolfe as a superman, but humanizes him by giving him some engaging weaknesses, as Conan Doyle had done with Sherlock Holmes. Archie Goodwin takes Watson's roles, but puts up with much less superciliousness from the Great Detective. As Baring-Gould and others have pointed out, Nero Wolfe physically resembles Sherlock's obese and indolent brother Mycroft. And the two authors share a set of priorities: One reads Conan Doyle and Stout for fine writing, good yarns, and fascinating characters, not to find out who did it.

Stout also looks back to Agatha Christie and Dorothy Sayers, among others, in letting readers experience vicariously the luxuries of the rich. As usual, the readers also get to watch the rich and powerful taken down a peg, so that they may go back to their humdrum lives feeling somewhat pleased with themselves.

◆ Related Titles ◆

The book most closely related to *Too*

Many Cooks in the Nero Wolfe series is *A Right to Die*. Paul Whipple, now a middle-aged professor at Columbia University, returns to find Wolfe and Archie essentially unchanged, and gets them involved in another case charged with racial tension. The two novels lend themselves admirably to comparative discussion.

◆ Adaptations ◆

Stout despised film and never authorized any cinematic or televised versions of Nero Wolfe.

For a television series, there was a two-hour pilot episode, loosely based on *The Doorbell Rang,* starring Thayer David as Nero Wolfe and Tom Mason as Archie Goodwin. Written and directed by Frank Gilroy, it was shown on ABC on December 18, 1979. The series eventually ran for one season on NBC: thirteen episodes, January 16, 1981 to August 25, 1981, with William Conrad as Wolfe and Lee Horsley as Archie.

◆ Ideas for Group Discussions ◆

It is tempting to play with trivia and quote one-liners when discussing Stout's Nero Wolfe books. Such amusements have their place; Stout was fond of them himself as a member of the Baker Street Irregulars. But there is a great deal to talk about, on several levels. Any of Nero Wolfe's pithy statements on women, racism, civic responsibility, or ethics could provide a starting point for reflection and vigorous debate. Archie Goodwin supplies another voice and another set of stimuli: Even when he is wrong, he manages to be interesting about it. Stout's blend of political liberalism and cultural conservatism is bound to incite readers to react.

Too Many Cooks vividly depicts American society almost sixty years ago; while some of Stout's opinions are strikingly modern, the novel is distant enough in time to be of historical value.

1. The murder victim seems to have richly deserved a knife in the back. Why is it necessary to capture and punish the killer of such a man? Will justice be served?

2. Several characters outside the circle of Les Quinze Maîtres consider their obsession with cuisine and their epic meals to be frivolous, if not worse. Certainly it could be considered a breach of good taste to eat so lavishly in an America still in the throes of the Depression. Does the book offer any viable defense of the gourmandizing?

3. Wolfe regards all women with suspicion; Archie surveys them with an appreciative eye, but with no intention of getting entangled. Are Stout's portrayals of the female characters distorted according to the quirks of his protagonists? Do they reflect typical attitudes of the time?

4. Wolfe is prepared to leave for home with the case unsolved, until the murderer takes a shot at him. Is he just being lazy and eccentric? Does his justification of his departure ring true?

5. Wolfe declares that the best way to deal with black men is to treat them *as* men, and he takes great pride in having learned more from them than the local sheriff had. Does he in fact approach them without adjusting for

their color?

6. As a naturalized citizen, Wolfe thinks and speaks at some length about his adopted country. How does Stout integrate Wolfe's pronouncements on the subject with the action of the novel?

7. Wolfe and Archie are outrageously high-handed in their dealings with the authorities, as usual. How do they get away with it? Should they get away with it?

8. Will the miniature society represented by the surviving members of Les Quinze Maîtres be able to recover from the disruption caused by the murder? Does the ending invite optimism about the order of society as a whole?

9. Wolfe's eccentric manner of living suits him well, and he has the verbal, intellectual, and financial resources to sustain it. Does he have anything of value to teach us about how to live?

Philip Krummrich
Drury College

TOO MANY MAGICIANS

Novel

1966

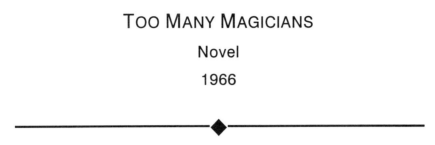

Author: Randall Garrett

◆ Characters ◆

Lord Darcy, Chief Investigator for the Duke of Normandy, is the main character of *Too Many Magicians*. Not a magician himself, he dominates the book by his authority and by his relentless powers of observation and deduction as the man responsible for investigating the murder of Sir James Zwinge, chief forensic sorcerer for the city of London and secretly the head of counterespionage for the Admiralty. Darcy is also an agent in the King's Secret Service. A Sherlock Holmes without the neuroses, Darcy can also be described as a G. K. Chesterton version of James Bond. Ruthlessness in pursuit is tempered by a sense of humor and sensible humility. Darcy, for example, shares none of the ascetic Holmes's habitual scorn of women. His "Dr. Watson," Master Sean O Lochlainn, is a more independent, powerful figure in his own right.

Master Sean is Darcy's technical expert out in the field. A forensic sorcerer of formidable talent and warm temper, he maintains the open-minded attitude necessary to keep up with Darcy and at the forefront of his discipline. Short and tubby, he is physically distinct from the tall, lean, and athletic Darcy.

Assisting them in the investigation is Commander Lord Ashley, who like Zwinge works for the Admiralty. Looking the classic seaman, Ashley is intelligent, brave, quick under fire but also reckless. Recklessness, like other excesses, may lead to compromise; no officer of the King can afford even the appearance of it. But even in his fall from grace, Ashley is limited in what mischief he is willing to do, at least in a short period of time. His fall is relatively recent; he is desperate but not cynical. He so abhors treason that he would rather become a murderer than be thought guilty of it.

Attending the convention in London where Zwinge is murdered is Master Ewen MacAlister, a weaseling little man who is eventually discovered to be more than a minor annoyance. While not guilty of the killing under investigation at the convention, he is, of the two criminals who come to light, the one who is genuinely evil. The fallen are no less individual in their state than the faithful; Ashley falls into bad circumstances and compounds them, but Master Ewen is under no duress to take up the practice of Black Magic and act as an agent for his country's enemies. His sole concern is for his own skin.

Minor characters who embody the novel's themes of responsibility, compassion, and bravery are the Dowager Duchess of Cumberland, Lord John Quetzal, and Tia Einzig. Mary, the Duchess, is a journeyman sorceress, a beautiful young widow, intelligent and vivacious, who is obviously more than the close friend of Darcy's that she appears in public. She lends her skills and influence to the investigation at crucial moments as an intelligent amateur. Lord John Quetzal du Moqtessuma de Mechicoe is a modest young sorcerer for all his noble blood and exceptional talent. He has bravely chosen a life as a hard-working forensic magician with a talent for detecting black sorcery, a capacity which will bring him into frequent contact with the most fallen and dangerous of criminals. Tia Einzig is an apprentice sorceress, a refugee from the Polish Hegemony. Her young life has been a difficult one; she is separated from family, ignorantly accused of Black Magic, and threatened even within the relative safety of the Angevin Empire by agents of the Polish government. Yet she still seeks to become a Healer, to work with the sick and suffering, when with her beauty and grace she could marry well and never have to work again.

Those minor characters who contrast, sometimes comically, the themes of responsibility, compassion, and bravery are the Marquis de London and Lord Bontriomphe. De London, who is Darcy's cousin, shares his gift for deduction but little else. The Marquis is a physically indolent, penurious bureaucrat who pulls the sublimely ridiculous stunt of jailing Master Sean for Zwinge's murder, to shift the expense of the investigation to the Crown and so embarrass his cousin. His information about the world outside his office is provided by the easy-going Lord Bontriomphe. Bontriomphe is a walking, talking sponge for experience, with a real gift for telling his story effectively. But he lacks any genuine ability to reason from the material he collects. During the course of the investigation he comes up with one impossible theory after another, to the amused exasperation of Darcy and company. For all the individual strengths of their peculiar gifts, as a pair the two Londoners can be as much of an obstacle as a help.

◆ Social Concerns ◆

The motivating force of this novel, typical of the murder-mystery genre, stems from society's desire for the rule of justice to be ascendant over the anarchy of crime. Garrett has taken this concept one step further by introducing the element of fantasy into his detective story, setting it in an "alternate earth" with alternative but quite logical rules, where the human need for justice and order still prevails. Although this fictional world has a kindlier history than the real world, *Too Many Magicians* is set in no utopia; its men and women have the same frailties, the same ill-luck, that entangle people in crime in the real world.

Individual responsibility for maintaining justice and order, an old-fashioned and unwritten code of conduct which might be labeled "honor," is strongly evident in the world of Lord Darcy. Christian chivalry did not die out, to be replaced, of necessity, by secular constitutional government, but continued to evolve in a world which never knew the fragmentation of Christendom. It is a world, while still divided into east and west along somewhat familiar lines, which never knew the Reformation or the Inquisition, Thomas Jefferson or Karl Marx, the Magna Carta or the American Revolution. It is a world in which the term "scientific revolution" applies not to material science, but to the laws of magic, which have brought quite different wonders and terrors to the modern world. It is a world where superior leadership has made a real difference in the quality of civilization.

That leadership has maintained sovereignty by respect for the people it rules, and a tradition of respect for the law. The historical point at which Garrett chose to have this civilization diverge from that of reality is quite important in this regard. Darcy's world is one where a superb warrior survived to become a good king at a crucial moment, preserving both a strong bloodline and a major achievement in the history of government. The warrior-king was Richard the Lion-Hearted, son of Henry II of England, and the greatest of the knights errant. Henry II is credited with the invention of an administrative apparatus to effectively carry on the King's Justice even after his death, something which no previous English king, however strong, had ever managed. In the real world Richard died young, and England was left to his younger brother John, who was so disreputable that his barons were forced to limit his power and that of future kings of England with the Magna Carta, starting a trend towards curtailing executive power and initiative that has continued to the present day. In Darcy's world Richard was brushed, but not taken, by death in a minor battle. The resulting long convalescence had a sobering effect on Richard, who instead of running off irresponsibly to the next available war and leaving the fate of his country in his brother's foolish hands, stayed home and preserved his nephew Arthur's claim to the throne. Arthur became a great king, preserving the Angevin Empire which would in time rule benevolently the territories of the British Isles, France, and New England and New France (North and South America). In Darcy's time (the 1960s) the Angevin Empire is eight hundred years old and still healthy.

Within the borders of a just and secure realm, new progress was possible. The discovery in the late thirteenth century of the analog equations by which the mind of man influences the universe — magic — by Saint Hilary of Walsingham, enabled the psychic healing and forensic arts to advance rapidly. The physical sciences remained mired in infancy, the province of amateurs and eccentrics only. Because of a lucky break in history, the forces in human society which heal and preserve, such as able leadership, good government, honest spirituality, and effective medicine, have a solid lead on those which tear and destroy, such as stupid or venal leadership, bellicosity, greed among the clergy, and neglect of learning. Therefore, Darcy's world is a frankly more wholesome place than the readers' for a variety of reasons that bear inspection, even study; though it is plain that the stories were written to amuse more than instruct, they do both uncommonly well.

◆ Themes ◆

Too Many Magicians explores two major themes common to the genre of detective fiction: the superiority of reason over impulse, and the variety of human responses to temptation. Reason is represented by the detective team of the novel: Lord Darcy, an investigator for the King's Justice, and his associate, forensic sorcerer Master Sean O Lochlainn. While Darcy has the superior gifts of deduction, and knowledge of self-defense, interrogation, and tactics, he must rely on Master Sean's scientific expertise and psychic gifts to gather the necessary evidence upon which to base his deductions. Neither can afford to let his imagination lead him far away from the paths of probability. For contrast, another investigator, Lord Bontriomphe, for all his remarkable memory for detail, and genuine narrative ability, makes himself look ridiculous doing just that. More importantly, neither Darcy nor Master Sean can afford to give way to impulse, for their exceptional abilities and power as King's officers would make them far more dangerous to society than the average man, should they ever decide to do wrong, or become lax in their duties.

Impulse is represented in the novel by the two criminals, Commander Lord Ashley and Master Ewen MacAlister. Ashley murders on impulse, desperate for the money he needs to pay off a gambling debt before it is exposed and he is discovered to be too reckless for promotion because of it. Master Ewen becomes involved in treason and attempted murder less out of desire for money than a desire to feel important, and he is no more reasonable in this impulse than Ashley is about money. Throughout the novel Master Ewen exposes himself as a vainglorious fool by thoughtless words or actions. Both men, like Darcy and Master Sean, hold positions of responsibility: Ashley, as an investigator for the Admiralty, and Master Ewen as a master sorcerer. Both men cause exceptional damage because their training enables them to plot mischief and conceal it from the ordinary eye.

Both heroes and villains in this novel are exposed to temptation, but the heroes help each other resist it, while the villains succumb to progressively worse temptations. Darcy can become imperious in his desire to run the perfect investigation, and at one point is reminded that he cannot order master Sean to do things against the master sorcerer's better judgment without breaking up the partnership. Darcy accepts this reminder with good grace, and Master Sean keeps the independent judgment which makes him of such value to Darcy. Ashley, a lone investigator, has more freedom than he can handle, with no partner of similar strength to spot warning signs of trouble. Master Ewen could not make a real friend to save his life, so there is little hope that he would learn temperance in time.

♦ Techniques ♦

Too Many Magicians is a "locked room" mystery, given a fresh twist by the introduction of the fantasy element. The impossible crime is committed, and because it occurs at a sorcerers' convention it would seem that a sorcerer must be the culprit. Because there are so many high-caliber suspects about, determining motive, method, and opportunity makes for a particularly Byzantine and absorbing puzzle.

Contrast is used playfully to draw the reader into the alternate world of the novel. Darcy's world is just similar enough to the reader's world for it to be comprehensible with an occasional paragraph explaining its history or technology. It is a world where the reader can feel at home, yet still be intrigued and amused by its unexpected parallels or differences.

Contrast between characters, or sets of characters, is used to emphasize the true nature of each. Darcy and Master Sean appear all the more dedicated and cogent for their comparison to the devious Marquis and his less-than-able assistant Bontriomphe. Lord Ashley's downfall is all the more sad for his likeness to Lord Darcy; but for a single flaw in his character, the Angevin Empire could have had a man of exceptional resourcefulness and daring in a key position to guard against its enemies, instead of accidentally doing their work for them. Master Ewen, for all his posturing as a Master of his guild, looks small compared to the two journeymen and one apprentice who risk their lives defying him and bringing him to justice.

◆ Literary Precedents ◆

Lord Darcy is a most fortunate imitation, flaunting his origins while transcending them. The parallels between Sherlock Holmes of Victorian London and Darcy of Angevin London are played up by Garrett, slipped in as an additional touch for devotees of Conan Doyle's character to enjoy. Darcy has, for example, his own "Watson" in the person of Master Sean O Lochlainn. He has the familiar skills of the nineteenth-century sleuth: the power of first-rate deductive reasoning, moments of insight, the understanding of human psychology that includes the abnormal side of the spectrum so often involved in bizarre crime, a handiness

with sword, gun, or fist, the ability to locate cabs and street urchins for message-carrying, and even an intimate knowledge of tobacco ash. But the familiar accouterments may also have the alternate-world twist; Darcy's Meerschaum pipe has a long straight stem, and his "Mycroft" is a cousin who is the Marquis of London, facts which defy the reader's expectations that Meerschaums are curved, and that London is governed by a mayor.

If it were Garrett's intention to set a Victorian-style detective loose in the streets of modern London without the obvious anachronisms bothering his readers, he has certainly found an audacious but internally consistent solution. He has had to set the familiar universe on its ear so that modern knight errant could be born into a world where his gentlemanly style is not a fading relic of a cherished past, but part of a living reality, a better world but still much in need of Darcy's gifts.

The sense of déjà vu is heightened by the homages to British detective fiction scattered through the Darcy series. There are suspicious similarities to G. K. Chesterton's Father Brown, Dorothy Sayers's Lord Peter Wimsey, Ian Fleming's James Bond, and Agatha Christie's Hercule Poirot. Like Chesterton's, Garrett's work shows religion at its best: fully integrated into everyday life, a reliable source of comfort and guidance to the weak and the strong alike, organized by reasonable men chosen for their compassion and insight. Garrett uses devices made famous by Christie in her Poirot adventures, such as the least-likely-suspect or the red herring; indeed, the title *Too Many Magicians* could easily be translated to *Too Many Red Herrings*. Although Lord Darcy, as a King's Officer, is spared the indignity of having to maintain a fatuous front to conceal his intelligence and drive, as must Sayers's Lord Peter among his vapid fellow-aristocrats in London of the 1920s, the two do share the common bond of knight errantry that goes back to Richard the Lion-Hearted himself. Too, the sleuths share a more modern view of women than earlier detectives, both as partners in work and in love. Finally, Garrett bows to the popularity of Fleming's secret agent 007, whose heyday was the 1960s, when most of the Darcy material was written. Like Bond, Darcy is handsome, clever, deadly when necessary, and thoroughly at home with counterintelligence techniques, although he fortunately lacks Bond's cruelty and licentiousness.

◆ Related Titles ◆

The premier story of the Darcy series is contained in *Murder and Magic* (1979), and establishes Darcy as the instrument of imperial justice to the high-born as well as the more humble. Darcy begins as the criminal investigator for Richard, the youthful Duke of Normandy, in "The Eyes Have It," which establishes Darcy's intuitive understanding of psychology and his willingness to consult scientific authorities to supplement it. By "The Muddle of the Woad" Darcy's reputation brings him to the attention of King John IV, the Duke's older brother, who gives Darcy occasional work involving international intrigue. The second collection of Darcy stories, *Lord Darcy Investigates* (1981), contains mostly international intrigue, as Darcy's gifts come into play more often to protect the Empire from more foreign threats than domestic ones.

Titles featuring Lord Darcy include: *Murder and Magic,* 1979, four short stories ("The Eyes Have It," 1964; "A Case of Identity," 1964; "The Muddle of the Woad," 1965; "A Stretch of the Imagination," 1973); *Lord Darcy Investigates,* 1981, four short stories ("A Matter of Gravity," 1974; "The Ipswich Phial," 1976; "The Sixteen Keys," 1976; "The Napoli Express," 1979).

Suzanne M. Munich

TOPPER

Novel

1926

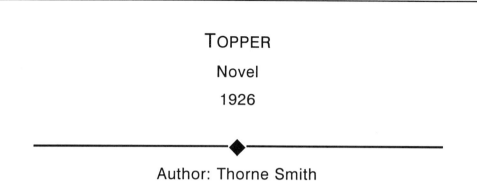

Author: Thorne Smith

◆ Social Concerns/Themes ◆

The novel *Topper* satirizes the newly developed upper middle class in American society: its pretension, hypocrisy, conformity, and insistence on conventional moral behavior. Like all of Smith's novels, it also attacks the Volstead act, which left America dry and dependent on homemade or illegally procured alcohol. Its major theme might be termed "immoral" regeneration, as the staid banker Topper is transformed from a conventional law-abiding citizen to a drunken playboy and potential adulterer. But it is purely escapist literature: For all of his mockery of bourgeoisie wealth and ways, Smith's joyful wickedness has meaning only within the confines of that class. The symbols of success are fast cars, beautiful women, expensive clothing, and dwellings with appropriately exclusive addresses. It is an exclusively white, Anglo-Saxon world, where all Irish are policemen, all blacks are servants, and all Italians sell food. Illicit sex is praised, no amount of drinking is excessive, and all those who hate the beautiful people are either envious or stupid. *Topper* mirrors the carefree, irresponsible world of the 1920s, which abhorred the Puritanical strain in American culture, but which never examined the consequences of a narcissistic, solipsistic lifestyle. The fantasy element is provided by the regenerated ghosts Marion and George Kerby, another irrational element to play against the seriousness and sobriety of the rational and respectable world of Cosmo Topper. However, the supernatural is not so much a theme as a *deus ex machina* to extricate Topper from his conventional lifestyle and introduce him to the joys of drinking and illicit sexuality.

◆ Characters ◆

In a word, the characters are stereotypes. Cosmo Topper is a stuffy banker as well as a henpecked husband; Mrs. Topper a shrew and the voice of conventional morality; Marion Kerby a witty and sexually vibrant representative of the flapper era; and her husband George a handsome playboy who uses his wealth only to pursue his own pleasure. The other two ghosts, Colonel Scott and Mrs. Hart, are of the same type, one generation removed. The others are what E. M. Forster called flat or one-dimensional characters: bell-hops, police, salespeople, secretaries. Character bows to situation in *Topper*, and the situations are always ludicrous and fantastic. All women are potential sex objects, all men potential philanderers. The characters function well in this fun-filled world, but as they move from one Smith novel to another, they tend to become formulaic, interchangeable, and repetitive.

◆ Techniques ◆

Smith's basic technique is one of contrast: the serious Topper and his conventional lifestyle against the flippant and reckless Kerbys, who (in life and in death) thumb their noses at the proprieties. As in most of Smith's novels, the attack on respectability involves a courtroom scene, where the forces of conformity and respectability are overrun by the absurdity of the situation. The intrusion of magic (in this novel the Kerby ghosts, and their ethereal companions Colonel Scott, Mrs. Hart, and their dog Oscar) makes a shambles of law and order and creates an opportunity for the sexual high jinks that are a major part of Smith's work. The dialogue is farcical, as the characters talk at cross-purposes, and confusion reigns. The novel is framed by the Kerby death car, which Topper buys at the beginning of the novel and almost loses his life in as a passenger at the end. It also marks out his journey from respectability and conformity to independence and a new sense of personal worth.

◆ Literary Precedents ◆

Smith's brand of humor in *Topper* and other comic novels has been compared to music hall comedy, Rabelais, P. G. Wodehouse, and F. Anstey (pseudonym for Thomas Anstey Guthrie, 1856-1934). The dialogue of mock confusion obviously owes much to the stand-up comedians of the music hall, but Smith's brand of humor in *Topper* borders on the prurient rather than the Rabelaisean. Perhaps H. L. Mencken's twitting of the Puritan conscience and excoriation of Prohibition also formed part of Smith's intellectual background. Like Smith, F. Anstey introduces magic into an otherwise rational world, with hilarious consequences, often threatening the breakup of engagements or marriages, just as Topper's marriage is threatened by the reckless behavior of the Kerby ghosts. Anstey's story "At a Moment's Notice" resembles *Topper* in that a respectable man is turned into a monkey after having an accident in a horse-drawn cab. He is made to appear ridiculous before a woman whom he would like to marry, and, like Topper, he awakens from a coma at the end of the story. Anstey, like Smith, also contrasts a severely constricted middle-class world with the madcap world of magic and transformation. He was probably the proximate source for Smith's peculiar type of comic fantasy.

◆ Related Titles ◆

The success of *Topper* prompted Smith to produce a sequel, *Topper Takes a Trip* (1931). The scene is shifted from New York to the Riviera, and Topper has almost reverted to his old respectable self. The novel is more episodic than *Topper*, and the encounters with authority and the sexually suggestive comic scenes do not enhance the contrast between respectability and playful high spirits as they do in the earlier novel. Topper also has the unique experience of cuckolding a ghost, for he commits "adultery" with Marion Kerby's ghost, even though he is constantly being pursued by the vengeful ghost of George Kerby. The novel is "framed" like *Topper*, in that Topper, in the opening and closing chapters, is gazing out of the window of his apartment on the Riviera.

The characters of *Turnabout* (1931) are somewhat more complex than in Smith's other satirical novels. Sally Willows is genuinely concerned about the fate of her oafish husband, and Tim gains sensitivity if not poise from his female experience. His simple honesty sets him apart from his wife-swapping colleagues, and makes it difficult for him to write the deceitful prose he must produce to make his living as an advertising copyist. Other characters are delightfully stereotypical: the gleefully malicious "Mr. Ram," the repulsive philanderer Carl Bently, the absurdly unjust Judge Clark, the charmingly amoral Claire Meadows, and Tim's pretentiously tiresome boss Mr. Gibber.

This intriguing novel combines a satire of upper-middle-class values with a mocking glance at a very modern concern: gender identification. Tim and Sally Meadows, a successful suburban couple, are dissatisfied with their lives, and each one feels that the other has an easier and happier lot. "Mr. Ram," an Egyptian statuette with human feelings and magical powers, sends them on a voyage of self-discovery by placing the soul of Tim in the body of Sally and shifting her soul to his body. Tim learns firsthand about the insults given to women when he is pursued by his wife's would be lover Carl Bently, and Sally learns the challenges and crudities of the aggressive male world when she tries to take Tim's place as an advertising executive (Smith's profession before he became a full-time writer). Tim actually has a baby, and experiences the humiliations and discomforts of the pregnant human female; he is even overpowered by the newly aggressive Sally when she tires of his complaints. Both Sally and Tim emerge from the experience with a new appreciation of each others' fate: Tim of the degrading and absurd treatment of women, Sally of the hypocrisies and incompetence of the executive suite. Much of the humor is very broad (Sally tries to strike up a conversation in the ladies' room, and Tim is smoking a cigar as he prepares to have "his" baby), but there is an uncharacteristic seriousness about Smith in this work: *Turnabout* is entertaining and hilarious, but comes closer than any other of Smith's works to becoming a serious novel of ideas.

Smith uses the ancient technique of physical transformation to produce psychological or personal change in his characters. The transformation causes a series of comic, absurd incidents that are enhanced by Smith's brand of vaudevillian double talk and risque humor. The forces of respectability are mocked by placing the transformed characters in ritualistic settings: the cocktail party, the church supper, the courtroom, the delivery room, the ladies' room. As in Topper, the humor is based on a series of contrasts between the banal realities of upper middle class life and the excitement of nonconformity; in *Turnabout*, the nonconformity is complete: After their outward forms have been restored at the end of the novel, Tim and Sally experience an inward transformation that makes them more sympathetic toward each other, and even less tolerant of the hypocritical society in which they find themselves.

The theme of physical transformation recalls the classical works of transformation, Ovid's *Metamorphoses* and Apuleius' *The Golden Ass*. F. Anstey's *Vice Versa* is very similar in technique to *Turnabout*, except that Anstey has a father exchange bodies with his son, instead of a husband with his wife. In both cases an exotic artifact provided by a relative has effected the change, and hilarious consequences result; again, both characters, after being returned to their respective bodies, have gained a new appreciation of the other's plight. While Anstey is more accepting of his social world than Smith, his work is also satirical of Victorian mores and employs broad contrasts to effect his social satire: an aging schoolboy and an adolescent father.

The technique of physical transformation is a staple of many of Smith's novels: from age to youth in *The Glorious Pool* (198434), from man to a variety of animals in *The Stray Lamb*, from plaster and stone to god and goddess in *The Night Life of the Gods*, from man to skeleton in *Skin and Bones* (1933). Many of these plots can also be traced to the tales of F. Anstey, particularly *The Tinted Venus*, *A Fallen Idol*, *The Brass Bottle*, and *The Talking Horse*.

◆ Adaptations ◆

Five of Smith's novels were made into movies: *Night Life of the Gods* (Universal, 1935), *Topper* (Metro-Goldwyn, 1937), *Topper Takes a Trip* (United Artists, 1938), *Turnabout* (United Artists, 1940), and *I Married A Witch* (based on *The Passionate Witch*, United Artists,

1942). There was also a sixth film, based on Smith's characters in the Topper novels, *Topper Returns* (United Artists, 1941). They drew measured praise from the critics, but were popular with audiences. *Night Life of the Gods* was praised for its use of special effects, *Topper* for its characterization. Mr. Ram's role was slightly expanded in *Turnabout*, and George Kerby was retained only in *Topper*. The old Topper films still appear on television, and occasionally in movie theaters. A popular television series by Loverton-Schubert productions appeared on the major networks from 1953-1955, and there was a disappointing made-for-TV film in 1979. *Topper* was at the center of a controversy about the colorization of classic black-and-white films.

John Mulryan
St. Bonaventure University

THE TORRENT

Novel

1900

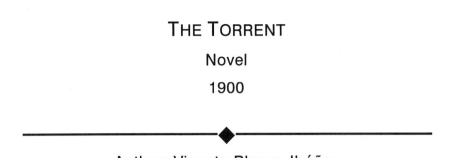

Author: Vicente Blasco Ibáñez

◆ Characters ◆

Several critics have suggested that Leonora, the female protagonist of *The Torrent*, closely resembles a Russian opera singer romantically linked with Blasco Ibáñez shortly before the writing of the book. Leonora, whether patterned on a real-life character or not, is a well developed melodramatic heroine: Born in Valencia, her free-thinking republican father, who was a doctor, abandons the region and moves to Milan where he wants his daughter to be trained in opera. After suffering untold misery, including rape, Leonora triumphs as a diva in Europe's opera houses. Recently widowed, she returns to her native Valencia, to her aunt's cottage, to recover from a life that has left her exhausted and alone. There she meets the young Rafael Brull, a deputy to the national parliament who falls madly in love with her. He is the son of a local *cacique* (political boss) and rich landowner. His widowed mother is doña Bernarda, a spiteful and domineering woman who, together with don Andrés, a political manager, attempts to control the young man and arrange for a more suitable marriage.

The reader is not surprised when the lovers' scheme to elope fails. Each character is drawn to represent a particular type, and Rafael, the male protagonist, is portrayed as feeble and cowardly. He is the weak link in the love relationship, yet he is a necessary figure if the Brull family is to maintain its power and prestige in future generations. As the heir, he chooses power and tradition over love and happiness.

◆ Social Concerns ◆

Like much of Blasco Ibáñez' early fiction, *The Torrent* is based on characters and situations that in many respects typify his native province of Valencia. This work differs from others in the Valencian cycle because of the author's choice of characters. His central concern here is with the family of a powerful local landowner and political boss rather than with the workers of the land. The family is autocratic, hypocritical, cruel, and self-serving. They are destined to perpetuate these qualities into future generations missing out on the opportunity to experience true love and happiness. On the political level, they will fail to secure and advance the future of the country.

The novel serves to expose the ruling class as rigid and ineffectual.

The general backdrop of this tale, as with others in this group, is the countryside around the city of Valencia. This book, in particular, takes place in the midst of its famed orange groves, inspiring the novel's original Spanish title, *Among the Orange Trees*. This earthly paradise, whose Moorish history is recounted in detail, is used by the author not only to celebrate nature and its beauty — in contrast with artifice — but also to exemplify energy and passion; the lovers are excited by the intoxicating scent of the orange blossoms, and their desire is consummated. Their love founders when society and convention conspire to put an end to their attachment.

◆ Themes ◆

The Torrent, the English title of the novel, refers to an important episode in the book based on a historical fact, a serious flood caused by the river Júcar, and the efforts of local farmers to make the waters subside. The lovers meet in this atmosphere and they fall in love; she is an outsider, an experienced and accomplished woman who represents freedom and passion; he is the heir to an important estate and political responsibilities who, early on, is seduced by the prospects of the fuller and more exciting life that the relationship promises. The hero, however, is unable to free himself from his own environment and accepts, almost without a struggle, the path chosen for him. He inherits his father's lands but also his politics and prejudices. In the process, he abandons his hopes and dreams, and the woman he loves. Society, portrayed here as traditional and repressive,

triumphs at the expense of the individual. The opportunities for freedom and renewal, which take the form of the woman from outside, are rejected and defeated. Nature, as the force capable of unleashing energy and love, must also be repressed just as the waters of the river must be contained.

◆ Techniques/Literary Precedents ◆

Blasco Ibáñez is a descriptive artist whose ability with the pen resembles that of an Impressionist painter. The geography, history, and landscape of the *huerta* are richly, eloquently, and colorfully depicted in *The Torrent*. The reader can easily partake of the strong scent of the orange flowers in full blossom that so affect the two lovers and can be impressed by the forceful narration of many of the scenes.

The characters of the novel are described with care and in detail. They are assigned traits that reveal spiritual characteristics: Leonora is blonde, tall, and pure — life's reverses notwithstanding. Rafael, youthful and handsome at first, degenerates into a bald, fat and ineffectual human being. The other characters, less developed than the two protagonists, are interesting as prototypes of provincial life. One of them, an old Cortes deputy who opposes Rafael, speaks eloquently in favor of policies advocated by Blasco himself. Today's reader can be easily engaged by the strong narrative line of the novel and will sympathize with the frustrations of the lovers; the unhappy end of the work, however, will neither surprise nor disappoint.

Blasco Ibáñez' early novels, *The Torrent* among them, are considered excellent examples of Naturalism, the literary movement whose main exponent was the French writer Émile Zola. Blasco was a staunch admirer of the French author. Blasco's interest in the plight of the lower classes; his detailed and accurate description of people and landscape, including the more unsavory traits in their character and their physical and moral shortcomings; his commitment to social justice; his belief in the importance of environment in the shaping of a person's character, are all instances of deliberate imitation of his much admired colleague. In *The Torrent*, there are also elements of *costumbrismo*, or a detailed and deliberate inclusion of local folklore and color. Last, but not least, some critics consider Blasco a good exponent of literary realism in his avoidance of the exotic, his democratic eye, and his use of the environment as a literary conceit.

◆ Related Titles ◆

Blasco Ibáñez was a hugely prolific writer. Aside from the novels he authored, he left several volumes of short stories and at least one play. Depending on their date of composition, these stories tend to resemble — both stylistically and thematically — the longer fiction written by Blasco. The collection of short stories entitled *La condenada* (1900), for example, belongs to the Valencian cycle. The main characters are poor, local types struggling to survive in a harsh social and economic environment. *Luna Benamor* (1919; original in Spanish, 1909), is perhaps the most famous of Blasco's short fiction volumes. The lead story of the collection, from which the book takes its name, revolves around the fortunes of star-crossed lovers unable to consummate their relationship because of

religious differences. It is reminiscent of *The Torrent*. The story takes place in North Africa, a locale chosen after Blasco visited the area. As in his longer fiction, geography and local customs figure prominently in the text. *The Old Woman of the Movies and Other Stories* (1926; *El préstamo de la difunta*, 1921) is the last collection of short fiction translated into English. It contains several cosmopolitan tales, as the author moves back and forth from Europe to America, not unlike the characters of *The Four Horsemen of the Apocalypse* (1918).

◆ Adaptations ◆

Please see the biographical entry on Blasco Ibáñez.

Clara Estow
University of Massachusetts-Boston

TOUGH GUYS DON'T DANCE

Novel

1984

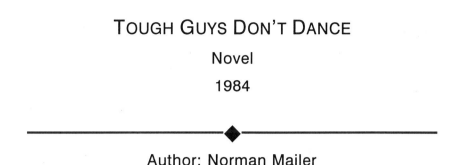

Author: Norman Mailer

◆ Social Concerns/Themes ◆

In most of Mailer's writings, both fiction and nonfiction, he has been concerned with the role of violence in American life. In his seminal essay, "The White Negro" (1957), he contrasted individual violence to the collective violence of the state. To Mailer, the state was capable of inflicting much more damage on individuals than individuals could inflict on themselves. In fact, for Mailer, an individual act of violence might even be a defensible rebellion against the repressive nature of society. Consequently, he has tended to create fictional heroes, such as Stephen Rojack in *An American Dream* (1965), who renew themselves through violence. In *Tough Guys Don't Dance*, Mailer reverses the usual order of things in his fiction. The novel begins with its hero, Tim Madden, wondering whether the severed head he discovers in his marijuana hideaway is the gory result of a drunken evening's debauchery which turned violent. Waking up with no memory of the night before, Madden fears he has given way to the wild impulses stimulated by his estranged wife, Patty Lareine. The violent side of himself sickens Madden. In order to make himself whole again, he sets out to discover what part he played not only in his wife's death but in the decapitation of another woman who resembled her and whom Madden met on the night that has been expunged from his memory.

◆ Characters ◆

Tough Guys Don't Dance is narrated in the first person by Tim Madden. The use of this voice is an effective way for Mailer to pursue the theme of identity and for Madden to discover what actually happened and what he is capable of as a man. It is Madden's quest to act honorably and courageously that is most important. His role model is his father, a stoical Irishman who fought hard for what he believed. His nemesis is his wife, a hard but beautiful blonde, who has tried to use him in pursuit of wealth and power.

The characters relate to each other as in a medieval romance, and Madden even refers to his wife as "my long lost medieval lady." Lareine, after all, means "the queen," and as in the Arthurian legend, Madden discovers she has had another lover, Deputy Police

Chief Alvin Luther Regency, a powerfully-built, maniacal rival. Complicating matters further for Madden is the lurking presence of his former schoolmate, Meeks Wardly Hilby III, who was also once married to Patty Lareine.

Clearly the underdog, and the one character who doubts both his probity and his sanity, Madden is meant to engage the reader's sympathies. He comes from immigrant stock, is a writer, and naturally the one to solve the mystery that threatens to engulf him. If Madden can make sense of the two murders, he can also begin to put his life back together — including his failed relationship with Madeleine Falco, his witty, tough counterpart who left him when he took up with Patty Lareine and who now finds herself mired in a bad marriage to the dangerous Regency.

◆ Techniques/Literary Precedents ◆

Mailer has clearly taken the mystery story as the model for his novel. It is his only work of fiction in which suspense plays a key part and the perpetrator of a crime must be discovered through detective work. As in a traditional mystery, each chapter thickens the atmosphere of ambiguity and at the same time provides several clues that hint at a solution to the crimes. The reader is faced with several questions: Did the same person kill both women? What was Madden's role in these murders? What exactly is Regency's interest in the case? Several vital facts are withheld from both Madden and the reader until late in the novel — such as Regency's affair with Patty Lareine and his marriage to Madden's former flame, Madeleine Falco.

Mailer departs from the traditional constraints of the murder mystery in his narrator's digressions into character analysis and metaphysical speculation. Madden believes, for example, that people live with two opposing souls, which make them capable of great good and great evil. The universe itself, in his opinion, is defined by a struggle between God and the Devil, and each human being, therefore, is a part of that conflict. This is why he can be his own suspect. Unlike the traditional mystery story, the detective in this case contemplates the possibility that he himself has committed the crime.

◆ Related Titles ◆

Tough Guys Don't Dance is a provocative variation of Mailer's earlier novels. Like Mikey Lovett in *Barbary Shore* (1951), Madden is an amnesiac trying to reconstruct his life and to remember an important event. Like Stephen Rojack in *An American Dream* (1965), Madden is beset by an ambivalent relationship with his wife. Both are wealthy women who dominate their men; both are women who express Mailer's concern with the fragility of the masculine ego. The women seem secure in their identities whereas the men struggle to find and maintain an identity, lacking the biological tie to life that makes women superior to men in this respect. Mailer has made this point in many interviews and in *The Prisoner of Sex* (1971), suggesting there is a willed, almost contrived quality to the male identity.

◆ Adaptations ◆

Mailer directed the 1987 film adaptation of the novel, which starred Ryan O'Neal and Isabella Rosselini. In the novel, Patty Lareine never actually appears; instead, she comes alive in Madden's sorrow over her departure and death. Since Mailer could not rely on a narrative voice in his screen adaptation, he introduced Lareine as a character. Initially, Mailer's plan was to rely only on dramatized action in the film, but in the end he was forced to use some voice-over narration to clarify Madden's point of view and certain plot elements. Most reviews of the film were negative, citing an uneven tone and unduly complicated plot. Reviewers wondered whether Mailer was intentionally parodying himself or taking himself too seriously. They also panned his direction of the film, pointing to a lack of cinematic rhythm, and faulted his writing, finding some of his more foreboding lines ludicrous.

Carl Rollyson
Baruch College
The City University of New York

TRACKS

Novel

1988

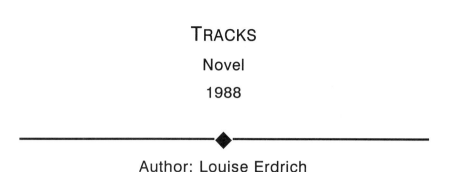

Author: Louise Erdrich

The most important character in *Tracks* is Fleur Pillager, a strong and beautiful woman, who seems to be a shaper of the forces of the land, particularly those of a lake near her home. Unlike Erdrich's previous novels in which nearly all the significant characters have a narrative voice, Fleur is seen only through two other characters: Nanapush, a wise, fun-loving tribal leader, and Pauline Puyat, a tormented mixed breed who envies Fleur's beauty and power. Nanapush's view of Fleur is friendly and caring; Pauline is fearful and shows a desire to humiliate a rival. Both views establish Fleur as an almost mythic figure. If Fleur spoke in her own voice, it would be harder for Erdrich to project Fleur's mythic dimension.

When Fleur succeeds in getting the money to pay her family's land fees and live the life of her ancestors, the test for her culture is whether she can find a traditional man — brave, responsible, and a good hunter — with whom to raise a family. Eli Kashpaw represents such a man, and the quality of their love is a measure of the tribe's success. The tribe feels and appreciates their symbolic role, as if Eli and Fleur were winning a victory for them through their love.

Pauline, who also loves Eli, disrupts the relationship by setting up a sexual liaison for Eli with a young girl whom she hopes will destroy his love for Fleur. The plot temporarily works, but it is the death of Fleur and Eli's baby and a crooked land deal by Eli's brother, Nector, that effectively ends Eli and Fleur's relationship.

Pauline is usually present for the negative crises in Fleur's life: her rape in Argus, the childbirth that results in death, and her dispossession from her land. Nanapush, on the other hand, vicariously participates in the love of Eli and Fleur, since he acts as Eli's confidant. Pauline's narrations are filled with horror, gloom, and perversity, while Nanapush is the source of nearly all of the novel's humor.

Margaret Kashpaw, Eli's mother, is an important character. Nanapush comes to love her, and he, along with Fleur, is betrayed by her. Since Margaret is proud and seems loyal, her swindle regarding the tax money is difficult to accept; she seems to have strength of character and honesty. When people such as this in a culture crack, little can be done to keep that culture together. Small wonder that Fleur attempts to kill herself. Unsuccessful, she eventually leaves the reservation with a cart, the same one we see her with in *The Beet Queen* (1986). Nothing is left in her culture to protect.

◆ Social Concerns/Themes ◆

In *Tracks* Erdrich deals not only with individual American Indian lives but the loss of a tribe's land and identity during a crucial period from 1912 to 1924. In the novel Native Americans are attacked by illnesses and hunger, and annual land fees and taxes cause many to lose their land and homes. Their ties to their ancestors are severed, and the mythic significance of the land is destroyed when loggers change its face.

While whites show ugly faces in *Tracks*, particularly in the rape of Fleur Pillager and her loss of home and land, the face of economic and governmental dispossession of the tribe is more Indian than white. Erdrich chooses to dramatize Native Americans undoing the lives of their kinsmen. Pauline Puyat, a mixed breed and one of the novel's two narrators, shows the terrible effects of white influence on her life, particularly that of the Catholic Church, which Pauline has absorbed along with the native American myths of place. Her tormented version of Christianity is more life-denying than the tribe's myths which focus on the land. To become a nun, Pauline denies her heritage, her language, her daughter, and her lover. Instead of a God of love we see a God of sexual torment, vindictiveness, envy, sadism, and pride. Other Native Americans betray their trust in exchange for white favors

as Bernadette does with the Agent; Nector and Margaret use money that others helped to raise to pay taxes on their land.

Probably even more pernicious is the corruption of love Erdrich presents in the novel. Fleur Pillager and Eli are the soul of the tribe. When their love is warped by the threat to the land, Fleur takes up a wandering existence. Even Nanapush, an old tribal leader and the other narrator of the novel, is betrayed by a longtime friend, Margaret, a woman he loves.

With so many victims it might seem as if *Tracks* is a reformist melodrama of innocent victims and evil victimizers. The losses here, however, are irreversible, and *Tracks* is more a tragedy than a political tract.

◆ Techniques/Literary Precedents ◆

As in much of Erdrich's work, the literary influence of Faulkner is evident. The friendly and hostile narrators of *Tracks* are reminiscent of the narrators that present a picture of Caddy in *The Sound and the Fury* (1929). Since the tribal vision of Nanapush and the jealous vision of Pauline both magnify Fleur's importance, the significance of her life becomes much greater as a result.

As Nanapush says, Fleur is the "funnel of our history," so what happens to her happens to the tribe. This substitution of character for tribe allows Erdrich to simplify and compress her story; Fleur's personal story translates into the tribe's story.

◆ Related Titles ◆

Tracks is part of a tetralogy that includes *Love Medicine* (1984), linked short stories; *The Beet Queen* (1986), novel; and *The Bingo Palace* (1994), novel.

While *Tracks* stands as an independent work, the novel gains in resonance when seen in the context of *Love Medicine* and *The Beet Queen*. The butcher shop and its owners, the Kozkas, and other characters, such as Russell Kashpaw, were introduced in *The Beet Queen*. The sadistic nun, Sister Leopolda of *Love Medicine*, who tortures Marie Lazarre, is none other than Pauline, one of the narrators of *Tracks*, and the girl she is torturing in *Love Medicine* is her own illegitimate daughter, the girl she tries to abort and unwillingly gives birth to in *Tracks*. Erdrich's newer novels seem to enlarge previous ones, deepening the texture of her fictional world.

In *Tracks* Erdrich has simplified her narrative perspective and her story line, creating a novel more symbolically compressed and unified than her earlier works. *Tracks* is a more painful book than its predecessors, and possibly more powerful.

◆ Ideas for Group Discussions ◆

Erdrich had great difficulty writing *Tracks*. She let the 400-page manuscript sit for ten years, publishing *Love Medicine* and *The Beet Queen* first, before she returned to the novel. What was probably difficult for her was that in *Tracks* she was establishing the origin or beginning of the dissolution of the tribe, the atomizing of its life. Since the novel explores how and why this happened, small wonder that Erdrich had such difficulty with the book. Politics and history compose the action of the novel; artistry sees that these are given

imaginative human representation. A good discussion needs to examine the causes of trouble the Chippewa experience and how Erdrich presents them.

1. While Native Americans participate in their own undoing in *Tracks*, whites are the originating cause. What acts by whites, either by contact or law, seem most pernicious in the imagined world of this novel?

2. Fleur Pillager does not have a voice in the narration of this novel, but she is certainly important to the tribe, in part through fear, in part through admiration. What do members of the tribe fear and admire about Fleur? How does her character seem to represent the tribe?

3. Nanapush's narrative is primarily oral; it is told to Lulu. Pauline's narrative is written. What is the effect of the continued juxtaposition of these narratives?

4. What is the effect of Pauline's Christianity on her? How does race connect to religion in this novel?

5. What does land seem to mean to the different Native Americans in this book?

6. Erdrich dramatizes many Native Americans aiding in their own destruction in *Tracks*. Why does she focus more on them than the originating white cause?

Craig Barrow
University of Tennessee at Chattanooga

TRADER TO THE STARS

Novellas

1964

◆

Author: Poul Anderson

◆ Characters ◆

Nicholas Van Rijn is the protagonist of all three novellas in *Trader to the Stars*. Although obese, he is strong, with a powerful sexuality and an alert and clever mind. In the first noveella "Hiding Place," he solves the mystery of the missing crew of a zoolike spaceship and wins the affection of a young woman who at the novella's end is sitting in Van Rijn's lap while wearing a "slit and topless blue gown which fitted like a coat of lacquer." The rugged Captain Bahadur Torrance of Van Rijn's own ship ends up with bruises after a brief battle with Van Rijn over the affections of the young woman.

Van Rijn is typical of Anderson's entrepreneurial heroes. Their dedication to commerce and to opening up new markets is accompanied by sturdy bodies and tremendous sex appeal. The women in their lives usually have to be content to share them, because the fertility of their minds is paralleled by their sexual drives. In contrast, government functionaries almost always have poor sex lives; their unimaginative minds are paralleled by impotence. However, Van Rijn and his kind are not exploitive brutes. Their sensitivity to the needs of others makes them successful merchants; this same sensitivity makes them thoughtful lovers. Some critics object to Anderson's entrepreneurial characters because they seem too self-absorbed, with underdeveloped personalities. On the other hand, general readers seem to find their use of wits to overcome enemies and other obstacles to be admirable as well as entertaining; and Van Rijn's low-key humor adds to his appeal.

◆ Social Concerns ◆

Trader to the Stars exemplifies Anderson's romantic view of human progress. In it, a cunning entrepreneur solves mysteries and figures out ways to establish mutually beneficial economic ties between his company and alien creatures in outer space. Where governments and ambassadors are ineffectual, the robust and dynamic merchant Nicholas Van Rijn succeeds because he pursues enlightened self-interest. For him and his kind, peace and friendly relations are necessary for successful economic enterprise. Therefore, Van Rijn resolves conflicts, makes friends, and turns a handsome profit.

The notion that free enterprise brings the greatest prosperity to the greatest number of people is a theme common to much of Anderson's fiction.

◆ Themes ◆

Trader to the Stars opens with remarks by "Le Matelot" (The Sailor), who declares in part: "Because today we are sailing out among the stars, we are more akin to Europeans overrunning America or Greeks colonizing the Mediterranean littoral than to our ancestors of only a few generations ago. We, too, are discoverers, pioneers, traders, missionaries, composers of epic and saga." This represents the principal theme of the book: that those who will travel in outer space will be frontiersmen. Some of these adventurers will be bandits, but others will be like Nicholas Van Rijn — daring people who use their wits to open up the universe to humanity and commerce.

◆ Techniques ◆

The novellas of *Trader to the Stars* are united by the character Nicholas Van Rijn and by the theme of opening up frontiers. Otherwise, they are notably different from one another. "Hiding Place" is a mystery; "Territory" is a tale of frontier adventure, with the tomahawk-wielding t'Kelans taking the place of American Indians; and "The Master Key" is told in the first person by an acquaintance of Van Rijn, whereas the others are third-person narratives. This last novella has Van Rijn making sense out of a report by employees of a disastrous trading mission.

Although "Hiding Place" follows the pattern of a mystery story, Anderson takes full advantage of its science-fiction setting. Van Rijn is confronted with the problem of a spaceship without a crew. The craft carries several encaged alien species in its hold, none of which is familiar to him. Van Rijn concludes that the crew must be trying to pass itself off as one of the menagerie, but his problem is then compounded: The only creature capable of working the ship's controls is unintelligent and incapable of understanding how to run the craft. Van Rijn's logical solution to the mystery establishes his ability to solve complicated problems and reveals him to be a character of depth and not simply a stereotypical adventurer. The story maintains suspense because Van Rijn and his crew need the alien ship because their own was damaged, and they must try to deal with a possibly hostile species that they cannot identify.

Like "Hiding Place," both "Territory" and "The Master Key" focus on problems that Van Rijn must solve with his wits. In "Territory," tension is maintained by the relationship between the pragmatic Van Rijn and the idealistic Joyce Davisson, who resists Van Rijn's sexual advances. Suspense is maintained by the uncertainties of their situation; the t'Kelans have become inexplicably hostile, and Van Rijn and Davisson must try to survive in an environment that is never warmer than forty degrees Celsius below zero, while they try to make peace with the natives. As the relationship between Van Rijn and Davisson slowly warms, the theme of trade as a way of securing peace is developed. Van Rijn eventually shows that all the good intentions of Davisson cannot substitute for mutually profitable trade. The t'Kelans are much more willing to believe that human beings want to profit from buying and selling t'Kelan products than they are that human beings have altruistic motives.

"The Master Key" is also a celebration of mind over brawn. Like Rex Stout's Nero Wolfe sifting through clues in his office, Van Rijn listens to the tale of a failed trading mission on a wild and mysterious planet. "The Master Key" features a complicated narrative technique. It is told in the first person by a guest at a gathering in Van Rijn's penthouse apartment near Chicago, but the narrator is not the focus of the story. Instead, he relates what two other guests, Per Stenvik and Manuel Felipe Gomez y Palomares, tell of their adventure among the Yildivans. Although Stenvik and Gomez are the focus of the story, Van Rijn's presence is always felt; he asks probing questions and urges Stenvik and Gomez to tell all. The complicated mix of storytellers enables Anderson to present diverse views of the events on the planet Cain, allowing for more than one plausible explanation for the violence that erupted between Yildivans and humans. In addition, each speaker reveals something of himself, which helps to advance one of Anderson's most disturbing themes — that his guests are like Yildivans, who are like wild animals, but most people are not wild and lovers of freedom; they are, instead, more akin to the Lugals, the intelligent domesticated animals of the Yildivans.

◆ Literary Precedents ◆

The fat and clever Nicholas Van Rijn belongs to a long line of cunning fat men, beginning with Count Fosco in Wilkie Collins's *The Woman in White*

(1859) and including Rex Stout's detective Nero Wolfe, the protagonist of mystery novels such as *Gambit* (1962). Such characters, often at once repellent and fascinating, have long appealed to popular audiences. In addition, the adventures surrounding Van Rijn are meant to advance Anderson's ideas about freedom and the common good. Authors have often followed the adventures of a single character to present their ideas about society. For instance, Jonathan Swift does so in *Gulliver's Travels* (1726), which features several different imaginary societies that represent Swift's social views. In tone and content, *Trader to the Stars* is distinctly literary, intending to engage the mind in thought as well as to entertain it, thus placing the book in the tradition of such fiction as Mark Twain's *A Connecticut Yankee in King Arthur's Court* (1889) and Samuel Butler's *Erewhon* (1872).

◆ Related Titles ◆

Trader to the Stars is part of an imaginary future universe that is often dubbed the "Technic History" by critics, although Anderson avoids such labels. Technic civilization is covered in two series of stories and novels. The first series focuses on the Polesotechnic League, a vast galactic trading organization, and it follows the adventures of Van Rijn and his protege, David Falkayn. The second and larger series focuses on the Terran Empire, which evolves a couple of centuries after the end of the Polesotechnic League. These complex series are notable for their sophisticated storytelling techniques and for their imaginative depth that reveals societies far more fully realized than in most science fiction.

Trader to the Stars comprises three novellas, part of a continuing series of short stories and novels about the Polesotechnic League. Other books in the series: *War of the Wing Men*, 1958, novel (reprinted as "The Man Who Counts" in *The Earth Book of Stormgate*); *The Trouble Twisters*, 1966, three novellas; *Satan's World*, 1969, novel; *Mirkheim*, 1977, novel; and *The Earth Book of Stormgate*, 1978, short stories.

◆ Ideas for Group Discussions ◆

Trader to the Stars is a good book to discuss in a writers' workshop. Beginning writers especially would benefit from studying the techniques used to create mystery and suspense in the book's three tales. Each story features some kind of mystery, each following to a degree the American tradition of mystery writing exemplified by the works of Dashiell Hammett and Rex Stout. In them, the main characters must survive in hostile environments, while coping with social ills (mostly brought with them), even as they try to make sense out of a mystery that features exotic characters (as in *The Maltese Falcon*, 1930) and complicated twists of plot in which friends and enemies are hard to tell apart. Because each story features similar background material, the differing techniques of each are easy to spot and identify.

Workshop members should note how the situation of the first story is such that the solution to the mystery is essential to the main characters' survival, thus creating tension, while the solution itself may reveal enemies not friends, thus creating suspense. In the second story, Anderson pairs off two appealing characters, one an idealistic heroine, the other a lovable rogue; his purpose is to present a case for pragmatism over idealism by showing how the idealist often takes little interest in finding out what the proposed beneficiaries of his or her charity really want or need. This could be dull stuff, but Anderson makes his theme an essential part of the mystery; one problem cannot be solved without the other being resolved. This makes the theme easy to digest. In the third story, Anderson uses multiple points of view, a technique often labeled "experimental" by literary critics. Yet, Anderson's uses of multiple points of view is not strained and its tone is not *avant garde*. Instead, the story is an absorbing tale of adventure and mystery. The multiple views allow for a more complete relating of the clues to the mystery than a single point of view would allow; thus they allow Anderson to let his reader in on all the essential evidence without resorting to authorial intrusion. Anderson has made the supposedly experimental technique an integral part of the mystery, thus putting it into the background where it does not intrude upon the plot. Master any one of these techniques, and one could well create a successful mystery; master the science fiction elements as well and — well, one could have a career like Anderson's.

For book clubs that are not workshops, *Trader to the Stars* has much fodder for discussions. For instance, the issue of Anderson's mixing of popular forms of fiction with topics customarily reserved for mainstream or even academic fiction could prove a controversial one. Does his mixing of his idiosyncratic social views with his efforts to entertain put off readers? Is he playing fair with readers who might at first think they have a casual read in store for them? He has a decidedly sanguine view of free enterprise; is this view accurate? Does actual history support his imaginary adventures of free marketeers in outer space?

Anderson's career itself is interesting to discuss. Not only does it span decades in which the popular audience for science exploded to capture a large portion of the general readership in America, but it shows definite steps of development. At first seemingly content to write mostly light reading, Anderson became more ambitious. The novel *The High Crusade* (1960) marked an advance in narrative complexity, as well as an adroit mixing of popular literary forms. *Trader to the Stars* not only mixes literary forms, it presents characters that represent social concepts. In it, Anderson adds thematic depth that caught the attention of literary critics; this depth may account for the book's enduring popularity. It represents Anderson's effort to simultaneously entertain and inspire contemplation. *Trader to the Stars* could generate an interesting discussion of what Anderson has done to expand his literary horizons as well as his audience: What elements in the book are repeated in Anderson's later work? Which of these elements could account for his currently high esteem among his fellow writers, even some of those who reject his social views?

1. You are isolated deep in unexplored space, perhaps doomed because your spaceship seems damaged beyond repair. You board an alien craft. What is the first thing you would do? Is it what Nicholas Van Rijn does? What are your first thoughts when confronted by the "Hiding Place"? Do you do what Van Rijn does? Would you take another approach to solving your problems?

2. Approach the mystery from another direction. You are a human being (pick your gender) transporting alien life forms, mostly animals, on a spaceship to a cosmic zoo or laboratory. Your craft is unarmed and is approached and about to be boarded by some unknown, bizarre, possibly dangerous creature — someone or something that you did not invite aboard. How do you hide yourself? How do you determine the intentions of your utterly alien visitors?

3. How valid is the point about pragmatism versus idealism in "Territory"?

4. In "Territory," is Joyce Davisson a well-developed character, or is she merely a mouthpiece for a point of view Anderson wishes to discredit?

5. Is "Territory" entertaining in spite of or because of its social theme? How well does the central problem of the story engage the mind and imagination? Does the social theme slip on by while the adventure has center stage?

6. Who in the discussion group figured out why the t'Kelans have become inexplicably hostile in "Territory" before it was revealed in the story?

7. A question that pops up now and again in science fiction is whether sentient alien beings would have souls. "The Master Key" presents a case of beings without religion — at least as human beings would conceive of it. Van Rijn says they have no souls. If there were sentient beings on other worlds, could they have souls? Would some, as "The Master Key" seems to suggest, have souls and others not? Does sentience require a soul?

8. In "The Master Key," the expedition members forego a chance to shoot up Yildivans who had treated them treacherously. Are their reasons for abstaining credible? Is it in keeping with Van Rijn's views on how to behave toward other cultures?

9. What are the prospects for another expedition among the Yildivans? Will humans and Yildivans constantly misunderstand one another, or can they build a mutually beneficial economic relationship? Is there any reason to believe that the Yildivans might have other cultures that believe in God? Is there reason to doubt that the Yildivans have any cultures that would include religious beliefs?

10. If the Yildivans have no souls, would it be a waste of time for missionaries to try to convert them? Why does Van Rijn seem unconcerned by this problem?

11. What makes Van Rijn an appealing character? Why would Anderson give him traditionally unheroic characteristics such as obesity and comical ways of speaking? Might the obesity be symbolic?

Kirk H. Beetz

TREASURE ISLAND

Novel

1883

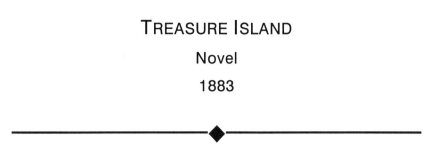

Author: Robert Louis Stevenson

◆ Characters ◆

Treasure Island is replete with eccentric and lively characters. The central group of "good" persons is made up of Jim Hawkins, the Squire, and the Doctor. Long John Silver is the leader of the opposing group, mostly the mutineers on the ship and on the island. However, there are the strange figures of Blind Pew, Billy Bones, Black Dog, Ben Gunn, and Israel Hands — each with enormous energy (often in the service of evil) and very distinctive features, both physical and behavioral.

It is Silver, however, whom the reader is likely to remember most vividly. Stevenson went to considerable effort to develop this crafty, quick-witted villain, giving him a charm that is seldom found in such a person. He also is provided with some positive features, which tend to cause him to be what E. M. Forster calls a "round" character: He speaks eloquently; he genuinely likes Jim (so far as he is able to like anyone but himself; his ego is formidable); and he avoids bloodshed when it is unlikely to bring profit. The fact that Stevenson based this character on his friend William Ernest Henley (who had been crippled, with one foot lost, since childhood) may have been responsible for the realism of Silver. As Stevenson wrote to Henley, he created Silver largely on the basis of his admiration for Henley's fortitude in withstanding the difficulties of his affliction. So, the peg-legged pirate lives on in countless plays, films, and television representations.

◆ Social Concerns ◆

As might be expected, the social concerns in *Treasure Island* are mostly of a historical nature. There is some straining of credulity when Squire Trelawny easily persuades young Jim Hawkins (who could be expected to engage in such a lively adventure as a search for buried treasure) and Dr. Livesy (who, as a prominent physician and local magistrate, would probably not have welcomed such a summons) to join him on the perilous voyage in search of the island where the treasure is supposed to lie buried. This acquiescence indicates the power of class and position at that time in Britain. A local squire possessed almost unlimited authority in his shire, and Trelawny's hasty resolution, while somewhat difficult to accept as realistic, represents the force that such a person could wield.

Not only does the Squire gain two loyal recruits, he also buys a ship and lines up a crew. For most of the rest of the text, the social differences between "gentle" folk (such as the Squire, the Doctor, and, by association, Jim) are to be found in behavioral matters: The "heroes" of the book are honest, dependable, and upright. Many of the lower-class persons, chiefly seamen, are crafty, undependable, and violent. Such a recognition and endorsement of these differences hardly sets Stevenson apart from the majority of authors of his time, but the novel depends heavily on them for plot and thematic effects.

◆ Themes ◆

Stevenson was quite unaware of the importance of his novel until some time after it was published. He regarded it as a "rattling" good tale that would attract young readers for its entertainment value. He had, however, created a morally complex (at least, for an adventure story) work. The fascinating figure of Long John Silver, certainly a villain as to intentions, dominates most of the novel, and his escape (with a bag of coins) at the end still brings some criticism down on Stevenson because the "bad" person (but one who, earlier in the story, saved Jim's life) is not punished.

For someone who admired courage and daring as much as Stevenson did, though, it is understandable that he would create a character who, while wicked in most of his actions, yet is charming, courageous, and clever. This certainly does not signify that Stevenson endorsed such behavior, but only that he recognized that people are often composed of varied traits. Moreover, for the rest of the characters, the moral is that honesty, bravery, and truthfulness will be rewarded and the lack of these traits punished — as is noted at the close, in regard to most of the mutineers: "Drink and the devil had done for the rest."

◆ Techniques ◆

The most notable strategy employed by Stevenson in this novel is the use of the "naive narrator" for most of the text. Jim Hawkins is young, impressionable, and human, but he is not stupid. Thus, he tells the story in a lively, relatively simple manner. This effect makes the perhaps excessively dramatic events in the plot more believable. Some of the plot is related by Dr. Livesy (those events which Jim could not witness), and it is to Stevenson's credit that these passages are written in a style befitting an older, more sophisticated speaker.

While the principal appeal of the book has always been its story line, Stevenson's evocation of setting, whether at the Admiral Benbow Inn and its environs, the good ship *Hispaniola*, or the island itself, is remarkable. Many readers may be familiar with the fact that the origin of the story was a map that Stevenson had drawn (and colored) for his stepson, Lloyd Osbourne. This may be one reason for the impressive accuracy Stevenson displays when explaining locations and narrating action in them. His grasp of nautical phenomena, founded on his early familiarity with lighthouse locations, is also admirable. The author understood tides, currents, weather, and other such factors related to seafaring activities.

All in all, the impression left with the careful is of a brisk tale told by someone who knows whereof he speaks.

◆ Literary Precedents ◆

Stevenson readily admitted that he depended on the works of other writers for much of the material in *Treasure Island*. Some of these writers were Washington Irving, Charles Kingsley, and "a parrot from Defoe, a skeleton from Poe, a stockade from Marryat." That he rose above the literary form of the "boys' book" (a tale intended to teach boys how to be men, including such romantic adventures as H. Rider Haggard's *King Solomon's Mines*, 1885) is now evident, but at the time many readers believed that Stevenson had simply added to the canon of such works. However, when so distinguished a person as William Gladstone, the Prime Minister of England, stated that he had sat up all night reading the book, one might agree that *Treasure Island* reaches far beyond any of its precedents.

◆ Adaptations ◆

The earliest adaptation of the novel was a silent version, produced by Vitagraph in 1908. In 1912, another silent production came out, made by Edison and directed by J. Searle Dawley. Perhaps the classic silent version starred Lon Chaney; it was produced by Twentieth Century Fox, directed by Maurice Tourneur, and appeared in 1920. The Metro-Goldwyn-Mayer adaptation was released in 1934; it was directed by Victor Fleming and starred the popular screen duo Wallace Beery and Jackie Cooper. A brilliant color version, pro-duced by Disney and directed by Byron Haskin, emerged in 1950. It starred British actor Robert Newton in what many film critics believe to be the finest portrayal of Long John Silver to reach the screen. Fifteen years later, UPA turned out an animated version, as did Australia, in 1970. Orson Welles appeared as Silver in a 1972 treatment, directed by Graham Hough. In 1990, Charlton Heston took on the Silver role in a production directed by Fraser L. Heston and co-starring Oliver Reed and Christopher Lee. The last example of a somewhat daring venture is a Muppet version of the classic, entitled "Muppet Treasure Island," starring Tim Curry as Silver and directed by Brian Henson; this adaptation appeared in 1996.

◆ Ideas for Group Discussions ◆

Since this work is so much more than an entertainment, discussion might profitably focus on the ways in which it exceeds the quality of other volumes of this type. Apart from the obvious elements of plot, characterization, setting, and theme, the matter of Stevenson's style might well be considered. He is still famous for the *mot juste*, the concrete image, and the rhythmical sentence. Examples could be noted and evaluated.

1. Which traits of Long John Silver impress you the most? Are they believably developed?

2. Is the passage, late in the novel, where Jim virtually sails the ship, fully credible? Could the problem in the plot be solved in a better way?

3. Does the greed for treasure in

many of the characters cause you to tend to reject them? Is the motivation in general adequate?

4. Do the figures of speech in the text really advance the mood and characterization of the novel? Are these images well thought out, or do they seem too contrived?

5. Does Dr. Livesy's part in the narration distract the reader from the concerns of Jim and his perceptions? Would it have been better for Stevenson to contrive to have Jim tell all of the plot?

6. Which of the colorful secondary characters — Gunn, Bones, Pew, Black Dog, etc. — seem to be the best developed and believable?

7. Since Stevenson admitted his dependence on other works of this type, can one fruitfully compare *Treasure Island* with such works as Marryat's *Masterman Ready* (1841) or some of Poe's tales?

8. The title which Stevenson had planned to affix to this text was *The Sea Cook* (clearly an allusion to Silver and an indication of the author's emphasis) — would that have been a better, more appropriate title?

Fred B. McEwen
Waynesburg College

A TREE GROWS IN BROOKLYN

Novel

1943

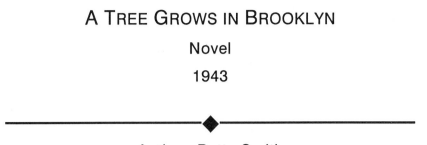

Author: Betty Smith

◆ Characters ◆

Francie Nolan is the protagonist of *A Tree Grows in Brooklyn*. Her parents endow her with two traits that enable her to conquer adversity: From her second-generation German mother, Katie, Francie inherits the strength, determination and indomitable sense of respectability that guide her into a future that holds promise; from her weak Irish father, Johnny, she inherits the ability to see and hear beauty in an ugly world. The foreground of the novel is full of strong female characters: Katie; Katie's solid, immigrant German mother; Katie's sisters; and Francie herself, whose strength increases as she learns to solve the problems of her young existence. It is she who convinces her father to connive to have her transferred to another, better neighborhood school. Although Francie is a good, obedient girl, her apparent passivity masks a will that eventually prevails over her domineering mother's. There is no real conflict, however, between mother and daughter. The values of hard work, education, cleanliness and decency are established as normative and Francie embraces them. Most of the male characters are weak and tend to inhabit the novel's background as biological, social and economic entities, but with no real importance. The women do not despise the men; rather, they accept their flawed husbands, brothers and fathers as necessities and move on with their lives. *A Tree Grows in Brooklyn* is Francie Nolan's quest for identity, an enactment of the central theme of the irrepressibility of life.

◆ Social Concerns ◆

Although Smith denied that she wrote a novel of social significance, there are societal themes in *A Tree Grows in Brooklyn*. The grinding desolation of urban poverty is closest to the surface and it is this, in all its naturalistic detail, that Smith concentrates on. However, she washes over the images of squalor with sentimentality, as in the figure of the tree: "It grew in boarded up lots and out of neglected rubbish heaps and it was the only tree that grew out of cement. It grew lushly but only in the tenement districts." Although mean and poor, Smith's Brooklyn teems with life, overflows with the irrepressible good nature of its main characters who refuse to be daunted by the squalor that always threatens to destroy them. Francie Nolan, the protagonist, resists the inadequacy of her life, insists on reading every book in the local library despite that fact that the librarian never once, over a period of six years, looks at her when Francie checks out a book. The Nolans fight against poverty by stuffing every grubby cent they can spare into a tin can nailed into the floor in a dark corner of their bedroom closet to insure future solvency. They also fight against their own hard circumstances, mainly that the father, Johnny Nolan, is a hopeless drunk who dies of alcoholism halfway through the novel, leaving his pregnant wife, Katie, Francie, and her younger brother, Neely, to carry on the battle from which he had withdrawn into alcohol. All around them are the tenement people, crude, careful, getting by on nickels and dimes, brawling, singing, pawning their overcoats until they can collect their next pay envelopes.

Another social concern is the integrity of the family unit, which closes ranks against outsiders, protecting and supporting its members without judging them. Even though Johnny Nolan is a drunk who must weave through his taunting neighbors to get home to his tenement flat, when he arrives there he is treated as the head of a family must be treated, with love, kindness and respect. Johnny is Francie's adored father who, with his physical beauty and innate Irish charm, has a special place, a haven, to come to every day. Katie, who cleans three other tenements to keep the family in rent and food money, is still jealous of the woman Johnny rejected for her when that woman shows up at his funeral. Johnny's alcoholism is viewed as a result of unfortunate circumstances, not something to censure him for.

What firmly anchors *A Tree Grows in Brooklyn* in popular fiction, however, is that its social significance is merely the background against which Francie's life unfolds. Smith was a playwright first and there is a real sense that the details of the poverty of tenement life in Brooklyn are placed carefully, like a set of props around a stage on which a girl cheerfully recites her part in an essentially comic play. Everything comes up, if not roses, at least ailanthus trees.

◆ Themes ◆

The central theme of *A Tree Grows in Brooklyn* is the great story of life triumphant against adversity, which probably accounts for its spectacular popularity. Francie Nolan is the protagonist in a *bildungsroman*. Francie's life grows as the symbolic tree grows, pushing through the cracks and rubble that oppress tenement life. She is eleven when the novel opens and seventeen at its close and she spends the intervening six years discovering who she is, that she is different from the other slum children and destined for a better life than they are. Since this is the coming-of-age of a girl rather than a boy in a novel about "serenity" nothing really bad is allowed to happen. For example, as Francie passes through puberty the shadow of sexual threat appears but is dispatched cleanly: Katie Nolan shoots the child molester who corners Francie in the dark, narrow tenement hallway, a deliriously satisfactory fictional device.

Using the conventional method of having Francie keep a diary, Smith shows the child inventing a role for herself in the world as a writer. On her voyage to self-discovery, Francie passes through occasional rough seas, but her exuberance never flags and the good ship Life carries her safely into port.

As a subsidiary theme, there is a somewhat hesitant representation of a Freudian family romance threaded through the story of the Nolans. Francie knows well that Katie loves Neely better than she loves Francie; and Francie adores her father who reciprocates in a hazy alcoholic way. To compound Francie's confusion, Neely inherits his father's handsome face and light-footed Irish grace (but not his tendency to drink) while Francie remains plain — not unattractive, but plain. This is not quite a version of Cinderella, nor do the Freudian/sexuality themes predominate. *A Tree Grows in Brooklyn* celebrates, in a sentimental way, the possibility of a good life developing in a mean environment, but the environment itself, Smith's Brooklyn, is, as Francie says, ". . . a magic city and it isn't real."

◆ Techniques ◆

A Tree Grows in Brooklyn is loosely constructed, anecdotal, digressive and episodic rather than carefully plotted. There is occasional foreshadowing, as in the saga of Francie's promiscuous Aunt Sissy's attempts to have a baby. Sissy finally succeeds after bearing nine stillborn infants and adopting one who turns out, it is hinted, to be her third husband's illegitimate child. But Smith is not interested in subtlety and most of her attempts at plotting are heavy-handed and obvious. Francie's development provides the book with its central structure and around this are stacked other related stories about the Nolan family and their neighbors. Almost all of this is told with energy and good humor. Smith writes in the plain style of the vernacular of Brooklyn with its slang and ungrammatical constructions. Even the omniscient narrator speaks in a simple, slangy way, injecting exclamatory statements to emphasize dramatic events and emotional responses. Much of the book is dialogue and although there is a sameness about the characters' speeches, there are enough action and signaling devices to keep the characters distinct. *A Tree Grows in Brooklyn* is the work of an amateur, in both senses of the word, and its lack of literary refinement, its simplicity and forward-marching, predictable story line make it both charming and ephemeral.

◆ Literary Precedents ◆

Because of its conventional coming-of-age theme, *A Tree Grows in Brooklyn* fits the *bildungsroman* genre, but it is a sentimental, simplistic example of the type. Its lack of serious literary achievement precludes it from formal critical commentary. Smith uses both realistic and naturalistic techniques, concentrating on sometimes exhaustive physical description of the economic poverty of her characters' lives, but she undercuts the effects of poverty by denying its importance and its repressive potential. Therefore, while it is tempting to cite Crane, Dreiser, or Howells as Smith's literary influences, and to suggest that Francie's mean environment has a deadening effect on her development, the novel's basically optimistic drive raises it from the lower depths and propels Francie merrily through the streets of Williamsburg.

A Tree Grows in Brooklyn is a woman's novel, and therefore it might be compared to the comic novels of Barbara Pym, whose Excellent Women (1952), for instance, also relies on the realistic description of reduced circumstances to depict the life of its heroine, Mildred Lathbury. But in Excellent Women the bleak, paralyzing details of middle-class life in postwar London function as a metaphor of the heroine's class status. The reader can feel the teacups and jumble sales constricting Mildred while simultaneously and properly confining her to her gentlewoman's place in a rigorously ordered social structure. Smith never develops the layered density of metaphor with her intentionally pathetic details. The reader knows, from the first paragraph, that Francie is destined for a happy future regardless of the pathos of her present circumstances.

◆ Related Titles ◆

Smith continued her story of the girl who grew up in Brooklyn in her succeeding three novels, Tomorrow Will Be Better (1948), Maggie-Now (1958), and Joy in the Morning (1963). In each, the central character is a young woman who, recognizing that she is different from the other tenement girls, knows she must control her life so that she succeeds in fulfilling the promise of that difference.

Tomorrow Will Be Better, although not a spectacular best seller like A Tree Grows in Brooklyn, nevertheless received fairly good reviews but dropped out of sight, perhaps because its heroine, Margy Shannon, temporarily fails in her quest for happiness. Margy chooses marriage as the only way to improve her life, but the marriage comes apart after she gives birth to a stillborn child and then realizes that her husband, while not quite homosexual, is at least sexually repressed. The homosexual theme had, as yet, not found a place in popular fiction that was designed to appeal to women at a time when they were occupied in building lives around the men who had just returned from fighting World War II.

Maggie-Now, the eponymous novel Smith published in 1958, constructs a heroine who attains a place for herself through marriage with the mysterious Mr. Bassett. Maggie-Now's struggle is not only against lower-middle-class poverty, but against the men who impinge on her life: her cantankerous, possessive father; her irresponsible brother; and Claude Bassett, who disappears from March to November during every year of their marriage until he dies. Maggie's strength, kindness, and fundamentally Christian ability to forgive allow her to maintain her sense of individuality and to build a rewarding life despite her problems.

Joy in the Morning, apparently the most autobiographical of Smith's four novels, takes the girl who grew up in Brooklyn to a college in the Midwest where she marries the Brooklyn boy who is enrolled there in law school. The novel describes the traditional difficulties of adjustment, money, pregnancy and childbirth that occur in the first year of their marriage. The girl, Annie, is the center of the book which is a continuation of A Tree Grows in Brooklyn. Annie is a thinly disguised Francie Nolan, transported to a world very different from Williamsburg, who nevertheless takes with her Francie's good-spirited ability to control and build a life. Joy in the Morning resembles the earlier book also in that it is an example of a similar genre, the *künstle-roman*; it traces Annie's development as a serious writer, from her first scribblings of dramatic dialogue to her recognition by the members of the English Department of the college, who criticize and praise her work.

◆ Adaptations ◆

Betty Smith and George Abbot wrote a musical comedy version of *A Tree Grows in Brooklyn* which played on Broadway in 1944. It was produced by Elia Kazan who then directed the movie version, Kazan's first feature film, released in 1945. The movie starred James Dunn as Johnny Nolan and Peggy Ann Garner as Francie. Reviewing it in *The Nation*, James Agee (with the caveat that he had not read the book) praised the movie for its attention to the details of poverty in the big city while damning it for not taking poverty seriously enough and for playing safe with the Freudian mother-son/father-daughter theme. However, Agee recommended that the movie not be dismissed by intelligent people who automatically dismiss best sellers. *Joy in the Morning* was made into a feature film starring Richard Chamberlain and Yvette Mimieux.

Janet Alwang
Penn State University

THE TRIAL

Novel

1925

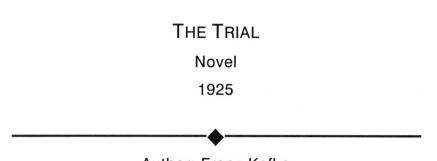

Author: Franz Kafka

◆ Characters ◆

Joseph K. is the central character of *The Trial*, although his perspective is not that of the novel itself. As with other figures out of Kafka's fiction readers know very little about Joseph K.'s life or habits. However, he is to all outward appearances a normal, relatively successful, minor bureaucrat working as a chief teller in a banking house. His life as a bachelor appears uneventful to the point of boredom. Once he is arrested his world changes in a nightmarish sort of way. He tries repeatedly to apply the everyday logic which has gotten him through life so far to order or explain or control what is happening to him. All fails and Joseph goes to his death never quite understanding what is happening to him.

The focus is so obsessively on Joseph that the subsidiary characters are easily overlooked. He runs into many figures in his quest to discover the source of his guilt. The most important is the Prosecuting Attorney, Hastler, who is everything Joseph K. is not, large, robust, powerful, gluttonous. He is in control, seems to know what is going on, has power over his life in ways

Joseph K. only dreams about. Hastler provides the perfect figure for him to try to emulate. It is part of the irony of the novel though that Joseph K. is so blind that he cannot see that the Prosecuting Attorney also lacks wisdom, a position only available to the reader.

There are a host of other figures who are featured only briefly in the labyrinthine text, most of them functioning as did their literary predecessors in *A Pilgrim's Progress* (1678), who test the quester or to impart to him some contradictory information or confusing advice. It is part of the structure of the text itself to invite interpretation, an impulse confirmed by the fiction's characters.

◆ Social Concerns/Themes ◆

The Trial deals with such themes as guilt, judgment, and retribution, and although Kafka studied law himself, the novel is not really about the legal system nor is it only about that portion of the legal system which complements or exacerbates a more complex and pervasive psychological phenomenon characteristic of the human psyche. The trial in this novel is an inner one brought about by the guilt Joseph K., the central character, experiences once he has been arrested. Although he is not accused of any particular crime, he assumes a mantle of guilt which produces a cycle of self-condemnations, which, in turn, produce his internal trial. Joseph K. goes to his death never really understanding what he is accused of but the reader learns that his "crimes" are more in the nature of omissions than commissions. Joseph K. is devoid of love, alienated from nature, and deprived of the consolations of art, literature, and music. Furthermore, he does not even realize that he is missing all of these things and that compounds his crime.

Joseph K. is not totally without self-awareness, but until his arrest he seems unable to act on it. By then, of course, it is too late. The trial stresses Joseph K.'s weakness not only before the law but also before his own consciousness. Indeed it is this very level of awareness, fed by his education and middle-class life, with its connections to those in higher places, which prevents one from seeing Joseph K. as some sort of Everyman. His experience is not everyone's; his life is of a privileged sort and the inability to use the opportunity that his status affords him is one of the most damaging accusations against him. Unlike the lower orders, Joseph K. should be able to do better than he does.

◆ Techniques ◆

One of the techniques most discussed in Kafka's fiction is his tendency to use parables, little stories which in their interpretation reveal the core meaning of the larger fictional whole in which they are set. By extension it is possible to see Kafka's longer prose works like *The Trial* as not only embodying parables within them but as being lengthy parables in themselves. This technique reinforces the main purpose behind the opacity of Kafka's plots and the indeterminacy of his characters; namely, to encourage, perhaps even force, interpretive readings of his prose. To this end Kafka wrote open-ended, convoluted, and often fragmentary works. It is interesting to note that he felt those stories which did have more conventional "endings" such as *The Metamorphosis* (1915) as botched affairs, lending themselves too easily to simple, i.e., single, readings.

One way to achieve such interpretive insistence is developed by the tension Kafka creates between the perception of Joseph K. and the narrator who is associated with him but who is able to see beyond him at the same time. Readers are given a privileged position to observe and judge the vision and the discrepancies between the two.

◆ Literary Precedents ◆

The Trial like Kafka's other novels defines a genre of its own. Although other authors have written about the labyrinth of the western legal system — Charles Dicken's *Bleak House* (1853) comes immediately to mind — no one has done so with quite the eerieness that Kafka employed. The emotional detachment of his prose also finds echos in the work of other European moderns such as Max Frisch or even more recently the late novels of Jerzy Kosinski, but no one really is able to maintain quite the same odd aloofness which is so characteristic of Kafka's writing.

The utter sense of futility and alienation which the various characters named "K" experience in his novels has really not been duplicated. Even the central character of Albert Camus's *The Stranger* (1942), seems a rather passionate by comparison.

All of this is not to say that Kafka wrote in a vacuum, but he did tend to set precedent rather than follow it, and that is why his writing remains so central to the study of literary modernism in the twentieth century.

◆ Related Titles ◆

Like all of the long prose works, *The Trial*, was not published during Kafka's lifetime, and therefore he was unable to provide his final imprimatur on the finished book. What changes he might have made to the manuscript version of the novel therefore remain speculative. That he probably would have done some revision is probable given his known working habits with those stories which were published while he was alive.

◆ Adaptations ◆

The Trial was filmed in 1963 by Orson Welles, produced by a French-Italian-German conglomerate, and reflects Welles' eccentric but always interesting approach to film. One critic has remarked that the movie is a bit muddled — but then so is Kafka's novel — and the international cast, including Welles playing the Prosecuting Attorney, seems at times, adrift. The film's interest focuses primarily on its director. Welles had a reputation as a filmmaker of the first order and even minor works directed by him have received considerable notice. The film

was plagued by production problems because of a scarcity of financing and reflects the shoestring budget on which it was shot.

However, Welles managed to capture the Kafkaesque quality of the novel through his film style which is elliptical and distancing as much as the prose style of the novel creates a barrier between text and reader. Welles' performance as the Prosecuting Attorney is wonderfully oblique, if at times bordering on self-parody, but Anthony Perkins as Joseph K. is a bit foggy as are at times the performances by Jeanne Moreau, Romy Schneider and Elsa Martinelli. Only Akim Tamiroff seems appropriately cringing and dislocated to be a part of the world of Kafka.

◆ Ideas for Group Discussions ◆

The elliptical nature of Kafka's narrative invites interpretation and no novel more so than *The Trial*. With its labyrinthine bureaucracy, governmental office upon governmental office, which leads nowhere, readers are constantly reminded of a drab and threadbare middle-European culture that the city of Prague perfectly evokes. K.'s descent into the nether world of the legal system provides ample means for raising a host of questions involving the law and its applications.

In addition, like his other longer works, *The Trial*, also seems to generate religious concerns. Is the magistrate really God? Is Joseph K.'s experience really a purgatory of sorts? These religious questions are also buttressed by the fact that the novel also raises lots of others that are religious in nature about the place of sin and innocence, pain and joy, suffering and redemption. The novel has on occasion been read as a quintessential existentialist work which balances freedom and responsibility against a deterministic universe which controls all human destiny.

1. What is the role of "justice" in this novel? How does this concept differ from legal questions of guilt and innocence?

2. To what extent is Joseph K. responsible for his predicament? A victim of forces beyond his control?

3. What do you make of the "unfinished" nature of the ending of the novel? How does this open-endedness extend our analysis of the fiction?

4. What is the role of the women in the novel? In what ways are they ministrative angels, avenging furies?

5. What is the place of the idea of "freedom" in the fiction? In the context of the narrative what does "freedom" mean?

6. Discuss the religious overtones of the novel. Do not be bound by conventional notions of religions but rather let your ideas flow from more broadly encompassing ideas of the "religious."

7. Why does Joseph K. keep pursuing his innocence? Why doesn't he just "plead out" his case?

8. In what ways is the title of the book an extended metaphor for modern life as Kafka envisioned it?

9. Why doesn't Kafka provide his narrative hero with some way out of his dilemma?

10. The image of the father plays a central part in Kafka's fiction. How does the role of the father figure work in this fiction, and what is the connection between the father and the law?

Charles L. P. Silet
Iowa State University

TRIPMASTER MONKEY: HIS FAKE BOOK

Novel

1989

◆

Author: Maxine Hong Kingston

◆ Characters ◆

Tripmaster Monkey: His Fake Book is concerned with the thoughts and feelings of a single character, Wittman Ah Sing, an unemployed artist and social critic one year out of college. Wittman is self-described as "the present-day USA incarnation of the King of the Monkeys" an allusion to the Monkey King of Chinese legend instrumental in bringing Buddha's Sutras to China. But Wittman is full of monkey business as well. His desire to integrate the orient and occident appears both mythic and melodramatic, both sincere and incredibly self-absorbed. In his search for unity and identity, he often berates and puzzles friends, prospective employers, and casual acquaintances alike. His character is not developed so much as revealed through a tangled series of internal monologues and harangues. The quest itself, not any particular insight, is what defines Wittman as quintessentially American.

Although not fully developed, the novel's secondary characters serve as intriguing, colorful foils who underscore the protagonist's confusion, ambivalence, anger, and sensitivity. Wittman's eccentric, imaginative old aunts, as well as his parents and grandmother, provide a glimpse of the world of the past which created him. His interaction with his co-workers, old friends, and new wife — they are married by a minister of the Universal Life Church traveling incognito to avoid the draft — highlight Wittman's pain and paranoia as well as his ambition, good humor, and need for synthesis.

◆ Social Concerns/Themes ◆

In 1782 in his collection of essays on American life, *Letters from an American Farmer*, Michel Crevecoeur posed the question, "What then is the American, this new man?" It is a question which has concerned American writers ever since. *Tripmaster Monkey; His Fake Book*, Kingston's novel of a young Chinese-American male roaming the streets of San Francisco in the early 1960s, adds another piece to the emerging picture of what this new man looks like. Through the antics and diatribes of Wittman Ah Sing, an unemployed would-be-poet full of allusions and illusions, the author poses a number of important questions about the nature of the relation between the individual and his community in America. Walt Whitman, "the poet that his father tried to name him after," once wrote: "One's-Self I sing, a simple separate person,/Yet utter the word Democratic, the word En-masse." The modern Wittman, too, is on a quest to reconcile self and society. The trouble is that he is not sure how he feels about either.

Wittman sees himself as an artistic loner, yet the reader sees him as a painfully self-conscious young man reaching out for understanding and acceptance while denying that he wants to belong to any society which fosters war, racism or materialism. Wittman is essentially an angry idealist whose frequent harangues reveal as much about his own prejudice and paranoia as they do about the ills of his society.

Wittman's anger toward society is both legitimate and melodramatic. It is appropriate for a young man sensitive to his times and to the tinge of racism in the attitudes and behavior of white America. His social activism takes the form of reading the German romanticist, Rainer Maria Rilke, to his fellow passengers on the bus and lecturing shoppers on the evils of keeping toy guns and using charge cards. His self-appointed mission is "to spook out prejudice."

Believing that "you have to be dumb to be happy on this Earth," Wittman would like to strike a pose as the self-sufficient artist: "If he could stand by himself alone, him and his cigarette, he would have perfected cool." But his need to belong, both to his community and to America as a whole, prevents such perfection. He remains exquisitely sensitive to social stereotypes, which suggests that he is an outsider despite his five-generation American ancestry.

Even the critical success of Wittman's marathon play, replete with ghosts, kung fu, fireworks, sixteenth-century Chinese warriors, senior citizen cancan dancers, Forest Dragon, and Horned Dragon, is not enough to pacify him. The final chapter, "One Man Show," consists of Wittman's explosive forty-page monologue to his predominantly Chinese-American audience explaining why they should be offended by the laudatory reviews which focus on the exotic oriental nature of his play in such terms as, "East meets West," "Sino-American theater," "snaps, crackles and pops like singing rice," "sweet and sour." "What's there to cheer about?" he taunts the audience, "You like being compared to Rice Krispies?" For Wittman, "There is no East here. West is meeting West. This was all West."

He resents labels such as "exotic" and "inscrutable," which he believes many Americans attach to all things oriental. "That's a trip they're laying on us," he harangues his audience, "because they are willfully innocent. Willful innocence is a perversion."

Yet Wittman is more a part of his culture than he realizes. He himself remains willfully innocent to the end. In his eagerness to claim America, while rejecting its excesses, Wittman reveals his own uncritical acceptance of a number of social stereotypes. His desire to rebel leads to an over-zealous admiration of any who appear more disenchanted than he. "What do you do down here with your extra time?" he asks the dope smoking former Yale Younger Poet in the stockroom. The reply, "Handle consciousness," causes Wittman to exclaim, "Hey, I do too. Me too. I want to do that too, man." Because he is "overawed by anyone who achieved more pain than he did, given average American conditions," Wittman lionizes the Beat writers of the 1950s. Jack Kerouac and Allen Ginsberg course their way through this novel side by side with sixteenth-century Chinese writers. Wittman-the-Cynic becomes Wittman-the-Romantic in his idealization of the recent past: walking with the beautiful Nanci Lee, he feels "the two of them making the scene on the Beach, like cruising in the gone Kerouac time of yore."

The pervasive nature of popular culture, suggested by repeated references to writers, movies, and folk heroes, is a recurring theme. Often Wittman and his friends define themselves by what movies they like or dislike and which poets they read. Kingston presents an array of names — from Dave Brubeck to Daniel Boone, Jesse James to Marilyn Monroe — to suggest the wide variety of popular culture as well as its influence on a young man's imagination. When hailing a cab, for example, Wittman finds that "his hand shot up like in the movies." As he slides into his girlfriend's Porsche, he recalls "James Dean had been killed in a Porsche, a silver Spyder. It was a risk car." Just as his reviewers are caught in East-West stereotypes, Wittman is caught in the surfeit of images of popular culture. His alienation and ambivalence toward society, as well as his search for acceptance, are presented vividly in the idiom and images of the post-Beat years in California.

♦ Techniques/Literary Precedents ♦

Tripmaster Monkey: His Fake Book is an unusual book in terms of both its narrative technique and its rich variety and odd mixture of images and allusions. It slides from objective description to interior monologue without warning or explanation. Allusions to literature, movies, and other aspects of popular culture cover a wide spectrum, William Shakespeare to Gary Snyder, Europa to Nabokov's *Lolita* (1955). The entire novel is a mix of logical narrative, stream of consciousness, *non sequiturs*, and a cascade of imagery, often for pages, drawn from sources as diverse as Chinese legends and Charlie Chaplin movies. The whirl of words and images, which seem to tumble over themselves, is both riveting and exhausting; readers may feel they are being flung from the ferris wheel to the roller coaster in Kingston's verbal carnival. Although at times disorienting, the sudden shifts in tone, point of view, imagery, and allusion ultimately provide a kaleidoscopic view of the diverse nature of modern society. Like George Seurat's Pointillist paintings, Kingston's novel must be viewed as a whole. She deliberately breaks conventional patterns and thwarts expectations. In Kingston's hands the novel is an elastic form which she stretches to suit her purposes.

Early twentieth-century writers provided a powerful example for defying the expected. Henry James, James Joyce, and William Faulkner broke with literary convention by refusing to be bound by a single, limited point of view. Each redefined and broadened the novelist's scope. The vivid language and antiromantic pose of the Beat writers of the 1950s, especially Allen Ginsberg and Jack Kerouac, can be felt throughout Kingston's book. But Wittman's attempts to romanticize the anger and antiestablishment views of the Beat writers betrays deeper feelings; his self-conscious detachment often highlights his desire for acceptance.

Perhaps the most useful literary

progenitor is the protagonist's name-sake, Walt Whitman, whose poetry embraces all aspects of American life and culture in language that is vivid, graphic, sensual, and imaginative. Anger, irony, passion, pity, and wonder are all part of Whitman's America. In its rich variety of images, unconventional subject matter, and strong sexual overtones, his poetry provides a model for Kingston's protagonist. Like the poet, Wittman Ah Sing wants to sing a "Song of Myself" that celebrates his individuality and ties him firmly into the American community.

◆ Related Titles ◆

Although in many ways it is very different in tone and technique from her earlier books, *Tripmaster Monkey: His Fake Book* continues Kingston's quest to explore what is unique about the American experience. The voice is different but the restless probing, the questioning, the humor, the pain, and the anger are similar. Like Kingston's autobiographies, her novel explores the values and norms of American society through the literature, legends, idioms, and parables of another culture. Such a juxtaposition requires a creative use of language and sudden shifts in point of view, which may be unsettling for readers expecting the flow of a conventional novel.

The novel succeeds, but on its own terms. The *Tripmaster Monkey: His Fake Book* lacks the structure provided by the autobiographical approach, as well as some of the immediacy and authority of the first-person perspective. Yet the rich imagery and the radical shifts from literary allusion to street jive ultimately result in revealing the confusion, anger and the idealism of a young man during an unsettled period of both his life and that of his country.

◆ Ideas for Group Discussions ◆

Fans of Kingston's use of fable and myth in contemporary settings will enjoy discussing her utilization of this technique in *Tripmaster*. The irony of Wittman's name will lead members of the discussion group into a comparison of the novel's main character with his American poet namesake. Individuals may find lively discussion regarding the theme of writing in general and how such creative activity works to form a frame for Kingston's work.

1. Compare and contrast Wittman's American aspects of personality with his Oriental aspects of personality.

2. In your opinion, how successful is Wittman's assimilation into the American culture? Conversely, how successful is his attempt to escape from his Oriental heritage?

3. What is the overall message regarding culture which Kingston wants her reader to carry away from this novel?

4. Discuss the symbolism in the book's title.

5. Discuss the effects upon the story-telling on the shifts in narrative point of view.

6. Make a list of all the allusions to occidental culture, such as of its writers, movies, etc., that you note in the novel. How do these allusions add to the theme of cultural mores?

7. Why or why don't you find Wittmann's internal dialogues successful in helping to define his character?

8. In your opinion, does the main character ever answer his self-imposed questions regarding his cultural identity? Find the scene which best illustrates this self-discovery.

9. Which minor characters are most important to Wittman's story, and why?

10. Discuss the success or failure of Kingston's novel to honestly embrace the difficulties encountered in the adoption of a foreign culture as one's own.

Danny Robinson
Bloomsburg University
[Ideas for Group Discussion
by Virginia Brackett,
University of Kansas]

TROPIC OF CANCER

Autobiographical Novel

1934

◆

Author: Henry Miller

◆ Characters ◆

The first-person narrator of *Tropic of Cancer* is really its only character. All of the "people" Miller describes are alive only in those moments that they are in the narrator's company. They are primarily sketches of attitudes, something like medieval humours, and they are seen entirely from the outside. Some of them are quite striking as caricature, particularly Van Norden, a portrait of the nonspiritual man as mechanical monster who is something of a psychic double for Miller's worst impulses. The closest thing to a real "character" is the city itself (Miller originally called his manuscript *Paris and Me*) and the most appealing human "characters" Miller meets are "alive" in the spirit of their art, like Matisse. The female "characters" are all especially dreadful clichés of a misguided, discredited male attitude toward sex which Miller uses to show the narrator's limited conditions of perception.

◆ Social Concerns ◆

Henry Miller's work is marked by his commitment to the principles of individual liberty and freedom of expression. Because his emphasis is on an erotic expression of these principles, his very strong feelings about the necessity to resist authoritarian social structures has often been misunderstood, but in *Tropic of Cancer*, Miller's anger at a society that has dehumanized its inhabitants flares with radiant light. Although the book is set in Paris, Miller's narrator finds himself amid a group of American and British proto-beatniks and European demi-bohemians who have been reduced to groping, desperate samples of human detritus. They have brought their native neuroses with them and the fabled City of Light cannot save them.

Miller's narrator is able to survive because he is responsive to the great art available for inspiration throughout the city and because he is still in touch with the beauty and purity of the natural world, represented here by the Seine river. He is unable to make a connection with a community of supportive fellow artists, but his adventures show him alternately raging at the effects of a destructive, inhuman social system and beginning to envision a place (a search which informs all of his writing) where a convergence of nature's beauty, artistic creativity, harmonious human relationships and sensory excitement might be the features of an ideal social landscape.

◆ Themes ◆

Miller's essential theme, the thread of which runs throughout his fiction, is the creation and preservation of artistic consciousness. The process by which Miller's own artistic "self" was forged is the subject of the books which follow *Tropic of Cancer* and cover the years before he left the United States for Europe. In *Tropic of Cancer*, after struggling with economic disaster, marital chaos and artistic impotence, Miller had finally recognized that, similar to Camus's *homme revolté*, he could find value in anything that the "self" does. Thus, instead of trying to adjust to the demands of a world which did not suit him, he realized that he could claim recognition for his embryonic artistic instincts, and that this would enable him to survive anything that an unpleasant environment might produce. This insight was like a shield which he drew around him, and with his wrath cutting forests of fakery like an axe, he moved through *Tropic of Cancer* untouched by the social decomposition around him.

◆ Techniques ◆

Miller's "autobiographical romances" or "auto-novels" must be seen as separate chapters in a multivolume "Book" of his life. The key to his method is Emerson's dictum that novels would give way to biography, which Miller quotes as an epigraph in *Tropic of Cancer*. Accordingly, his major writing might be divided into a quartet including *Tropic of Cancer, Black Spring* (1938), *The Colossus of Maroussi* (1941), and *Big Sur and the Oranges of Hieronymus Bosch* (1957) in which he is essentially an observer or commentator, and a triad including *Tropic of Capricorn* (1939), *Sexus* (1949), and *Nexus* (1960), in which he is an actor involved in the creation of his artistic consciousness. *Tropic of Cancer* is the first book in this sequence, and it displays the artist/hero as fully formed, confident of his power and judgment, and the voice in which he speaks is a product of this certainty. Its tone is striking, singular, and somewhat daunting in regard to people and society, sensitive and enraptured about art and nature.

The book itself is not exactly a novel; it is more like a journal of a year in a surreal city, a packet of sketches, a rough collection of essays, an assemblage of anecdotes and poems. It has fifteen sections, and except for a brief excursion to Dijon near the conclusion, it is set entirely in Paris, or in the narrator's mind. The span of time covered is rather elastic and conventional chronology is confounded.

◆ Literary Precedents ◆

Like Whitman's *Leaves of Grass* (1855), *Tropic of Cancer* does not really have any precedents in American literature. The travel journal and the picaresque early novel, might be vague ancestors and some of the tales of Boccaccio or Chaucer are not too distant relations. Specific features of Miller's work do have precedents, like the lists which resemble those of Rabelais, or the catalogues found in Emerson. Ideas from Andre Breton's surrealist manifesto are present, and some of Rimbaud's *symboliste aesthetique* might be detected, but ultimately, this book is a mutant and basically, it belongs to a category of one.

◆ Related Titles ◆

Because *Tropic of Cancer* is a part of a multibook sequence, Miller purposely withholds some very important elements of his art from the narrative. To balance the bleak landscape of *Tropic of Cancer,* Miller reaches back to a utopian vision of the past in descriptions of his early childhood in *Black Spring* (1938), and then sets both the Attic landscape of Greece ("land of light") and the rugged terrain of Big Sur as correctives from the natural world in *The Colossus of Maroussi* (1941), and *Big Sur and the Oranges of Hieronymus Bosch* (1957). In addition, the full scale of the social disaster which *Tropic of Cancer* delineates is measured by the rapid decline of the men and women Miller describes from *Black Spring* to *Tropic of Cancer,* and by the vision of another "Paris" which Miller offers in some of the chapters of *Black Spring.* Perhaps most important, the complex nature of his relationship with women is reduced to debased sensuality in *Tropic of Cancer* because Miller was not ready to explore it more fully. The record of his struggles with his ego impulses, sensory desires and romantic dreams is the subject of the books in the triad, and the reasons behind choices he made in writing *Tropic of Cancer* become more clear from the perspective of that account.

◆ Adaptations ◆

The rights to film *Tropic of Cancer*
were bought by producer Joseph E. Levine in 1962 and the book was made into a film by Joseph Strick in 1965, with Rip Torn playing the character who is ostensibly "Henry Miller" and Ellen Burstyn in the role of his wife June. The film is a botch, with the normally excellent Torn playing "Miller" as a crazed satyr with no artistic sensibility. As Paulene Kael remarked, it is "so much less than the book that it almost seems deliberately intended to reduce Miller . . . to pipsqueak size." One cannot help but wonder what might have happened if Miller had not turned down Stanley Kubrick's offers in 1958 — "holding out for the day when we really have freedom of expression."

Leon Lewis
Appalachian State University

TROPIC OF CAPRICORN

Autobiographical Novel

1939

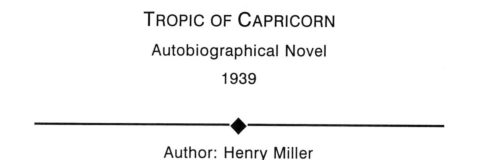

Author: Henry Miller

◆ Characters ◆

As is always the case in Miller's auto-novels, it is the narrative consciousness and sensibility of the author that is the only real "character" in the book. However, the woman he refers to as Mara/Mona, drawn from June Edith Smith, his second wife, is the most completely examined other "person" in his work. He tells the reader almost nothing about her in *Tropic of Capricorn*, introducing her at first as a near-mythic creature, as much legendary Goddess as earthly woman, but in *Sexus* and *Nexus*, as he tells the story of the origin of their romance, their eventual marriage and the eventual dissolution of their relationship, Mona (as she is finally called) evolves into a fascinating, mysterious woman who the author never ceases to love in some way but is never able to really understand. The shifting emphasis on chords of power, rage and empathy as the couple's relationship progresses is never resolved into full harmony. Miller cannot fully understand either the woman who is at the center of his life, or his own psychosexual responses to her. As he begins to realize that the enormous energy generated by their relationship is crucially connected to his creative powers, he becomes increasingly desperate to achieve some kind of insight which will give him direction for action.

◆ Social Concerns ◆

The theme of the triad which begins with *Tropic of Capricorn* is the struggle to shape artistic perception into narrative consciousness; to mold and transmute personal experience into the revelation of artistic expression. Before he was able to begin *Tropic of Cancer* in Paris in 1930, Miller spent a decade in New York City where he gradually learned to refine his energy for creative expression from a maelstrom of physical and emotional currents surging in diverse directions. This story began with Miller's last attempt at regular employment when he took a job as the manager of a Western Union office. His description of the hilarious chaos and numbing cruelty of the Cosmodemonic Telegraph Company — his metaphor for modern industrialized America — explains his final alienation from a conventional way of life. This is matched by a kind of alienation from the self as he turns to escape from his economic failures in an excess of sensory indulgence ("On the Ovarian Trolley") and an increasing reliance on the fantasy of extended interior monologues. When he meets the woman who becomes the focus of what he calls a "great tragedy of love" at the conclusion of *Tropic of Capricorn*, his desire for a romantic experience which would completely transcend the mundane aspects of his life carries him out of the social realm entirely and into a world of passion, awe and mental instability. *Sexus* and *Nexus* chart his course through this new and strange landscape.

◆ Techniques ◆

Tropic of Capricorn has two narrative modes. The long opening section that desscribes Miller's experiences with the Cosmodemonic Telegraph Company is written with a kind of heightened realism, combining vivid description of the woeful "messengers" Miller hired with Miller's reactions to the disasters that afflict their lives. This part is a high-energy construct in which Miller's mixture of anger and amusement is presented in a relentless series of anecdotes and incidents that gather momentum through an increasing tension built with the datalogue of failure Miller is developing. The utilization of wrath — expressed in a narrative voice that pulses with almost uncontrollable irritation — to resist the circumstances of a world devoid of personal warmth or social support is one of Miller's favorite stylistic devices.

When Miller moves from the Cosmodemonic world (that is, the external realm of economic oppression and social scorn) to an escape into rampant sensuality and/or the regions of his mental landscape, Miller alternates between descriptions of sexual activity written with a kind of erotic power that is responsible for his reputation as a writer of pornographic/obscene books and passages that also indicate a suspension of the rational faculties as images from the subconscious drift across a not entirely in focus mental screen. In this part of *Capricorn*, there is a degree of bitterness rarely seen in Miller's work since he is trying to show how his narrator has been damaged by cultural calamaties and personal miscalculations and weaknesses. The surreal quality of the images of sensual excess and psychic disorganization emphasizes the extremes of desperation that his protagonist is experiencing.

The last part of *Capricorn* introduces the woman who is at the center of Miller's triad, the agent responsible for the protagonist's experience of the "rosy crucifixion," which is the subject of *Capricorn*, *Sexus* and *Nexus*. The effect she has on the narrator is extraordinary, and while he doesn't develop her "character" beyond her initial appearance, the impact of her introduction is designed to be overwhelming. Miller's account of his first version of June Smith is like an extended lyric poem, an inspired tribute and love letter to a woman who combines apparently human and divine attributes. It is written in a rhapsodic tone that is a testament to her qualities and to her ability to inspire the author. And beyond this, Miller is trying to make a statement about the nation where a woman like this exists. "She is America on foot, winged and sexed," he says, likening the ethos of a vast, unruly, dynamic country metaphorically to the woman who incarnates its spirit of awesome energy and mysterious and dangerous terrain.

◆ Literary Precedents ◆

Miller's determination to explore the psyche is an example of one of literature's most basic and enduring archetypes. His interest in the work of Carl Jung undoubtedly influenced him in his soul-analysis and his mental voyage is patterned after the dark-night-of-the-soul ordeal. On the other hand, his erotic honesty has no parallel in American literature, although works by Remy de Gourmont, Jacques Casanova, and others are appropriate precedents. His quest for self-discovery, however, is clearly akin to Thoreau's journals, and his concentration on the self recalls Whitman's poetry, especially the very aptly titled "Song of Myself." Miller is also, like Whitman, eternally about to set foot on the open road, and in this, he is a precursor of Jack Kerouac and other Beat writers whose work contains many elements of erotic exploration, social commentary, personal introspection and wild language — the primary components of Miller's own literary voice.

◆ Related Titles ◆

Tropic of Capricorn is extended and continued with the novels *Sexus* (1949) and *Nexus* (1960) (see also separate entitled *The Rosy Crucifixion*).

Leon Lewis
Appalachian State University